W9-BIL-890

QUALITY CONTROL AND APPLICATION

Bertrand L. Hansen

The Hansen Group, Management Consultants
University of Toronto

Prabhakar M. Ghare

Virginia Polytechnic Institute
and State University

PRENTICE-HALL, INC., Englewood Cliffs, New Jersey 07632

Library of Congress Cataloging-in-Publication Data

Hansen, Bertrand L. (date)
Quality control and application.

Bibliography: p.
Includes index.
1. Quality control—Statistical methods.
I. Ghare, P. M. II. Title.
TS156.H33 1987 658.5′62 86-4966
ISBN 0-13-745225-X

Editorial/production supervision and interior design: *Nancy Menges*
Cover design: *Wanda Lubelska*
Manufacturing buyer: *Rhett Conklin*

Printed in the United States of America

10 9 8 7 6 5 4 3 2 1

ISBN 0-13-745225-X 025

PRENTICE-HALL INTERNATIONAL (UK) LIMITED, *London*
PRENTICE-HALL OF AUSTRALIA PTY. LIMITED, *Sydney*
PRENTICE-HALL CANADA INC., *Toronto*
PRENTICE-HALL HISPANOAMERICANA, S.A., *Mexico*
PRENTICE-HALL OF INDIA PRIVATE LIMITED, *New Delhi*
PRENTICE-HALL OF JAPAN, INC., *Tokyo*
PRENTICE-HALL OF SOUTHEAST ASIA PTE. LTD., *Singapore*
EDITORA PRENTICE-HALL DO BRASIL, LTDA., *Rio de Janeiro*

This book is dedicated
to George Geoffrey Hansen
and to the memory of
Mrs. Janhavi Ghare

CONTENTS

PREFACE xiii

PART I 1

1 QUALITY CONTROL IN PERSPECTIVE 1

Quality of Design 3
Quality of Conformance to Design 3
Quality of Performance 3
Growth of Quality Control 4
Illustrative Application: Quality of Design 5
Quality of Conformance to Design: Process Monitoring 10
Quality of Conformance to Design: Acceptance Sampling 14
Quality of Performance: Reliability 16
Management of Quality 18
Quality and Productivity 19
About This Book 19

2 FUNDAMENTALS OF STATISTICS AND PROBABILITY IN QUALITY CONTROL 21

Events and Probability 22
Laws of Probability 23
Event Space, Distribution, and Frequency 26
Expectations and Moments 28
Some Distributions Useful in QC Studies 30
Hierarchy of Approximations 40
Probability Functions in Practice 43
Graphic Representation of a Frequency Distribution 45
Estimates and Their Distributions 47
Hypothesis Testing 50
Type I and Type II Errors 53
Run Length of a Monitoring Process 57
Degrees of Freedom 60
Significance Tests 62
Significance Tests for Sample Averages: *t* Tests 65
t Tests for Significance of Differences Involving Proportions 69
Tests for the Significance of Differences Between Variances 71

PART II 80

3 STATISTICAL CONTROL OF PROCESSES 80

Illustration of Variability in Materials, Machines, and People 80
Statistical Inference of Process Variability 84
Variation Over Time Versus Natural Variation of the Process 88
Basic Form of the Control Chart 88
Use of the Control Chart 91
Development of a Control Chart 93
Causes for Investigation 94

Responsibilities for Chart Maintenance and Adjustment Action 95

Process Sampling 95

4 CONTROL CHARTS FOR VARIABLE QUALITY CHARACTERISTICS 98

Basics of a Control Chart 99

Use of Control Charts 101

Charts for Variable Quality Characteristics 102

Derivation of Control Chart Factors 105

Starting a Control Chart 106

Process Not Stable During the Base Period 109

Control Chart During the Monitoring Period 112

5 SPECIAL PROCEDURES IN PROCESS CONTROL 120

Control Charts for $\overline{X}$ and s 120

Control Charts for Individual Measurements 123

Warning Limits 128

Moving Average and CUSUM Charts 131

6 PROPERTIES OF CONTROL CHARTS 143

Operating Characteristic of a Control Chart 143

Computing the OC Curve 145

OC Curve and the Subgroup Size 147

Run-Length Distribution in Quality Control 149

Average Run Length for $\overline{X}$ Charts 151

Use of Warning Limits 154

OC Curve and Average Run Length 159

Production of Defective Items Before a Shift in Process Average Is Detected 160

7 CONTROL CHARTS FOR ATTRIBUTES 164

Percentage Control Chart or p Chart 165

Job Shop Process Quality Control 169

Job Shop Application of Attributes Control 171
Defects Control Chart 178
Application of Defects Per Unit Control 179
Attributes Chart for Quality Troubleshooting 181
Attributes Chart for Performance Control 183
Index Chart for Performance Control 184
Demerit Rating System 190
Possible Applications of Performance Rating 193

8 PROCESS CAPABILITY ANALYSIS 199

Determination of Process Capability 199
Determination of Process Capability: Using Sample Observations 203
Single-Range Method 206
Adjustment for Within-Study Trend 208
Design Specifications and Tolerances 209
Process Capability and Tolerances 210
Tolerances for Subassemblies 211
Setting Tolerances for Intermediate Steps in Production 213
Interference and Tolerance of Fit 215

PART III 222

9 INTRODUCTION TO QUALITY ASSURANCE AND ACCEPTANCE CONTROL 222

Objectives of Acceptance Control 222
Responsibilities for Assuring Quality 223
Receiver-Producer Relationships (In-Plant, Interdivision, and Intercompany) 224
Fallacies of the Spot-Check Method of Sampling 225
Hypothesis Testing in Acceptance Control 227
Operating Characteristic of a Sampling Plan 228
Rectifying Inspection 230
Average Outgoing Quality 231

Total Inspection under Rectifying Inspection 232
Double and Multiple Sampling 233

10 LOT-BY-LOT ACCEPTANCE SAMPLING BY ATTRIBUTES 236

Construction of the OC Curve of an Attributes Single Sampling Plan 237
Development of a Simple Attributes Sampling Plan 241
Analysis and Interpretation of the Operating Characteristic Curve 243

11 ACCEPTANCE PROCEDURES BASED ON AQL 245

Circumstances for Using AQL 246
A Brief History 247
Applicability of AQL Procedures 248
Initial Decisions 248
Specification of the AQL 249
Specification of Inspection Level 251
Normal, Tightened, and Reduced Inspection 252
Single, Double, and Multiple Sampling Plans 252
Description and Use of Tables 255
Producer's Risk and OC Curves 257
Criteria for Administration 258
Inspection Records and Estimated Process Average 260
Acceptance Procedure for Defects 262
Using MIL-STD-105D for Defects 263
Total Amount of Sampling Inspection 264
Administrative Procedures for Submission and Resubmission of Lots 266

12 OTHER ACCEPTANCE PROCEDURES 271

Indifference Quality Acceptance Procedures 272
Dodge-Romig Tables 275
Estimating Process Average 277
Sequential Acceptance Procedures 278

Demerit Sampling 283
Audit Sampling for Quality Assurance 288

13 CONTINUOUS ACCEPTANCE SAMPLING BY ATTRIBUTES 291

Advantages of Continuous Sampling 292
Moving Lots 292
Historical Note 294
MIL-STD-1235 (ORD) 294
Description of Continuous Acceptance Procedures 296
Tightened and Reduced Inspection Plans 303
Effectiveness of Continuous Sampling 304
Plans for Specific AOQL 306

14 ACCEPTANCE PROCEDURES FOR VARIABLE CHARACTERISTICS 317

Applicability of Acceptance Sampling by Variables 317
Variables Sampling Plan 318
Operation of a Variables Sampling Plan 319
MIL-STD-414: Sampling Procedures and Tables for Inspection by Variables for Percent Defective 321
Design of Variables Sampling Plans 327

PART IV 332

15 DESIGN FOR QUALITY ASSURANCE 332

Quality Engineering 332
Planning for Quality and Reliability 333
The Preaward Quality Survey 334
Other Planning Responsibilities 336
Evaluation of Quality and Reliability 337
Elements of a Tool, Gage, and Test Equipment Control Program 340

16 QUALITY ASSURANCE METHODS AND STANDARDS 348

Product Quality Value Analysis 349
Classification of Defects Procedure 351

Specification of Inspection Method 355
Setting Standard Quality Levels 357
Classification of Demerits 364
Illustration of Classification of Demerits 365
Experimental Standard Quality Levels 366

17 QUALITY, PRODUCTIVITY, AND ECONOMY 368

Budgetary Control of Quality Costs 369
Control of Quality Costs in Engineering 373
Economic Optimization of Quality Control 373
Economic Choice of a Sampling Plan 374
Simple Illustration of Game Theory Applied to an Inspection Problem 378

18 ORGANIZING FOR QUALITY AND PRODUCTIVITY 381

Objectives of an Enterprise 382
Management Guidelines for Improving Quality and Productivity 382
Structure of an Organization 383
Division of Work and Functionalization 384
Organization for Quality and Productivity 388
Traditional Quality Organization 388
Quality Control Circles 391
Example of a New Quality Control Circle Program 397
Kanban System 399

19 RELIABILITY 410

Distributions Encountered in Controlling Reliability 411
Mean Time to Failure 415
Exponential Failure Density 418
Estimation of MTTF: Exponential Failure Density 419
Weibull Failure Density 422
Achievement of Reliability 423
Designing for Reliability 424
Reliability Measurement and Tests 428

Use of Handbook H108 429
Sequential Acceptance Procedures Based on MTTF 435
Maintenance and Reliability 439

BIBLIOGRAPHY 443

APPENDIX 445

INDEX 535

PREFACE

The main objective of this book is to present an exposition of the techniques of quality control in a form easily usable by the practitioner. The presentation of each method is brief, allowing for a larger selection of methods and examples to be included in a book of moderate length.

The book is organized in four parts. Part I introduces the basic concepts of quality control and the necessary background information on statistics and probability. Part II describes the techniques for monitoring quality and maintaining quality during processing and production operations. Part III presents a variety of acceptance control procedures. Part IV is devoted largely to the management of quality and also includes a brief discussion of product reliability.

Many case applications have been retained from the original text, *Quality Control: Theory and Applications*, by Bertrand L. Hansen. While references may not always be the most recent, and products described in some of the cases no longer in use, we make no apologies for carrying them over. Like good management, good quality control is never out of date.

The major changes from the original text are as follows:

1. The concepts of "run length" and "average run length" for any control procedure are introduced. The practitioner needs to be aware that no technique can guarantee instantaneous detection of an "out of control" condition. The quantity of unsatisfactory product produced is a direct function of the time required for detection. Two special tables have been included to assist the analysis of average run lengths.

2. The productivity/quality link is introduced. Productivity improvement methods conventionally described as Q. C. Circles and Kanban are presented with a discussion of their implications for product quality.
3. All statistical background material is included in condensed form in a single chapter, Chapter 2. The statistical techniques used in quality control are presented in a "how to" fashion and their theoretical development is limited.
4. A large number of examples have been included and there are over 200 practical exercise problems.

We wish to thank Dr. Shakuntala Ghare (the co-author's wife) and Dr. Wolter Fabrycky for their continuing encouragement. Dr. Donald R. Jensen and Dr. Ezey Dar-El, respectively, deserve special expressions of appreciation for their contributions to the authors' further understanding of statistics and productivity. Also, there are many authors whose works are either quoted or paraphrased in the book. Although they are too numerous to be named individually, we would like to acknowledge the kindness of these authors and their publishers for permission to use material. Finally, Mrs. Joni Chambers and Ms. Nancy Menges, respectively, deserve special thanks for their patient work in typing the manuscript and carrying the editing process through the various stages to the final product.

Bertrand L. Hansen
Prabhakar M. Ghare

one

QUALITY CONTROL IN PERSPECTIVE

One can find many definitions for quality assurance. For example, the definition quoted from the National Symposium on Reliability and Quality Control, 1959 is: "Quality assurance is a broad term used to include both quality control and quality engineering." With this definition one must define both quality control and quality engineering before obtaining a definition of quality assurance. In the authors' view, quality assurance is a much broader term than is indicated by the definition above. In this book it embraces all the methods used by an interested party to assure the quality of product or performance. Thus it is an all-inclusive definition. The methods that may be used to assure quality are many. They include, in addition to quality control and quality engineering, methods of assuring the quality of a product already manufactured or work already completed.

Although the word *quality* has different connotations when used by different people, all definitions of quality include a central concept. The quality of a product is satisfactory when the product is able to satisfy the needs of the consumer. The production of a product of high quality involves many intermediate steps. The design engineer must be able to translate the stated needs of the consumer into an engineering design, including specifications and tolerances. The production engineer must design a production process that will be able to produce a product meeting these specifications and tolerances. The production manager has the responsibility of actually producing the product. The purchasing officer must furnish the necessary raw materials and energy. The personnel officer must furnish workers having the appropriate skills. A quality inspector must test and evaluate the product being produced. Finally, feedback from the consumer is essential. In many instances the "initially stated needs" do not reflect what the consumer actually wants. It is not that the consumer does not know what he or she wants. It is that the consumer is unable to translate these wants into language understood by the design engineer. After the product is actually produced, the consumer can identify exactly the modifications needed to make it perfectly satisfactory.

Quality control is a name given to the collection of management techniques and devices used to manage, monitor, and control all these steps in the production of a product of desired quality. Quality control is more than a paper empire. It is more than a set of statistical formulas and tables for acceptance and control. Indeed, it is more than the departmental unit responsible for quality control. To an enlightened management it must represent a business investment which, as any other investment, should show a proper return to justify its existence. The control of quality is the responsibility of everyone in the enterprise. Whatever work is performed by a person or a machine, the person doing the work or operating the machine is the one who can most effectively control quality or make information available that the quality desired cannot be attained, so that remedial action can be taken.

Between 1965 and 1985 most American business enterprises have come to accept this enlightened approach to quality control. In this period American business faced increasing competition, both at home and abroad, from products of higher quality and lower cost coming from other industrialized nations. Leading this competition were West Germany and Japan. Japan, in the decade of the 1980s, has come to represent the ideal in both high quality and low cost. To fight back, American and other Western business enterprises are increasing their efforts in the area of *quality control* to improve quality and *productivity* to lower costs. Although this book emphasizes quality control, the authors recognize and would like the readers to recognize the quality control–productivity connection. In addition, we include the outline of some management techniques, both American and Japanese, that highlight this connection.

Ultimately, the person who has the most influence for good or bad over the worker, whether the work is production or administration, is the first-line supervisor. Thus the supervisor becomes the hub around which the total quality control effort revolves. Top-level management can be completely sold on quality control, but its efforts will go for naught if the supervisor is not aware of its worth. Competent statisticians and quality control engineers can be performing their calculations in a vacuum simply because the supervisor has not encouraged control of quality by the worker.

QUALITY OF DESIGN

The quality of the design of a product is concerned with the stringency of the specifications for manufacture of the product. For example, a part that has a drawing tolerance of ∓ 0.0001 would be considered to have a better quality of design than another with a tolerance of ∓ 0.010. Generally, the greater the requirement for strength, fatigue resistance, life, function, and interchangeability of a manufactured item, the better the quality of design. Needless to say, the design should be the simplest and least costly which will still meet the customers' preference requirement.

Quality of design is greatly influenced by the market for the product. For example, the market for ballistic missiles consists of the various procurement agencies of the Department of Defense, and the quality they desire in their designs is well known. In contrast, it is common knowledge that many consumer items are manufactured to fail early because of style changes.

QUALITY OF CONFORMANCE TO DESIGN

Conformance quality is concerned with how well the manufactured product conforms to the original design requirements—that is, generally speaking, how well quality is controlled from materials procurement through shipment and storage of finished goods. Quality control, as it has been known and used in the past, has been closely associated with conformance quality. Also, it has been this area in which most of the sampling and statistical techniques have been used.

QUALITY OF PERFORMANCE

When the product is put to work, how it performs depends on both the quality of design and the quality of conformance. It can be the best design possible but poor conformance control can cause poor performance. Conversely, the best conformance control in the world cannot make a product function properly if the design is not right. Thus a continuing feedback system is necessary for providing quality information to act as a basis for decision making regarding the optimizing of a quality product. The key word here, in each case, is *optimum*, which does not necessarily mean the most stringent quality requirement, but the *best* in the sense that it will yield the greatest long-term return on the investment in quality control.

The quality process is not the responsibility of any single organizational element or unit. It requires contributory functions from many organizational units of various levels within the corporation. In general it can be said that top management, accounting, "quality control," and information processing units are concerned with sponsoring, promoting, controlling, and coordinating the quality effort. Research and development, sales, and engineering are concerned with assessing the consumers' needs and designing products and process. Production engineering, tool engineering, purchasing, and manufacturing are concerned with producing a product that satisfies the specifications as economically as possible. These functions are described in Table 1.1.

GROWTH OF QUALITY CONTROL

The earliest records of the beginning of quality control go back to 1924, when Walter A. Shewhart of Bell Telephone Laboratories first applied a statistical quality control chart to manufactured product. Subsequently, Shewhart authored a book, *Economic Control of Quality of Manufactured Product*, published in 1931 by D. Van Nostrand Company, Inc., New York. The objective explicitly put forth in the title was *economic* control. It is unfortunate that many of the later applications of statistical techniques to the control of quality have been anything but economical. The early 1940s saw development and use of sampling tables for acceptance inspection,[1] plus publication of military sampling tables and endorsement of their use by the armed services.[2] The latter culminated in Military Standard 105D, which is used widely both within and outside the government for acceptance sampling inspection by attributes.[3] Also, the Department of Defense (DOD) has published Military Standard 414 for acceptance sampling by variables[4] and has standards for single- and multiple-stage continuous sampling for inspection by attributes.[5]

By the very nature of voluminous procurement activities, the defense agencies have always had great influence on the promulgation and use of quality control techniques both directly and indirectly. A substantial percentage of the gross national product is represented by defense expenditures. When the total chain-of-events effect of insistence on requisite quality is

[1] H. F. Dodge and H. G. Romig, *Sampling Inspection Tables—Single and Double Sampling* (New York: John Wiley & Sons, Inc., 1944).

[2] Both the Army and the Navy used sampling tables for acceptance.

[3] Military Standard 105D, *Sampling Procedures and Tables for Inspection by Attributes*, National Technical Information Service, Washington, D.C.

[4] Military Standard 414, *Sampling Procedures and Tables for Inspection by Variables for Percent Defective*, National Technical Information Service, Washington, D.C.

[5] Military Standard 1235-ORD, *Sampling Procedures and Tables for Inspection by Variables for Percent Defective*, National Technical Information Service, Washington, D.C.

TABLE 1.1 Business Functions and Their Responsibilities for Quality

Top management	Quality control	Accounting	Research	Sales and marketing
Top-level support and encouragement of quality effort	Quality assurance plus promotion, coordination, and control of entire quality effort	Measurement of quality costs and quality effort	Quality of research—proper design and analysis of experimental data	Selling a quality product and providing information on field performance
Design engineering	**Tool engineering**	**Production engineering**	**Purchasing**	**Manufacturing**
Designing a quality product and changing the design to achieve optimum quality condition	Providing quality tools, jigs, and fixtures	Providing a quality production process	Quality of conformance of purchased goods: feedback of quality information	Quality conformance in manufacturing, semifinished, and finished goods; feedback of quality information

considered, it is possible to attribute to the procurement agencies of the Department of Defense a large measure of the credit for the development of quality control. Indeed, the growth of quality control can be compared directly to the changing attitudes of defense agencies toward the role of quality control in its procurement activities. During World War II and the Korean War the emphasis was on the *use* of the techniques by the various inspection agencies of DOD. Following the Korean War the emphasis shifted to *promotion* of the use of quality control techniques by the supplier, accompanied by *assurance* methods used by the inspection agencies of DOD. Currently, the emphasis has shifted to *life cycle*, which is concerned with the quality during the entire cycle of need assessment–design–production–use–maintenance–performance of a product.

ILLUSTRATIVE APPLICATION: QUALITY OF DESIGN[6]

This case has been selected to set the stage for the book. It shows that the application of quality control does not necessarily have to involve extensive administrative burden or unusual skills. It is intended to show that quality

[6] Contributed by A. G. Tashjian, Chief Engineer, Cleveland Welding Division, American Machine and Foundry, Cleveland, Ohio.

control is a philosophy and an attitude rather than just an elaborate system. The systems help to attain the desired attitudes and philosophy but are not ends in themselves. The case history (with the authors' comments in parentheses) shows what *can* result from a questioning attitude about quality; the savings and benefits, direct and indirect, to many departmental units, resulting from just one small practical application of quality control. The case is first presented as a problem for study. Following it are the results of a project study. Subsequently, the same product, in combination with some hypothetical data (shown in Table 1–3), is used to illustrate how the principles and techniques described in this book can be used for effective quality control.

The item for study, a spacer band for dual truck rims (Figure 1.1), has been produced by the company for many years. The current volume is approximately 200,000 units per year, representing about $220,000 in sales. Price competition for the item is vigorous. The item is manufactured from commercial-quality C-1010 hot-rolled strip steel $4\frac{3}{4}$ in. wide by 0.105 in. thick by 118 in. long. The manufacturing operations for the item are as follows:

1. Shear to length and stamp.
2. Pickle.

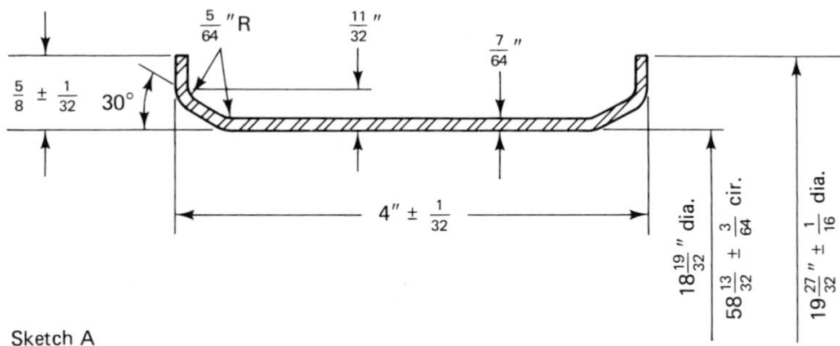

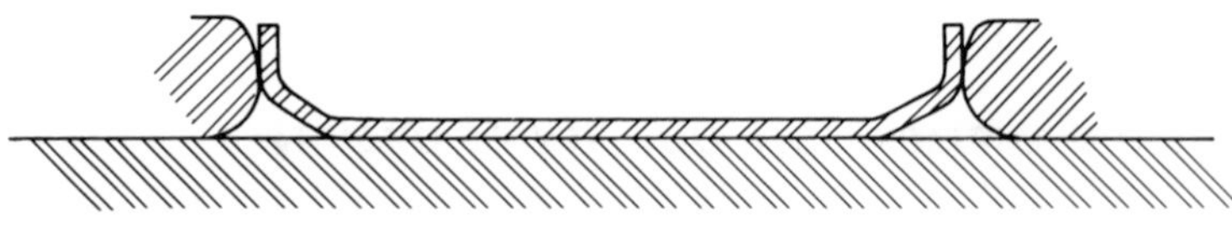

Figure 1.1 Sketch of spacer band.

3. Form (circle).
4. Flash weld.
5. Rough burr (remove weld flash).
6. Finish burr (remove flash).
7. First roll (partial shape).
8. Second roll (final shape and edge roll).
9. Expand.
10. Inspect 100% and transfer to conveyor.
11. Galvanize.

The cost per operation is approximately 1 cent per unit.

The item is used to space dual truck rims assembled on five- or six-spoke wheels. The fit is supposed to be reasonably snug. The assembler would normally mount the spacer in the flash-weld area between spokes. There appears to be no problem in holding to any of the dimensions.

The manufacturing operations are continuous at the rate of approximately 250 units per hour up to the galvanize operation. However, the material is stacked after the expand operation. The inspection instruction requires 100% inspection at this point. One acceptance inspector is stationed at this operation. The in-process inventory at this point may vary from one day's to several weeks' supply. However, in the event of rejection, the costs of galvanizing and extra handling on rejected units are saved. There is no storage space problem.

The welding practice and tooling appear to be satisfactory. The welding cycle is automatic but there has been some trouble in slippage during welding upset.

It is agreed by all parties that the most serious defects in this item would be defective material and cracked welds. The other characteristics have not been separated into serious and nonserious categories.

The acceptance standard for flash trim has been to insist on flush to approximately 0.005 in. projection. The production department has adhered to this standard rigidly, and based on this standard, which has not varied for years, has insisted that it is absolutely necessary to trim in two steps. There has been no attempt to verify the necessity for this requirement, nor has there been any examination of competitors' quality performance on flash-weld trims.

Inspection data have been collected and filed, but the records have not been examined to determine outgoing quality. Questions to the inspection foreman about quality receive the answer "pretty good."

Production operators work on the standard hour plan. They have an implied responsibility for quality; however, they rely completely on the inspector to sort out defective units.

Results of a Quality Control Project Study

First, inspection records for the previous six months were examined. The quality average for the period was 2.4% defective, with more than 60% of the defectives caused by poor workmanship on flash-weld removal. About 20% of the defectives were caused by cracked welds.

Next, the dimensions and tolerances were examined and considered to be generally acceptable. Several questions were raised about the $\frac{5}{8}$ in. by $\frac{1}{32}$ in. dimension:

1. Is a maximum dimension necessary since the edge "fits the wind" and is necessarily a function of mill strip width and centering of the piece during rolling to shape?
2. Is an unnecessary operation being performed to control a nonfunctional surface and, if so, is there a potential material savings in as-purchased width?

Discussion with production supervisors revealed that the second rolling was being performed to control the maximum leg height. To obtain the opportunity costs here, it was decided to reduce purchased width by $\frac{1}{8}$ in. and authorize tooling change to eliminate the first rolling.

Next, a trip was made to the consumer's assembly line to determine whether the flash-weld trim acceptance requirement of 0.005 in. to flush projection was actually required. Units of competitors' product were also examined. The consumer stated that 0.030-in. projection of the outside and 0.020-in. projection on the inside surface would be acceptable. With such an acceptance standard, both engineering and production agreed that a single burring operation would suffice. Recommendations were made that new-type welding dies be authorized and new flash trim inspection standards be adopted.

Representatives from inspection, production, and quality control were called together to establish the defect descriptions and to develop a classification of defects for the spacer band.

The station of inspection prior to galvanizing appeared to be satisfactory. In case of rejection, costs of galvanizing and extra handling on rejected units would be saved. The defect categories were defined as follows:

Group 1: defects likely to cause serious functional trouble during usage and/or complaints by customers likely to seriously endanger quality reputation or cause loss of business

Group 2: defects likely to cause minor inconveniences only at assembly and/or minor customer complaints easily adjusted and routine

Group 3: defects not reducing usability or likely to cause customer complaints

The characteristics on the spacer band were assigned to the categories in accordance with the group defect descriptions (Table 1.2). Acceptable quality levels (AQLs) were arbitrated with cost, function, assembly, and customer complaints being the principal items considered.

TABLE 1.2

Group 1: AQL 0.15%	Group 2: AQL 1.5%	Group 3: AQL 4.0%
Cracked welds Defective steel	Leg height minimum Width minimum Circumference maximum and minimum Flash trim I.D.	Flash trim O.D. Width minimum Surfaces defects Stamping

The inspection lot size was initially established as one-half shift's production—about 1000 units—with the provision that when sufficient quality data for analysis became available, an increase in lot size would be given serious consideration. Single sampling was specified for ease of administration. Also, several lots were "dry run" before the plan was put into full use. Machine operators were fully briefed on the operation of the plan.

Results of Operation of the Sampling Plan

All tooling changes were installed and inspection instructions issued. A compilation was made after the first 50 lots sampled. One lot was sorted for group 1 (cracked welds) and group 2 (flash trim I.D.). The balance of the lots were acceptable on first submission. The group quality averages, based on sampling to date, were as follows: group 1, 0.08%; group 2, 1.10%; and group 3, 1.00%.

As a direct result of the project, the following changes were made:

1. Material size was revised from $4\frac{3}{4}$ in. width to $4\frac{5}{8}$ in. width, resulting in a material savings of 0.23 lb. per unit.
2. One manufacturing operation (first rolling) was eliminated immediately.
3. One manufacturing operation (rough burr) will be eliminated soon.
4. Welding die changes have reduced weld cracks 50%.
5. Inspection labor hours have been reduced 80%.

The above, translated into annual savings, yields:

Inspection labor	$1625.00
Direct labor	2000.00
Material	4000.00
Reduced rework (estimated)	500.00
Total	$8125.00

In addition, \$2000.00 opportunity cost savings will be realized if single burring is successful.

In manufacturing costs the savings equal \$0.05 per unit. When overhead profit is added, it can readily be seen that real progress has been achieved in an effort to remain competitive in a period of rising costs.

The immediate costs involved in the installation of the plan and improvements are as follows:

New welding dies	\$ 125.00
Roll rework	300.00
Rearrangement of line	100.00
Project cost	500.00
Total	\$1025.00

First-year net savings equaled \$7100.00. No customer complaints were received. Salespeople can quote lower prices if necessary. Production was not disturbed. Quality is better. Production and inspection now work together.

QUALITY OF CONFORMANCE TO DESIGN: PROCESS MONITORING

The design and the drawings specify exactly alike dimensions for all spacer bands to be produced. However, the production process usually is not good enough to produce all spacer bands with identical dimensions. For any specific dimension such as "width of spaces" there would always be some small variations. Small variations would not make the spacer bands unsatisfactory but larger variations might. Some simple statistical tools can be used to answer the question: Are the variations large enough to affect the performance of the spacer bands? Shewhart control charts provide a simple but effective tool to determine the answer. In any manufacturing process the variations may either be due to a chance or random pattern inherent in the process or may be due to an external identifiable cause that can be discovered and avoided in the future. A control chart delineates the range of variations that are not likely to occur due to chance causes. Consequently, any variation in this range would have an external cause and quality control engineers can proceed to identify it.

For example, if the probability distribution of a characteristic is normal with mean μ and standard deviation σ, the probability of the observed value of this characteristic being larger than $\mu + 3\sigma$, solely due to chance causes, is about 0.005, or 1 in 200. If the characteristic is larger than $\mu + 3\sigma$, significantly more frequently than 1 in 200, say 1 in 4, the quality control engineer has reason to believe in the existence of some external cause. In quality control parlance the limit $\mu + 3\sigma$ is called a *control limit* and the existence of an external cause is called *process out of control.*

The procedures and techniques for using these control charts are described in detail in Chapters 3 and 4. However a simplified introduction to these techniques can be given using the characteristic "width of spacer band" as an example. A sample of 5 spacer bands out of 250 produced is inspected each hour. The observations for two shifts, 16 hours, are given in Table 1.3.

The specifications for the width of the spacer band are 4 ∓ 0.040 in. To obtain the values in Table 1.3, the following procedure is followed:

1. The width of each band is measured as the deviation from 4.000 in. in units of one thousandth of an inch.
2. The range R is calculated as the difference between the largest observation in the sample and the smallest observation in the sample.
3. The average $\overline{X}$ is calculated as the arithmetic average of five observations in the sample:

$$\text{Average of samples} = \overline{\overline{X}} = \frac{240}{16} = 15$$

$$\text{Average of ranges} = \overline{R} = \frac{400}{16} = 25$$

TABLE 1.3 Observations of Widths of Spacer Bands

Sample Number	Average Width, $\overline{X}$	Range, R
1	18	28
2	35	30
3	−1	24
4	−3	18
5	9	30
6	10	24
7	19	40
8	13	32
9	13	36
10	15	16
11	11	24
12	21	20
13	19	20
14	34	32
15	12	14
16	15	12
Total	240	400

Using expressions given later in the book, the control limits are calculated as

$$\text{UCL}_{\overline{X}} = 15 + 0.58 \times 25 = 29.5$$

$$\text{LCL}_{\overline{X}} = 15 - 0.58 \times 25 = 0.5$$

$$\text{UCL}_R = 2.11 \times 25 = 52.75$$

$$\text{LCL}_R = 0 = 0$$

Figure 1.2 shows plots of observed average sample widths and observed ranges of sample values together with the corresponding control limits. These are called *$\overline{X}$ and R charts*, sometimes referred to as *Shewhart charts*. The production supervisor can use the information presented by the charts for monitoring the production process.

1. Four points, samples 2, 3, 4, and 14, lie outside the control limits on the $\overline{X}$ chart. None of the points lie outside the control limits on the R chart.
2. The manufacturing process appears to be out of control for averages, $\overline{X}$, and in control for ranges, R. Had the process been in control, the proportion of points outside the control limits would have been only 1 in 200. Here the proportion is 4 of 16, or 25%.

Based on this information the supervisor can proceed to do two things: (1) assess the capability of the process itself, and (2) search for causes leading to the process being out of control.

To assess the capability of the process, an estimate of σ, the standard deviation, can be obtained from the average range (Table A7 in the Appendix).

$$\sigma = \frac{\overline{R}}{d_2}$$

$$= \frac{25}{2.326}$$

$$= 10.748$$

If the process can be maintained in control with a standard deviation of 10.748, the *natural tolerances* of this process is approximately "mean ± 32.25." So, when in control, the process is capable of producing items within the *stated tolerances* of "mean ± 0.040."

The desired mean, as per specifications, is 4.000 or 0 on the transformed scale. The estimated mean width of spacers based on these 16 samples is 15. With a mean of 15 and natural tolerances of "mean ± 32.25," most of

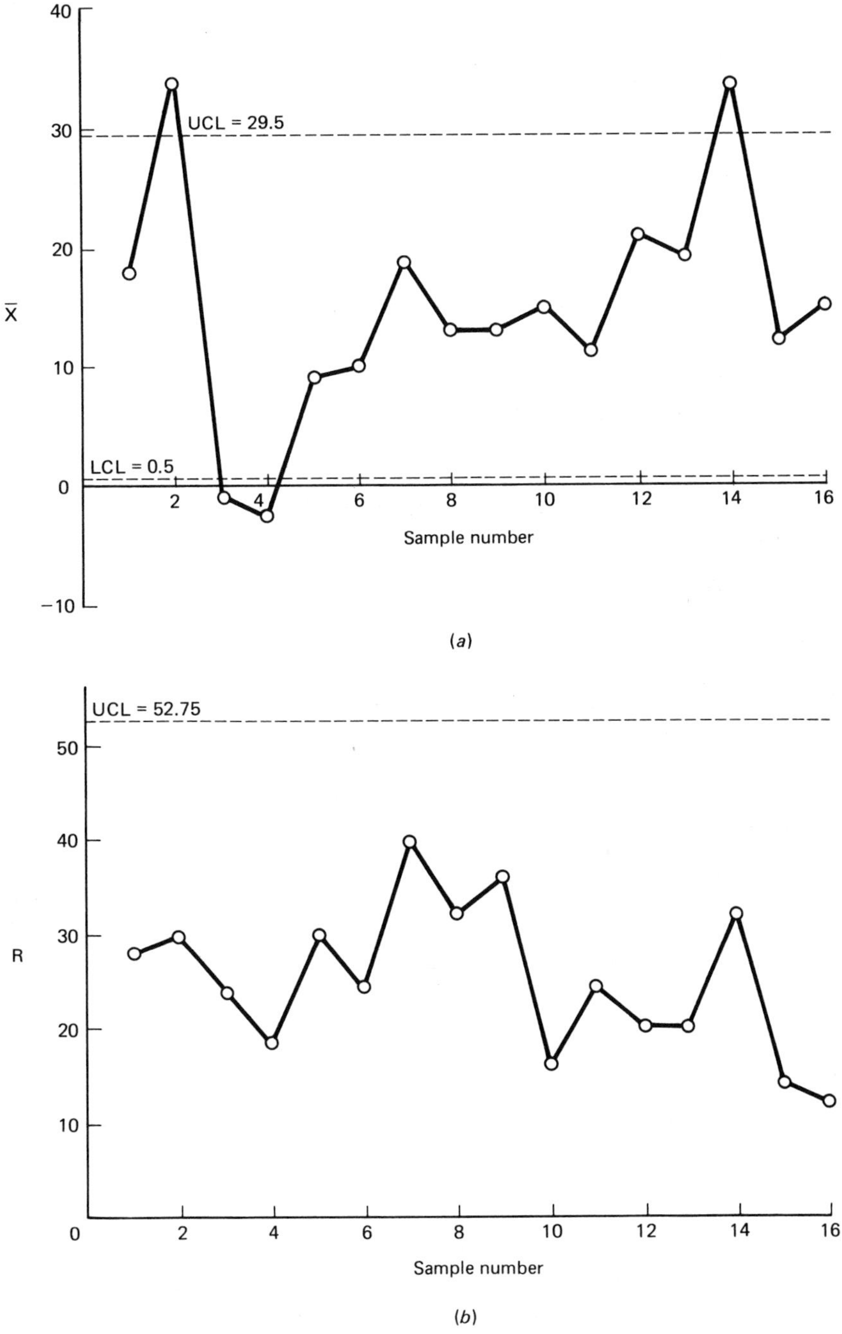

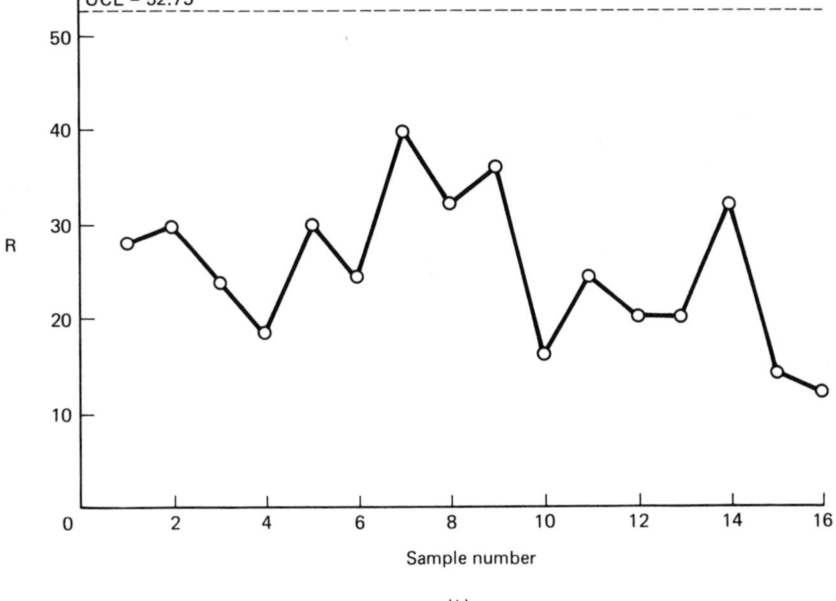

Figure 1.2 Control chart for spacer band production: (a) plot of average sample widths, $\overline{X}$ chart; (b) plot of sample ranges, R chart.

the product would be within the range −17.25 to +47.25. The acceptable range is −40 to +40. The production of unsatisfactory spacers can be avoided by lowering the mean from 15 to the desired 0. With a mean of 0 and natural tolerances, most of the product would be within the range −32.25 to +32.25, well within the acceptable range.

The supervisor can reach the conclusion that the process of manufacturing spacers is capable of producing product of acceptable quality. However, three conditions must be met to reach this objective:

1. The causes for the out-of-control situation for samples 2, 3, 4, and 14 must be determined and corrected.
2. The process mean must be lowered to 0.
3. The process must remain in control.

QUALITY OF CONFORMANCE TO DESIGN: ACCEPTANCE SAMPLING

The production supervisor of the department that produces the spacers can use control charts or similar techniques to monitor the quality of the spacers as these are being produced. At this stage timely modifications and adjustments can be made to assure the production of high-quality product.

This procedure, called *process monitoring*, is not available to the purchaser. Typically, the purchaser would be a buyer for a truck assembly plant. The buyer has the responsibility of furnishing spacers that meet the requirements of wheel assembly. Once a lot, say several boxes, of spacers is received from the parts manufacturer, the buyer's options are limited. The lot can be accepted as such, rejected totally, or returned to the manufacturer for replacement of defective spacers and resubmission. To reach the appropriate decision, the buyer can use one of two alternative methods.

1. *100% inspection or "screening."* Here a decision is based on the inspection (and testing if needed) of every spacer received.
2. "*Acceptance sampling*." Here only a small sample is inspected. A decision concerning the lot is reached on the basis of information gathered from this sample.

The advantage of acceptance sampling over screening lies mainly in the reduced cost (and time) of inspection. A properly designed acceptance sampling would lead to decisions that can be reliable under most conditions, but not perfect. A typical acceptance sampling procedure involves determining a sample size and the critical number of defects in the sample. Assume that the spacers are shipped in boxes containing 1000 units each and the consumer, a truck assembly plant, considers "1% defective" as acceptable. The buyer can obtain an acceptance sampling procedure by referring to MIL-STD-105D, which is a source book widely used for this purpose (and described in more detail in Chapter 11). The "sampling plan" is given as $n = 80$ and $c = 2$. The acceptance sampling procedure implied by this plan is as follows. Take a sample of 80 spacers from each box and test these 80 spacers. If 2 or less are found defective, accept the box. If 3 or more are found defective, reject the box.

The chances of a box being accepted would obviously depend on the quality or the fraction that is defective. If all spacers in a box are good (i.e., the quality is 0% defective), it is obvious that the box would be accepted. There is no way of finding 3 defectives in the sample if there are none in the box.

As the fraction that is defective increases, the chances of acceptance decrease. To illustrate this, consider three levels: 1%, 2%, and 10%. If the product is 1% defective, how many defectives would be found in a sample of 80? The box contains 1% or 10 defectives in all. The number that would be picked up in the sample would depend on the laws of probability. The applicable law in this case is called *Poisson law*. More about this law is presented in Chapter 2. Using Poisson law, it can be estimated that if the sampling is performed 1000 times, the sample will have 0 defectives 449 times, 1 defective 360 times, and 2 defectives 144 times. The remaining 47 times the sample will have 3 or more defectives and the box will be rejected. Hence the probability that a box with a quality of 1% will be accepted is 95.3%. Similar computations will yield the probability of acceptance at other levels of quality (Table 1.4). Figure 1.3 shows the probability that a box would be accepted as a function of the quality of product in the box. Such a curve is called the *operating characteristic* of the sampling procedure.

It can be noted that whenever the product subjected to this sampling plan is of the acceptable quality level of 1% or better, the probability of acceptance is very high, 95% or higher. Even product slightly inferior (e.g., 2%), has a fairly good chance of being accepted—78%. When the product is significantly poor (e.g., 10%), it is almost sure to be rejected; the probability of acceptance is only 1.4%. It is desirable for a sampling plan that it provide adequate protection to both the producer and the consumer (i.e., the seller

TABLE 1.4 Sampling Summary

Quality	1%	2%	10%
Pr(0 defectives in sample)	449	202	0
Pr(1 defective in sample)	360	323	3
Pr(2 defectives in sample)	144	258	11
Pr(3 or more defectives in sample)	47	217	986
Probability of acceptance	95.3%	78.3%	1.4%

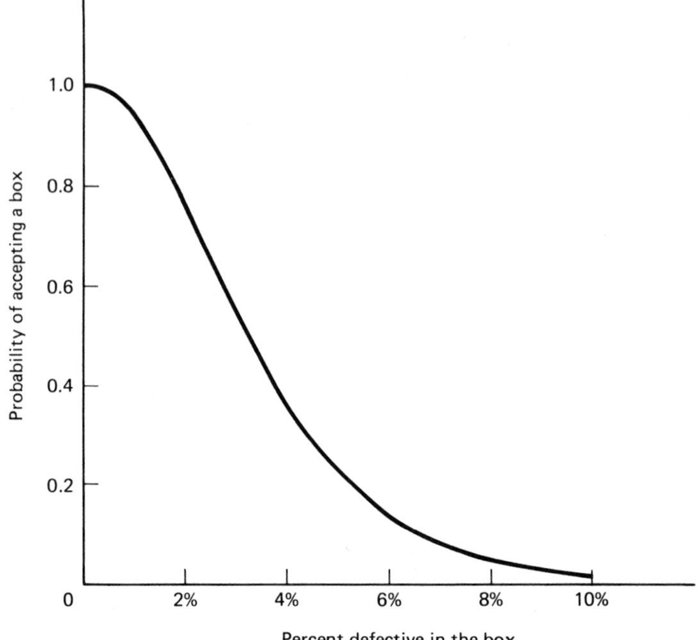

Figure 1.3 Operating characteristic curve of a sampling procedure.

and the buyer). When the producer produces "good-quality" product, the probability of the lots being rejected should be low. On the other hand, the consumer needs assurance that the probability of "poor-quality" lots being accepted should also be low.

QUALITY OF PERFORMANCE: RELIABILITY

Once the product is accepted by the buyer and put into operation, either by itself or as a part of a larger assembly, the quality of performance would be judged by how long the product gives useful service. This is indicated by the word *reliability*. When two items are observed a certain time t after being put in service, the item that has a higher probability of still being in satisfactory operation would be considered more reliable. In some instances it is both possible and desirable to base the acceptance sampling procedures on reliability of the product.

A department store uses a large number of light bulbs. Records maintained for two lots of 1000 bulbs each purchased from competing suppliers of light bulbs showed the results given in Table 1.5.

It is possible to relate the percentage of bulbs still operating with the probability that any bulb selected at random would still be operating. In

TABLE 1.5 Bulb Performance

Hours	Percentage of Bulbs Still in Operation	
	Supplier A	Supplier B
0	100	100
200	92	98
400	85	96
600	71	93
800	59	88
1000	43	80
1200	34	71
1400	25	61
1600	17	52
2000	12	46

other words, the two curves in Figure 1.4 can be viewed as the reliability patterns of the bulbs supplied by the two suppliers. The product from supplier B is clearly superior, as it is more reliable at every period of measurement.

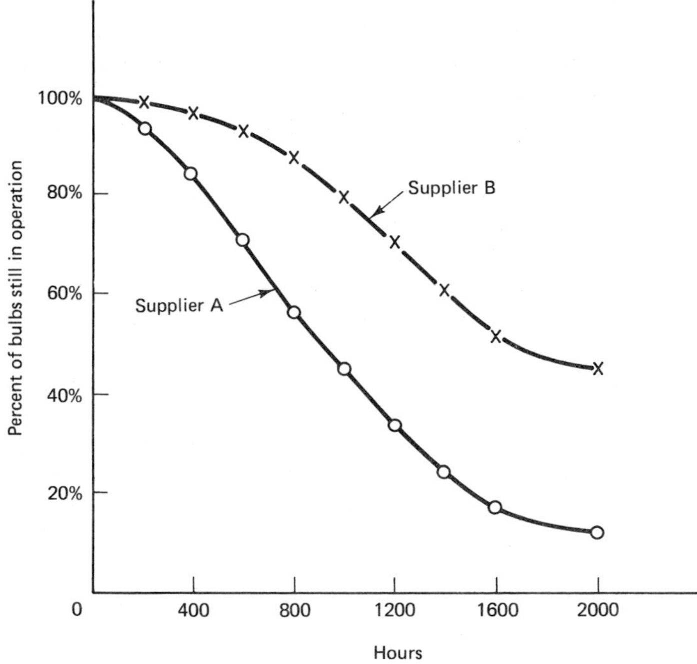

Figure 1.4 Lifetimes of light bulbs from two suppliers.

MANAGEMENT OF QUALITY

A modern corporation is an intricate web of myriads of small and large decisions and their communication and implementation. All aspects of the output from such a corporation, quality among them, depend on how these decisions are arrived at and the structure of the network of communication and implementation. Eventually, persons at all levels within the corporation, from chairman to production-line worker, have some influence on the final quality.

The influence of the worker is obvious. Quality control techniques or management systems or management goals do not produce high-quality product. Only motivated and well-trained workers using proper equipment and materials can produce high-quality product. Any effort to improve quality that overlooks the worker is bound to fail.

The junior management, such as line supervisors, are the last link in the communication of the decisions and first link in their implementation. If these persons feel apprehensive about any decision, or do not understand the relevance of the decision, the implementation of these decisions is likely to be inadequate or incorrect or both. For the purposes of quality control it is imperative that these persons understand the techniques used—not necessarily all the statistics and mathematics in the background but at least the mechanical application of the techniques along with the goal and objective of each technique used should be familiar. They should not feel that the quality control engineer is one more boss to be satisfied and placated. On the other hand, they should be able to look on the quality control engineer as a person to help them identify and correct quality problems in "their" line or shop.

The middle management, from section supervisors to plant and division managers, are persons responsible for all the decision making for the normal operations. The four key ingredients in the production of high-quality product—motivation, training, equipment, and materials—all depend on these decisions. The quality of the final product can only be as good as these decisions.

The top management, from vice presidents to the chairman of the board, usually do not get involved in the day-to-day operational decisions. The number of hours in a day being limited, any involvement in such operational decisions would detract these top managers from their principal function, which is strategic decision and policymaking for the whole corporation. Their role in quality improvement is (1) to set the policy guidelines, (2) to create an atmosphere within the corporation which encourages and nurtures better decision making by the middle managers, and (3) to structure the corporation so that the communication and implementation of these decisions is facilitated.

It is properly said that in a corporation "quality is everybody's job."

QUALITY AND PRODUCTIVITY

Productivity is an index for measuring the efficiency with which a production process converts input resources into usable output. A worker in a widget plant works for 8 hours. These 8 labor hours constitute an input resource. If the worker produces 80 widgets during the day, these widgets would be considered as the output. The production system, called the "widget plant," takes in 8 labor hours as input and converts these into 80 widgets as output. If some improvement in production method leads to an increase in the output from 80 to 100, the production system can be said to have become more productive. The productivity index has increased from 10 widgets/labor hour to 12.5 widgets/labor hour.

Productivity and quality are very closely related. In some sense these two are two alternative ways of looking at the same thing, the efficiency of the conversion of input resources. Both have the same objective: to obtain "more usable output" from the same expenditure of input resources. The only difference is that the study of productivity puts more emphasis on the word "more" and the study of quality emphasizes the word "usable." Assume that the widgets production mentioned in the preceding paragraph was such that only 75% of the widgets produced were usable. When the production increased from 80 to 100, the quantity of usable widgets increased from 60 to 75. If, instead of improving the production, the quality were to be improved from 75% usable to 100% usable, the quantity of usable widgets would have increased from 60 to 80.

Because productivity and quality are closely related efforts, to improve one usually leads to an improvement in the other. Two productivity improvement techniques are described later in this book. One, quality control circles, attempts to improve worker involvement in the management of the workstation. The second, the kanban system, attempts to achieve a steady, "no-rush" production system. It would be obvious that the effect of these productivity improvement techniques on resulting product quality would certainly be positive. A worker who feels that he or she can have some influence over correcting problems at his or her workstation and has assurance that there would always be an adequate amount of time for every job would naturally produce better quality product.

ABOUT THIS BOOK

This book is designed with a specific objective of providing an overall understanding of the problems and solution techniques involved in the four areas of quality: quality of design, quality of conformance to design both in process monitoring and acceptance sampling, quality of performance, and management of quality. The book does not attempt to provide a thorough knowledge of the basic mathematics and statistics behind these techniques. Nor does it attempt to describe basic research. However, the authors acknowledge that some knowledge of fundamentals of statistics and probability is essential for any practitioner of quality control. In this light, Chapter 2 gives an overview of these fundamentals. The chapter may be considered superfluous and may be skipped by persons who already possess substantial knowledge in the fields of statistics and probability. For others, this chapter would provide the necessary introductory background.

The rest of the book is divided into three parts. Part II deals with the process monitoring aspects of quality of conformance to design. It describes how the different types of control charts are developed. It also attempts to help the reader in the interpretation of the information provided by these charts. Part III deals with the acceptance sampling aspects of quality of conformance to design. Here the emphasis is directed to the sampling procedures developed by the U.S. Department of Defense. The plans developed by this department, called Military Standards, do provide a source of easily accessible and reliable sampling procedures, and their application is by no means limited to military uses. Part IV deals with the quality of design as well as the quality of performance, more emphasis being given to the latter. This part also deals with the management of quality and the interrelated roles of quality and productivity.

The parts are essentially independent of each other and may be studied in any order. Persons needing the overview of statistics and probability in Chapter 2 also have two alternatives. The first is to study Chapter 2 in its entirety before proceeding to Parts II, III, and IV. The second is to start reading Parts II, III, and IV, returning intermittently to Chapter 2 as the need arises.

two

FUNDAMENTALS OF STATISTICS AND PROBABILITY IN QUALITY CONTROL

A quality control manager is continually facing a question about the status of the operation of the production process. Is the production process running as it should? Or has there been some deviation from the normal operation? Does this deviation warrant corrective action? This determination is crucial to the efficient control of quality. If any deviation goes undetected or uncorrected, the quality of the product will deteriorate. If, on the other hand, the manager overcorrects or gets in the habit of taking corrective action when not needed, the costs will increase without any benefit to quality.

Techniques based on *statistics* and *probability* are used to assist the manager to reach a correct decision about this crucial question. This chapter presents the basic principles of statistics and probability that are necessary to develop these techniques. Obviously, this treatment of statistics and probability is by no means complete. It is not intended to be. It is presented here to give quality control professionals some elementary background in these areas. Persons interested in the study of statistics and probability in depth would find that there are a large number of excellent books covering every level of understanding, from basic to advanced to state-of-the-art. A sampling of these books is listed as a part of the bibliography.

These techniques are fundamental in any quality control program. These can be used mechanically without a full understanding of the principles of statistics and probability. Sometimes it is sufficient to teach only the use of the techniques, especially to quality control operators or production operators who maintain quality control data. In many academic programs the first course in quality control is devoted solely to these techniques and is called *statistical quality control*. As viewed in this book, quality control is the sum of all control activities, direct or indirect, designed to produce high-quality product. In this sense statistical quality control is a subset of quality control.

EVENTS AND PROBABILITY

An event is characterized by two elements, the time of occurrence of the event and the descriptive data describing the event. For example, the fact that an item produced by an automatic press at 3:23 P.M. on Monday, January 15, 1984 had a length of 3.638 in. is an event. It has both the time of occurrence and descriptive data. After the occurrence the event is known with certainty. Before the occurrence the descriptive data can only be guessed. The word "probability" is used to express the degree of faith one has that a stated event will occur. Clearly, after the fact, the probability of any event is either 1 or 0 because the event either has or has not taken place. Before the fact, the probability is some level between 1 and 0. For the event described earlier, after the item is produced, the length of the item produced is fixed; it is either 3.638 in. or some length other than 3.638 in. Symbolically, this is expressed as

$\Pr(x = 3.638)$ = probability that the variable x denoting the length of the item has a value 3.638

$$= \begin{cases} 1 & \text{if the length is, in fact, 3.638} \\ 0 & \text{if the length differs from 3.638} \end{cases}$$

Before the fact, the observer does not know with any certainty what the length is going to be. An estimation or a guess has to be made based on prior knowledge of the operation of the machine and of items produced by it. If the estimation is that the length is 3.638 for 3 of each 5 items produced, the statement can be expressed as

$$\Pr(x = 3.638) = \frac{3}{5}$$
$$= 0.60$$
$$= 60\%$$

In this book the word *probability* will be used exclusively to denote probability before the fact.

In general, probability is a number between (and including) the values 0 and +1. For any event A,

$$0 \leq \Pr(A) \leq 1$$

Many times the principle of "unknown events being equally likely" is used to obtain the estimate of probability. This principle was first initiated by the French mathematician Laplace in the early nineteenth century. To illustrate this principle, consider a bowl that contains 3 green balls and 9 red balls. A person is blindfolded and asked to pick one ball. According to this principle, each of the 12 balls is equally likely to be picked. The probability that any specific ball will be picked is $\frac{1}{12}$. The probability that the ball that is picked will be red is $9 \times \frac{1}{12}$, or $\frac{9}{12}$, or 75%.

This concept of probability is called the *relative frequency concept of probability*. In this sense probability is the ratio

$$\text{probability} = \frac{\text{number of outcomes leading to the event}}{\text{number of all possible outcomes}}$$

LAWS OF PROBABILITY

Definition. The *conditional probability* $\Pr(A \mid B)$ is the probability of event A occurring, if we know that the event B has occurred.

Conditional probability can be illustrated as follows. A box contains 100 plastic pieces. Of these

30 pieces are round and red.
20 pieces are round and green.
40 pieces are square and red.
10 pieces are square and green.

When a blindfolded person selects one piece, the probability that the piece is round is 0.50, as there are 50 round pieces out of 100. However, if it is already known that the piece is green, the conditional probability that the piece is round is 0.667, as there are 20 round green pieces out of 30 green pieces.

$$\begin{aligned} A &= \text{event that the piece is round} \\ B &= \text{event that the piece is green} \\ \Pr(A) &= 0.50 \\ \Pr(A \mid B) &= 0.667 \end{aligned}$$

Definition. Two events A and B are said to be *statistically independent* of each other if $\Pr(A \mid B) = \Pr(A)$ and $\Pr(B \mid A) = \Pr(B)$.

Evidently, the events of the piece selected being round and being green are not statistically independent.

Definition. Two events A and B are said to be *statistically dependent* if they are not statistically independent.

This statistical dependence does not imply any physical dependence or any cause-and-effect relationship. On the other hand, physical dependence or cause-and-effect relationship does imply statistical dependence.

Definition. $\Pr(A \cdot B)$, read as *probability of A and B*, is the probability that both the events A and B will occur.

$\Pr(A + B)$, read as *probability of A or B*, is the probability that either A, or B, or both the events will occur.

$\Pr(A^c)$, read as *probability of A complement*, is the probability that the event A will not occur.

Algebra of Probabilities

The definitions stated above lead to certain rules of algebra that would be followed by probability statements.

Complementary rule:

$$\Pr(A + A^c) = 1$$

$$\Pr(A \cdot A^c) = 0$$

Commutative rule:

$$\Pr(A + B) = \Pr(B + A)$$

$$\Pr(A \cdot B) = \Pr(B \cdot A)$$

Associative rule:

$$\Pr(A + (B + C)) = \Pr((A + B) + C)$$

$$\Pr(A \cdot (B \cdot C)) = \Pr((A \cdot B) \cdot C)$$

Distributive rule:

$$\Pr(A \cdot (B + C)) = \Pr((A \cdot B) + (A \cdot C))$$

$$\Pr(A + (B \cdot C)) = \Pr((A + B) \cdot (A + C))$$

Conditional rule:

$$\begin{aligned}\Pr(A \cdot B) &= \Pr(B \mid A) \cdot \Pr(A)\\ &= \Pr(A \mid B) \cdot \Pr(B)\end{aligned}$$

Mutually Exclusive Events

If events A and B are mutually exclusive (i.e., occurrence of one precludes the occurence of the other), then

$$\Pr(A + B) = \Pr(A) + \Pr(B)$$
$$\Pr(A \cdot B) = 0$$

Simple Quality Problems as Probability Problems

Many problems in the detection of quality deterioration can be studied as problems of determining the nature of a random event. This section shows how several problems that occur frequently in quality evaluation may be stated as probability problems. When properly formulated, the application of probability algebra enables the analyst to obtain the solutions.

Example 2.1

The specifications for a certain item require that it be at least 4.00 cm long. An operator produces 10 units during one hour, 3 of which are shorter than 4.00 cm. An inspector selects 2 units at random for measurement. What is the probability that the inspector will detect the production of short items?

Mathematically stated, the problem becomes: What is the probability that at least one of the 2 units inspected is short? Let

$$A = \text{event that first unit is short}$$
$$B = \text{event that second unit is short}$$

Then

$$\begin{aligned}
\text{event at least 1 unit is short} &= \text{(event that first unit is short) or} \\
&\quad\ \text{(event that first unit is regular size} \\
&\quad\ \text{and event that second unit is short)} \\
&= A + A^c \cdot B \mid A^c \\
\text{probability of detection} &= \Pr(A + A^c \cdot B \mid A^c) \\
&= \Pr(A) + \Pr(A^c \cdot B \mid A^c) && \text{Mutually exclusive events} \\
&= \Pr(A) + \Pr((B \mid A^c) \mid A^c) \cdot \Pr(A^c)) && \text{Conditional rule} \\
&= \Pr(A) + \Pr(B \mid A^c) \cdot \Pr(A^c) && (B \mid A^c) \mid A^c = B \mid A^c \\
&= \frac{3}{10} + \frac{3}{9} \cdot \frac{7}{10} \\
&= \frac{9 + 7}{30} = \frac{8}{15}
\end{aligned}$$

Example 2.2

Three separate safety valves are provided for a chemical reaction vessel. Probability that valve X will function properly is 0.9, that of valve Y is 0.8, and valve Z is 0.7. What is the probability that exactly two valves will function? (The valves function independently of each other.)

Let X, Y, Z = events that valve X, Y, and Z will function, respectively. Three possible ways in which exactly two valves will function are:

1. $X \cdot Y \cdot Z^c$
2. $X \cdot Y^c \cdot Z$
3. $X^c \cdot Y \cdot Z$

Probability two valves will function

$$\begin{aligned}
&= \Pr(X \cdot Y \cdot Z^c + X \cdot Y^c \cdot Z + X^c \cdot Y \cdot Z) \\
&= \Pr(X \cdot Y \cdot Z^c) + \Pr(X \cdot Y^c \cdot Z) + \Pr(X^c \cdot Y \cdot Z) \\
&= \Pr(X) \cdot \Pr(Y) \cdot \Pr(Z^c) \\
&\qquad + \Pr(X) \cdot \Pr(Y^c) \cdot \Pr(Z) \\
&\qquad\qquad + \Pr(X^c) \cdot \Pr(Y) \cdot \Pr(Z) \\
&= (0.9)(0.8)(0.3) + (0.9)(0.2)(0.7) + (0.1)(0.8)(0.7) \\
&= 0.398
\end{aligned}$$

EVENT SPACE, DISTRIBUTION, AND FREQUENCY

The random outcomes of any process or decision are all random events. The set of all these events is called the *event space*. For example, when a person enters a lottery only two possible events can occur, W = win and L = lose. The event space is the set of two events $\{W, L\}$. When a die is thrown, any one of the six sides may be up. If these are numbered 1 through 6, the event space would be the set of six events $\{1, 2, 3, 4, 5, 6\}$. A spindle turned on a lathe can have a diameter in the range 1.365 to 1.375 cm. In this case every real number in the range 1.365 to 1.375 represents a possible event. The event space is the set of all events corresponding to every real number in this range. This event space can be considered as *continuous* and *infinite*, whereas the event spaces for the throwing of a die or entering lottery are *discrete* and *finite*.

When every event in an event space is described by a number, it is called a *numerically valued event space*. In the examples stated, the lottery does not produce a numerically valued event space, whereas the spindle does. The outcomes of a numerically valued event space are considered to be different *values* of a *random variable*. In the case of the spindle, the random variable D = diameter is said to have values in the range 1.365 to 1.375, and each event in the event space is described when the random variable D has some stated numerical value. In the analysis of quality control problems it is necessary to deal exclusively with random variables rather than events. Although "probability distribution" is defined in this section for events only, the distributions of random variable will be used in subsequent sections and chapters.

Definition. The set of probabilities of all events in an event space is called the *probability distribution* for that event space.

Probability distribution is usually of interest when the event space is numerically valued. However, event spaces that are not numerically valued can also have probability distribution. For example, in the case of a lottery, the probability distribution may possibly be given as $P(W) = 0.0001$, $P(L) = 0.9999$. This is a complete probability distribution.

Definition. A function that assigns a value to the probability of every event in the event space is called a *probability function*.

Hence the probability function of the outcomes of throwing a die are

$$\Pr(x = k) = \frac{1}{6} \qquad \text{for } k = 1, 2, 3, 4, 5, \text{ or } 6$$

For continuous event spaces, many times there exists a function $f(\cdot)$, defined for all real numbers x that describe the event space, which satisfies the relation

$$\Pr(k \leq x \leq m) = \int_k^m f(x)\, dx$$

The function $f(\cdot)$ is called the *probability density function* (PDF) of the probability function $\Pr(\cdot)$. As all integrations of $f(\cdot)$ must be probabilities, the function $f(\cdot)$ must satisfy three requirements.

1. $f(x) \geq 0$ for all x in the event space.
2. $\int_{-\infty}^{\infty} f(x)\, dx = 1$.
3. $f(x) = 0$ for all x outside the event space.

Similarly, the probability function must also satisfy the requirements that

1. $\Pr(E_i) \geq 0$ for every event E_i in the event space.
2. $\Pr(U(E_i)) = 1$ where $U(E_i)$ is the set of all events in the event space.
3. $\Pr(E_j) = 0$ for every event E_j outside the event space.

These requirements can be used to test whether a function can qualify as either a probability function or a probability density function.

Example 2.3

Can the function $f(\cdot)$ given by equation (2.1) be a probability density function?

$$\begin{aligned} f(x) &= x - x^2 \qquad 0 \le x \le 2 \\ &= 0 \qquad \text{otherwise} \end{aligned} \tag{2.1}$$

The answer is no because $f(x)$ is negative for $x > 1$.

Example 2.4

Can the function $\Pr(\cdot)$ given by equation (2.2) be a probability function?

$$\begin{aligned} \Pr(x) &= \frac{x}{15} \qquad \text{for} \quad x = 1, 2, 3, 4, 5 \\ &= 0 \qquad \text{otherwise} \end{aligned} \tag{2.2}$$

Here the first and third conditions are satisfied. To test the second condition, the probability of $U(E_i)$ can be determined.

$$\begin{aligned} \Pr(U(E_i)) &= \Pr(x = 1) + \Pr(x = 2) + \Pr(x = 3) + \Pr(x = 4) + \Pr(x = 5) \\ &= \frac{1}{15} + \frac{2}{15} + \frac{3}{15} + \frac{4}{15} + \frac{5}{15} \\ &= 1 \end{aligned}$$

Hence this function can qualify as a probability function.

Definition. When a continuous event space consists of all the real numbers in the range from a minimum value k to a maximum value m, the integral

$$\int_k^t f(x)\, dx = F(t) \qquad k \le t \le m$$

is called the *cumulative probability function* at t. For a discrete event space the *cumulative probability function* is given by the sum

$$\sum_{j=k}^{t} \Pr(x = j)$$

EXPECTATIONS AND MOMENTS

The *expectation* or *expected value* of a function $h(x)$ of a random variable is defined as

$$\begin{aligned} E[h(x)] &= \int h(x)\, f(x)\, dx \qquad \text{if } x \text{ is continuous} \\ &= \sum h(x) \Pr(X = x) \qquad \text{if } x \text{ is discrete} \end{aligned} \tag{2.3}$$

The statement above implies that if x is a random variable having a probability density function $f(x)$ or $\Pr(X = x)$ and the values of the function $h(x)$ are observed over a long period of time, the values so observed, on average, will have a value given by equation (2.3).

Although an expectation can be defined and calculated for most functions, expectations of two types of functions are of interest in the study of quality control.

1. Expectation of powers of x such as x, x^2, x^3. These are called *moments* of x. The moment of most significance is the first moment or the expectation of x itself. This value, $E(x)$, is usually represented by the letter μ and referred to as the *mean* of the random variable x.

Definition

$$\text{mean} = E(x) = \mu_x \tag{2.4}$$

2. Expectations of the powers of the difference, $x - \mu$, such as $(x - \mu)$, $(x - \mu)^2$, $(x - \mu)^3$, and so on. These are called as *central moments.* The central moment of most significance is the *second central moment* or the expectation of $(x - \mu)^2$. This value, $E[(x - \mu)^2]$, is usually represented by the symbol σ^2 and referred to as the *variance* of the random variable x.

Definition

$$\text{variance} = E[(x - \mu)^2] = \sigma_x^2 \tag{2.5}$$

Mean and variance describe two of the salient characteristics of the distribution of any random data; mean is a measurement of the *central tendency* and variance is a measurement of the *variability*. An alternative measurement of the variability is the square root of the variance or σ. This measure is called the *standard deviation* of the random variable x.

It must be remembered that the moments as defined in this section are the moments for the entire probability density function, that is, the *population* all possible occurrences of all the feasible values of x.

Two important relations within expectations:

1. If k is a constant, then $E[k \cdot h(x)] = k \cdot E[h(x)]$.
2. If $h_1(x)$ and $h_2(y)$ are two functions of variables x and y, then $E[h_1(x) + h_2(y)] = E[h_1(x)] + E[h_2(y)]$.

Both the relations can be proven by expressing the expectation as integration.

These relations can be used to determine the means and variances of the sums of random variables.

$$\begin{aligned}\mu_{(x+y)} &= E(x + y) = E(x) + E(y) \\ &= \mu_x + \mu_y\end{aligned} \tag{2.6}$$

$$\begin{aligned}\mathrm{Var}_{(x+y)} &= E(x + y - \mu_x - \mu_y)^2 \\ &= E(x + y - \mu_x - \mu_y)^2 \\ &= E(x - \mu_x)^2 + E(y - \mu_y)^2 + 2E[(x - \mu_x)(y - \mu_y)] \\ &= \mathrm{Var}_x + \mathrm{Var}_y + 2\,\mathrm{Cov}_{(x,y)}\end{aligned} \tag{2.7}$$

$$\mathrm{Var}_{(k\cdot x)} = k^2\,\mathrm{Var}_x$$

$$\mu_{\overline{x}} = E\left(\frac{1}{n}\sum_{i=1}^{n} x_i\right) = \frac{1}{n}\sum_{i=1}^{n} E(x_i) = \frac{1}{n}\cdot n\mu_x = \mu_x \tag{2.8}$$

$$\begin{aligned}\mathrm{Var}_{\overline{x}} &= E[(\overline{x} - \mu_{\overline{x}})^2] \\ &= E\left[\frac{1}{n}\cdot\sum (x_i - \mu)^2\right] \\ &= \frac{1}{n^2}\sum E(x_i - \mu)^2 \\ &= \frac{1}{n^2}\sum \mathrm{Var}_x = \frac{1}{n^2}\cdot n\,\mathrm{Var}_x \\ &= \frac{1}{n}\mathrm{Var}_x\end{aligned} \tag{2.9}$$

SOME DISTRIBUTIONS USEFUL IN QC STUDIES

Hypergeometric Distribution

If an urn[1] contains N balls, of which n are red and the remainder $N - n$ are green, and a sample of y balls is selected from this urn, it is possible that some of these balls are red. The number x of red balls in the sample is a random variable that is discrete and has values within the range 0 and y.

Define events

E = selecting y balls out of N balls

E_1 = selecting x red balls out of n red balls

E_2 = selecting $y - x$ green balls out of $N - n$ green balls

[1] Statisticians always like to keep balls in an urn. A more common bowl or other container can be used instead without affecting the mathematical development in any manner.

Event E occurs whenever a sample of size y is selected. Joint event "E_1 and E_2" occurs when exactly x out of the y balls are red.

Probability of x

$$\begin{aligned} &= \Pr(x) \\ &= \frac{\text{number of ways in which } E_1 \text{ and } E_2 \text{ can occur}}{\text{number of ways in which } E \text{ can occur}} \qquad (2.10) \\ &= \frac{\binom{n}{x}\binom{N-n}{y-x}}{\binom{N}{y}} \end{aligned}$$

In the expression on the right hand side of equation 2.10 the symbol $\binom{p}{q}$ represents the number of combinations of p things taken q at a time. This number of combinations is calculated as

$$\binom{p}{q} = \frac{p!}{q!(p - q)!} \qquad (2.11)$$

where $p!$ is "p factorial" or the product of terms p, $p - 1$, $p - 2$ on up to 1.

$$\begin{aligned} \Pr(x) &= \frac{\binom{n}{x}\binom{N-n}{y-x}}{\binom{N}{y}} \\ &= \frac{n!(N - n)!y!\,(N - y)!}{x!(n - x)!(N - n - y + x)!(y - x)!N!} \end{aligned} \qquad (2.12)$$

Example 2.5

If the urn contains 10 balls out of which 4 are red and a sample of 3 balls is selected, what is the probability that exactly 1 of these will be a red ball?

Here $N = 10$, $n = 4$, $y = 3$, and $x = 1$.

$$\Pr(x) = \frac{\binom{n}{x}\binom{N-n}{y-x}}{\binom{N}{y}}$$

or

$$\begin{aligned} \Pr(1) &= \frac{\binom{4}{1}\binom{6}{2}}{\binom{10}{3}} = \frac{4!}{1!3!}\cdot\frac{6!}{2!4!}\cdot\frac{3!7!}{10!} \\ &= \frac{6!7!}{3!2!10!} = \frac{6 \times 5 \times 4}{2 \times 10 \times 9 \times 8} \\ &= \frac{1}{12} \end{aligned}$$

The hypergeometric distribution is the natural and basic distribution applicable for most of the situations encountered in quality control. When a consumer purchases large quantities of certain items, it might be uneconomical to inspect each and every one of these items. Inferences would have to be reached on the basis of *sampling inspection*. A sampling inspection problem can be illustrated as follows.

Example 2.6

A company purchases resistors in large quantities. The producer usually packs these in boxes of 1000 units. Specifications require that fewer than 1% be defective items. For test purposes the company may instruct the inspector to take a sample of 20 resistors from each box and test each once. If the product as shipped is 1% defective, what is the probability that the inspector will find no more than 1 defective?

$N = 1000$, $n = 10$ (1% of 1000), and $y = 20$.

$$\text{required probability}^2 = \Pr(0) + \Pr(1)$$

$$= \frac{\binom{10}{0}\binom{990}{20}}{\binom{1000}{20}} + \frac{\binom{10}{1}\binom{990}{19}}{\binom{1000}{20}}$$

$$= 0.97$$

If the inspector does actually find 2 or more defectives, he/she would be justified in concluding that the product is not 1% defective as specified but contains a higher percentage of defective items. The inspector can then reject the shipment.

The nature of this distribution, unfortunately, makes it almost impossible to create easily usable tables of values; each probability has to be calculated individually using the tedious long multiplications. For this reason the hypergeometric distribution is rarely used in quality control applications even though it is natural. In most situations an appropriate approximating distribution is used.

Binomial Distribution

If a series of N tests are conducted and the result of each test is either a "success" with a probability of α or a "failure" with a probability of $1 - \alpha$, and the results of these tests are independent of each other, what is the probability that exactly x of these tests will be "successes"?

Suppose that $N = 3$ and $x = 1$. If the three tests are viewed as a sequence, there are three separate ways in which only one shows a success. These three ways are FFS, FSF, and SFF. In general, exactly x successes out of N tests can occur in $\binom{N}{x}$ different ways.

Since the tests are independent, the probabilities of separate events can be multiplied to yield the probability of the joint event. Hence the probability of x successes and $N - x$ failures is given by

$$\alpha^x(1 - \alpha)^{N-x}$$

[2] This probability has been computed using a Poisson approximation, which is explained later in this chapter.

The probability that exactly x out of N tests will be successes is then given by

$$\Pr(x) = \binom{N}{x}\alpha^x(1 - \alpha)^{N-x} \tag{2.13}$$

This distribution is called *binomial distribution* since the probability of x is exactly the $(x + 1)^{\text{th}}$ term in the binomial expansion of

$$[(\alpha) + (1 - \alpha)]^N$$

As a corollary it can be seen that the sum of the probabilities for all possible values of x, from 0 to N, is 1.

$$\begin{aligned}\sum_{x=0}^{N} \Pr(x) &= \sum_{x=0}^{N} \binom{N}{x}\alpha^x(1 - \alpha)^{N-x} \\ &= [(\alpha) + (1 - \alpha)]^N \\ &= 1^N = 1\end{aligned}$$

Example 2.7

If a fair coin is tossed six times, what is the probability that a "head" will show on exactly two tosses?

Here $N = 6$ and $x = 2$. As the coin is fair, the probability of a head is 0.5 or $\alpha = 0.5$.

$$\begin{aligned}\Pr(2 \text{ heads}) &= \binom{N}{x}\alpha^x(1 - \alpha)^{N-x} \\ &= \binom{6}{2}(0.5^2)(0.5^4) \\ &= \frac{6!}{2!4!}\left(\frac{1}{2}\right)^6 \\ &= \frac{15}{64}\end{aligned}$$

Figure 2.1 shows the complete distribution of the random variable x, the number of heads out of six tosses of a fair coin.

The binomial distribution is encountered in quality control in two different ways. First, it is the natural distribution where one considers the quality of items being produced sequentially. Here each item produced is a new test. Second, it can be used as an approximation of the hypergeometric distribution. A limited number of bionomial distribution values has been tabulated. However, in most situations it is not too difficult to compute the values individually.

Poisson Distribution

Whenever the probability of a certain event occurring is very small in any specific instance, but the number of possible instances is exceedingly

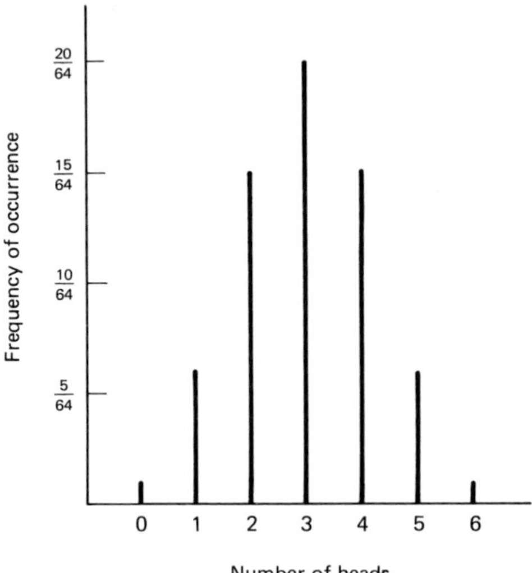

Figure 2.1 Number of heads out of six tosses of a fair coin.

large, the distribution of the occurrences is described by the Poisson distribution,

$$\Pr(x) = \frac{e^{-\lambda}\lambda^{x}}{x!} \tag{2.14}$$

where λ is a constant. A classic example of Poisson distribution has been the study of the number of soldiers in the Prussian army suffering from the kick of a mule. The probability of a mule kicking a soldier was very low, as mules, by nature, are very docile animals. On the other hand, the number of soldiers in the Prussian army was very large.

Cumulative probabilities under Poisson distribution are tabulated in Table A3.1. Approximate values can be found from the modified Thorndyke chart illustrated in Figure 2.2. This graph gives the probability of x or fewer "successes" in a sample of n when the average proportion of success is p. Under these conditions the parameter λ is given by

$$\lambda = n \cdot p$$

The Poisson distribution also finds application in quality control in two ways. First it gives a good approximation, under certain conditions, of the binomial distribution. The second application is illustrated by the following example.

Example 2.8

A supplier supplies a large quantity of item CXB-12, and in the past it has been noted that 1% of these items are defective. If a sample of 100 units of CXB-12 is inspected, what is the probability that exactly 3 will be found defective?

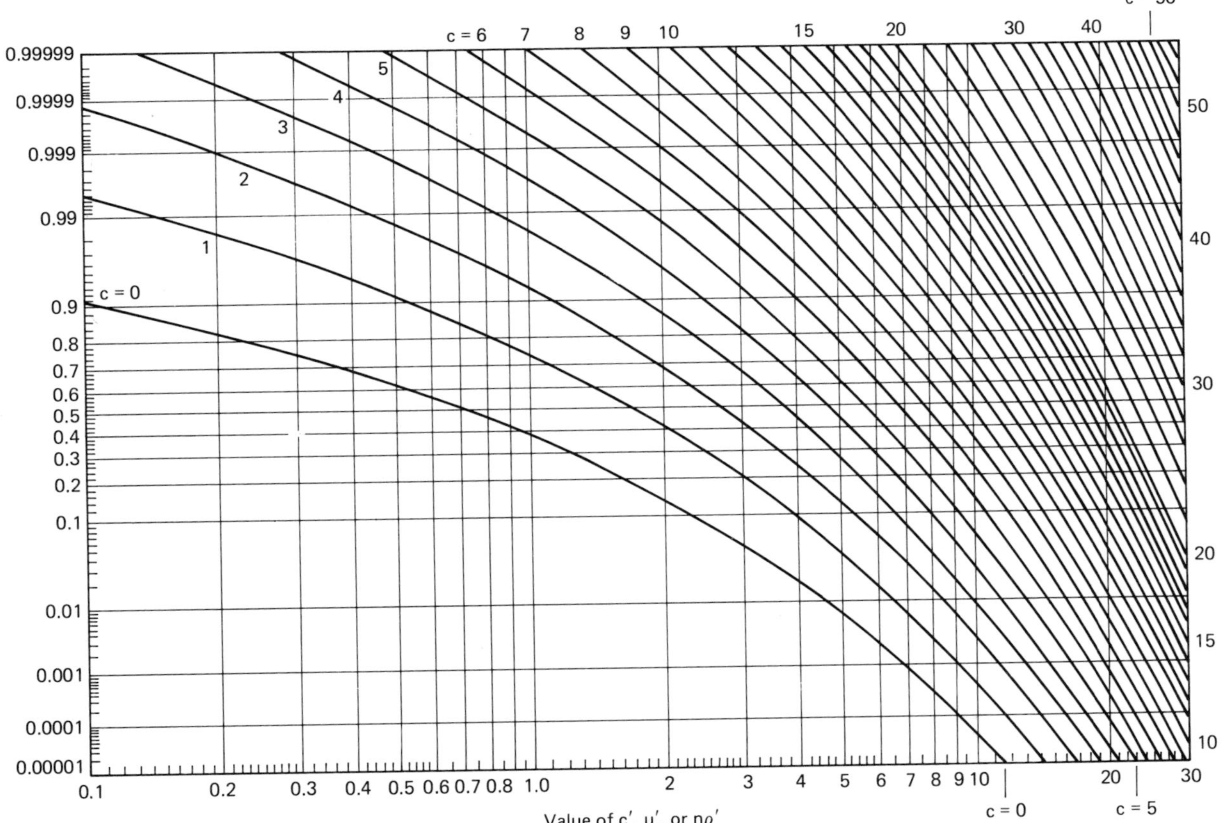

Figure 2.2 Thorndike chart showing cumulative probability curves for the Poisson distribution. [From H. F. Dodge and H. G. Romig, *Sampling Inspection Tables* (New York: John Wiley & Sons, Inc.). Reprinted with permission.]

$$\lambda = n \cdot p = 100 \times 1\% = 1.00$$

$$\Pr(3) = \frac{e^{-\lambda} \cdot \lambda^x}{x!}$$

$$= \frac{e^{-1} \cdot 1^3}{3!}$$

$$\approx 0.062$$

Normal Distribution

Early in the nineteenth century the German mathematician Carl Friedrich Gauss observed that a large class of natural phenomena exhibit a distribution characterized by the following:

1. The probability of occurrence increases as the variable approaches the mean value and decreases as it deviates from the mean value.
2. Occurrences above and below the mean are equally probable.
3. Although most deviations from the mean are small, extremely large deviations are possible but very, very rare.

A probability function with these characteristics appears as the bell-shaped function shown in Figure 2.3. Gauss showed this function to have the mathematical form

$$f(x) = \frac{1}{\sqrt{2\pi}\,\sigma} e^{-(x-\mu)^2/2\sigma^2} \tag{2.15}$$

where μ and σ are constants (parameters). Both e and π have the usual meaning from traditional mathematics (e = base of natural logarithms = 2.71828. π = ratio of circumference to diameter = 3.1416 . . .). This distribution is called the normal distribution, as it can *normally* be expected to occcur, or as Gaussian distribution, after its inventor.

In quality control studies normal distribution is useful in three ways. First, it can be expected to be present when some quality characteristics are measured for a product.[3] Second, under certain conditions it can become a handy approximation for the binomial distribution and an approximation, once removed, for hypergeometric distribution. Finally, it can be shown that the distribution of average characteristic values in large samples tends to follow the normal distribution regardless of the distribution of the data origin of the samples. (There are certain conditions that must be met. These are explained in a later section.)

[3] The frequency distribution of "diameter" shown as a histogram in Figure 2.7 is a normal distribution.

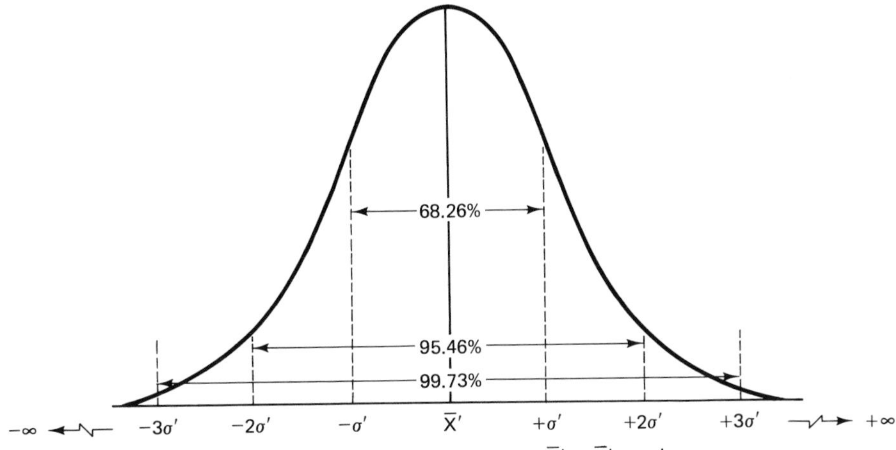

Area (percent of observations) from $\bar{X}'$ to $\bar{X}' + k\sigma'$

k	Percent of observations	k	Percent of observations	k	Percent of observations
0.0	0	1.4	41.92	2.8	49.74
0.1	3.98	1.5	43.32	2.9	49.81
0.2	7.93	1.6	44.52	3.0	49.86
0.3	11.79	1.7	45.54	3.1	49.90
0.4	15.54	1.8	46.41	3.2	49.93
0.5	19.15	1.9	47.13	3.3	49.95
0.6	22.57	2.0	47.73	3.4	49.96
0.7	25.80	2.1	48.21	3.5	49.97
0.8	28.81	2.2	48.61	3.6	49.98
0.9	31.59	2.3	48.93	3.7	49.98
1.0	34.13	2.4	49.18	3.8	49.99
1.1	36.43	2.5	49.38		
1.2	38.49	2.6	49.53		
1.3	40.32	2.7	49.63		

Figure 2.3 Normal or Gaussian density of function.

Because of its extensive usefulness, the normal distribution is extensively tabulated both as

$$f(x) = \frac{1}{\sqrt{2\pi}\,\sigma} e^{-(x-\mu)^2/2\sigma^2}$$

and as the cumulative function

$$\phi(x) = \int_{-\infty}^{x} f(x)\,dx$$

As a special case, if the mean $\mu = 0$ and the variance $\sigma^2 = 1$, then

$$f(x) = \frac{1}{\sqrt{2\pi}} e^{-x^2/2}$$

This variable x is said to have a *standard normal distribution*. The variable x is called a *standard normal variate*. It is easy to see that if a variable y has the probability density function

$$f(y) = \frac{1}{\sqrt{2\pi}\,\sigma} e^{-(y-\mu)^2/2\sigma^2}$$

then the variable $z = (y - \mu)/\sigma$ is a standard normal variate and

$$f(z) = \frac{1}{\sqrt{2\pi}} e^{-z^2/2}$$

The distribution function of z is a function only of the variable itself and does not involve any parameters. Tables A1 and A2 give the cumulative probability values and the density function of the standard normal variate. These values can be used to obtain the corresponding values for any variable with a normal distribution and specific values of mean and variance.

Example 2.9

A machine fills a jar with a measured amount of coffee. The weight of coffee in each jar has a normal distribution with a mean of 510 g and the standard deviation 4 g. What is the probability that a jar picked at random will contain less than 500 g of coffee?

Let y = weight of coffee in a jar. Then

$$f(y) = \frac{1}{\sqrt{2\pi}\cdot 4} e^{-(y-510)^2/2(4)^2}$$

The quantity

$$z = \frac{y - 510}{4}$$

will have standard normal distribution

$$f(z) = \frac{1}{\sqrt{2\pi}} e^{-z^2/2}$$

When y is 500, z is $(500 - 510)/4$ or -2.5. Therefore,

$$\Pr(y \le 500) = \Pr(z \le 2.5) = \int_{-\infty}^{2.5} f(z)\,dz$$

This quantity is tabulated in Table A1 as 0.0048. The probability that a jar picked at random will contain less than 500 g of coffee is 0.0048.

Exponential and Weibull Distributions

Normal, binomial, and Poisson distributions are used extensively in quality control studies. Two other distributions, the exponential and Weibull, are found useful when the quality of performance is measured in terms of the reliability of the product. The exponential distribution is given by

$$f(x) = \frac{1}{\theta} e^{-x/\theta} \qquad \text{for } x \geq 0$$

and

$$F(x) = 1 - e^{-x/\theta}$$

Figure 2.4 shows the form of exponential density functions. The Weibull distribution is given by

$$f(x) = \frac{\beta}{\alpha}\left(\frac{x - \gamma}{\alpha}\right)^{\beta - 1} \exp\left[-\left(\frac{x - \gamma}{\alpha}\right)^{\beta}\right] \qquad \text{for } x \geq \gamma$$

and

$$F(x) = 1 - \exp\left[-\left(\frac{x - \gamma}{\alpha}\right)^{\beta}\right]$$

The three parameters, α, β, and γ are called the *scale parameter, shape parameter,* and *location parameter*, respectively. Depending on the values of these parameters, the Weibull density function can adopt a wide variety of forms. These are shown in Chapter 19.

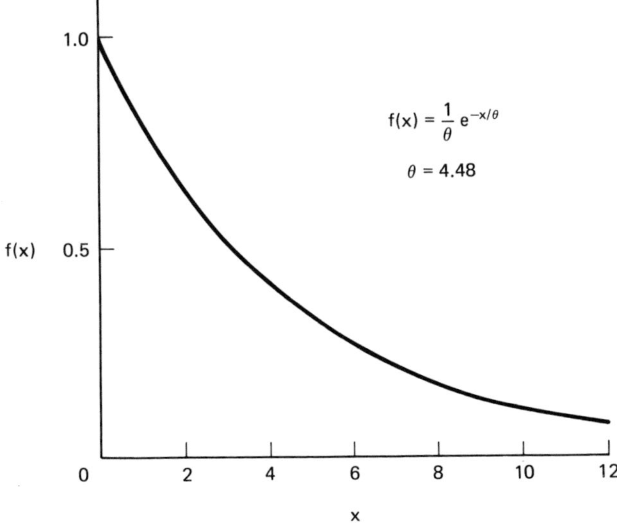

Figure 2.4 Exponential density function.

HIERARCHY OF APPROXIMATIONS

As indicated earlier, hypergeometric distribution is the natural and basic distribution applicable for almost all situations encountered in quality control. The population consisting of all the product either produced or purchased is finite, samples inspected are not too small, and each unit has a binary characteristic, either "satisfactory" or "not satisfactory." However, the use of hypergeometric distribution is not easy for practicing engineers. It is almost impossible to create readily available and usable tables. Each probability has to be calculated separately and involves the computations of several factorials. To avoid these complexities, a hierarchy of approximations is used. First hypergeometric distribution is approximated by Binomial distribution. Then binomial distribution is approximated by either Poisson distribution or normal distribution (Figure 2.5).

Approximation 1

Whenever the size of the sample y is extremely small in relation to N, that is, the population before sampling N is approximately equal to the population after sampling $N - y$ the hypergeometric probability function

$$\Pr(x) = \frac{\binom{n}{x}\binom{N-n}{y-x}}{\binom{N}{y}}$$

can be approximated by the binomial probability function

$$\Pr(x) = \binom{y}{x}\alpha^x(1 - \alpha)^{y-x}$$

where the parameter $\alpha = n/N$.

Although strictly speaking, the approximation can be used only when y is "extremely small" in relation to N, as a practical matter, the approximation can be successfully used whenever y is less than 10% of N.

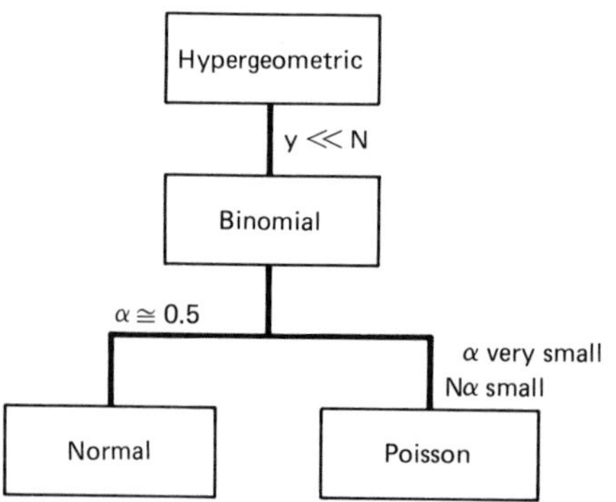

Figure 2.5 Hierarchy of approximations.

Approximation 2

Whenever the parameter α is approximately equal to 0.5, the binomial probability function

$$\Pr(x) = \binom{N}{x}\alpha^x(1 - \alpha)^{N-x}$$

can be approximated by the normal density function

$$f(x) = \frac{1}{\sqrt{2\pi}\sigma} \exp\left[-\frac{1}{2}\left(\frac{x - \mu}{\sigma}\right)^2\right]$$

where the parameters μ and σ^2 are equal to $N\alpha$ and $N\alpha(1 - \alpha)$, respectively.

Here again, although α should be approximately 0.5, the approximation can be used without excessive loss of accuracy over a very wide range of α from 0.1 up to 0.9.

Approximation 3

Whenever the parameter α is very small and/or $N\alpha$ is a small number, the binomial probability function

$$\Pr(x) = \binom{N}{x}\alpha^x(1 - \alpha)^{N-x}$$

can be approximated by Poisson probability function

$$\Pr(x) = \frac{e^{-x}\lambda^x}{x!}$$

where parameter $\lambda = N\alpha$.

As a matter of practical convenience, Poisson approximation to binomial is used in all the situations where normal approximation cannot be used.

Approximation 4: Central Limit Theorem

This last approximation does not approximately describe a hypergeometric distribution. It describes the approximate behavior of the probability distribution of the average value of a sample from any population. This approximation is usually stated as a theorem called the *central limit theorem*.

Theorem. If $x_1, x_2, \ldots, x_n$ are n samples taken from a population having a finite mean μ and a finite variance σ^2, and if $\bar{x}$ represents the average $(x_1 + x_2 + \cdots + x_n)/n$, the quantity

$$\xi = \frac{\bar{x} - \mu}{\sigma/\sqrt{n}}$$

has an approximate normal distribution with mean 0 and variance 1 when n is sufficiently large.

TABLE 2.1 Frequency Distribution

Interval	Designation	Frequency
0–0.15	1	0
0.15–0.25	2	13
0.25–0.35	3	91
0.35–0.45	4	226
0.45–0.55	5	316
0.55–0.65	6	t249
0.65–0.75	7	90
0.75–0.85	8	15
0.85–1.00	9	0

The term "n is sufficiently large" is rather vague. How large a value of n should be in order to yield a "reasonably good" approximation would depend on the probability distribution of the population of x. If the distribution of x is approximately bell-shaped and symmetric, the central limit theorem yields a reasonably good approximation for n as small as 4. Fortunately for application to quality control studies, most of the situations of manufactured items fall in this category. This implies that control procedures can be based on the behavior of the averages of small samples even though the distribution of the characteristic itself is not completely understood.

To demonstrate the central limit theorem, 1000 samples of 6 random numbers were selected from a uniform distribution having a range from 0 to

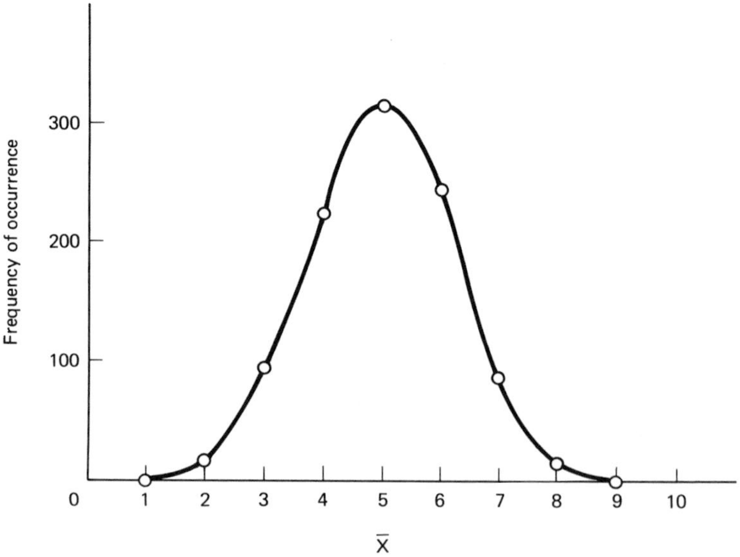

Figure 2.6 Illustration of the central limit theorem.

1 (Table 2.1). Figure 2.6 shows the frequency distribution of the average values for these 1000 samples.

PROBABILITY FUNCTIONS IN PRACTICE

In manufacturing processes many of the characteristic dimensions of the product are random variables. Only in rare instances is it feasible to obtain exact probability density functions for these variables using simple logic (as in the case of the throwing of a single die). Usually, it becomes necessary to obtain an estimate of the function by observing a small sample of actual production.

A typical example of how a probability density function can be estimated is described next. Table 2.2 is a listing of raw data obtained from the outside-diameter measurements of a sample of 100 machined parts. The reference to machined parts is used here to make the analysis more meaningful to the student. It is to be understood that the same principles will apply regardless of the commodity produced or whether measurement is in inches, centimeters, foot-pounds, kilograms per square centimeter, pH numbers, ohms of resistance, or whatever. The determining factor is whether or not the measurement is of the continuous type.

Not much can be inferred from data in this form. A frequency *array* of the data from high to low would be an improvement. Table 2.3 shows

TABLE 2.2 Raw Data Obtained from Measurement of 100 Machined Parts (+0.3800)

0.0024	0.0043	0.0024	0.0048	0.0022
0.0036	0.0066	0.0025	0.0033	0.0025
0.0029	0.0036	0.0032	0.0019	0.0044
0.0036	0.0031	0.0041	0.0035	0.0035
0.0040	0.0034	0.0048	0.0042	0.0041
0.0025	0.0020	0.0048	0.0041	0.0021
0.0019	0.0038	0.0037	0.0039	0.0051
0.0029	0.0034	0.0033	0.0035	0.0025
0.0058	0.0037	0.0032	0.0045	0.0041
0.0050	0.0037	0.0039	0.0031	0.0022
0.0041	0.0025	0.0056	0.0024	0.0033
0.0026	0.0025	0.0036	0.0046	0.0019
0.0043	0.0048	0.0053	0.0032	0.0034
0.0057	0.0024	0.0036	0.0019	0.0036
0.0007	0.0032	0.0044	0.0037	0.0027
0.0037	0.0021	0.0035	0.0011	0.0034
0.0037	0.0043	0.0021	0.0043	
0.0048	0.0040	0.0045	0.0028	
0.0045	0.0039	0.0028	0.0039	
0.0024	0.0025	0.0021	0.0041	
0.0030	0.0027	0.0029	0.0048	

TABLE 2.3 Frequency Array of Data (×10.000 and +0.3800) from Table 2.2

<table>
<tr><td>70</td><td></td><td>47</td><td></td><td>24</td><td>||||</td></tr>
<tr><td>69</td><td></td><td>46</td><td>|</td><td>23</td><td></td></tr>
<tr><td>68</td><td></td><td>45</td><td>|||</td><td>22</td><td>||</td></tr>
<tr><td>67</td><td></td><td>44</td><td>||</td><td>21</td><td>||||</td></tr>
<tr><td>66</td><td>|</td><td>43</td><td>||||</td><td>20</td><td>|</td></tr>
<tr><td>65</td><td></td><td>42</td><td>|</td><td>19</td><td>||||</td></tr>
<tr><td>64</td><td></td><td>41</td><td>𝍸 |</td><td>18</td><td></td></tr>
<tr><td>63</td><td></td><td>40</td><td>||</td><td>17</td><td></td></tr>
<tr><td>62</td><td></td><td>39</td><td>||||</td><td>16</td><td></td></tr>
<tr><td>61</td><td></td><td>38</td><td>|</td><td>15</td><td></td></tr>
<tr><td>60</td><td></td><td>37</td><td>𝍸 |</td><td>14</td><td></td></tr>
<tr><td>59</td><td></td><td>36</td><td>𝍸 |</td><td>13</td><td></td></tr>
<tr><td>58</td><td>|</td><td>35</td><td>||||</td><td>12</td><td></td></tr>
<tr><td>57</td><td>|</td><td>34</td><td>||||</td><td>11</td><td>|</td></tr>
<tr><td>56</td><td>|</td><td>33</td><td>|||</td><td>10</td><td></td></tr>
<tr><td>55</td><td></td><td>32</td><td>||||</td><td>9</td><td></td></tr>
<tr><td>54</td><td></td><td>31</td><td>||</td><td>8</td><td></td></tr>
<tr><td>53</td><td>|</td><td>30</td><td>|</td><td>7</td><td>|</td></tr>
<tr><td>52</td><td></td><td>29</td><td>|||</td><td>6</td><td></td></tr>
<tr><td>51</td><td>|</td><td>28</td><td>||</td><td>5</td><td></td></tr>
<tr><td>50</td><td>|</td><td>27</td><td>||</td><td>4</td><td></td></tr>
<tr><td>49</td><td></td><td>26</td><td>|</td><td>3</td><td></td></tr>
<tr><td>48</td><td>𝍸 |</td><td>25</td><td>𝍸 ||</td><td>2</td><td></td></tr>
</table>

this array from high to low with the occurrences of each measurement tallied as many times as it appears in the raw data.

The frequency array, although an improvement over the simple listing, is still not sufficient to yield an estimate of the probability density function. To obtain this estimate, proceed as follows.

1. Prepare a grouped frequency distribution tally sheet with the headings "class interval," "tally," f, d, fd, and $f(d)^2$ (see Table 2.4).
2. Determine the range of the data. For this example, the range $= 66 - 7 = 59$.
3. Divide the range found in step 2 by a number such that the answer lies between 10 and 20. (It is emphasized that this is a guide. Sometimes as few as 7 or as many as 30 groups are acceptable.) For the example here, $59/5 = 12$.
4. Select from the following preferred list the number nearest the number used. The number thus selected will represent the size of the class interval to be used. Preferred intervals are 1, 2, 3, 5, 7, 10, 15, or any higher multiple of 5. For the example in question, 5 is the interval used.

TABLE 2.4 **Grouped Frequency Distribution Tally Sheet for Example Data**

<table>
<tr><th>Class Interval</th><th>Tally</th><th>f</th><th>d</th><th>fd</th><th>fd^2</th></tr>
<tr><td>65–69</td><td>|</td><td>1</td><td>+7</td><td>+7</td><td>49</td></tr>
<tr><td>60–64</td><td></td><td>0</td><td>+6</td><td>+0</td><td>0</td></tr>
<tr><td>55–59</td><td>|||</td><td>3</td><td>+5</td><td>+15</td><td>75</td></tr>
<tr><td>50–54</td><td>|||</td><td>3</td><td>+4</td><td>+12</td><td>48</td></tr>
<tr><td>45–49</td><td>𝍸 𝍸</td><td>10</td><td>+3</td><td>+30</td><td>90</td></tr>
<tr><td>40–44</td><td>𝍸 𝍸 𝍸</td><td>15</td><td>+2</td><td>+30</td><td>60</td></tr>
<tr><td>35–39</td><td>𝍸 𝍸 𝍸 𝍸 |</td><td>21</td><td>+1</td><td>+21</td><td>21</td></tr>
<tr><td>30–34</td><td>𝍸 𝍸 𝍸</td><td>14</td><td>0</td><td>0</td><td>0</td></tr>
<tr><td>25–29</td><td>𝍸 𝍸 𝍸</td><td>15</td><td>−1</td><td>−15</td><td>15</td></tr>
<tr><td>20–24</td><td>𝍸 𝍸 ||</td><td>12</td><td>−2</td><td>−24</td><td>48</td></tr>
<tr><td>15–19</td><td>||||</td><td>4</td><td>−3</td><td>−12</td><td>36</td></tr>
<tr><td>10–14</td><td>|</td><td>1</td><td>−4</td><td>−4</td><td>16</td></tr>
<tr><td>5– 9</td><td>|</td><td>1</td><td>−5</td><td>−5</td><td>25</td></tr>
<tr><td></td><td></td><td>$\Sigma f = n = 100$</td><td></td><td>$\Sigma fd = +55$</td><td>$\Sigma fd^2 = 483$</td></tr>
</table>

5. Write the limits of each interval in descending order in the class interval column of the tally sheet. This, along with the other step, has already been done in Table 2.4. The limits of an interval are the highest and lowest values of the interval. Begin at the top with the highest interval and continue until the interval containing the lowest observation is included.
6. Tally the observations in the appropriate class interval. The array of Table 2.3 was used for illustration purposes only, so this tallying will be accomplished from the raw score data.
7. Count the tally marks for each interval and write the result in the f column.
8. Divide each number in column f by the total number of tallies, Σf. This is the estimated probability density function. This function is also called the frequency distribution function, as it indicates the relative frequency of occurrence in each interval.

GRAPHIC REPRESENTATION OF A FREQUENCY DISTRIBUTION

The visual picture of the density function can be refined in several ways. Figure 2.7 shows several types of graphic expression appropriately labeled. Figure 2.7a is a *histogram*; Figure 2.7b shows both an actual estimated *polygon*

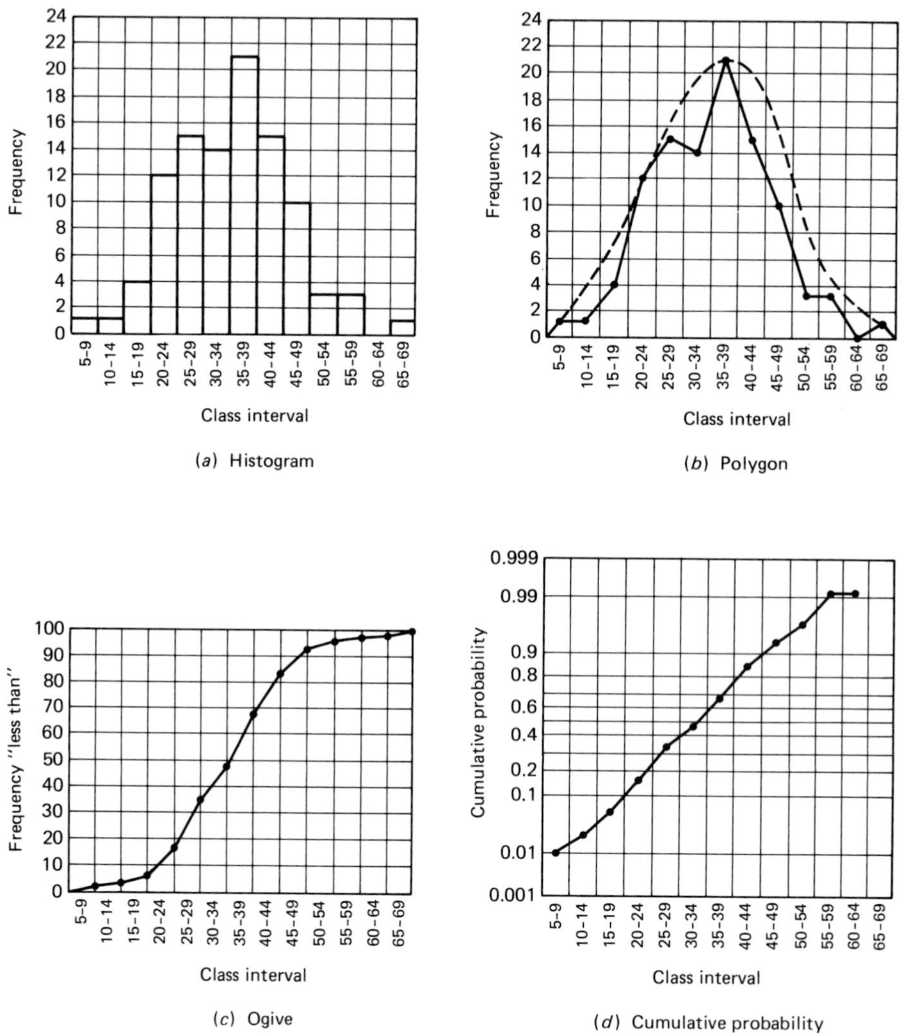

Figure 2.7 Graphs of example data.

and a smoothed "could possibly be" estimate of the function. Figure 2.7c shows the cumulative frequency of observations being in intervals below each class interval.

$$\text{cumulative probability} = \frac{\text{sum of frequencies less than interval upper limit}}{\text{number of observations}}$$

This type of curve is called an *ogive* or a "less than" curve. In Figure 2.7d, the vertical scale is adjusted so that the cumulative probability of a *normal* probability function will appear as a straight line. Distributions similar to normal, as in the case of this example, will *approximate* a straight line.

In graphing or constructing grouped frequency distributions, the student is cautioned to observe the interval limits carefully. Note that in the example the limits for each interval are 65–69, 60–64, 55–59, and so on. Properly, there is no overlap of the interval limits. Observe also that the interval labeled "69–65" includes all observations from 69.5 to 64.5. A check on the maintenance of proper interval size may be obtained by avoiding overlap and by successive subtraction of the interval size from the previous interval limit. Comparison to Table 2.4 will serve to clarify this.

ESTIMATES AND THEIR DISTRIBUTIONS

Parameters and Their Distributions

Both histograms and smoothed frequency polygons give a very rough estimate of the frequency function. To obtain better and more usable estimates of the frequency function or probability function, it becomes necessary to use more formal mathematical methods. Each frequency or probability function involves three types of elements:

1. Random variables
2. Known numbers or constants
3. Unknown elements that are not random variables

The last category of elements are called *parameters*. For example, the binomial probability function is given as

$$\Pr(x) = \binom{N}{x} \alpha^x (1 - \alpha)^{N-x}$$

Here x is the random variable, 1 is a known number, and both N and α are "unknown elements that are not random variables" or parameters. In this sense binomial is a two-parameter function. Similarly, Poisson is a one-parameter function with parameter λ.

The observed data can be used to obtain the estimates of these parameters if an assumption can be made about the type or form of the frequency function. Every time a random characteristic is observed, it is an event governed by the frequency distribution function of the random variable measuring the characteristic. The set of all possible events is called as the *population* or *universe*. ("Population" is not the same thing as the event space described earlier. Why?) The observed data form a subset of this population and are called a *sample*. The parameter values of any frequency of probability function relate to the population. The estimates of these values obtained from the sample are called *estimates, estimators,* or *sample parameters*. These are usually indicated by attaching the symbol ˆ. For example, $\hat{\phi}$ is one estimate of the unknown parameter ϕ. The estimation can be either in the form of *point estimation*, which gives a specific value for an estimate as $\hat{\alpha} = 0.3$, or *interval estimation*, as

$$0.25 \le \hat{\alpha} \le 0.40$$

Point Estimation

A random sample $x_1, x_2, \ldots, x_n$ is selected from a process with distribution function $f(x, \theta)$. A function h where

$$\hat{\theta} = h(x_1, x_2, x_3, \ldots, x_n)$$

is used to obtain an *estimate* $\hat{\theta}$ of the unknown parameter value θ. The function h is called as an *estimator function* or simply *estimator*. An example of an estimator is the sample average used to estimate the mean of a normal distribution:

$$x_i \sim N(\mu, \sigma^2)$$

$$\hat{\mu} = \frac{1}{n} \sum_{i=1}^{n} x_i$$

It should be noted that the estimate $\hat{\theta}$ is a function of the sample values $x_1, \ldots, x_n$. Consequently, $\hat{\theta}$ itself is a random variable and has a probability distribution of its own. For any given sample the value $\hat{\theta} - \theta$ can be called the *error of estimation*. Criteria for evaluating a function h as an estimator can be stated as follows:

1. The estimator should be unbiased or the expected value $E(\hat{\theta} - \theta)$ of the error should be zero.
2. The estimator should be consistent, or

$$\lim_{n \to \infty} E[(\hat{\theta} - \theta)^2] = 0$$

3. The variance of the estimator should be as small as possible.

Some Useful Estimator Functions

The parameters for the three distributions, normal, Poisson, and binomial, can be estimated from sampled observations using the estimator functions given below. In each case $x_1, x_2, \ldots, x_n$ represents a sample of observations.

Normal Distribution

Parameter μ is estimated by $\bar{x} = (1/n) \sum_{i=1}^{n} x_i$. This estimator is an unbiased, consistent, and minimum-variance estimator.

Parameter σ^2 is estimated by two estimator functions. The first function is $s^2 = (1/n) \sum (x_i - \bar{x})^2$ and the second is $\hat{\sigma}^2 = [1/(n-1)] \sum (x_i - \bar{x})^2$. Neither satisfies all three requirements for a good estimator. s^2 is biased and $\hat{\sigma}^2$ is not minimum variance. Both are used according to convenience.

Poisson Distribution

Parameter λ is estimated by

$$\frac{1}{\bar{x}} = \frac{n}{\sum_{i=1}^{n} x_i}$$

This estimator is unbiased, consistent, and minimum variance.

Binomial Distribution

In the case of binomial distribution, the observations x_i are each either 0 or 1. Parameter α is estimated by $\bar{x} = (1/n) \sum_{i=1}^{n} x_i$. The sample size n is taken as the parameter N.

Distributions of Functions of Sample Observations

The distributions of estimator functions as well as other functions of sample values become very valuable in analysis and estimation problems. Some of the more important distributions of functions of sample values are stated below. The development is omitted to save space.

1. If $x_1, x_2, \ldots, x_n$ is a sample from a normal population with mean μ and variance σ^2, the distribution of $\bar{x} = (1/n) \Sigma x_i$ is normal with mean μ and variance σ^2/n.
2. If $x_1, x_2, \ldots, x_n$ is a sample from a normal population with mean μ and variance σ^2, the function

$$u = \sum_{i=1}^{n} \left(\frac{x_i - \mu}{\sigma} \right)^2$$

has a chi-square distribution with n degrees of freedom. The chi-square density function is given by

$$f(u) = \frac{1}{[(n/2) - 1]!} \times \frac{1}{2^{n/2}} u^{(n/2)-1} e^{-(u/2)} \qquad \text{for all } u \geq 0$$

Chi-square distribution has been extensively tabulated and is described in Table A4.

3. If $x_1, x_2, \ldots, x_n$ is a sample from a normal population with mean μ and variance σ^2 and s^2 is an estimate of σ^2 obtained as

$$s^2 = \frac{\sum (x_i - \bar{x})^2}{n}$$

then the ratio $(x_i - \mu)/s$ follows a Student's t distribution with n degrees of freedom. The Student's density function is given by

$$h(t) = \frac{[(n - 1)/2]!}{\sqrt{n\pi}\,[(n - 2)/2]!} \times \frac{1}{[1 + (t^2/n)]^{(n+1)/2}} \tag{2.17}$$

For very large values of sample size n, Student's t density function approaches the form of a normal density function. Student's t distribution has been tabulated and shown in Table A5.

4. If u and v are two random variables distributed chi-square with n and k degrees of freedom, respectively, their ratio

$$F = \frac{u/n}{v/k} = \frac{ku}{nv}$$

follows the F distribution with n and k degrees of freedom. The F distribution is considerably complex, but has been tabulated for practical use and is given in Table A6.

HYPOTHESIS TESTING

A *hypothesis* is a statement about the statistical characteristics of a process or a physical thing. A hypothesis is a conjecture. For example, if a farmer observes the weights of several hogs on his farm he would know, with certainty, the actual average weight of the hogs that he observed. He can go a step further and conjecture that the average weight of all hogs on his farm is k kilograms. In the scientific process he would then have to test this hypothesis against an alternative hypothesis.

Null Hypothesis H_0: average weight $= k$ kilograms

Alternative hypothesis H_1: average weight $\neq k$ kilograms

It is important that the hypothesis to be tested, H_0, is stated before any test data are collected. If this caveat is not observed, the results are likely to be biased.

A *test* is a statistical procedure for determining the validity of a hypothesis. In a statistical test, the first step is to decide on the size of the sample to be observed. The observations from this sample are called *test data*. A function of the test data called a *test statistic* is used as the basis of the test. If the value of the test statistic falls outside a stipulated range, there are reasons to reject the hypothesis. If not, there are not sufficient grounds to reject the hypothesis. Acceptance of a hypothesis is very difficult using the statistical procedures by themselves. However, for most purposes "not rejecting a hypothesis" is a workable substitute for "accepting a hypothesis."

The essential steps in hypothesis testing are the following.

1. Formulate the null hypothesis. The farmer would consider his hog-fattening program a success if the average weight is 200 kg. If he suspects that the fattening program is not a success, he can test the hypothesis

   $$H_0: \mu = 200 \text{ kg}$$

   against an alternative

   $$H_1: \mu < 200 \text{ kg}$$

   A rejection of the null hypothesis would verify his suspicions. If the null hypothesis is not rejected, the farmer can rest assured that his fears are without basis.
2. Specify the maximum probability α that the test will reject the null hypothesis when it is true. This choice is usually based on a trade-off between costs of testing and those of an incorrect conclusion.
3. Define a test statistic and the probability distribution of this test statistic under the assumption that H_0 is true. This is the most important step. The validity of hypothesis testing depends largely on proper implementation of this step.

   As the farmer is interested in a hypothesis about the mean, an acceptable statistic would be $\bar{x}$, the average weight of hogs in a sample of n hogs. We may further assume that the weights of hogs are distributed normal with mean μ and variance σ^2.
4. Determine the rejection region. This is a region such that if H_0 is true, the probability of the observed value of test statistic occurring within this region is less than the value α selected in step 2. The exact location of this region would be determined by the distribution of the statistic chosen, in this case $\bar{x}$.
5. Conduct the test. The farmer would select n hogs at random from the herd, weigh each, and find the average weight $\bar{x}$.
6. Reach a conclusion. If the rejection region for average weight of 12 hogs was determined to be values under 187 kg (Figure 2.8), a conclusion can be reached by comparing the observed value with this rejection region. If the actual average weight of 12 hogs were 198 kg, the farmer does not have enough grounds to reject the null hypothesis. He should not feel that the hog-fattening program is a failure.

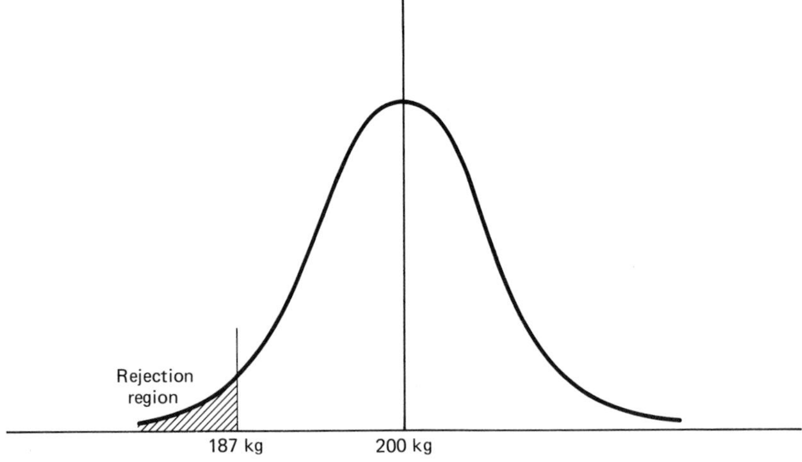

Figure 2.8 Rejection region for testing a hypothesis.

Example 2.10

This example demonstrates a one-sided test of a characteristic having a normal distribution with known variance. Consider a characteristic whose probability distribution is normal with mean μ and variance σ^2. It is assumed that the variance is known and we need to test the hypothesis

$$H_0: \mu = k$$

against an alternative hypothesis

$$H_1: \mu > k$$

Further, we want to limit the probability of not accepting H_0 when it is in fact true to some number α. A statistic that can be used for this test is $\bar{x}$, the average of a sample of n observations. If H_0 is true, the distribution of this statistic is also normal, with mean $\mu = k$ and variance σ^2/n. Next we define a critical region, that is, the region that would indicate a rejection of H_0. To limit the probability that a true hypothesis is rejected to α, the critical region R must satisfy the relation

$$\Pr(\bar{x} \in R \mid H_0 \text{ true}) = \alpha$$

Since we are not concerned with μ being smaller than k (the alternative hypothesis is $\mu > k$), the critical region is selected to be the region from some value x_c to infinity. Then

$$\Pr(\bar{x} > x_c \mid \mu = k) = \alpha$$

or

$$\Pr(\bar{x} < x_c \mid \mu = k) = \Phi\left(\frac{x_c - k}{\sigma/\sqrt{n}}\right)$$

$$= 1 - \alpha \tag{2.18a}$$

or

$$x_c = k + \phi_{1-\alpha} \frac{\sigma}{\sqrt{n}} \tag{2.18b}$$

TYPE I AND TYPE II ERRORS

It is not certain that the conclusion from a test would be identical to the actuality, which is usually unknown. In actuality the hypothesis H_0 may be "true" or "not true." The test conclusion could be to either "reject" or "not reject" the hypothesis. If the conclusion is to reject a hypothesis that is not true or not to reject a hypothesis that is true, there is no error. In other cases the conclusion of the test would be in error. There are two types of errors:

Type I error: the error of rejecting a true hypothesis
Type II error: the error of not rejecting a hypothesis that is not true

These four possibilities can be shown schematically as shown below (√ indicates no error in the conclusion).

		Conclusion	
		Do Not Reject	Reject
Actuality	H_0 True	√	Type I error
	H_0 Not True	Type II error	√

For any test the probabilities of making the two types of error are represented by the symbols α and β, respectively.

$$\Pr(\text{type I error}) = \alpha$$

$$\Pr(\text{type II error}) = \beta$$

Power of a Test

The objective of a test is to discriminate between two hypotheses, one true and the other not true. This objective can be reached by many different ways (i.e., through many different tests). For example, when testing a hypothesis about a characteristic having a normal distribution with known variance,

$$H_0\colon \mu = 3.0 \text{ cm}$$

against an alternative hypothesis,

$$H_1\colon \mu = 3.5 \text{ cm}$$

there can be several ways of designing a test with $\alpha = 0.05$. Although all these tests would have the same probability of giving a signal (i.e., rejecting H_0) when H_0 is true, the behavior of these tests would differ when the H_0 is not true (H_1 is true).

Example 2.11

Figure 2.9 shows two possible tests for testing the hypothesis with the same probability of type I error. The test in Figure 2.9a is a one-sided test where hypothesis H_0 is rejected whenever the observation is above the limit U_1. The test in Figure 2.9b is

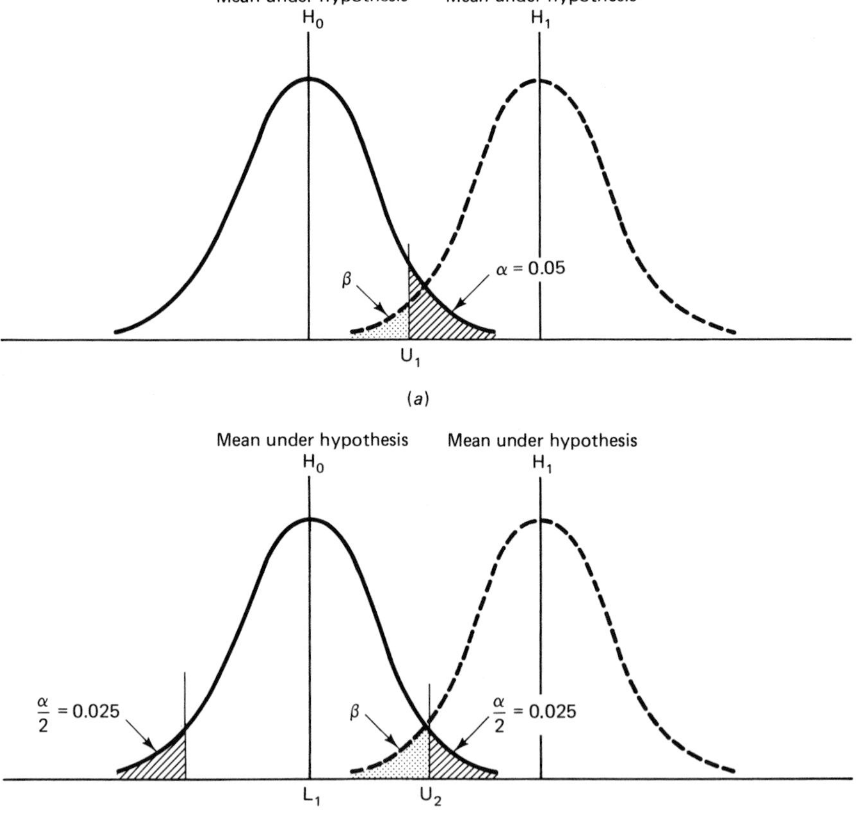

Figure 2.9 Two alternative tests for testing the hypothesis $H_0\colon \mu = 3.0$ against $H_1\colon \mu = 3.5$.

a two-sided test where hypothesis H_0 is rejected whenever the observation is either above the limit U_2 or under the limit L_1. Although the type I error is the same for both tests, the type II error is significantly different. Approximate values of these two errors are as follows:

Test	α	β
1	0.05	0.03
2	0.05	0.15

Obviously, test 1 is a better test than test 2. For a single sample, test 1 is better able than test 2 to detect an out-of-control situation. It is said that "test 1 is a more powerful test than test 2."

Definition. The quantity $1 - \beta$ is called the *power* of a test.

This definition is usually used for distinguishing between tests with the same level of significance (i.e., the same α). Further, for any test, β and consequently the power would depend on the difference between what constitutes an "in control" and an "out of control" state of the production process. In the example $\mu = 3.0$ in. denotes the "in control" state and $\mu = 3.5$ in. denotes the "out of control" state. The difference is 0.5 in. If this difference were to increase to 1.5 in. and the new alternative hypothesis becomes H_1: $\mu = 4.5$ in., any "out of control" condition would be detected with a higher probability. In other words, the power of a test will increase and β will decrease.

Definition. The operating characteristic curve (OC curve) of a test is a graph showing β as a function of the "difference" between the null and the alternative hypotheses (i.e., the designations of "in control" and "out of control" state; see Figure 2.10).

Definition. The power function of a test is a graph showing the power, $1 - \beta$, as a function of the "difference" (Figure 2.11).

In Example 2.11, test 1 was seen to be more powerful than test 2 when the common α was 0.05 and the difference was 0.5 in. If test 1 were more powerful than test 2 for any common α and for any difference, it would have been considered to be "uniformly more powerful" than test 2.

Definition. A test θ is called the *uniformly most powerful test* within a class of tests τ if (a) $\theta \in \tau$ and (b) θ is uniformly more powerful than any other test $\phi \in \tau$.

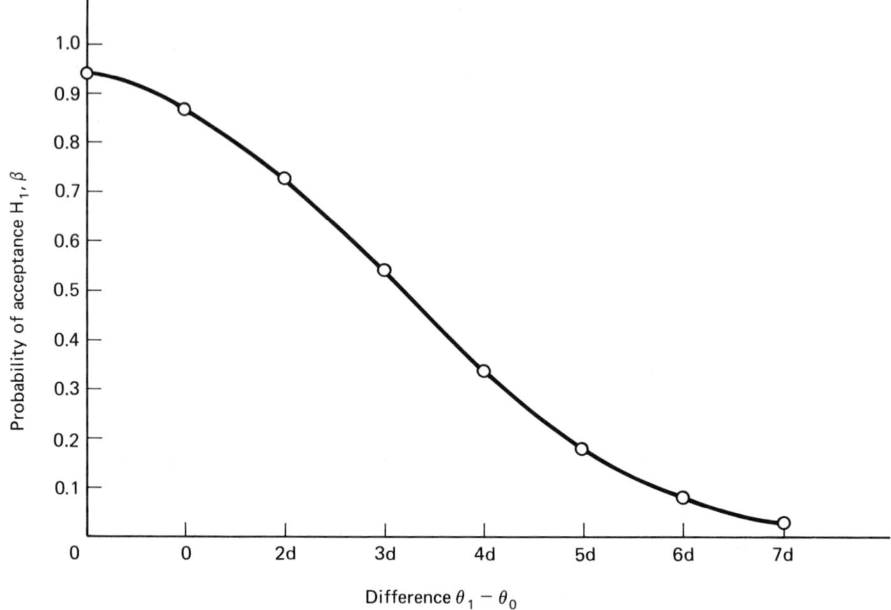

Figure 2.10 Operating characteristic curve of a test.

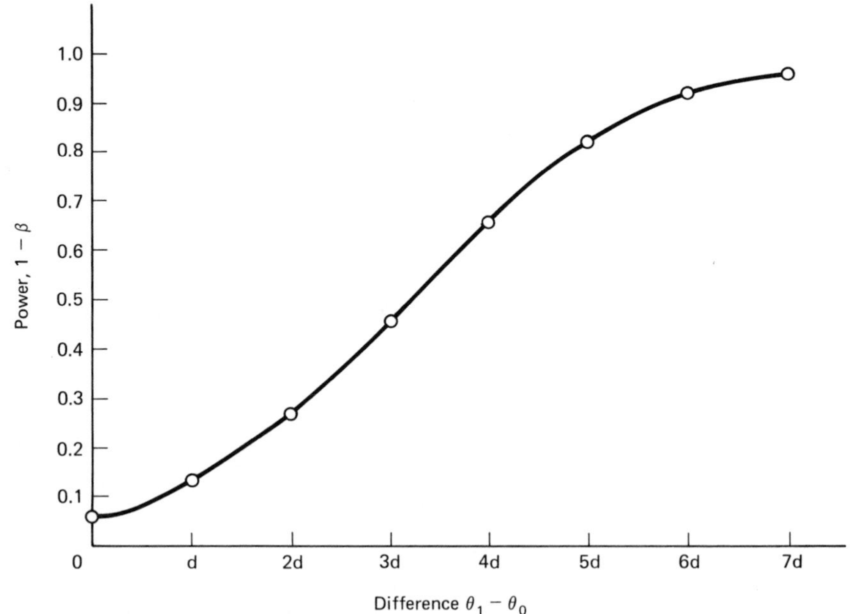

Figure 2.11 Power function of a test.

A test that is uniformly most powerful within a class is "optimal" in a weak sense. A stronger sense of optimality is obtained when the class τ is the class of all tests. An alternative way of defining optimality in a strong sense is based on the run-length distribution.

Definition. A test is *optimal in the strong sense* when its run length is stochastically smallest under specified conditions.

RUN LENGTH OF A MONITORING PROCESS

The monitoring of a production process would normally involve the following steps.

1. Observation and measurement of the characteristic for a sample size of $n, y_1, y_2, \ldots, y_n$
2. Computation of a control statistic D as a function of these observations:

$$D = \phi(y_1, y_2, \ldots, y_n)$$

3. Determination of the PDF of D, $h(D)$, when the process is in control
4. Determination of the significance level α and the selection of an acceptance region R such that

$$\Pr(D \in R) = 1 - \alpha$$

5. A signal whenever the control statistic D is outside the acceptance region R

These five steps can collectively be referred to as a *monitoring process*. A control chart is clearly a monitoring process. In the following discussion and in subsequent discussions, the term "monitoring process" will be used in this sense. It should not be confused with a *production process*, which produces product and is being monitored.

A *run* would be the number of samples observed until the first signal is given. When the first through $(j - 1)$th samples do not generate a signal but a signal is given by the jth sample, there is a run of length j. For a monitoring process the run length j would be a random variable and its probability distribution, $h(J) = \Pr[j \leq J]$, would be called a *run-length distribution*. The run-length distributions of monitoring processes, when the production process is in control, are of special interest.

Theorem. When the successive values of the control statistic are independent, the run-length distribution is a geometric distribution.

For a monitoring process the significance level α is specified and the distribution of the control statistic is predetermined. For any sample k,

$$\Pr(D_k \in R) = \alpha$$

Since the successive values $D_1, D_2, \ldots, D_j$ are independent, the probability of getting a signal on the jth sample, but not before that, is given by

$$\Pr(\text{run length} = j) = (1 - \alpha)^{j-1} \tag{2.19}$$

Hence the run-length distribution $h(J)$ is given by

$$\begin{aligned} h(J) &= \Pr(j \leq J) \\ &= \sum_{j=1}^{J} (1 - \alpha)^{j-1} \\ &= \alpha \frac{1 - (1 - \alpha)^J}{1 - (1 - \alpha)} \\ &= 1 - (1 - \alpha)^J \end{aligned} \tag{2.20}$$

Figure 2.12 shows the form of a geometric distribution.

Definition. A random variable U is said to be *stochastically larger* than a random variable V whenever for every t, $\Pr(U > t) \geq \Pr(V > t)$.

Let $G(t, \alpha)$ be a geometric distribution with argument t and parameter α:

$$G(t, \alpha) = 1 - (1 - \alpha)^t$$

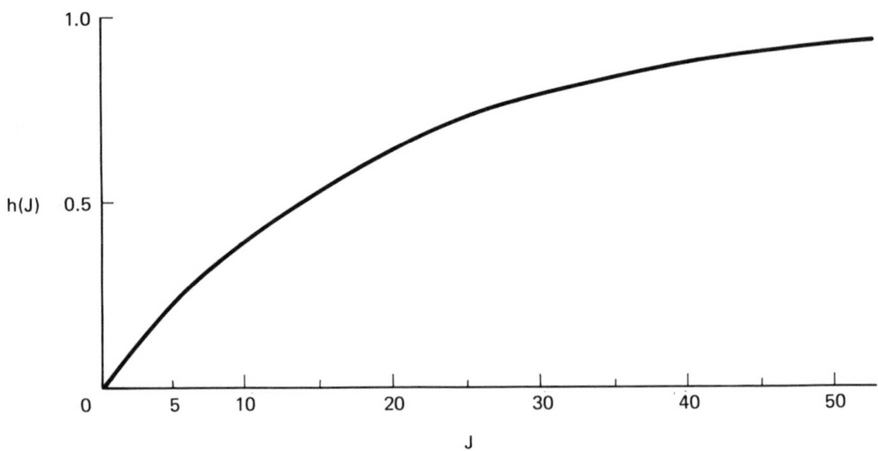

Figure 2.12 Run-length distribution (geometric) for $\alpha = 0.05$.

Theorem. The family of a geometric distribution $G(t, \alpha)$; $\alpha \in (0, 1)$ is stochastically decreasing in α.

Let U_1 and U_2 be two random variables having geometric distributions $G(t_1, \alpha_1)$ and $G(t_1, \alpha_2)$, and let $\alpha_1 < \alpha_2$.

$$\Pr(U_1 > t) = 1 - G(t_1, \alpha_1)$$

$$= (1 - \alpha_1)^t$$

$$\Pr(U_2 > t) = 1 - G(t, \alpha_2)$$

$$= (1 - \alpha_2)^t$$

Since $\alpha_1 < \alpha_2$,

$$(1 - \alpha_1) > (1 - \alpha_2)$$

and

$$(1 - \alpha_1)^t > (1 - \alpha_2)^t$$

or

$$\Pr(U_1 > t) > \Pr(U_2 > t)$$

This implies that U_1 is stochastically larger than U_2. This holds for all pairs α_i, α_j as long as both α_i and α_j are within the range 0–1.

Theorem. If a random variable U is stochastically larger than another random variable V, then

1. $E(U) \geq E(V)$.
2. $F_U(t) \leq F_V(t)$ for all t.

Part 1 is intuitive. For part 2 it is easy to see that

$$\Pr(U > t) \geq \Pr(V > t)$$

as U is stochastically larger.

$$1 - F_U(t) \geq 1 - F_V(t)$$

or

$$F_U(t) \leq F_V(t)$$

This relation is usually expressed as "the probability distribution of V is bounded from below by the probability distribution of U" or alternatively, as "the variable U has dominance over the variable V." The relation is shown in Figure 2.13.

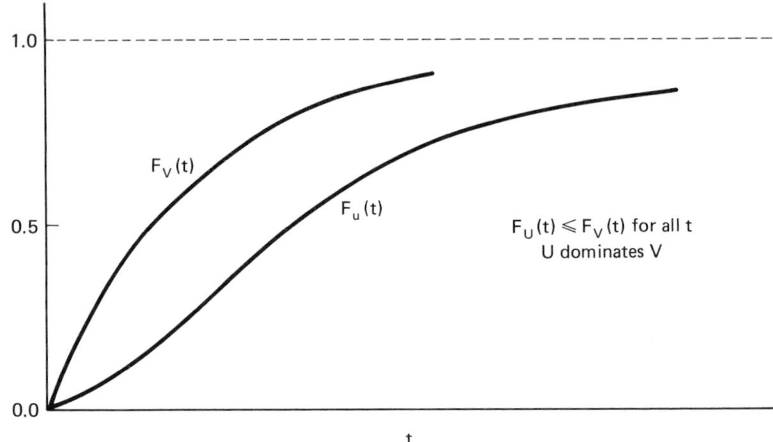

Figure 2.13 Statistical dominance.

DEGREES OF FREEDOM

In any problem involving n variables, some k of these variables may be dependent on the remaining $n - k$ variables. In such cases only $n - k$ variable values may be chosen freely. Once these are chosen, the t values of k dependent variables are fixed and cannot be freely chosen. One may think of degrees of freedom as (n − the number of fixed values), or alternatively, as the number of free choices.

Example 2.12

Let $X_1 + X_2 + X_3 = +10$. Any two of the variables X_1, X_2, or X_3 may be assigned values at will (two free choices = two degrees of freedom) but once two have taken on values, the value of the third variable is fixed. Letting

$$X_1 = -50 \qquad \text{and} \qquad X_3 = +35$$

the value of X_2 is fixed at +25 in order to have

$$X_1 + X_2 + X_3 = +10$$

This should be evident immediately, but practice with a few examples may be convincing. For another example, it will be recalled that the denominator of the formula for the root mean square was $(n - 1)$. The computation of the mean, $\overline{X}$, from the $(\Sigma X)/n$ is unbiased, but the computation of σ is biased unless the number of free choices is considered. Given three deviations of X from $\overline{X}$ and with

$$(X - \overline{X})_1 = 10 \qquad (X - \overline{X})_2 = 5$$

the value of $(X - \overline{X})_3$ is fixed at −15 because one of the properties of the mean, $\overline{X}$, is that the sum of the deviations about the mean must equal zero.

Thus

$$10 + 5 - 15 = 0$$

and degrees of freedom $= (n - 1) = 2$.

Table 2.5a gives the row and column sums of a small two-by-two table. The circled value in the table of Table 2.5b shows a freely assigned value. With this value assigned the other values in the table are fixed as shown. Thus, for this arrangement there is one degree of freedom; that is,

$$n - 3 = 4 - 3 = 1$$

degree of freedom.

TABLE 2.5 Illustration of df for Two-by-Two Table

(a)

			Total
			7
			3
Total	4	6	10 / 10

(b)

			Total
	(2)	5	7
	2	1	3
Total	4	6	10 / 10

In the four-by-four table of Table 2.6 the free assignment of nine values fixes the other seven values. The reader may wish to check this with a few hypothetical practice problems.

There are occasions when it is desired to compare the variability within columns to the variability between columns. This is what the $\overline{X}$ and R chart combination measures. The $\overline{X}$ chart measures the variability between sub-

TABLE 2.6 Illustration of df for Four-by-Four Table

		Column 1	2	3	4	Total
Row	I	+1	+1	+1	Fixed at 0	+3
	II	+2	−1	+1	Fixed at +1	+3
	III	−2	+2	+5	Fixed at −3	+2
	IV	Fixed at +3	Fixed at 0	Fixed at −2	Fixed at +3	+4
	Total	+4	+2	+1	+1	+12 / +12

group samples (columns), while the R chart measures the within-subgroup (column) variability. Using Table 2.6 for calculation of number of degrees of freedom, the between-column df can be calculated from either the totals of the columns or their averages. Working with the totals, it is seen that three column totals may be freely assigned, with the other fixed by those freely assigned and the table total. The within-column df is 12; that is, there are four columns each, of which can be assigned three freely chosen values

$$n - 4 = 16 - 4 = 12$$

By mentally omitting the column and row totals leaving only the table total, the df for the entire table is seen to be

$$n - 1 = 16 - 1 = 15$$

The df information for this type of analysis is given in Table 2.7. It will be noted that the between-column df plus within-column df equal the total df.

TABLE 2.7 Illustration of df for within-Column and between-Column Variation

Variation	df	Remark
Between columns	3	Number of totals minus one
Within columns	12	n minus number of columns
Total	15	$n - 1$

SIGNIFICANCE TESTS

When a hypothesis explicitly defines one specific value of parameters involved, it is referred to as a *simple hypothesis*. In a testing of H_0: $\theta = \theta_0$ against H_1: $\theta = \theta_1$, both the null and alternative hypotheses are simple hypotheses. A result of rejecting the null hypothesis would be in favor of the alternative hypothesis and would lead to increased belief in the alternative hypothesis.

If the alternative hypothesis had been H_1: $\theta < \theta_0$, it would not be a simple hypothesis. In this case the test would only be an attempt to answer the question: Is the observed value of θ significantly smaller than θ_0? Such tests can be called *significance tests*. A significance test can be called a *one-tailed test* if the rejection region is at only one extreme of the range of test statistic values; if the rejection region is at both extremes, the test can be called *two-tailed* (Figure 2.14).

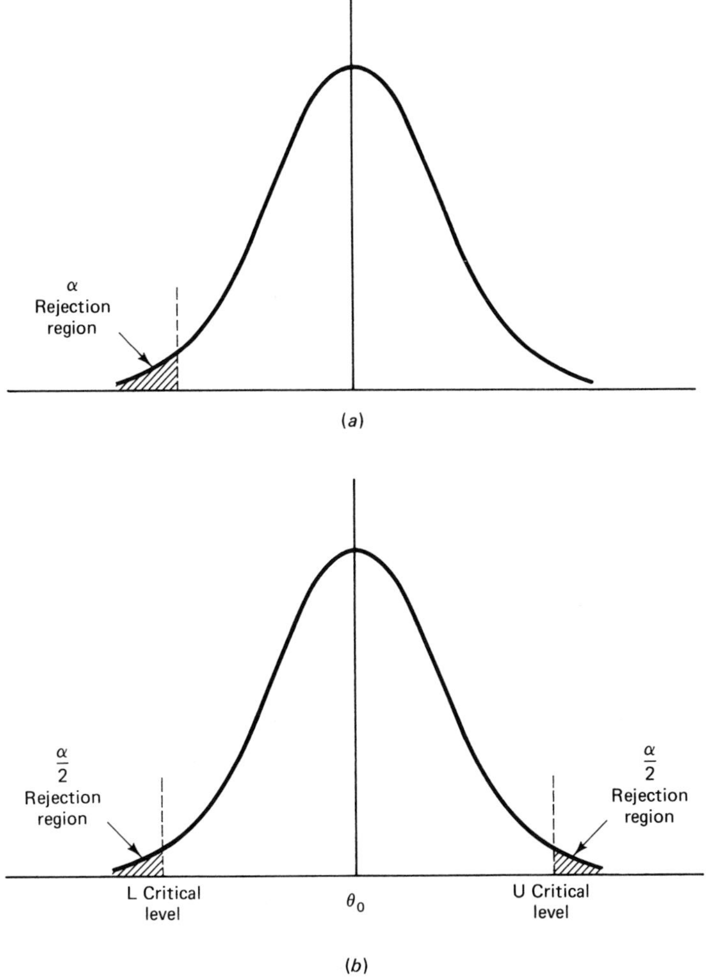

Figure 2.14 (a) One-tailed test (H_0: $\theta = \theta_0$, H_1: $\theta < \theta_0$); (b) Two-tailed test (H_0: $\theta = \theta_0$, H_1: $\theta \neq \theta_0$).

Significance tests are useful in evaluating proposed new methods, treatments, or projects. A project can be considered successful when the results are significantly better than the results before the project was undertaken. The probability of type I error or α is called the *significance level*. The null hypothesis states that there is no difference between the results before and after the proposed project. The test described in Example 2.13 is a significance test.

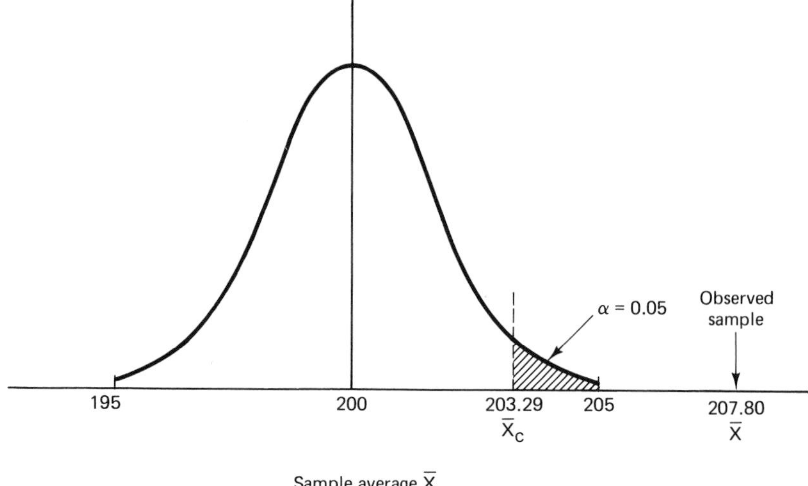

Figure 2.15 Test of significance in Example 2.13.

Example 2.13

From past experience a farmer knows that the average weight of hogs after a nine-month fattening program is 200 kg with a standard deviation of 10 kg. A new feed has arrived on the market and is being advertised as superior for fattening hogs. To verify the authenticity of this claim, the farmer runs a test by using the new feed for a sample of 25 hogs. Let $\bar{x}$ be the average weight of the hogs at the end of the fattening program.

Here the null hypothesis is H_0: $\mu = 200$ kg against the alternative H_1: $\mu > 200$ kg.

Let $\alpha = 0.05$. This is a one-sided test of a characteristic, weight of a hog, with known variance. The distribution of the test statistic $\bar{x}$ is approximately normal with mean 200 kg and standard deviation $10/\sqrt{25}$ or 2 kg. From Table A1 the 0.95 probability gives the critical level $\bar{x}_c$ as mean + 1.645 standard deviations.

$$\bar{x}_c = 200 + 1.645 \times 2$$
$$= 203.29 \text{ kg}$$

After the test the average weight is found to be 207.80 kg (Figure 2.15). The null hypothesis is rejected and it is concluded that the new feed has superior hog-fattening properties. It is customary to say that this conclusion is reached at the "5% level of significance."

The next two sections describe a number of variations of significance tests applicable in a variety of industrial situations.

SIGNIFICANCE TESTS FOR SAMPLE AVERAGES: t TESTS

Significance of a Sample Mean from a Standard: Variance Known

When the variability is known and is stable, only the average need be computed for the significance test.

Example 2.14

Assume that a sample of 10 from a process with known σ' of 5 yields an average Brinell hardness of 197. The specification standard for the average of a sample of 10 is 200. With 0.01 as the chosen significance level, is the null hypothesis accepted or rejected on the basis of these data?

When the variance is known, the distribution of the sample mean is normal and the distribution of t is standard normal. Standard normal is a special case of Student's t distribution with df $= \infty$.

$$t = \frac{(\overline{X} - \overline{X}')\sqrt{n}}{\sigma'}$$

For the sample data the expression becomes

$$t = \frac{(197 - 200)\sqrt{10}}{5} = 1.89$$

The one-tailed t value associated with a probability of 0.01 for df $= \infty$ is 2.326. Since the computed t value is less than the chosen significance level of t, the null hypothesis is not rejected. That is, it is assumed that 197 is not significantly different from 200.

Significance of a Sample Mean from Standard: Variability Unknown

When the variability is unknown and must be estimated from a sample, the sample estimate of variability must be corrected to yield an unbiased estimate of the population variability. The correctness factor is $\sqrt{n/(n - 1)}$, which is multiplied by σ estimated from the sample. The t expression reduces to

$$t = \frac{(\overline{X} - \overline{X})\sqrt{n - 1}}{\sigma'}$$

Assuming that the variability was unknown and had to be calculated from the data above (assume that $\sigma = 5$ also) the solution for t would yield

$$t = \frac{(197 - 200)\sqrt{9}}{5} = 1.80$$

As might be expected, a greater actual deviation is required for significance inference when the variability is unknown. Here also the null hypothesis is not rejected.

Significance of a Difference between Two Sample Means: Variances Known and Equal

For testing for the difference between two means, the distribution of $(\overline{X}_1 - \overline{X}_2)$ is used. Assuming X_1 and X_2 to be statistically independent,

$$\sigma(\overline{X}_1 - \overline{X}_2) = \sigma(\overline{X}_1 + \overline{X}_2) = \sqrt{(\sigma_{\overline{X}_1})^2 + (\sigma_{\overline{X}_2})^2}$$

$$\sigma(\overline{X}_1 - \overline{X}_2) = \sqrt{\frac{\sigma'^2}{n_1} + \frac{\sigma'^2}{n_2}} = \sigma \sqrt{\frac{1}{n_1} + \frac{1}{n_2}}$$

and the t expression reduces to

$$t = \frac{|\overline{X}_1 - \overline{X}_2|}{\sigma' \sqrt{\dfrac{1}{n_1} + \dfrac{1}{n_2}}}$$

Example 2.15

As an example of this test of significance, assume that lot identification of two lots has been lost and it is desired to test whether the two lots are significantly different in Brinell hardness. The chosen significance level is 0.05 because the cost of being wrong is small. The data obtained from samples taken from each lot are as follows:

	Lot 1	Lot 2
$\overline{X}$	300	296
n	80	120
σ	14	14

These data give the value of test statistic t as

$$t = \frac{|300 - 296|}{14 \sqrt{\dfrac{1}{80} + \dfrac{1}{120}}} = 2.0$$

The test here is for the difference between two means, so the two-tailed test must be used. The difference is not unidirectional as it is in the case of comparing a mean to a standard. For the two-tailed test, Table A5 is entered from the bottom. The t value for a significance level $= 0.05$ and df $= \infty$ is 1.96. Since the computed t is greater than the significant t ($2.0 > 1.96$), the null hypothesis is rejected. In other words, the inference is that the difference between the hardness of these two lots is significant.

Significance of a Difference between Two Sample Means: Equal but Unknown σ′

Quite often the variance is unknown. If the variance of two test populations is unknown but is believed to be the same (same processing method, materials, and so on), a weighted estimate can be obtained from the calculated σ values of each sample. This weighted estimate then replaces σ′ in the formula above. The weighted estimate

$$(\sigma_w) = \frac{n_1\sigma_1^2 + n_2\sigma_2^2}{n_1 + n_2 - 2}$$

Since there are two sample estimates of the variability, two degrees of freedom are lost. Also, the σ of the larger sample has a greater weight than that of the smaller. Using the $\overline{X}$ and n hardness data from the known σ′ example above, with $\sigma_1 = 17$ and $\sigma_2 = 12$, solution of the t formula yields

$$t = \frac{|\overline{X}_1 - \overline{X}_2|}{\sqrt{\dfrac{n_1\sigma_1^2 + n_2\sigma_2^2}{n_1 + n_2 - 2}\left(\dfrac{1}{n_1} + \dfrac{1}{n_2}\right)}}$$

$$= \frac{|300 - 296|}{\sqrt{\dfrac{(80)(17)^2 + (120)(12)^2}{80 + 120 - 2}\left(\dfrac{1}{80} + \dfrac{1}{120}\right)}} = 1.94$$

From Table A5 the two-tailed t value for 198 df is the same as ∞ df. Using the same significance level as that used in the previous example, 0.05, the table t value is 1.96. Since the calculated t is less than the table t ($1.94 < 1.96$) the null hypothesis is accepted at the 0.05 significance level. In other words, it is inferred that there is no significant difference between the average hardness of the two lots.

Significance of Difference between Sample Means: Data from Paired Specimens; Variance Unknown

Often it is impossible to exclude undesired variables that will affect the test results. One way of handling this is by randomizing the data in an experiment designed for analysis of variance. Another way is to minimize the effect of extraneous variables by pairing test specimens for treatment.

Example 2.16

In a weather test of corrosion resistance coatings, the effects of different intensities of sunlight, moisture, pressure, and so on, may be minimized by placing paired specimens in different atmospheres for testing. Assume that paired corrosion resistance tests of coating types I and II yielded the data shown in Table 2.8 (in hours before appearance of corrosion). On the basis of the evidence, is the difference between the two types of coatings significant?

The two additional columns are for the difference and squared difference between the paired specimens. To test for the significance between averages where the data are obtained from paired specimens, it is necessary to compare the average difference to the measure of variability of the average difference. The average difference is the average of the third column, which is equal to

$$\frac{\sum (\mathrm{I} - \mathrm{II})}{n} = \frac{6}{6} = 1.0$$

The measure of variability is the standard error of the average difference. Denoting $\overline{D}$ as the average difference and σ_D as the standard deviation of the difference yields the expression for t of $\overline{D}/\sigma_D$. σ_D is calculated from $\sigma_D \sqrt{n}$, where

$$\sigma_D = \sqrt{\frac{n \sum D^2 - (\sum D)^2}{n(n-1)}}$$

Thus

$$t = \frac{\overline{D}(\sqrt{n})}{\sqrt{\dfrac{n \sum D^2 - (\sum D)^2}{n(n-1)}}}$$

with df $= n - 1$. Only one degree of freedom is lost here because there is only one estimate, variability. For the example paired data,

$$t = \frac{(1)(\sqrt{6})}{\sqrt{\dfrac{6(26) - (6)^2}{6(5)}}} = 1.22$$

TABLE 2.8 Sampling Data

Paired Specimen	Type I	Type III	$D = \mathrm{I} - \mathrm{II}$	$D^2 = (\mathrm{I} - \mathrm{II})^2$
1	12	10	+2	4
2	8	9	−1	1
3	15	12	+3	9
4	11	13	−2	4
5	9	7	+2	4
6	17	15	+2	4
			$\sum D = 6$	$\sum D^2 = 26$

Even at a very liberal level of significance of 0.20 (one that is almost never used), the two-tailed table value of t is greater than the calculated t; that is, at $(n - 1) = \text{df} = 5$, t from Table A5 is 1.282, which is greater than 1.22. Thus the inference is that there is insufficient evidence for believing that there is significant difference between the two types of coatings. The null hypothesis is accepted.

t TESTS FOR SIGNIFICANCE OF DIFFERENCES INVOLVING PROPORTIONS

Significance of a Difference between a Proportion and a Standard (*n* Large)

In the event that tables of the binomial probabilities are not available, the normal curve can be used for testing the significance of a difference between a proportion and a standard based on the normal approximation to the binomial distribution.

Example 2.17

As an illustration, assume that the standard for a process has been set at $p' = 0.02$. A sample of 400 taken from a lot produced by the process shows a fraction defective, p, of 0.04. Is the difference between p and p' significant at the 0.5% level?

For testing deviation of a proportion from a standard, the test statistic t is

$$t = \frac{p - p'}{\sigma_p} = \frac{p - p'}{\sqrt{\dfrac{p'(1 - p')}{n}}}$$

with $\text{df} = \infty$. As such,

$$np' = 400(0.02) = 8 > 5$$

so the normal approximation is appropriate:

$$t = \frac{0.04 - 0.02}{\sqrt{\dfrac{0.02(1 - 0.02)}{400}}} = 2.86$$

The one-tailed 0.5% level of t for $\text{df} = \infty$ from Table A5 is 2.576. Since the computed $t = 2.86$ is greater than significant t of 2.576, the null hypothesis is rejected and the inference is that the difference is significant.

Sometimes it may be preferred to calculate the above in terms of *numbers* of defectives rather than fraction defective. Then, using the same data and conditions,

$$t = \frac{np - np'}{\sqrt{np'(1 - p')}} = \frac{16 - 8}{\sqrt{8(1 - 0.02)}} = 2.86$$

as would be expected.

Significance of a Difference between a Proportion and a Standard (n large and p' Small)

As the quantity np' gets smaller, the binomial begins to approximate the Poisson.

Example 2.17 Continued

Given the same data as in Example 2.17 except that $n = 50$ instead of 400, then from Table A3.1, when the true number defective (np') is 1.0, the probability of an np of 2 or greater is 0.08. (This is obtained by subtracting the value in the $c = 2$ column of Table A3.1 from 1000 and converting to a decimal fraction.) Thus in this case the null hypothesis is accepted because the level of significance of 0.005 (0.5%) is far in excess of the 0.08 obtained from Table A3.1. This would be expected, as n is much smaller than it was for the previous illustration.

Significance of a Difference between Number of Defects in a Sample and the Number Specified by a Standard

Table A3.1 can also be used for significance testing when it can be assumed the Poisson is the underlying distribution. The distributions of number of defects and defects per unit follow the Poisson law. Hence this law may be used for testing for the significance of sample deviations from a standard number of defects.

Example 2.18

The standard number of defects per unit for paint flaws on a refrigerator door is set at 0.5. A sample of 10 is selected from the process at random. This sample yields a total of 10 paint flaws. Is this occurrence of defects sufficient to reject the null hypothesis at the 5% level? In the solution, 0.5 is located in the c' column of Table A3.1. This value is actually u'; that is, c'/n where $n = 1$. The value of u from the sample of 10 is $c/n = 10/10 = 1$. The table value for $c' = 0.5$ and $c = 1$ is 910. This value is subtracted from 1000 and converted to the probability expression of 0.09. Since 0.09 is greater than the significance value of 0.05, the null hypothesis is accepted and no significance of a difference is inferred. This test is widely used as a basis of acceptance procedures for quality control.

Significance of a Difference between Two Proportions (n_1 and n_2 Large and $np' > 5$ in Each Sample)

The standard error of the difference (or sum) considered previously in this chapter for tests of the differences between means may also be used for testing for the significance of a difference between two proportions when normal approximation is appropriate. The test statistic is

$$t = \frac{p_1 - p_2}{\sqrt{\frac{n_1p_1 + n_2p_2}{n_1 + n_2}\left(1 - \frac{n_1p_1 + n_2p_2}{n_1 + n_2}\right)\left(\frac{1}{n_1} + \frac{1}{n_2}\right)}}$$

with df $= \infty$. The denominator is the weighted estimate of $\sigma_{p_1 - p_2}$ making the formula look more complicated than it really is.

Example 2.19

A lot has been sampled by both the producer and the consumer. The producer took a sample of 200 from the lot and found eight defective units. The consumer also selected a sample from the same lot and found that in a sample of 300 there were 24 defective units. Is there a difference between their results at the 0.05 level of significance? Designating the result p_1 as that of the producer and p_2 that of the consumer and substituting the values into the equation yields

$$t = \frac{0.08 - 0.04}{\sqrt{\frac{8 + 24}{200 + 300}\left(1 - \frac{8 + 24}{200 + 300}\right)\left(\frac{1}{200} + \frac{1}{300}\right)}} = 1.79$$

The two-tailed t value for significance of 0.05 from Table A5 is 1.96. 1.96 is greater than 1.79, so the null hypothesis is accepted. The inference is that there is no significance between the two proportions at the 5% level of significance.

TESTS FOR THE SIGNIFICANCE OF DIFFERENCES BETWEEN VARIANCES

All the significance tests considered prior to this point have involved averages. It may be that the deviation of a sample dispersion measure is significantly different from a standard dispersion measure. For instance, a golfer may average 75 strokes for 18 holes with a usual range of ± 5. Suppose that he changes his swing to reduce the range to ± 3 while still averaging 75. Alternatively, a change in swing might increase the range to ± 7 while still averaging 75. In the former case, the question is whether the change in swing reduced the variability significantly; in the latter, whether it increased the variability significantly. The average has not changed, so it is of no importance here. A test known as the chi-square (χ^2) is used for testing this type of difference.

Significance of a Difference between Sample Variance and a Standard

When the average is assumed not to have changed, the test for variance involves the ratio

$$\frac{n\sigma^2}{\sigma'^2}$$

where n is the sample size, σ'^2 is the standard variance, and σ^2 is the sample variance.

Example 2.20

In a heat-treating process the strength of the item is measured by periodic samples of three tests each. The range of values in the sample is used to obtain an estimate of standard deviation σ' as

$$\hat{\sigma}' = \frac{\overline{R}}{d_2}$$

where $\overline{R}$ is the average range and d_2 is a constant given in Table A7. This process has a long recorded history and $\overline{R}$ has stayed fairly constant at 6000 psi. The estimate for standard deviation is

$$\hat{\sigma}' = \frac{6000}{1.693} = 3544 \text{ psi}$$

A new heat-treating process being tested gave an estimated value for standard deviation σ of 1750 psi based on six samples of three tests. Is the new process significantly better than the existing process at the 1% level?

When (1) the underlying distribution is normal or is approximately normal based on the central limit theorem, and (2) the mean of this distribution is assumed not to have changed, the test statistic

$$u = \sum_{1}^{n} \left(\frac{x_i - \mu}{\sigma'} \right)^2$$

has a chi-square distribution with n degrees of freedom. Using $\overline{X}$ as an estimate of μ, the degrees of freedom is $n - 1$. The statistic u reduces to

$$u = \frac{n\sigma^2}{\sigma'^2}$$

To test the hypothesis H_0: $\sigma^2 = \sigma'^2$ against the alternative H_1: $\sigma^2 < \sigma'^2$, the lower tail 1% level or the level for $\chi^2_{0.99}$ for a chi-square distribution with 5 degrees of freedom can be used. From Table A4, $\chi^2_{0.99}$ for df $= 5$ is 0.554.

For the observed sample

$$u = \frac{6(1750)^2}{(3544)^2} = 1.46$$

As the observed value u is larger than $\chi^2_{0.99}$, the null hypothesis cannot be rejected. The inference is that the improvement of the process is not significant.

Significance of Difference between Sample Variances from Two Samples

Consider two samples from a normal population, with sample sizes n and k and sample variances σ_1^2 and σ_2^2, respectively. Then the statistics

$$u = \frac{n\sigma_1^2}{\sigma'^2}$$

and

$$\nu = \frac{k\sigma_2^2}{\sigma'^2}$$

would be distributed chi-square with $n - 1$ and $k - 1$ degrees of freedom, respectively. The ratio of these chi-square-distributed random variables is expressed as

$$\frac{(k - 1)u}{(n - 1)\nu} = (k - 1)n \cdot \frac{\sigma_1^2}{\sigma'^2} \cdot \frac{1}{n - 1} \cdot \frac{\sigma'^2}{k\sigma_2^2}$$

$$= \frac{(k - 1)n}{(n - 1)k} \cdot \frac{\sigma_1^2}{\sigma_2^2}$$

This ratio would be distributed F with $n - 1$ and $k - 1$ degrees of freedom, respectively. The ratio, incidentally, is approximately equal to the ratio of sample variances. As a matter of convention the larger sample variance is always designated as σ_1^2 (numerator) and the smaller as σ_2^2 (denominator).

Example 2.21

Assume that it is desired to test for the difference between two sample variances at the 0.01 level of significance.[4] The reason for the test is to see whether the variability of the first shift is significantly different from that of the second on an operation where it is necessary to control the variability of yield strength. The first shift had higher production, so a larger sample was selected. The two tests yielded the following data:

	Test 1 (First Shift)	Test 2 (Second Shift)
Sample size, n	9	5
Variance, σ^2	9,000,000 psi^2	1,000,000 psi^2

In applying the F test, the greater variance is always the numerator and the smaller the denominator. The value of F for this example may be shown conceptually by Figure 2.16. $F = 9$ is *not* significant at the 0.01 level since the critical F value associated with this level is 14.80. Had the 0.05 level been chosen, it would have been significant since the critical F value associated with the 0.05 level is 6.04. The F table, Table A6, is entered with $df_1 = 8$ at the top and $df_2 = 4$ from the side. The critical values of F at 0.05 and 0.01 levels of probability are 6.04 and 14.8, respectively.

[4] The variance (square of the standard deviation) of each sample has been computed from the formula

$$\sigma^2 = \frac{\Sigma (X - \overline{X})^2}{n - 1}$$

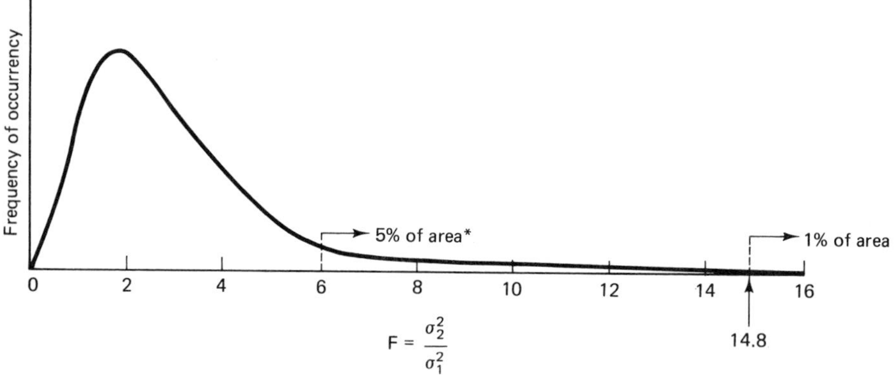

Figure 2.16 Approximate distribution of F statistic for (4, 8) degrees of freedom.

PROBLEMS

2.1. An urn contains 20 red balls and 40 black balls. A second urn contains 30 green balls and 30 black balls.

(a) When a ball is picked from the first urn, what is the probability that it is a red ball?

(b) When a ball is picked from the second urn, what is the probability that it is a green ball?

(c) When one ball is picked from each urn, what is the probability of picking one red ball and one green ball?

(d) When one ball is picked from each urn, what is the probability of picking either a red ball or a green ball or both?

(e) When one ball is picked from each urn, what is the probability of picking exactly one black ball?

(f) When one ball is picked from each urn, what is the probability of picking at least one black ball?

2.2. Mario is considering a coast-to-coast trip in his new car. The probability of a new tire surviving the whole trip is 0.8. What is the probability of at least one tire failing during the trip?

2.3. In a single throw of a six-sided die, what is the probability of coming up with the number 5? When two dice are used, what is the probability of coming up with a total of 8?

2.4. It is said that a famous Hollywood director used three cameras to shoot some of his complicated scenes. The probability of a camera recording such a scene is ⅓. What is the probability of a complicated scene taking place without being recorded?

2.5. A deck of cards consists of 52 cards (4 suits of 13 cards each). Cardplayer C picks a card at random. Then cardplayer D picks a card at random. What is the probability that both cards come from the same suit?

2.6. A probability density function is given as $f(x) = Ax - Bx^2$ for the range $0 \leq x \leq 2$. Determine the values of A and B.

2.7. If x, the life of an automobile tire in miles of travel, is a continuous random variable with a probability density function

$$f(x) = \frac{1}{30{,}000} e^{-x/30{,}000} \qquad 0 < x < 0$$
$$= 0 \qquad \text{otherwise}$$

(a) What is the probability of the tire surviving the first 20,000 miles?
(b) Assuming that it has survived the first 20,000 miles, what is the probability of the tire surviving another 5000 miles?

2.8. Let x be a discrete random variable with the probability function

$$\Pr(x) = a - \frac{1}{2x} \qquad x = 1, 2, 3, 4$$
$$= 0 \qquad \text{otherwise}$$

(a) Determine the value a so as to make the function above a legitimate probability function.
(b) Using the value of a, find $\Pr(x \le 3)$.

2.9. Prove the following using the definition of the expectation of a function $h(x)$ for both continuous and discrete cases.
(a) $E(cx) = cE(x)$
(b) $E(cx + d) = cE(x) + d$
(c) $E(cx + dy) = cE(x) + dE(y)$
where x and y are random variables and c and d are constants.

2.10. Prove that $\text{Var}(x) = E(x^2) - [E(x)]^2$.

2.11. For the variable x in Problem 2.8, determine $E(x)$, $E(x^2)$, and $\text{Var}(x)$.

2.12. For a six-sided die, if x represents the number showing up when the die is cast, what is the expected value of x?

2.13. In a casino card game each player receives a card after placing a bet of $25. If the next card revealed by the dealer is of the same suit, the player wins $60 (in addition to getting back his bet). If the next card is of a different suit, the player loses his bet. In the long run, who would profit from this game, the casino or the player?

2.14. A box contains 6 green marbles and 3 blue marbles. Four marbles are chosen at random. What is the probability that 2 out of these 4 marbles are blue?

2.15. A service station has received 100 units of spare parts, 20 of which are suspected to be defective. If a random sample of 5 units is taken from the box, what is the probability of exactly 1 item being defective in the sample?

2.16. A TV station wanted to interview some delegates attending a party convention. Out of the total delegates, it is assumed that 40% are conservatives, 30% moderates, and the remaining, liberals. If 4 persons are picked at random for the interviews, what is the probability that more than 1 is a conservative?

2.17. A fair die is thrown 5 times. What is the probability that "6" will show up exactly 2 times?

2.18. In a trial, let the probability of success be p. Show that, in a sequence of trials, the probability of scoring first success exactly on the nth trial is

$$p(1 - p)^{n-1}$$

This is known as *geometric distribution.*

2.19. Suppose that the number of accidents occurring on a highway during one day is a Poisson random variable with $\lambda = 2$. Calculate:

(a) The probability that exactly 2 accidents occur on a given day.

(b) The probability that more than 1 accident occurs on a given day.

2.20. The number of customers arriving at a checkout counter is a Poisson random variable with mean rate of 6 per hour. What is the probability that during a given hour not more than 2 persons arrive at the counter?

2.21. In a certain production unit, 8% of the tools manufactured turn out to be defective.

(a) Determine the probability that in a random sample of 10 tools, exactly 3 will be defective. Use the binomial distribution.

(b) Using the Poisson approximation to binomial distribution, recompute the probability above. Compare the two answers.

2.22. A manufacturing company estimates that, on average, 1 out of 600 items manufactured is defective. In a sample of 1200 items, what is the probability that exactly 3 items are defective? Use the Poisson approximation.

2.23. The diameter of a cylinder is assumed to be normally distributed with mean 3.5 in. and variance 0.012. What is the probability that a cylinder picked up at random has a diameter of larger than 3.65 in?

2.24. The distribution of points scored in a certain test is assumed to be normal with mean 80 and variance 25. What percentage of the students scored 70 or less?

2.25. Assume that the distribution of the random variable x is standardized normal. Calculate:

(a) $\Pr(x \leq 2.5)$

(b) $\Pr(x \geq 1.67)$

(c) $\Pr(-2.0 \leq X \leq 2.0)$

(d) t, such that $\Pr(x \leq t) = 0.97$

2.26. In a class of 50 students, the points scored on an exam are as follows:

34	49	56	63	69
37	51	56	63	72
39	52	56	64	72
42	53	57	64	73
42	54	58	64	73
44	54	58	65	77
45	54	61	66	79
46	55	61	67	80
46	55	62	67	84
48	56	62	68	88

Obtain:

(a) The grouped frequency distribution.

(b) A histogram showing points versus frequency.

(c) A polygon with actual estimated frequency and a smoothed estimate of the probability function.

(d) An ogive curve.

2.27. A box contains 5 balls which are marked 3, 5, 7, 9, and 11, respectively. Each time two balls are taken out, their numbers are noted and replaced. Consider all possible samples of this population. Compute:

(a) The mean of the population.

(b) The standard deviation of the population.

(c) The mean of the sample means.

(d) The standard deviation (standard error) of the sample means.

2.28. It is assumed that the diameter of a certain cylinder is normally distributed with mean 5.00 cm and variance 1.10. If a sample of size 100 is taken for inspection, find the distribution of the sample mean $\overline{X}$. What is the probability that a sample mean is greater than 5.2 cm?

2.29. It is assumed that ball bearings manufactured at a production unit have a mean diameter of 2.2 cm and standard deviation of 0.70 cm. Determine the distribution of the sample means. What is the probability that a given sample mean falls between 2.0 and 2.35 cm?

2.30. In 100 tosses of a fair coin, what is the probability that the number of heads lies between 45 and 55?

2.31. The diameter of ball bearings manufactured in a company is assumed to be normally distributed with variance 0.5. In a sample of 30 bearings, the sample mean is 2.3 in. Using $\alpha = 0.05$, test the hypothesis that the mean μ is 2.1 in. against an alternative that μ is not equal to 2.1 in.

2.32. In Problem 2.31, suppose that the null hypothesis is $\mu = 2.1$ and the alternative hypothesis is $\mu > 2.1$. Do the data support the null hypothesis or an alternate hypothesis?

2.33. The IQ of the students in a school is assumed to be normally distributed with variance 6400. For a random sampling of 50 students, the mean is 120. The dean has claimed that the average IQ of the school is 155. For an α value of 0.05, check whether the dean's claim may be accepted or not.

2.34. The deflection of a horizontal beam under a given vertical stress is assumed to be normally distributed with variance 6.2. The hypothesis to be tested is

$$H_0 = 4.0 \text{ mm}$$

$$\text{against } H_1 > 4.0 \text{ mm}$$

A sample of size 5 yields an average deflection of 4.25 mm. For $\alpha = 0.10$, would you accept the null hypothesis?

2.35. If for Problem 2.34., the variance of the population is not known but the sample variance is estimated to be 0.2, would you accept the null hypothesis for an α value of 0.05?

2.36. The average grades obtained in two classes, A and B, in an examination are to be compared. Assume that the variances of the two populations are known and both are assumed to be equal to 7200. A random sampling of 50 students' tests from each class yields a mean grade of 75 and 87, respectively. If the null hypothesis states that the two means are equal, verify whether the data support the null hypothesis. Assume that the populations are normally distributed and that $\alpha = 0.05$.

2.37. An automobile assembly plant would like to purchase piston rods from two suppliers. A key dimension for these rods is the diameter of the bushing for a piston pin. These diameters for the rods from both the companies are normally distributed and their variances known and assumed to be equal. The estimated σ values are available. The data are as follows:

	Company	
	A	B
Mean	3.45	3.51
σ^2	0.005	0.004
n	40	35

The plant can use the rods from both suppliers simultaneously only if, statistically, there is no difference between the two means. Should the plant go ahead with its plans or not? (Assume that $\alpha = 0.025$.)

2.38. A consumer advocate wants to compare the performances of cars manufactured by two companies. One of the criteria used is the time taken by the cars to pick up speed from 0 to 60 mph. It is assumed that the times are normally distributed with equal variances; however, only the estimated values are available for σ^2. The results of the tests are as follows:

	Car 1	Car 2
μ, mean time for 0–60	9.6 sec	11.4 sec
σ^2	1.1	1.2
n	20	20

The hypothesis test is set up as

$$H_0: \mu_1 = \mu_2$$

$$H_1: \mu_1 < \mu_2$$

Are there sufficient grounds to reject H_0?

2.39. Lifetimes of two types of vacuum tubes are to be compared for any significant difference between them. Under the identical voltage and temperature conditions, eight tubes of each type yielded the following lifetimes expressed in hours:

Type 1	Type 2
1010	1040
980	1000
880	870
900	965
1205	1185
1060	1030
870	860
990	990

For an α level of 0.025, verify the contention that there is a significant difference using the method of paired specimens.

three

STATISTICAL CONTROL OF PROCESSES

Most production and management systems involve a combined utilization of materials, machines, and people. The functions of any one or all of these components of the industrial combination may range from simple to complex. However, *each* of these components has some *inherent* or *natural variability*, the causes of which cannot be isolated, plus unnatural variability which can be isolated and therefore controlled to a certain irreducible economic minimum.

ILLUSTRATION OF VARIABILITY IN MATERIALS, MACHINES, AND PEOPLE

Assume that this illustration involves a multiple-spindle drilling operation on a casting. The casting is placed in a jig and secured. The drill press operator spins the handle and six drills make holes in the casting. The drills are bottomed with a short dwell time, after which the handle is returned to the normal hover position. Now, what are the possible sources of variation? First, the material of which the casting is made will have some variability from unit to unit. Some units will be harder than others. Some may have more porosity than others. The dimensions will vary from unit to unit. The causes for material variation may be many, including inadequate purchased materials or quality assurance, poor material specifications, *immediate* need of materials regardless of quality, lowest purchase price rather than minimum cost delivered to the shop floor, reciprocity, or any of a number of causes.

One frequent cause of poor quality of purchased materials, if such exists, probably results from the vendor's lack of knowledge of what the buyer *really* wants. There is often a double standard; (1) the material specification, and (2) what the buyer will take for the sake of expedience. An analogous situation exists in the shop with the worker on the machine, that is, (1) the working drawings, and (2) what his or her supervisor will okay—again for the sake of expedience.

The second source of variation is the machine. Every process, precision or not, has a certain capability range within which it will operate. The limits of this range are known as the *natural limits* of the process. This natural range of variability is also often referred to as *process* or *machine capability*. A process is defined to be any employment of resources for the purpose of production, the products of which may be tangible or intangible. Contrasted to the natural limits are *specification* or *drawing* limits. These limits are most often arbitrary since the objectives of the design of the product determine what they will be. At least this is the way it should be. Very often, however, the design limits are arbitrary without proper consideration of the objectives of the design or the needs of an economical production procedure. This, in turn, leads to the formation of the double standard, namely, what is desired and what will be accepted.

Attempts to control the process to a range of variability that is narrower than its natural range are courting indecision, frustration, and unjustified expense. If the process is incapable of acceptable operation within design limits, there are but three alternative courses of action open to the decision maker: (1) separation of nonconforming from conforming product, (2) employment of a more precise process, and (3) change in the design of the product. The choice of which alternative to use must be an economic one. There may be occasions when the first alternative is justified, but there are many more occasions when poor production planning and expedience are reasons for its use. The second alternative may involve a substantial investment in new equipment, a different machine load, or subcontracting to more precise production processes. Quite often, through careful machine loading and scheduling, more precise equipment may be released for use as needed. It is just as economically faulty to tie a highly precise process to an imprecise design as the reverse. The third choice, and one that may be most difficult to achieve, is a change in design. Indiscriminate change in design can wreak havoc in a planned production operation, but a justified relaxation in design requirements can mean the difference between profit and loss. The costs of screening inspection, scrap, and rework may be viewed as opportunity costs, that is, unnecessary costs that can be reduced or eliminated through proper planning and control. Conversely, a merited tightening in design requirements can mean increased demand for a quality product. In any case, the objective should be optimum design at minimum total cost.

The problem is compounded in this drill press example by the number of drills. Each drill, in effect, represents a separate process producing something—a drilled hole. If there are four quality characteristics of depth, width, radius, and surface finish for each hole, there are $6 \times 4 = 24$ possible sources of machine variation. There will be many analogous situations to this in continuous process and job shops which, with a little reflection, will come to the mind of the reader.

The third source of variation, man, is the most variable of them all. People's decisions and actions directly affect the extent of variability and the other sources—materials and machines. For an example of the variability contributed by people, the production of the quality characteristic "depth of drilled hole" will serve.

Setup approval inspection of the first piece in machine shop work is quite common. Also quite common is a perpetuated habit pattern of staying on the side of "maximum metal." This habit pattern reflects a natural desire to stay on the rework side since metal is comparatively easy to remove and very difficult and expensive to put back on. The latter almost always means a scrapped unit. To make the example more meaningful, suppose that the drawing requirements for depth of drilled hole is 1.000 ± 0.002 in. and 50 units are to be produced. The operator experiments and sets the stop on the drill, so that the first unit produced at this setting gives a depth reading of 0.999. The operator is very satisfied with this setting since he reasons that it is on the shallow (maximum metal) side, and if the minimum dimension is not reached owing to undetected tool wear, the defective units can always be reworked.

This is quite a natural reasoning on his part, for he is not responsible for determining the economics of screening inspection, reworking, or scrapping. He operates the drill at the same setting, then checks the tenth unit for depth again. To his alarm the depth reading is now right on the nominal, so he resets the drill to produce a hole 0.001 in. less—what he believes to be 0.999 in.—and then makes the entire run at this setting. Figure 3.1 pictures the results of the machine operator's actions.

What the operator had not considered was the natural variability of the process. The first measurement was no more an indication of the *true* level of the process than the fifth or the tenth of any other individual reading. The first measurement gave an indication of 0.999 in., and without any adjustment at all, the second reading indicated 1.000 in. As a matter of fact, although he thought the setting was on the maximum metal side, it was really quite close to the nominal, as shown by the compressed readings of the original process (Figure 3.1b). After measurement of the tenth unit, his adjustment of -0.0001 in. actually caused the process to produce defective material (Figure 3.1c).

Note two interesting features of Figure 3.1: (1) the data collected on the unit series chart of Figure 3.1c, when compressed, give the appearance of a normal-type distribution, and (2) based on visual evidence alone, the

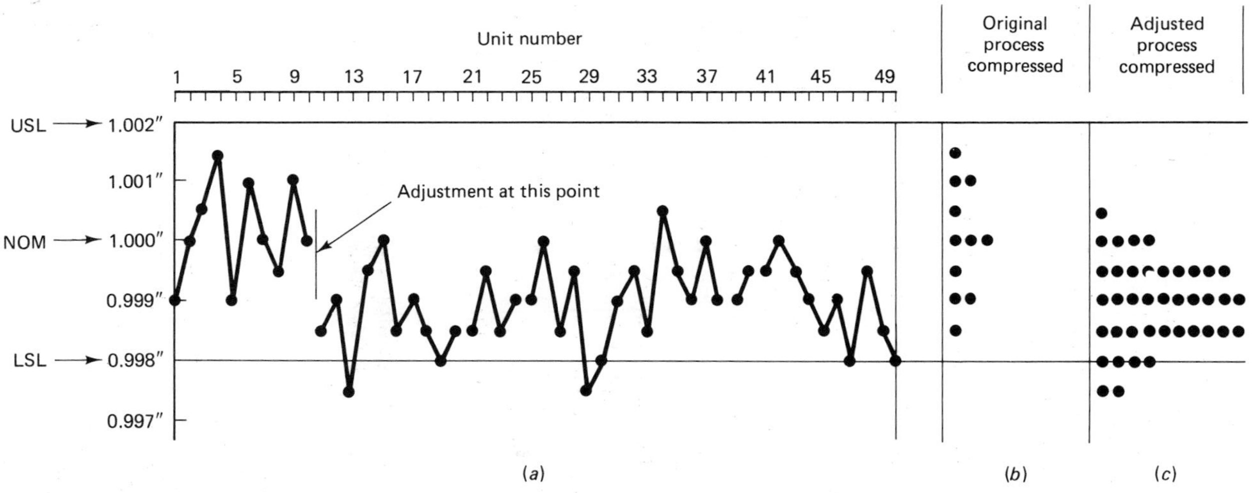

Figure 3.1 Results of indiscriminate adjustment of process.

process appears capable of producing within drawing limits if centered properly and then left alone. Thus it is seen how man, with his indiscriminate adjustment, actually makes the entire process more variable than it would be if materials and machine were the only varying elements of the process. Add to this the indecisive and brush-fire actions of the other two "m's," management and methods, and the benefits possible through graphic control become more obvious. It is appropriate to reiterate the basic principle of efficient process control, which says: *Unless there is a compelling reason to act otherwise; leave the process alone.*

STATISTICAL INFERENCE OF PROCESS VARIABILITY

The control of a process begins with the understanding of the variability of the process itself (Figure 3.2). The product characteristics would reflect all the process variabilities. For example, the characteristic "depth of drilled hole" exhibits variability which results as a culmination of all the variabilities, those of material, machine, or man, entering in the process of drilling the holes. Hence for a proper understanding of the variability of the entire process, it becomes essential to monitor some important (or significant) characteristic of the product.

Let x denote the measurement of the output characteristic. x is a random variable and its probability density function $f(x)$ is a function of all the variabilities [and probability density functions (PDFs)] of the resources entering the production process. An estimate of the PDF $f(x)$ then becomes the basis of the understanding of the behavior of the production process.

The procedure for controlling a process would involve the following steps:

1. Estimating the PDF of an important quality characteristic of the output. Preferably, this should be the same characteristic that is subject to the stated "specifications."

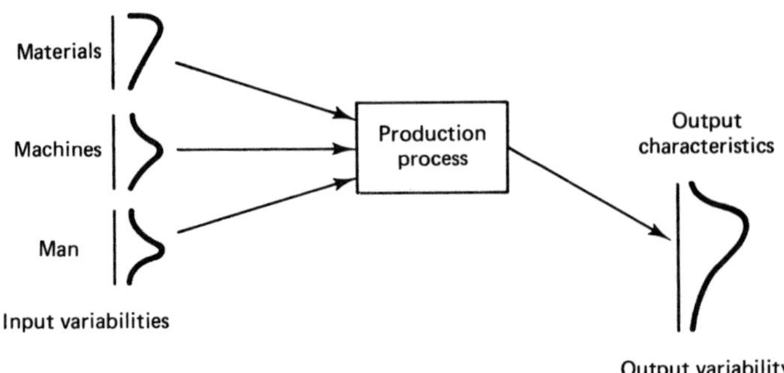

Figure 3.2 Variability of process output.

2. Based on this estimate, attempting to answer the question: Is the product (or an acceptable proportion of the product) satisfactory and conforming to the specifications? If the answer is "yes," the process is said to be "in control" and no further action is necessary.
3. If the answer is "no," the next question to be answered is: Can the answer in step 2 be changed to "yes" under the most beneficial adjustments to the process? If the answer to this question is "no," the process capability is inadequate to produce products satisfactorily conforming to the specification. In this case any of the three options indicated in the preceding section (separation of product, change of process, or change of design) would have to be adopted.
4. If the answer in step 3 is "yes," the final step is the determination of appropriate adjustments to the process.

These steps can be represented schematically as shown in Figure 3.3.

To illustrate this stepwise procedure, the operation of the same multiple-spindle drilling machine is considered. The measurements represented in Figure 3.1 include some units prior to adjustment and some units produced after the adjustment. To avoid any effect of adjustments, another set of 15 units produced sequentially without any intervening adjustments is chosen for this illustration (Table 3.1).

Quality characteristic	Depth of drilled hole
Specifications	1.000 ± 0.002 in. or 1000 ± 2 in thousandths of inches
Production date	1/17
Units produced between	9:30 and 9:52 A.M.

To facilitate the estimation of the PDF, two assumptions are made:

Assumption 1. The form of probability distribution is "normal distribution."

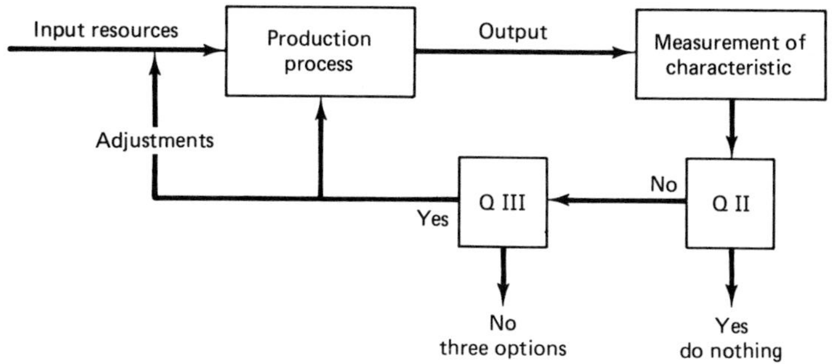

Figure 3.3 Steps in the control procedure.

TABLE 3.1

Unit Number	Adjusted Depth*	$x - \bar{x}$
1	0.3	−0.5
2	−0.5	−1.3
3	1.4	0.6
4	1.2	0.4
5	1.0	0.2
6	−1.4	−2.2
7	0.7	−0.1
8	2.0	1.2
9	0.4	−0.4
10	1.8	1.0
11	0.5	−0.3
12	1.5	0.7
13	0.8	0.0
14	0.5	−0.3
15	1.5	0.7

* Adjusted depth indicates "(actual depth in inches × 1000) − 1000."

Assumption 2. There is no change in the PDF during the production span or between 9:30 and 9:52 A.M.

Referring to Chapter 2, the estimates of the two parameters μ and σ^2 of the assumed normal distribution are given by

$$\begin{aligned}\text{estimate of } \mu &= \hat{\mu} = \bar{x} \\ &= \sum_{1}^{15} \frac{x_i}{15} \\ &= 0.8 \\ \text{estimate of } \sigma^2 &= \hat{\sigma}^2 \\ &= \sum_{1}^{15} \frac{(\bar{x} - x_i)^2}{14} \\ &= 0.79357\end{aligned}$$

It follows that the estimate of σ is given by

$$\begin{aligned}\text{estimate of } \sigma &= \hat{\sigma} \\ &= \sqrt{\hat{\sigma}^2} \\ &= 0.89\end{aligned}$$

This completes the first step and the estimated PDF is "normal distribution with mean 0.8 and standard deviation 0.89."

For step 2, the product is considered satisfactory if more than 98% of the product meets the specifications. The two specification limits +2 and −2 are related to the estimated PDF in the following manner:

$$\text{upper specification limit} = +2.00$$
$$= +0.8 + \left(\frac{1.2}{0.89}\right)0.89$$
$$= \hat{\mu} + 1.348\,\hat{\sigma}$$
$$\text{lower specification limit} = -2.00$$
$$= +0.8 + \left(\frac{-2.80}{0.89}\right)0.89$$
$$= \hat{\mu} - 3.146\,\hat{\sigma}$$

Refering to Table A1, the probability that any unit selected at random, when the variability of production is, in fact, as per estimated PDF, would be outside the upper specification limits is 8.883%. The probability of being outside the lower specification limit is 0.083%. Clearly, the answer to the question in step 2 is "no," as more than 2% of the product is likely to violate one or the other specification limit.

The question in step 3 cannot usually be answered by statistical inference alone; it becomes necessary to include intuition and knowledge of the working of the production process. In this case, the form of the PDF is assumed to be "normal." From the shape and the symmetry it can be deduced that the proportion of units not conforming to specifications is minimized when the process mean is centered between the two specification limits. In other words, the most beneficial adjustment would be for $\hat{\mu}$ to be centered between +2 and −2, or 0.00 instead of the observed 0.8. After such adjustment,

$$\text{upper specification limit} = +2.00$$
$$= 0.00 + 2.247\hat{\sigma}$$
$$\text{lower specification limit} = -2.00$$
$$= 0.00 - 2.247\hat{\sigma}$$

Referring to Table A1, the probability that a unit produced after the adjustment would violate either specification limit is 1.232%. The total proportion of units not conforming to specifications would be 2 × 1.232 = 2.464%. The answer to the question in step 3 is also "no." The existing production process is not capable of delivering product so that more than 98% of the product would meet the specifications. The management would have to choose between the three options of separation of satisfactory product through inspection or change of process or change of product design.

VARIATION OVER TIME VERSUS NATURAL VARIATION OF THE PROCESS

Figure 3.1a is actually a time-series chart with the horizontal scale expressed as a unit series. The horizontal axis could just as well have been labeled "time" and scaled accordingly. Because of the short run of the example, the true effect of variation over time is not evident. In any run long enough for process deterioration to occur, the natural variation will be confounded by the deterioration. The basic reason for control is to detect undesirable deterioration in the process and to correct for it with minimum economic loss. Figure 3.4 shows that a control chart loses most of its value if the data are collected without regard to time. If the product produced during all time units is mixed together prior to the data collection and then charted, the plottings when compressed as in Figure 3.1 would show a distribution with wide dispersion even though the process capability is considerably better than the drawing requirements. This leads to a rule that natural process capability can be determined only when the effects of deterioration are excluded or at least minimized. There is also a corollary rule as follows: It serves no purpose to chart data of missed product. The chart will almost always show control.

BASIC FORM OF THE CONTROL CHART[1]

A control chart is a device for testing whether the probability pattern is stable or changing over time. In describing the statistical inference about process variability, the words "process in control" were used to designate a production process that can produce a satisfactory proportion of product conforming to the specifications. In other words "in control" implies that the pattern of variability of the process does not change over time and the process is capable of meeting the specifications. When used in connection with the control charts, the concept of being "in control" is limited to the process variability being stable without regard to the process capability.

There are many types of control charts for different control situations involving different patterns of variability. However, all have a few characteristics in common and are interpreted in the same manner. In each case the control chart is a test of a hypothesis, there is a separate control chart for each parameter of the distribution being studied and the chart itself is a

[1] It has been stated that the purpose of the control chart is to detect undesirable deterioration of the process. Deterioration can have many causes—a wearing tool bit, contamination, progressive dilution of a chemical agent, fatigue, and so on. In general, the type of deterioration that proceeds from level to level as indicated by Figure 3.1 is fairly easy to detect and adjust. (This is the pattern exhibited by tool wear.) Dispersion deterioration is harder to correct: that is, the deterioration which results from a change in the *capability* of the process. As a rule, the former may be corrected by a simple adjustment of the level of the process. The latter generally involves an engineering job.

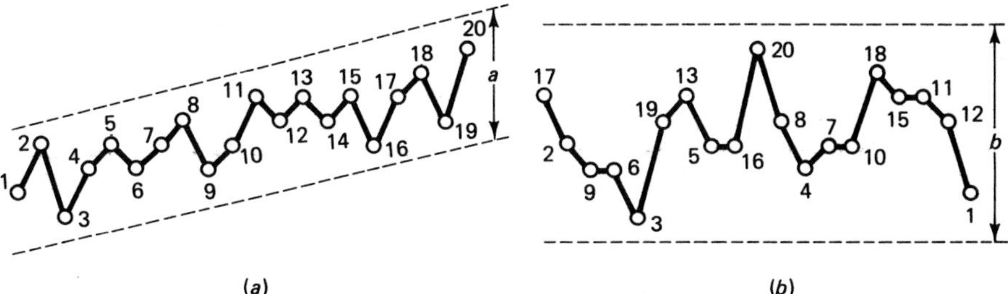

Figure 3.4 Comparison of patterns resulting from sample-time charting a trend during production and the same well-mixed units at incoming inspection: (a) natural dispersion of the process with level uncontrolled; (b) apparent dispersion of the process resulting from loss of sample-time control.

time-series representation of the critical regions of this test on a time-series scale.

In the illustration of the multiple-spindle drilling operation the probability distribution is assumed to be normal. To test the hypothesis that the mean of this distribution is stable, a control chart is created in the following manner.

$$\text{Null hypothesis:} \qquad H_0\text{: } \mu = 0.8$$

$$\text{Alternative hypothesis:} \quad H_1\text{: } \mu \neq 0.8$$

Since only the mean is being tested, it is assumed that σ is constant at 0.89. If H_0 is true, the observed depths x would be distributed normal with mean 0.8 and standard deviation 0.89. Consequently, the probability that any observation would either be over $\mu + k\sigma$ or less than $\mu - k\sigma$ would be the small shaded area illustrated in Figure 3.5 marked $\alpha/2$. Or if the region

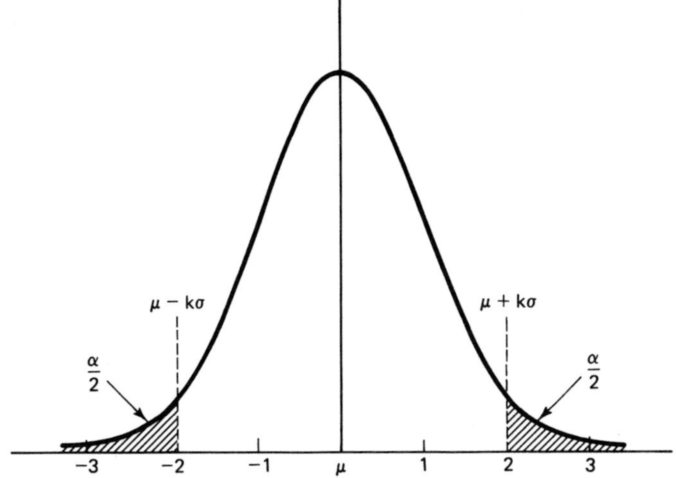

Figure 3.5 Critical region with probability of type I error = α.

outside the limits $\mu + k\sigma$ and $\mu - k\sigma$ is chosen as the critical region, the probability of type I error (error of rejecting H_0 when H_0 is true) is α. Table A1 can be used to obtain α for a stated k or to obtain k for a desired α.

If k is chosen as 2.0, α is 4.56%. Control limits are the boundaries of this critical region. If the pattern of variability is stable, these limits will be identical for all observations. On a time-series chart these limits would appear as a horizontal line, as shown in Figure 3.6.

In this example $k = 2$:

$$\begin{aligned}\text{upper control limit} &= \mu + 2\sigma \\ &= 0.8 + 2(0.89) \\ &= 2.58 \\ \text{lower control limit} &= \mu - 2\sigma \\ &= 0.8 - 2(0.89) \\ &= -0.98\end{aligned}$$

The complete control chart is shown in Figure 3.7. It can be seen that unit 6 is below the lower control limit. For the selected level of significance, $\alpha = 4.56\%$, and the size of the observed sample, the number of units that would be expected to be outside the control limits, is (15)(4.56)/100, or less than 1. Hence the hypothesis of the pattern of variability (specifically the "mean") being stable during the production time has to be rejected.

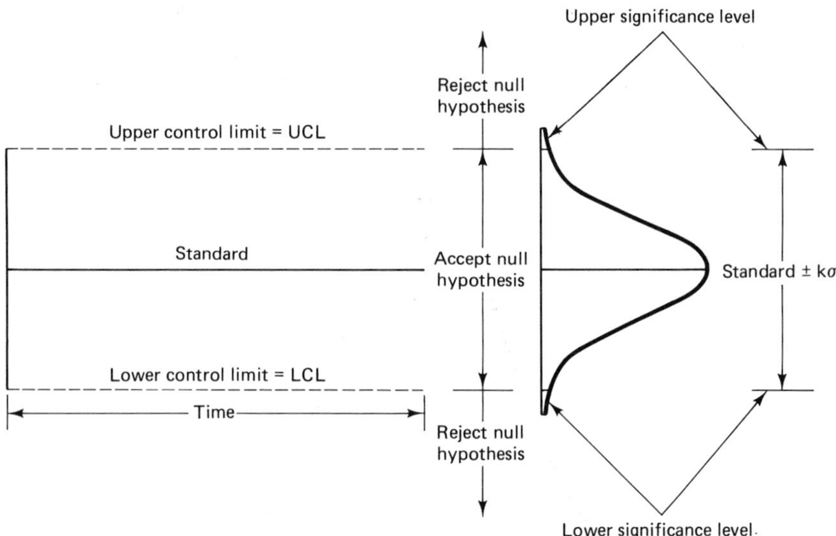

Figure 3.6 Comparison of control limits to confidence interval and significance levels.

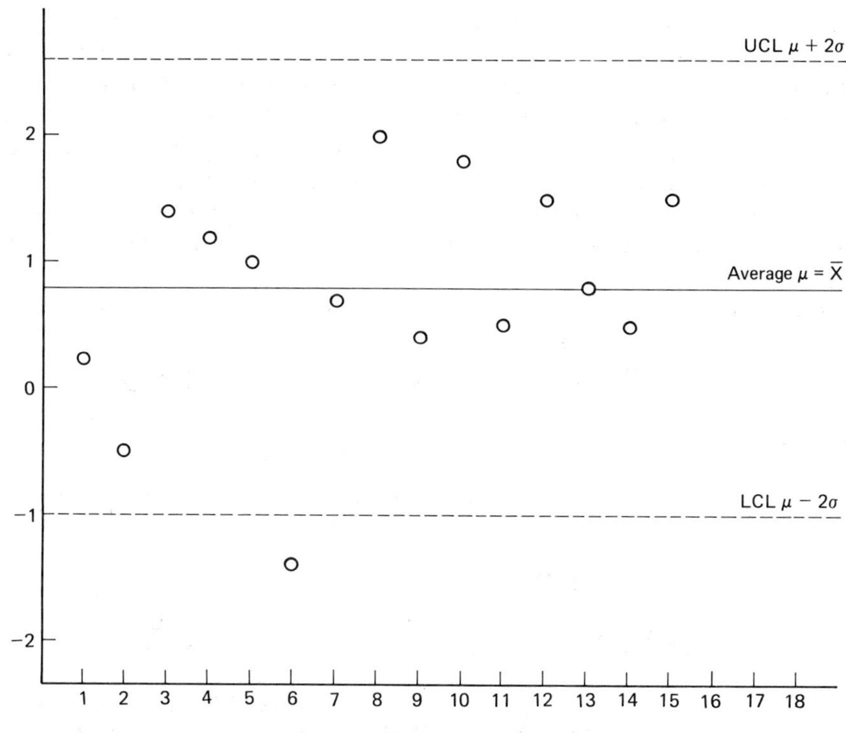

Figure 3.7 Simple control chart.

USE OF THE CONTROL CHART

The control limits are decision limits which inform the interpreter *when* he or she should investigate. The placement of the control limits, as determined by the selected k value, will reflect the interpreter's willingness to accept a certain probability of being wrong in making the decision. If the k is set at 3, a plotted value at or beyond the control limit directs the interpreter to reject the null hypothesis at the 0.0013 (half of 0.26%) significance level for each limit. The odds of being wrong in making this decision will be only 26 in 10,000 for both limits, and 13 in 10,000 for a single limit. The area beyond $\mu \pm 3\sigma$ is approximately equal to 0.0026. This value $k = 3$ is commonly used in most applications of control charts.

The control chart acts as a powerful stimulant for improvement and deterrent for indiscriminate adjustment. The rejection of the hypothesis of process being stable occurs only when there is a strong reason to believe that something has gone astray. The process is left alone until some symptom of abnormality indicates that an investigation for the cause of the abnormal condition is justified. Because of their powerful psychological effect for improvement, control chart symptoms should receive proper attention. If the chart is not maintained properly or its symptoms of abnormality not investigated for cause, it would be better to remove it. Otherwise, shop cynicism toward charts will develop and they will be looked on as management's playthings. This cynicism will introduce other problems not necessarily related to quality control alone. However, a properly maintained chart will do much good in any shop or administrative organization. It is very difficult for a person or group of persons to ignore a prominently displayed

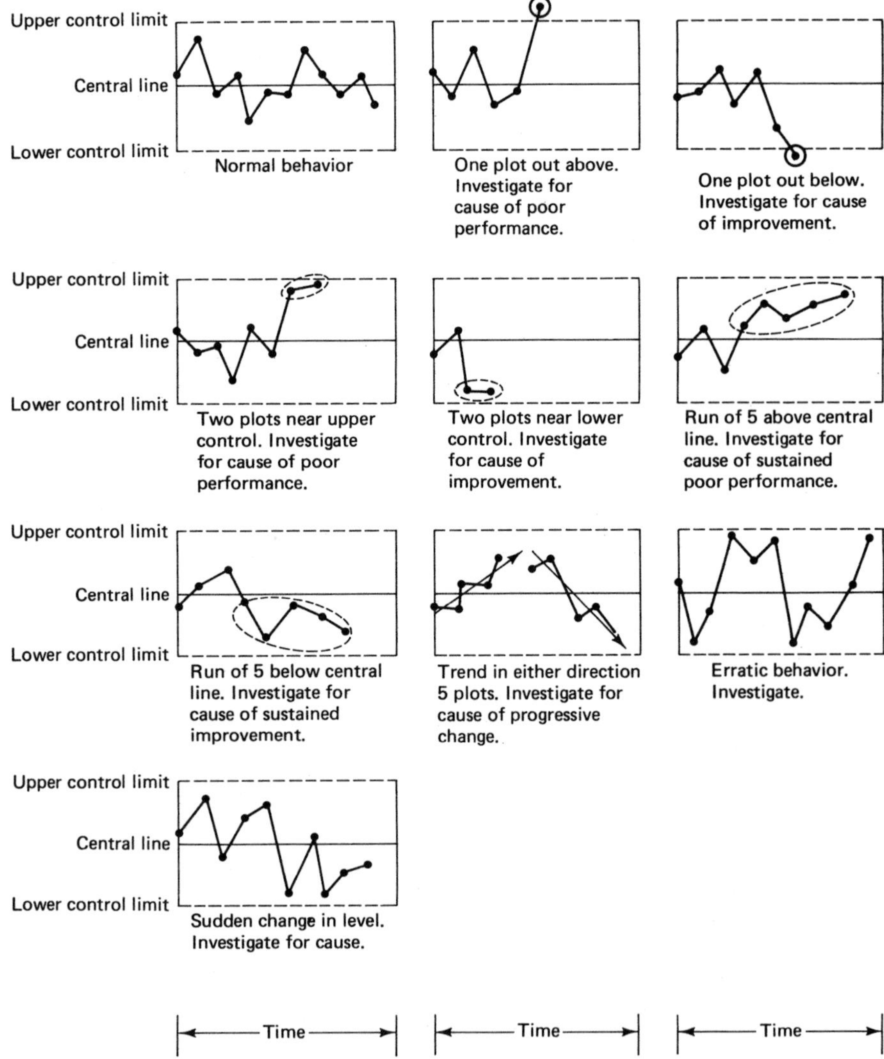

Figure 3.8 Control chart evidence for investigation. Percent defective format used for illustration.

achievable standard. It is against human nature. Conversely, it is also against human nature to continually strive to achieve a standard that is virtually impossible in the light of current performance. There is a breaking point, which varies with personalities of course, where employees become frustrated and cynical because of inability to achieve the standard. Such a condition reflects not on the worker but on management. Figure 3.8 shows some more typical indications of abnormalities.

DEVELOPMENT OF A CONTROL CHART

Process control using control charts typically involves two phases. A process being "in control" implies that the probability distribution pattern of the process output does not vary significantly over time. For example, consider the characteristic "depth of drilled hole x." A control chart would be a test of the hypothesis that the probability distribution of x is *stationary* (does not vary significantly over time); more specifically, the mean of the distribution is a constant.

$$H_0\colon \mu_x = \mu_0$$

In general, the numerical value of μ_0 will not be known. The first phase, called the *base period*, is used for estimating the parameters such as μ_0. The estimated values would be used for the subsequent period, called a *monitoring period*.

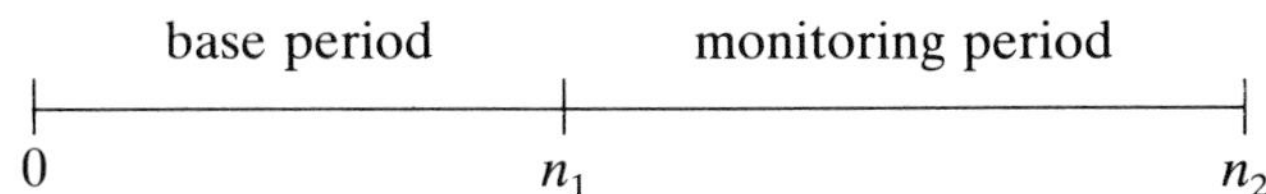

Phase 1: Base-Period Analysis

Let $\bar{x}_i$ = the average observed value of the characteristic during the ith sample; this is the test statistic

α = specified type 1 error

n_1 = number of samples in the base period

$$\hat{\mu}_0 = \frac{1}{n_1}\sum_{1}^{n_1} \bar{x}_i$$

= estimate of mean obtained during base period

$g(\cdot)$ = conditional distribution of $\bar{x}$ given mean equals $\hat{\mu}_0$

$G(\cdot)$ = cumulative of $g(\cdot)$

Hypothesis being tested in the base period:

$$H_0\colon \mu_x = \hat{\mu}_0$$

against

$$H_1\colon \mu_x \neq \hat{\mu}_0$$

The hypothesis is rejected if $G(\bar{x}_i) < \alpha/2$ or $G(\bar{x}_i) > 1 - \alpha/2$ for any sample i during the base period. Acceptance of H_0 implies that the process is in control during the base period; and the process mean equals $\hat{\mu}_0$.

Phase 2: Monitoring-Period Analysis

The estimate $\hat{\mu}_0$ obtained during the base period is continued to be used during the monitoring period. Hence the same distribution $G(\cdot)$ would continue to be used.

Hypothesis being tested in the monitoring period:

$$H_0\text{: } \mu_x = \hat{\mu}_0 \text{ from the base period}$$

against

$$H_1\text{: } \mu_x \neq \hat{\mu}_0$$

The hypothesis is rejected if $G(\bar{x}_j) < \alpha/2$ or $G(\bar{x}_j) > 1 - \alpha/2$ for any sample j during the monitoring period. As long as the hypothesis continues to be accepted, the process is said to be in control. For the purpose of testing this hypothesis, a set of control limits may be used.

At the lower control limit: $G(\bar{x}) = \alpha/2$.
At the upper control limit: $G(\bar{x}) = 1 - \alpha/2$.

Procession through these two phases will be demonstrated by an example in the next chapter. Any rejection of the hypothesis would be indicated by the terms (1) process out of control, (2) a signal from the control chart, or (3) lack of control.

CAUSES FOR INVESTIGATION

Once the control chart pattern has indicated that investigation for the cause of nonrandom variation is merited, the investigation may reveal any of the following:

1. The deviating condition is a *random* variation even though only expected to occur k times in 1000; that is, there appears to be no assignable cause for its occurrence. Properly, then, the deviating condition should be considered when setting the next standard.
2. The deviating condition has a determinable cause that cannot be eliminated. For example, cyclic or seasonal activity cannot be eliminated. They should be planned for in any future control situations either as expected deviations or, if the cycle or season has any appreciable length, as cyclic or seasonal standards.

3. The deviating condition is determinable and caused by faulty data collection. Faulty data collection could mean an unreliable gage as well as a misplaced decimal in calculation or plotting of the chart.
4. The deviation has a determinable cause that is due to one or more of the resources: man, machine, or material.

Control charting involves both short- and long-term decision making. The short-term decision occurs when investigative action is taken as a result of an indicated symptom of abnormality on the control chart. The long-term decision results from the effect a decision to include or exclude certain data has on the future standard and control limits.

In general, the investigation during the base period indicates the *capability* of the process. This knowledge can be used to indicate what is achievable in subsequent periods if satisfactory process control is maintained.

RESPONSIBILITIES FOR CHART MAINTENANCE AND ADJUSTMENT ACTION

Many companies make the quality control department responsible for chart maintenance. This may be necessary in the early stages of chart application, but usually the ultimate objective should be to make the producing unit responsible for chart maintenance and decision making. Primarily, the control chart is a tool for *process control.* Sound organizational principles demand that the unit supervisor have the responsibility and the necessary tools to control the process. The control chart is one of the most valuable of the tools and the supervisor should therefore be encouraged to utilize it and be responsible for its upkeep. The exclusive use and maintenance of the control chart by the quality control department connotes a punitive measure and the tendency will be for the processing unit to resist and ignore the valuable information the chart contains.

PROCESS SAMPLING

A process may be sampled for two purposes: (1) control of the process, and (2) acceptance of the products of the process. In the latter case the objective is to obtain a *representative* sample of the product processed since the previous sampling period, so sample units are selected from the production process in a stratified, random manner. In the former case the objective is *control*, and units should be selected so as to yield minimum within-sample variation and maximum between-sample variation.

One might ask about the effect of observer bias here. Operator bias should be at a minimum since, properly utilized, the control chart is a tool for his use just the same as one of the tools in his toolbox. If cyclic bias is suspected, the time of selection of *each sample* may be randomized. Generally, the purpose of acceptance sampling is to assure quality *after* the units have been manufactured. Control sampling should be designed to obtain the fastest possible indication of a deviating condition.

PROBLEMS

3.1. The following tensile strength readings were taken from a line processing steel after heat treatment.

Date	Strength (1000 psi)	Date	Strength (1000 psi)
1	95.5	16	93.0
2	96.5	17	87.5
3	90.5	18	96.5
4	100.0	19	98.0
5	97.0	20	96.0
6	93.5	21	98.5
7	90.0	22	94.0
8	89.5	23	96.5
9	92.5	24	98.0
10	96.5	25	92.0
11	97.0	26	93.8
12	99.5	27	96.0
13	91.0	28	94.0
14	102.0	29	95.0
15	87.0	30	94.5

(a) Estimate the mean and the standard deviation of the tensile strength.
(b) Determine the upper and lower control limits using $k = 2.5$. Is the process stable?
(c) Draw a chart similar to Figure 3.7.
(d) What inference can you draw from the chart?

3.2. Packages of Torino frozen pizzas are labeled "net wt. 800 g." A sample of 30 pizzas were removed from the packages and weighed.
(a) Assuming that the weights are distributed normal, estimate the mean and the variance.
(b) What percentage of the packages would be more than 10 g. underweight?
(c) Determine the upper and lower control limits using $k = 2$.
(d) Is the production process "in control" (in the sense of process variability being stable)?

Package Number	Weight	Package Number	Weight
1	789	16	795
2	771	17	794
3	800	18	792
4	800	19	786
5	798	20	805
6	804	21	798
7	809	22	809
8	787	23	793
9	799	24	791
10	795	25	811
11	794	26	802
12	800	27	816
13	791	28	782
14	807	29	784
15	802	30	793

four

CONTROL CHARTS FOR VARIABLE QUALITY CHARACTERISTICS

A variable quality characteristic is one that can be measured on a variable scale of values. Because the magnitude of deviation can be determined by variables measuring instruments, more information about the quality characteristic under examination can be obtained. As one might suspect, this added information can be obtained only at more expense. In general, variables measuring instruments cost more at original purchase, cost more to maintain, and cost more to use. Frequently, though, the investment required is well worth the added information obtained and the reduction in inspection that is possible.

Some familiar examples of variable characteristics are temperature, pressure, tensile strength, hardness, and acidity. The gages used to measure these variable characteristics are also more or less familiar. Frequently characteristics normally considered attributes are susceptible to conversion to a variables scale. One example is taste rating. In addition to grading the taste of a food or beverage as good or bad, point values for gradations of good and bad can be assigned for variable-type grading.

Probably the most commonly used variable characteristics quality control method is the control chart. Although a very powerful tool of quality control, it has received a disproportionate amount of attention in the literature as well as in academic and industrial training courses. The heavy concentration on the method has resulted in its being applied in many situations where it is not economically justified. It is a control device that should be used only on a very small percentage of the total quality characteristics. Nevertheless, when it is justified, it is a very powerful and effective tool for quality control in-process.

BASICS OF A CONTROL CHART

A control chart is designed to be a simple graphical technique to monitor and control a single-variable quality characteristic. The objective is to obtain an estimate of the principal parameter that describes the variability of this characteristic and then use the techniques of hypothesis testing to determine if the process is in control. In the multiple-spindle operation described in Chapter 3, "depth of drilled hole" was considered as the single, most significant characteristic. The production process of "drilling" would be considered stable and "in control" whenever the variability of "depth of drilled hole" is stable.

Let x_i denote the depth of hole in the ith item produced and let μ and σ^2 be the mean and variance of the random variable x_i. If a sample of n items is observed (i.e., the value of x_i is measured for each of these n items), the probability distribution of the average of the depths, $\bar{x}$, would be approximately normal, according to the central limit theorem. For $\bar{x}$ the mean and variance would be μ and σ^2/n, respectively.

If the drilling process is stable, then for all samples, each consisting of n items, the average of observed depths $\overline{X}$ would be consistent with the implied probability distribution: normal with mean μ and variance σ^2/n. On the other hand, finding several values of $\overline{X}$ to be inconsistent (too large or too small) would give reason to suspect that the process is no longer stable.

For any sample j, $\overline{X}_j$ can be treated for consistency using the technique of hypothesis testing. Let the desired value of the mean be μ_0. The null hypothesis would be "drilling process is operating as it should." Under this hypothesis the mean μ would be equal to μ_0. The alternative hypothesis would be "drilling process is out of control" or mean μ is not equal to μ_0.

Null hypothesis: H_0: $\mu = \mu_0$

Alternative hypothesis: H_1: $\mu \neq \mu_0$

If the null hypothesis H_0 is true, the observed values of $\overline{X}$ would be distributed normal with mean μ and standard deviation $\sigma/\sqrt{n}$. Consequently, the probability that any $\overline{X}$ would either be over $\mu_0 + k\sigma/\sqrt{n}$ or less than $\mu_0 - k\sigma/\sqrt{n}$ would be the small shaded area illustrated in Figure 4.1. Let $\alpha/2$ denote the small shaded area on each side. If a decision rule is set up so that H_0 is rejected when any sample value $\overline{X}_j$ is in the shaded area, the probability that H_0 would be rejected when it in fact was true is $\alpha/2 + \alpha/2$ or α. This is the type I error.

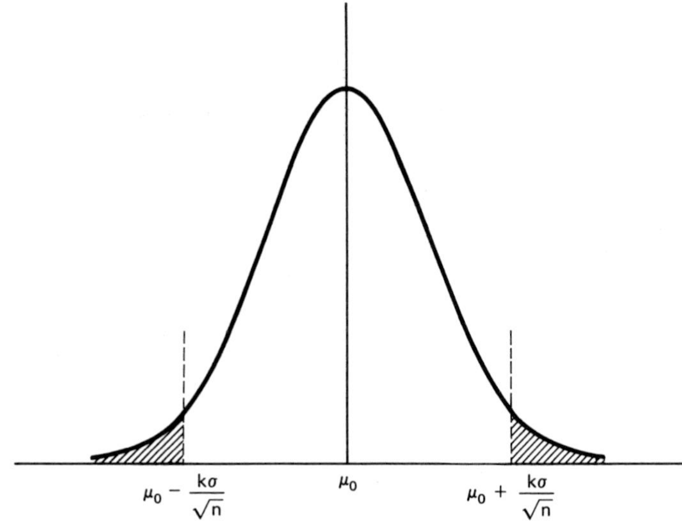

Figure 4.1 Probability density of $\overline{X}$ under H_0.

For example, let $\mu_0 = 0.8$, $n = 1$, $\sigma = 0.89$, and $k = 2$. Then

$$U = \mu_0 + \frac{k\sigma}{\sqrt{n}}$$

$$= 0.8 + \frac{2(0.89)}{\sqrt{1}}$$

$$= 2.58$$

$$L = \mu_0 - \frac{k\sigma}{\sqrt{n}}$$

$$= 0.8 - \frac{2(0.89)}{\sqrt{1}}$$

$$= -0.98$$

For the value $k = 2$, the probability α can be obtained from Table A1 as 4.56%. The decision rule for determining the stability of the process would be as follows. "Take a sample of 1 item. Measure the depth of the hole drilled. If the depth is within the limits -0.98 to 2.58, accept the hypothesis. If the depth is either less than -0.98 or more than 2.58, reject the hypothesis."

If H_0 is accepted, the implication is that the process is in control. If it is rejected, the implication is that the process is not in control. The limits U and L are called *upper* and *lower control limits*, respectively. Using this decision rule, the probability that a process would be declared as "out of control" when in fact it was "in control" is only 4.56%.

The limits U and L can be used repeatedly for monitoring the process

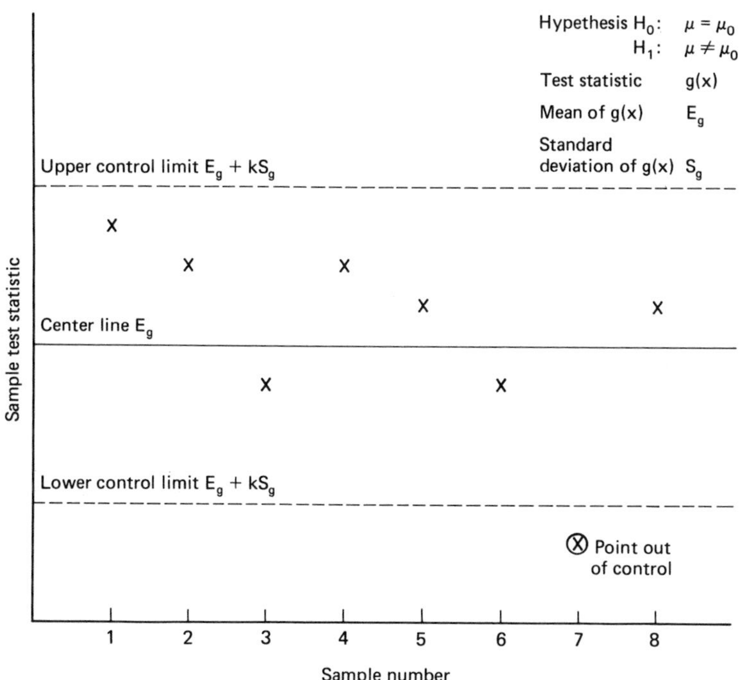

Figure 4.2 Basic control chart.

using samples from the continuing production. To facilitate the evaluation, a chart is prepared as shown in Figure 4.2. This chart is called a *control chart*. The value of the estimator, in this case $\overline{X}$, for each sample is plotted on the chart. As long as the plotted value is within the two control limits U and L, the conclusion is "the process is in control." For sample 7, the value of $\overline{X}$ is outside the control limits, leading to a conclusion "the process is not in control."

USE OF CONTROL CHARTS

It can be seen from Figure 4.1 that the probability of making a type I error (i.e., concluding H_0 to be false when in fact it is true), depends on the choice of k. Table 4.1 gives the maximum probability of this error (in percent) under differing assumptions about the probability distribution function of the estimate.

Condition 1. The PDF is approximately normal.

Condition 2. The distribution is symmetric about the mean and its variance is finite.

Condition 3. The variance is finite.

The control limits are decision limits that inform the interpreter *when* to investigate. The placement of the control limits, as determined by the

TABLE 4.1 Probabilities of Type I Error under Different Assumptions about PDF

k	Condition 1	Condition 2	Condition 3
2	4.55	11.1	25.0
2.5	1.24	7.1	16.0
3	0.26	4.9	11.1
3.5	0.05	3.6	8.2

selected k value, will reflect the interpreter's willingness to accept a certain probability of being wrong in making the decision. If the k is set at 3, a plotted value at or beyond the control limit directs the interpreter to reject the null hypothesis at the 0.0013 (half of 0.26%) significance level for each limit. The odds of being wrong in making this decision will be only 26 in 10,000 for both limits and 13 in 10,000 for a single limit. The area beyond $\mu \pm 3\sigma$ is approximately equal to 0.0026. This value $k = 3$ is commonly used in most applications of control charts.

CHARTS FOR VARIABLE QUALITY CHARACTERISTICS

When quality characteristics are measured for a sample of items, in most instances it can be assumed that the central limit theorem would be applicable and the average of the measured values would be approximately normally distributed. Two parameters, mean μ and variance σ^2, are needed to fully describe the normal distribution. Consequently, two charts are needed for the control of any variable characteristics, one to monitor the estimator of mean and one to monitor the estimator of variability.

Estimator of the mean:

$$\overline{X} = \frac{1}{n} \sum_{i=1}^{n} x_i$$

Estimators of variability:

$$R = x_i(\max) - x_i(\min)$$

$$\hat{\sigma} = \sqrt{\frac{1}{n} \sum_{i=1}^{n} (x_i - \overline{x})^2}$$

These pairs of charts are usually referred to as *$\overline{X}$ and R charts* or *$\overline{X}$ and $\hat{\sigma}$ charts*. The control limits are usually set at $k = 3$; that is,

upper control limit = mean of the estimator
+ 3 standard deviations of the estimator

lower control limit = mean of the estimator
− 3 standard deviations of the estimator

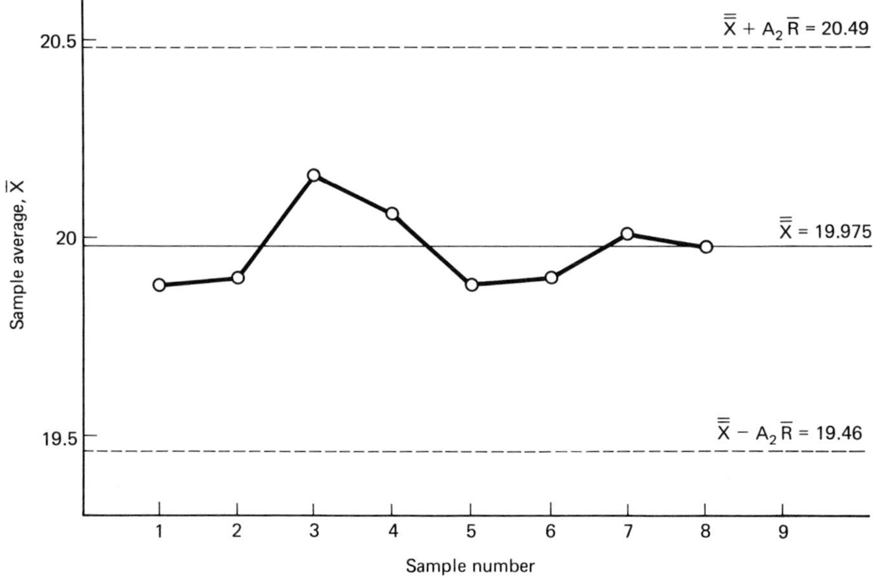

Figure 4.3 $\overline{X}$ chart.

Example 4.1

The length of a bolt is specified at 20 mm. Semiautomatic equipment is used to produce these bolts. Samples of 5 bolts taken from each hour's production produced results shown in Table 4.2. Figures 4.3, 4.4, and 4.5 show the $\overline{X}$, R, and $\hat{\sigma}$ charts for these eight sample observations. Because of the simplicity of the computations involved, $\overline{X}$ and R charts are much more prevalent than $\overline{X}$ and $\hat{\sigma}$ charts.

TABLE 4.2 Sampling Data

	Sample Bolt Length						
Hour	1	2	3	4	5	$\overline{X}$	R
1	19.5	19.8	19.6	20.4	20.1	19.88	0.9
2	20.1	19.8	20.3	19.7	19.6	19.90	0.7
3	20.0	20.4	20.5	19.9	20.0	20.16	0.6
4	19.9	20.4	20.3	20.1	19.7	20.08	0.7
5	19.8	19.2	19.7	20.4	20.3	19.88	1.2
6	20.3	20.0	19.4	20.2	19.6	19.90	0.9
7	19.6	20.7	20.3	19.8	19.7	20.02	1.1
8	20.4	19.4	19.8	20.4	19.9	19.98	1.0
						159.80	7.1

$$\text{Average of the averages } \overline{\overline{X}} = \frac{159.80}{8} = 19.975$$

$$\text{Average of the ranges } \overline{R} = \frac{7.1}{8} = 0.8875$$

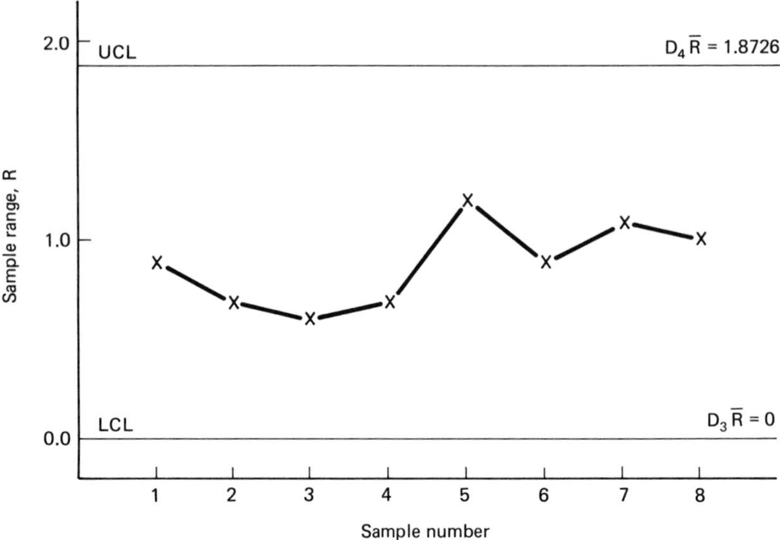

Figure 4.4 *R* chart.

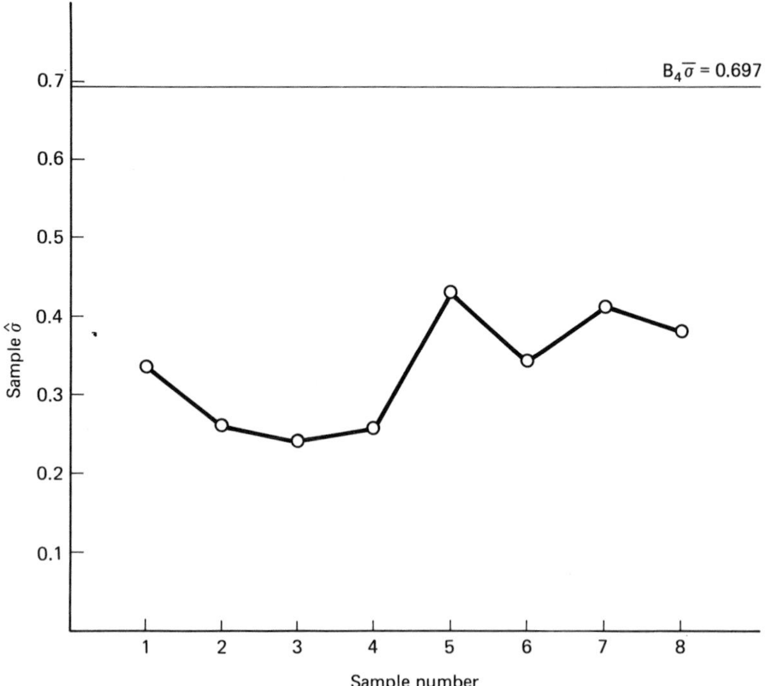

Figure 4.5 $\hat{\sigma}$ chart.

DERIVATION OF CONTROL CHART FACTORS

The control limits in any of the three types of control charts are aimed at $k = 3$ or 3 times the standard deviation of the estimators. In constructing the charts in practice, both for the base period and for the monitoring period, precomputed factors are used for calculating the control limits for averages of small samples ($\overline{X}$), ranges of small samples (R), or the sample standard deviations $\hat{\sigma}$.[1] These factors are assigned symbols and the factors are tabulated in Table A8.

Let μ and σ^2 denote the parameter of the characteristic X. Using the approximating distributions of $\overline{X}$, R, and $\hat{\sigma}$, it can be seen that

mean of $\overline{X} \simeq \mu \simeq$ average of $\overline{X}$ (denoted as $\overline{\overline{X}}$)

standard deviation of $\overline{X} \simeq \dfrac{\sigma}{\sqrt{n}}$

mean of $R \simeq \overline{R}$

standard deviation of range does not have a simple approximation

mean of $\hat{\sigma} \simeq \sigma$

standard deviation of $\hat{\sigma} \simeq \dfrac{\sigma}{\sqrt{2n}}$

The factors for computing control limits are defined as follows:

c_2 = factor to estimate σ from $\hat{\sigma}$

$\overline{\sigma}$ = average of $\hat{\sigma}$

$$c_2 = \frac{\overline{\sigma}}{\sigma}$$

d_2 = factor to estimate σ from $\overline{R}$

$$= \frac{\overline{R}}{\sigma}$$

A_1 = factor to determine "3 times the standard deviation of $\overline{X}$" from $\overline{\sigma}$

$$3 \cdot \frac{\sigma}{\sqrt{n}} \simeq A_1 \cdot \overline{\sigma}$$

upper control limit for $\overline{X}$ chart $= \overline{\overline{X}} + A_1\overline{\sigma}$

lower control limit for $\overline{X}$ chart $= \overline{\overline{X}} - A_1\overline{\sigma}$

[1] The symbols $\hat{\sigma}$ and s are used to denote the same quantity. Both the symbols are used in this book.

A_2 = factor to determine "3 times the standard deviation of $\overline{X}$" from $\overline{R}$

$$3 \cdot \frac{\sigma}{\sqrt{n}} \simeq A_2 \cdot \overline{R}$$

upper control limit for $\overline{X}$ chart $= \overline{\overline{X}} + A_2\overline{R}$

lower control limit for $\overline{X}$ chart $= \overline{\overline{X}} - A_2\overline{R}$

B_3 = factor to determine the lower control limit for $\hat{\sigma}$ chart

lower control limit $= B_3\overline{\sigma}$

B_4 = factor to determine the upper control limit for $\hat{\sigma}$ chart

upper control limit $= B_4\overline{\sigma}$

D_3 = factor to determine the lower control limit for R chart

lower control limit $= D_3\overline{R}$

D_4 = factor to determine the upper control limit for R chart

upper control limit $= D_4\overline{R}$

These factors have been extensively computed and tabulated when the probability distribution of X is approximately normal. Most of the variability encountered in production processes justifies an assumption of approximate normality. This makes it easy to adapt these tabulated values of factors c_2, d_2, A_1, A_2, B_3, B_4, D_3, and D_4 to the determination of the control limits.

STARTING A CONTROL CHART

Three critical decisions need to be made before any control chart technique can be initiated. These are decisions regarding the sample size, base period, and level of significance and are explained for the $\overline{X}$ and R charts as an example.

Sample Size

This is the size n or the number of units included in each sample. According to the central limit theorem (Chapter 2), the distribution of the sample average $\overline{X}$ is approximated by a normal distribution and the approximation gets better when the sample size n increases. For this reason one would prefer a large sample size. On the other hand, if the production covered by a single sample is to be homogeneous, it is desirable that very little time be involved and that the sample size n be small. Generally, the choice of sample size involves a trade-off between these two considerations. Most commonly, the values 4 or 5 are used as sample sizes. In the case of most industrial products the sample averages from samples of size 4 or 5 provide an acceptable application of the central limit theorem. From a practical point of view it is not difficult to find an average and a range in a sample of 4 or 5 and most operators are capable of this simple arithmetic. In many cases the charts can be updated daily (or every shift) by the operators themselves.

Base Period

A control chart is a monitoring process and involves a hypothesis test for each and every sample. As long as the hypothesis is not rejected, the conclusion is that the process is in control. This test of hypothesis necessarily requires the knowledge of the conditional distribution of $\overline{X}$:

$$g(\overline{X} \mid H_0 \text{ is true})$$

in other words, the distribution of $\overline{X}$ when the process is operating in a stable and normal manner. In most cases this distribution is not known when the control chart is started and a number of samples are observed solely for the estimation of this distribution. The number of initial samples in the base period should be enough to yield a satisfactory estimate of the distribution $g(\overline{X} \mid H_0$ is true) and consequently the critical region for the acceptance or rejection of H_0. Usually, at least 20 samples are included in the base period before the estimates are considered satisfactory.

To determine if the process has been stable during the base period all the sample averages observed in the base period are tested against the critical region from the estimated conditional distribution. The process would be considered stable if none indicates the rejection of H_0.

Level of Significance

This is the maximum probability of type I error or α. The choice of α determines the critical region. For $\overline{X}$ charts, using normal approximation, the most commonly used acceptance region is $\hat{\mu} \pm 3\hat{\sigma}$, where $\hat{\mu}$ and $\hat{\sigma}$ are the estimates of the mean and variance of $\overline{X}$ obtained from the base period. This gives a value of $\alpha = 0.0027$, or 0.27%.

$\hat{\mu} = \overline{\overline{x}} =$ average of all $\overline{X}$ values

$\hat{\sigma} = A_2\overline{R}$ where $\overline{R}$ is the average of ranges and A_2 is a factor dependent on the sample size n

$$\text{Acceptance region:} \quad \overline{\overline{X}} \pm A_2\overline{R}$$

Control Chart in the Monitoring Period

Once the acceptance region is determined for the base period and it is determined the process is stable, a chart is prepared for monitoring the process. Three horizontal lines are drawn on graph paper.

Line at $\overline{\overline{X}} + A_2\overline{R}$	upper control limit (UCL)
Line at $\overline{\overline{X}}$	central line (CL)
Line at $\overline{\overline{X}} - A_2\overline{R}$	lower control limit (LCL)

The values of sample averages $\overline{X}$ are plotted sequentially for all samples during the monitoring period. Whenever any value is above the UCL or below the LCL, a "signal" is said to be given. A signal indicates the rejection of H_0 and a conclusion that the process is not in control.

A second chart is maintained for monitoring the variability. This chart has two horizontal lines.

Line at $D_4\overline{R}$	upper control limit (UCL_R)
Line at $D_3\overline{R}$	lower control limit (LCL_R)

The sample ranges R are plotted on this chart.

Example 4.1 (Continued)

For Example 4.1, if the first 8 hours are considered as the base period, the lines for the monitoring period can be calculated using the factors A_2, D_3, and D_4 from Table A8.

For sample size 5:

$\overline{\overline{X}}$ in the base period	19.975
$\overline{R}$ in the base period	0.8875
A_2	0.58
D_3	0
D_4	2.11

For the monitoring period:

$$\overline{X} \text{ chart: upper control limit } = \overline{\overline{X}} + A_2\overline{R}$$

$$= 19.975 + 0.58(0.8875)$$

$$= 20.49$$

$$\overline{X} \text{ chart: central line } = \overline{\overline{X}}$$

$$= 19.975$$

$$\overline{X} \text{ chart: lower control limit} = \overline{\overline{X}} - A_2\overline{R}$$
$$= 19.975 - 0.58(0.8875)$$
$$= 19.46$$
$$R \text{ chart: upper control limit} = D_4\overline{R}$$
$$= 2.11(0.8875)$$
$$= 1.8726$$
$$R \text{ chart: lower control limit} = D_3\overline{R}$$
$$= 0(0.8875)$$
$$= 0$$

These limits have been shown on the charts in Figures 4.3 and 4.4, respectively. (The reader can verify the limits on the $\hat{\sigma}$ chart in Figure 4.5 as $B_4\overline{\sigma}$ and $B_3\overline{\sigma}$, respectively).

PROCESS NOT STABLE DURING THE BASE PERIOD

In Example 4.1, the sample $\overline{X}$ and R values for the base period were within control limits as shown in Figures 4.3 and 4.4. This implies that the process would have been declared "in control" if the same control limits were used for both the base period and monitoring period. In other words, the base-period observations were consistent with the parameters estimated from the same observations. This indicates stability of the production process. When the production process is stable, control limits obtained from base-period observations can dependably be used during the monitoring period.

If any of the $\overline{X}$ or R values during the base period were outside the control limits, it would indicate probable lack of stability of the process. When the process is not stable in the base period, the validity of using control limits for the monitoring period would be questionable. Monitoring would require "the control limits that would have been obtained if the process were stable." If the instability during the base period is inherent in the process itself (worn-out equipment, poor quality of materials), it is best to abandon the base-period results and reinitiate after the inherent causes have been corrected. If the instability is due to the newness of the product or process and/or the operators not being familiar with the product, the control limits can be derived as follows.

1. If time permits and the observations are not very expensive, a new base period can be started. The process would probably have stabilized by this time.
2. Check if the process is stable if the "out-of-control-limits" observations are eliminated.

In order to be able to adopt option 2, the following procedure is used:

Step 1. Start with a base period of at least 25 samples.

Step 2. Calculate $\overline{X}$ and $\overline{R}$. Calculate the control limits.

Step 3. Check the R chart. If all observations are within control limits, go to step 4. If some observations are outside the upper control limit, remove the corresponding samples from the base period and go to step 2.

Step 4. Check the $\overline{X}$ chart. If all observations are within control limits, go to step 5. If some observations are outside either control limit, remove the corresponding sample from the base period. If the base period has 15 or fewer samples left, abandon the base period. Otherwise, go to step 2.

Step 5. Extend the control limits to the monitoring period.

Example 4.2

A soft drink is sold in bottles marked 325 ml. The bottles are filled by an automatic machine. Samples of 5 bottles taken every 15 minutes of production during the first shift produced the results shown in Table 4.3. The measurement x is the number of milliliters over 300. The range is in milliliters. Initial tentative values of control limits are obtained for this base period.

$$\overline{\overline{X}} = \frac{\Sigma \overline{X}}{30} = \frac{776.9}{30} = 25.90$$

$$\overline{R} = \frac{\Sigma R}{30} = \frac{144}{30} = 4.8$$

TABLE 4.3 Sampling Data

Sample Number	$\overline{X}$	R	Sample Number	$\overline{X}$	R
1	29.0	11	16	23.8	4
2	25.0	8	17	27.0	5
3	26.0	5	18	28.4	3
4	25.2	5	19	25.4	7
5	25.4	3	20	26.2	6
6	28.0	4	21	27.0	5
7	26.0	5	22	26.0	5
8	27.0	4	23	28.0	3
9	24.8	7	24	26.4	6
10	21.4	4	25	27.3	4
11	23.9	3	26	24.0	4
12	24.1	5	27	22.6	2
13	27.0	4	28	28.0	6
14	26.8	6	29	24.4	5
15	26.4	2	30	26.4	3

From Table A8 for a sample size 5, $A_2 = 0.58$, $D_3 = 0$, and $D_4 = 2.11$.

$$\text{upper control limit for } R = D_4\,\overline{R} = 2.11 \times 4.8$$
$$= 10.13$$
$$\text{lower control limit for } R = 0$$
$$\text{upper control limit for } \overline{X} = \overline{\overline{X}} + A_2\,\overline{R} = 25.9 + (0.58 \times 4.8)$$
$$= 28.68$$
$$\text{lower control limit for } \overline{X} = \overline{\overline{X}} - A_2\,\overline{R} = 25.9 - (0.58 \times 4.8)$$
$$= 23.12$$

According to step 3, all ranges are compared with these tentative limits. Sample 1 is above the UCL (see Figure 4.6). This means that the process is not stable during the base period. Sample 1 is dropped from the data set. New tentative limits are obtained for the remaining 29 samples.

$$\overline{\overline{X}} = \frac{\sum \overline{X}}{29} = \frac{747}{29} = 25.76$$

$$\overline{R} = \frac{\Sigma R}{29} = \frac{133}{29} = 4.59$$

$$\text{upper control limit for } R = 2.11 \times 4.59$$
$$= 9.68$$
$$\text{lower control limit for } R = 0$$

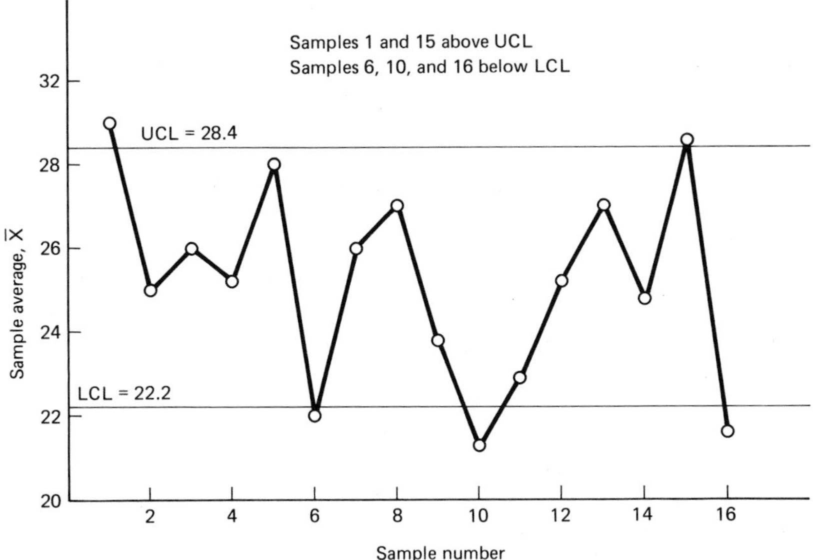

Figure 4.6 Control chart when process is not stable in the base period.

$$\text{upper control limit for } \overline{X} = 25.76 + (0.58 \times 4.59)$$
$$= 28.42$$
$$\text{lower control limt for } \overline{X} = 25.76 - (0.58 \times 4.59)$$
$$= 23.10$$

Returning to step 3, all ranges are compared with these tentative limits. All ranges are within control limits. Going to step 4, all $\overline{X}$ values are compared with the control limits. Samples 10 and 27 are below the LCL. These two are dropped from the data set. New tentative limits are obtained for the remaining 27 samples.

$$\overline{\overline{X}} = \frac{703}{27} = 26.03$$

$$\overline{R} = \frac{127}{27} = 4.70$$

$$\text{upper control limit for } R = 2.11 \times 4.70$$
$$= 9.92$$
$$\text{lower control limit for } R = 0$$
$$\text{upper control limit for } \overline{X} = 26.03 + 0.58 \times 4.70$$
$$= 28.76$$
$$\text{lower control limit for } \overline{X} = 26.03 - 0.58 \times 4.70$$
$$= 23.30$$

Returning to steps 3 and 4, it is observed that all 27 ranges and $\overline{X}$'s are within their respective control limits. The base-period data set has 27 samples. It is possible to conclude that the control limits would hold if the process were to remain in control. In conclusion, these limits, 28.76 and 23.30 for $\overline{X}$ and 9.92 and 0 for R, are extended to the monitoring period. At the same time attempts are initiated to determine possible causes for the lack of control for samples 1, 10, and 27.

CONTROL CHART DURING THE MONITORING PERIOD

Once the control limits are established during the base period, these can be used during the monitoring period to test the hypothesis "the process is stable (i.e., in control)." Once set, the control limits are not altered during the monitoring period until a signal is given (i.e., a sample observation indicates the process being out of control and the hypothesis is rejected). A signal would necessitate the investigation of causes that may be responsible for the out-of-control status. This investigation may lead to two possible decisions. (1) The probable cause is considered random and not likely to be repeated. In this case the process is left alone and the control limits on the charts are left unaltered. (2) The probable cause requires a corrective action. If a corrective action is taken, the previous control chart is abandoned and a new base period is initiated.

Example 4.1 (Continued)

During the monitoring period the observation of 8 samples gave the results shown in Table 4.4. The $\overline{X}$ and R control charts during the monitoring period are shown in Figures 4.7 and 4.8. The first six samples indicate that the process continues in control. Sample 7 indicates that the process is out of control on $\overline{X}$ chart. An out-of-control status can be indicated on either chart. An in-control process must be in control on both charts. If the investigation of the causes for the out-of-control status (sample 7) leads to a corrective action this chart would be abandoned and a new base period would be initiated.

TABLE 4.4

Sample Number	$\overline{X}$	R
1	19.95	0.9
2	19.80	0.7
3	20.32	1.3
4	20.04	1.0
5	19.86	0.8
6	20.08	0.7
7	20.60	1.2
8	20.12	0.9

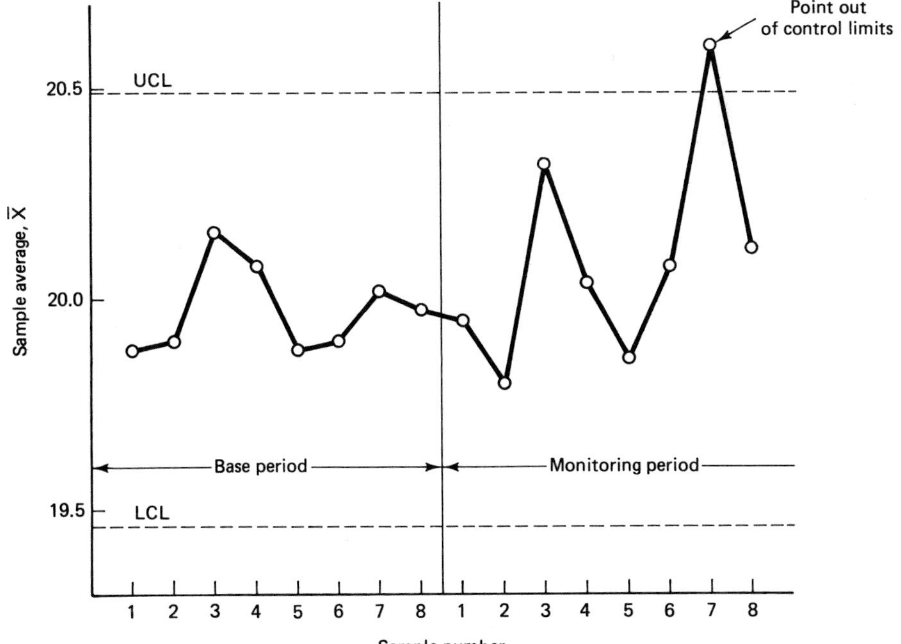

Figure 4.7 $\overline{X}$ chart in the monitoring period.

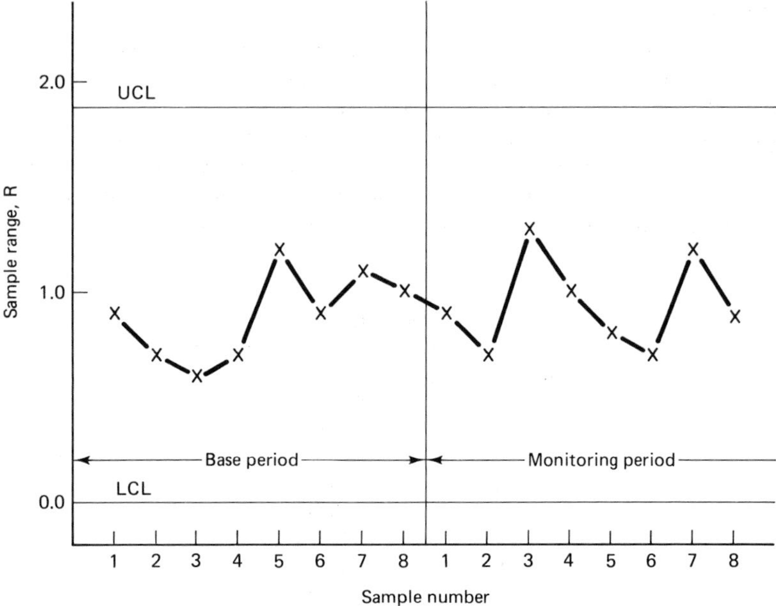

Figure 4.8 *R* chart in the monitoring period.

PROBLEMS

4.1. A chocolate manufacturer produces individually wrapped chocolates. Each chocolate has a nominal weight of 30 g printed on the wrapper. For quality control, a sample of 3 chocolates is inspected each 10 minutes of production. The process is considered out of control (i.e., H_0 is rejected) whenever the sample average $\overline{X}$ falls outside 2.5σ limits on both sides of the desired mean $\mu = 30$ g. It is assumed that the standard deviation σ is 0.25 g and the sample average $\overline{X}$ is distributed normal when the process is in control. For the sample observed at 9:10 A.M. the average weight $\overline{X}$ is 30.39 g.

(a) Is the null hypothesis H_0 rejected?

(b) What is the probability, α, of H_0 being rejected when in fact H_0 is true?

4.2. What would be the answers to Problem 4.1 if the control limits were set at 3σ instead of 2.5σ on both sides of μ?

4.3. Control charts are to be set for $\overline{X}$ and R for the width of an automobile part. The sample size is 5. $\overline{X}$ and R are calculated for each sample after 20 samples, $\Sigma\,\overline{X} = 309.5$ and $\Sigma\,R = 22.38$.

(a) Determine the control limits for $\overline{X}$ and R charts assuming that $k = 3$.

(b) Estimate σ, the standard deviation.

4.4. Control charts are to be maintained on the pH value of a newly developed shampoo. The sample size is 4. After 25 samples, $\Sigma\,\overline{X} = 175.5$ and $\Sigma\,R = 13.7$. For $k = 3$, determine the control limits for $\overline{X}$ and R charts.

4.5. Set up $\overline{X}$ and R control charts using 3σ limits and the following data:

sample size = 6

number of samples observed = 20

$\sum \overline{X} = 308.8$

$\sum R = 40.6$

4.6. Set $\overline{X}$ and R control charts using 3σ limits and the following data:

sample size = 8

number of samples observed = 15

$\sum \overline{X} = 146.25$

$\sum R = 22.64$

4.7. Control charts for $\overline{X}$ and $\hat{\sigma}$ are to be set up for the power output of an engine. The sample size is 5 and 25 samples are observed. $\Sigma \overline{X} = 1885.0$ HP and $\Sigma \sigma = 88.0$. Determine the control limits for $\overline{X}$ and $\hat{\sigma}$ charts.

4.8. An automobile manufacturer wants to set up control charts for the diameter of pistons. The following data are given:

$n = 6$

number of samples = 20

$\sum \overline{X} = 71.8$ in.

$\sum \sigma = 2.32$

Set up the $\overline{X}$ and $\hat{\sigma}$ control charts.

4.9. For Problem 4.8, the manufacturing division wants to discard any piston whose diameter falls outside 3.5 ± 0.150 in. Assuming normal distribution of the piston diameters, what fraction of the pistons would be scrapped when the production process is in control?

4.10. For the item described in Problem 4.6, the specifications are 10.0 ± 0.65. Assuming that the process is in statistical control, to what extent is the process able to meet the specifications?

4.11. An automobile part has to conform to the specifications 5.0 ± 0.15, failing which it must be scrapped. The data gathered by the quality control department are as follows:

$n = 5$

number of samplings = 20

$\sum \overline{X} = 100.2$

$\sum \sigma = 4.8$

Assuming that the process is in control, what percentage of the total parts produced actually fell outside the control limits?

4.12. The following data refer to 20 samples of 5 pistons each observed during the base period.

Sample	$\overline{X}$	R	Sample	$\overline{X}$	R
1	2.6	13	11	4.8	13
2	1.6	8	12	1.4	8
3	3.4	12	13	3.4	7
4	1.6	12	14	3.2	6
5	2.0	7	15	5.6	6
6	4.4	18	16	4.6	6
7	3.6	15	17	3.4	7
8	4.6	8	18	2.8	4
9	3.8	17	19	5.6	8
10	3.2	12	20	2.2	6

The observed variable X is 1000 (Diameter—3.475 in.). Determine the upper and lower control limits for the X and R charts during the base period. Plot the two charts.

4.13. Do the charts in Problem 4.12 indicate whether the process is in control during the base period? How would you explain the difference between the first part of the R chart (samples 1–11) and the second part (samples 12–20)?

4.14. $\overline{X}$ and R charts are maintained for the tensile strength of polyester fiber. It is estimated that the mean strength is 90 kg with a standard deviation 2 kg. The sample size is 7 and the control limits are at $\overline{X} \pm 3\delta$. A change in the composition of one of the chemicals used in the process increases the mean strength to 92.5 kg with no change in the standard deviation. If the charts are not readjusted, what percentage of sample averages would fall outside the upper control limit on

(a) the $\overline{X}$ chart?

(b) the R chart?

4.15. Quality control is to be maintained for a battery. During the base period, 25 samples were taken, each with a size of 4. For the 25 samples in the base period, $\Sigma\,\overline{X}$ = 130.25 V, $\Sigma\,R$ = 7.25.

(a) Determine the control limits to be used during the monitoring period.

(b) During the monitoring period, the first three samples, each with a sample size of 4, yielded $\overline{X}$ as 5.01, 5.51, and 5.35 V. Determine if any of these three samples was outside the control limits.

4.16. In Problem 4.6, for the first 4 samples during the monitoring period the $\overline{X}$ values were 10.28, 9.04, 10.4, and 9.4. Determine if any of these sample averages was outside the control limits.

4.17. Refer to Problem 4.4. After the control charts were set up, the quality of the shampoo was being monitored. A particular sample with its sample size 4 yielded 5.4, 7.3, 7.1, and 7.8 pH values. Based on this sample, what can be said about the process with respect to its $\overline{X}$ and R control charts?

4.18. Control charts are maintained on the temperature tolerance of a certain thermostat. During the base period, 15 samples, each with a size of 6, were tested.

The testing yielded $\Sigma \overline{X} = 3079.8°C$ and $\Sigma R = 294$. During the monitoring period, the same sample size was maintained and a particular sample yielded 199.6, 206.5, 215.4, 214.3, 209.2, and 203.9°C, respectively. Is the process in control?

4.19. Refer to Problem 4.18. A sudden shift in the process changes the mean temperature by d. Assuming that the variance σ remains the same and that the new $\overline{X}$ is also normally distributed, what proportion of the points would be expected to fall beyond the upper control limit? The sample size is maintained as 6.

(a) Solve the problem for $d = +7°$.

(b) Solve the problem for $d = -1°$.

4.20. Refer to Problem 4.7. A disturbance occurs in the process which decreases the mean $\overline{X}$ by 1.0σ. Assuming that the normal characteristic of $\overline{X}$ is preserved and σ remains the same, what percentage of points are expected to fall outside the control limits? Assume that the sample size during the monitoring period is 6.

4.21. The quality control division at Hightek, manufacturers of photocopiers, wants to monitor the length of a certain cylinder. During the base period they inspected 20 samples, each sample of size 4. The data are as follows:

62.0	62.5	65.0	64.0
57.4	61.9	58.9	65.6
57.7	61.2	60.6	59.3
60.5	60.9	59.8	62.7
63.2	63.4	59.9	63.3
60.6	61.2	59.8	62.2
65.5	64.9	62.9	64.3
63.4	63.5	60.1	59.8
66.1	65.9	63.7	62.8
58.1	57.8	57.6	61.2
61.1	62.3	62.2	58.7
62.4	63.1	60.0	60.2
59.9	59.6	57.4	61.3
60.4	59.4	59.5	58.3
61.1	63.2	57.8	59.2
62.8	62.4	59.8	60.4
61.9	62.1	63.1	59.1
60.3	60.8	62.2	61.6

62.8	63.1	60.6	63.4
60.2	59.8	59.9	62.0

What control limits should be used for the $\overline{X}$ and R charts during the subsequent monitoring period?

4.22. A cable insulation manufacturing company wants to monitor the diameter of cable insulators. During the base period 25 samples are observed; the sample size is 4. The measurements of individual diameters are as follows:

4.9	4.8	5.1	5.4
5.0	5.8	5.3	5.3
4.4	4.7	4.8	4.6
4.6	5.8	5.4	4.9
5.2	5.3	6.1	5.2
5.0	5.9	5.8	4.8
4.3	4.6	4.7	4.5
4.9	4.9	5.5	5.7
5.9	6.4	6.1	6.5
5.3	5.9	6.1	4.8
4.6	4.6	5.3	5.0
5.3	5.8	5.4	5.1
4.9	5.3	5.2	5.7
5.2	5.4	4.6	5.5
5.4	4.8	4.2	5.1
4.6	4.4	4.9	5.1
5.7	5.4	5.0	4.8
5.1	4.3	5.7	5.8
5.9	6.4	6.2	6.1
5.0	5.1	4.5	4.8
4.9	5.9	5.3	5.2
5.4	5.9	4.4	5.0
5.2	4.7	5.7	5.8
4.0	4.8	5.1	5.8
5.3	5.8	6.0	6.3

It is proposed to set up control limits on $\overline{X}$ and R with 3σ limits.

(a) Is the process stable during the base period?

(b) If the process is not stable, what necessary action would you recommend to set up the control limits during this base period?

4.23. $\overline{X}$ and R control charts are to be maintained on a certain dimension in a heavy machines company. Twenty samples each with a size of 4 were observed. The readings are given below. Assuming that $k = 3$, set up control limits for $\overline{X}$ and R charts.

9.5	10.2	10.4	9.8
9.9	11.7	12.1	10.3
10.4	12.1	11.8	11.7
10.9	10.5	10.5	10.2
10.7	12.4	12.4	11.7
7.7	9.2	9.2	9.4
11.4	9.5	9.6	11.2
11.9	12.1	10.7	11.4
9.9	9.8	12.1	10.3
10.0	10.4	11.6	10.1
11.3	11.9	10.4	9.1
9.2	9.7	10.9	11.5
10.2	10.3	10.9	11.0
9.9	11.7	10.1	10.7
12.0	11.4	10.8	11.6
11.0	8.8	9.6	9.9
9.5	9.3	9.9	10.4
10.9	11.5	11.2	11.8
8.6	9.4	9.9	9.7
9.5	9.4	9.9	9.7

five

SPECIAL PROCEDURES IN PROCESS CONTROL

When the quality characteristic is variable, $\overline{X}$ and R charts are the most commonly used device for process control. Similarly, when the quality characteristic is discrete, p, c, and u charts are most commonly used. (These charts are described in Chapter 7.) However, in certain situations it may be advisable (or obligatory) to use some variations of these procedures. This chapter describes some of these variations.

CONTROL CHARTS FOR $\overline{X}$ AND s[1]

In the development of $\overline{X}$ and R charts the range R of a subgroup is used as an estimator of the standard deviation σ of the population. An alternative indicator of σ is the standard deviation s of the subgroup. When $x_1, x_2, \ldots, x_m$ are the measurements in a subgroup, the quantity s is calculated as

$$s = \sqrt{\frac{\sum_{i=1}^{m} (x_i - \overline{X})^2}{m}} \tag{5.1}$$

When s is used to estimate σ, the two charts for process control would be (1) an $\overline{X}$ chart, where the control limits are based on s, and (2) an s chart. Compared to $\overline{X}$ and R charts, the use of $\overline{X}$ and s charts involves significantly

[1] These are the same charts referred to in Chapter 4 as $\overline{X}$ and $\hat{\sigma}$ charts. These are illustrated in more detail here.

more computation. Further, $\overline{X}$ and s charts are applicable only when the underlying distribution of the quality characteristic is approximately normal. If there is any suspicion that this distribution differs significantly from normal, it is advisable not to use $\overline{X}$ and s charts.

To set up $\overline{X}$ and s charts, m subgroups of n items each are observed during the base period. For each subgroup the quantities $\overline{X}_i$ and s_i are calculated. Then the averages of these are used to obtain the estimates of mean μ and standard deviation σ.

$$\overline{\overline{X}} = \frac{\overline{X}_i + \overline{X}_2 + \cdots + \overline{X}_m}{m} \tag{5.2}$$

$$\bar{s} = \frac{s_1 + s_2 + \cdots + s_m}{m} \tag{5.3}$$

The factors A_1, B_3, and B_4 tabulated in Table A8 are used to obtain the trial control limits.

$$\text{central line for } \overline{X} \text{ chart} = \overline{\overline{X}}$$

$$\text{upper control limit for } \overline{X} \text{ chart} = \overline{\overline{X}} + A_1\bar{s}$$

$$\text{lower control limit for } \overline{X} \text{ chart} = \overline{\overline{X}} - A_1\bar{s}$$

$$\text{upper control limit for } s \text{ chart} = B_4\bar{s}$$

$$\text{lower control limit for } s \text{ chart} = B_3\bar{s}$$

If all the subgroups in the base period are "in control" with respect to these trial limits, the process is considered to be in control and the limits continued for the monitoring period.

Example 5.1

The diameter of a machine part is specified to be 3.750 ± 0.015. In the base period 20 subgroups of size 5 were tested. The results are given in Table 5.1 [*Note:* The tabulated values are 1000(diameter − 3.700).] For each subgroup $\overline{X}$ and s are calculated (Table 5.2). For a sample of 5 the factors A_1, B_4, and B_3 are 1.60, 2.09, and 0, respectively.

$$\text{central line for } \overline{X} \text{ chart} = 47.55$$

$$\begin{aligned}\text{upper control limit for } \overline{X} \text{ chart} &= 47.55 + 1.6(5.527)\\ &= 56.39\end{aligned}$$

$$\begin{aligned}\text{lower control limit for } \overline{X} \text{ chart} &= 47.55 - 1.6(5.527)\\ &= 38.71\end{aligned}$$

$$\begin{aligned}\text{upper control limit for } s \text{ chart} &= 2.09(5.527)\\ &= 11.55\end{aligned}$$

TABLE 5.1 Test Data

Subgroup	1	2	3	4	5
1	42	40	46	55	48
2	50	43	32	51	53
3	46	44	58	46	47
4	59	52	48	45	47
5	37	34	43	49	59
6	53	58	49	56	36
7	47	51	49	40	46
8	47	38	45	44	43
9	49	40	40	53	40
10	54	40	56	51	50
11	54	48	51	48	48
12	44	51	36	47	57
13	63	46	47	40	62
14	40	45	45	52	59
15	62	41	44	45	49
16	56	45	55	45	54
17	54	44	37	47	56
18	49	44	44	43	44
19	44	46	47	44	42
20	42	44	55	48	52

TABLE 5.2 Calculations

Subgroup	$\overline{X}$	s	s^2
1	46.2	5.23	27.35
2	45.8	7.67	58.83
3	48.2	4.99	24.90
4	50.4	4.95	24.50
5	44.4	8.93	79.74
6	50.4	7.81	60.99
7	46.6	3.72	13.84
8	43.4	3.01	9.06
9	44.4	5.53	30.58
10	50.2	5.53	30.58
11	49.8	2.40	5.76
12	47.0	7.01	49.14
13	51.6	9.22	85.01
14	48.2	6.61	43.69
15	48.2	7.35	54.02
16	51.0	4.93	24.30
17	47.6	6.88	47.33
18	44.8	2.13	4.54
19	44.6	1.74	3.03
20	48.2	4.83	23.33
	$\overline{\overline{X}} = 47.55$	$\bar{s} = 5.527$	$\Sigma s^2 = 700.52$

$$\text{lower control limit for } s \text{ chart} = 0$$

$$\text{estimated } \sigma \text{ for the process} = \frac{\bar{s}}{c_2} = \frac{5.527}{0.8407} = 6.57$$

The $\overline{X}$ and s charts are shown in Figure 5.1.

Equation (5.3) is useful when all subgroups are of the same size and the underlying distribution is normal. In the general case an alternative way of calculating $\bar{s}$ is usually preferable:

$$\bar{s} = \sqrt{\frac{n_1 s_1^2 + n_2 s_2^2 + \cdots + n_m s_m^2}{n_1 + n_2 + \cdots + n_m}} \tag{5.4}$$

When equation (5.4) is used to calculate $\bar{s}$, the factors from Table A8 cannot be used. However, control limits can be obtained from the fact that the quantity

$$(\overline{X} - \overline{\overline{X}}) \Big/ \bar{s} \sqrt{\frac{1}{\bar{n}} + \frac{1}{m}}$$

follows a t distribution with $(m \cdot \bar{n})/(m + \bar{n}) - 1$ degrees of freedom. When all samples are of the same size n, these quantities become

$$(\overline{X} - \overline{\overline{X}}) \Big/ \bar{s} \sqrt{\frac{1}{n} + \frac{1}{m}} \quad \text{and} \quad \frac{m \cdot n}{m + n} - 1$$

respectively.

CONTROL CHARTS FOR INDIVIDUAL MEASUREMENTS

If the operators are not familiar with the quality control methods, they are likely to be confused when the average measurement of a sample $\overline{X}$ is plotted instead of each individual measurement. Consider two samples of five items each. The nominal size is 3.10.

Sample 1: individual measurements

3.10, 3.12, 3.10, 3.10, 3.00

$\overline{X} = 3.08 \qquad R = 0.12$

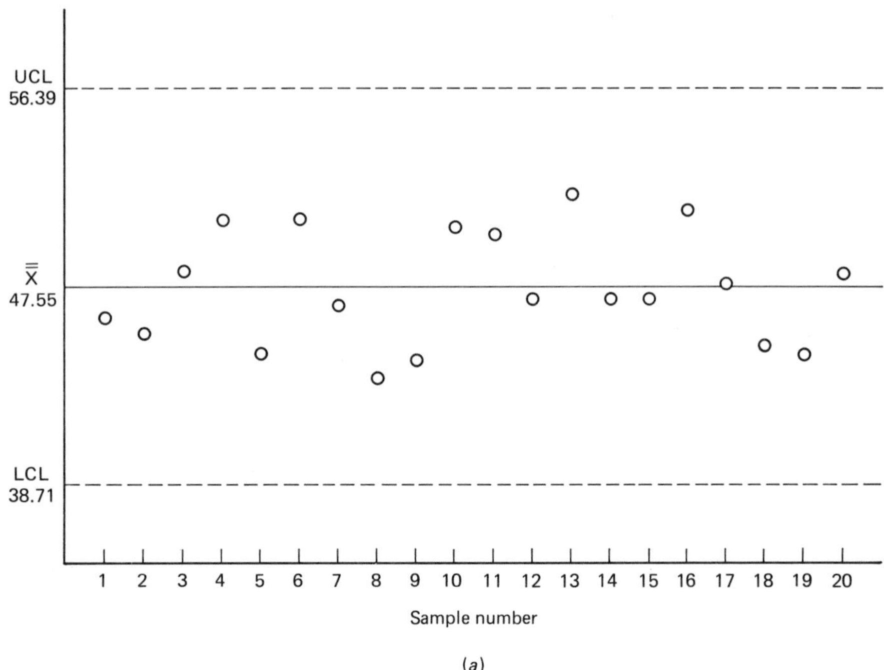

(*a*)

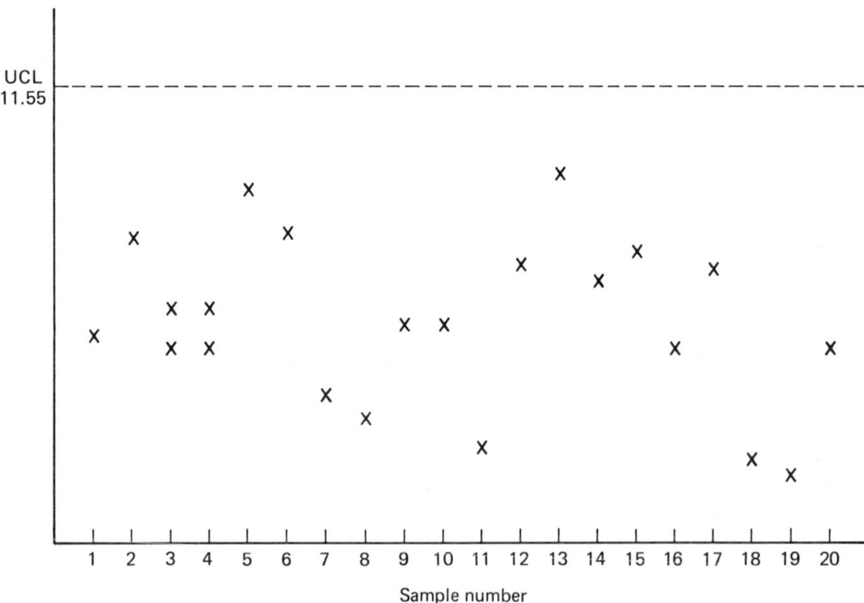

(*b*)

Figure 5.1 (a) $\overline{X}$ chart; (b) s chart.

Sample 2: individual measurements

$$3.04, 3.06, 3.08, 3.10, 3.12$$

$$\overline{X} = 3.08 \qquad R = 0.08$$

To the uninitiated, sample 1 may appear to be better since 3 out of 5 items are exactly of nominal size. Sample 2 has only one item of nominal size. Further, both samples indicate the same mean. It is quite difficult to understand that sample 1 represents a wider variation than sample 2.

Charts where individual measurements are plotted, even when accompanied by specification limits, are distinctly inferior to the conventional $\overline{X}$ and R charts. Of course, individual measurement charts are better than "no charts at all." The best procedure for avoiding confusion and misunderstanding is to conduct training sessions for the operators describing the basics of $\overline{X}$ and R charts. If plotting of individual measurements is unavoidable, the damage can be minimized by (1) plotting individual measurements on the conventional $\overline{X}$ chart, or (2) plotting individual measurements and circling the median for emphasis.

For illustration the first five subgroups from Example 5.1 are used. Figure 5.3 shows the plotting of the individual measurements on the conventional $\overline{X}$ chart.

Example 5.1 (Continued)

If the assumption of the underlying normal distribution is not considered valid, equation (5.4) can be used to calculate $\bar{s}$:

$$\bar{s} = \sqrt{\frac{\sum s_i^2}{m}}$$

$$= \sqrt{\frac{700.52}{20}} = 5.918$$

$n = 5$ and $m = 20$

$$\text{Degrees of freedom} = \frac{20 \times 5}{20 + 5} - 1$$

$$\text{Quantity } \sqrt{\frac{1}{n} + \frac{1}{m}} = \sqrt{\frac{1}{5} + \frac{1}{20}}$$

$$= 0.5$$

$$\overline{\overline{X}} = 47.55$$

Therefore, $(\overline{X} - 47.55)/(5.918)(0.50)$ has a t distribution with 3 degrees of freedom. To calculate control limits with $\alpha = 0.05$, the quantity $t_{0.025,3}$ can be obtained from Table A5.

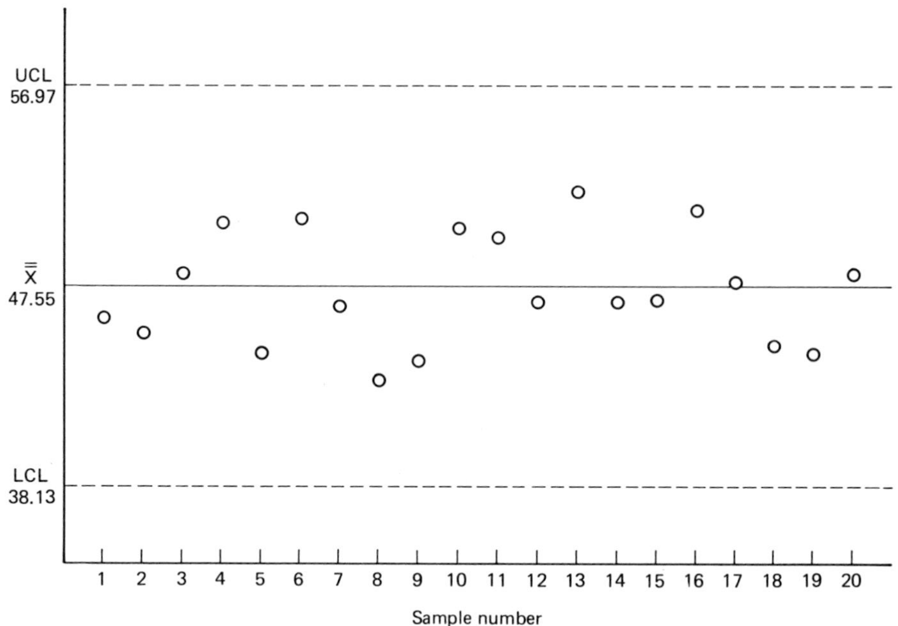

Figure 5.2 $\overline{X}$ chart with control limits based on t distribution.

$$t_{0.025,3} = 3.182$$

$$\begin{aligned} \text{upper control limit} &= 47.55 + (3.182)(5.9182)(0.5) \\ &= 47.55 + 9.42 \\ &= 56.97 \\ \text{lower control limit} &= 47.55 - (3.182)(5.918)(0.5) \\ &= 38.13 \end{aligned}$$

The $\overline{X}$ chart is shown in Figure 5.2.

The procedure for using the medians is described by Clifford.[2]

Let

$$\tilde{x}_i = \text{median of sample } i$$

$$\tilde{\tilde{x}} = \text{median of the medians}$$

$$m(R) = \text{median of the ranges}$$

[2] P. C. Clifford, "Control Charts without Calculations," *Industrial Quality Control*, Vol. 15, No. 11, 1959.

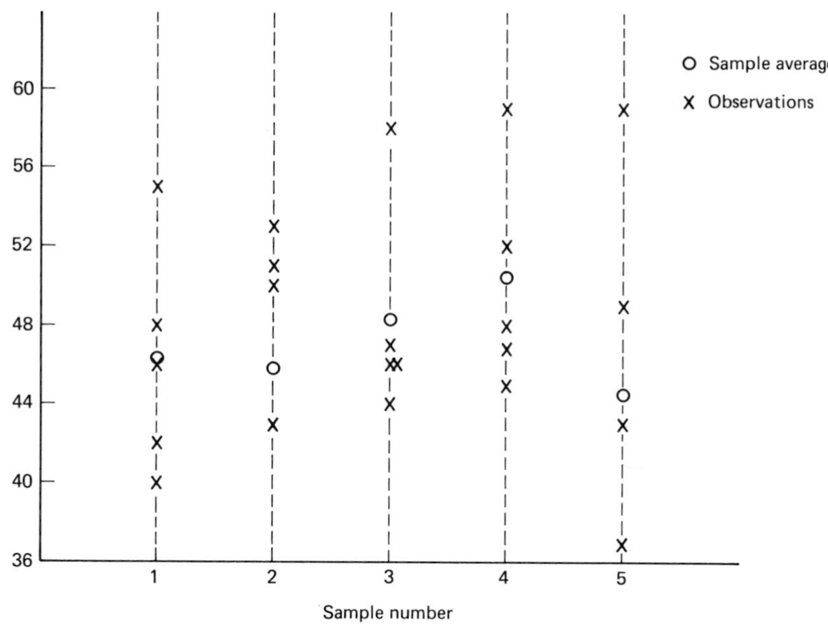

Figure 5.3 Plotting individual observations.

The upper and lower control limits are calculated as

$$\text{upper control limit} = \tilde{\bar{x}} + \tilde{A}_2\, m(R)$$

$$\text{lower control limit} = \tilde{\bar{x}} - \tilde{A}_2\, m(R)$$

The factor $\tilde{A}_2$ has been tabulated by Clifford in the article cited. Table 5.3 gives some selected values. More values may be found in Table A10. For the data in Example 5.1, the medians and ranges are shown in Table 5.4.

$$n = 5 \qquad \tilde{A}_2 = 0.712$$

$$\begin{aligned}\text{upper control limit} &= \tilde{\bar{x}} + \tilde{A}_2\, m(R)\\ &= 47 + 0.712(14.5)\\ &= 47 + 10.324\\ &= 57.324\\ \text{lower control limit} &= \tilde{\bar{x}} - \tilde{A}_2\, m(R)\\ &= 47 - 10.324\\ &= 36.676\end{aligned}$$

Figure 5.4 shows the plotting of a median control chart.

TABLE 5.3 Selected Values for A_2

n	$\tilde{A}_2$
3	1.265
5	0.712
7	0.520
9	0.419

TABLE 5.4

Subgroup	$\tilde{x}$	Range	Subgroup	$\tilde{x}$	Range
1	46	15	11	48	6
2	50	21	12	47	15
3	46	14	13	47	23
4	48	14	14	45	19
5	43	25	15	45	21
6	53	22	16	54	11
7	47	11	17	47	19
8	44	9	18	44	6
9	40	13	19	44	5
10	51	16	20	48	13
					$\bar{\tilde{x}} = 47$
					$m(R) = 14.5$

WARNING LIMITS

The control limits on a conventional $\overline{X}$ chart give a signal indicating that the process may be out of control. Under normal distribution and the usual 3 standard deviation control limits, the probability of a false signal is only 0.0027. This means that the quality control engineer can be reasonably sure that the process is out of control if a signal does occur. The engineer is not sure when the signal does not occur. Even after the process has shifted out of control, a signal may not be forthcoming immediately. To guard against undue delay in detection, some experts advise the use of *warning limits*. Warning limits are situated inside the usual control limits. Observing a point outside the warning limits but still inside the control limits indicates that the process needs to be watched carefully.

Some persons find the use of warning limits confusing. They prefer the definitiveness of a single set of limits on the chart. This preference stems from the ignorance of the principles of probability. Consider warning limits set at 2 standard deviations from the mean. If the null hypothesis is true and the process is in control, the probability that any sample observation would be between the warning limits is 95.54%. For the control limits this

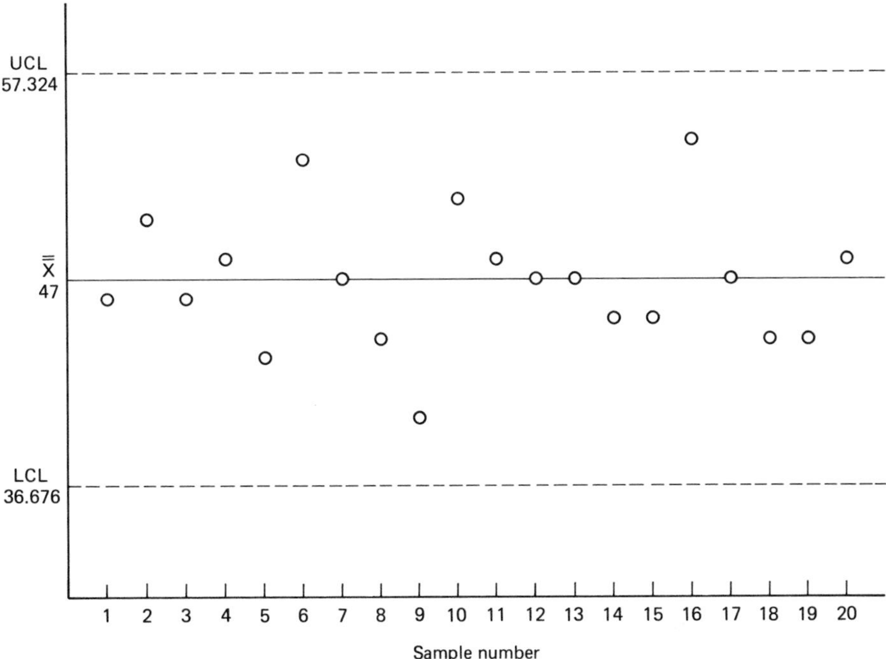

Figure 5.4 Median chart.

probability is 99.73%. For a process in control, the chance for getting a warning but not a signal is only 99.73 − 95.54, or 4.19%. On the other hand, if the process is drifting out of control, the chances of catching this drift improves by using the warning limits. The improvements by the use of warning limits are demonstrated further in Chapter 6.

It must be remembered that the warning limits are just that, warning limits. A single observation outside these limits should not cause any great concern. Nor should the engineer start looking for instability in the process. It is only an alert. If several succeeding samples are inside the warning limits, there is nothing to worry about. In any manufacturing plant the rule should always be: *Leave the process alone unless there is a definite reason.*

If the process gives a warning and the next sample also gives a second warning, things are pretty bad. The probability of two successive samples being outside the warning limits is very small.

Let x_1 and x_2 be the two events of observed sample values being outside 2-standard-deviation warning limits. Then

$$\Pr(x_1) = 1 - 0.9554 = 0.0446$$

$$\Pr(x_2) = 0.0446$$

As x_1 and x_2 are independent events,

$$\begin{aligned}\Pr(x_1 \text{ and } x_2) &= \Pr(x_1) \times \Pr(x_2)\\ &= (0.0446)(0.0446)\\ &= 0.001989\end{aligned}$$

This probability is smaller than the probability of getting a signal from 3-standard-deviation control limits, which is 0.0027.

Example 5.1 (Continued)

Consider the application of 2σ warning limits to the data in Table 5.1. The warning limits are:

$$\begin{aligned}\text{upper warning limit} &= \overline{\overline{X}} + 2\hat{\sigma}\\ &= \overline{\overline{X}} + 2\left[\frac{1}{3} \cdot (1.6)\bar{s}\right]\\ &= 47.55 + 2\left[\frac{1}{3}(1.6)(5.527)\right]\\ &= 47.55 + 5.90\\ &= 53.45\\ \text{lower warning limit} &= \overline{\overline{X}} - 2\hat{\sigma}\\ &= 47.55 - 5.90\\ &= 41.65\end{aligned}$$

Comparing these limits with the $\overline{X}$ values in Table 5.2, it is seen that no warnings are issued during this period. Figure 5.5 shows the 2σ warning limits.

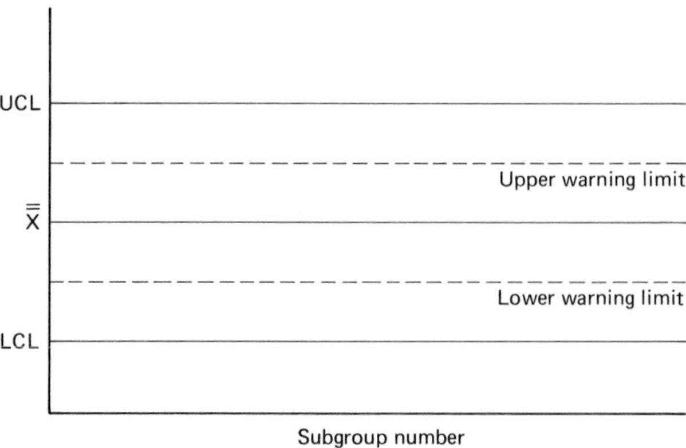

Figure 5.5 Warning limits for $\overline{X}$ chart.

MOVING AVERAGE AND CUSUM CHARTS

The usual $\overline{X}$ chart uses information from only one sample at a time. When a sample value of $\overline{X}$ is plotted, all the information from the preceding sample observations is lost. Such a procedure keeps the operation simple but is somewhat less efficient in tracking any changes developing in the process mean μ. For the treatment of information contained in the past observations, there are four possible courses of action:

1. Use no past data.
2. Use all past data.
3. Use only a small (but constant) number of past observations.
4. Use only the recent sequence of observations that may indicate a change in μ.

The conventional or Shewhart types of control charts follow option 1, leading to a simple but less efficient procedure. Paradoxically, option 2 also leads to a less efficient procedure. The reason is that the recent data are combined with a large amount of data in the past when the process had been operating "in control." A small amount of recent "out of control" data may be completely overwhelmed by the long sequence of "in control" data, thus preventing the detection of a shift in the process mean μ. Option 2 is not used in any control charts. Option 3, which is based on the use of the most recent r sample observations, is used in *moving average* (or *moving sum*) *charts*. Here the efficiency of detection of shifts in the process average will depend on r. Option 4 forms the basis of *CUSUM charts*. In many respects it is similar to the use of moving average charts. However, the number r is not fixed but is a random number based on the values of most recent observations. Further moving average charts are usually used for moving averages of individual observations. *CUSUM* charts, on the other hand, are usually used for subgroup averages or $\overline{X}_i$'s.

Moving Average Charts

Moving average and accompanying moving range charts are usually applied to individual observations. To distinguish this from conventional $\overline{X}$ and R charts having the same subgroup size, it must be remembered that in $\overline{X}$ and R charts for each sample a new subgroup of size r is selected at random, whereas in moving average charts all items are observed and each consequent group of r observations is called a *subgroup*. The procedure for obtaining the moving average and moving range is illustrated in Table 5.5.

TABLE 5.5 Data for the Moving Average and Moving Range

Hour	Concentration of C (%)	5-Hour MA	5-Hour MR
1	6.5		
2	11.0		
3	11.5		
4	7.0		
5	5.0	8.20	6.5
6	5.8	8.06	6.5
7	5.7	7.00	6.5
8	6.6	6.02	2.0
9	8.1	6.24	3.1
10	12.1	7.66	6.4
11	8.7	8.24	6.4
12	7.8	8.66	5.5
13	7.5	8.84	4.6
14	12.8	9.78	5.3
15	10.6	9.48	5.3
16	14.3	10.60	6.8
17	12.7	11.58	6.8
18	12.8	12.64	3.7
19	15.4	13.16	4.8
20	14.0	13.84	2.7
21	19.8	14.94	7.1
22	21.0	16.60	8.2
23	23.2	18.68	9.2
24	24.2	20.44	10.2

Example 5.2

In a chemical reaction two chemicals, A and B, react to form a third chemical, C. The concentration of C in the resulting mixture is monitored hourly. The plant operates continuously on a 24-hour basis. Five-hour moving averages and moving ranges are used for control purposes. The concentration of C must be at least 10% for the plant to operate with no loss. Higher values indicate more efficient conversion and more profitable operation.

$$MA_i = \frac{1}{r}\left(\sum_{j=0}^{r-1} X_{i-j}\right)$$

$$MR_i = \max_{j=0}^{j=r-1} X_{i-j} - \min_{j=0}^{j=r-1} X_{i-j}$$

For the observations 7, 8, 9, 10, and 11,

$$MA_{11} = \frac{5.7 + 6.6 + 8.1 + 12.1 + 8.7}{5}$$

$$= 8.24$$

$$MR_{11} = \text{Max}(5.7, 6.6, 8.1, 12.1, 8.7)$$

$$- \text{Min}(5.7, 6.6, 8.1, 12.1, 8.7)$$

$$= 12.1 - 5.7 = 6.4$$

In this example it is possible to employ only a single lower control limit of 10%. As a general practice, however, the same control limits as in the conventional $\overline{X}$ and R charts can be used. Figure 5.6 shows the moving average and moving range charts, including the conventional limits.

Moving average and moving range charts have limited application when the production is discrete. It is obvious that observing each item is expensive. However, in certain types of manufacturing these charts are very useful for two reasons. First, the operation itself may be continuous, as in most chemical processes. Second, the industry practice may require the observation and recording of each periodic item of data. This record is then readily available for quality control.

CUSUM Charts[3]

The CUSUM chart was originally proposed during the 1950s. The chart uses a moving sum. This sum includes only that recent sequence of data which indicates a possible change in the process mean. In general, CUSUM charts are more efficient in detecting small shifts in process average. The advantage of the CUSUM chart over the conventional $\overline{X}$ chart is described in Chapter 6.

To understand the basic principles of CUSUM charts, a simple case is considered where it is necessary only to detect a shift to higher values of the process mean.

Null hypothesis: H_0: $\mu = \mu_0$
Alternative hypothesis: H_1: $\mu = \mu_1$ where $\mu_1 > \mu_0$

$\overline{X}_i$ denotes the average of the ith subgroup as usual. When the process is in control and μ_0 is true, the quantity

$$Z_i = \overline{X}_i - \mu_0$$

[3] This description of CUSUM charts is adopted with permission from working notes prepared by Marion Reynolds of the Statistics Department at Virginia Polytechnic Institute and State University, 1984. These notes form a part of a proposed textbook.

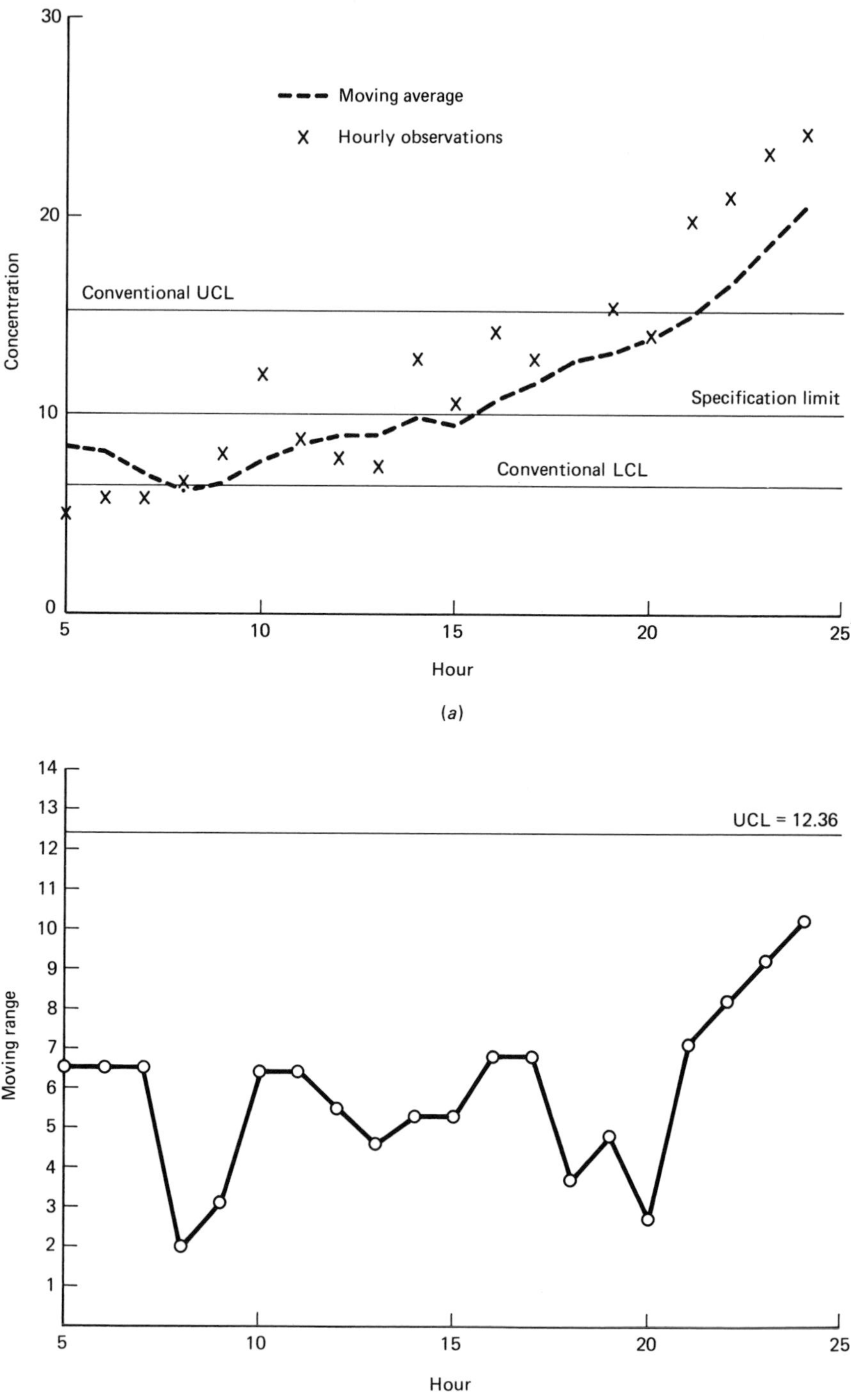

Figure 5.6 (a) Moving average chart; (b) moving range chart.

would be a random variable with an expected value of zero. Another quantity,

$$y_i = Z_i - d \qquad d > 0$$

would also be a random variable but with a negative expected value. The *cum*ulative *sum* (CUSUM, for short) of y_i would tend to move in a downward direction as long as H_0 is true (Figure 5.7).

$$Y_k = \sum_{i=1}^{k} y_i$$

If the process shifts to the "out of control" state and H_1 is true, the expected value of y_i would no longer be $-d$.

$$\begin{aligned} E(y_i | H_1) &= E[(\overline{X}_i - \mu_0 - d) | H_1] \\ &= E(\overline{X}_i | H_1) - \mu_0 - d \\ &= \mu_1 - \mu_0 - d \end{aligned}$$

Since $\mu_1 > \mu_0$, it is possible to choose a value d that makes $E(y_i | H_1)$ positive. Reynolds[4] recommends a value

$$d = \frac{\mu_1 - \mu_0}{2}$$

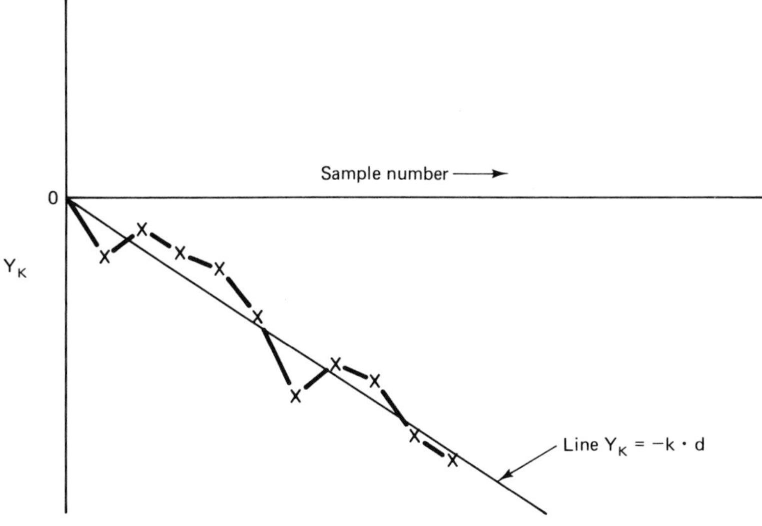

Figure 5.7 Probable values of Y_k when H_0 is true.

[4] Ibid.

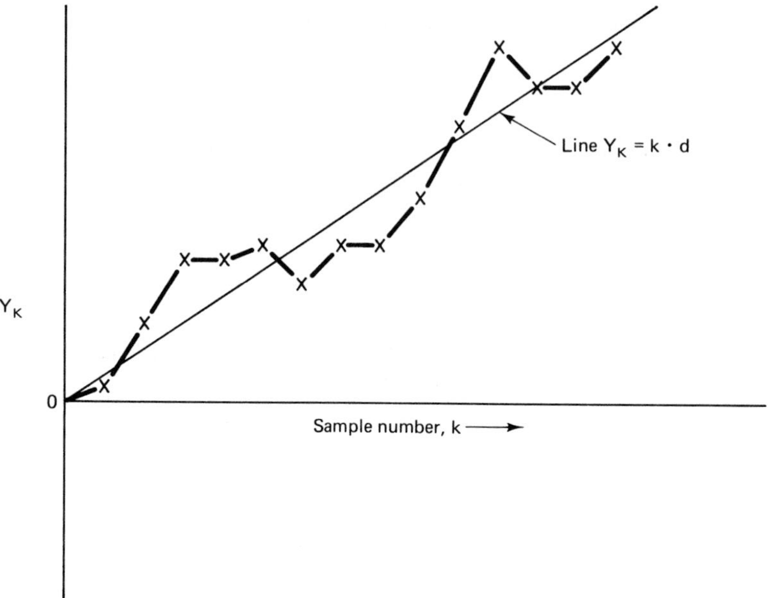

Figure 5.8 Probable values of Y_k when H_0 is false.

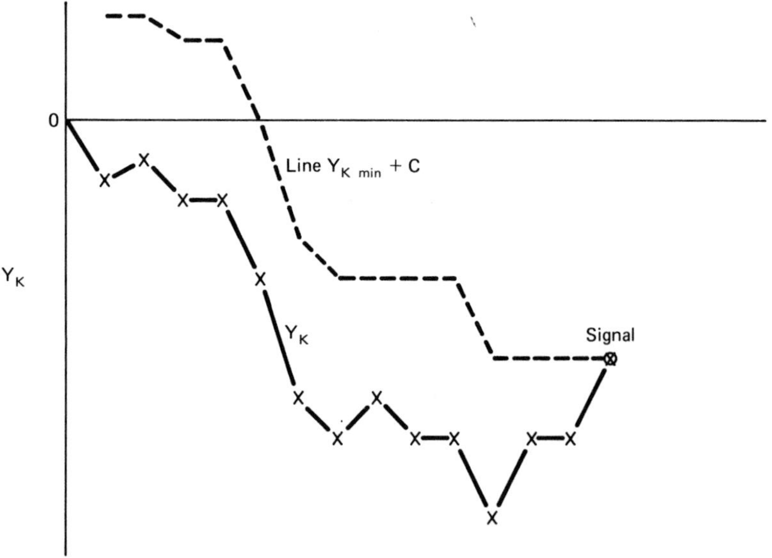

Figure 5.9 Generation of signal on a CUSUM chart.

This value makes $E(y_i | H_1) = d$, which is positive. The cumulative sum of y_i would tend to move in an upward direction as long as H_1 is true (Figure 5.8).

A CUSUM chart is a plot of the cumulative sum Y_k. As long as Y_k is generally decreasing, the process is left alone and sampling continued. Whenever there is a significant upturn in the plot of Y_k, a signal is given that the process is going out of control. This signal is based on an increment c. Thus if the most recent value of Y_k exceeds a previous minimum level of Y by c units, a signal is given. This is illustrated in Figure 5.9. The choice of c is somewhat arbitrary.

Example 5.3

The nominal diameter of the piston is 2.996 in. The upper tolerance limit is 3.002 in. From a long history of the production of this type of piston, the standard deviation is known to be 0.0028 in. The process would be considered unsatisfactory if the mean increases to 2.998 in. Control charts are maintained to detect this shift from nominal 2.996 in. to 2.998 in. Thirty subgroup averages are given in Table 5.6. The values in the table are scaled as $(\overline{X}_i - 2.990) \times 10{,}000$.

Using the same scaling as in Table 5.6, we obtain the following:

$$\begin{aligned} \text{nominal diameter} &= (2.996 - 2.990) \times 10{,}000 \\ &= 60 \\ \text{upper tolerance} &= (3.002 - 2.990) \times 10{,}000 \\ &= 120 \\ \text{diameter after shift} &= (2.998 - 2.990) \times 10{,}000 \\ &= 80 \\ \text{standard deviation} &= 0.0028 \times 10{,}000 \\ &= 28 \end{aligned}$$

When the mean diameter is nominal,

$$\begin{aligned} Z &= \frac{120 - 60}{28} \\ &= 2.14 \end{aligned}$$

The fraction of production exceeding the upper tolerance is 0.0162, or 1.62%. When the mean diameter has shifted,

$$\begin{aligned} Z &= \frac{120 - 80}{28} \\ &= 1.43 \end{aligned}$$

TABLE 5.6 Subgroup Averages

Subgroup Number	$\overline{X}_i$	Subgroup Number	$\overline{X}_i$
1	20	16	37
2	56	17	97
3	39	18	17
4	42	19	80
5	77	20	95
6	21	21	96
7	27	22	96
8	23	23	102
9	12	24	95
10	100	25	90
11	97	26	76
12	37	27	88
13	98	28	90
14	60	29	65
15	12	30	102

The fraction of production exceeding the upper tolerance is 0.0764, or 7.64%.

Conventional control chart:

$$\overline{\overline{X}} = 64.73$$

factor A for σ-known control charts with subgroup size of 5 = 1.34

$$\begin{aligned} \text{upper control limit} &= \overline{\overline{X}} + A\sigma' \\ &= 64.73 + (1.34 \times 28) \\ &= 64.73 + 37.52 \\ &= 102.25 \end{aligned}$$

Although two subgroups 23 and 30 come close to the upper control limit, no definite signal is given by the conventional control chart (without any warning limits).

CUSUM chart: For a CUSUM chart the parameters d and c are selected as follows:

$$\text{Null hypothesis:} \quad H_0: \mu = 60$$

$$\text{Alternative hypothesis:} \quad H_1: \mu = 80$$

$$d = \frac{\mu_1 - \mu_0}{2} = \frac{80 - 60}{2} = 10$$

$$c = 6 \times d = 60 \qquad \text{(this choice is somewhat arbitrary)}$$

$$\begin{aligned} y_i &= \overline{X}_i - \mu_0 - d \\ &= \overline{X}_i - 60 - 10 \\ &= \overline{X}_i - 70 \end{aligned}$$

Values of y_i and $Y_k = \sum_i y_i$ are shown in Table 5.7.

TABLE 5.7 Computations for CUSUM Chart

Sample Number	$\overline{X}_i$	y_i	Y_i	$c + \min Y_i$	Sample Number	$\overline{X}_i$	y_i	Y_i	$c + \min Y_i$
1	20	−50	−50	+10	16	37	−33	−368	−308
2	56	−14	−64	−4	17	97	+27	−341	−308
3	39	−31	−95	−35	18	17	−53	−394	−334
4	42	−28	−123	−63	19	80	+10	−384	−334
5	77	+7	−116	−63	20	95	+25	−359	−334
6	21	−49	−165	−105	21	96	+26	−333*	−334
7	21	−49	−214	−154	22	96	+26	−307*	−334
8	23	−47	−261	−201	23	102	+2	−275*	−334
9	12	−58	−319	−259	24	95	+25	−250*	−334
10	100	+30	−289	−259	25	90	+20	−230*	−334
11	97	+27	−262	−259	26	76	+6	−224*	−334
12	37	−33	−295	−259	27	88	+18	−206*	−334
13	98	+28	−267	−259	28	90	+20	−186*	−334
14	60	−10	−277	−259	29	65	−5	−191*	−334
15	12	−58	−335	−275	30	102	+32	−159*	−334
	$\overline{\overline{X}} = 47.67$					$\overline{\overline{X}} = 81.73$			

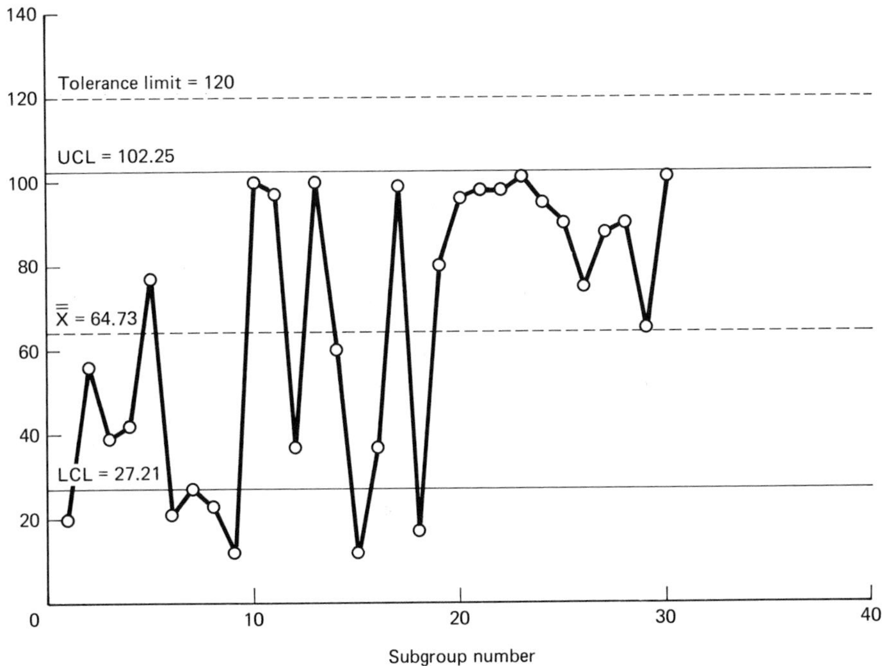

Figure 5.10 Conventional $\overline{X}$ chart for Example 5.3.

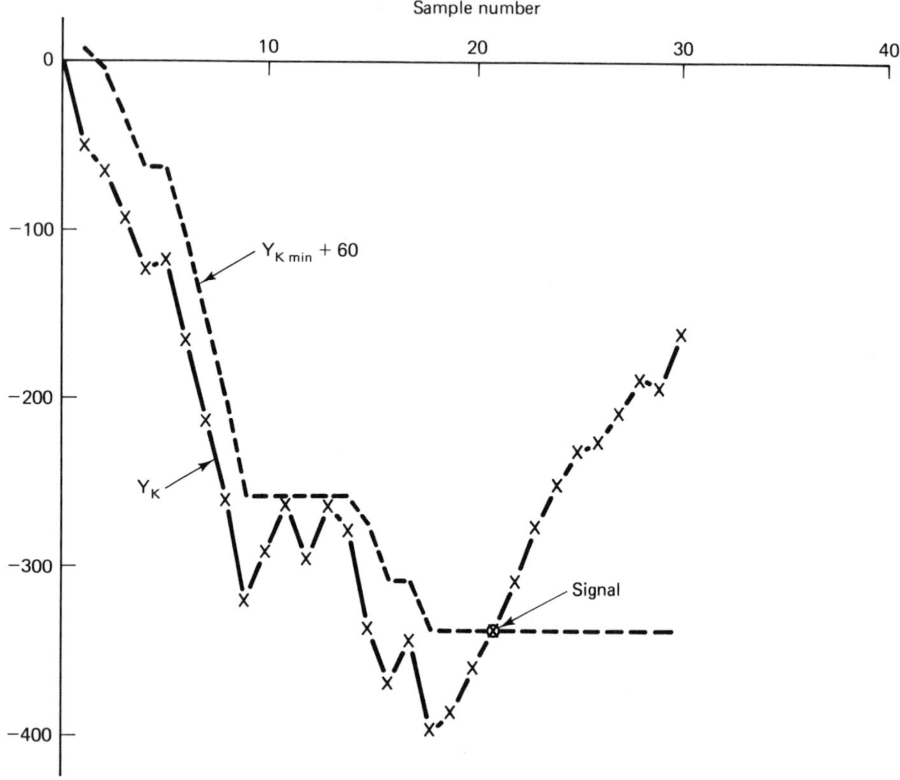

Figure 5.11 CUSUM chart for Example 5.3.

The CUSUM chart signals the shift with the twenty-first subgroup. From that point the chart remains above the signal level. Figures 5.10 and 5.11 show the conventional $\overline{X}$ chart and the CUSUM chart, respectively. That a shift had actually taken place can be inferred by comparing the average of the first half of the data, 47.67, to the average of the second half of the data, 81.73.

PROBLEMS

5.1. Set up $\overline{X}$ and S control charts using 3σ control limits, given that sample size = 6, number of samples = 20, $\Sigma\,\overline{X} = 234.2$, and $\Sigma\,S = 11.4$.

5.2. Refer to the data in Problem 4.22. There is no reason to assume that the observations are distributed normal. Set up $\overline{X}$ and S charts without the normal assumption.

5.3. For the data in Problem 4.23, determine the control limits for $\overline{X}$ and S charts (a) with normal distribution assumption, and (b) without normal distribution assumption.

5.4. Plot the $\overline{X}$ and S charts for the data in Problem 4.21. Also, plot $\overline{X}$ and R charts for the same data. What conclusion can you draw about the process being in control during the base period?

5.5. The quality control department requested the supervisors for three shifts to observe and report on a sample of items produced in each shift. Through a clerical error no sample size was designated. The three supervisors used three different sample sizes. The observations for the first week were as follows:

	I	20.00	20.50	20.50	21.00		
Monday	II	20.00	19.50	19.00	21.00	20.50	
	III	20.00	17.50	20.50	17.50	19.00	18.25
	I	18.50	17.75	21.00	20.75		
Tuesday	II	18.75	18.00	19.00	20.50	20.00	
	III	19.50	20.00	19.25	20.75	19.50	18.75
	I	20.50	21.00	21.50	21.50		
Wednesday	II	21.25	17.75	18.50	18.25	19.75	
	III	20.00	20.25	22.00	19.25	19.00	18.75
	I	21.00	20.00	19.50	21.25		
Thursday	II	20.75	19.25	20.25	19.75	19.50	
	III	19.50	22.50	21.25	21.00	18.50	20.00
	I	21.00	19.50	20.00	20.50		
Friday	II	20.50	18.00	18.50	21.00	21.50	
	III	23.25	18.50	19.00	21.25	20.75	18.75

Determine the control limits that would be used for $\overline{X}$ and S charts for the three shifts. Use equation (5.4).

5.6. Construct a median chart for the data in Example 4.1.

5.7. Construct a median chart for the data in Problem 5.5. (To obtain samples of equal size, treat the sixth observation of the third shift as the fifth observation of the first shift for each day.)

5.8. The following data show the average strength and the range of samples of 5 plastic helmets selected from each hour's production.

Hour	$\overline{X}$ (kg)	R (kg)	Hour	$\overline{X}$ (kg)	R (kg)
1	495.5	12.8	13	489.0	15.2
2	493.0	13.2	14	493.5	11.6
3	496.0	15.3	15	488.4	11.8
4	497.5	8.3	16	495.5	7.6
5	490.5	7.4	17	491.0	8.4
6	496.0	8.8	18	497.0	7.3
7	500.0	13.2	19	494.5	8.7
8	498.0	7.3	20	490.5	9.8
9	497.0	8.4	21	487.5	9.8
10	496.6	9.2	22	489.4	11.2
11	493.4	10.2	23	488.0	10.8
12	498.0	12.3	24	486.5	12.5

Plot $\overline{X}$ and R charts. Plot mean $\pm$ 2.5σ warning limits on the chart. Identify any warnings.

5.9. A control chart uses control limits at mean $\pm$ 2.5σ and warning limits at mean $\pm$ 2.0σ. What is the probability that a sample observation will generate a warning but no signal?

5.10. Plot a moving average chart, using subgroup size 5, for the tensile strength data in Problem 3.1.

5.11. Plot a moving average chart, using subgroup size 4, for the weights of frozen pizzas in Problem 3.2.

5.12. For the soft drink bottles in Example 4.2 it would be considered unsafe if the process average volume of liquid in the bottles were to exceed 327.5 ml. It is desired to test the hypothesis

$$H_0\text{: } \mu = 325.90$$

against

$$H_1\text{: } \mu = 327.50$$

Construct a CUSUM chart using $d = 6 \times c$.

5.13. Construct a CUSUM chart for Problem 5.12 after changing the alternative hypothesis to

$$H_1\text{: } \mu = 324.30$$

six

PROPERTIES OF CONTROL CHARTS

Control charts are used to monitor processes, usually production processes. As a monitoring device, a control chart needs to satisfy two conflicting requirements. 1) If the process is in fact out of control, the chart should signal this as quickly as possible. An early signal would minimize the production of unsatisfactory units. 2) If the process is in fact in control, any signal from the chart would be a false signal. Such false signals should be infrequent. The control chart should permit an in-control process to operate for long periods of time without giving a false signal.

The operation of a control chart is a test of the hypothesis that the process is in control. Two properties of this test of hypothesis indicate the extent to which a control chart can meet the two seemingly conflicting requirements mentioned above. These properties are (1) power of the test, and (2) run length of the test. Both of these properties are described in Chapter 2 in general terms. In this chapter these properties are discussed specifically in reference to control charts for variable characteristics.

OPERATING CHARACTERISTIC OF A CONTROL CHART

Example 6.1

The lengths of bolts being manufactured are monitored using an $\overline{X}$ chart. If the upper control limit, central line and lower control limit are 20.5 cm, 20 cm, and 19.5 cm, respectively, the use of the charts amounts to a test of the hypothesis

$$H_0\text{: } \mu = 20 \text{ cm}$$

against an alternative hypothesis

$$H_1: \mu \neq 20 \text{ cm}$$

If the process is in control and the mean length of the bolts being produced is exactly 20 cm, the hypothesis H_0 would be true. The probability that the average length $\overline{X}$ for any sample of five bolts would be between the upper and lower control limits would be $1 - \alpha$, the probability of accepting a hypothesis that is true. This probability would be 0.9974 if 3σ limits are used and the distribution of the sample averages is normal.

If there is a change in the production process and the mean length changes from 20 cm to 20.5 cm, H_0 is no longer true. If the average length of a sample falls within the control limits, H_0 may still be accepted. This would be a type II error, the error of accepting a hypothesis that is not true. The probability of this event is the probability that the control chart does not signal when it really should signal.

It can be seen from Figure 6.1 that the probability β is approximately 0.5 when the mean length has changed from 20 to 20.5. A change of 0.5 cm in μ has decreased the probability of acceptance from 0.9975 to 0.5.

In a similar manner, the probability of acceptance of a sample would change according to the change in the underlying production process. In other words, the probability of acceptance of a sample, β, would be a function of the "difference" between the actual mean and the mean under hypothesis H_0. This function is shown in Figure 6.2. The nature of the curve in Figure 6.2 can be deduced from Figure 6.1. If the difference becomes smaller, the production process gets closer to the condition H_0 being true and the probability of acceptance is higher. If the difference becomes larger, the prob-

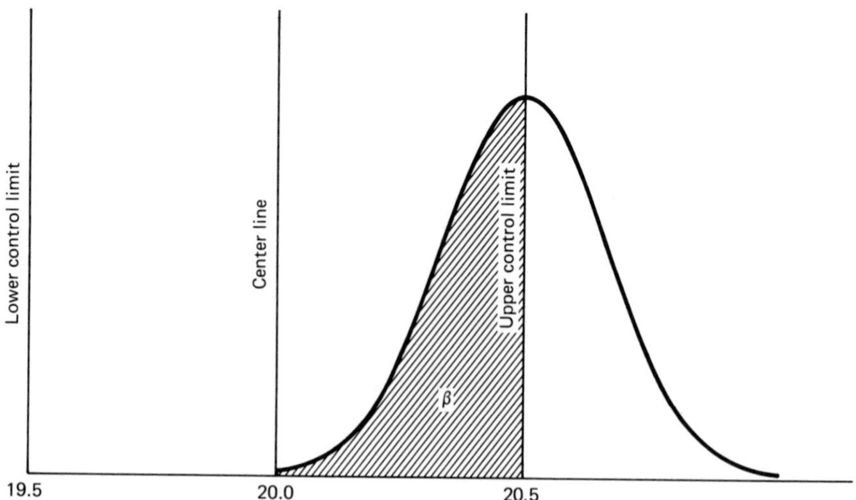

Figure 6.1 Probability of type II error when there is a change in the mean of the process.

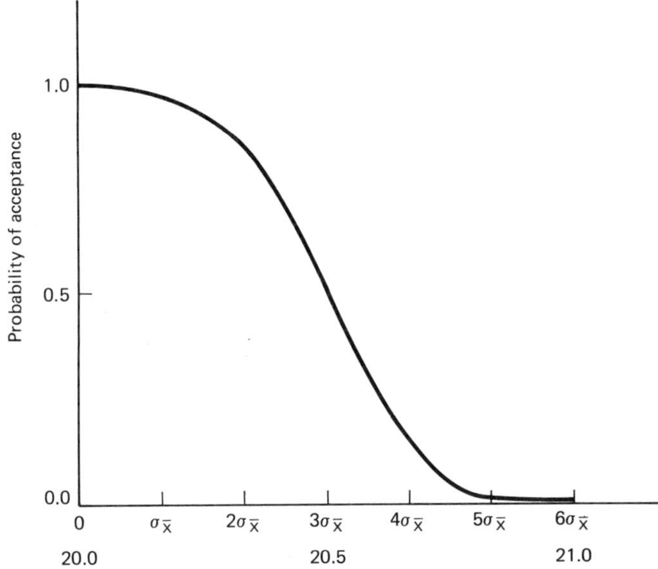

Figure 6.2 Operating characteristic curve of an $\overline{X}$ chart.

ability of acceptance is lower. The control chart would quickly signal when the difference is large, and vice versa.

The curve in Figure 6.2 is called the *operating characteristic curve* of the control chart. The function describing the operating characteristic curve can be stated as follows:

1. When difference $d = 0$, probability of acceptance $= 1 - \alpha$.
2. When difference $d \neq 0$, probability of acceptance $= \beta$.

A complementary function giving the probability of rejection is called the *power function* of the control chart. Figure 6.3 gives the power function corresponding to the operating characteristic curve in Figure 6.2.

COMPUTING THE OC CURVE

A simple step-by-step procedure for computing the OC curve for any control chart is described below.

Step 1. Start with the given control limits and the value of k. In the numerical example

$$\text{UCL} = 20.5$$

$$\text{LCL} = 19.5$$

$$k = 3$$

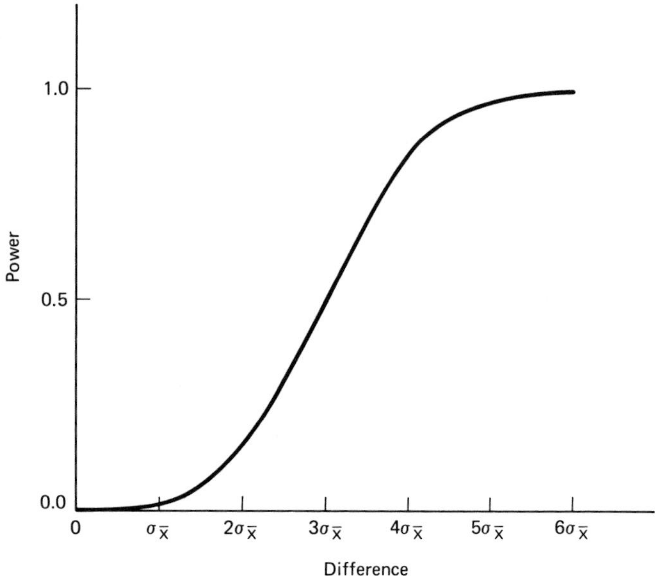

Figure 6.3 Power function of an $\overline{X}$ chart.

Step 2. Estimate the standard deviation of $\overline{X}$ as (UCL − LCL)/2k:

$$\sigma_{\overline{X}} = \frac{20.5 - 19.5}{2 \times 3}$$

$$= 0.1667$$

Step 3. Select the difference d. A convenient set of values for d is given by the multiples of (UCL − LCL)/2k or $\sigma_{\overline{X}}$. The values of 0, $\sigma_{\overline{X}}$, $2\sigma_{\overline{X}}$, $3\sigma_{\overline{X}}$, $4\sigma_{\overline{X}}$, $5\sigma_{\overline{X}}$, and $6\sigma_{\overline{X}}$ would usually suffice.

Step 4. For the selected difference, determine the position of control limits relative to the new mean. For example, $d = 0.1667 = \sigma_{\overline{X}}$.

$$\text{new mean} = 20.1667$$

$$\text{UCL} = 20.5$$

$$= 20.1667 + \frac{20.5 - 20.1667}{0.1667} \times 0.1667$$

$$= 20.1667 + 2\sigma_{\overline{X}}$$

$$\text{LCL} = 19.5$$

$$= 20.1667 + \frac{19.5 - 20.1667}{0.1667} \times 0.1667$$

$$= 20.1667 - 4\sigma_{\overline{X}}$$

UCL is located at mean $+2\sigma$ and the LCL at mean -4σ.

Step 5. Compute the probability of acceptance using the cumulative normal probability tables (Table A1).

$$\text{probability of acceptance} = \phi(\text{UCL}) - \phi(\text{LCL})$$
$$= \phi(+2) - \phi(-4)$$
$$= 0.9773 - 0$$
$$= 0.9773$$

Step 6. Repeat steps 4 and 5 for the entire set of differences (see Table 6.1).

OC CURVE AND THE SUBGROUP SIZE

The computational procedure clearly indicates that the probability of acceptance for any difference depends on the relation between d and $\sigma_{\overline{X}}$. Whenever the ratio $d/\sigma_{\overline{X}}$ is large, the probability of acceptance is low. Whenever the ratio $d/\sigma_{\overline{X}}$ is small, the probability of acceptance is high, reaching a maximum when $d/\sigma_{\overline{X}}$ is 0.

Since $\sigma_{\overline{X}} = \sigma/\sqrt{n}$, an increase in the value of sample size n would decrease $\sigma_{\overline{X}}$ and consequently increase $d/\sigma_{\overline{X}}$. Larger sample sizes make the OC curve of the control chart sharper, whereas smaller sample sizes make the OC curve flat.

Example 6.2

$$\mu \text{ under } H_0 = 12.0$$
$$\sigma = 1.20$$

TABLE 6.1 Computations for the Probability of Acceptance

Difference, $^*\sigma_{\overline{X}}$	UCL, $^*\sigma_{\overline{X}}$	LCL, $^*\sigma_{\overline{X}}$	ϕ(UCL)	ϕ(LCL)	Pr(A)
0	+3	−3	0.99865	0.00135	0.9973
1	+2	−4	0.9773	0	0.9773
2	+1	−5	0.8413	0	0.8413
3	0	−6	0.5000	0	0.5000
4	−1	−7	0.1587	0	0.1587
5	−2	−8	0.0228	0	0.0228
6	−3	−9	0.00135	0	0.00135

TABLE 6.2

	Sample Size		
	2	5	9
$\sigma_{\overline{X}}$	0.849	0.537	0.40
UCL	14.547	13.611	13.20
LCL	9.453	10.389	10.80

Three different sample sizes are considered: $n = 2$, $n = 5$, and $n = 9$ (Table 6.2). Figure 6.4 gives the OC curves for the three control charts.

This relation between the OC curve and the sample size permits the determination of the minimum sample size that will give specified protection. The desired protection can be stated in terms of the probability of detecting a certain shift in the process mean. This is illustrated by Example 6.3.

Example 6.3

$$\mu \text{ under } H_0 = 30$$

$$\sigma \text{ (known)} = 0.60$$

It is desired that if there is a shift in the process mean of 1.0, the control chart should detect it with a probability of 0.95 when the first sample is inspected after the shift (see Figure 6.5).

$$\text{probability of detection} = 0.95$$

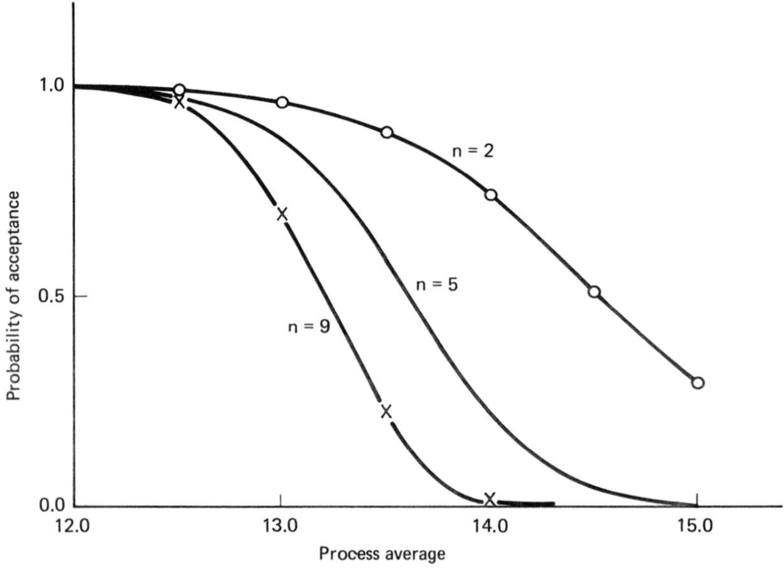

Figure 6.4 OC curves of control charts with subgroup sizes 2, 5, and 9.

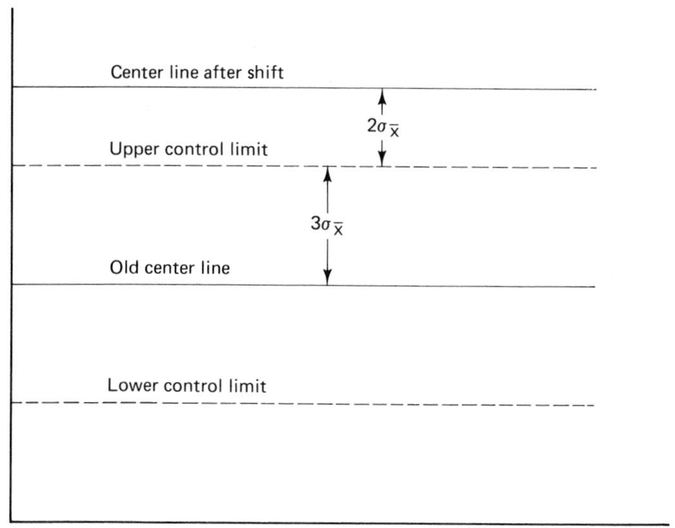

Figure 6.5 Probability of detecting a shift.

$$\text{probability of acceptance} = 0.05$$

$$\text{UCL} = \mu + 3\sigma_{\overline{X}} = 30 + 3\sigma_{\overline{X}}$$

UCL relative to the mean after the shift should yield the probability of acceptance of 0.05:

$$\phi\frac{\text{UCL} - 31}{\sigma_{\overline{X}}} = 0.05 \qquad \text{or} \qquad \frac{\text{UCL} - 31}{\sigma_{\overline{X}}} = -2$$

Hence $\text{UCL} = 31 - 2\sigma_{\overline{X}}$. Therefore,

$$30 + 3\sigma_{\overline{X}} = 31 - 2\sigma_{\overline{X}}$$

$$5\sigma_{\overline{X}} = 1$$

$$\sigma_{\overline{X}} = 0.2$$

But $\sigma_{\overline{X}} = \sigma/\sqrt{n} = 0.6/\sqrt{n}$;

$$n = \left(\frac{0.6}{0.2}\right)^2 = 9$$

The sample size should be 9 or larger to give the desired protection.

RUN-LENGTH DISTRIBUTION IN QUALITY CONTROL

A desirable property of any monitoring process is that it should detect any out-of-control situation as quickly as possible, yet leave the production process alone when it is in control. In other words, the monitoring process should generate signals as quickly as possible if the production process is out of control and as late as possible if the production process is in control.

The foregoing property implies that the run-length distribution, when the process is in control, should be stochastically as large as possible. When two monitoring processes P and Q operate with the same significance level α, the process P would be a better choice if its run-length distribution, $H_p(t_1, \alpha)$, dominates the alternative run-length distribution, $H_Q(t_1, \alpha)$.

At the same time, if the process is out of control, the run length should be as small as possible. Run length provides a basis for comparing alternative procedures for monitoring production processes. Briefly the guidelines for selecting monitoring procedures would be as follows:

1. When the alternative hypothesis (i.e., out-of-control status of the production process) is either not known or not specifically defined, select the monitoring procedures with stochastically longest run length when the process is in control.
2. When the alternative hypothesis is well defined and specific and the run lengths for two monitoring procedures, when the production process is in control, are stochastically equal, select the monitoring procedure with stochastically shorter run length when the process is out of control.

Let

t = time interval between samples (assumed constant)

c = production rate

n = sample size

r = run length

This implies that in any sampling interval, $c \cdot t$ units are produced. Of these, n units chosen at random will be used for monitoring (e.g., for plotting a control chart). The signal will be given after r samples. In other words, $c \cdot t \cdot r$ units will be produced by the time a signal is given. As indicated earlier, if the process is in control, this quantity should be as large as possible. If the process is not in control, the product would likely be defective and the total quantity $c \cdot t \cdot r$ should be as small as possible.

The behavior of any monitoring procedure can be described in terms of its run-length distribution. However, it is usually not necessary to observe the entire distribution. It is sufficient to know the average run length (ARL) or the mean of the distribution. A procedure with a shorter ARL would indicate a stochastically shorter run length as long as it can be assumed that the successive samples are statistically independent. This assumption holds for most control chart applications as well as acceptance sampling procedures.

If θ is the probability of rejecting the null hypothesis for any sample and the samples are independent, the run-length distribution is geometric distribution (see Chapter 2),

$$\Pr(r \leq R) = 1 - (1 - \theta)^R \tag{6.1}$$

The mean of this distribution is given by

$$E(r) = \text{ARL}$$
$$= \frac{1}{\theta} \tag{6.2}$$

AVERAGE RUN LENGTH FOR $\overline{X}$ CHARTS

Case 1: Mean and the Variance Are Known

When a process is in operation for a fairly long time and is operating in control, a large number of observations are available. The mean and variance of the process estimated from these large number of observations can usually be assumed to imply that the mean and variance are known. The control limits in this case would be

$$\text{UCL} = \mu + \frac{3\sigma}{\sqrt{n}}$$

$$\text{LCL} = \mu - \frac{3\sigma}{\sqrt{n}}$$

Let d be the shift or the change in the mean of the process. Then the hypotheses being tested can be written as

$$H_0\text{: } d = 0$$

$$H_1\text{: } d \neq 0$$

The shaded areas in Figure 6.6 represents the probability of rejection of the null hypothesis θ. Values of θ and ARL are given in Table 6.3. Table A12 gives ARL values for other sample sizes.

Case 2: Mean Known, $\overline{R}$ Used to Estimate Variance

When $\overline{R}$ is used to estimate σ, the relation between these quantities is

$$\overline{R} = d_2\sigma \qquad \text{or} \qquad \sigma = \frac{\overline{R}}{d_2}$$

Using this estimate of σ, the probability of rejecting the null hypothesis θ can be calculated as in Figure 6.6. For a sample size of 5 the values of θ

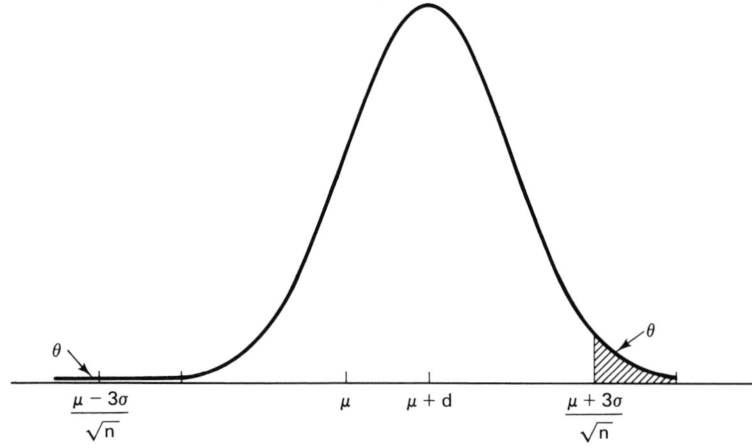

Figure 6.6 Probability of rejecting a null hypothesis; $d = 0$.

TABLE 6.3 Values of θ and ARL for Control Chart with Sample Size 5

d/σ	θ	ARL
0	0.0027	370.4
0.1	0.0034	298.3
0.2	0.0057	175.6
0.5	0.02994	33.4
1.0	0.22245	4.5
1.5	0.6281	1.6
2.0	0.92951	1.1
3.0	0.99193	1.0

TABLE 6.4 Values of θ and ARL for Control Chart with Sample Size 5

$d\overline{R}$	θ	ARL
0	0.0027	370.4
0.1	0.00659	151.6
0.2	0.02506	64.5
0.5	0.3449	11.9
1.0	0.9580	1.043

and ARL are given in Table 6.4. Table A13 gives ARL values for other sample sizes.

Example 6.4

$\overline{X}$ and R control charts are maintained for the tensile strength in pounds per square inch of steel reinforcement rods. The subgroup size is 5. After 30 subgroups $\Sigma R = 18{,}000$ and $\Sigma \overline{X} = 429{,}000$. The subgroups used in the base period indicate statistical control. The control limits computed in the base period are used during the monitoring period. If the average strength changes to (a) 14,180 or (b) 14,000, how long would it take to detect the shift? (See Figure 6.7).

$$\overline{R} = \frac{\Sigma R}{30}$$

$$= \frac{18{,}000}{30} = 600$$

$$\hat{\mu} = \overline{\overline{X}} = \frac{\Sigma \overline{X}}{30}$$

$$= \frac{429{,}000}{30} = 14{,}300$$

(a)

$$d = 14{,}300 - 14{,}180 = 120$$

$$\frac{d}{R} = \frac{120}{600} = 0.2$$

From Table 6.4, ARL for subgroup size 5 and $d/\overline{R} = 0.2$ is 64.5. On an average, 65 samples would be examined before the shift is detected.

(b)

$$d = 14{,}000 - 14{,}300 = 300$$

$$\frac{d}{\overline{R}} = \frac{300}{600} = 0.5$$

From Table 6.4, ARL for subgroup size 5 and $d/\overline{R} = 0.5$ is 11.9. On an average, 12 samples would be examined before the shift is detected.

Case 3: $\overline{\overline{X}}$ Used to Estimate the Mean, $\overline{R}$ Used to Estimate the Variance

The exact distribution in this case is a Student's t distribution. It is possible to construct an ARL table similar to Table 6.4 based on this distribution. However, in most applications in manufacturing the underlying dis-

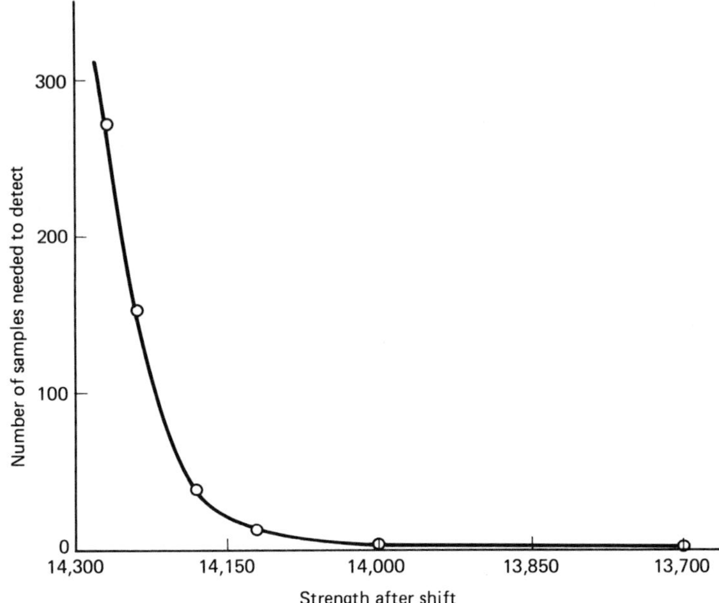

Figure 6.7 Run length as a function of shift.

tribution of characteristics being observed is close enough to a normal distribution, so that when the base period is sufficiently large, more than 20 subgroups, Table 6.4 can be used for this case.

USE OF WARNING LIMITS

Conventional $\overline{X}$ and R charts are very efficient in detecting large shifts. If the shift is small, it is not easy to detect it with $\overline{X}$ chart. This is seen from the large average run lengths needed when d/σ or $d/\overline{R}$ are small. For example, if the process mean changes from μ to $\mu + 0.5\sigma$, the new mean is still within the control limits based on the old mean. Table 6.3 indicates that it would take 33.4 samples of 5 units each before this shift can be detected.

The use of warning limits combined with the control limits can reduce the time required to detect small shifts. For this purpose a signal is given when either of two conditions holds.

1. A sample $\overline{X}$ value is outside the control limits.
2. Some number r of consecutive $\overline{X}$ values are outside the warning limits but still inside the control limits.

The use of warning limits in this fashion makes the derivation of average run length quite complicated. As the decision depends not only on the most recent sample but on the most recent r samples, the run-length distribution is not a geometric distribution. One possible approach is to formulate the problem as a Markov process. However, this approach is beyond the intended scope of this book.

In the simple case when r is 2, it is possible to give a simple derivation of the average run length.[1] In this case a signal is given whenever two consecutive sample $\overline{X}$'s are outside the warning limits or any sample $\overline{X}$ is outside the control limit.

Let the states 0, 1, and 2 be defined as

State 0. Most recent $\overline{X}$ is inside the warning limits.

State 1. Most recent $\overline{X}$ is outside the warning limits but inside the control limits.

State 2. Most recent $\overline{X}$ is outside the control limits.

Let

$$p_0 = \text{probability of state 0}$$

$$p_1 = \text{probability of state 1}$$

$$p_2 = \text{probability of state 2}$$

Further, let L_0, L_1, and L_2 be the average run lengths when the process is in state 0, 1, and 2, respectively. Obviously, $L_2 = 0$. Starting in state 1, L_1 can be calculated as follows. After taking one more sample the new state can be either 0, 1, or 2. If the new state is 0, an average run length of L_0 would be needed to generate a signal. If the new state is 1, a signal is generated, as there are two consecutive $\overline{X}$ values in state 1. If the new state is 2, a signal is generated, obviously.

Hence

$$\begin{aligned} L_1 &= \text{next sample} + (\text{probability of state 0}) \times L_0 \\ &= 1 + p_0 L_0 \end{aligned} \tag{6.3}$$

Starting in state 0, L_0 can be calculated as follows. After one more sample, the new state can be 0, 1, or 2. If the new state is 0, an average run length of L_0 would be needed to generate a signal. If the new state is

[1] This derivation is adopted from working notes prepared by Marion Reynolds of the Statistics Department at Virginia Polytechnic Institute and State University. These notes form part of a proposed textbook.

1, an average run length of L_1 would be needed to generate a signal. If the new state is 2, a signal is generated. Hence

$$\begin{aligned} L_0 &= \text{next sample} + (\text{probability of state 0}) \times L_0 \\ &\qquad + (\text{probability of state 1}) \times L_1 \qquad (6.4) \\ &= 1 + p_0 L_0 + p_1 L_1 \end{aligned}$$

Substituting the value of L_1 from equation (6.3) yields

$$L_0 = 1 + p_0 L_0 + p_1(1 + p_0 L_0)$$

or

$$L_0 = \frac{1 + p_1}{1 - p_0 - p_1 p_0} \qquad (6.5)$$

Example 6.5

$\overline{X}$ charts have been maintained for a certain characteristic. It is assumed that σ is known. Warning limits are set at $\mu + 2\sigma$ and $\mu - 2\sigma$. Subgroup size is 5. Calculate the average run length (a) when the process is in control and $\overline{\overline{X}} = \mu$, and (b) if the process mean suddenly shifts to $\mu + 0.5\sigma$. Figure 6.8 shows the probability distribution of the characteristic for part (a) of the example. Figure 6.9 shows the probability distribution of the characteristic for part (b) of the example.

Because of the shift in the process mean, the location of the warning limits and control limits will not be symmetrical with respect to the new mean. By definition

$$p_0 = \Pr(\text{LWL} \le \overline{x} \le \text{UWL})$$

$$p_0 + p_1 = \Pr(\text{LCL} \le \overline{x} \le \text{UCL})$$

$$p_0 + p_1 + p_2 = 1$$

For part (a),

$$p_0 = \Pr\left(\mu - \frac{2\sigma}{\sqrt{5}} \le \overline{x}_i \le \mu + \frac{2\sigma}{\sqrt{5}}\right)$$

$$= 0.9545$$

$$p_0 + p_1 = \Pr\left(\mu - \frac{3\sigma}{\sqrt{5}} \le \overline{x}_i \le \mu + \frac{3\sigma}{\sqrt{5}}\right)$$

$$= 0.9973$$

Hence

$$p_1 = (p_0 + p_1) - p_0$$

$$= 0.0428$$

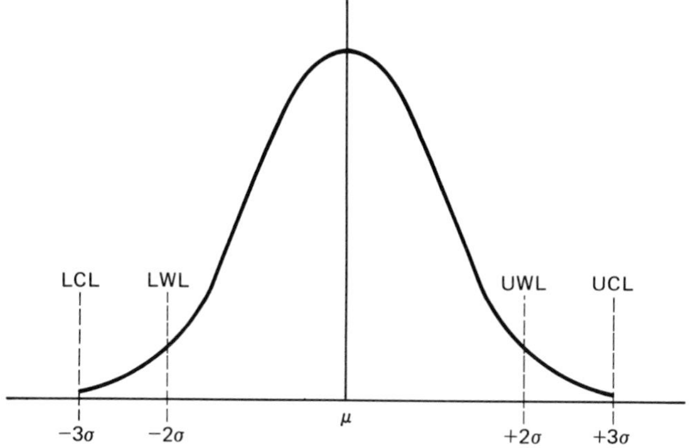

Figure 6.8 Process in control.

and

$$p_2 = 1 - (p_0 + p_1)$$
$$= 0.0027$$

Substituting these values in equation (6.3) gives ARL,

$$L_0 = \frac{1 + 0.0428}{1 - 0.9545 - (0.9545)(0.0428)}$$
$$= 224.4$$

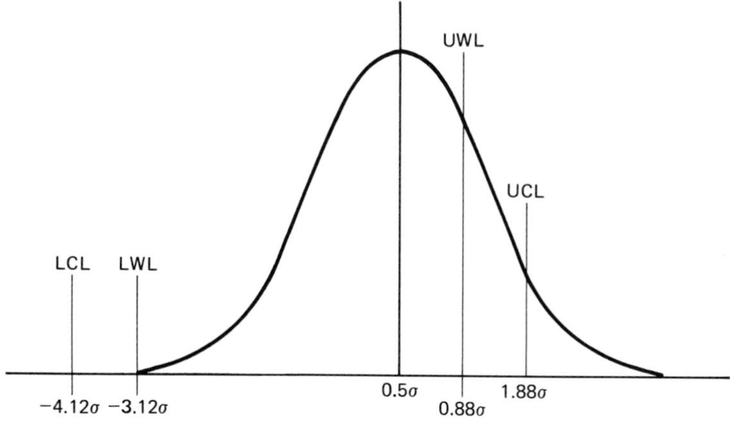

Figure 6.9 Process mean shift to $\mu + 0.5\sigma$.

For part (b) new mean $= \mu + 0.55$

$$\text{lower control limit} = -0.5\sigma - \frac{3\sigma}{\sqrt{5}}$$

$$= \frac{-1.118\sigma}{\sqrt{5}} - \frac{3\sigma}{\sqrt{5}}$$

$$= \frac{-4.118\sigma}{\sqrt{5}}$$

$$\text{lower warning limit} = -0.5\sigma - \frac{2\sigma}{\sqrt{5}}$$

$$= \frac{-3.118\sigma}{\sqrt{5}}$$

$$\text{upper warning limit} = -0.5\sigma + \frac{2\sigma}{\sqrt{5}}$$

$$= \frac{0.882\sigma}{\sqrt{5}}$$

$$\text{upper control limit} = -0.5\sigma + \frac{3\sigma}{\sqrt{5}}$$

$$= \frac{1.882\sigma}{\sqrt{5}}$$

As in part (a),

$$p_0 = \Pr(\text{LWL} \le x \le \text{UWL})$$

$$p_0 + p_1 = \Pr(\text{LCL} \le x \le \text{UCL})$$

For part (b),

$$p_0 = \Pr\left(\mu - \frac{3.118\sigma}{\sqrt{5}} \le \overline{X}_i \le \mu + \frac{0.882\sigma}{\sqrt{5}}\right)$$

$$= 0.81114 - 0.00091$$

$$= 0.81023$$

$$p_0 + p_1 = \Pr\left(\mu - \frac{4.118\sigma}{\sqrt{5}} \le \overline{X}_i \le \mu + \frac{1.882\sigma}{\sqrt{5}}\right)$$

$$= 0.97004 - 0$$

$$= 0.97004$$

$$p_1 = (p_0 + p_1) - p_0$$

$$= 0.97004 - 0.81023$$

$$= 0.15981$$

Substituting these values in equation (6.5) gives ARL,

$$L_0 = \frac{1 + 0.15981}{1 - 0.81023 - (0.81023)(0.15981)}$$
$$= 19.23$$

These average run lengths with warning limits can be compared with average run lengths without warning limits for the same subgroup size (Table 6.5).

OC CURVE AND AVERAGE RUN LENGTH

An OC curve is a description of the probability of the acceptance of the null hypothesis for any one sample observation. In other words, it is the probability that the control procedure will not give a signal. If θ denotes the probability of giving a signal and successive samples are considered independent, the two functions describing (1) the OC curve and (2) the ARL can be written as

$$\text{function describing the OC curve} = 1 - \theta$$

$$\text{function describing ARL} = \frac{1}{\theta}$$

Figure 6.10 shows the two functions for a subgroup size of 5.

As the shift in the process average d/σ increases, the control procedure has increasing possibility of detecting the shift and giving a signal

$$\text{As } \frac{d}{\sigma} \rightarrow \infty \qquad \theta \rightarrow 1$$

As θ, the probability of giving a signal approaches 1, the OC curve function $1 - \theta$ approaches zero and the ARL function $1/\theta$ approaches 1. It is logically obvious that a run length cannot be less than 1, as no signal can be given without the first sample.

TABLE 6.5 Average Run Lengths for Sample Size 5

	ARL	
d/σ	Without Warning Limits	With Warning Limits
0	370.4	224.4
0.5	33.4	19.23

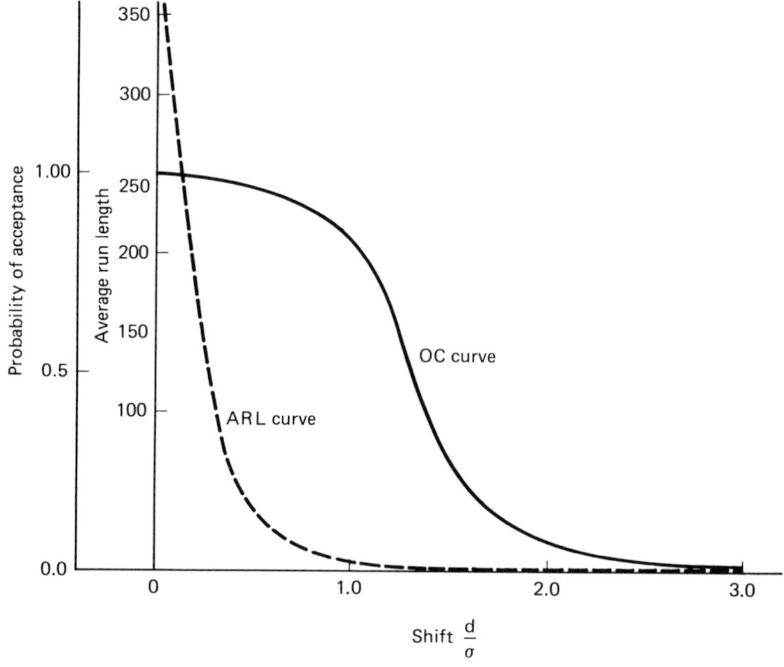

Figure 6.10 ARL and OC curves for sample size 5.

PRODUCTION OF DEFECTIVE ITEMS BEFORE A SHIFT IN PROCESS AVERAGE IS DETECTED

When the specification limits for the dimensions are known and the natural standard deviation of the production process can be estimated, it would be possible to minimize the production of defective items by proper setting of the process average. For normal operations the process average is set 3 or more standard deviations away from the specification limits. For one-sided specifications, this presents no problem. For two-sided specifications, at times, there might be need for a trade-off. In either case there exists a "best" setting for the process average, and this setting can be determined in a straightforward fashion.

If there is an unplanned shift in the process average away from this "best" setting, the fraction of production that does not meet the specification would increase. When the run length of the control procedure is long, the production process continues to produce at a higher fraction defective for a longer time. The effect is the production of a larger number of defective items. The motivation for having a shorter run length, when the process is out of control, is the control and reduction of the number of defective items produced. The shorter run length, however, has its price. First, there is an increase in the frequency of false signals when the process is in control. Second, the device used to obtain a shorter run length, such as use of warning limits or larger subgroup sizes, would increase operational costs. This trade-off is illustrated in Example 6.6.

Example 6.6

The length of a screw being produced on a semiautomatic machine is subject to a single upper specification limit L. The natural standard deviation of the process is σ. For normal operation the average is set at $L - 3\sigma$. There is a 10% risk of a sudden shift of the process average to $L - 2.5\sigma$ (a shift of 0.5σ). Three types of $\overline{X}$ charts are proposed as possible ways of detecting this shift: (a) conventional chart with subgroup size 5, (b) chart with warning limits, subgroup size 5, and (c) conventional chart with subgroup size 9. The cost per sample is \$0.50, \$0.70, and \$0.90 per sample for the three plans. The cost of investigating a false signal is \$300. The production rate is 2000 screws per sampling period and the penalty cost of shipping a defective screw is \$0.10.

Under normal setting the specification limit is at process average + 3σ. The fraction that would be defective is obtained from Table A1 as 0.00135. As 2000 screws are produced each sampling period, the expected number of defective screws is 2000×0.00135, or 2.7 screws. After the shift the specification limit would be only 2.5σ from the new process average. The fraction defective will increase to 0.0062. The expected number of defective screws will be 2000×0.0062, or 12.4 screws. The effect of not detecting the shift would be permitting the shipment of $12.4 - 2.7$, or 9.7 additional defective screws.

From the ARL tables the average run lengths for the three plans are calculated as follows:

	d/σ	(a)	(b)	(c)
Normal operation	0	370.4	224.4	370.4
After shift	0.5	33.4	19.23	14.97

$$\begin{aligned}\text{Total cost} &= \text{expected cost of false signal} \\ &\quad + \text{expected cost of inspection} \\ &\quad + \text{expected cost of defective product} \\ &= \text{EC}_1 + \text{EC}_2 + \text{EC}_3\end{aligned}$$

Expected cost of a false signal EC_1:
Probability that the operation is normal = 0.9. Hence

$$\begin{aligned}\text{EC}_1 &= (0.9)(\text{probability of a signal})(300) \\ &= \frac{270}{\text{ARL}} \qquad \text{when } d = 0\end{aligned}$$

	(a)	(b)	(c)
EC_1	0.7289	1.2032	0.7289

Expected cost of inspection and charting EC_2:

	(a)	(b)	(c)
EC_2	0.50	0.70	0.90

Expected cost of defective product:
Probability of a shift 0.10. Hence

$$EC_3 = (0.10)(\text{ARL})(9.7)(0.10)$$
$$= 0.097 \text{ ARL}$$

	(a)	(b)	(c)
EC_3	3.2398	1.8653	1.4521

Combining all three costs yield Table 6.6. Introduction of warning limits reduces the total cost for sample size 5. However, best results are provided by increasing the sample size to 9.

TABLE 6.6 Expected Costs of Three Proposed Plans

	a	b	c
EC_1	0.7289	1.2032	0.7289
EC_2	0.5000	0.7000	0.9000
EC_3	3.2398	1.8653	1.4521
Total	4.4687	3.7685	3.0810

PROBLEMS

6.1. 20 samples of size 5 taken during the base period yielded the following values:

$$\overline{\overline{X}} = 235.9 \text{ cm} \qquad \overline{R} = 10.8 \text{ cm}$$

Compute the operating characteristic curve of the control chart resulting from these values.

6.2. Production is started to produce a newly designed component. To monitor the length, $\overline{X}$ and R charts are started based on 25 subgroups of four items each. For these 25 subgroups $\Sigma\, \overline{X} = 500$ cm and $\Sigma\, R = 153.2$ cm. Determine the 3σ control limits. What is the probability that a shift of 2 cm in the process average would be detected on the first subgroup observed after the shift?

6.3. In Problem 6.2, what is the probability of detecting the shift within first four subgroups after the shift?

6.4. In Problem 6.2, what would be the average run length before a shift of 0.8 cm would be detected? (Use interpolation within the ARL tables.)

6.5. The average length of a feed regulator produced during a steady operation is 18.0 cm. The standard deviation is assumed to be known and equal to 0.1 cm.

It is proposed to use an $\overline{X}$ control chart to monitor the length. What should be the size of the subgroups if a shift of 0.2 cm is to be detected with a probability of 0.90 when the first subgroup is inspected after the shift?

6.6. What should be the sample size if the probability of detection after the first subgroup, in Problem 6.5, were (a) increased to 0.99? (b) decreased to 0.8?

6.7. Control charts are maintained on the weight of an item. After a base period of 30 samples of size 3, $\Sigma\,\overline{X} = 12930$ g and $\Sigma\,R = 123$ g.

(a) Compute the control limits and estimate the standard deviation of the item weights. (Assume that base period observations indicate the process to be in control.)

(b) If the process average of the weights shifts to 433 g, how long will it take to detect the shift using the control limits in part (a)?

6.8. The standard deviation of the holding strength of certain type of nails is known to be 8 lb. Using conventional $\overline{X}$ charts with sample size 10, samples being taken each hour, how long will it take to detect a shift of 4 lb in the process average?

6.9. Base period data are given as: 20 samples of size 6, $\overline{\overline{X}} = 153.3$, $\overline{R} = 12.65$, process in control. In addition to the control limits at $\mu \pm 3\sigma_{\overline{X}}$ warning limits are set at $\mu \pm 2.5\sigma_{\overline{X}}$. Calculate the average run length (a) when the process is in control and (b) if the process average shifts to 158.5.

6.10. The specification for the weight of an item is 1380 $\pm$ 25 g. Base-period analysis based on 30 samples of 5 items each indicates that process average is 1400 g with standard deviation 8 g.

(a) What percentage of product is defective?

(b) At what level of the process average would the production of defectives be minimized?

(c) Assume that 300 units are produced in each sampling period; how many defective items would be expected in the production during the base period?

(d) If the process average is set at the optimum level determined in part (b) and it shifts back to 1400-g level, on the average how many defective units would be produced before the shift is detected?

(e) What would be the answer to part (d) if the shift is to the 1384 g instead of 1400 g?

seven

CONTROL CHARTS FOR ATTRIBUTES

The term *attribute*, as used in quality control, is the property a unit of product has of being either good or bad, that is, the quality characteristic of the unit is either within the specified requirements or it is not. Attributes-type inspection is usually associated with *go/no-go gages*. For example, a plug gage divides the units inspected into two groups: units within specifications and units outside specifications. Visual inspection for paint separates units into two categories: good and bad. There are many opportunites for typing errors on a typewritten sheet. After the letter is written, there are two attributes to the letter: the correct type and the incorrect type. A worker is either tardy for work or is not tardy. A man either has an accident or he does not have one. The either-or situation is always typical of attributes measurement. A chart constructed for control of this type of quality measurement is known as an *attributes chart*. It is a very valuable tool for general process quality control, for pointing up troublesome quality characteristics, and for presenting quality information to management.

Control of quality in process involves the rationalization of many quality objectives to those which will provide the best return on the quality control labor hours invested. The quality control tool which will do the job at optimum total quality cost is the one that should be used. The attributes chart is recommended highly as a primary tool for *gross* process quality control and for presenting quality information to management and the public. Also, it should be used extensively for isolating troublesome areas early in the development of the quality control program.

PERCENTAGE CONTROL CHART OR p CHART

One of the most popular control charts used is the percentage control chart or p chart. It is highly adaptable and can be used for attribute characteristics. Each unit being produced has a certain probability p' of being defective or not being within specified requirements. If out of n units produced x are defective, the random variable x will have a binomial distribution given by

$$\Pr(x) = \binom{n}{x}(p')^x(1 - p')^{n-x}$$

The objective of percentage control chart is to estimate and control p'. An estimate of p' is given by the fraction defective p found in the sample

$$p = \frac{x}{n}$$

The distribution of p is approximately normal when either (1) p' is less than 0.1, or (2) n is large. Alternatively, the measure "defects per 100 units," $100p'$, can be used in place of fraction defective p. The distribution of $100p$ is also approximately normal.

For p:

$$\text{mean} = p'$$

$$\text{variance} = p'\frac{1 - p'}{n}$$

For np:

$$\text{mean} = np'$$

$$\text{variance} = np'\ (1 - p')$$

The construction of control chart follows the variables control chart described in Chapter 4. During the base period:

1. m samples are observed. These need not be of the same size, n_i is the sample size, and p_i the observed fraction defective in the ith sample.
2. The weighted average $P_w = \Sigma(n_i \cdot p_i)/\Sigma\, n_i$ is used as the estimate of p' and the central line for the control chart.
3. The control limits used for the ith period are $p_w \pm 3\sqrt{p_w(1 - p_w)/n_i}$. For defects per 100 units the control limits are

$$100p_w \pm 300\sqrt{\frac{p_w(1 - p_w)}{n_i}}$$

During the monitoring period:

1. A sample of size n_j is observed.
2. The control limits for the jth period are obtained as

$$p_w \pm 3 \sqrt{\frac{p_w(1 - p_w)}{n_j}}$$

where p_w from the base period is used.

Example 7.1

Table 7.1 gives the results of inspection of a certain product during three weeks in December. The "fraction defective, p" and "defects per 100 units, $100p$" can easily be computed as shown in Table 7.2. Considering these three weeks in December as the base period,

$$p_w = \frac{\Sigma\, n_i p_i}{\Sigma\, n}$$

$$= \frac{66}{6000} = 0.011$$

$$\text{control limits} = p_w \pm 3 \sqrt{\frac{p_w(1 - p_w)}{n_i}}$$

$$= 0.011 \pm 3 \sqrt{\frac{0.011(1 - 0.011)}{400}}$$

$$= 0.011 \pm 0.016$$

$$\text{UCL} = 0.011 + 0.016 = 0.027$$

$$\text{LCL}^1 = 0.011 - 0.016 = 0$$

Table 7.2 indicates that two points, Dec. 6 and Dec. 13, are outside the control limits. The objective of the base-period analysis is to establish what standard is achievable. Of the two points outside the "normal" behavior, it may be possible to determine the specific cause for higher number of defectives on Dec. 13. If this cause is not likely to recur, the point is removed from the base-period analysis. The cause of the Dec. 6 out-of-control point is not determinable. As it forms a part of the general system of chance causes, the point represents a "normal" situation and is retained in the analysis. A control chart with an achievable standard is established excluding Dec. 13.

[1] Whenever the lower control limit is negative for "fraction defective" or "defects per units," it is taken to be zero.

TABLE 7.1 Inspection Results

Date	Number Inspected	Number Defective
Dec. 3	400	2
4	400	5
5	400	0
6	400	14
7	400	3
10	400	0
11	400	1
12	400	0
13	400	18
14	400	8
17	400	6
18	400	0
19	400	3
20	400	0
21	400	6

TABLE 7.2 Defects Computation

Date	Number Inspected, n	Number Defective, np	Fraction Defective, p	Percent Defective, $100p$
Dec. 3	400	2	0.0050	0.50
4	400	5	0.0125	1.25
5	400	0	0.0000	0.00
6	400	14	0.0350	3.50
7	400	3	0.0075	0.75
10	400	0	0.0000	0.00
11	400	1	0.0025	0.25
12	400	0	0.0000	0.00
13	400	18	0.0450	4.50
14	400	8	0.0200	2.00
17	400	6	0.0150	1.50
18	400	0	0.0000	0.00
19	400	3	0.0075	0.75
20	400	0	0.0000	0.00
21	400	6	0.0150	1.50
	$\Sigma n = 6000$	$\Sigma np = 66$		

$$p_w = \frac{\Sigma\, n_i p_i}{\Sigma\, n_i}$$

$$= \frac{48}{5600} = 0.0086$$

$$\text{control limits} = p_w \pm 3\sqrt{\frac{p_w(1 - p_w)}{n_i}}$$

$$= 0.0086 \pm 3\sqrt{\frac{0.0086(1 - 0.0086)}{400}}$$

$$= 0.0086 \pm 0.0138$$

$$\text{UCL} = 0.0086 + 0.0138 = 0.0224$$

$$\text{LCL} = 0.0086 - 0.0138 = 0$$

This value of p_w can be used during the monitoring period. If the sample size during the monitoring period remains 400, the control limits can also be extrapolated to the monitoring period. If the sample size changes, new control limits can be computed. For example, if the size changes to 500, the control limits would be

$$0.0086 \pm 3\sqrt{\frac{0.0086(1 - 0.0086)}{500}}$$

$$= 0.0086 \pm 0.0124$$

$$\text{UCL} = 0.021$$

$$\text{LCL} = 0$$

Figure 7.1 shows the control chart during the base period using the revised control limits. When the number inspected varies, as it often does in 100% inspection, individual control limits reflecting the changes are needed. Figure 7.2 shows the construction of a percent defective control chart where the sample size is not constant during the base period. Since such varying control limits require as many control limit calculations as there are samples inspected, it is quite common to use the average number inspected for n. Averaging is permissible when the range between numbers inspected is not too great. If most of the numbers inspected are clustered around a certain value and a few are not, separate control limits may be calculated for the few. Generally, if the range is less than 40% of the average number inspected, and certainly less than 20%, averaging may be permitted. Justification for this simplification lies in the square-root reduction. For example, the average of 120 and 80 is 100. The approximate square roots of 120 and 80 are 11 and 9, respectively. A difference of 40 in the squares represents a difference of 2 in the square roots. Of course, averaging of numbers inspected results in an average control limit from which different inferences may be drawn, depending on the number inspected. The numbers inspected of Figure 7.2 vary too much, so separate control limits are properly placed. Note that control

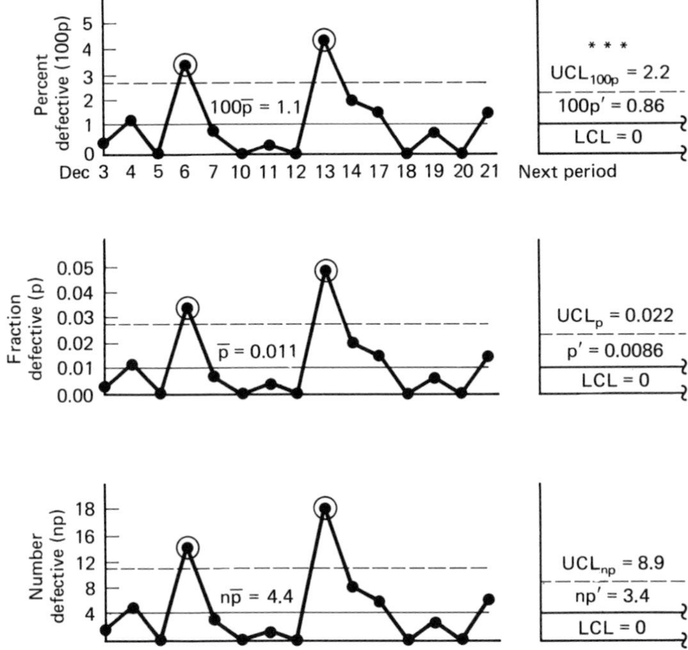

Figure 7.1 Control charts during the base period.

limits are not extended, as is $100p_w$. Of course, when n is unknown and expected to vary, control limits cannot be extended.

JOB SHOP PROCESS QUALITY CONTROL

A frequent objection to the percent defective control chart is the number required to be inspected to obtain any realistic inferences about control or lack of it. On the surface this would seem to eliminate it from control consideration by many job shops which process runs characterized by their small quantities—say between 1 and 20. Some authorities say that if p is small, n should be large enough that there is a good chance of obtaining defective units in the sample. Otherwise, the occurrence of one defective would throw the chart out of control. To illustrate, suppose that the standard is set at $100p' = 0.50$. The n required to yield an average of just one defective per sample would be 200, that is,

$$n = \frac{np'}{p'} = \frac{1.0}{0.005} = 200$$

Lot number	Number inspected, n	Number defective, np	Fraction defective, p	Percent defective, 100p
1	500	6	0.0120	1.20
2	600	9	0.0150	1.50
3	600	4	0.0067	0.67
4	300	9	0.0300	3.00 *
5	300	3	0.0100	1.00
6	600	3	0.0050	0.50
7	200	1	0.0050	0.50
8	500	2	0.0040	0.40
9	200	1	0.0050	0.50
10	200	2	0.0100	1.00
	$\Sigma n = 4000$	$\Sigma np = 40$		

$$100p_w = \frac{100\ \Sigma np}{\Sigma n} = \frac{100(40)}{4000} = 1.0$$

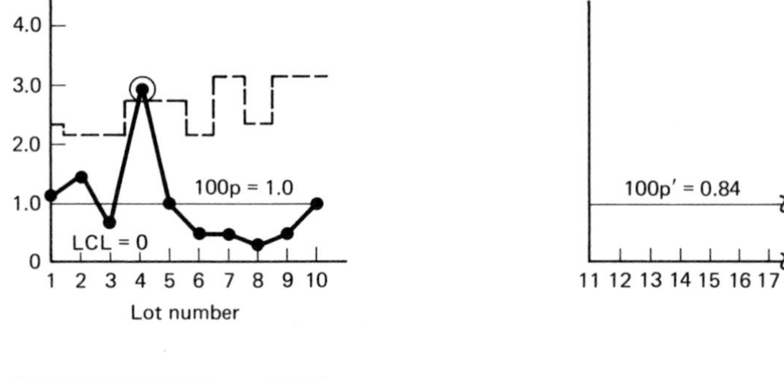

$$3\sqrt{100p_w(100 - 100p_w)} = 3\sqrt{1(99)} = 29.8$$

$\sqrt{200} = 14.14$ $\qquad \sqrt{500} = 22.36$

$\sqrt{300} = 17.32$ $\qquad \sqrt{600} = 24.50$

n	Control limits for 100p
200	1.0 ± 2.12
300	1.0 ± 1.72
500	1.0 ± 1.33
600	1.0 ± 1.22

*Cause of out-of-control point determined. Should not occur again. Data for lot number 4 excluded to yield revised

$100p_w = 100(31)/3700 = 0.84$

Figure 7.2 Construction of percent defective chart for different sample sizes.

With the use of a number inspected, say 10, using the median of the usual job lot range, the average number of defectives per number inspected would be 0.05; that is,

$$p'n = 0.005(10) = 0.05$$

The conventional upper control limit in number of defectives with

$$p'n = 0.05$$

would be

$$0.05 + 3\sqrt{0.05(0.995)} = 0.72$$

Obviously, the occurrence of defectives in the number inspected is either going to be zero or some other whole number. The occurrence of one defective (which must occur occasionally if 0.50 is a realistic standard) will be considered out of control. Common sense signifies that this occurrence *must* happen occasionally. Actually, in job shops, setup and other problems associated with short runs will make the expectancy of defectives much higher, but the example illustrates a point.

JOB SHOP APPLICATION OF ATTRIBUTES CONTROL[2]

What recourse does the job shop have? Frank Caplan, Jr. of Westinghouse Electric Corporation suggests that nonconformance be expressed as defective inspection points rather than defective units of a particular item of product.

The system reported was devised because most of the lot sizes produced ranged from 1 to 20. Operations included forging, casting, machining, and hand rework. Such operations constitute a majority of practices in American job shops. The two most important points of the program adopted were (1) operators were producing inspection points rather than parts, (2) the control was not to be punitive in nature.

Figure 7.3 illustrates a page of the notebook carried by each inspector for this system. The machine number, how many points had been accepted during the shift, the proper shift to be credited with these points, and the number of deviating points found were required to be recorded. These daily sheets were collected from all inspectors and tabulated on floor charts similar to Figure 7.4. The charts were posted so that they could be seen and showed the number of defects found, number of inspection points examined for each shift, cumulative defects, and inspection points over a two-week period. Numbers defective out of control on the high side were circled in red, on the low side in green. The posted results presented a clear picture of the quality

[2] Frank Caplan, Jr., "Process Control in a Job Shop," *Industrial Quality Control*, November 1958, pp. 16–18.

INSPECTION DAILY TOTAL						
	PARTS PROCESSED BY					
Machine number	First shift		Second shift		Third shift	
	Insp. points	Deviations	Insp. points	Deviations	Insp. points	Deviations
326			97	2		
417			116	14		
83			17	0		
205			263	1		
641			121	4		

J. George — INSPECTOR; AREA Lathe; 2 — SHIFT; 3/2/56 — DATE

Figure 7.3 Inspection daily total sheet. (From Frank Caplan, Jr., "Process Control in a Job Shop," *Industrial Quality Control*, November 1958, pp. 16–18. Reprinted with permission.)

effort of each department. Charts similar to Figure 7.5 were posted in the offices of the general supervisors to show the quality results of the previous day for each supervisor. Similar charts that recapped the operations of each general supervisor were posted in the office of the superintendent.

The result of the application of the system was to make it healthy for the supervisor to investigate every unusual deviation immediately for the answers to the questions that would inevitably come from above. The results of these investigations were recorded on a supervisor's deviation report (Figure 7.6). Any disagreements about responsibilities were adjudicated by the general supervisor.

Figures 7.7 and 7.8 show the quality control reports issued monthly to show departmental standings and the defect figures chargeable to various causes. Thus quality improvement effort could be concentrated where the return would be maximized.

		First shift				Second shift				Third shift			
Machine number	Date	$\bar{P}$%	3/1	3/2	3/15	$\bar{P}$%	3/1	3/2	3/15	$\bar{P}$%	3/1	3/2	3/15
326	No. defects	1.4	1	0		2.0	0	2		2.4	1	–	
	No. inspections		49	101			86	97			51	–	
	Total defects		1	1			0	2			1	1	
	Total inspections		49	150			86	183			51	51	
417	No. defects	2.3	3	0		5.0	5	(14)		3.6	(8)	1	
	No. inspections		84	89			67	116			101	28	
	Total defects		3	3			5	(19)			(8)	(9)	
	Total inspections		84	173			67	183			101	129	
83	No. defects	6.9	1	0		4.2	1	0		.6	0	0	
	No. inspections		9	19			14	17			13	8	
	Total defects		1	1			1	1			0	0	
	Total inspections		9	28			14	31			13	21	
205	No. defects	2.1	3	3		2.5	4	1		1.5	0	–	
	No. inspections		147	188			214	263			204	–	
	Total defects		3	6			4	5			0	0	
	Total inspections		147	335			214	477			204	204	
641	No. defects	.05	0	(1)		.4	0	(4)		1.0	0	4	
	No. inspections		178	178			88	121			19	162	
	Total defects		0	1			0	(4)			0	4	
	Total inspections		178	356			88	209			19	181	

Figure 7.4 Floor chart for tabulation of inspection results. (From Frank Caplan, Jr., "Process Control in a Job Shop," *Industrial Quality Control*, November 1958, pp. 16–18. Reprinted with permission.)

QUALITY CONTROL CHART

Month March.

Shift	$\bar{P}$%	Date	3/1	3/2	3/3	3/4	3/5	3/6	3/	/26	3/27	3/28	3/29	3/30	3/31	
1	2.2	No. defects	8	4												
		No. inspections	467	575												
		Total defects	8	12												
		Total inspections	467	1,042												
2	2.8	No. defects	10	21												
		No. inspections	469	614												
		Total defects	10	31												
		Total inspections	469	1,083												
3	2.1	No. defects	9	5												
		No. inspections	388	198												
		Total defects	9	14												
		Total inspections	388	586												
Total	2.3	No. defects	27	30												
		No. inspections	1,324	1,387												
		Total defects	27	57												
		Total inspections	1,324	2,711												

Figure 7.5 Supervision chart. (From Frank Caplan, Jr., "Process Control in a Job Shop," *Industrial Quality Control*, November 1958, pp. 16–18. Reprinted with permission.)

FOREMAN'S DEVIATION REPORT				
Area: Lathe	Machine or operation number: 641	Date: 3/2/56	Shift: 2	No. of deviations: 4
Part number and name: 304B627 Shaft.				

Operator error		Non-operator error	
Cause of defect	X	Cause of defect	X
Faulty machine operation		Prior operation	
Measurement error		Machine	
Poor set-up		Planning	
Misread print		Engineering	
Wrong tool	X	Heat treat	
Other (specify)		Tooling	X
		Material	
Operator: 114		Other (specify)	
Shift: 2		Specific cause of defect: (i.e. gage design, computation of stack-up in planning, etc.) Wrong tool provided	

Comments: Operator asked for special tool at tool cab___, wrong one issued___, he didn't check it, but used it.

Action taken to prevent recurrence: Discussed with operators, tool room supervisors, and tool room attendants.

Disposition of part(s): Scrap

Foreman and shift at deviation location	Foreman and shift responsible	General foreman's approval
J. Deron 2-Lathe	H. Brown 2 Tool room	P. R. Sloan.

Figure 7.6 Supervisor's deviation report. (From Frank Caplan, Jr., "Process Control in a Job Shop." *Industrial Quality Control*, November 1958, pp. 16–18. Reprinted with permission.)

QUALITY CONTROL CHART

Shift 2 — Month March.

Area	$\bar{P}$%	Date	3/1	3/2	3/3	3/4	3/5	3/6	3/	/26	3/27	3/28	3/29	3/30	3/31
Lathe	2.3	No. defects	27	30											
		No. inspections	1,324	1,387											
		Total defects	27	57											
		Total inspections	1,324	2,711											
Mills-drills	3.7	No. defects	41	4											
		No. inspections	864	162											
		Total defects	41	45											
		Total inspections	864	1,026											
Sheet metal	10.4	No. defects	(49)	44											
		No. inspections	326	465											
		Total defects	(49)	93											
		Total inspections	326	791											
Totals	4.1	No. defects	290	271											
		No. inspections	7,219	6,437											
		Total defects	290	561											
		Total inspections	7,119	13,656											

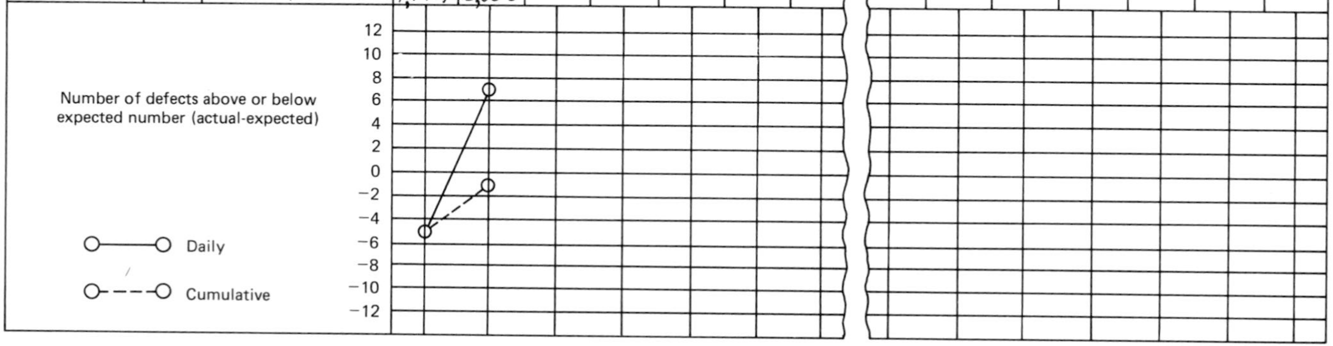

Number of defects above or below expected number (actual-expected)

12, 10, 8, 6, 4, 2, 0, −2, −4, −6, −8, −10, −12

O——O Daily

O- - -O Cumulative

Figure 7.7 Departmental data and overall control chart. (From Frank Caplan, Jr., "Process Control in a Job Shop," *Industrial Quality Control*, November 1958, pp. 16–18. Reprinted with permission.)

QUALITY CONTROL CHART

Shift | Month March

Cause	$\bar{P}$%	Date	3/1	3/2	3/3	3/4	3/5	3/6	3/	/26	3/27	3/28	3/29	3/30	3/31	
Operator	6.8	No. defects	229	188												
		Total defects	229	477												
Machine	4.6	No. defects	25	67												
		Total defects	25	92												
Planning	.45	No. defects	4	0												
		Total defects	4	4												
Tooling	.8	No. defects	0	1												
		Total defects	0	1												
Vendor	5.9	No. defects	31	15												
		Total defects	31	46												
Engineering	.6	No. defects	1	0												
		Total defects	1	1												
Total	4.1	No. defects	290	271												
		No. inspections	7,219	6,437												
		Total defects	290	561												
		Total inspections	7,219	13,656												

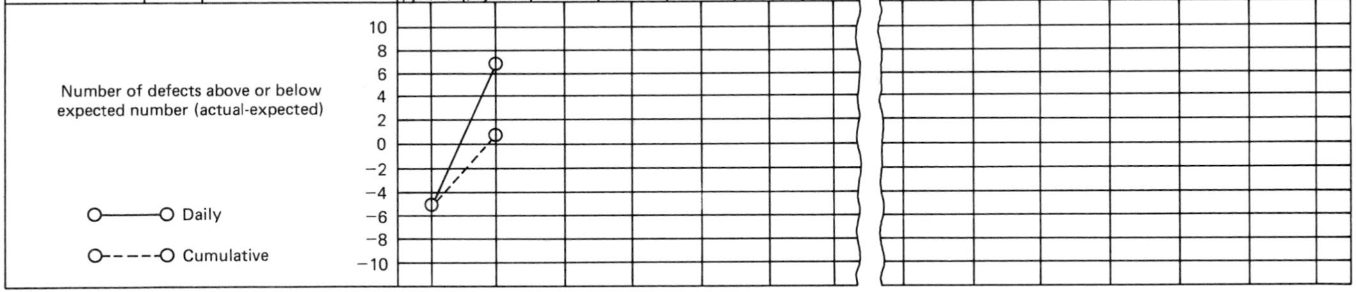

Number of defects above or below expected number (actual-expected)

10, 8, 6, 4, 2, 0, −2, −4, −6, −8, −10

O——O Daily

O- - - -O Cumulative

Figure 7.8 Defect-cause control chart. (From Frank Caplan, Jr., "Process Control in a Job Shop," *Industrial Quality Control*, November 1958, pp. 16–18. Reprinted with permission.)

Mr. Caplan pointed out that meetings were held with supervisors, union representatives, and inspectors present to ensure that everyone was informed of the program and its goals. Although there was some distrust initially, this soon disappeared and was replaced by a spirit of cooperation.

One could point to some small liberties taken with theory, but such would ignore the really significant contribution here—that of providing job shops with a practical method of control where none was apparent before. The approach fits the situation. It tempers the idealistic desires with what can be attained practically through psychological effects. The end result is probably pretty close to the minimum total quality cost solution desired.

DEFECTS CONTROL CHART

Defects (or any other occurrence of interest) may be charted in a similar manner to percent defective. The condition for use of number of defects as an expression of nonconformance is that the area of opportunity for occurrence of a defect should be fairly constant from unit of inspection to unit of inspection. A unit of inspection can be 1 unit, 10 units, 100 units, or any quantity chosen. Two types of control charts can be developed. If the unit remains fairly constant from period to period, the chart may be in terms of defects per unit. This is called the c chart. An alternative method is to use the ratio $\Sigma\, c$, the total number of defects to n number of units, for example, number of paint imperfections per 100 square inches of painted surface. Such a chart is called a u chart, where $u = \Sigma\, c/n = \bar{c}$. The denominator of the ratio may be expressed in any way desired: square inches, square feet, hundreds of square feet, and so on. This freedom of choice means that different numbers of units may be inspected, and the expression of noncomformance converted to a common denominator provided that the possibilities for occurrence of a defect are high in relation to the number of defects that actually do occur and the area of opportunity for defect occurrence stays reasonably constant from inspection unit to inspection unit.

The probability distribution of both c and u would be Poisson with the parameter c'. Even though Poisson is not as closely approximated by normal as is the binomial, a normal approximation is used nevertheless. It is practical, simple to use, and the errors involved are usually insignificant.

For the c-chart:

$$\text{mean} = c'$$

$$\text{variance} = c'$$

$$\text{estimate of } c' \text{ is given by } \bar{c} \text{ from the base period}$$

$$\text{control limits} = \bar{c} \pm 3\sqrt{\bar{c}}$$

For the u chart:

$$\text{mean} = c'$$

$$\text{variance} = \frac{c'}{n}$$

estimate of c' is given by $\overline{u}$ $(\Sigma\, c_i / \Sigma\, n_i)$ from the base period

$$\text{control limits} = \overline{u} \pm \sqrt{\frac{\overline{u}}{n_i}}$$

APPLICATION OF DEFECTS PER UNIT CONTROL

Herschell R. Harrison[3] of Collins Radio Company in Cedar Rapids, Iowa, relates the use of the defects chart for assembly control. Collins Radio Company manufactures and assembles complex electrical equipment. Many orders for equipment are for quantities of 100 or less. Thus much the same conditions apply as in the previous case except for the type of product manufactured.

At Collins Radio, the industrial engineering department designates where inspection will be conducted in the assembly line. A $\overline{c}$ chart (same as a u chart) is maintained at each station. It shows the number of units checked daily and the number of errors discovered by type (see Figure 7.9). The charts are analyzed for defect concentrations and inspection efforts are centered on the attributes that fail most frequently.

The quality control department maintains trend charts for each section. These charts are constructed by counting all possible errors per time period on equipment at each inspection station and dividing this quantity into the quality average for the same time period. This gives an index of performance of the section and one that properly allows for the complexity of the product handled by the section. It makes it possible to compare one supervisor's quality effort to another's.

A report is sent up to top management each week. This report shows the quality level of each job and contains a listing of the production and inspection supervisors in the order of quality produced during the previous week.

With reference to Figure 7.9, note that u is used as the measure of defects,

$$u = \frac{\Sigma\, c}{n}$$

[3] H. R. Harrison, "Statistical Quality Control Will Work on Short Run Jobs," *Industrial Quality Control*, September 1956, pp. 8–11.

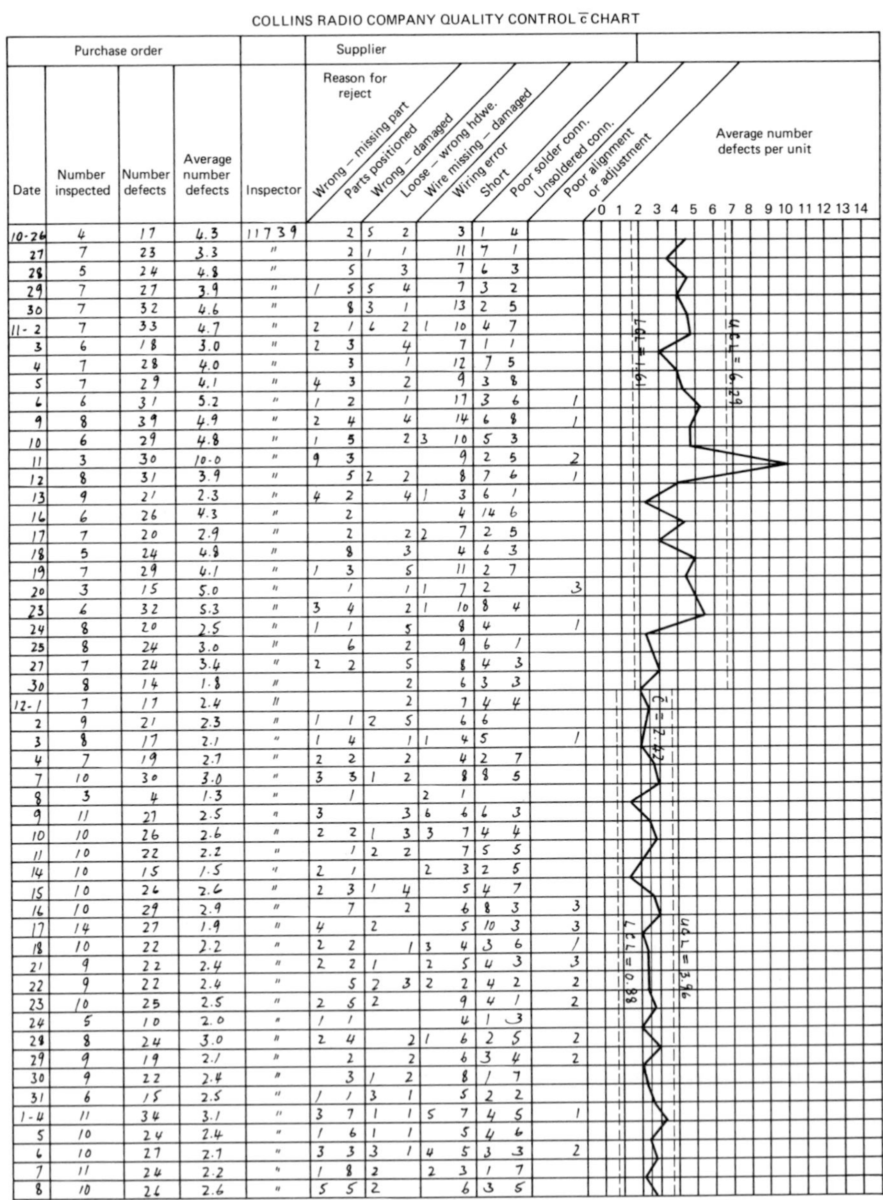

Date	Number inspected	Number defects	Average number defects	Inspector	Wrong – missing part	Parts positioned	Wrong – damaged	Loose – wrong hdwe.	Wire missing – damaged	Wiring error	Short	Poor solder conn.	Unsoldered conn.	Poor alignment or adjustment
10-26	4	17	4.3	11739		2	5	2		3	1	4		
27	7	23	3.3	"		2	1	1		11	7	1		
28	5	24	4.8	"		5		3		7	6	3		
29	7	27	3.9	"	1	5	5	4		7	3	2		
30	7	32	4.6	"		8	3	1		13	2	5		
11-2	7	33	4.7	"	2	1	6	2	1	10	4	7		
3	6	18	3.0	"	2	3		4		7	1	1		
4	7	28	4.0	"		3		1		12	7	5		
5	7	29	4.1	"	4	3		2		9	3	8		
6	6	31	5.2	"	1	2		1		17	3	6		1
9	8	39	4.9	"	2	4		4		14	6	8		1
10	6	29	4.8	"	1	5		2	3	10	5	3		
11	3	30	10.0	"	9	3				9	2	5		2
12	8	31	3.9	"		5	2	2		8	7	6		1
13	9	21	2.3	"	4	2		4	1	3	6	1		
16	6	26	4.3	"		2				4	14	6		
17	7	20	2.9	"		2		2	2	7	2	5		
18	5	24	4.8	"		8		3		4	6	3		
19	7	29	4.1	"	1	3		5		11	2	7		
20	3	15	5.0	"		1		1	1	7	2			3
23	6	32	5.3	"	3	4		2	1	10	8	4		
24	8	20	2.5	"	1	1		5		8	4			1
25	8	24	3.0	"		6		2		9	6	1		
27	7	24	3.4	"	2	2		5		8	4	3		
30	8	14	1.8	"				2		6	3	3		
12-1	7	17	2.4	"				2		7	4	4		
2	9	21	2.3	"	1	1	2	5		6	6			
3	8	17	2.1	"	1	4		1	1	4	5			1
4	7	19	2.7	"	2	2		2		4	2	7		
7	10	30	3.0	"	3	3	1	2		8	8	5		
8	3	4	1.3	"		1			2	1				
9	11	27	2.5	"	3			3	6	6	6	3		
10	10	26	2.6	"	2	2	1	3	3	7	4	4		
11	10	22	2.2	"		1	2	2		7	5	5		
14	10	15	1.5	"	2	1			2	3	2	5		
15	10	26	2.6	"	2	3	1	4		5	4	7		
16	10	29	2.9	"		7		2		6	8	3		3
17	14	27	1.9	"	4		2			5	10	3		3
18	10	22	2.2	"	2	2		1	3	4	3	6		1
21	9	22	2.4	"	2	2	1		2	5	4	3		3
22	9	22	2.4	"		5	2	3	2	2	4	2		2
23	10	25	2.5	"	2	5	2			9	4	1		2
24	5	10	2.0	"	1	1				4	1	3		
28	8	24	3.0	"	2	4		2	1	6	2	5		2
29	9	19	2.1	"		2		2		6	3	4		2
30	9	22	2.4	"		3	1	2		8	1	7		
31	6	15	2.5	"	1	1	3	1		5	2	2		
1-4	11	34	3.1	"	3	7	1	1	5	7	4	5		1
5	10	24	2.4	"	1	6	1	1		5	4	6		
6	10	27	2.7	"	3	3	3	1	4	5	3	3		2
7	11	24	2.2	"	1	8	2		2	3	1	7		
8	10	26	2.6	"	5	5	2			6	3	5		

Figure 7.9 Chart for average defects. (From H. R. Harrison, "Statistical Quality Control Will Work on Short Run Jobs," *Industrial Quality Control*, September 1956, pp. 8–11. Reprinted with permission.)

For the first period from October 26 through November 30, the total number of defects was 640. The total number inspected was 162, hence

$$\overline{u} = \frac{\Sigma\, c}{\Sigma\, n} = 3.95$$

Base-period upper and lower control limits were placed at

$$\overline{u} \pm 3\sqrt{\frac{\overline{u}}{n}}$$

where n represents the average number inspected—in this case 6.5. There was no standard set for the period December 1 through January 8 since another base-period chart analysis was made on the basis of the results obtained during the period. Of course, there is no limit to the number or lengths of base-period analyses that may be made. It is emphasized, however, that this is an *ex post facto analysis*. It merely records and analyzes that which has happened in the past. The true value of the control chart lies in its standard and decision limits for control of *current* quality performance. The base-period analysis is performed strictly for the purpose of estimating past performance so that achievable standards and natural decision limits may be established.

ATTRIBUTES CHART FOR QUALITY TROUBLESHOOTING

Ideally, the control chart for defects or defectives should have a data collection portion to point up the quality characteristics which are causing trouble. Whether such a device is maintained in conjunction with the chart or separate from it, such maintenance is urged very strongly. Much of the value of the data collection process is lost if the troublesome points are not isolated for special consideration. This is directly relevant to the management by the exception principle of investigating only the exceptional cases to preclude more occurrences of the bad and to press for continuance of more occurrences of the good.

If the attributes chart shows that the majority of the trouble is caused by a few quality characteristics, as it will, the economic effect of these problems can be determined and necessary action taken. More often than not, the distribution of defects within a unit of product will approximate the Poisson. Figure 7.10 shows the discrete and cumulative distributions of incidental defects. By expressing the data in cumulative fashion, meaningful statements about the distribution of defects can be made. For example, reference to Figure 7.10 shows that 70% of the defect observations occurs in only 20% of the quality characteristics. Also, half of the characteristics account for about 95% of the defects. In purchasing and engineering this type of analysis is

Characteristic number	Number of observations	Cumulative number of observations	Cumulative percent of observations
110	215	215	38.5
101	182	397	71.2
107	84	481	86.2
109	45	526	94.2
108	14	540	96.8
102	10	550	98.6
106	5	555	99.4
104	3	558	100.0
105	0	558	100.0
103	0	558	100.0

(*a*)

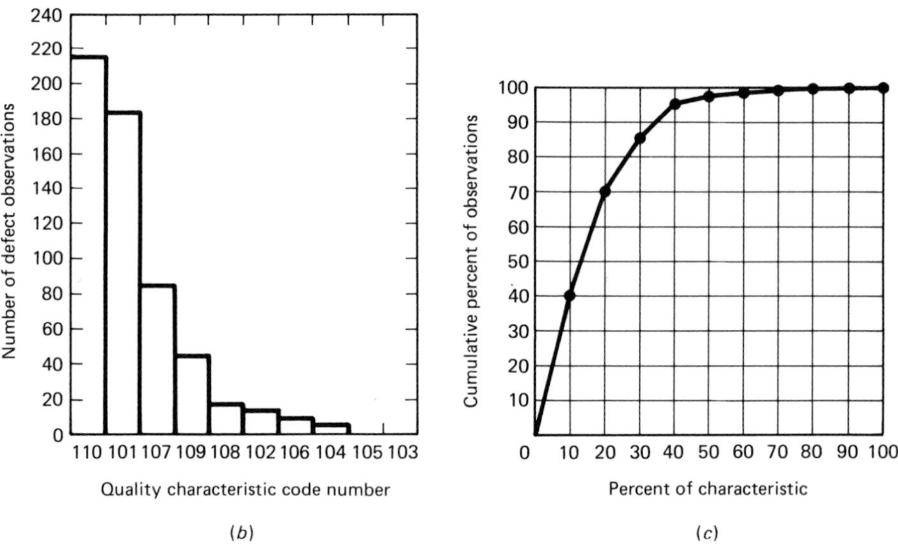

Figure 7.10 Graphical distribution analysis of incidental defect data of Figure 11-8: (a) calculation table; (b) distribution of defect observations by characteristic code numbers; (c) distribution of cumulative percent of observations by percent of characteristics.

referred to as *value analysis*. The items are analyzed to determine the most important from the standpoint of contributed value. Applied to quality, it may be referred to as *quality value analysis*. If an economic analysis indicates a more precise control is justified, possibly application of a variables type control chart is warranted. Or it may be that certain designs, suppliers, or equipment should be changed. In a nutshell, quality value analysis pinpoints areas for further analysis, evaluation, and control.

ATTRIBUTES CHART FOR PERFORMANCE CONTROL

The attributes chart is ideal for performance measurement and control of quality or any other event that can be expressed either as a percentage or a number of events. Figure 7.11 is an illustration of how the attributes chart is used for performance control. Here the subject for performance measurement and control is the quality of incidental characteristics on the Willys Jeep.

The historical portion of the chart is a condensed, weighted average of the data for the period indicated. Management wants to know: Where were

Sample number	1452	1453	1454	1455	1456	1457	1458	1459	1460	1461	1462	1463	1464	1465	1466	
Sample size = n	5	5	5	5	5	5	5	5	5	5	5	5	5	5	5	
Characteristic	Number of defects by characteristic															
101	7	4	5	4	2	9	7	4	9	7	6	4	4	5	4	
102	1					1	1		1	1						
103																
104																
105																
106			1					1		1						
107	2	3	4	5	4	2	1	2	2	2	4	3	3	2	3	
108	1														2	
109	1		1	2	2	2	3	1	2	2		4	4	2	2	
110	10	11	8	8	6	8	6	9	5	5	10	4	4	8	4	
No. def. = c or np	22	18	19	19	14	23	20	17	17	19	18	20	15	17	15	
100u	440	360	380	380	280	460	400	340	340	380	360	400	300	352	300	

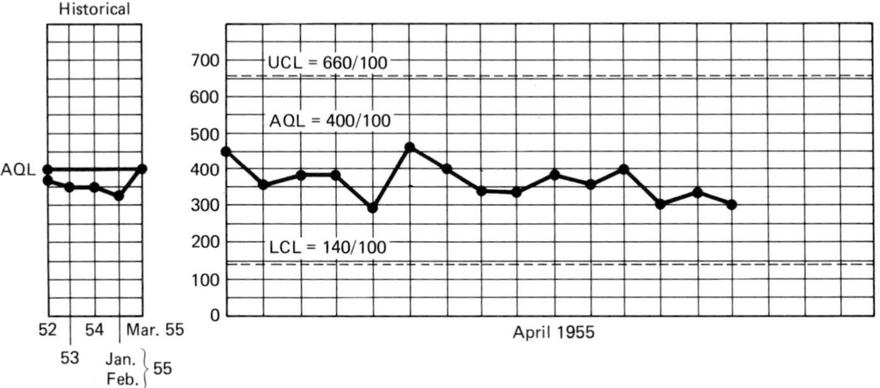

Figure 7.11 Defects per 100 units performance control chart.

we when we started the project? The historical portion of the chart answers this question. The AQL (acceptable quality level) is the standard—in this example 400 defects per 100 units. The right-hand portion of the chart shows how current performance compares with the standard and at what deviations decision to investigate for cause should be made. The upper portion of the chart shows which defects are occurring and what their normal level is so that decisions about them may be made. Spottiness checks may be made by testing for significant deviations of number of defects for any of the characteristics.

INDEX CHART FOR PERFORMANCE CONTROL

A performance chart may be maintained for occurrence of a single event, a group of events, or all of a possible number of events. Grouping events into categories of seriousness is often a reasonable compromise between the high administrative cost of individual-event control and the low information furnished by the total events chart. Many users have found the grouped-events chart with the accompanying data information, as in Figure 7.11, to be a practical and economical compromise for most situations.

When presenting vendor and departmental quality performance information to management, it becomes cumbersome to present data involving many different standards and performances from many different producers. In such cases an index control chart is very helpful. The co-author[4] has devised a simple little index system which converts percentage estimates into standard performance ratings using a universally familiar scale of values. For example, consider the data in Table 7.3 obtained from inspection records of two outside vendors (A and B) and three in-plant production departments (C, D, and E), all manufacturing different products but which use approximately the same tooling and equipment.

If a responsible manager were to examine only the first three columns in Table 7.3, he would have to relate the performance of the third column to the standard of the second column considering also the number inspected. Of course, this can be done and an informed manager would immediately apply a significance test to each to find the deviation in standard error units and thus obtain a standardized deviation measure. To be effective as an information medium, this measure must then be interpreted, which automatically presumes knowledge of statistics. Very few persons using control chart methods have intimate understanding of statistics, but almost all remember their schooldays when below 70 represented failure and 100 was tops. It would seem approriate, then, to convert the plus and minus standard error

[4] B. L. Hansen, *Sampling Aids for Management Control* (Cleveland, Ohio: American Management Institute, Inc., 1959).

TABLE 7.3 Inspection Data

Producer	Specified Quality Standard (% defective)	Actual Quality Estimate—One Month's Inspection	Number Inspected	k	Standard Rating	Action
A	1.0	0.60	800	+1.2	91	None
B	0.65	0.95	1200	−1.2	79	None
C	4.0	3.0	4200	+3.1	100+	Reduce inspection
D	1.5	1.3	7150	+1.4	92	None
E	2.5	4.5	700	−3.3	70−	Tighten inspection

units to the 70-to-100 grading system. The simple conversion is shown in Figure 7.12.

It is convenient here to use two calculation nomographs constructed for use with this performance rating system. Figures 7.13 and 7.14 are used for computing σ_{100p} or σ_{100u} and the numerical performance ratings. The first

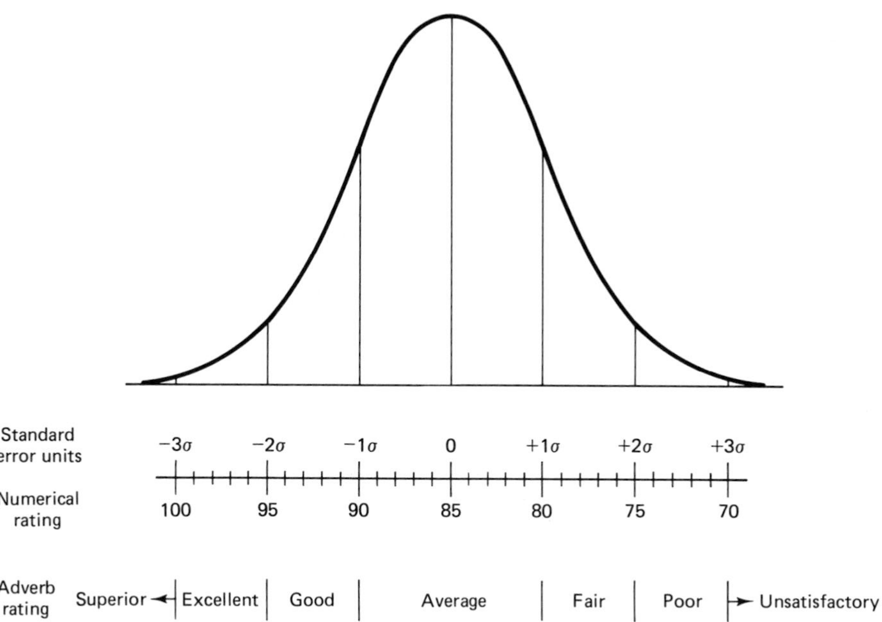

Figure 7.12 Conversion of standard error (k) units to numerical ratings (index percentages).

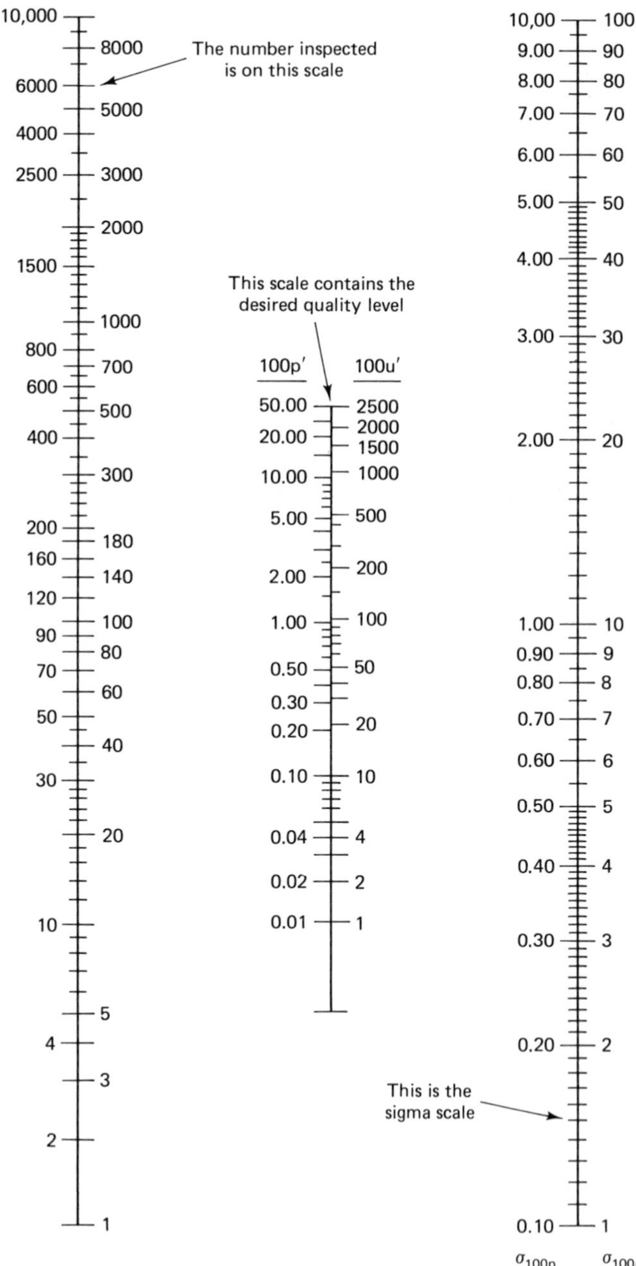

Figure 7.13 Nomograph for computing σ_{100p} and σ_{100u}. (Reprinted from *Sampling Aids for Management Control* with full permission.)

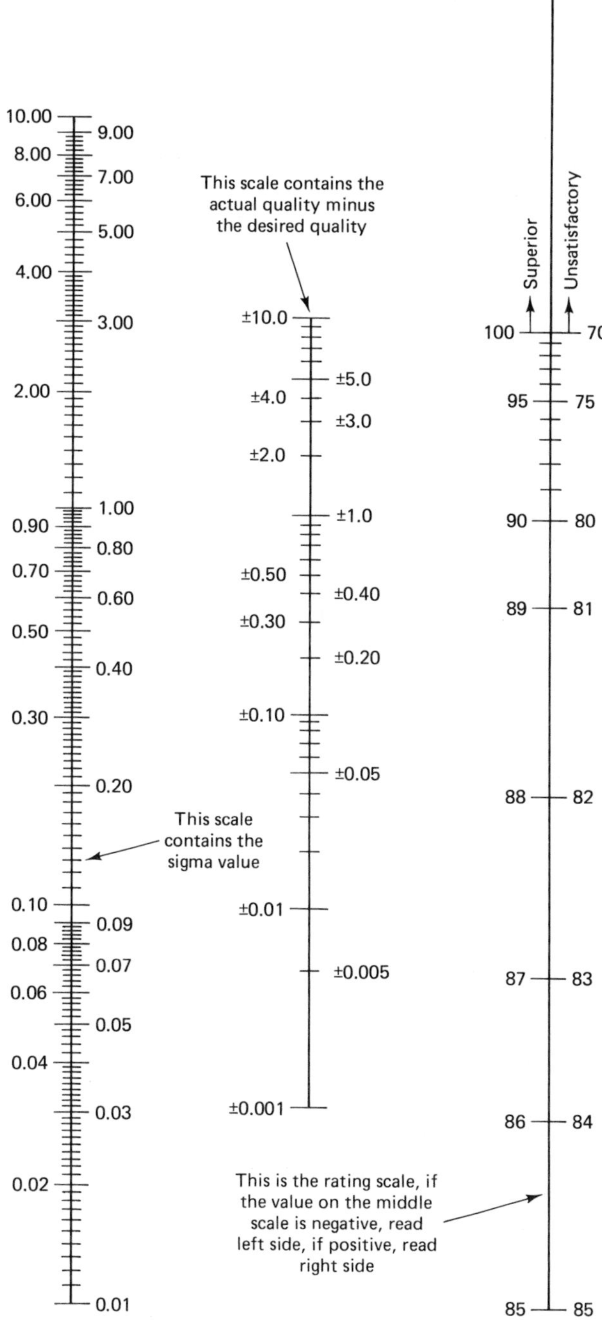

Figure 7.14 Nomograph for computing performance rating. (Reprinted from *Sampling Aids for Management Control* with full permission.)

example of producer A will be used to show the step-by-step process for obtaining the performance rating:

1. On the nomograph of Figure 7.13, lay a straightedge across the left scale at 800 (the number inspected) and at 1.0 ($100p'$) on the left side of the middle scale. The intersecting point on the left side of the right scale is σ_{100p}. For this example, $\sigma_{100p} = 0.35$. Note that Figure 7.13 computes

$$\sigma_{100p} = \frac{\sqrt{100p'(100 - 100p')}}{\sqrt{\text{number inspected}}}$$

and

$$\sigma_{100u} = \frac{100\sqrt{u'}}{\sqrt{\text{number inspected}}}$$

2. On the nomograph of Figure 7.14 lay a straightedge on the left scale at $\sigma_{100p} = 0.35$ and across the middle scale at the value yielded by subtracting the desired quality from the actual quality. For this example, the actual quality ($100\,\bar{p} = 0.60$) minus the desired quality ($100p' = 1.0$) is -0.40. The intersecting point on the right-hand scale is 91. Note that Figure 7.14 computes

$$\frac{100\bar{p} - 100p'}{\sigma_{100p}} \qquad \frac{100\bar{u} - 100u'}{\sigma_{100u}}$$

and translates the resulting k value into the numerical performance rating.[5]

Figure 7.15 illustrates the application of this standardized performance rating method to the control of product furnished by producer A. The same control can be applied to all other producers. Interpretation and evaluation by management is facilitated because the standard, upper, and lower control limits are always 85, 100, and 70, respectively—the same for all producers. A cumulative chart was also prepared to show the effect of accumulated data. Just as in law, where weight of evidence is important, the accumulated evidence of quality finally pushes producer A over the 100 mark into the reduced (or audit) inspection zone. The method may be used for any situation where occurrence of events can be expressed as a fraction, percentage, or number of events. The same procedure is followed exactly.

[5] The nomograph was constructed specifically for percent defective quality and *a* defects per hundred unit scale was added. Figure 7.14 will not suffice for some defects per hundred units cases, since the sigma scale upper limit is 10. There will be occasions when $\sigma_{100u} > 10$. In such instances the computation formula will have to be used.

Performance rating data for producer A

Month	Actual quality level (100p)	Number inspected	Standard rating	* Cumulative rating
Jan.	0.60	800	91	91
Feb.	0.70	900	90	92
Mar.	0.85	1300	89	92
Apr.	0.55	450	90	93
May	0.65	750	90	95
Jun.	0.80	950	89	96
Jul.	0.72	650	89	97
Aug.	0.93	1000	88	96
Sep.	0.58	1250	92	98
Oct.	0.65	1400	92	99
Nov.	0.62	1150	92	100
Dec.	0.70	1720	91	100+

*The cumulative rating is based on the weighted average of the cumulative actual quality levels $(\Sigma W \cdot 100p)/(\Sigma W)$. For example, for the month of May $(\Sigma W \cdot 100p)/(\Sigma W) = 2950/4200 = 0.70$. The desired quality level $100p'$ is 1.0, ΣW is 4200 and $100\overline{p} - 100p' = 0.70 - 1.0 = -0.30$. From the nomographs the cumulative rating for May is 95.

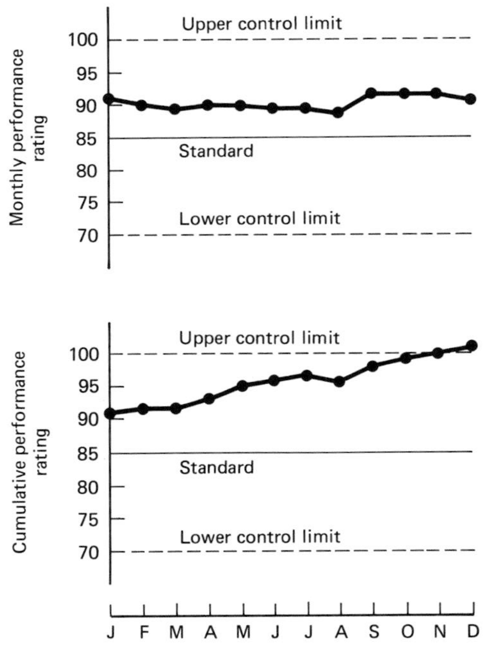

Figure 7.15 Performance control chart.

There are other proprietary quality performance rating systems in vogue.[6] All use the same principles of development and interpretation. If one is learned, the others can be assimilated very easily.

DEMERIT RATING SYSTEM

An index of performance is valuable, but it has the same limitations as the attributes control chart. Chief among these is the requirement for maintaining a chart on individual characteristics or categories of characteristics having like seriousness. One method that has received some favor is the *demerit rating system*. The demerit method may be used for performance control by itself just as the attributes chart, or it may be used in conjunction with one of the index performance rating systems.

Dodge and Torrey have documented the use of the demerit system as a check inspection and demerit rating plan.[7] It is a valuable plan in its entirety and potential users would do well to investigate the technique further.

The demerit system requires that defect types be weighted according to seriousness. In the Dodge–Torrey plan, defects are placed in categories A, B, C, and D with weights of 100, 50, 10, and 1, respectively. The number of demerits for a period

$$D = 100d_{\mathrm{A}} + 50d_{\mathrm{B}} + 10d_{\mathrm{C}} + d_{\mathrm{D}}$$

where d_{A}, d_{B}, d_{C}, and d_{D} are the number of class A, B, C, and D defects, respectively, found during the period

$$U = \frac{D}{n}$$

where n is the number of units inspected during the period.

For control of quality, a standard quality level is computed,

$$U_s = 100u_{\mathrm{a}} + 50u_{\mathrm{b}} + 10u_{\mathrm{c}} + u_{\mathrm{d}}$$

[6] R. L. Pappas, "The Ampex Quality Rating System," *Industrial Quality Control*, March 1957, pp. 9–11. G. Georgis, "An Application of the Bendix Vendor Quality Rating System to a Small Plant," *Industrial Quality Control*, March 1957, pp. 12–13. This article features a vendor rating slide rule for use with the Bendix system. S. J. Wilson, "A Missiles Seriousness and Complexity Vendor Rating System," *Industrial Quality Control*, June 1958, pp. 15–17. J. Schneider, "A Vendor Quality Conformance Procedure," *Industrial Quality Control*, September 1958, pp. 10–13.

[7] H. F. Dodge and M. N. Torrey, "A Check Inspection and Demerit Rating Plan," *Industrial Quality Control*, July 1956, pp. 5–12. The basic features of this plan have been adopted by the Atomic Energy Commission and by certain guided missile and business machine manufacturers.

where u_a, u_b, u_c, and u_d are the defects-per-unit values for class A, B, C, and D defects, respectively.

A standard variance factor is computed,

$$C_s = (100)^2 u_a + (50)^2 u_b + (10)^2 u_c + u_d$$

The equation for the control limits for a demerits-per-unit chart is

$$U_s \pm 3\sigma_u$$

where

$$\sigma_u = \sqrt{\frac{C_s}{n}}$$

An index system may be used where it is desired to measure performance to different demerit standards. The *demerit index* is the ratio of observed demerits to expected demerits ($I = D|nU$), so the standard quality level is always 1. Control limits are

$$1 \pm 3\sigma_I$$

where

$$\sigma_I = \frac{nC_s}{nU_s} \quad \text{or} \quad \frac{\sigma_u}{U_s}$$

When the types of product in a given category have different standard values, the demerit index for the category is a weighted average of the indexes for the types included. The general equation for an overall demerit index is

$$I_o = \frac{\Sigma\, W_i I_i}{\Sigma\, W_i}$$

where W_i = weight for the ith type
I_i = index for the ith type
Σ = sum over all types

The general equation for the standard deviation of the overall demerit index is

$$\sigma_{I_o} = \frac{1}{\Sigma\, W_i}\sqrt{\Sigma\left(\frac{W_i^2 C_{s_i}}{n_i (U_{s_i})^2}\right)}$$

where C_{s_i} = standard variance factor for the ith type
U_{s_i} = standard quality level for the ith type
n_i = sample size for the ith type for the period of control

The 3σ control limits are $1 \pm 3\sigma_{I_o}$.

Figure 7.16 is a composite illustration of the construction of a demerit chart. The usual control chart interpretations are used to determine whether investigation for cause is worthwhile.

A single demerit rating will not suffice completely for *true* control of quality but will usually be satisfactory if individual characteristics do not

X, Y and Z type relays – unmounted
monthly demerit rate

Type of defect	Demerit weight	Number defects June	Number defects J-A	Number defects Sept.	Number demerits June	Number demerits J-A	Number demerits Sept.
A	100	0	1	0	0	100	0
B	50	0	2	0	0	100	0
C	10	5	10	6	50	100	60
D	1	1	4	3	1	4	3
			Total demerits		51	304	63
			Sample size, n		232	240	165

$$\text{Demerits per unit} = \frac{\text{Demerits}}{\text{Number relays in sample}} = \quad 22 \quad 1.27 \quad 0.38$$

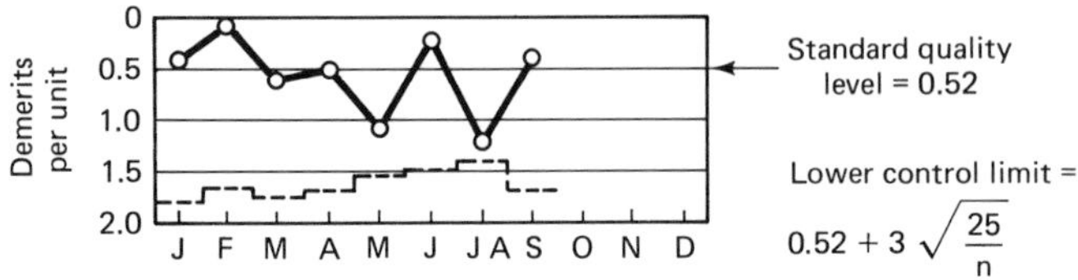

X, Y and Z type relays – unmounted
quality standards

Defects class	Demerits per defect, w	Contributions to standards: Defects per unit, u	Demerits per unit	(Demerits)^2 per unit
A	100	0.0014	0.140	14.00
B	50	0.0034	0.170	8.50
C	10	0.0205	0.205	2.05
D	1	0.0097	0.010	0.01
		Total	0.525	24.56
		standards:	$U_s = 0.52$	$C_s = 25$

$U_s = w_A u_A + w_B u_B + w_C u_C + w_D u_D$, and
$C_s = w_A^2 u_A + w_B^2 u_B + w_C^2 u_C + w_D^2 u_D$
Rounded to two significant figures

Figure 7.16 Typical summary of inspection results and control chart with computation of quality standards U_s and C_s. (From H. F. Dodge and M. N. Torrey, "A Check Inspection and Demerit Rating Plan," *Industrial Quality Control*, July 1956. This figure is a composite of Figures 2 and 3 in the article.)

exhibit nonconformance and if the index is within the control limits and not a part of a significant run or trend.

The authors of the demerit system propose a standard index of 1 instead of 85, as in this author's system. Any index is satisfactory as long as the appropriate reference base is established in the interpreter's mind.

Using the example data for the months of June, July–August, and September of Figure 7.16 for illustration, the performance ratings and the necessary calculations to obtain them are given by Table 7.4. Calculation of k values and conversion with the scale of Figure 7.14 are shown. Figure 7.14 could be used once observed minus standard and the standard error in demerits per hundred units have been determined. Both the left and middle scales of Figure 7.14 may be multiplied by the same amount, enabling its use no matter what the input data may be.

POSSIBLE APPLICATIONS OF PERFORMANCE RATING

In general, any attributes-type measurement will be amenable to performance rating. Even variables information may be converted to a percentage statement which can then be converted to a performance rating. Thus there is really very little in the way of performance which cannot be rated easily. A few of the work and administrative areas of effort, in addition to quality and errors, to which performance rating can be applied are idle time, absenteeism, tardiness, schedule adherence, safety performance, payment of invoices, and inventory stockouts. Of course, there are many other direct applications in addition to many of the opportunity type, that is, the type of application which depends on one's ingenuity in devising a method that provides the *opportunity* to use this method.

TABLE 7.4 Conversion of Figure 7.6 Data to Standardized Performance Rating Using Figure 7.14 Conversion Scale

Month	Demerits per 100 Units	Observed Minus Standard	Standard Error = $100\sqrt{\frac{25}{n}}$	k	Standardized Performance rating
June	20	−32	32.7	−0.92	90
July–Aug.	127	+75	32.2	+2.33	73
Sept.	38	−14	38.8	−0.36	87

PROBLEMS

7.1. The following data were taken from the daily records of inspection of a relatively simple mass produced component. These data were accumulated as the components were produced.

Date	Number Inspected	Number Defective
March 10	1,200	4
11	1,300	5
14	1,250	7
15	1,175	6
16	1,400	8
17	1,350	8
18	1,300	5
21	1,350	9
22	1,400	10
23	1,250	7
24	1,200	16
25	1,150	8

Use these data for computing a base period control chart for percent defective. If there are out-of-control points, assume that they are not cyclic in nature, that their causes have been determined, and such causes have been eliminated. What would be a realistic standard to set for the quality of immediate future production of this component? Where should 3σ control limits be placed? Assume that the average percent defective of the next period were 0.72%. Is the average percent defective significantly different from the standard at the 1% level of significance?

7.2. An electronic consumer products company produces control switches to be used in desktop computers. The following data describe inspection results for these switches during the month of May 85.

Date	Fraction Defective	Date	Fraction Defective
1	5.5	16	11.6
2	8.3	17	7.4
3	6.0	20	6.3
6	5.2	21	5.0
7	4.5	22	5.4
8	6.2	23	7.5
9	5.8	24	7.6
10	7.3	27	5.2
13	4.6	28	6.3
14	6.8	29	5.8
15	7.8	30	6.2
		31	6.0

All fractions are expressed as "percent of daily production." Compute a percent defective control chart using 3σ control limits.

7.3. Wooden pallets manufactured in a plant are inspected on a 100% basis. Compute 3σ control limits applicable to each shift.

	Shift	Number of Pallets	Defective Pallets
Monday	1	138	3
	2	140	5
	3	124	1
Tuesday	1	137	2
	2	143	6
	3	122	0
Wednesday	1	136	4
	2	148	5
	3	125	1
Thursday	1	138	3
	2	150	3
	3	124	2
Friday	1	136	4
	2	145	6
	3	123	0

7.4. Using the data in Problem 7.3, determine the central line $\overline{p}$ and 3σ control limits for three separate control charts for shifts 1, 2, and 3.

7.5. On the following Monday, shift 3 produces 125 pallets, of which 3 are defective. Would this be considered an event that should be investigated:
(a) Using control limits computed in Problem 7.3?
(b) Using control limits computed in Problem 7.4?

7.6. Construct a base-period 100μ chart (expressed as defects per 100 units) from the following data obtained from original inspection of all characteristics on a complex item of equipment. Because of the large number of characteristics, the expectancy of defects per unit is high, although it is unlikely that any one characteristic would have more defects than others.

Lot Number	Sample Size	Total Defects in Sample	Defects per 100 Units
1	10	15	150
2	10	17	170
3	10	12	120
4	10	16	160
5	10	14	140
6	10	5	50
7	10	14	140
8	10	11	110
9	10	9	90
10	10	10	100

7.7. Household refrigerators are inspected for minor imperfections (defects) in the enameled finish. Each refrigerator is considered as a separate lot.

Lot Number	Capacity	Defects
1	17	16
2	17	14
3	17	19
4	17	28
5	17	15
6	17	22
7	17	21
8	17	12
9	17	23
10	17	25
11	12	9
12	12	7
13	12	9
14	12	11
15	12	8
16	12	10
17	12	11
18	12	9
19	12	9
20	12	7

Determine the trial control limits and prepare a c chart for these data.

7.8. **(a)** Is it appropriate to have a single control chart for 17- and 12-ft refrigerators in Problem 7.7?

(b) During the subsequent period the company expects to continue producing both 17- and 12-ft models. However, the mix (how many of each type) is not known in advance. Which of the following policies would you recommend?

(i) Use a single control chart

(ii) Use a single central line with different control limits for each model.

(iii) Use separate control charts for each model.

7.9. Magnesium I-beams are being extruded and cut into 3-ft lengths. As they are cut, they are inspected visually for surface defects and inspected internally for subsurface flaws by means of an ultrasonic detector. Each beam is considered a unit. As they are inspected, the number of defects noted in each is recorded in the order that the beams are produced. The following figures show the tabulation of 24 consecutive units:

Lot Number	Number of Defects	Lot Number	Number of Defects
1	33	13	28
2	27	14	33
3	17	15	36
4	22	16	43
5	19	17	28
6	28	18	30
7	31	19	20
8	38	20	17
9	24	21	23
10	12	22	27
11	41	23	12
12	18	24	15

Make a c chart for these data. Is the process stable? What value of c' would you suggest as a standard for the following period?

7.10. A hosiery manufacturer uses a control chart based on defects found in every 100 pairs of stockings. During a month (25 working days) 10,800 pairs of a certain type of stockings were produced and inspected. The total number of defects observed was 360. The daily production varied from 200 to 900 pairs. Determine the central line for a $100u$ chart and set up formulas for determination of 3σ control limits. What are the control limits when the production is (a) 400 pairs; (b) 900 pairs?

7.11. For the data in Problem 7.9, determine the 0.025 and 0.975 probability limits. Use Table A3.1 to find these control limits.

7.12. Using Figures 7.13 and 7.14, compute the ratings of the following vendors, who are submitting lots being inspected to a quality standard of 1.0%.

Vendor	Number Inspected	Number Defective
A	5000	60
B	600	4
C	2500	21
D	8500	92
E	2500	20
F	4000	30

7.13. Product supplied by vendor X has been monitored for six months. The desired quality for this product is 0.5% ($p = 0.005$).

Month	Number Inspected	Observed Quality	Standard Rating	Cumulative Rating
April	1200	0.58		
May	1000	0.3		
June	1500	0.46		
July	1100	0.37		
August	1000	0.40		
September	1200	0.42		

Compute the charts for monthly and cumulative performance ratings.

7.14. Construct a demerits per unit base period control chart for the following data using weights of 50, 10, 5, and 1, for critical, major, minor, and incidental defects, respectively.

Month	Sample Size	Critical	Major	Minor	Incidental
1	4	1	3	2	5
2	4	0	2	4	7
3	4	0	1	3	7
4	4	0	2	1	4
5	4	0	3	5	5
6	4	0	2	3	4
7	4	0	0	4	6
8	4	1	1	1	2
9	4	0	1	3	4
10	4	0	2	2	6

Are any points out of control? What would be a realistic standard for the next period?

7.15. Complete the following table. The standard demerits per unit is 68 and C_s = 1600.

n	Month	Demerits /units	Observed Standard	Standard Error	k	Performance Rating
5	1	20				
6	2	96				
7	3	73				
8	4	52				

eight

PROCESS CAPABILITY ANALYSIS

Process capability analysis is a basic step in any quality control program. Actually, process capability analysis is an attempt to analyze the extent to which the product produced by the process can conform to the design. This analysis gives an estimate of the highest quality level that can possibly be achieved by the process as it is set up. Quality capability analysis is often called *process* or *machine* capability. The latter, of course, is more confining and refers only to the capability of machinery, where the term *process* includes machines and any other type of process used, including human beings. The purpose of capability analysis is to determine the *natural variation* of a process when the effects of all extraneous factors not contributing to the process have been minimized.

Besides the natural variation, there are two factors that would influence the capability of a process: first, the *tolerances* and *specifications* in the design of the product, and second, the same tolerances and specifications *as these relate to the production*.

DETERMINATION OF PROCESS CAPABILITY

Process capability can be determined either at the beginning of the project through a pilot or preliminary study, or it can be monitored on a continuing basis during production. Process capability may be defined as the range of variation that will include *almost all* the product coming out the process.

When the assumption of normal probability distribution is valid, 99.73% of the product measurements would lie in the range of mean ± 3 standard deviations. Since the normal assumption is valid for most processes and 99.73% does represent "almost all," this range of 6 standard deviations is commonly used as the range of natural variation.

When making the preliminary study it is important to minimize the effects of factors essentially extraneous to the study. Such factors are unnatural material variations, process adjustments, and process deterioration. Hence homogeneous materials should be used, no process adjustments should be made during the study, and if within study process deterioration exists, the effect should be calculated and subtracted.

When these conditions have been noted and accounted for, a process capability study may be made by gathering the required data—at least 50 observations and preferably 100 or more if possible—and computing the standard deviation of these data:

$$\text{process capability} = 6\sigma \tag{8.1}$$

This range of natural variation does indicate what fraction of the production would be considered defective. This is shown in Figure 8.1. Obviously, the quality of the product can be improved by altering the process setting. The best quality attainable or the smallest fraction defective that can be achieved by manipulating the process setting can be called the *capability of the process*.

Example 8.1

A workstation performs the "rough-turn" operation on a machine component. The specifications for this operation ask for a diameter in the range 0.505 ± 0.005 in.

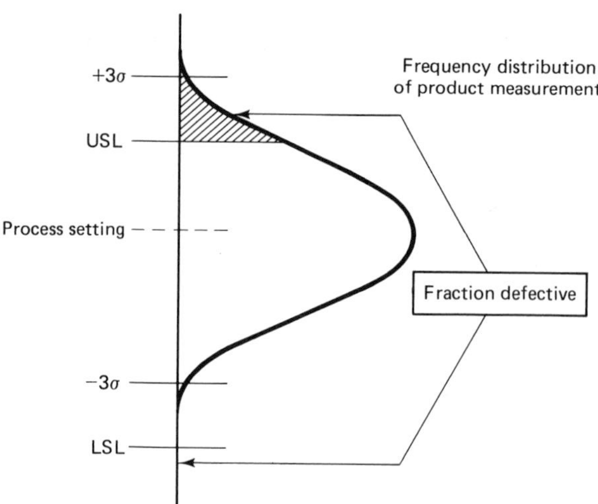

Figure 8.1 Quality of the product from a process.

After the setup of the process, a preliminary study was made by measuring the diameter of the first 100 pieces produced. Tool wear was believed to be negligible during the study.

Table 8.1 shows the computation of process capability. From the computation it is seen that the process setting is at 0.50825 and the number of defective pieces are (a) 15 above the upper specification limit and (b) 0 below the lower specification limit. The fraction defective is 15 out of 100, or 15%. If the process setting is moved to the nominal value of 0.505, the fraction defective can be calculated as follows:

$$\begin{aligned} \text{USL} &= 0.505 + 0.005 \\ &= 0.505 + \frac{0.005}{0.00227}(0.00227) \\ &= \overline{X} + \frac{0.005}{0.00227}\sigma \\ &= \overline{X} + 2.2\sigma \end{aligned}$$

TABLE 8.1 Computation of Process Capability of Rough-Turn Operation, Workstation 17

Observation	Tally	f	d	fd	$f(d)^2$
0.516	1	1	+9	+9	81
0.515		0	+8	0	0
0.514	1	1	+7	+7	49
0.513	111	3	+6	+18	108
0.512	11	2	+5	+10	50
0.511	~~1111~~ 111	8	+4	+32	128
USL → ———	———————				
0.510	~~1111~~ ~~1111~~ 1	11	+3	+33	99
0.509	~~1111~~ ~~1111~~ ~~1111~~	15	+2	+30	60
0.508	~~1111~~ ~~1111~~ ~~1111~~ 111	18	+1	+18	18
0.507	~~1111~~ ~~1111~~ ~~1111~~ ~~1111~~ 11	22	0	0	0
0.506	~~1111~~ ~~1111~~ 11	12	−1	−12	12
NOM → 0.505	1111	4	−2	−8	16
0.504	11	2	−3	−6	18
0.503		0	−4	0	0
0.502		0	−5	0	0
0.501		1	−6	−6	36
LSL → ———	———————				

$$\sum f = n = 100 \qquad \sum fd = +125 \quad \sum fd^2 = 675$$

$$\bar{X} = \bar{X}_d + i\left(\frac{\Sigma fd}{n}\right) = 0.507 + 0.001\left(\frac{125}{100}\right) = 0.50825$$

$$\sigma = i\sqrt{\frac{\Sigma fd^2}{n} - \left(\frac{\Sigma fd}{n}\right)^2} = 0.001\sqrt{\frac{675}{100} - \left(\frac{125}{100}\right)^2} = 0.00227$$

$$\text{Process capability} = 6\sigma = 6(0.00227) = 0.01362$$

Similarly,

$$\text{LSL} = \overline{X} - 2.2\sigma$$

The proportion that would be below $\overline{X} - 2.2\sigma$ and above $\overline{X} + 2.2\sigma$ can be obtained from Table A1 as 0.0139. Therefore, the best quality or smallest fraction defective is 2(0.0139), or 2.78% defective.

It is obvious that the process is not capable of meeting the stipulated specifications. The range computed according to equation (8.1) is 6×0.00227, or 0.01362. The specified range is $(0.505 + 0.005) - (0.505 - 0.005)$, or 0.010. Ideally, the range of the process should be no greater than three-fourths of the specified range. This arbitrary rule of thumb allows for the fact that process conditions will not always be held constant as in this preliminary study.

With the capability of each piece of equipment in the overall process known (or estimated through a preliminary study), jobs can be *quality scheduled* more efficiently. Jobs with tighter tolerances can be assigned to machines with lesser variation range. Of course, knowing the capability of the equipment will not always eliminate the necessity for using a process that will produce defective pieces because of stringent specification requirements. However, the extent of deficiency can be calculated in advance and the steps taken with full knowledge of the consequences. When a process has been shown to be incapable of producing the great majority of units within specification requirements, there are four alternative courses of action that may be taken:

1. Use a difference process.
2. Change the specification requirements.
3. Screen (100% inspection) for removal of defective units.
4. Leave alone.

The first alternative may involve rescheduling and loading, the purchase of new equipment, or subcontracting to an outside source with more precise equipment. In many cases the second alternative is logical, but it is traditionally difficult to get design changes in the relaxation direction. Nevertheless, this second alternative should be considered very thoroughly, for it often involves the least total cost. The third should be considered if the cost of inspection is low in comparison to the cost of the other alternatives. The fourth may be resorted to when the unit cost is very low, inspection cost relatively high, and the cost (tangible and intangible) of a defective unit in the field is low.

DETERMINATION OF PROCESS CAPABILITY: USING SAMPLE OBSERVATIONS

An alternative method for determining process capability, when the process is already in operation, is to use the information from samples of product being produced. Whenever control charts are maintained, most of the information needed for determination of process capability is available. If the charts are for $\overline{X}$ and R, the quantity $\overline{R}$, the average of sample ranges, can be used to determine the process capability. When the charts are for $\overline{X}$ and s, the quantity $\overline{s}$, the average of sample standard deviations, can be used.

The average of the ranges of small samples taken from a population is directly related to the population standard deviation. The average range is larger, however, so it must be adjusted by a factor to yield an efficient estimate of σ'. The factor to be used is given by the d_2 column of Table A7.

If small samples of, say, five are taken repeatedly from a population with known standard deviation, the ranges relative to standard deviation

$$\frac{R}{\sigma'}$$

will distribute as shown by Figure 8.2. The factor d_2 is the average of the ratios and for samples of 5 is equal to 2.326. For smaller samples d_2 will be smaller, and for larger samples d_2 will be larger.

$$d_2 = \frac{\overline{R}}{\sigma'} \quad \text{or} \quad \sigma' = \frac{\overline{R}}{d_2} \tag{8.2}$$

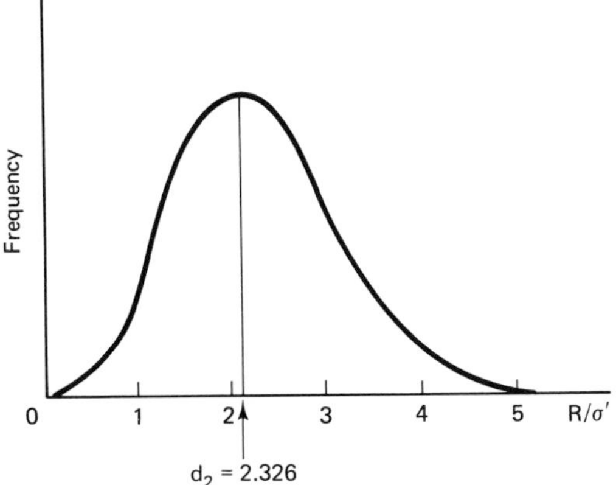

Figure 8.2 Distribution of range relative (R/σ') for samples of five each.

Sample readings																					
	X_1	.505	.513	.506	.509	.510	.508	.506	.511	.509	.506	.507	.507	.510	.506	.507	.512	.506	.507	.508	.511
	X_2	.508	.507	.504	.508	.506	.510	.506	.508	.509	.511	.509	.514	.508	.509	.507	.508	.510	.507	.508	.507
	X_3	.507	.505	.512	.509	.506	.513	.508	.507	.508	.507	.511	.507	.507	.509	.509	.506	.516	.509	.507	.513
	X_4	.511	.510	.511	.509	.507	.503	.510	.507	.507	.509	.508	.509	.505	.507	.506	.510	.509	.507	.509	.506
	X_5	.511	.510	.510	.507	.508	.506	.508	.507	.509	.507	.508	.510	.508	.511	.508	.508	.506	.505	.508	.510
ΣX		2.542	2.545	2.543	2.542	2.537	2.540	2.538	2.540	2.542	2.540	2.543	2.547	2.538	2.542	2.537	2.544	2.547	2.535	2.540	2.547
Ave. = $\overline{X}$ =		.5084	.509	.5086	.5084	.5074	.508	.5076	.508	.5084	.508	.5086	.5094	.5076	.509	.5076	.5088	.5094	.507	.508	.5099
High X =		.511	.513	.512	.509	.510	.513	.510	.511	.509	.511	.511	.514	.510	.511	.509	.512	.516	.509	.509	.513
Low X =		.505	.505	.504	.507	.506	.503	.506	.507	.507	.506	.507	.507	.505	.506	.506	.506	.506	.505	.507	.506
Range = R =		.006	.008	.008	.002	.004	.010	.004	.004	.002	.005	.004	.007	.005	.005	.003	.006	.010	.004	.002	.007

$$\overline{R} = \frac{\Sigma R}{m} = \frac{0.106}{20} = 0.0053$$

m = number of samples

$$\sigma' = \frac{\overline{R}}{d_2} = \frac{0.0053}{2.326} = 0.00228$$

$$\text{Process capbility} = 6\sigma' = \frac{6\overline{R}}{d_2}$$

$$= \frac{6(0.0053)}{2.326} = 0.0137$$

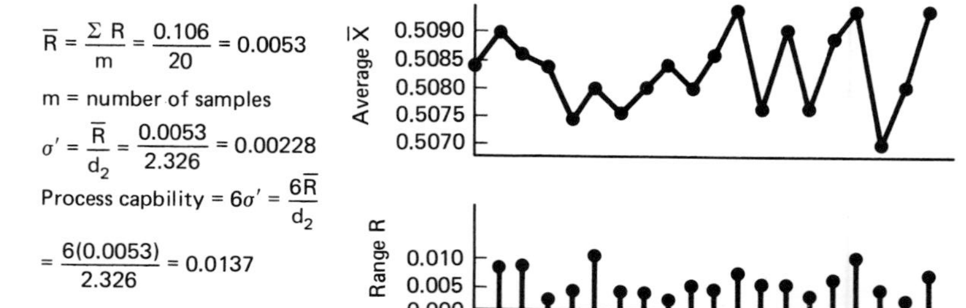

Figure 8.3 Calculation of process capability using the average range method.

Example 8.2

This example uses the same data as in Example 8.1. Figure 8.3 shows the calculation of process capability using the average range. For samples from a population, the sample standard deviation s is also directly related to the population standard deviation σ'. As seen in Chapter 2, the quantity

$$\frac{(n - 1)s^2}{\sigma^2}$$

is distributed with a chi-square distribution with $n - 1$ degrees of freedom. The expected value k of the distribution in Figure 8.4 can be used to estimate σ from observations of s.

$$\begin{aligned}\frac{s}{\sigma} &= \sqrt{\frac{1}{n - 1}\,\frac{(n - 1)s^2}{\sigma^2}} \\ &= \frac{1}{\sqrt{n - 1}}\sqrt{\frac{(n - 1)s^2}{\sigma^2}}\end{aligned} \tag{8.3}$$

The expected value of s/σ is approximated by the relation

$$\begin{aligned}E\left(\frac{s}{\sigma}\right) &\simeq \frac{1}{\sqrt{n - 1}}\sqrt{k} \\ E(s) &\simeq \frac{1}{\sqrt{n - 1}}\sqrt{k}\,\sigma\end{aligned} \tag{8.4}$$

Using the average of standard deviations as an estimator of $E(s)$,

$$\begin{aligned}\bar{s} &\simeq \frac{1}{\sqrt{n - 1}}\sqrt{k}\,\sigma \\ &= c_2\sigma\end{aligned} \tag{8.5}$$

The quantity c_2 is tabulated in Table A7.

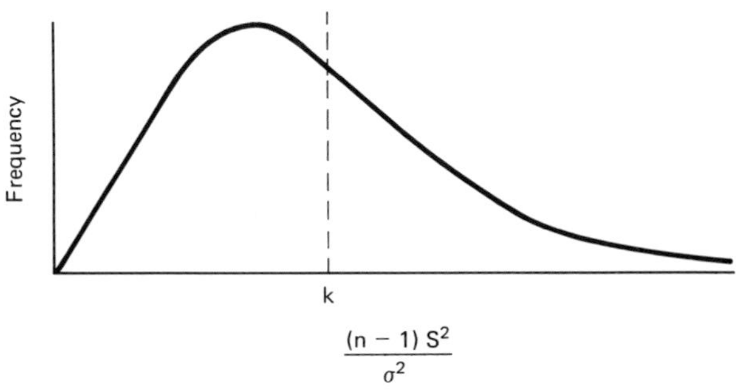

Figure 8.4 Distribution of sample variance for samples for a normal population.

Example 8.3

We continue to use the observation in Example 8.1 to illustrate the estimation of process capability using $\bar{s}$. The value s for each sample is computed according to the equation

$$s^2 = \frac{\Sigma (x_i - \bar{x})^2}{n - 1}$$

where x_i are individual observations, $\bar{x}$ is the sample average, and n is the sample size. Table 8.2 shows the estimation of process capability using $\bar{s}$.

SINGLE-RANGE METHOD

A rough estimate of process capability may be obtained from the range of a single large sample from a process in statistical control. In this case it is not necessary to make any assumption regarding the distribution of the population, nor is it necessary to estimate the population standard deviation. When

TABLE 8.2 Estimation of Process Capability Using $\bar{s}$

Sample Number	$s \times 10^3$	Sample Number	$s \times 10^3$
1	2.332	11	1.356
2	2.757	12	2.577
3	3.072	13	1.625
4	0.800	14	1.744
5	1.497	15	1.020
6	3.406	16	2.039
7	1.497	17	3.666
8	1.549	18	1.265
9	0.800	19	0.632
10	1.789	20	2.577

$$\Sigma s = 0.038$$

$$\bar{s} = \frac{0.038}{20}$$

$$= 0.0019$$

C_2 for sample size 5 is 0.8407

$$\sigma = \frac{\bar{s}}{C_2} = \frac{0.0019}{0.8407} = 0.00226$$

$$\text{process capability} = 6\sigma = 6 \times 0.00226$$

$$= 0.01356$$

the process is in control, a sample of size n is selected and the range of the sample values is obtained. The proportion of total product that would be within the observed range of the sample is calculated using the following relationship.

Theorem. The density of random variable q, which is the fraction of the total population lying within the observed range of a sample of size n is given by

$$f(q) = n(n - 1)q^{n-2}(1 - q) \tag{8.6}$$

Using this density function, the least proportion that would be expected to be within the observed range can be calculated for any desired level of confidence. Table 8.3 shows some selected values for confidence levels of 90%, 95%, and 99.73%.

Applying the single range method to the data in Example 8.1 yields

$$\text{range} = 0.516 - 0.501$$
$$= 0.015$$
$$\text{sample size } n = 100$$

From Table 8.3 it can be stated with 95% confidence that at least 95.2% of the product would be within this range.

Example 8.4

The single-range method yields rough estimates for small samples. However, when the production is based on automatic and/or computer-controlled machines, large samples become available in a short period of time. In such cases the single-range

TABLE 8.3 Percent of Production from a Process in Control Having a Stated Probability of Lying Within the Observed Range of a Sample of Size n

Sample Size	Probability		
	0.90	0.95	0.9973
10	66.2	60.4	42.0
20	81.8	78.2	65.6
50	92.4	90.8	84.8
100	96.0	95.2	92.0
200	98.0	97.6	96.0
500	99.2	99.0	98.2
1000	99.6	99.5	99.2

method would give satisfactory estimates. Electric light bulbs are being assembled by automatic machines. A sample of 500 bulbs is tested for power consumption.

Specified power consumption	60 W
Maximum power consumption	60.8 W
Minimum power consumption	59.4 W

From Table 8.5 it can be stated with 90% confidence that at least 99.2% of the product would be within the range 59.4 to 60.8 W. Also, there is 99.73% confidence that 98.2% of the product would be within this range. In other words, there is less than a 10% chance that 0.8% of the product would be "defective" (outside the range) and the chance of finding 1.8% defectives is less than 0.27%.

ADJUSTMENT FOR WITHIN-STUDY TREND

If there is a trend or change in the level of process average, it may appear that the process has a larger variation than it actually does. Referring to Figure 8.5, it is obvious that the variation would appear to be large when the relatively smaller values in the first subgroup are compared with the larger values in the last subgroup. The results are likely to be erroneous when all subgroups are lumped together in a single sample: for example, computing the standard deviation as in Table 8.1 or using the single-range method. However, since the variation within samples can be minimized in the average range method, this method more or less automatically corrects for trend.

Example 8.5

The data for this example are taken from a case history in the co-author's files. The case in point concerns control of the pitch diameter on an external thread. A thread roll indicator with a unit of measure 0.00025 in. was used for measurement. The specification requirement was 0.3720 ± 0.0018 in. The data were coded by setting 0.3720 equal to zero on the gage and multiplying each reading by 100,000. Thus a reading of +0.00100 on the gage appears as 100 on Figure 8.5. If one is willing to accept eight ranges of five each, the process capability, with trend excluded, is 210, which is less than 3/4(360); therefore, the process is considered capable.

It must be remembered that this is the *best* the process is capable of doing. The best figure of 210 for a production run of any size would actually be meaningless. In other words, it may be more realistic to correlate process capability with run size in those cases where an immediate severe trend is inevitable.

When the trend changes within a single run leads to the possibility of some product going out of the specifications, it is obligatory that the process average must be reset. Naturally, the run size would be reduced accordingly.

The best method of estimating the effect of trend on process capability is to find the "slope" or the rate at which $\overline{X}$ changes, on an average, between samples. A regression line fitted to the $\overline{X}$ chart in Figure 8.5 indicates an increase of 10 between consecutive samples. Obviously, the range is going to increase by this amount. If the process capability is to remain satisfactory, it must remain below 3/4(360), or 270.

X_1 =	100	100	175	50	150	150	200	125		
X_2 =	100	125	200	125	175	150	150	175		
X_3 =	125	125	125	175	175	50	175	150		
X_4 =	125	150	150	175	175	200	200	225		
X_5 =	150	75	175	150	175	200	200	225		
ΣX =	600	575	825	675	850	750	925	900		
$\bar{X}$ =	120	115	165	135	170	150	185	180		
X_{H1} =	150	150	200	175	175	200	200	225		
X_{LOW} =	100	75	125	50	150	50	150	125		
R =	50	75	75	125	25	150	50	100		

$$\bar{R} = \frac{\Sigma R}{m}$$
$$= \frac{50 + 75 + 75 + 125 + 25 + 150 + 50 + 100}{8}$$
$$= 81.25$$

Process capability $= \frac{6\bar{R}}{d_2} = \frac{6(81.25)}{2.326} = 210$

Total tolerance = 360. $6\sigma' = 210 < \frac{3}{4}\ 360$; therefore process is capable.

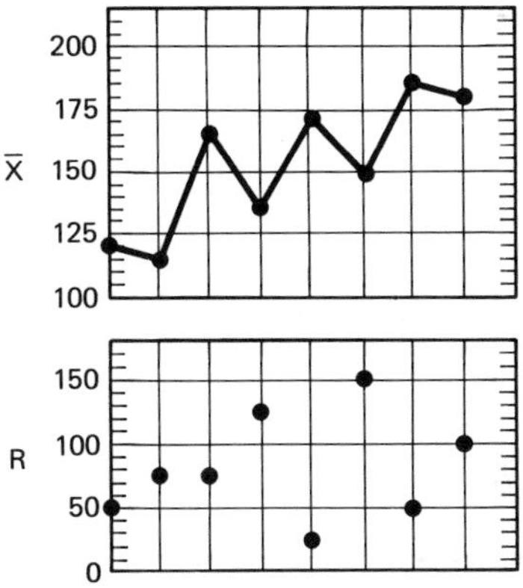

Figure 8.5 Average range calculation of process capability when trend exists.

So the maximum range permissible would be given by

$$\frac{6\bar{R}}{d_2} = 270 \qquad \text{or} \qquad \bar{R} = \frac{270(2.326)}{6}$$
$$= 104.67$$

$\bar{R}$ computed without trend adjustment is 81.25. Hence the maximum permissible deviation due to the trend is 23.42. In other words, two changes in $\bar{X}$ ($2 \times 10 = 20$) would be sustainable. However, the process would have to be reset before the third increase due to the trend. The proper run size for this product would equal the production during three sampling periods.

DESIGN SPECIFICATIONS AND TOLERANCES

There are three major steps in the production of any item: design, production, and inspection. Specifications are usually set in the design phase. An effort is made during production to conform to these specifications. Inspection is necessary to evaluate the extent to which the production conforms to the design specifications. The words "specifications" and "tolerances" are sometimes used interchangeably. However, it must be noted that *tolerances* refer to physical dimensions only. *Specifications* are more general and refer to all characteristics of the product process as well as raw materials. Tolerances are included within the specifications.

The fundamental basis of all specifications is the function desired of the product. No design engineer would wish to jeopardize the function. The desire to be absolutely certain about the functional capability of the product may lead to overdesign. For example, the top of a desk designed to support a 40-kg personal computer must be strong enough to support the weight without bending or cracking. However, specifying 2-cm-thick nickel–chromium steel plate would be ridiculous. The plate would perform the function easily but would be prohibitively expensive (besides creating the further problem of supporting weight of the plate).

In setting up the specifications, the design engineer must keep in mind two factors in addition to the function of the product:

1. The item must be capable of being produced.
2. In any normal production there are random variations.

If the process capability is not adequate, the desired tolerances would not be satisfied. If relaxing the tolerances to the extent that would be within the capability of the process would not endanger the function of the product, it is always prudent to relax. In Example 8.1 the specifications are stated as 0.505 ± 0.005 in. The permissible range is 0.01 in. The natural range of the process is 0.014 in. If the specifications are relaxed to 0.505 ± 0.007 in., the process is capable of producing the product. The operation is stated as "rough turning," implying that a finishing operation is to follow. The product is not going directly to the consumer and the final function would not be jeopardized by the relaxation. The only question to consider would be: Would the relaxation, in any way, impair the finishing operation? If the finishing operation is not going to be impaired, a lot of costly equipment replacement and process redesign would be saved by relaxing the tolerances.

The random variations, or the probability distributions of these variations, determine the capability of a process. When the product undergoes several steps during production and consists not of a single item but an assembly of several components, the variations have great influence on the ability of the final product to conform to the specifications.

PROCESS CAPABILITY AND TOLERANCES

If the design engineer is familiar with the "natural variation" of the process that would be used to manufacture the product, the task of setting appropriate specifications would be considerably simplified. In the absence of any information, the design engineer is likely to set the specifications as tight as possible, anticipating that "The manufacturing department is going to complain regardless of what I do. They always complain." Knowing the estimated process capability the engineer can avoid designing a product that can not be produced without producing a larger number of defective items. It is also highly desirable that the design engineer be familiar with the basic principles of statistics to facilitate the understanding and interpretation of the process capability studies.

One common misunderstanding involves the results of a process capability study. It must be remembered that the only definite information contained in these results pertains to what the process cannot do. There is very little definite information about what the process can do. For example, in Example 8.1 it is estimated that the standard deviation of the process is 0.00227 in. Based on this information, it is concluded positively that the process would always produce 97.22% satisfactory product. The only positive conclusion is that the fraction defective will not be less than 2.78%. What the process would be producing would depend on whether:

1. The assumption of normal distribution is valid.
2. The process can be held in control for a long period of time.
3. There is no tool wear.
4. The quality of raw materials is uniform.
5. There is no operator error.

The statements based on the single-range method are somewhat more definite. However, these also depend on the repetition of the exact study conditions during the manufacture.

The information from the results of any process capability study must be combined with judgment based on the possible differences in operating conditions during the study and during actual manufacture. The rule of thumb of setting a tolerance range at 75% of natural range of the process is one of the attempts to allow for such differing conditions.

TOLERANCES FOR SUBASSEMBLIES

Subassemblies are formed by combining two or more components. The aggregate dimension of the subassembly would be the sum of individual component dimensions. Consider a subassembly of four components, A, B, C, and D (Figure 8.6). The total length of the subassembly is the sum of the length of A, B, C, and D. The function of the subassembly would dictate that this length be within same specification limits.

$$L(S) = L(\mathrm{A}) + L(\mathrm{B}) + L(\mathrm{C}) + L(\mathrm{D}) \tag{8.7}$$

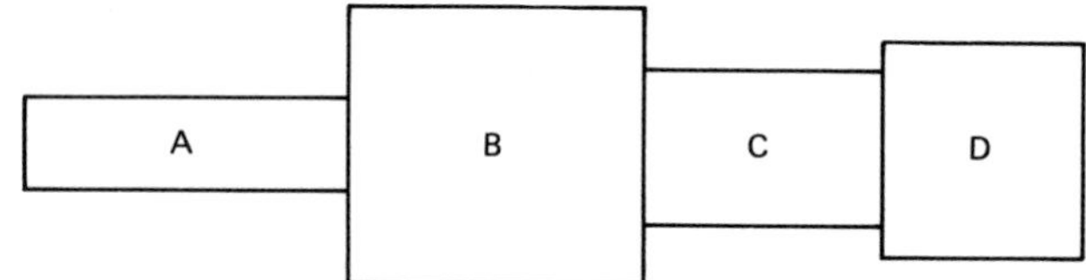

Figure 8.6 Subassembly of four components.

This relationship raises two types of questions. First, if the natural variation of each component dimension is known, what would be the variation in the dimension of the subassembly? Second, if the entire subassembly is subject to the same tolerance limits, what would be the tolerance limits for the partial subassemblies? Examples 8.6 and 8.7 indicate the general procedures for answering these questions. As a basis for these procedures, it is necessary to refer to two relations stated in Chapter 2.

If x_1 and x_2 are two independently distributed random variables, the variances of the sum $x_1 + x_2$ and the difference $x_1 - x_2$ are given by

$$\sigma^2_{x1+x2} = \sigma^2_{x1} + \sigma^2_{x2} \tag{8.8}$$

$$\sigma^2_{x1-x2} = \sigma^2_{x1} + \sigma^2_{x2} \tag{8.9}$$

It is important to note that the variance of the difference $x_1 - x_2$ is the same as the variance of the sum $x_1 + x_2$.

Example 8.6

A subassembly, shown in Figure 8.6, consists of four components, A, B, C, and D. A process capability study has revealed the information given in Table 8.4 about the processes producing these components. It is the policy of the department to set the specification limits at ± 3 standard deviations. What would be the specification limits for the components and the subassembly?

The computation of the specification limits for the components is straightforward (Table 8.5).

TABLE 8.4 Component Data

Component	Nominal Dimension	Standard Deviation
A	1.86	0.003
B	2.30	0.002
C	1.95	0.003
D	0.40	0.002
Subassembly	6.51	

TABLE 8.5 Specification Limits

Component	Upper Specification Limit	Lower Specification Limit	Tolerance Range
A	1.869	1.851	0.018
B	2.306	2.294	0.012
C	1.959	1.941	0.018
D	1.406	1.394	0.012
		Sum of tolerances =	0.060

If σ_A^2, σ_B^2, σ_C^2, σ_D^2, and σ_S^2 represent the variances of the four components and the subassemblies, respectively, then from equation (8.8) (using 1/100-in. units),

$$\sigma_S^2 = \sigma_A^2 + \sigma_B^2 + \sigma_C^2 + \sigma_D^2$$

$$= 3^2 + 2^2 + 3^2 + 2^2$$

$$= 26$$

or

$$\sigma_S \simeq 5.1 \qquad \text{or} \qquad 0.0051 \text{ in.}$$

Hence for the subassembly,

nominal size = 6.51 in.

standard deviation = 0.0051 in.

upper specification limit = 6.5253

lower specification limit = 6.4947

tolerance range = 0.0306

Persons not familiar with the laws of statistics sometimes mistakenly believe that the tolerance range for the subassembly would be the sum of the tolerance ranges for individual components. It certainly is not so, as demonstrated by this example. Here the tolerance range for the subassembly is approximately only one-half of the sum of component tolerance ranges.

SETTING TOLERANCES FOR INTERMEDIATE STEPS IN PRODUCTION

Example 8.6 indicates that the tolerance range for a subassembly is smaller than the sum of the tolerance ranges of individual components. If components A, B, C, and D are produced independent of each other and assembled, the natural tolerance of the subassembly would be 0.0306, as indicated. The assembly workstation can operate satisfactorily if the specified tolerance range is 0.040.

The situation is somewhat different when the subassembly is achieved in stages. For illustration purposes it is assumed that the assembly is performed at three workstations:

Workstation 1 (C and D)	CD
Workstation 2 (B and CD)	BCD
Workstation 3 (A and BCD)	ABCD

Example 8.6 continued.

If the subassembly ABCD is assembled in three workstations and the specified tolerance range for the subassembly is 0.040, what tolerance ranges need to be specified for the three workstations?

The problem is best solved in a backward sequence. For workstation 3 the specified tolerance range is the same as the tolerance range for ABCD (i.e., 0.040). At workstation 3 there is an assembly of two components, A and BCD. From equation (8.8),

$$6\sigma_{\mathrm{BCD}} = \sqrt{(6\sigma_{\mathrm{ABCD}})^2 - (6\sigma_{\mathrm{A}})^2} \tag{8.12}$$

or

$$T_{\mathrm{BCD}} = \sqrt{T_{\mathrm{ABCD}}{}^2 - T_{\mathrm{A}}^2} \tag{8.13}$$

σ_{A} under normal manufacture is given as 0.003. Under the specified tolerance range of 0.040, the maximum permissible value of σ_{ABCD} is (1/6)(0.040). An alternative way of using equation (8.11) is to state it in terms of "6σ," the tolerance range, instead of σ:

$$6\sigma_{\mathrm{BCD}} = \sqrt{(6\sigma_{\mathrm{ABCD}})^2 - (6\sigma_{\mathrm{A}})^2} \tag{8.12}$$

or

$$T_{\mathrm{BCD}} = \sqrt{T_{\mathrm{ABCD}}{}^2 - T_{\mathrm{A}}^2} \tag{8.13}$$

where T_x = tolerance range of x
T_{ABCD} = 0.040 specified
T_A = 0.018 natural

Substituting these values in equation (8.13) yields

$$\mathrm{T}_{\mathrm{BCD}} = 0.0357$$

This means that a tolerance range of 0.0357 must be specified for the workstation in order that workstation 3 can meet its specification tolerance range.

Similarly, at workstation 2,

$$T_{\mathrm{CD}} = \sqrt{T_{\mathrm{BCD}}^2 - T_{\mathrm{B}}^2}$$

$$T_{\mathrm{BCD}} = 0.0357 \text{ calculated}$$

$$T_{\mathrm{B}} = 0.012 \text{ natural}$$

Substitution given the value of T_{CD}:

$$T_{CD} = 0.0336$$

A tolerance range of 0.0336 must be specified for workstation 1.

An alternative tabular method of computation is illustrated in Table 8.6. The final specified tolerance range is reduced from 0.040 to 0.033.

INTERFERENCE AND TOLERANCE OF FIT

Many subassemblies involve a mating of two components. Component A fits inside the opening provided in component B. Examples are engine block and piston, shaft and bearing or nut and socket wrench. In each case, unduly loose fit—component A too small relative to the opening in B—would lead to inefficient operation. At the other extreme, interference (i.e., component A larger than the opening in B) would prevent the operation all together.

Let the nominal diameter of cylinder bore be 3.00 in. and the nominal diameter of piston be 2.98 in. Then the nominal gap would be

$$\text{gap} = \frac{1}{2}\,(\text{diameter of bore} - \text{diameter of piston})$$

$$= \frac{1}{2}\,(3.00 - 2.98)$$

$$= 0.01, \text{ or 10 units of 1/1000 in.}$$

If the variables G, B, and P are defined as 2 times the gap, diameter of the bore, and diameter of the piston, respectively, equation (8.9) will give

$$\sigma_G = \sigma_B^2 + \sigma_P^2$$

Let $\sigma_B = 2.2$ units and $\sigma_B = 3.4$ units.

$$\sigma_G = \sqrt{2.2^2 + 3.4^2} = 4.05 \text{ units}$$

The standard deviation for each side of the gap would be 2.025 units.

TABLE 8.6 Calculations for Specified Tolerance Range at Intermediate Workstations

Workstation	Tolerance Range Specified, x	Tolerance Range Work Added, y	Tolerance Range Input, $\sqrt{x^2 - y^2}$
3	0.033	0.018	0.0276
2	0.0276	0.012	0.0249
1	0.0249		

The interference level would be some level such that a smaller gap would lead to excessive friction, which will prevent the engine from functioning. Let the interference level be 4 units. At the other extreme there would be a level beyond which a larger gap will cause loss of pressure and reduced power from the engine. Let this level be 15 units. For the gap,

$$\text{mean} = 10$$

$$\text{standard deviation} = 2.025$$

$$(\text{gap} < 4) \qquad \text{interference}$$

$$(\text{gap} > 15) \qquad \text{loose fit}$$

Figure 8.7 shows the probability distribution of the gap.

The problem faced by a manufacturer where a plant produces both A and B and the assembly can be stated as follows. What is the risk that the person at the assembly workstation would randomly pick up a piece A and a piece B, causing either interference or loose fit? There are the two shaded areas in Figure 8.7. Numerical values of these risks can be calculated assuming a normal distribution. For interference the standardized normal variate

$$z_i = \frac{4 - 10}{2.025} = -2.96$$

$$\text{risk of interference} = 0.0015$$

$$= 0.15\%$$

For loose fit the standardized normal variate

$$z_l = \frac{15 - 10}{2.025} = 2.47$$

$$\text{risk of loose fit} = 0.0068$$

$$= 0.68\%$$

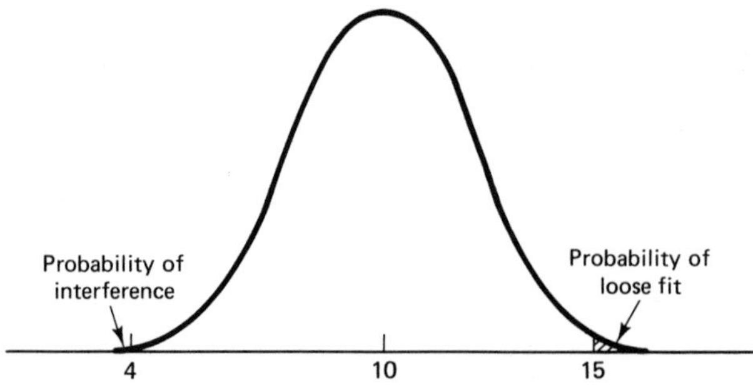

Figure 8.7 Probability distribution of a gap between piston and cylinder bore.

These risks would be acceptable under most conditions. If the risks are too large to accept, these can be reduced to a certain extent by 100% inspection. However, this is usually accompanied by the high cost of scrapping and rework.

The manufacturer who does not control both components and the assembly operation has fewer options. An illustration of this type is described by Example 8.7.

Example 8.7

Acme Tool Company produces socket wrenches to be used by mechanics in automobile repair facilities. Acme can control only the opening between the "flats" for any size socket. The nuts are produced or purchased independently by various automobile manufacturers.

From a study of commercially available 1/2-in. nuts, the distribution of the width of the nut between "flats" is estimated as

$$\text{mean width} = 0.75 \text{ in.}$$

$$\text{standard deviation} = 0.0015 \text{ in.}$$

Most mechanics would consider a clearance of 0.003 as interference and clearance in excess of 0.010 as loose fit. The manufacturing process used to produce the sockets has a natural standard deviation of 0.0015 in. What should be the nominal size for the opening between flats?

If x is the nominal clearance, the nominal size of opening would be $0.75 + x$. The standard deviation of the clearance would be given by equation (8.9) as

$$\sigma_x = \sqrt{0.0015^2 + 0.0015^2}$$

$$= 0.00212$$

The permissible range between the interference level 0.003 and the loose-fit level 0.010 is 0.007, or $3.3\sigma_x$. The probability of "either interference or loose fit"

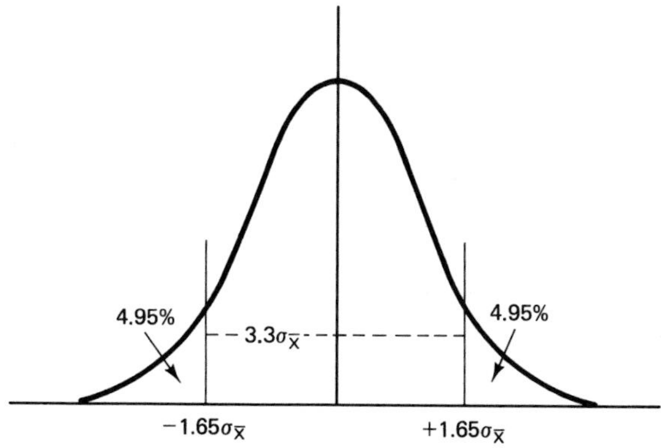

Figure 8.8 Effect of centering the mean of the distribution of socket widths.

would be minimized by locating the mean of the distribution halfway between the two levels as shown in Figure 8.8. For this choice,

$$x = \frac{0.003 + 0.010}{2}$$

$$= 0.0065$$

The nominal opening between flats is 0.7565 in. The risk of interference and the risk of loose fit are each 4.9%. Acme Tool Company can reduce one of the risks only at a cost of increasing the risk on the other side.

PROBLEMS

8.1. A machine is working to a specification of 0.258 ± 0.004 in. A study of 50 consecutive pieces is made, yielding the following results (values are in thousandths of an inch in excess of 0.250 in. and the data are broken into 10 groups of 5):

1	2	3	4	5	6	7	8	9	10
12	13	12	11	9	7	7	8	11	6
10	6	6	16	8	13	6	7	10	9
12	10	7	12	7	10	11	10	12	12
11	9	8	11	9	10	9	10	10	8
15	10	13	10	6	9	9	11	15	4

Make a frequency distribution of the data. Calculate the process capability from $\overline{X}$ and σ. Does it appear that the machine is capable of meeting the specification requirements? What is the present percent defective? Compute the average and the range of each subgroup. Compute the grand average and the average range. Compare the process capability by the $\overline{R}$ method with the standard deviation method.

8.2. Perform the same operations as in Problem 8.1 for the following data from parts made to the same specification by another machine (data selected at intervals over several days' production):

1	2	3	4	5	6	7	8	9	10
6	7	7	8	10	10	14	9	12	13
4	6	7	10	12	8	8	13	10	15
3	7	6	8	7	8	9	7	13	12
5	3	8	6	7	6	12	11	13	17
5	4	6	7	8	8	10	9	11	13

Which of the two machines has better process capability? On what do you base your conclusion? Could you explain the apparent trend in the results from the second machine?

8.3. Use the $\overline{R}$ method to determine the process capabilities of the two machines in Problems 8.1 and 8.2.

8.4. Use the $\overline{s}$ method to determine the process capabilities of the two machines in Problems 8.1 and 8.2.

8.5. The specifications for the diameter of an item are 3.00 ± 0.020 cm. An automatic production line was set up to produce this item. First, 1000 items produced by the line were measured. The largest diameter was 3.018 cm and the smallest was 2.996 cm. Is the production line capable of meeting the specifications? What probability statement can be made about the fraction of production that may be expected to be "defective"?

8.6. Determine the process capabilities of the two machines in Problems 8.1 and 8.2 using a single-range method for all 50 observations treated as a single sample. Compare this with the results obtained in Problems 8.1 through 8.4. Would you consider the single-range method as a satisfactory procedure to compare the two machines? Why?

8.7. Twenty samples of 5 items each from the production of an aircraft component were selected at random. The thickness of each item was measured with a micrometer to the nearest ten-thousandth of an inch. The specifications for the item were: upper limit, 1.5100, and lower limit, 1.5050. Unit of measurement is (size − 1.5000) × 10,000.

Sample Number	1	2	3	4	5
1	72	104	79	19	77
2	56	87	33	42	34
3	56	73	22	60	45
4	44	80	54	74	72
5	102	26	48	58	44
6	83	107	91	62	57
7	47	66	53	58	67
8	88	50	84	69	62
9	57	47	41	46	47
10	13	30	10	05	27
11	16	30	52	35	51
12	46	27	63	34	30
13	49	62	78	87	71
14	71	67	85	72	65
15	71	58	69	70	71
16	67	69	70	94	86
17	37	25	40	80	73
18	26	50	82	75	101
19	62	84	49	39	97
20	54	62	73	87	56

Determine the process capability using $\overline{S}$.

8.8. The following values of $\overline{X}$ and R were obtained from samples of five items taken each hour of production.

Sample Number	$\overline{X}$	R	Sample Number	$\overline{X}$	R
1	20	4	9	51	5
2	28	7	10	53	13
3	33	5	11	57	5
4	32	10	12	57	8
5	35	11	13	65	10
6	41	12	14	60	10
7	44	10	15	65	9
8	48	4	16	70	6

Determine the process capability. If the specifications for this item are: maximum 120, minimum 0, determine the appropriate setting of $\overline{X}$ at the start of a production run. What would be the optimum production run, expressed as hours of production?

8.9. The average clearance specified between two mating components is 0.003 cm. The distribution of the diameters of the two components is assumed to be normal.

	Mean	Standard Deviation
Inner diameter of A	8.003	0.0006
Outer diameter of B	8.000	0.0014

If the assembly is random, what is the probability of interference? What should be the average inner diameter of A to reduce the probability of interference below 0.1%?

8.10. A subassembly of four components is assembled at three workstations.

Workstation 1	A and B	AB
Workstation 2	AB and C	ABC
Workstation 3	ABC and D	ABCD

A process capability study has indicated the following information about the production of the four components:

Component	Nominal Size	Standard Deviation
A	3.16	0.004
B	6.84	0.006
C	8.24	0.005
D	1.76	0.007
	20.00	

If the tolerance range for the subassembly is 0.080, what tolerance ranges need to be specified for the three workstations?

8.11. If the assembly order for the subassembly in Example 8.6 is changed as shown, what would be the tolerance ranges at each workstation?

Workstation 1	B and C	BC
Workstation 2	BC and D	BCD
Workstation 3	A and BCD	ABCD

8.12. If in Example 8.7 the definition of "loose fit" is given as 0.015 instead of 0.010, what should be the nominal opening between flats? What is the risk of loose fit?

nine

INTRODUCTION TO QUALITY ASSURANCE AND ACCEPTANCE CONTROL

Acceptance control may be defined as the sum of the measures taken by a receiver to assure the quality of product or work offered by a producer. Acceptance control may be applied by a consumer to products furnished by a vendor, by a finished goods inspection department to products furnished by the production departments, by an auditor to records furnished by an accounting department, by an industrial engineer to work performance, by a buyer to the systems and procedures of quality control used by the producer, and in general, in any situation where the definition above applies.

Acceptance control procedures need to protect the interests of both the receiver and the supplier without unnecessarily favoring one over the other. The receiver should not be subjected to excessive risk of receiving inferior product. At the same time the supplier should not be subjected to the risk of having good-quality product being rejected.

OBJECTIVES OF ACCEPTANCE CONTROL

There are two principal objectives of acceptance control: (1) to assure the quality of a particular unit or group of units submitted for acceptance, and (2) to assure that quality characteristics over the long term will meet with the

TABLE 9.1 Acceptance Control Measures

Acceptance Techniques	Control Techniques
A. 100% inspection B. Certification C. Sampling techniques 1. Lot-by-lot acceptance sampling by attributes a. Single sampling b. Double sampling c. Multiple sampling (truncated sequential) d. Sequential sampling 2. Continuous acceptance sampling by attributes a. Single stage b. Multistage 3. Acceptance sampling by variables a. Known variability plans b. Unknown variability plans 4. Audit sampling a. Of product submitted b. Of producer's control	A. Approval of producer's quality assurance system and procedures, including: process inspection and control methods; gage approval and control methods; acceptance inspection methods; inspection and test records; control of drawings, specifications, and engineering changes; lot identification controls; material controls B. Approval of producer's purchase control method C. Recording and measuring quality progress of the producer D. Rating of producers and vendors

quality standards. The application of the former, in a large measure, ensures the latter. The more prevalent measures used to assure quality of accepted product may be categorized as shown in Table 9.1.

RESPONSIBILITIES FOR ASSURING QUALITY

In general, the responsibility for assuring acceptance quality lies with the receiver. The responsibility for controlling quality lies with the producer. However, in a sense, the receiver has long-term control responsibilities. By applying the various lot acceptance techniques above, the receiver exerts a form of indirect quality control. A producer cannot afford to have many lots of product rejected. The costs of rejection are simply too high for all parties concerned. Thus the lot quality requirements imposed on the producer by the receiver *force* consideration and use of quality control methods. Too often, the method used is 100% inspection merely because it is expedient. One hundred percent inspection, used indiscriminately, is expensive for both parties. In the long run, the receiver pays for a good portion of the unnecessary expense incurred by a producer. Ultimately, the receiver recognizes this and either asks for price cuts or seeks alternative suppliers. Change in suppliers is, in itself, an expensive process. In summation, most of the arguments are *for* establishment of a sound quality relationship between receiver and producer—one that is based on the use of scientific methods of quality control and assurance and which gives the maximum assurance of quality of product and performance.

RECEIVER–PRODUCER RELATIONSHIPS (IN-PLANT, INTERDIVISION, AND INTERCOMPANY)

In order for there to be a good working relationship between receiver and producer on quality matters, it is necessary for the receiver to continually promote the use of scientific methods of quality control. Passing this off with the statement "how he does it is his business" is ignoring completely the increases in costs incurred by such action. It is in the interest of the receiver to promote these methods because, over the long term, it will give the most return on the investment.

Figure 9.1 graphically depicts the quality relationships that exist between the various receivers and producers of product with the total business picture. The relationships depicted indicate that no functions or organizations are completely devoid of one or the other responsibilities. In the case of reciprocal relationships, the receiving and production may be nearly equal. In small companies and divisions it may be necessary for a separate quality assurance agency responsible to the top manager to do all the promoting and specifying of quality assurance methods to be used. Good quality control

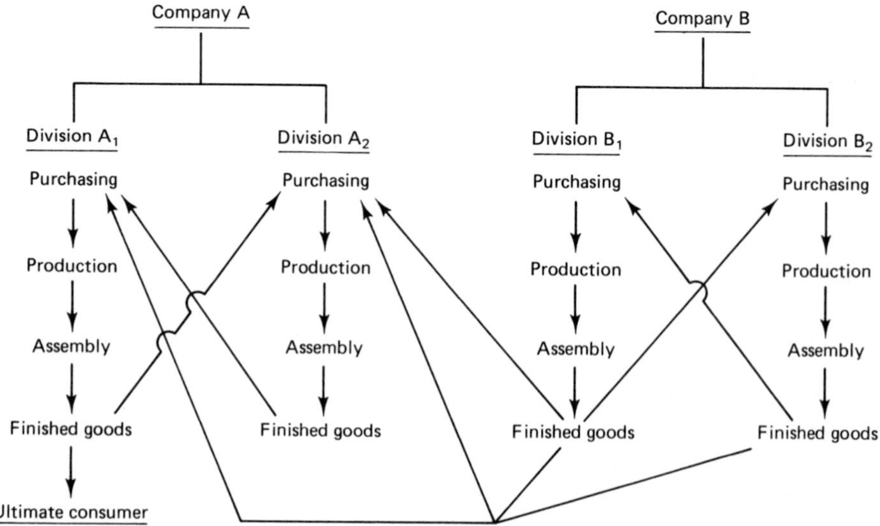

Figure 9.1 Flow of product from producer to receiver (→).

experience can be pretty expensive; therefore, the staffing of every department with this experience would be economically unwise. In very large companies and divisions, these relationships *do* exist and quality control personnel are necessary in all departments.

Possible flow of a hypothetical product might be as follows. Purchasing of division A_1 receives components from finished-goods inspection departments of divisions A_2 and B_2. Purchasing of division A_1 furnishes these components to production of division A_1. Production does further work on them and furnishes them to assembly of A_1. The assembly is sent to finished goods for final inspection. From there it goes to the ultimate consumer. At each of the receiving points some assurance of the incoming quality is necessary. The optimal condition is achieved when the receiver has maximum confidence that no incoming inspection of any kind is required for determining the quality of product. At the other extreme, the receiver finds it necessary to inspect every unit in order to assure quality.

Unfortunately, in all but a few cases, the optimum condition is difficult to attain. However, the emphasis should be toward this objective and away from the other extreme. This means that one or more of the sampling methods will be necessary for assuring quality at each of the receiving points. Determining which method to use is a matter for quality engineering to decide. The decision should involve a choice between the different approved methods rather than a choice between 100% inspection and a so-called *spot check*. Also, it should not be a situation where the quality control engineer has to argue for a replacement of 100% inspection by some approved sampling method. Unfortunately, this has too often been the case. Rather, it should be a consideration of *all* the tools available, resulting in a choice of those which are the most logical. Sometimes 100% inspection can be the most logical method to use, but when selected in this manner rather than as an expedient, a true job of quality control engineering is performed.

When the decision not to use 100% inspection is made in favor of sampling, which type of sampling method to use is dependent on many factors. In any case, the *percentage spot check* should be eliminated from any consideration as a sampling method.

FALLACIES OF THE SPOT-CHECK METHOD OF SAMPLING

Spot-check inspection, as usually practiced, consists of either a percentage check of material from the process in the ratio $1/n$ (where n is every tenth, twentieth, one-hundredth unit, etc., selection being dependent on the desired frequency of spot-check inspection) or a random check, the frequency of which varies with the amount of trouble encountered. The percentage method and the random check are, in fact, approved sampling methods but only when the risks to both producer and recever in the use of the plan have been analyzed. This analysis of risks is what differentiates scientific sampling from the spot check.

Often, in spot-check inspection for acceptance, the decision to curtail acceptance is based on the discovery of one defective unit. As a result, and to rectify the situation, it is common practice to screen all units produced between the inspected defective unit and the preceding inspected unit. The inadequacy of such a sampling plan is immediately apparent. Given a group of units, half of which are defective, a sample of 1 taken therefrom will show a defective about half the time and a good unit about half the time. With the acceptance number as zero, it is evident that about half the product must undergo a screening inspection. In addition to this added work load, what about the defective units that were accepted because a good unit was selected as the sample? In the analysis of the plan, each of the groups of units from which a sample of 1 is selected may be considered as a lot. The "lots" will average about 50% defective. The half of the "lots" that undergo screening inspection should, theoretically, be free of defectives. The "lots" that were accepted are, on the average, 50% defective so the overall improvement in quality amounts to 25%; that is, the quality of outgoing product is 25% defective.

Quantifying the illustration to clarify it, assume a lot of 1000 units, 500 of which are defective, and a sampling frequency of 1/100. On the average, half of the samples (5) will show defective units, resulting in about 500 units undergoing screening inspection. Assuming that defective units are replaced with good units, the outgoing quality of this portion of the total number is 0% defective. Thus the overall improvement amounts to a removal of 25% of the defective product; that is, the average outgoing quality is 25% defective. This is a heavy price to pay both in inspection time and defective product accepted and the damage to producer–receiver relations is incalculable. In practice, quality will usually not be this bad, but no matter what the quality, the spot check (without complete risk analysis) simply will not discriminate efficiently between good and bad lots. If the incoming quality is very good, it would be almost as efficient and certainly far less costly to have no inspection at all.

Wherever possible, the lot-by-lot method, where the sampling risks have been analyzed, and where avoidance of lot rejections is the stimulus for quality improvement, is to be preferred. In those situations where 100% inspection by the receiver is deemed necessary, the receiver must recognize that he is taking over the responsibility for quality from the producer and, as a result, the production of quality is not likely to get any better. In any case, the optimum condition is achieved when the producer recognizes his responsibilities with respect to quality and takes the necessary measures to control quality, so the receiver has maximum assurance of quality.

HYPOTHESIS TESTING IN ACCEPTANCE CONTROL

All acceptance techniques involve the statistical test of a hypothesis. In the process of inspecting or testing a sample of units from a lot offered by the supplier, the receiver attempts to determine whether the quality of the entire lot is acceptable. This determination amounts to the test of a hypothesis (null hypothesis).

H_0: The quality of the product is satisfactory.

Against an alternative hypothesis

H_1: The quality is not satisfactory.

When the test is arranged in this fashion, the receiver is saying in effect: "I would believe the quality of the product is satisfactory unless there is overwhelming statistical evidence to the contrary."

Expressing the quality of product quantitatively as "fraction defective," the receiver may indicate a satisfactory quality level as $\frac{1}{2}\%$ or $q = 0.005$. Then the hypothesis test in acceptance control involves testing the null hypothesis

$$H_0\text{: } q = 0.005$$

against

$$H_1\text{: } q > 0.005$$

A type I error or the error of rejecting a null hypothesis when it, in fact, is true involves the rejection of a lot that, in fact, is satisfactory. The receiver specifies an appropriate level α which this error should not exceed.

If X represents the event of observing a specific test result from a sample, the conditional probability of X

$$\Pr(X \mid H_0 \text{ is true}) \geq 1 - \alpha$$

If the receiver considers $\frac{1}{2}\%$ defective a satisfactory quality and would prefer to limit the type I error to 5%, a workable test of the hypothesis can be performed in the following manner. A sample of size n is tested. If c or fewer defective items are found in this sample, the hypothesis is accepted and the lot is considered satisfactory. If $c + 1$ or more items are found defective, the hypothesis is rejected (and so is the product). As the number of items in each lot is large, a sample size n is taken as 50 items. When H_0 is true and q is 0.005, the expected number of defective items in the sample is

$$\begin{aligned} c' &= n \times q \\ &= 50 \times 0.005 \\ &= 0.25 \end{aligned}$$

The probability distribution of the items found defective within the sample is approximately Poisson distribution. When the mean is 0.25, the probability of obtaining 1 or 0 defective items is (from the cumulative probabilities of Poisson distribution in Table A3.1) 0.974. The probability of type I error is 2.6%. This is somewhat smaller than desired 5% but is definitely acceptable.

The complete procedure for hypothesis testing would be to inspect a sample of 50 items from a large lot and if only 1 or none are found defective, the lot is considered satisfactory and accepted. This entire procedure is called *acceptance sampling*, and the pair of numbers n and c are together referred to as a *sampling plan*.

OPERATING CHARACTERISTIC OF A SAMPLING PLAN

Using any sampling plan (n, c) the probability that a particular lot will be accepted will naturally depend on the quality of the lot. If the lot that contained N items had a quality q, the actual lot would contain Nq defective items. The remaining $N - Nq$ items would be good items. When a sample of n items is selected from this lot, it may contain some defective items, say x. In the selection x defective items are chosen out of a total Nq defective items and $n - x$ good items are chosen out of the remaining $N - Nq$ good items. Therefore, the probability distribution of x would be a hypergeometric distribution given by (see Chapter 2)

$$\Pr(x) = \frac{\binom{N-Nq}{n-x}\binom{Nq}{x}}{\binom{N}{n}}$$

The expected value of x, or the average number of defective items found in the sample, would be nq. Whenever the lot size N is very large relative to sample size n and the fraction q is very small (i.e., under 0.05), the complex hypergeometric distribution can be approximated by the more easily manageable Poisson distribution with the same expected value, or

$$\lambda = nq$$

In most commercial and industrial applications of quality control these two conditions, N very large relative to n and q under 0.05, are always present. So Poisson distribution is almost always used as a valid but simple approximation.

$$\Pr(x) = \frac{\lambda^x e^{-\lambda}}{x!} \qquad \text{where } \lambda = nq$$

$$= \frac{(nq)^x e^{-nq}}{x!}$$

Probability that a lot with quality q will be accepted would be the probability that the observed number of defective items x will be less than or equal to the critical number c:

$$\begin{aligned}\Pr(\text{accept}) &= \Pr(x \leq c) \\ &= \Pr(0) + \Pr(1) + \cdots + \Pr(c - 1) + \Pr(c)\end{aligned}$$

Another interpretation of this equation is that the probability of acceptance is the same as the cumulative probability up to c for a Poisson distribution with parameter $\lambda = nq$. These cumulative probabilities are tabulated for pairs of values of c and λ in Table A3.1.

Since the probability of acceptance of a lot is a function of sample size n, critical number c, and the lot quality q, when a sampling plan is specified (i.e., n and c are fixed), the probability of acceptance is a function of q. This functional relationship between probability of acceptance of a lot and its quality level q is called the *operating characteristic* of the sampling plan. The relationship is usually presented in a graphical fashion as a curve with q represented on the horizontal axis and Pr(Accept) on the vertical axis. The curve is called the *operating characteristic curve* or *OC curve* of the sampling plan. Figure 9.2 shows the OC curve for the sampling plan $n = 50$, $c = 1$.

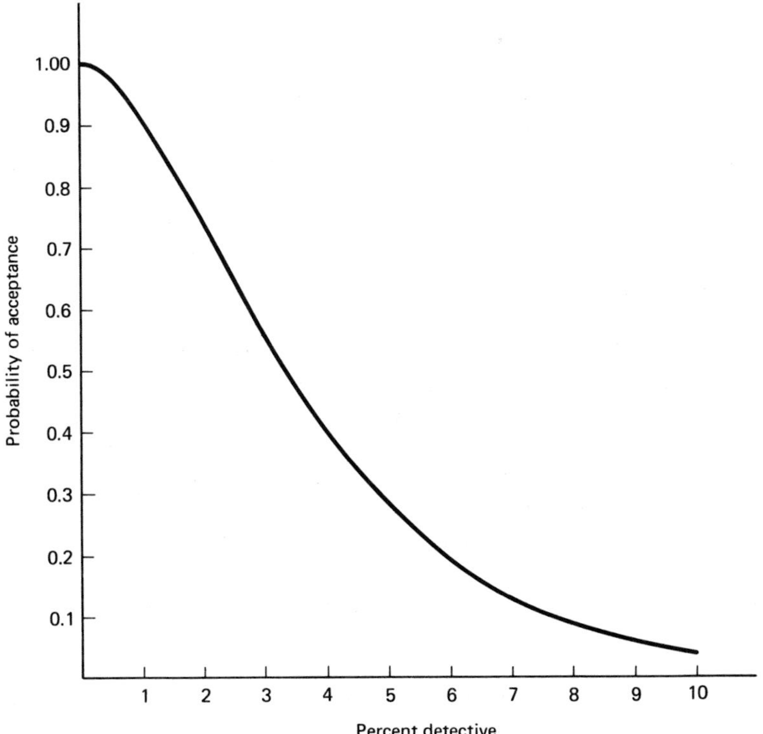

Figure 9.2 Operating characteristic curve for sampling plan: $n = 50$, $c = 1$.

A step-by-step procedure for constructing an OC curve for any specified sampling plan is described in Chapter 10. It is easy to see that every OC curve would have five specific points on the curve.

Point 1: Pr(accept) = 1.0, q = 0. This point affirms that if the lot contains no defective items, it will always be accepted.

Point 2: Pr(accept) = 1 − α, q = *acceptable quality* q_1. This point assures that the probability of type I error, or the error of not accepting a lot with acceptable quality, is α. This point is called the *producer's risk point.*

Point 3: Pr(accept) = 0.5, q = *indifference quality* q'. This point defines the quality level for which the probability of acceptance and rejection are the same. Effectively, the supplier and consumer are both taking the same risk.

Point 4: Pr(accept) = β, q = *unacceptable quality* q_2. This point assures that the probability of type II error, or the error of accepting a lot of unacceptable quality, is β. This point is called the *consumer's risk point.*

Point 5: Pr(accept) = 0, q = 1.00. This point affirms that if all items in the lot are defective, the lot would never be accepted.

RECTIFYING INSPECTION

When a lot is rejected, the consumer has a choice. The lot can be returned to the supplier and the supplier is asked to send a substitute lot, of, hopefully, better quality. Alternatively, the lot can be inspected 100%. This procedure of inspecting each and every item in the rejected lots is called *rectifying inspection.* The supplier is expected to replace all defective items found. Compared to the first alternative of returning rejected lots entirely, rectifying inspection is more expensive, as a larger number of items have to be tested. However, there are two advantages: first, the quality of the product accepted is improved as the lots undergoing rectifying inspection contain no more defective items, and second, there is no interruption of supplies.

The choice between these two alternatives is usually dictated by the nature of usage of items immediately after receipt. If the product is being used in a continuous manufacturing process or is being resold without much delay, rectifying inspection is preferable. Both the improvement of quality and continuity of supply become critical factors. If, on the other hand, the product is being stored in a warehouse, the lower cost of returning rejected lots becomes very attractive. All military standard plans described in Chapter 11 involve returning rejected lots.

The question of who bears the additional cost of rectifying inspection needs to be resolved at the time of negotiating the contracts for the supplies. Like the transportation costs or taxes, the contract should specify the exact division of the proportion of the costs to be borne by the supplier and the consumer. Very costly litigations can result from any misunderstanding about this division of costs.

AVERAGE OUTGOING QUALITY

One advantage of rectifying inspection is an improvement in the quality of the product received. When L lots of N items each are subjected to acceptance sampling using a sampling plan (n, c), the quality improvement can be calculated using the following analysis. Let q be the quality of lots as presented by the supplier and $P(a)$ be the corresponding probability of acceptance using sampling plan (n, c).

Of the L lots $L \cdot P(a)$ will be accepted. This means that all the defective items in these lots will still be present in the product accepted. As each lot contains N items and the quality is q, there would be $N \cdot q$ defective items in each lot and $(L \cdot P(a) \cdot (N \cdot q)$ defective items will be accepted. $L(1 - P(a))$ lots will undergo a rectifying inspection. Each and every defective item will be tested and replaced by a serviceable item. There will be no defective items accepted:

total number of defective items accepted

$$\begin{aligned} &= L \cdot P(a) \cdot N \cdot q + L(1 - P(a)) \cdot N \cdot 0 \\ &= L \cdot P(a) \cdot N \cdot q \end{aligned}$$

As the total number received is $L \cdot N$, the quality of the product received

$$\begin{aligned} q' &= \frac{\text{number of defective items received}}{\text{number of items received}} \\ &= \frac{L \cdot P(a) \cdot N \cdot q}{L \cdot N} \\ &= P(a) \cdot q \end{aligned}$$

The quality q' is called the *average outgoing quality* of the sampling plan (n, c) and q is referred to as the *incoming quality*.

Example 9.1

Consider the sampling plan (50, 1) discussed earlier. Let the incoming quality be 4% defective.

$$\begin{aligned} nq &= 50 \times 0.04 \\ &= 2 \end{aligned}$$

$$P(a) \text{ from Table A3.1} = 0.406$$

$$\begin{aligned} q' &= P(a) \cdot q \\ &= 0.406 \times 0.04 \\ &= 0.01624 \end{aligned}$$

The quality improvement is from the incoming quality of 4% defective to the average outgoing quality of 1.624% defective.

Figure 9.3 shows the relationship between the incoming quality and the average outgoing quality for the sampling plan (50, 1). The maximum reached by this curve represents the worst possible outgoing quality for any level of incoming quality. In a way this limit, the worst outgoing quality, represents the poorest quality of product accepted or the maximum risk faced by the consumer. This limit is called the *average outgoing quality limit* (AOQL); the entire curve is conventionally called the AOQ curve.

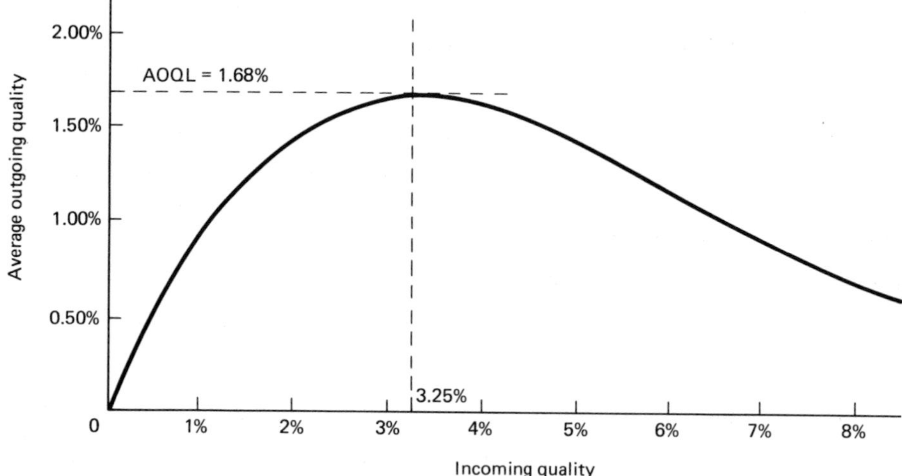

Figure 9.3 Average outgoing quality for sampling plan: $n = 50$, $c = 1$.

TOTAL INSPECTION UNDER RECTIFYING INSPECTION

The quality improvement from rectifying inspection is not free; it comes at the cost of extra inspection (and testing) of all the items in the rejected lots. Each lot subjected to a sampling plan (n, c) would require the inspection of n items. However, a fraction $1 - P(a)$ of the lots would be rejected. After rejection, the remaining $N - n$ items in the lot would have to be inspected. Hence

total effort of inspection

$$= n \text{ items in the sampling inspection}$$
$$+ (1 - P(a))(N - n) \text{ items in the rectifying inspection}$$
$$= n + (1 - P(a))(N - n)$$
$$= nP(a) + N(1 - P(a))$$

This quality is called the *average total inspection* (ATI).

Example 9.2

To illustrate ATI, the same sampling plan (50, 1) and incoming quality (4%) is used. The lot size N is 1000. Then the average total inspection is

$$\begin{aligned} \text{ATI} &= nP(a) + N(1 - P(a)) \\ &= (50 \times 0.406) + 1000(1 - 0.406) \\ &= 20.3 + 594 \\ &= 614.3 \end{aligned}$$

Under rectifying inspection an average of approximately 614 items is inspected from each lot. This can be compared with only 50 items being inspected in acceptance sampling without rectifying inspection.

DOUBLE AND MULTIPLE SAMPLING

The sampling plan $n = 50$, $c = 1$ is called a *single sampling plan* because a decision either to accept or to reject the lot is reached after the inspection of a single sample. In a *double sampling plan* the decisions possible after the inspection of the first sample would be (1) to accept the lot, (2) to reject the lot, or (3) to take the second sample. There are only two possible decisions after the inspection of the second sample: (1) to accept the lot or (2) to reject the lot. A double sampling plan is defined by the following parameters.

For the first sample:

$$\begin{aligned} n_1 &= \text{sample size} \\ c_1 &= \text{acceptance number} \\ r_1 &= \text{rejection number} \end{aligned}$$

For the second sample:

$$\begin{aligned} n_2 &= \text{sample size} \\ c_2 &= \text{acceptance number} \\ r_2 &= \text{rejection number} \end{aligned}$$

The acceptance number c_2 is the number of permissible defectives in both (first and second) samples taken together. Obviously, $r_2 = c_2 + 1$ in order to ensure a definite decision after the second sample. The operation of a double sampling plan is illustrated in the next example.

Example 9.3

A double sampling plan is given as

$$\begin{array}{lll} n_1 = 80 & c_1 = 0 & r_1 = 3 \\ n_2 = 80 & c_2 = 3 & r_2 = 4 \end{array}$$

The operating procedure under this plan would be as follows. First, take a sample of 80 units. If the inspection of this sample reveals 0 defectives, accept the lot. If it reveals 3 or more defectives, reject the lot. If the number of defectives is either 1 or 2, take a second sample of 80 units. If, after inspection of the second sample, the total number of defectives found in the first and second samples is 3 or less, accept the lot. Otherwise, reject the lot.

Assume that the quality of product submitted for inspection (incoming quality) is 2% defective. What is the probability that this product would be accepted?

$$p = 0.02 \qquad n_1 p = n_2 p = 80 \times 0.02$$
$$= 1.6$$

From Table A3.1 for $np = 1.6$, the probabilities given in Table 9.2 are obtained. [*Note*: The probabilities in Table A3.1 are cumulative probabilities, i.e., $\Pr(x \le c)$. To obtain $\Pr(x = c)$ it is necessary to get the difference between $\Pr(x \le c)$ and $\Pr(x \le c - 1)$.]

Probability of acceptance on the first sample $= \Pr(x = 0) = 0.202$. Acceptance after second sample can come about in two different ways.

A. 1 defective in first sample and (2 or less) in the second sample.
B. 2 defectives in the first sample and (1 or less) in the second sample.

$$\Pr(A) = 0.323 \times 0.783$$
$$= 0.2529$$
$$\Pr(B) = 0.258 \times 0.525$$
$$= 0.1355$$
$$\text{overall probability of acceptance} = 0.202 + 0.2529 + 0.1355$$
$$= 0.5904$$

Multiple sampling plans having k levels operate along the same line. After the inspection of the first through $(k - 1)$th samples there are three possible decisions: to accept, to reject, or to take the next sample. After inspection of the last sample there are only two possible decisions, to accept or to reject the lot. In Example 9.3 the sample sizes n_1 and n_2 are both 80. This is not a requirement for either double sampling or multiple sampling plans. However, MIL-STD-105D, which is the most common source for

TABLE 9.2 Probabilities of Acceptance

c	$\Pr(x = c)$	$\Pr(x \le c)$
0	0.202	0.202
1	0.323	0.525
2	0.258	0.783
3	0.138	0.921

sampling plans, has a convention of keeping all samples of the same size. This standard also uses only seven-level plans under multiple sampling. The standard is described in greater detail in Chapter 11.

PROBLEMS

9.1. A single sampling plan is given as $n = 15$, $c = 1$. What would be probabilities of acceptance of lots that are 3%, 6%, 10%, and 18% defective?

9.2. A single sampling plan is given as $n = 120$, $c = 3$. What is the indifference quality? What is the quality of a lot that has 95% probability of acceptance?

9.3. A lot 5% defective is submitted to a single sampling plan with rectifying inspection, $n = 120$, $c = 3$. What is the average outgoing quality?

9.4. Calculate the average total inspection for the lot in Problem 9.3.

9.5. A product is purchased in lots of 600 each. Three alternative plans are proposed for sampling inspection; (1) $n = 32$, $c = 1$; (2) $n = 50$, $c = 2$; and (3) $n = 80$, $c = 3$. Calculate the AOQ and ATI under each plan if the incoming quality is 2% defective. What plan minimizes ATI? Which plan gives the best AOQ? Which plan would you choose?

9.6. A double sampling plan is given as $n_1 = 100$, $c_1 = 1$, $n_2 = 100$, $c_2 = 3$. Compute the probability of acceptance for a lot 2% defective.

9.7. If rectifying inspection is used along with the plan in Problem 9.6 and the lot size is 3000, what would be the AOQ and ATI? (*Note*: Rectifying inspection is initiated after any rejection. If the lot is rejected on the first sample, a second sample is not taken but rectifying inspection is started immediately.)

9.8. If a single sampling plan and a doubling sampling plan offer the same risk protection, what would be the advantages and disadvantages of choosing the double sampling plan?

9.9. Analyze the producer–receiver relationships discussed in this chapter to identify advantages and disadvantages.

9.10. A manufacturer purchases components from three suppliers. The manufacturer uses an ad hoc sampling plan. Under this plan 10% of each lot is inspected. If 1 or 0 defectives are found, the lot is accepted. Suppliers X, Y, and Z ship their product in lots of 100, 1000, and 10,000, respectively.

(a) What is the indifference quality implied for each supplier?

(b) Is this plan fair to all suppliers?

ten

LOT-BY-LOT ACCEPTANCE SAMPLING BY ATTRIBUTES

This type of sampling applies particularly in situations where a multiple number of units are presented for inspection in static form at essentially one geographic location and where the inspection is for attributes type (go/no go) characteristics. Currently, it is the most widely used method of lot acceptance sampling—primarily because it is efficient, easy to understand, and easy to apply. Also, consumers recognize that whenever possible, it is preferable to require vendors to submit material in static lots rather than as continuous product. The requirement of providing "lots" of units of product contributes to homogeneity and through awareness of the cost of lot rejection provides maximum motivation for the vendor to submit only units of good quality.

Usually, with lot-by-lot inspection there is agreement between the producer and receiver that (1) lots accepted by the sampling plan will be accepted as is except for defective units found in the samples from all lots which will be replaced by good units, (2) rejected lots will be returned to the producer for rectification, and (3) the resubmitted lot will be inspected only for those defects causing original rejection or any other defects that might have been caused by the rectification process. There are variations of these agreements. Some receivers will use the option of screening the rejected lots and charging these costs back to the producer. This option is exercised most often when the material is urgently needed. In either case the objective is to make the producer bear the cost of rectification.

Single or multiple samples may be selected from a lot for determination of lot quality. The derivation of a simple single sampling plan will be considered first to develop understanding of risk determination. In single sampling by attributes a representative sample is drawn from the lot and the decision to accept or reject the lot is based on the results of the one sample.

The sample plans for lot-by-lot acceptance which consist of the sample size n and the acceptance number c are based on Poisson distribution of defective units in the lot. It will be recalled that the Poisson approximates the binomial when $p' \leq 0.10$ and $np' < 5$. The binomial will be the underlying distribution in most attributes sampling situation, so it is perfectly logical to make an approximation and use Poisson distribution instead.

CONSTRUCTION OF THE OC CURVE OF AN ATTRIBUTES SINGLE SAMPLING PLAN

A typical single sampling plan is $n = 300$ and $c = 5$ (n = sample size and c = acceptance number). This can be interpreted as a direction to take a representative sample of 300 for inspection; to accept if there are 5 or less defectives in the sample, and to reject if there are more than 5. The decision to accept or reject is made solely on the results of the single sample. What are the risks to producer and receiver in using this plan? A convenient way to express the risks graphically is the operating characteristic curve of a sampling plan (see Chapter 9). The curve will be derived here to show the method of development of an OC curve for any sampling plan.

The step-by-step method for deriving the OC curve for a single sampling plan is as follows:

1. Set up table headings and the P_α column as follows:

n	np'	p'	P_α	$P_\alpha P'$
			0.98	
			0.95	
			0.70	
			0.50	
			0.20	
			0.05	
			0.02	

where n = sample size

np' = number defective

p' = fraction defective

P_α = probability of acceptance

$P_\alpha p'$ = AOQ = average outgoing quality

The chosen values of P_α will give ordinate values which, when coordinated with p' values to be derived, will yield the OC curve.

2. Search Table A3.1 under the given c value until the desired P_α (or closest value to desired P_α) is located. (If the exact value is not found, the value in the P_α column should be changed to correspond to the one from the table.)
3. Place the np' value associated with the selected P_α in the np' column.
4. Divide the np' value by n. This will give the p' coordinate of P_α for the OC curve.

Example 10.1

Determine the OC curve of the single sampling plan

$$n = 300 \qquad c = 5$$

1. *Table construction*:

n	np'	p'	P_α	$P_\alpha p'$
300			0.98	
300			0.95	
300			0.70	
300			0.50	
300			0.20	
300			0.05	
300			0.02	

2. *Finding np' and p'*. Search through Table A3.1 under $c = 5$ discloses a P_α value of 0.983. This is the closest value to 0.98. The np' value associated with a P_α value of 0.983 is 2.0. This value of np', when divided by $n = 300$, yields a p' value of 0.0067. The same procedure is followed for each of the other P_α values until the table is completed.

n	np'	p'	P_α	$P_{\alpha p'}$ = AOQ
300	2.0	0.0067	0.983	0.0065
300	2.6	0.0087	0.951	0.00827
300	4.4	0.0147	0.72	0.0106
300	5.6	0.0187	0.512	0.00957
300	7.8	0.025	0.210	0.00526
300	10.5	0.035	0.05	0.00175
300	12.0	0.04	0.02	0.0008

The $P_{\alpha p'}$ column is provided to give the necessary ordinate values for the graphing of an AOQ (average outgoing quality) curve, with p' again being the abscissa and $P_\alpha p'$ the ordinate. Figure 10.1 shows both of these curves as plotted from the data in the table above. The reader will note that the arbitrarily chosen P_α points enable the construction of smooth curves.

Several points on the two curves have been identified. These have been selected because they represent the usual identifying points in the derivation

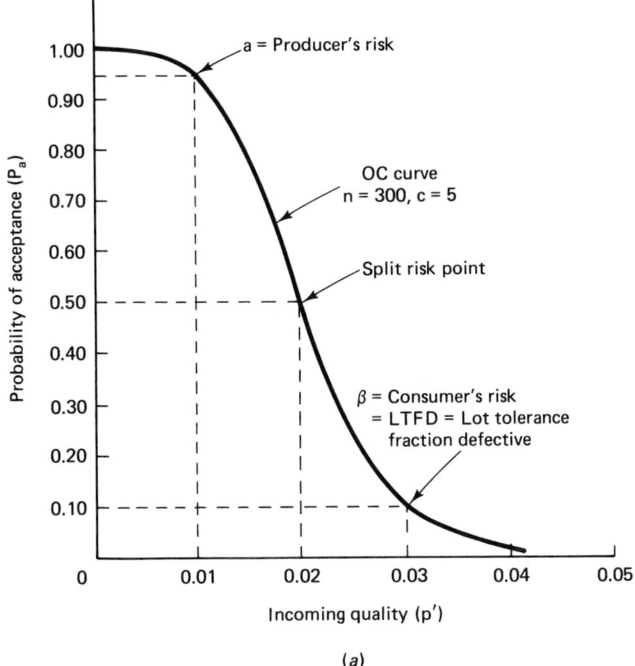

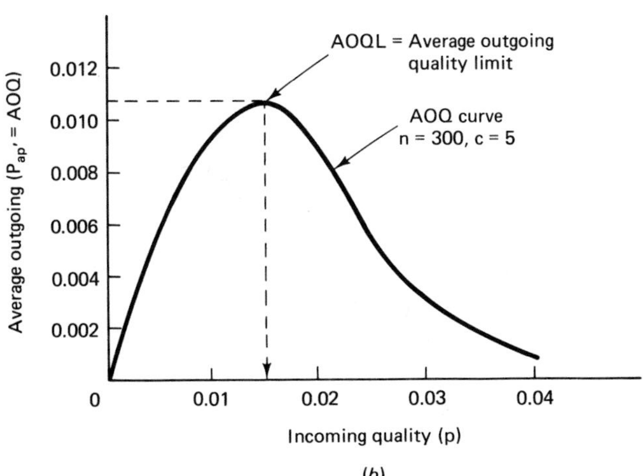

Figure 10.1 (a) Operating characteristic (OC) and (b) average outgoing quality (AOQ) curves for the sampling plan $n = 300$, $c = 5$.

of sampling plans. They are:

α = producer's risk = risk of rejection of product which should be satisfactory (usually set at $P_\alpha = 0.95$, thus $\alpha = 0.05$; α is the probability of type I error)

β = consumer's risk = risk of acceptance of product which is definitely unsatisfactory (usually set at $P_\alpha = 0.10$, thus $\beta = 0.10$; β is the probability of type II error)

AOQL = average outgoing quality limit = maximum average outgoing quality as a result of the application of the plan and the rectification measures prescribed earlier

point of indifference = indifference quality (p') where the producer and consumer take the same risks in the application of the plan

It is conventional to identify plans in terms of performance. It is immediately evident that the assured performance is designated by reference to a point on either the OC curve or the AOQ curve. For example, the plan $n = 300, c = 5$, in terms of expected performance is identified in the following ways:

α *plan:* $p'_\alpha = 0.0083$

β *plan:* $p'_\beta = 0.03 = \text{LTPD}$[1]

AOQL *plan*: $p'_{\text{AOQL}} = 0.015$

Point of indifference plan: $p'_{0.50} = 0.0095$

The plan is the same. It is the method of defining the plan that varies here. A plan is specifically defined when the p' values at the α and β points are specified. LTPD (lot tolerance percent defective) and AOQL standards are used in the well-known Dodge–Romig tables discussed in more detail later. The α plans are also called AQL (acceptable quality level; AQL = $p'\alpha$). AQL is almost universally accepted as a basis for sampling plans and all the plans included in the military standards (MIL-STD-105D or ABC Standard) are based on AQL.

Now that the different risk points on the operating characteristic have been defined, it may be helpful to derive a single sampling plan where the sample size and acceptance number are undetermined. First, an engineering judgment must be made regarding the α and β points of the curve. Assume, for example, that it is desired to set the producer's risk ($\alpha = 0.05$) such that

[1] The quality level or proportion of defective units in the lot when $\beta = 0.10$ is called *lot tolerance percent defective* (LTPD).

submitted inspection lots of quality 1% defective will be rejected 5% of the time, and the consumer's risk ($\beta = 0.10$) such that lots 6% defective will be accepted no more than 10% of the time. What single sampling plan will meet these requirements?

DEVELOPMENT OF A SIMPLE ATTRIBUTES SAMPLING PLAN

When two points on the OC curve of a sampling plan are specified, it is possible to design a plan that comes closest to meeting these requirements. Usually, the two points specified are the producer's risk point and the consumer's risk point.

Example 10.2

Design a sampling plan that will come close to the following:

$$p_1 = 0.01 \qquad \alpha = 0.05$$

$$p_2 = 0.06 \qquad \beta = 0.10$$

If the sampling plan is (n, c) at the producer's risk level, with $n \cdot p_1$ being the expected number of defectives in the sample, the probability of acceptance should be $1 - \alpha = 0.95$.

Table A3.2 gives the values of np needed to yield a desired probability of acceptance for different critical numbers. The row headings are the critical numbers c and the column headings are the probabilities of acceptance $p(\text{A})$. A portion of the table is repeated here:

c	0.95	0.10
0	0.05	2.3
1	0.35	3.9
2	0.82	5.3
3	1.37	6.7

The entry 0.35 indicates that for a critical number $c = 1$ to reach a probability of acceptance of 0.95, the value of np must be 0.35.

This table is very useful in designing a sampling plan. If $c = 0$ for the desired plan, then

$$R = \frac{p_2}{p_1} = \frac{np_2}{np_1} = \frac{np \text{ for probability of acceptance } 0.10}{np \text{ for probability of acceptance } 0.95} = \frac{2.3}{0.05} = 46$$

However, the ratio R desired is only 6:

$$R = \frac{p_2}{p_1} = \frac{0.06}{0.01} = 6$$

Obviously, $c = 0$ would not give a satisfactory sampling plan. Trying other critical numbers will give:

c	R
0	46
1	11.1
2	6.5
3	4.9

$c = 2$ gives the ratio nearest the desired value of 6. Using $c = 2$, the sample size calculated at the producer's risk point is

$$n = \frac{np_1}{p_1} = \frac{0.82}{0.01} = 82$$

The sample size calculated at the consumer's risk point is

$$n = \frac{np_2}{p_2} = \frac{5.3}{0.06} = 88$$

These two values are not the same, as the ratio R does differ from 6. However, it is imperative that the critical number c be an integer. A compromise is made to accept a sample size 85 (average of 88 and 82).

The sampling plan $n = 85$, $c = 2$ would be the plan that comes closest to specifications. For this plan at quality level $p_1 = 0.01$, α is 0.055 and at quality level $p_2 = 0.06$, β is 0.10. The complete OC curve is shown in Figure 10.2.

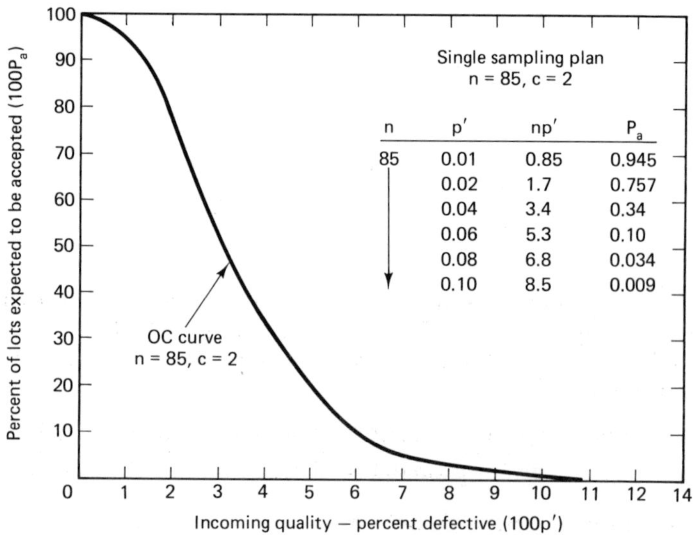

Figure 10.2 Operating characteristic curve and calculations of single sampling attributes plan to meet $100\,p'_{\alpha 0.05} = 1\%$, $100\,p'_{\beta 0.10} = 6\%$.

ANALYSIS AND INTERPRETATION OF THE OPERATING CHARACTERISTIC CURVE

Comparison of the two OC curves of Figures 10.1 and 10.2 shows that despite the greater number of sample defectives allowed by the plan of Figure 10.1, it is a *better* acceptance plan in that it provides more favorable risks to the consumer. This does not necessarily say that it is better from an economic standpoint, but the risks of accepting product of quality worse than desired (assuming that $100p'_{\alpha 0.05} = 1.0$ is the standard) are less with this plan. The plan of Figure 10.2 will accept lots that are 6% defective about 10% of the time. The plan of Figure 10.1 will accept virtually no lots of 6% defective quality. Yet each plan has almost the same standard quality requirement of 1% defective.

Curious readers may ask why any defectives are allowed in the sample at all. Figure 10.3 answers this question effectively. The sampling plans of curves (a), (b), and (c) are all zero-defective plans. Yet there are radically different risks involved. Also, plans with zero defectives usually penalize the producer more than plans allowing one or more defectives. Zero-defective plans are characterized by concave-upward trends. As more and more defectives are allowed in the sample, the curves resemble reverse S curves. However, even though more defectives are allowed in the samples, they provide better risks to both the producer and consumer. For the consumer the most important factor in the use of sampling is the *absolute* size of the sample. The larger the sample, the less the risk taken by the consumer. In

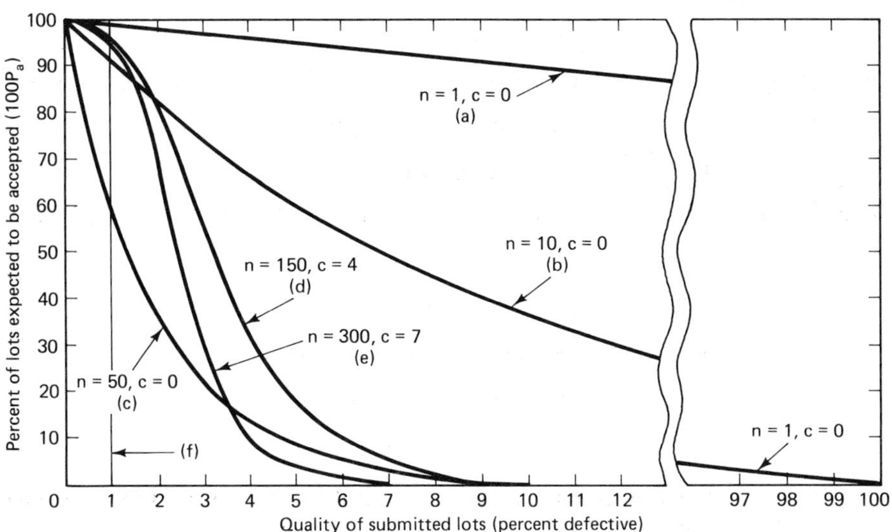

Figure 10.3 Comparative OC curves, zero acceptance plans, and $100\,p'_{\alpha 0.05} =$ 1% defective plans.

contrast, allowance of one or more defectives in the same sample results in less risk of rejection for the producer. Comparison of curves (d) and (e) dramatically illustrates this. Curves (d) and (e) are plans that allow defectives in the sample. Both have essentially the same producer's risk; however, because curve (e) has a larger sample size than curve (d), less risk is taken by the consumer. Curve (f) is the ideal OC curve. This sampling plan accepts all lots 1% or better and rejects all lots worse than 1% defective. This curve is unattainable with sampling. However, as the sample size increases, the OC curve comes closer and closer to this ideal.

PROBLEMS

10.1. Construct OC and AOQ curves for the following single sampling plans:

(a) $n = 10, c = 1$
(b) $n = 50, c = 2$
(c) $n = 100, c = 4$
(d) $n = 200, c = 2$

Locate the following points for each of the plans:

(i) $\alpha = 0.05$
(ii) $\beta = 0.10$
(iii) Indifference quality
(iv) AOQL

10.2. Design a single sampling plan that will be close to the following requirements:

$$p_1 = 0.02 \qquad \alpha = 0.05$$

$$p_2 = 0.06 \qquad \beta = 0.08$$

10.3. Design a single sampling plan that will be close to the following requirements:

$$p_1 = 0.02 \qquad \alpha = 0.05$$

$$\text{LTPD} = 0.09$$

10.4. Design a single sampling plan that will be close to the following requirements:

$$p_1 = 0.01 \qquad \alpha = 0.03$$

$$\text{point of indifference} = 0.12$$

10.5. Develop four sampling plans that bracket the points

$$p_1 = 0.03 \qquad \alpha = 0.05$$

$$p_2 = 0.15 \qquad \beta = 0.10$$

Calculate the average total inspection for each of these plans if the incoming quality is 0.08.

eleven

ACCEPTANCE PROCEDURES BASED ON AQL

AQL stands for *acceptable quality level*. It is the quality level that the consumer considers acceptable. When an acceptance procedure is based on AQL, the result is a clear decision either to accept or to reject the lot. There is no rectifying inspection. When AQL is stated as a certain level, say 0.4%, the consumer is effectively informing the producer that lots with a higher fraction of defective items are likely to be rejected with a high probability. The procedure only specifies the producers risk. The consumer does not undertake to carry out any rectifying inspection, nor would he or she believe in any rectifying inspection by the producer.

Acceptance procedures used by the U.S. Department of Defense are based primarily on AQL. As this department is probably the largest consumer in the world, the procedures followed by the department are emulated by other industries and government agencies both in the United States and abroad. These procedures are referred to as the ABC Standard or MIL-STD-105D. The latter term is used in this chapter, although the terms are interchangeable.

MIL-STD-105D has become the standard for AQL-based inspection procedures for all industry. Other plans, equally good, are available but none have achieved the popularity of MIL-STD-105D. Its use in most government procurement contracts accounts in part for its popularity. Aside from this, however, it contains a collection of sampling plans which are relatively easy to select, apply, and interpret. Also, when used in conjunction with its companion document, "Administration of Sampling Procedures for

Acceptance Inspection," it becomes a very complete procedure for administering a lot-by-lot acceptance sampling-by-attributes operation.

CIRCUMSTANCES FOR USING AQL

Rectifying inspection, where rejected lots are inspected 100% and all defective items replaced by good items, does improve the quality of product that is actually used. However, there is a price to be paid in the form of increased inspection. When the producer and the consumer are elements of the same organization, there are few problems; a trade-off can be achieved. On the other hand, when the producer and the consumer represent two different organizations, with conflicting interests, rectifying inspection gives rise to several problems. Some of these problems are described here.

First, who should bear the cost of additional inspection? The producer is not likely to accept the cost of additional inspection performed by the consumer, as this amounts to the acceptance of costs over which the producer has no control and no way of even measuring them properly. At the same time, the consumer is unlikely to accept the results of any rectifying inspection done by the producer. After all, the acceptance procedures are installed to protect the interests of the consumer and would be redundant if the consumer can have so much faith in the producer. Further, the consumer is not likely to carry out the inspection and bear the costs, as this amounts to the consumer paying for the poor quality produced by the producer.

The second factor is psychological. When the consumer performs rectifying inspection and returns (or destroys) only the defective items, there is little incentive for the producer to improve quality. The psychological impact of the rejection of entire lot or lots is impressive. It puts pressure on the producer to attempt to determine the causes of poor quality and make adequate corrections.

The third problem involves the wording and legal satisfaction of contracts. When the product submitted for inspection is 2% defective and each lot contains 100 items, for every accepted lot there are on an average 2 defective and 98 good items. The consumer has contracted to pay for good items. Should the consumer pay for only 98 items? The producer can argue that some defects are unavoidable. Is the price not already adjusted to reflect this fact?

Adoption of AQL does not resolve the legal dilema. If a lot of 100 items 4% defective is rejected, on an average there are 4 defective and 96 good items in the rejected lot. When the consumer contracts for the purchase of good items, there is no legal basis for refusal to pay for 96 good items. In any case there is need for careful wording of the contracts for purchase and supply.

In actual practice the choice of acceptance procedures, whether based on AQL or on rectifying inspection, is a result of negotiations between the producer and the consumer. In general, it can be said that AQL-based procedures favor the consumer, and procedures based on rectifying inspection favor the producer. It is a falacy that rectifying inspection procedures protect the consumer by limiting the average outgoing quality. If the AOQL is set at 2% defective, the actual outgoing quality is fairly close to the limit of 2%. Specification of a limit usually spells out how far a person can go and still be within legal limits. It is similar to the situation of paying taxes. When income tax is made payable *not later than April 15*, most people take it to mean *not later than April 15 but no earlier than April 14*.

In general, when the producer has a strong negotiating position, rectifying inspection would be included in the acceptance procedures. The strong position may be the result of monopoly or a large advantage of size or financial strength. One example of this type was the giant American Telephone and Telegraph Company (predecessor to all the "Bell Telephone" companies) supplying telecommunication equipment to small businesses and individuals.

When the consumer has a strong negotiating position, as a result of the same factors of monopoly, size, or financial strength, the consumer can elect to use an AQL-based acceptance procedure. The U.S. Department of Defense amply qualifies as a consumer with a strong negotiating position, and naturally developed their own AQL-based procedures of MIL-STD-105D.

A BRIEF HISTORY

Acceptance based on statistical sampling was first introduced to the Ordnance Department of the U.S. Army during World War II. Acceptance procedures were developed by a group of civilian statisticians and engineers organized for this purpose.[1] Bell Telephone Laboratories and Columbia University were principal sources. Initially, the Army and Navy had their own tables of acceptance sampling procedures. When the armed forces were unified in a single Department of Defense, the Navy tables were adopted as Joint Army-Navy Standard 105 (JAN-ATD-105) in 1949.

A revision of these tables in 1950 led to the publication of MIL-STD-105A. Succeeding revisions in 1958, 1961, and 1963 were designated as MIL-STD-105B, MIL-STD-105C, and MIL-STD-105D.

The last standard was adopted by a working group from the United States, Britain, and Canada engaged in developing a common standard. As a common standard, MIL-STD-105D is also recognized as the ABC Standard (*A*merica, *B*ritain, *C*anada) or ABC-STD-105.

[1] This group laid the foundations of most of the theoretical developments in statistical quality control. However, the publication of these works was delayed until after the war was over.

APPLICABILITY OF AQL PROCEDURES

AQL-based acceptance procedures are applicable to acceptance inspection by attributes (generally lot by lot) for parts, components, subassemblies, assemblies, and end items. It may also be used in administrative situations where the appropriate conditions apply: for example, in audit sampling for such things as record-keeping accuracy, accounts receivable, work load, inventory, and so on. Inspection may be applied at delivery destination or at the point of production or supply. It may be used for acceptance purposes at various stages of manufacture or completion of the product.

INITIAL DECISIONS

Prior to the introduction of any acceptance procedure based on AQL, it is necessary to arrive at certain preliminary decisions. These decisions would indicate the choice of an acceptance sampling plan best suited for the situation.

1. *Acceptable quality level (AQL).* As this quality level is acceptable to the consumer, it is desirable that the producer not face an unduly high risk or rejection of product of this quality or better.
2. *What constitutes a defect or a defective item?* A clear specification of what constitutes a defective item would be desirable for both consumer and producer and should be included, as far as possible, in the purchase contract. This specification also determines the technical process used for the inspection of an item and consequently the inspection cost per item inspected.
3. *Fraction of any incoming product to be inspected or the relative amount of inspection.* If n items are inspected from a lot of N items, the fraction inspected is n/N. In general, for a constant value of α (producer's risk) the fraction n/N will decrease as N increases. When N is kept constant, the fraction will generally increase as β (consumer's risk) decreases. A third factor affecting the amount of relative inspection is the cost of inspection. A higher cost per item inspected would indicate the choice of a smaller fraction being inspected.

In military standards, the relative inspection is specified in the form of an inspection level. For any stated inspection level, plans are specified that keep the fraction inspected n/N approximately the same. The response of each sampling plan would depend on the AQL. In each case, if the quality of the incoming product submitted for inspection is exactly at the AQL, the probability of acceptance is 95%. In this level of type 1 error, $\alpha = 5\%$ has been used as the basis for all the versions of MIL-STD-105D and its predecessors. The shape of the OC curve also depends on the relation between

AQL and the fraction inspected n/N. When AQL is small, quality is high and there are fewer defective units. To obtain adequate protection for both consumer and producer, the fraction inspected needs to be large. Looking at it another way, if the relative inspection is set at a certain level it would be adequate up to a certain AQL. At higher qualities (smaller AQL's) the protection can be maintained either at consumer risk point or producer risk point but not at both. Figure 11.1 shows operating characteristic curves for a fixed fraction inspected, $n/N = 10\%$, for different AQL levels. Note that all curves indicate the probability of acceptance is 95% when the quality of incoming lots equals AQL. However if the quality of incoming lots deteriorates to five times AQL, the response is strikingly different at different AQLs. Using 0.10 AQL curve the probability of acceptance at 0.5% incoming quality is 54%. Using 2.0% AQL curve the probability of acceptance at 10.0% incoming quality is close to 0%.

SPECIFICATION OF THE AQL

MIL-STD-105D defines AQL as "nominal value expressed in terms of percent defective or defects per hundred units, whichever is applicable, specified for a given group of defects (or individual defect)." This is a rather broad definition. It has also been referred to as the "maximum percent defective (or defects per hundred units) which may be tolerated as a quality average." This is a more precise definition but somewhat erroneous in the respect that it is recognized that there may be brief periods when the quality is worse than standard. A more accurate definition would be that it is the "quality level where the producer takes a comparatively small risk of rejection of product of quality equal to or better than the AQL." The risk of rejection may vary between a fraction of 1% and 20%. In general, plans with acceptance number zero increase the producer's risk of rejection.

The specification of the AQLs is closely related to the task of inspection planning. It is properly a part of quality engineering. It is sufficient to say here that before AQLs can be specified, it is first necessary to determine the characteristics to be inspected, to break these characteristics down into inspection stations, to classify characteristics at each station according to the seriousness of a defect (critical, major, minor, and/or other desired classification), to specify expression of nonconformance as percent defective or defects per 100 units at each station for each class of defects or for individual defects. This must be followed by the specification of AQLs as governed by the foregoing and certain other considerations, such as the following: cost of inspection versus cost of rejection, design requirements, producer's average quality, demand for the product, consumer complaints, and so on. Also, there should be a continuing review of AQL values for possible change to ensure that they are consistent with quality needs.

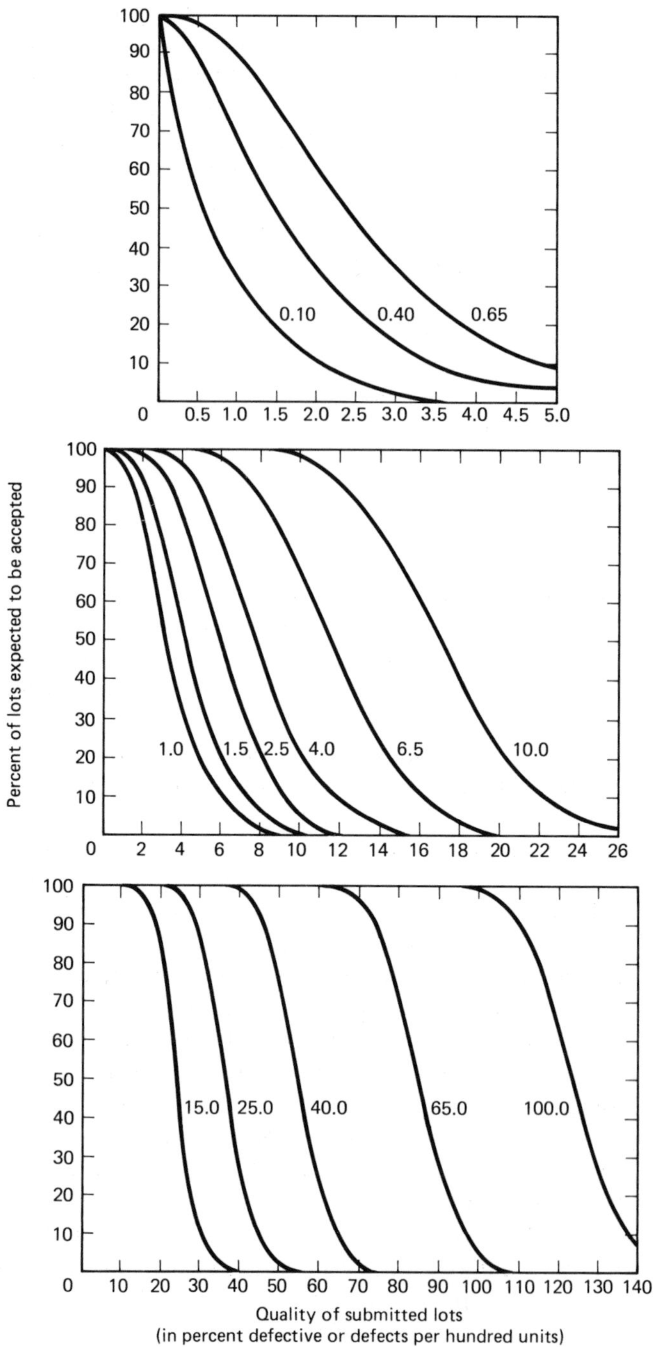

Figure 11.1 Operating characteristic curves for single sampling plans with the same fraction inspected for different AQLs.

The AQLs of MIL-STD 105D range from 0.015 to 1,000.0 approximately in geometric progression. Expression of nonconformance may be in defects per 100 units for all AQLs, or in percent defective for AQLs of 10 or below.

SPECIFICATION OF INSPECTION LEVEL

It has been stated that the most important factor in sampling is the absolute size of the sample. *Inspection level* is the term used to indicate the relative amount of inspection performed. Different levels of inspection provide approximately the same protection to the producer when he is submitting material of acceptable quality, but they provide different protections to the consumer.

MIL-STD-105D provides for seven levels of inspection. These are called *general inspection levels* I, II, and III and *special inspection levels* S-1, S-2, S-3, and S-4. For most products only general inspection levels are used, with special inspection levels being reserved for products where the tests are very expensive or are "destructive tests" (i.e., the item is no longer usable after being tested). The relative amount of inspection increases in this order. S-1 provides the minimum relative inspection, then S-2, S-3, S-4, I, II in increasing order and general inspection level III provides the maximum relative inspection.

Within the general inspection levels, considering level II as a norm, the relative amount of inspection provided by the three levels is approximately as shown in Table 11.1.

TABLE 11.1 Comparison of Inspection Levels

General Inspection Level	Relative Amount of Inspection
I	One-half of norm
II	Norm
III	Twice the norm

General inspection level II is the usual level used. Actually, the provision of inspection levels is somewhat superfluous in the sense that MIL-STD-105D allows an inspection administrator considerable latitude in the selection of sampling plans. It states that a different sample size code letter than that shown in Table A14.1 may be used at the discretion of the consumer. In effect, this can be regarded as an establishment of other levels of inspection. It is appropriate to state here that the risks afforded by a particular sampling plan are of prime importance as a prerequisite for its selection.

Factors affecting the choice of an inspection level are varied and should be balanced against one another before a decision is reached. The particular inspection plan under consideration must be judged by the protection it will give against accepting bad lots and rejecting good lots: that is, by critical review of the operating characteristics of the sampling plans under consideration.

NORMAL, TIGHTENED, AND REDUCED INSPECTION

No sampling plan provides perfect discrimination between good and bad inspection lots. There is always some risk of accepting an inspection lot with quality worse than the AQL or of rejecting an inspection lot with quality better than the AQL. The plans in MIL-STD-105D are designed so that, on normal inspection, they will accept nearly all lots submitted whose quality is equal to the AQL and a fairly high percentage of lots whose quality is slightly worse than the AQL. Protection against continuing to accept lots of worse quality than desired is obtained by shifting to a more severe sampling plan when there is sufficient evidence that the average quality is worse than the AQL. This is generally done without increasing the sample size, and the shift is not made until the quality average is sufficiently worse than the AQL to assure that the difference is not caused by a chance fluctuation in sampling. When the quality history is sufficiently good, economies may be realized by utilizing reduced sampling. This procedure also permits the concentration of inspection on products where attention is most needed. In effect, it may be said that the benefit of the doubt is given to the producer until the weight of evidence is so heavy as to demand a more severe plan.

Change to tightened inspection results in an improved consumer risk thus protecting the buyer from continued acceptance of lots worse than the AQL. Essentially, a shift to tightened inspection is a shift to a tighter AQL.

Change to reduced inspection results in a drastically increased consumer risk. However, if the evidence indicates that the quality is better than the AQL and would not change for the worse, reduced inspection provides inspection economies and psychological benefits. The criterion used for any change is the quality history supplemented by the industrial environment of current and immediate future production.

For a product with no significant previous history, acceptance procedure starts with normal inspection. Normal inspection is continued as long as the quality of product submitted is close to AQL. A significant deviation from this quality level will indicate a need for a change to either tightened or reduced inspection.

SINGLE, DOUBLE, AND MULTIPLE SAMPLING PLANS

MIL-STD 105D provides for single, double, or multiple sampling plans. In a multistage sampling plan the difference between acceptance and rejection numbers is not limited to 1. If acceptance and rejection numbers for a sampling plan are C and R, respectively, there can be three possible outcomes of inspection.

1. If $x \leq C \Rightarrow$ accept.
2. If $x \geq R \Rightarrow$ reject.
3. If $C < x < R \Rightarrow$ take the next sample.

In the last level of sampling the difference between C and R is exactly 1. Thus the third condition can never be satisfied and there is no next sample. The last level is provided by the first sample in single sampling, second sample in double sampling, and nth sample in n-level sampling.

For any AQL single, double, or multiple sampling plans can be designed to provide approximately the same OC curve and provide approximately the same protection for producer and consumer. The only differences in different types of sampling plans come from different needs for inspection and the psychological effects of appearing to permit a second, third, or more chances for product not immediately accepted.

In general, double sampling plans require less average inspection than do single sampling plans. Multiple sampling plans require less average inspection than do single or double sampling plans. The savings in the amount of inspection for double or multiple plans is greatest for lots of very good or very bad quality. For lots of marginal quality, however, double sampling plans sometimes require more average inspection than do single sampling plans. The savings of inspection is not much for tight AQLs and small sample sizes, but may be considerable in other cases. Some of the factors to be considered follow.

Administration. Single plans are simplest to administer. Multiple plans are the most difficult. The latter requires better trained inspectors and the results are more difficult to audit.

Lot information. The larger sample size of single sampling plans furnishes more information for long-term quality average determination.[2]

Lot availability for sample selection. If it is difficult to obtain additional samples because of lot movement or other reason, single sampling may be the preferable alternative.

Sample-size variation. Double and multiple plans require provisions for variable work load. If a variable work load cannot be tolerated, single sampling must be used.

Marginal quality influence. Marginal quality reduces the inspection savings of multiple plans. Figure 11.2 contains curves that indicate the average amount of inspection for the three types of sampling plans taken

[2] This is because only first sample results are used for quality average computations and records.

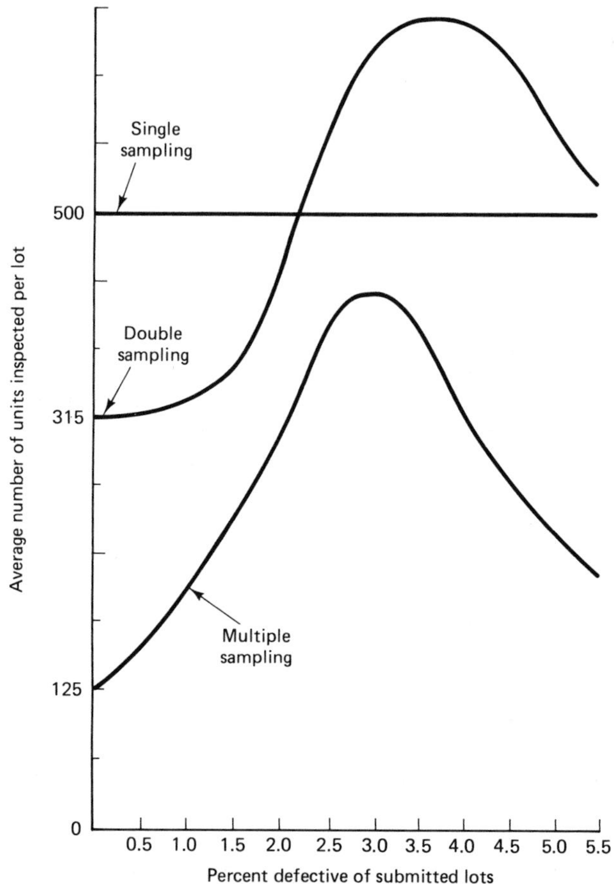

Figure 11.2 Comparison of average number of units inspected under single, double, and multiple sampling.

from the table for code letter N, AQL = 1.5. The graphs for the double and multiple sampling plans indicate that the maximum average number of units inspected occurs for the marginal quality above the AQL.

Acceptance number of zero. For single sampling plans with zero as the acceptance number, there are no matching double or multiple plans. Hence only single sampling can be used.

Unit inspection cost. If the cost of inspection is high, the savings in inspection cost with double or multiple sampling may preclude the use of single sampling. However, for low inspection cost the savings from smaller samples may be more than offset by the greater administrative difficulties encountered.

Psychological considerations. Double and multiple plans *appear* to give the producer another chance. Actually, the OC curves are essentially the same. Thus the protection afforded the producer against lot rejection does not change with the *type* of sampling.

DESCRIPTION AND USE OF TABLES

The tables for obtaining sampling plans are reproduced in the Appendix as Tables A14.1 through A14.10. These are called *master tables*. There is one master table for normal, tightened, and reduced inspection of each type. For example, Table A14.5 is the master table for normal-inspection double sampling plans. The row headings for this (and all other) master tables are sample size and code letter, and the column headings are AQL. The AQL values range from 0.01 up to 1000 in the progression 1, 1.5, 2.5, 4, 6.5, 10, ... These numbers are in approximate geometric progression. Values of AQL from 0.10 through 10 are expressed as percent defective or defects per 100 units; values above 10 are expressed as defects per 100 units only.

In each row there are two numbers, giving the sizes of the first and second samples. For code letter H both samples are of size 32. In each column there are two subcolumns: Ac, the acceptance number, and Re, the rejection number. For AQL 2.5 (2.5% defective) and code letter H, the acceptance and rejection numbers are given as follows:

		Ac	Re
First	32	1	4
Second	32	4	5

These numbers indicate the following double sampling plan for normal inspection when the code letter is H and the AQL is 2.5. First take a sample of size 32. If only 1 defective (or none) is found, accept the lot. If 4 or more defectives are found, reject the lot. If 2 or 3 defectives (more than 1 and less than 4) are found, take a second sample of size 32. If the total number of defectives in both samples is 4 or less, accept the lot. If it is 5 or more, reject the lot.

Table A14.1 gives the sample-size code letters. In this table the rows are lot or batch sizes and the column headings are the seven inspection levels. The inspection level is specified by the user. It is understood that general inspection level II is used when none is specified. For a lot of size 400 and general inspection level II, the code letter is H. (Size 400 falls within the range 281–500.)

In this case the relative inspection is 32/400, or 8%, for the first sample and the same for the second sample. In MIL-STD-105D the relative inspection decreases with increasing lot size. Had the lot size been 400,000 instead of 400, the code letter would have been P. The first and second samples would each have been 500. The relative inspection would be only 500/400,000, or 0.125%.

Tables A14.11 and A14.12 give the average outgoing quality limits for normal and tightened inspections, respectively. Table A14.13 gives the limit numbers to be used in reduced inspection.

MIL-STD-105D also includes the OC curves and average sample number curves for many sampling plans, but these are not reproduced here.

Example 11.1

Single sampling is to be used with special inspection level S-1 and AQL 4%. If the lot size is 750, what are the criteria for acceptance under normal inspection? If the product submitted for inspection is 6% defective, what is the probability of acceptance?

The lot size 750 is in the range 501–1200 and the code letter for inspection level S-1 in Table A14.1 is C. Entering the master table for normal-inspection single sampling, the sample size corresponding to code letter C is 5. In row C under AQL 4.0, no sampling plan is given but an arrow ↑ indicates that a plan at the top of the arrow may be used. Therefore, the sampling plan to be used is:

Sample Size	Ac	Re
3	0	1

When the product is 6% defective, the average number of defectives in the sample or np' is 3×0.06, or 0.18. Entering Table A3.1 for cumulative Poisson probabilities gives the probability of finding no defectives is 0.836. This is the probability of acceptance of the product submitted.

Example 11.2

A manufacturer receives preformed plastic covers in lots of 3000. The manufacturer wishes to use a double sampling plan from MIL-STD-105D with inspection level II and AQL of 0.65%. What are the criteria for acceptance under normal inspection? What is the probability that a lot 3.0% defective would be accepted?

The lot size is in the range 1201–3200 and the code letter for inspection level II in Table A14.1 is K. Entering the master table for normal-inspection double sampling, the sampling sizes corresponding to code letter K are 80 and 80. In row K under AQL 0.65 the sampling is found as:

	Sample Size	Ac	Re
First	80	0	3
Second	80	3	4

A lot would be accepted on first sample if there are no defectives in the first sample. It can be accepted on a second sample in two ways; either "1 defective in first sample and 2 or less in second sample" or "2 defectives in first sample and 1 or less in second sample."

When the incoming quality is 3.0% defective, the average number of defectives in either sample or np' is 80 × 0.03, or 2.4. Table A3.1 for cumulative Poisson probabilities gives the following:

$$\Pr(x \le 0) = 0.091 \qquad \Pr(x = 0) = 0.091$$
$$\Pr(x \le 1) = 0.308 \qquad \Pr(x = 1) = 0.217$$
$$\Pr(x \le 2) = 0.570 \qquad \Pr(x = 2) = 0.262$$
$$\Pr(x \le 3) = 0.779 \qquad \Pr(x = 3) = 0.209$$

Pr(0 defectives in first sample) = 0.0910
Pr(1 defective in first sample and 2 or less in second sample)
= 0.217 × 0.570 = 0.1237
Pr(2 defectives in first sample and 1 or less in second sample)
= 0.262 × 0.308 = 0.0807

Total 0.2954

The probability of acceptance of a lot 3.0% defective is 0.2954.

PRODUCER'S RISK AND OC CURVES

There are three types of sampling plans: single, double, and multiple. However, for every combination of code letter and AQL, these plans have approximately the same OC curve and offer the same risks for the producer. Sampling plans for code letter K and AQL of 1.0 under normal inspection are used to illustrate this.

From the master tables the plans obtained are as shown in Table 11.2. Figure 11.3 illustrates the OC curves for these plans. It is worth noticing

TABLE 11.2 Sampling Plans

	Sample Size	Ac	Re
Single sampling (Table A14.2)	125	3	4
Double sampling (Table A14.5)	80	1	4
	80	4	5
Multiple sampling (Table A14.8)	32	*	3
	32	0	3
	32	1	4
	32	2	5
	32	3	6
	32	4	6
	32	6	7

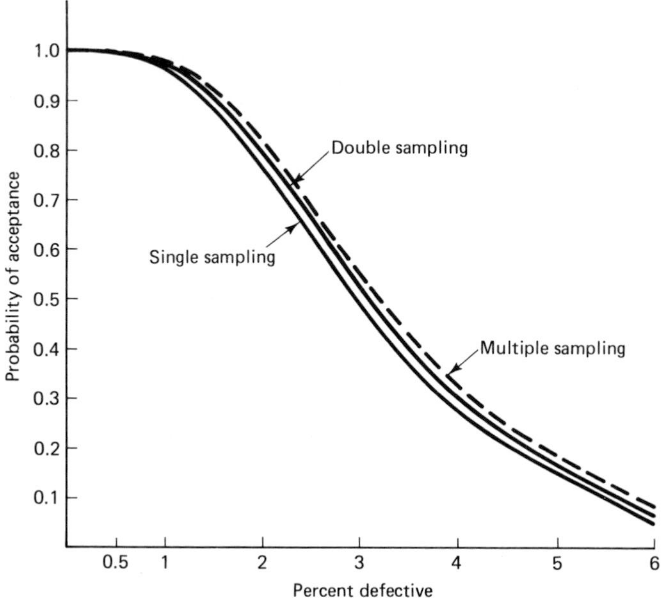

Figure 11.3 OC curves for single, double, and multiple sampling plans for code letter.

that all three curves are essentially the same and each has a probability 0.95 of accepting the lots with a designated AQL of 1.0.

CRITERIA FOR ADMINISTRATION

Unless otherwise indicated by a supplier's quality history, *normal* inspection is used at the start of a contract. The conditions that would favor *tightened* inspection at the start of a contract would include:

1. The supplier has had difficulties on prior contracts for the same item, or similar item, in meeting the prescribed AQLs.
2. The supplier has had no previous experience in manufacturing the item or similar items.
3. A survey of the supplier's production facilities prior to the start of production indicates the use of tightened inspection because of a likelihood that substandard quality will be produced.
4. Previous experience with reliable suppliers shows the need for using tightened inspection due to initial difficulties in manufacturing the item.

The only factor that might favor the use of reduced inspection at the start of the contract is the fact that the supplier has recently completed a contract on reduced inspection or is currently producing the same or similar item on reduced inspection. It should be stressed that when the use of reduced inspection may be justified due to recent completion of a contract on reduced inspection, it may be employed only if advantage can be taken of its economies in the significant savings of inspection labor hours with an insignificant loss in quality assurance to the consumer.

Normal inspection is used as long as the quality of product submitted is close to the AQL. If the quality is consistently better, reduced inspection may be used. If the quality is sufficiently worse than the AQL, tightened inspection should be instituted. The conditions for an indicated change are as follows:

1. The preceding 10 lots or batches (or more as indicated by the note to Table VIII[3]) have been on normal inspection and none has been rejected on original inspection.
2. The total number of defectives (or defects) in the samples from the preceding 10 lots or batches (or such other number as was used for condition a above) is equal to or less than the applicable number given in Table VIII. If double or multiple sampling is in use, all samples inspected should be included, not "first" samples only.
3. Production is at a steady rate.
4. Reduced inspection is considered desirable by the responsible authority.

It has been observed that it is wise to institute reduced inspection only when the entire inspection station qualifies. Otherwise, the administrative burdens overshadow the economies supposedly gained from the reduced sample sizes.

Normal inspection must be reinstated if any one of the following conditions occurs while reduced inspection is in effect:

1. A lot or batch is rejected.
2. The estimated quality average is greater than the AQL.
3. Production becomes irregular or delayed.
4. A lot or batch is "not accepted" under reduced inspection. The condition "not accepted" occurs in some reduced sampling plans when these plans include an area or indecision. To explain the code K, AQL 1.0 reduced single sampling plan is used.

Code Letter	Sample Size	Ac	Re
K	50	1	4

[3] Table VIII is the same as Table A14.13.

Under this sampling plan a sample with 2 or 3 defectives would be "not accepted." When this happens, the lot or batch being inspected is accepted but reduced inspection is discontinued.

5. Reduced inspection is no longer considered desirable by the responsible authority.

When normal inspection is being used, a suspicion that the quality of product being submitted is deteriorating leads to more stringent tightened inspection. If the quality level is at or above AQL, almost all the lots would be accepted. If the quality deteriorates, some lots would start being rejected. The condition for an indicated change to tightened inspection is as follows.

(a) When normal inspection is in effect, tightened inspection shall be instituted when 2 out of 5 consecutive lots or batches have been rejected on original inspection. For the purpose of this condition, any lot being accepted after resubmission is considered as rejected.

When tightened inspection is in effect, the condition for requalification for normal inspection is as follows:

(b) When tightened inspection is in effect, normal inspection shall be instituted when five consecutive lots or batches are accepted on original inspection.

Example 11.3

A product is being inspected under normal-inspection single sampling with code letter H and AQL 2.5 (i.e., sample size 50, Ac = 3, and Re = 4). The numbers of defectives found in the samples from the first 10 lots were 0, 1, 0, 2, 1, 1, 0, 2, 0, and 1, respectively. Does the supplier qualify for reduced inspection?

Since all 10 samples had fewer than 3 defectives, none would be rejected on original inspection and condition (1) is satisfied.

The total number inspected in these 10 samples is $50 \times 10 = 500$. The limit number given in Table A14.13 for 500 samples units and AQL 2.5 is 7. The total number of defectives found in the 10 samples is $0 + 1 + 0 + 2 + 1 + 1 + 0 + 2 + 0 + 1 = 8$. This exceeds the limit number and condition (2) is not satisfied.

The supplier does not qualify for reduced inspection.

INSPECTION RECORDS AND ESTIMATED PROCESS AVERAGE

MIL-STD-105D does not specifically require keeping historical records or computing process average. However, for quality history purposes, it is necessary to compile and maintain data regarding the sampling procedure used and the inspection results. The inspection record should include complete identification of the product or operation inspected, changes in degree of inspection, the inspection level, whether single, double, or multiple sampling was used, the AQL for each class of defects, lot size, whether or not the lot was previously submitted, the sample size, the number of defects or defectives found in the first sample for each class of defects, and whether or not the lot was accepted or rejected.

The estimated process average is the average percent defective or average number of defects per 100 units of product submitted by the supplier for original inspection. The original inspection is the first inspection of a particular quantity of product as distinguished from the inspection of product which has been resubmitted after prior rejection. The estimated process average should be computed for each defect or class of defects for which an AQL has been established. Its purpose is to furnish the accepting agency with a continuing record of quality of a producer so that decisions regarding changes in degree of inspection may be made. The true process average is almost never known, but an estimate may be made from the average results of previous lots. The precision of the estimate will depend on both the average and the total number of units included in the computation of the average. There are two formulas which are used for computation. It matters not whether nonconformance is expressed in percent defective or defects per 100 units. The formulas below are expressed in percent defective. For defects per 100 units' computation, simply insert "defects" in place of defectives.

When inspection lots vary considerably in size, it is necessary to compute a quality average that is weighted by lot size:

$$\text{Process average for } k \text{ lots} = \frac{100(p_1N_1 + p_2N_2 + \cdots + p_kN_k)}{N_1 + N_2 + \cdots + N_k}$$

$$\text{where } p_j = \frac{\text{number of defectives in first sample of the } j\text{th inspection lot}}{\text{number of units in first sample of the } j\text{th inspection lot}}$$

$$N_j = \text{number of units in the } j\text{th inspection lot}$$

When inspection lots do not vary appreciably in size, the following formula may be used:

$$\text{process average for } k \text{ lots} = \frac{100(p_1 + p_2 + \cdots + p_k)}{k}$$

When single sampling is used, the entire sample should be inspected even though the rejection number may be reached before the sample has been completely inspected. The same holds true for the first samples of double or multiple sampling. This procedure yields a quality average that is unbiased. The results of resubmitted lots should be excluded from any quality average computations, as should the results of lots that are considered to be abnormal. However, care must be taken not to exclude data unless it is known definitely that the data arose under abnormal conditions which are not likely to be encountered again. A statistical significance test can be used for the determination of an abnormal condition.

The frequency of computation of quality averages will depend on several factors. When samples are large, the number of samples included may be small. When samples are small, the number of samples included should be large. Also, new averages should be computed whenever it is suspected that a significant change has occurred in the quality of product submitted. It is wise to specify a minimum number of samples with the option of recomputation at any time that a change is suspected.

Example 11.4

Determine the estimated process average for the product in Example 11.3 from the first 10 lots inspected.

Using the second formula, we obtain

$$\text{process average} = \frac{100(p_1 + p_2 \cdots p_k)}{k}$$

Here $k = 10$ and $p_j = \dfrac{\text{number of defects in the } j\text{th sample}}{50}$

$$\text{process average} = \frac{100(\text{sum of all defectives})}{10 \times 50}$$

$$= \frac{100 \times 8}{500} = 1.6$$

The estimated process average is 1.6% defective.

ACCEPTANCE PROCEDURE FOR DEFECTS

An item is considered *defective* when the characteristic being measured does not satisfy the specifications for the characteristic. Sometimes specifications are given for a multitude of characteristics each with a different degree of importance. Obviously, in an automobile the specification for the power developed by engine would be considerably more important than the specification for number of stitches per inch for the seat cover. It is essential to classify the characteristics according to the importance of meeting the specifications.

MIL-STD-105D defines four classes of defects: critical, major, minor A, and minor B. A *critical defect* gives rise to an unsafe operating condition or prevents the functional performance of the unit. A *major defect* is not critical but is still capable of reducing materially the useful performance of the unit. *Minor defect A* has only a minor effect on the performance, and *minor defect B* has little or no effect on the performance.

Although MIL-STD-105D is initially stated in terms of defectives, it can be used for inspection based on defects as well. The only change necessary is to substitute "defects per 100 units" for "percent defective" as the measure of AQL. In the tables AQL values of higher than 10 are only interpreted as "defects per 100 units." Of course, it would be absurd to think of an AQL more than 100 "percent defective," but an AQL of more than 100 "defects per 100 units" can be feasible.

USING MIL-STD-105D FOR DEFECTS

In MIL-STD-105D the defects are classified according to the definitions in the preceding section and then acceptance criteria are applied separately for each class. Usually, the sample size, which is determined only by lot size and inspection level, is the same for all classes. Hence one sample can be used for acceptance procedure for all classes and the lot is rejected if it merits rejection for any one class. Because of differing importance of failures in different classes, the AQL is different. Critical characteristics are usually inspected fully (100%). Other classes would have increasing AQL according to decreasing importance of defects.

To illustrate, an imaginary item having 26 characteristics is considered. Nonconformance to specification in characteristics 1 through 4 gives rise to major defects, in characteristics 5 through 16 gives rise to minor defects A, and in the remaining characteristics gives rise to minor defects B. The item is supplied in boxes each containing 1440 units. The AQL is 1.0 for major defects, 2.5 for minor defects A, and 10 for minor defects B. When general inspection level II is used, the code letter is determined as K. For normal-inspection single sampling the acceptance criteria become: "In a sample of size 125,

Major defects: accept if ≤ 3, reject if ≥ 4.
Minor defects A: accept if ≤ 7, reject if ≥ 8.
Minor defects B: accept if ≤ 21, reject if ≥ 22."

If one of the samples, when inspected for all 26 characteristics, shows the following results: major defects, 5; minor defects A, 6; and minor defects B, 16, the lot is rejected on the basis of major defects even though it is acceptable on the basis of both minor defects A and B.

Example 11.5

A product submitted for inspection under the inspection plan described above has a process average quality of 1.0 for major defects, 3.0 for minor defects A, and 12.0 for minor defects B. What is the probability of acceptance of this product?

The product must be acceptable under all three criteria. Probability of acceptance can be calculated separately for each class of defects.

For major defects:

$$\begin{aligned} np' &= 125 \times \frac{1}{100} \\ &= 1.25 \\ \text{probability of acceptance} &= \Pr(x \le 3 \mid np' = 1.25) \\ &= 0.9615 \end{aligned}$$

For minor defects A:

$$\begin{aligned} np' &= 125 \times \frac{3}{100} \\ &= 3.75 \\ \text{probability of acceptance} &= \Pr(x \le 7 \mid np' = 3.75) \\ &= 0.9623 \end{aligned}$$

For minor defects B:

$$\begin{aligned} np' &= 125 \times \frac{12}{100} \\ &= 15.0 \\ \text{probability of acceptance} &= \Pr(x \le 21 \mid np' = 15) \\ &= 0.947 \end{aligned}$$

Normally, the three classes of defects can be assumed to be statistically independent of each other. Hence the probability that the product would be accepted is the product of probabilities of acceptance in each class:

$$\begin{aligned} \text{probability of acceptance of the lot} &= 0.9615 \times 0.9623 \times 0.947 \\ &= 0.876 \end{aligned}$$

TOTAL AMOUNT OF SAMPLING INSPECTION

In a single sampling plan a fixed sample is taken and inspected. For example, in the plan for code letter K, AQL = 1.0, and normal inspection described earlier, the sample size for single sampling is 125. This means that 125 items will be inspected from every lot. This is not the case with multiple sampling. For double sampling, the sample size is given as 80 for the first sample and 80 for the second sample. If a decision is reached on the first sample, either to accept or reject, there will be no second sample. In this case only 80 items will be inspected from that particular lot. If a decision is not reached on the first sample, the second sample would be needed and the number of items inspected would be 80 + 80 = 160. *Average sample number* (ASN) is the average number that may be expected to be inspected. Obviously, ASN would be a function of the incoming quality p.

Example 11.6

Compare the ASNs for single and double sampling plans for normal inspection, code letter K, and AQL 1.0 if the incoming quality is 2.0.

The plans are as follows:

	Sample Size	Ac	Re
Single sampling	125	3	4
Double sampling	80	1	4
	80	4	5

For single sampling:

$$\begin{aligned} \text{ASN} &= \text{sample size} \\ &= 125 \end{aligned}$$

In double sampling, for each sample:

$$\begin{aligned} np &= 80 \times 0.02 \\ &= 1.6 \end{aligned}$$

From Table A3.1 the probability of finding k defects is found as follows:

k	$P(k)$
0	0.202
1	0.323
2	0.258
3	0.138
4 or more	0.079

$$\begin{aligned} \text{probability of reaching a decision on the first sample} &= P(0) + P(1) + P(4 \text{ or more}) \\ &= 0.604 \\ \text{probability of taking a second sample} &= 1 - 0.604 = 0.396 \\ \text{ASN for double sampling} &= 80 + 0.396(80) \\ &= 111.68 \end{aligned}$$

It can be seen that there is a small saving in inspection when double sampling is used. The saving is even more significant for multiple sampling.

It is important not to confuse ASN with ATI, average total inspection, described in Chapter 10. ATI includes both sampling inspection and rectifying inspection of rejected lots. ASN is for sampling inspection only.

MIL-STD-105D does not provide for rectifying inspection. Most of the government agencies using these plans follow the principle of returning the rejected lots to the supplier. However, these plans are very widely used by industries in the private sector. Some of these industries may prefer to use rectifying inspection together with the plans from MIL-STD-105D. For their purposes, ATI, AOQ, and AOQL values can be computed for any plan using the methods described in Chapter 10.

ADMINISTRATIVE PROCEDURES FOR SUBMISSION AND RESUBMISSION OF LOTS

Whenever possible, lots should be submitted for inspection in static form, that is, completed product insofar as the particular inspection is concerned. The application of lot-by-lot plans to moving product is unwieldy and generally unsatisfactory. It is to be avoided if possible. Arrangements for the formation of inspection lots should include provision for identification and segregation of an inspection lot. Maintenance of lot identity will assure that acceptance or rejection is made on the collection of units from which the sample was drawn. Moreover, the selection of representative samples depends on the proper identification of the lot. Maintaining lot identity will prevent mixture of rejected product with other production not yet inspected, or inspected product awaiting shipment. The simplest way of maintaining lot identity is by physical segregation. This facilitates the disposition of the inspected product, whether the decision is one of acceptance or of rejection. In case acceptance is made, segregated material is most easily earmarked for shipment. In case rejection is made, rejected product can be screened for resubmittal, if such action is warranted or desired. Otherwise, the material can be marked for return to the supplier.

The quality of accepted product depends, to a great extent, on how inspection lots are formed. The average quality of accepted product will be better if inspection lots are formed without mixing product of different quality. In practice this is attained by forming *rational* lots. Rational lots consist of product from essentially the same origin. They may be formed, generally, by combining product produced only from the same batches of raw materials, components, or subassemblies; combining the output manufactured by the same production or assembly line with the same molds, dies, patterns, and so on; and combining product turned out during a unit of time, such as an hour, day, shift, or other period of time. All of this means that insofar as practicable, homogeneity of lots should be the objective in lot formation.

Rational lot formation may not be possible, or even advisable. Large lots require less proportional inspection. Also, the larger samples from large lots enable better representation of quality and provide less risk to the consumer. The possibility of rejection of a large lot creates a forceful incentive for the producer to submit only good-quality lots. The availability of inspection staff may play a large part in the determination of lot size. Frequently, a compromise will be necessary. When economic considerations necessitate the formation of large nonhomogeneous inspection lots, an effort must be made to separate the product in each inspection lot into homogeneous sublots. These sublots represent what would have been individual rational inspection lots if it had not been necessary to combine them into one large inspection lot in order to reduce the cost of inspection. It is then possible to select a sample in such a way as to represent more accurately the quality of the inspection lot. For example, suppose that an inspection lot has been formed from the combined output of three production shifts in the following proportions: shift 1: 50%; shift 2: 25%, shift 3: 25%. The sample would then be drawn from each of the sublots in the same proportion.

In practice it is advisable to limit the spread of inspection lot size to a relatively small range. Shifting from one lot size range to another results in a change in the inspection work load required. If this cannot be controlled, it may be preferable to set a definite inspection plan and stick with it regardless of the lot size.

The methods of drawing samples have been covered in Chapter 2. Either random or systematic sampling may be used, but samples should be chosen fairly in order to represent the lot truly. If sublots are formed, the subsample sizes should be proportional to the sublot sizes.

Occasionally, circumstances will arise that require taking special precautions to avoid bias in the taking of samples. Such occasions arise when obviously defective units appear in a lot or sublot presented for inspection. Usually, this occurs with visual inspection. When such units appear, they should be suitably identified but should not be removed until after a sample has been selected. Selection of a sample to determine acceptability of the lot and for quality average computation should proceed so that each unit in the lot, including obvious defectives, has an equal chance of being included in the sample. An impersonal and objective method of selection should be employed, such as the use of a table of random numbers.

Whenever resubmission of lots is permitted, the lot that has once been rejected should never be resubmitted "as is." If it were resubmitted, the only effect would be an increase in the probability of accepting a lot with inferior quality. It is definitely not in the interest of the consumer. MIL-STD-105D explicitly states that lots or batches that are found not acceptable on the first inspection can be resubmitted only after all units are examined by the supplier and defective units either repaired or replaced by good units.

PROBLEMS

11.1. Given the following information, select and extract the proper sampling plans from MIL-STD-105D.

Plan	Inspection Level	Type of Sampling	Degree	AQL	Lot Size
1	II	Single	Normal	0.15	55
2	II	Double	Tightened	1.0	400
3	I	Single	Reduced	150.0	4,000
4	III	Single	Tightened	0.40	200
5	II	Multiple	Normal	0.65	10,000
6	III	Multiple	Tightened	0.25	70
7	II	Single	Normal	400.0	1,500
8	II	Single	Tightened	6.5	30

11.2. John Smith Co. has a contract with you to deliver 60,000 assembly components at any time during the next three months. You have specified in the contract that the quality standard is an AQL of 4.0 in accordance with MIL-STD-105D. John Smith Co. is adjacent to your plant, so delivery costs are negligible. The end-item acceptance inspectors at John Smith Co. are pretty astute and know that the average outgoing quality will be about 8%. Election is made to submit material in lots of 500 rather than the entire 60,000 at one time. Why?

11.3. Single sampling is to be used with general inspection level II and AQL 0.65%. The lot size is 5000. If the product has an average quality 0.5%, what is the probability of acceptance under reduced inspection?

11.4. If the product quality in Problem 11.3 shifts to 1%, what is the probability that (after the first sample is inspected):

(a) Reduced inspection will be continued?

(b) The lot will be accepted and normal inspection reinstated?

(c) The lot will be rejected?

11.5. What fraction of the total product submitted for inspection is being inspected in plans 1, 3, and 4 in Problem 11.1?

11.6. In Problem 11.3, determine the probability of acceptance of a lot 0.8% defective under:

(a) Normal inspection.

(b) Tightened inspection.

11.7. In acceptance sampling using MIL-STD-105D, double sampling is used with code letter M and AQL 0.40.

(a) What are the acceptance criteria under normal, reduced, and tightened inspection?

(b) What is the most likely range of the lot size?

(c) What is the probability that a lot with quality 0.5 would be accepted under tightened inspection?

(d) What is the probability that a lot with quality 0.3 would be "not accepted" under reduced inspection?

11.8. MIL-STD-105D does not provide for rectifying inspection. However, a supplier to a government agency uses plans from MIL-STD-105D together with rectifying inspection to inspect finished product before it is shipped. The supplier uses double sampling, inspection level II, AQL 1.0, and lot size 5000. If the process average quality is 1.5%, what is AOQ?

11.9. A product is being inspected using single sampling, code letter J, and AQL 1.0. The numbers of defectives found in first 10 lots were 3, 1, 2, 2, 4, 0, 1, 1, 0, and 1. What decision to initiate/continue the normal/tightened/reduced inspection would be taken after each sample inspection?

11.10. The inspection of 10 consecutive lots of product using the plan in Problem 11.9, normal inspection, showed 0, 0, 0, 1, 0, 0, 1, 0, 1, and 0 defects, respectively. Does the product supplied qualify for reduced inspection?

11.11. From the following information, determine what action should be taken regarding degree of inspection. Assume that all other conditions of MIL-STD-105D have been satisfied and that only the following need be considered:

Case	Current Inspection Degree	Number Inspected	Quality Average	AQL	Action
I	Tightened	1,200	6.2	6.5	
II	Reduced	20,000	4.6	4.0	
III	Normal	12,000	0.04	0.15	
IV	Normal	9,500	1.9	1.5	
V	Reduced	500	0.87	0.65	
VI	Normal	180	4.02	1.5	
VII	Tightened	475	1.7	1.5	
VIII	Reduced	3,800	98.0	100.0	
IX	Normal	2,765	0.00	0.15	

11.12. The classification of defects in a circuit board includes 8 defects classified as major, 10 as minor A, and 9 as minor B. These boards are purchased in lots of 8000. Determine a double sampling plan for normal inspection under general inspection level II using AQL of 0.4 for major defects, 1.0 for minor A, and 1.5 for minor B defects.

11.13. If the circuit boards produced by a manufacturer have an average quality level of 0.5 for major defects, 0.8 for minor A, and 1.0 for minor B, what would be the probability that a lot inspected under the inspection plan in Problem 11.12 will be accepted?

11.14. A certain type of ammunition is liable to have 10 types of defects, of which 2 are major and the rest are minor A. The product is purchased in lots of 2000. Determine the normal and tightened plans for single sampling, general inspection level II, if the AQL for major defects is 0.4 and that for minor A is 1.0. If the process average quality is 0.8 and 2.5, respectively, what is the probability that tightened inspection will be initiated after first two samples? What is the probability that a lot will be accepted under tightened inspection?

Note: For Problems 11.15 through 11.18, assume that rectifying inspection is in effect.

11.15. Single sampling is used with inspection level S-4, lot size 12,000, and AQL 1.5. Determine the AOQL and ASN values for normal and tightened inspection.

11.16. Determine the AOQL for normal inspection for plan in Problem 11.14. Comment on the propriety of using this plan.

11.17. Determine the ASN and ATI for the plan in Problem 11.12. Assume that the process average equals AQL.

11.18. Determine the AOQL and ASN for the plan in Problem 11.13. Assume that the process average is 80.

11.19. Determine the multiple sampling normal inspection plan, general inspection level I, for lots of size 40,000 and AQL = 1.0. What is the ASN for this plan if the process average is 2.0?

twelve

OTHER ACCEPTANCE PROCEDURES

The choice of a sampling plan is effectively a decision to adopt an *operating characteric curve*. The tables of acceptance sampling plans are designed to conform to a specific point on the OC curve and to approximate the curve as closely as possible elsewhere. There are three important points on any OC curve and separate tables can be generated to emphasize each of these points.

> *Point 1:* $q = q_1$, $P(A) = 1 - \alpha$ (α *is usually* 0.05). The quality q_1 may be called an *acceptable quality level*. Procedures emphasizing this point are said to be based on AQL.
>
> *Point 2:* $q = q_2$, $P(A) = 0.5$. The quality q_2 may be called an *indifference quality level*. Procedures emphasizing this point are said to be based on indifference quality.
>
> *Point 3:* $q = q_3$, $P(A) = 0.1$. Here the value of the probability of type II error is specified as exactly 10%. The quality q_3 may be called *lot tolerance percent defective*. Procedures emphasizing this point are said to be based on LTPD.

In each type of procedure the tables may be designed either to limit the worst quality in the accepted product, AOQL, or the total cost of inspection indicated by ATI. MIL-STD-105D procedures are based on AQL. A separate chapter was devoted to these procedures because of its almost universal acceptance. The instruction for administration of the military standard make it flexible enough to fit almost any situation where sampling inspection by attributes is indicated. Other types of plans are described in this chapter. The treatment of each type of acceptance procedure is brief. The discussion of each is not intended to be complete as to its use or development. Rather, an overall view of these procedures is provided so that these may be available for application in special situations logically warranting such applications.

Procedures based on indifference quality and LTPD were developed by two industrial giants: first, by Philips Gloelampenverke in Holland and second, by American Telephone and Telegraph in the United States. *Sequential sampling* provides procedures with variable sample sizes, and *demerit sampling* provides simplified procedures applicable when multiple characteristics are to be inspected at the same time.

INDIFFERENCE QUALITY ACCEPTANCE PROCEDURES

The indifference quality point, point 2, on the OC curve exhibits exactly equal probabilities of acceptance and rejection. The risk can be said to be split evenly between the producer and the consumer.

The quality standard of MIL-STD-105D is an AQL which is, roughly, at the 0.95 probability of acceptance. Dodge–Romig has two basic quality standards: the LTPD at $\beta = 0.10 =$ consumer's risk, and the AOQL. Tables which specify standards that split the risks has also been designed. Representative of the split risk concept is the *Philips standard sampling system*.[1] In this system the standard quality or *point of control* corresponds to point 2 in Figure 12.1. Table 12.1 shows the table used by the Philips company in Holland. An appreciable part of the system's value is in its compactness and simplicity. Single sampling is used for all lots of size 1000 or less, double sampling for larger lots. With double sampling the second sample is twice the size of the first. Since the risks are split, there is no such thing as tightened inspection. The OC curves of these plans all pass roughly through the point of control at $P_\alpha = 0.50$. As with all plans, those with larger sample size and rejection number combinations give better operating characteristic curves.

Another interesting feature of Table 12.1 is the inverse relationship between specified quality and sample size. An increase in specified quality is associated with a decrease in sample size. This would make sense to the practical inspector on the grounds that the poorer the quality that can be tolerated, the less attention should be devoted to it. It also makes sense viewed from economic considerations. If a poorer quality level can be tolerated, it follows that more error in sample inference can be tolerated. This justifies smaller samples.

[1] H. C. Hamaker, J. J. M. Jaudin Chabot, and F. G. Willemze, "The Practical Application of Sampling Inspection Plans and Tables," *Philips Technical Review*, Vol. 11 (June 1950), pp. 362–370.

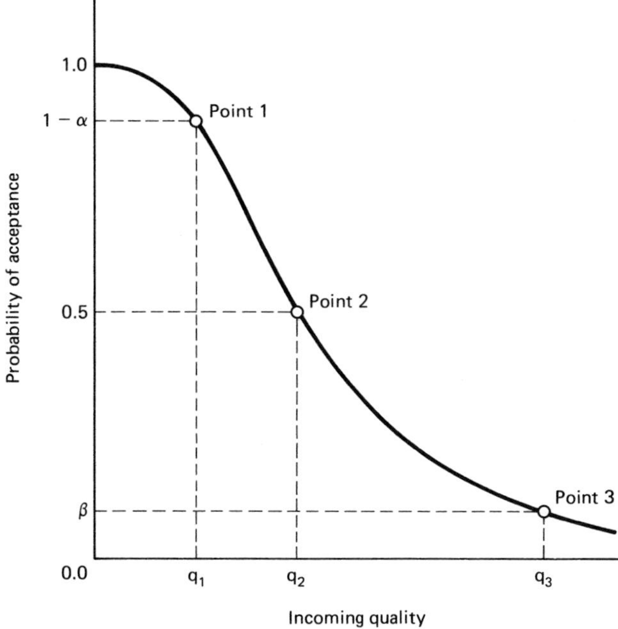

Figure 12.1 Important points on an OC curve.

If Poisson probabilities may be assumed applicable, a simple formula[2] may be used for designing families of plans for specified quality levels with P_α of standard quality equal to 0.50. The formula is

$$n = \frac{c + 0.67}{P'_{0.50}}$$

Assume a standard quality of $P'_{0.50}$ equal to 0.01 (i.e., 1%) and an acceptance number of zero ($c = 0$). The formula yields

$$n = \frac{0 + 0.67}{0.01} = 67$$

By varying c in the formula a complete family of plans may be constructed (Table 12.2).

Example 12.1

Determine an indifference quality sampling plan for lots of 1000 and indifference quality 2% (a) using Philips standard tables, and (b) using the simple formula.

[2] From E. L. Grant and R. S. Leavenworth, *Statistical Quality Control*, 5th ed. (New York: McGraw-Hill Book Company, 1980). The authors give credit for this relationship to G. A. Campbell, writing in the *Bell System Technical Journal* in 1923.

TABLE 12.1 Philips Standard Sampling System*

Lot Size \ Point of Control		0.25%		0.5%		1%		2%		3%		5%		7%		10%	
		n	c	n	c	n	c	n	c	n	c	n	c	n	c	n	c
Single sampling	20–50	A		A		A		30	0	20	0	13	0	10	0	7	0
	51–100	A		A		60	0	30	0	20	0	13	0	10	0	7	0
	101–200	A		100	0	60	0	35	0	55	1	35	1	25	1	17	1
	201–500	175	0	100	0	135	1	75	1	55	1	35	1	40	2	25	2
	501–1,000	225	0	225	1	150	1	85	1	85	2	55	2	55	3	35	3

Lot Size		0.25%			0.5%			1%			2%			3%			5%			7%			10%		
		n_1	c_1	c_2	n_1	c_1	c_2	n_1	c_1	c_2	n_1	c_1	c_2	n_1	c_1	c_2	n_1	c_1	c_2	n_1	c_1	c_2	n_1	c_1	c_2
Double sampling	1,001–2,000	330	0	1	150	0	1	110	0	2	55	0	2	45	0	3	25	0	3	30	1	5	22	1	5
	2,001–5,000	425	0	2	200	0	2	135	0	3	70	0	3	70	1	5	45	1	5	55	2	10	40	2	10
	5,001–10,000	525	0	3	260	0	3	220	1	5	110	1	5	125	2	10	75	2	10	75	3	15	55	3	15
	10,000–20,000	875	1	5	440	1	5	380	2	10	190	2	10	180	3	15	110	3	15	100	4	20	70	4	20
	20,000–50,000	1,500	2	10	750	2	10	540	3	15	270	3	15	240	4	20	140	4	20	120	5	25	85	5	25
	50,000–100,000	2,200	3	15	1,100	3	15	700	4	20	390	4	20	290	5	25	175	5	25	145	6	30	105	6	30

* *A* means inspect entire lot. Second sample $n_2 = 2n_1$.

Source: H. C. Hamaker, J. J. M. Jandin Chabot, and F. G. Willemze, "The Practical Application of Sampling Inspection Plans and Tables," *Philips Technical Review*, Vol. II (June 1950), pp. 362–370. Reprinted with permission.

TABLE 12.2 Family of Plans

c	n	c	n	c	n
0	67	4	467	8	867
1	167	5	567	9	967
2	267	6	667	10	1,067
3	367	7	767	11	1,167

(a) From Table 12.1 for lot size 1000 and IQL 2%, the sampling plan is $n = 85$, $c = 1$.

(b) $p'_{0.50} = 0.02$ and $c = 1$ [keeping the same acceptance number as in part (a)]:

$$n = \frac{c + 0.67}{p'_{0.50}}$$

$$= \frac{1.67}{0.02} = 83.5$$

$$= 84 \quad \text{after rounding}$$

This example shows the closeness of the approximation in using the simple formula.

DODGE–ROMIG TABLES

H. F. Dodge and H. G. Romig developed acceptance sampling procedures as well as complete sets of tables of sampling plans in the early 1920s. Although originally intended for internal use by the Bell Telephone System,[3] these tables were released for use by general public in the form of a book[4] published in 1944. These tables are based on LTPD, or point 3, on the OC curve. The tables refer to the quality represented by LTPD as P_t. The book contains four sets of tables.

1. Single sampling lot tolerance tables
2. Double sampling lot tolerance tables
3. Single sampling AOQL tables
4. Double sampling AOQL tables

The tables do not provide for multiple sampling. The first two sets include

[3] Before 1983, almost all regional telephone companies in the United States were subsidiaries of the giant corporation American Telephone and Telegraph Company. The network formed by these companies was usually referred to as the "Bell Telephone System" named after the inventor of the telephone, A. G. Bell.

[4] H. F. Dodge and H. G. Romig, *Sampling Inspection Tables—Single and Double Sampling* (New York: John Wiley & Sons, Inc., first edition 1944, second edition 1959).

one table each for eight values of P_t. These are

0.5%, 1.0%, 2.0%, 3.0%, 4.0%, 5.0%, 7.0%, and 10.0%

The next two sets include one table each for 13 values of AOQL. These are

0.1%, 0.25%, 0.5%, 0.75%, 1.0%, 1.5%, 2.0%, 2.5%, 3.0%, 4.0%, 5.0%, 7.0%, and 10.0%

The two types of tables are complementary in the sense that the lot tolerance tables give the AOQL for each plan in the table, and vice versa. The sampling plans in Dodge–Romig tables attempt to minimize the *average total inspection* (ATI) or the *average fraction inspected* (AFI) in each lot. The tables assume 100% inspection of rejected lots but do not mandate this procedure.

One example from each of the four sets is included in the Appendix as:

Table A17.1	Single Sampling Lot Tolerance Table, P_t = 5.0%
Table A17.2	Double Sampling Lot Tolerance Table, P_t = 5.0%
Table A17.3	Single Sampling AOQL Table, AOQL = 2.0%
Table A17.4	Double Sampling AOQL Table, AOQL = 2.0%

Use of Dodge–Romig Tables

Two examples are used to illustrate the use of Dodge–Romig tables. In all these tables, the rows are indicators of lot size and there are six columns indicating estimated process averages. Both lot sizes and estimates of process averages are expressed as ranges. Each intersection of row and column gives the specific sampling plan as well as the other base index (i.e., lot tolerance tables give AOQL values and AOQL tables give P_t).

Example 12.2

Dodge–Romig single sampling lot tolerance plan with P_t = 5.0% is being used. The lot size is 750 and the estimated process average is 1.3%. What are the criteria for acceptance? If the lot actually submitted has a quality 3.0%, what is the probability of accepting the lot?

The single sampling lot tolerance table with P_t = 5.0 is Table A17.1. The lot size 750 is in the range 601–800 and the estimated process average is in the range 1.01–1.50. The intersection of row 601–800 and column 1.01–1.50 gives the sampling plan as

n	c	AOQL
130	3	1.2

The lot would be accepted if 3 or fewer defectives are found in a sample of 130 items. The AOQL for this plan would be 1.2%.

When the product is 3% defective, the average number of defectives in the sample, or np', is 130 × 0.03, or 3.9. Using Table A3.1 for cumulative Poisson distribution, the probability of finding 3 or fewer defectives is 0.453.

Example 12.3

For the product described in Example 12.2, what are the criteria for acceptance if a 2% AOQL double sampling plan is to be used?

The double sampling AOQL table AOQL = 2.0% is Table A17.4. The lot size 750 is in the range 601–800 and the estimated process average is in the range 1.21–1.60. The intersection of row 601–800 and column 1.21–1.60 gives the sampling plan as

Trial 1		Trial 2			
n_1	c_1	n_2	$n_1 + n_2$	c_2	P_t
38	0	82	120	4	7.3

In double sampling plans in Dodge–Romig tables, the number c_2 represents the cumulative total of defectives. It is interesting to compare plans in Examples 12.2 and 12.3. In Example 12.2 the plan indicates acceptance only if 3 or fewer defectives in 130 items. In Example 12.3, however, after both samples 4 defectives are permitted in 120 items. The plan in Example 12.3 is a less exacting plan. This is to be expected as both AOQL (2.0 against 1.2) and P_t (7.3 against 5.0) are higher.

ESTIMATING PROCESS AVERAGE

Dodge–Romig sampling plans are designed to be the most appropriate plans when incoming product quality is within some stated limits. The plans will need minimum ATI when based on the correct range of process average quality. Hence it becomes very important to obtain a good estimate of process average quality before selecting a sampling plan.

Manufacturing processes that are in operation for a long time usually do not present any problems in this respect. Historical data usually provide an excellent basis for estimating process average quality. For newer processes there are two possible ways of obtaining good estimates:

1. A fraction-defective control chart is maintained over a sampling base period of 20–30 lots. If this chart indicates the process to be in control, the centerline of the chart would indicate the process average quality. This estimate can be used as a basis for the determination of Dodge–Romig sampling plans. (The chart itself may be continued as a process monitoring chart.) This alternative can be used only by the manufac-

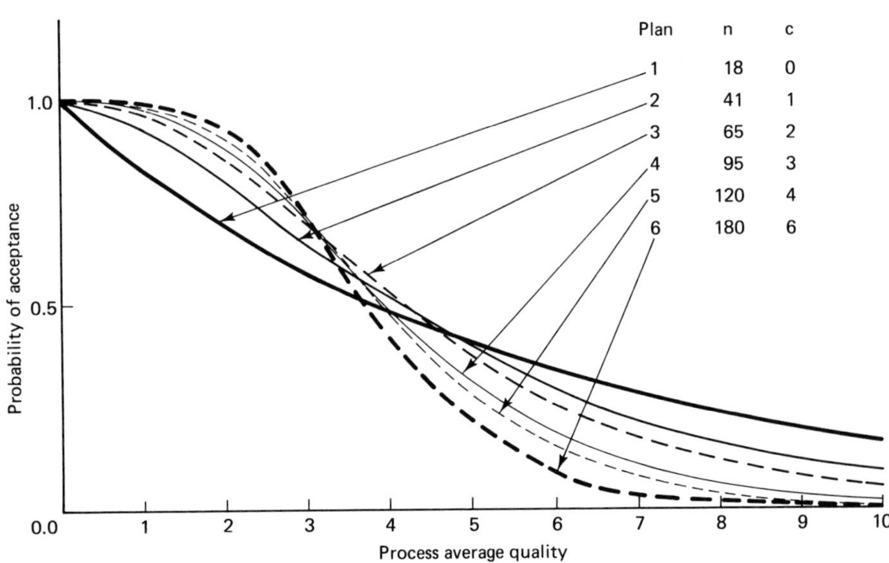

Figure 12.2 Effect of process average quality assumption on the OC curves of sampling plans from Dodge-Romig tables.

turer or a consumer having access to the manufacturer's production information.

2. The second alternative can be used by a consumer who does not know (or does not have faith in) the supplier. In this case a preliminary assumption of process average quality is used to determine a trial sampling plan. The AQL provides a good starting point. This trial plan is used for a predetermined number of lots. The results from these sample inspections give a better estimate of the process average quality. In this case care must be taken to use the data from the first samples only. In other words, data from second samples, resubmissions, and rectifying inspection are not included in the computation of process average.

The effect of the process average quality assumption on the OC curve of the plan selected from Dodge–Romig tables is shown in Figure 12.2.

SEQUENTIAL ACCEPTANCE PROCEDURES

In single sampling the sample size is fixed definitely by the plan. In double sampling the number of units inspected is determined in part by the plan and in part by the results of the sampling process. The minimum number of sample units possible in double sampling is n_1, but the sampling results determine whether additional sampling units need be inspected. Sequential sampling takes maximum advantage of the latter by basing the acceptance, rejection, or continue-sampling decisions completely on the results of the sampling process. The sequential decision-making process may be presented graphically by linear equations for the acceptance and rejection lines with the continue-inspection zone between these two lines (see Figure 12.3a). In operation, as each unit is inspected, one of the three decisions is made. Theoretically, inspection could go on indefinitely, so it is common practice to truncate the sampling process by fixing a limiting value where the lot is either accepted or rejected. This truncation results in a plan similar to multiple sampling plans. The similarity is shown by comparison of a sequential plan and a multiple sampling plan that have the same p_1 and p_2 values (see Figure 12.3d and e).

The concept of sequential decision making after each item being inspected is based on the *sequential probability ratio test* (SPRT) developed by Abraham Wald.[5] A simplified version of the logic behind SPRT is presented here; more exact development can be found in the book by Wald.

Acceptance sampling is basically a test of the hypothesis

$$H_0\colon p = p_1 \text{ or good quality}$$

against an alternative

$$H_1\colon p = p_2 \text{ or poor quality}$$

If ϕ is the event of having found d defectives after n items have been examined, the conditional probabilities of ϕ are

$$\Pr(\phi \mid H_0) = p_1^d(1 - p_1)^{n-d} = x$$

$$\Pr(\phi \mid H_1) = p_2^d(1 - p_2)^{n-d} = y$$

If the quality of the product offered is p_1, the lot should be accepted. For an acceptable lot,

$$x \geq 1 - \alpha$$

$$y \leq \beta$$

These can be combined as a single condition:

$$\text{ratio } \frac{x}{y} \geq \frac{1 - \alpha}{\beta}$$

Similarly, for an unacceptable lot

$$x \leq \alpha$$

$$y \geq 1 - \beta$$

[5] Abraham Wald, *Sequential Analysis* (New York: John Wiley & Sons, Inc., 1947).

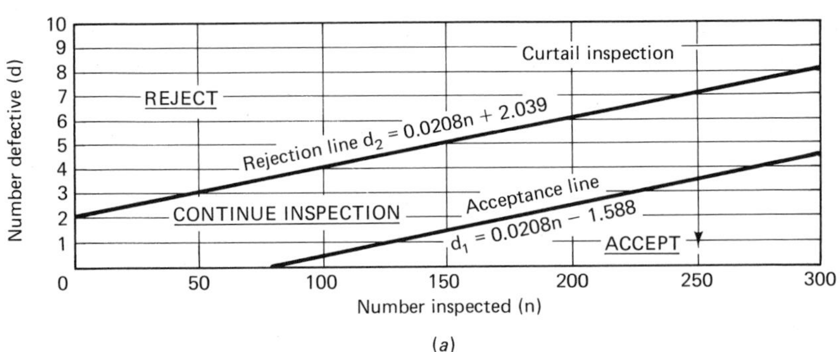

(a)

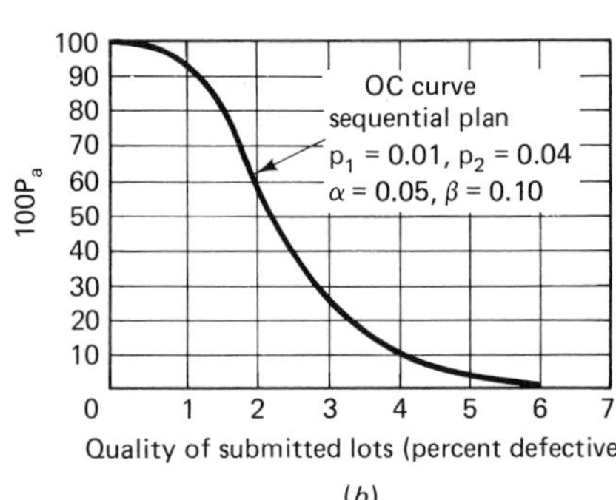

(b)

Truncated sequential plan
AQL = 1.0%

Sample size	Acceptance number	Rejection number
0-50	*	3
51-75	*	4
76-100	0	4
101-125	0	5
126-150	1	5
151-175	1	6
176-200	2	6
201-225	2	7
250	6	7

(d)

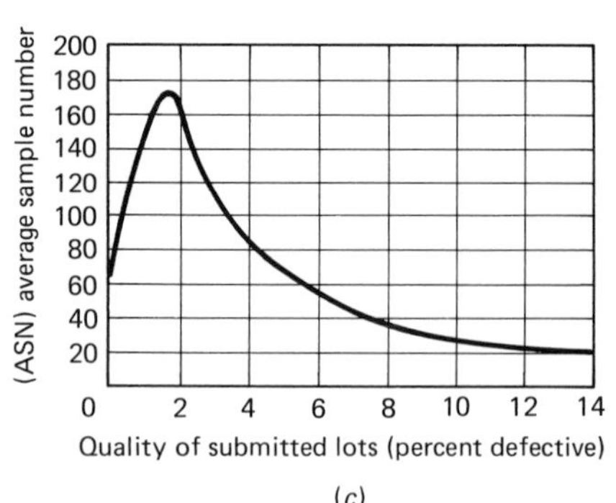

(c)

MIL-STD-105D multiple sampling
plan code letter L. AQL = 1.0%

Sample size	Acceptance number	Rejection number
50	*	4
100	1	5
150	2	6
200	3	7
250	5	8
300	7	9
350	9	10

(e)

Figure 12.3 (a) Graphic representation of sequential plan example; (b) operating characteristic of the plan; (c) ASN curve for the plan; (d) numerical sample range expression of the plan; (e) matched OC curve multiple plan from MIL-STD-105D.

These can also be combined in the same manner as

$$\text{ratio } \frac{x}{y} \leq \frac{\alpha}{1 - \beta}$$

The ratio x/y is called the *probability ratio*:

$$\frac{x}{y} = \left(\frac{p_1}{p_2}\right)^d \left(\frac{1 - p_1}{1 - p_2}\right)^{n-d}$$

The analysis of a lot is obtained by plotting this ratio after inspection of each item. As soon as the ratio exceeds the acceptance constant $(1 - \alpha)/\beta$, the lot is accepted. If the ratio becomes smaller than the rejection constant $\alpha/(1 - \beta)$, however, the lot is rejected.

For practical use the probability ratio test is simplified algebraically so that the plotting is done on a graph of d versus n, avoiding computation of the actual probability ratio. The acceptance and rejection constants become two parallel lines, as seen in Figure 12.3a.

Example 12.4

For the design of sequential sampling plans it is necessary to specify p_1, p_2, α, and β. For this example assume that the specifications are $p_1 = 0.01, p_2 = 0.04, \alpha = 0.05 (P\alpha = 0.95)$, and $\beta = 0.10$. The two linear equations, using the conventional notation are:

$$\text{Rejection line:} \quad d_2 = sn + h_2$$

$$\text{Acceptance line:} \quad d_1 = sn - h_1$$

Without going into the derivation, the formulas necessary for finding the parameters of s, h_1, and h_2 so that these linear equations may be solved for various n are as follows:

$$h_1 = \frac{b}{g_1 + g_2}$$

$$h_2 = \frac{a}{g_1 + g_2}$$

$$s = \frac{g_2}{g_1 + g_2}$$

where $g_1 = \log \dfrac{p_2}{p_1}$

$$g_2 = \log \frac{1 - p_1}{1 - p_2}$$

$$a = \log \frac{1 - \beta}{\alpha}$$

$$b = \log \frac{1 - \alpha}{\beta}$$

Note: Logarithms in these expressions are "base 10" logarithms.

The solution for the parameters of s, h_1, and h_2 proceeds as follows:

$$g_1 = \log \frac{0.04}{0.01} = \log 4 = 0.6021$$

$$g_2 = \log \frac{0.99}{0.96} = 0.0128$$

$$a = \log \frac{0.90}{0.05} = 1.2553$$

$$b = \log \frac{0.95}{0.10} = 0.9777$$

$$h_1 = \frac{0.9777}{0.6149} = 1.588$$

$$h_2 = \frac{1.2553}{0.6149} = 2.039$$

$$s = \frac{0.0128}{0.6149} = 0.0208$$

The rejection line is set at

$$d_2 = 0.0208n + 2.039$$

and the acceptance line at

$$d_1 = 0.0208n - 1.588$$

An operating characteristic curve for this plan can be constructed from three points. Two points have already been provided by the design, that is,

$$p_1 = 0.01, \quad p_2 = 0.04, \quad \alpha = 0.05, \quad \text{and} \quad \beta = 0.10$$

When the lot fraction defective is equal to s, the probability of acceptance of a lot of this quality is $h_2/(h_1 + h_2)$. Figure 12.3b shows the OC curve for this plan constructed from these three points.

As with all plans where multiple or sequential sampling is involved, the average sample number inspected is of importance. The ASN curve of a sequential plan may be constructed from the relationships shown in Table 12.3.[6]

The curve for the example sequential plan drawn from four points is shown by Figure 12.3c. Figure 12.3d and e compare the sampling plans of Example 12.4 and the multiple plan for code letter L of MIL-STD-105D for AQL = 1.0. These two plans have OC curves that are fairly well matched. The similarity between the two plans is immediately evident. The sequential plan has been arbitrarily truncated at 250; the multiple plan at 350. Actually,

[6] For a development of these relations, see Acheson J. Duncan, *Quality Control and Industrial Statistics* (Homewood, Ill.: Richard D. Irwin, Inc., 1955).

TABLE 12.3 **Construction of the Sequential Plan**

When p' Is Equal to:	The Average Sample Number ASN Is:
0	$\dfrac{h_1}{s}$
p_1	$\dfrac{(1 - \alpha)h_1 - ah_2}{s - p_1}$
s	$\dfrac{h_1h_2}{s(1 - s)}$
p_2	$\dfrac{(1 - \beta)h_2 - \beta h_1}{p_2 - s}$
1	$\dfrac{h_2}{1 - s}$

the sequential plan should proceed by units instead of groups of units as shown by Figure 12.3d. However, the decision values for acceptance and rejection remain essentially the same for number inspected within the ranges shown. Probably, in the multiple plan, certain concessions were made, resulting in the slight differences in sample sizes and acceptance numbers. For example, at $n = 100$, the multiple plan acceptance and rejection numbers of 1 and 5, respectively, could be obtained by setting the limiting values at the halfway point between numbers. Thus the acceptance line value at $n = 100$ is >0.5 and <1. The rejection line value at $n = 100$ is >4 and <5.

DEMERIT SAMPLING[7]

The basis of *demerit sampling* is the combination of many differing types and categories of defects into a single measure of demerit. This measure of demerit can be used to develop acceptance sampling plans. Such plans may be of value where complex assemblies are purchased and where a single measure of acceptance or rejection is desired. Recall that in the normal use of attributes sampling, characteristics are classified according to the seriousness of a defect. Such classifications may result in the formation of several categories with different acceptable quality levels for each category. Of course, this requires keeping records and control by category. The assignments of demerits to each category eliminates much of the record keeping and provides *one* measure of quality performance.

The development of a satisfactory acceptable quality level for a number of demerits depends to a great extent on the quality history of the particular

[7] Demerit sampling is based on the demerit rating system developed by H. F. Dodge and M. N. Torrey and described earlier in Chapter 7.

TABLE 12.4 Quality History

Defect Class	Total Defects	Defects/Unit	Demerits/Unit	Variance/Unit
A	113	0.00113	0.113	11.3
B	280	0.0028	0.140	7.0
C	5,100	0.051	0.510	5.1
D	43,000	0.430	0.43	0.43
			1.193 $= U_s$	23.83 $= C_s$

item for which a plan is being designed. In the numerical example used to illustrate the acceptance procedures with demerit sampling, it is assumed that sufficient historical data are available.

Example 12.5

A complex item being procured on a regular basis is subject to four types of defects and the weights (assigned according to the prospective effect of the defects in the use of the product) are 100 for defects of type A, 50 for type B, 10 for type C, and 1 for type D. The past history of inspection of 100,000 items revealed the quality history shown in Table 12.4.

The demerit measure U_s is defined as

$$U_s = 100U_A + 50U_B + 10U_C + U_D$$

and the standard variance C_s is defined as

$$C_s = (100)^2U_A + (50)^2U_B + (10)^2U_C + U_D$$

Thus it is seen that the totals of 1.193 and 23.93 above equal U_s and C_s, respectively.

The allowable number of demerits per sample of size n is set at

$$nU_s + 3\sqrt{nC_s}$$

and action limits are set at

$$nU_s + 4\sqrt{nC_s}$$

nU_s is the expression for acceptable demerit quality level for the *sample* of size n. $\sqrt{nC_s}$ is the expression for the demerit standard deviation of the *sample* of size n.

Assume further that lots of size 50 are to be submitted for inspection. From each lot a sample of 10 will be selected. If the number of demerits in the sample exceeds the *allowable* number of demerits per sample, the lot will be rejected. If the number of demerits in the sample exceeds the *action* number, the lot will be rejected and, in addition, tightened inspection will be instituted. Figure 12.4 shows this sampling plan expressed in the form of a control chart.

Sampling inspection tables for demerit acceptance inspection have been developed for use with particular items. An example of such a table is given by Table 12.5. Note that this table provides for acceptance controls on a number of like defects. It also specifies tighter allowable and action demerit

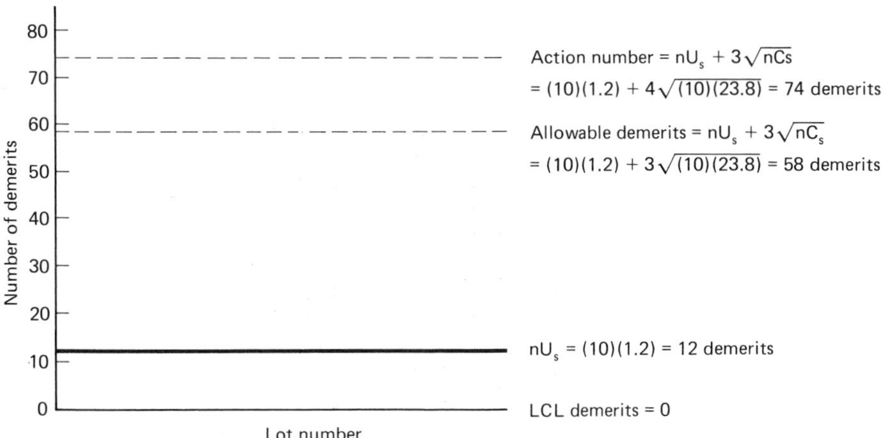

Figure 12.4 Graphic expression of sampling plan $N = 50$, $n = 10$, acceptable number of demerits = 58.

numbers for resubmitted lots. The former ensures against spotty occurrences of like defects, whereas the latter is analogous to using the tightened inspection in MIL-STD-105D for resubmitted lots.

Instead of setting an arbitrary sample size and the allowable number of demerits at three standard deviations, as is done above, it is possible to derive an acceptance number and sample size using the normal distribution. For example, assume that an acceptance agency is willing to take a 5% risk that lots having more than 4 demerits per unit will be accepted. Assuming that U_s and C_s of the example above apply, what sample size is necessary?

Procedure. Let k = normal deviate at significance level of 0.05, and U = demerits/unit at significance level = 4. The normal deviate for demerits per sample is

$$k = \frac{nU - nU_s}{\sqrt{nC_s}}$$

Solving for n yields

$$n = \frac{C_s k^2}{U - U_s}$$

Substituting for U_s and C_s gives us

$$n = \frac{(23.8)(1.645)^2}{4 - 1.2} = 23$$

The sampling plan now becomes $n = 23$, accept on 92 demerits in a sample of 23. For reducing and tightening inspection, the principles used in MIL-STD-105D may be followed.

TABLE 12.5 Quality Assurance Inspection Procedure

Lot Sizes				Nonconformance Criteria											
Level of Inspection				New Production Material						Reacceptance Material					
				Like Defects				Grouped Defects		Like Defects				Grouped Defects	
				Allowable Like Defects in Sample						Allowable Like Defects in Sample					
I Reduced	II Normal	III Tightened	Sample Size	A	B	(C)	(D)	Allowable Demerits in Sample	Action Limit (Demerits)	A	B	(C)	(D)	Allowable Demerits in Sample	Action Limit (Demerits)
1*	1*	1*	1	0	0	0	1	9	12	0	0	0	1	11	15
2*	2*	2*	2	0	0	0	2	13	17	0	0	1	2	16	21
3–5*	3*	3*	3	0	0	0	3	16	21	0	0	1	3	20	26
6–12†	4*	4*	4	0	0	1	4	19	24	0	0	1	4	24	31
13–35	5–14†	5*	5	0	0	1	4	21	28	0	0	1	5	27	35
36–50	15–18	6*	6	0	0	1	4	24	30	0	0	2	5	30	38
51–70	19–24	7*	7	0	0	1	4	26	33	0	0	2	5	33	42
71–90	25–32	8*	8	0	0	1	4	28	36	0	0	2	5	36	45
91–110	33–40	9–10†	9	0	0	1	4	30	38	0	0	2	5	38	48

111–140	41–50	11–12†	10	0	0	1	4	32	40	0	0	2	5	41	51
141–200	51–70	13–18	12	0	0	2	4	35	45	0	0	3	5	46	57
201–270	71–100	19–24	14	0	0	2	4	39	49	0	0	3	5	50	63
271–350	101–130	25–32	16	0	0	2	4	42	53	0	0	3	6	55	68
351–450	131–160	33–40	18	0	0	2	4	45	57	0	0	4	6	59	73
451–610	161–220	41–55	21	0	1	3	4	50	62	0	1	4	7	65	80
611–850	221–310	56–75	25	0	1	3	5	56	69	0	1	5	8	73	89
851–1,250	311–450	76–110	30	0	1	3	5	62	77	0	1	5	9	82	100
1,251–1,800	451–640	111–160	36	0	1	4	6	70	86	0	1	6	10	93	112
1,801–2,450	641–880	161–220	42	1	1	4	7	78	95	1	1	7	11	103	124
2,451–3,300	881–1,200	221–300	49	1	1	5	8	86	105	1	1	8	13	114	137
3,301–4,350	1,201–1,550	301–390	56	1	1	5	8	94	114	1	1	8	14	125	150
4,351–5,650	1,551–2,000	391–510	64	1	1	6	9	103	125	1	1	9	16	138	164
5,651–7,200	2,001–2,500	511–640	72	1	2	6	10	112	135	1	2	10	17	150	178
7,201–9,100	2,501–3,250	641–820	81	1	2	7	11	121	146	1	2	11	19	163	193
9,101–11,250	3,251–4,050	821–1,010	90	1	2	7	12	131	156	1	2	12	20	176	207
11,251–14,000	4,051–5,000	1,011–1,250	100	1	2	8	13	141	168	1	2	13	22	190	223
14,001–20,000	5,001–7,300	1,251–1,830	121	1	2	9	15	161	191	1	2	15	25	219	255

* Inspect all units.

† Minimum lot size shall be 12, unless otherwise authorized.

AUDIT SAMPLING FOR QUALITY ASSURANCE

The objective of audit sampling by the consumer is to assure that the producer's process quality and acceptance control systems are operating effectively. Any effective auditing system requires that some audit sampling be performed. Such sampling for audit purposes is usually done by attributes. Either the inspection system is good or it is not good; gauge control is good or it is not good; materials control is good or it is not good; inspection is according to procedure or it is not according to procedure; and so on.

In this type of acceptance control the consumer usually must make a positive inference of conformance or nonconformance on the basis of a comparatively small sample. Of course, large samples can be selected. However, it is assumed that sufficient evidence of the supplier's ability to produce a quality product was obtained before the decision to use audit sampling was put into effect. Such evidence would be a long history of good quality, efficient processing equipment, good control and inspection procedures adequately spelled out, and so on. In determining whether the system is good or not good, the consumer must audit all the components of the system. In many cases the components of the quality control system will have units of output by which particular components can be measured quantitatively. For example, the producer maintains quality average records at the various stations of inspection. Also, the producer might (and should) maintain records of gauge inspections. Up-to-date maintenance of drawings is another example of a system component that can be measured quantitatively. Errors of excluding new changes and obsoleting the old can be measured on a numerical scale.

In audit sampling the problem becomes one of making a decision whether the sample selected for audit agrees with a standard or the producer's findings or whether it does not. Of course, since sampling is involved, any inference made must be at some chosen level of significance.

Two types of significance tests may be involved in audit sampling. One type is where the consumer desires to determine whether the producer's quality is up to standard or not. The other type is where the consumer desires to determine how closely his sampling results agree with the results of the producer. Any significance level desired may be chosen for making the decisions, in effect, to accept or reject the system component being measured. Of course, economic considerations should determine the level to use, but in the absence of definitive cost elements, a significance level of 5% is recommended. This is setting a fairly high risk of making a rejection decision when one should not be made. It is justified, however, when one considers the continual risks of acceptance assumed by the consumer when he is not performing inspection for acceptance himself.

Significance tests are covered in detail in Chapter 2.

PROBLEMS

12.1. Determine a Philips standard sampling plan for a lot size of 750 and point of control 3%. What is the probability that a 5% defective lot would be accepted under this plan?

12.2. **(a)** Determine a Philips standard sampling plan for a lot size of 1600 and indifference quality 2%.

(b) Determine a double sampling plan for normal inspection, general inspection level II for a lot size of 1600 and AQL 0.65%.

(c) Compare the ASN for the two plans if the incoming quality is (i) 0.3%, (ii) 0.65%, and (iii) 2%.

12.3. Plot the OC curves for the two plans in Problem 12.2.

12.4. A consumer is concerned about the possibility of accepting product with 5% or more defectives. Two possible plans are suggested: (1) a Philips standard plan with point of control 3%, and (2) a Dodge–Romig single sampling 2% AOQL plan. The lot size is 800 and the assumed process average is 1%. Which of the two plans would provide better protection to the consumer?

12.5. Process average is estimated as 0.95% and lot size is 900. Determine a 5% LTPD Dodge–Romig single sampling plan. What fraction of incoming product is inspected under sampling inspection? If the incoming product quality is actually 1%, what is the outgoing quality?

12.6. Determine the 2% AOQL Dodge–Romig double sampling plan for a lot size of 900 and an estimated process average of 0.95%. If the incoming product quality is actually 1%, what is the outgoing quality? What is the ASN? What is AFI?

12.7. An item is purchased in lots of 5000. For consumer's risk of 10% at lot tolerance 5%, the Dodge–Romig tables give the following alternative plans depending on the estimated process average:

(a) $n = 105, c = 2$
(b) $n = 160, c = 4$
(c) $n = 235, c = 7$

Compare the average total inspection and outgoing quality from these three plans if the incoming product is actually 0.4% defective.

12.8. A government agency purchases large quantities of a small item from a manufacturer. The lot size is 1200. When the item is received, the agency uses a single sampling plan to inspect the product. This plan is obtained from MIL-STD-105D based on AQL 0.65 and general inspection level II. When the item is manufactured, it is subjected to a sampling/rectifying inspection before it is shipped. The manufacturer uses a 2% AOQL Dodge–Romig plan with the assumption that process average quality equals AQL stated by the agency.

(a) What is the average quality of product shipped to the agency if the actual production quality is 0.65%?

(b) What is the average quality of product shipped to the agency if the actual production quality is 1.1%?

(c) What is the probability that the agency will accept the product in each case?

12.9. If the actual production quality of the product in Problem 12.8 is 1.1%, what is the probability that a lot will be accepted by the agency if the lot is:

(a) Accepted under manufacturer's inspection and shipped without rectifying inspection?

(b) Rejected under manufacturer's inspection and shipped after rectifying inspection?

12.10. Design a sequential sampling plan for the following specifications: $\alpha = 0.05$, $\beta = 0.10$, $p_1 = 0.02$, and $p_2 = 0.08$. Sketch the OC curve and the ASN curve for this plan.

12.11. Solve Problem 12.10 using $p_1 = 0.005$ and $p_2 = 0.02$. Notice that the ratio p_2/p_1 is the same for both problems. Comment on the effect of this on the OC curve.

12.12. **(a)** Design a sequential sampling plan for the following specifications: $\alpha = 0.05$, $\beta = 0.10$, $p_1 = 1.5\%$, and $p_2 = 5\%$.

(b) Determine a 5% LTPD Dodge–Romig single sampling plan with estimated process average $= p_1$ for a lot size of 600.

(c) Determine a normal-inspection single sampling plan for lot size 600 and inspection level II from MIL-STD-105D using AQL $= p_1$.

(d) Compare the ASN for plan in part (a) with the sample sizes for plans in parts (b) and (c).

12.13. Draw the OC curves for the three plans in Problem 12.12.

12.14. Given standard levels of U_s and C_s to be 5.00 and 25.00, respectively, with defect classes A, B, C, and D having weights 100, 50, 10, and 1, respectively, design a demerit acceptance sampling plan. Set the allowable number of demerits at a normal deviate of $k = 3$ and the tightened action limit at $k = 4$. Samples of 5 each are to be taken from lots of 50 each.

12.15. Design a single sampling plan, using U_s and C_s from Problem 12.14, that would have a 5% chance of accepting a lot with $U = 12$.

thirteen

CONTINUOUS ACCEPTANCE SAMPLING BY ATTRIBUTES

In operation, continuous sampling is an acceptance–rectification inspection procedure that involves alternative periods of 100% inspection and sampling inspection. Essentially, the product is sampled off the line in a prescribed ratio f until a defect is found. The finding of one or more defects, depending on the plan used, is the signal for 100% inspection to begin. Sampling is resumed when a certain number i of successive defect-free units have been inspected. The average outgoing quality is improved during the screening phase as a result of finding the defect during the sampling phase.

There are two basic types of continuous sampling inspection. The first is known as single-level or single-stage continuous sampling. The second type is termed multistage or multilevel continuous sampling. In the single-stage type the sampling is confined to a specified frequency f which is determined by factors to be discussed immediately. In the multistage type the sampling frequency is relaxed as merited by the quality being produced. Thus one or more stages of inspection frequency f are used.

The most important feature of continuous sampling inspection is the elimination of the need for inspection lot formation. In many production situations, the formation of a lot or bank of units interferes seriously with the smooth flow of the product through the production line to completion. It also adds substantially to the producer's in-process inventory investment.

ADVANTAGES OF CONTINUOUS SAMPLING

Acceptance procedures based on continuous sampling provide many advantages over lot-by-lot acceptance procedures.

1. There is no need to form lots of inspection. This means that there is no interruption of production.
2. The product can be delivered as soon as it is produced. This is very important when the items are expensive and represent a large investment of working capital.
3. The need for storage space for forming the lots is eliminated.
4. In general, the cost of inspection is lower for continuous-sampling procedures.
5. The production department receives the information about defects as soon as one is observed. This facilitates the determination of causes and possible corrective actions.

In one application of continuous sampling, the savings were startling.[1] Minneapolis-Honeywell switched from job lot to mass production in the manufacture of the modern round thermostats. The shift from lot-by-lot inspection to continuous sampling inspection resulted in the following savings:

1. A 40% increase in production with no increase in personnel
2. A 35% cut in total production labor hours per unit
3. A 70% reduction in salvage labor per unit—from 39.5 labor hours per 1000 good units to 11.8
4. An 80% improvement in quality; critical and major defect rates dropped from 4% to 0.7%
5. An 87% reduction (from 400 ft to 50 feet) in the movement of thermostats by hand truck.
6. The elimination of eight in-process storage areas. By eliminating the storage of lots awaiting inspection, the time lag of inspection decisions on acceptability of units was in turn eliminated and standards for consistent inspection decisions were established.

MOVING LOTS

Attempts have been made, notably by the government, to apply lot-by-lot inspection to continuous-production situations. For the most part these attempts have not been completely satisfactory. Applying a very broad inter-

[1] Alan L. MacLean, "Continuous Sampling Inspection–Key to This Company's Mass Production," *Factory*, February 1955, pp. 114–117.

pretation of MIL-STD-105D, samples may be selected from moving product. This results in the formation of a *moving lot*. Aside from the obvious complication of where such a lot begins and ends, other problems are introduced.

> The most serious of these, when it occurred, was the expense entailed in recovering rejected material. With product continuously in motion and being allowed to pass the station until proved rejectable, part or nearly all of the material involved in a lot might have passed through one or more subsequent processing operations by the time the reject number was reached. As a result, product would have to be unpacked, disassembled, removed from the production line, placed in a segregated area, or handled otherwise at considerable cost following the rejection decision. It might be thought that the expense involved in this situation is less a concern of the government [consumer] than the contractor [producer]. The presumption of such an argument is "Well, if the contractor doesn't want the expense of unloading the product from a boxcar, he should keep the quality high enough to prevent rejection." The fallacy in this attitude is twofold:
>
> 1. Often the government owns the material and is paying the entire operating expense on a direct reimbursement basis. In other words, some of the largest contracts are of the cost-plus-fixed-fee type.
> 2. Even if the material were not government-owned, the increased costs occasioned by this kind of handling still have a tendency to be reflected in the price paid by our government for the product. Renegotiation clauses, waivers, prices for additional quantities of the material, etc., all afford the contractor a means to recoup such costs if they must be temporarily absorbed by him.[2]

Another disadvantage is the practice of *cutting off* lots. Such practice results from the approach to, or reaching of, the rejection number before the predetermined lot size has been reached. Rejection of a moving lot at an intermediate production inspection station can cause chaos. Portions of the lot may already be packaged and in the boxcar. Other portions may have undergone additional manufacturing, assembly, and preparation for storage. At the other end of the lot, units may be in the first stages of manufacture or not even started yet. The most obvious expedient is to cut off the lot and form a new one as soon as the acceptance number is approached or reached. The undesirable features of such an expedient should be evident immediately. A lot will never be rejected, no matter how defective it is. Even worse, and as a direct result of the elimination of the possibility of lot rejection, the average outgoing quality will be substantially the same as the incoming quality. Also, there will be absolutely no stimulus for the improvement of incoming

[2] R. L. Storer, "The Use of Continuous Sampling in Ammunition Procurement," *Industrial Quality Control*, May 1956, pp. 48–54. Reprinted by permission.

quality. With no stimulus for improvement, the chances are that quality will get worse and assume a generally unsatisfactory level.

HISTORICAL NOTE

The single-stage type of continuous-sampling plan was first introduced by H. F. Dodge in 1943.[3] This plan is termed CSP-1. Later H. F. Dodge and M. N. Torrey[4] introduced two variations of this single-stage plan, termed CSP-2 and CSP-3. In 1959, the Department of Defense published an interim handbook entitled "Inspection and Quality Control Handbook (Interim) H107." This handbook included the plans developed by Dodge and Torrey as well as a modification introduced by Navy, designated CSP-A.

The concept of multistage continuous sampling was discussed by many statisticians. However, formal acceptance sampling based on multistage continuous sampling was first described by G. J. Lieberman and H. Solomon.[5] In 1958, these multistage plans were incorporated in the Department of Defense handbook, "Handbook H106: Multi-level Continuous Sampling Procedures and Tables for Inspection by Attributes."

In 1962, Handbooks H106 and H107 were combined to form a single standard, MIL-STD-1235 (ORD). Normally, continuous acceptance sampling plans are only designated by AOQL. However, to be consistent with MIL-STD-105D, the plans in MIL-STD-1235 (ORD) are designated in terms of both AQL and AOQL.

MIL-STD-1235 (ORD)

Just as MIL-STD-105D is a very valuable source for acceptance sampling procedures in lot-by-lot inspection, MIL-STD-1235 (ORD) provides a source for acceptance sampling procedures when production is continuous. Each sampling plan in the standard is given as two numbers, i and f. The number i indicates the number of consecutive items that need to be found acceptable during the phase of 100% inspection to qualify the production for a fractional inspection phase. The number f is the fraction inspected during such phase. As the standard was created by combining Handbooks H106 and H107, the administrative procedures in MIL-STD-1235 (ORD) follow these handbooks.

[3] Harold F. Dodge, "A Sampling Inspection Plan for Continuous Production," *Annals of Mathematical Statistics*, Vol. 14 (1943), pp. 264–279.

[4] CPS-2 is treated in Harold F. Dodge and Mary N. Torrey, "Additional Continuous Sampling Plans," *Industrial Quality Control*, March 1951, pp. 7–11.

[5] G. J. Lieberman and H. Solomon, "Multi-level Continuous Sampling Plans," *Annals of Mathematical Statistics*, Vol. 26 (1955), pp. 686–704.

However, these are some modifications introduced to make these standards consistent with MIL-STD-105D.

Some administrative decisions are necessary prior to the adoption of MIL-STD-1235 (ORD).

1. Administration, in most cases meaning the Department of Defense, must decide who is to make the inspection. Usually, the 100% inspection is left with the producer and the receiving agency performs only the sampling inspection. However, any other combination can be admissible as long as it is decided beforehand.
2. Administration must be satisfied that (a) production is really continuous, (b) the process is capable of producing homogeneous product, and (c) ample inspection facilities exist for rapid 100% inspection.
3. Characteristics and procedures for measurement must be clearly defined.
4. The degree of relative inspection should be specified. As in MIL-STD-105D, MIL-STD-1235 (ORD) provides for different levels of inspection. However, only three levels of inspection, general inspection levels I, II, and III, are provided.

To ensure a quick response to any production defects detected, the standard provides for two ways of terminating acceptance of a product. When the acceptance is terminated, the producer is forced to determine the causes for unsatisfactory production and take corrective action.

First, the standard provides for verifying inspection at the option of the consumer. This inspection is in addition to the screening or 100% inspection and sampling inspection. For verifying inspection a sampling rate f used in the particular sampling plan or some other fraction satisfactory to the consumer may be used. All items actually inspected during the normal acceptance procedure are subjected to a verifying inspection at the rate f. If the plan being used is $i = 20$ and $f = 0.2$, the sampling inspection would be applied to 0.2, or one-fifth, of the units during the sampling inspection phase after 20 consecutive good items during 100% inspection phase. The items inspected during verifying inspection would be determined as follows:

Total number produced	520
Produced during 100% inspection	20
Produced during sampling inspection	500
Inspected during 100% inspection	20
Inspected during sampling inspection	100 (500×0.2)
Total inspected	120
Items to be verified	24 (120×0.2)

If screening inspection is in progress and the verifying inspection detects one critical defect or two noncritical defects separated by fewer than 50 good units, acceptance of the product is terminated. If sampling inspection is in progress and the above-mentioned defects are detected, the inspection reverts to 100% inspection.

The second way of acceptance being terminated is if 100% inspection is in progress and a total of L items are inspected without qualifying for sampling inspection. The standard includes tables for limiting values L for each type of sampling plan. Not qualifying for sampling inspection (i.e., not finding i consecutive good items) indicates that the average quality of production is poor.

Whenever acceptance is terminated, all items being processed are subjected to 100% inspection and resubmitted as a lot to be inspected separately under MIL-STD-105D. The inspection of resubmitted product is performed separately from the routine inspection of the product under the continuous-sampling plan.

The standard contains four classes of sampling plans: CSP-1, CSP-2, CSP-A, and CSP-M. These are described in more detail in the next section. As in MIL-STD-105D, a code letter is determined according to the production rate and inspection level. This code letter is then used to enter the proper master table to obtain the sampling plans. If the four classes of sampling plans, only CSP-1 and CSP-A can be used for critical defects.

Some representative tables from H106 and H107 included in MIL-STD-1235 (ORD) are shown as Tables A16.1 through A16.10. These include a table for the determination of code letters (A16.1), tables for CSP-1 and CSP-2 (A16.2 through A16.5), table for CSP-A (A16.6), and tables for CSP-M for two sampling frequencies $f = \frac{1}{2}$ and $f = \frac{1}{3}$ (A16.7 through A16.10).

DESCRIPTION OF CONTINUOUS ACCEPTANCE PROCEDURES

Single-Stage Plan CSP-1

In CSP-1 the inspection begins by screening the product in the order of production (or as near to it as possible) until i number of successive defect-free units pass the station. As soon as this qualification is met, sampling in the frequency of f is invoked. The sampling at the chosen frequency continues until a sample unit with a defect is discovered. Immediately, the screening phase is resumed and continued until the qualification requirement of i successive defect-free units is achieved again. Normally, the plan is used for a single defect; that is, the plan is applied for acceptance and rectification of quality in individual characteristics. It may, however, be applied to an entire class of characteristics. Figure 13.1 is a flowchart depicting the operation of CSP-1 as applied to individual defects and to classes of defects.

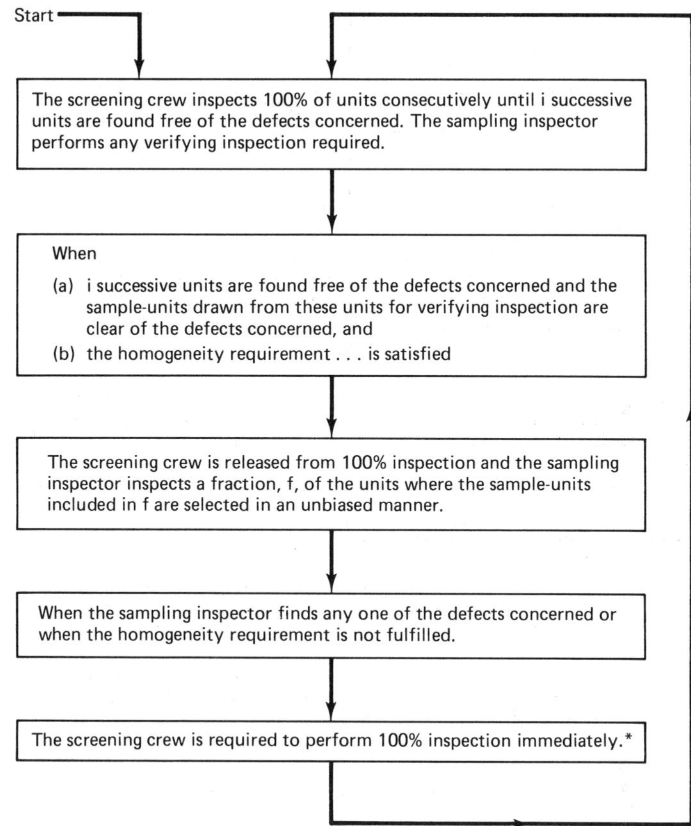

Figure 13.1 Procedure for CSP-1 plans. [From "Single Level Continuous Sampling Procedures and Tables for Inspection by Attributes," *Supply and Logistics Handbook H107* (Washington, D.C.: U.S. Government Printing Office, April 30, 1956).]

Single-Stage Plan CSP-2

CSP-2 operates the same as CSP-1 except that the finding of a defect does not immediately trigger a return to 100% inspection. Instead, the finding of a defect is a signal to the inspector to continue sampling at the same frequency, but at that point, to start keeping count of the number of sample units inspected after finding of the defect. If the next i number of *sample units* are free of the defect, the sampling may be continued as before. If, however, a defect is encountered during the latter phase, 100% inspection must be invoked immediately upon the finding of the defect. Figure 13.2 is

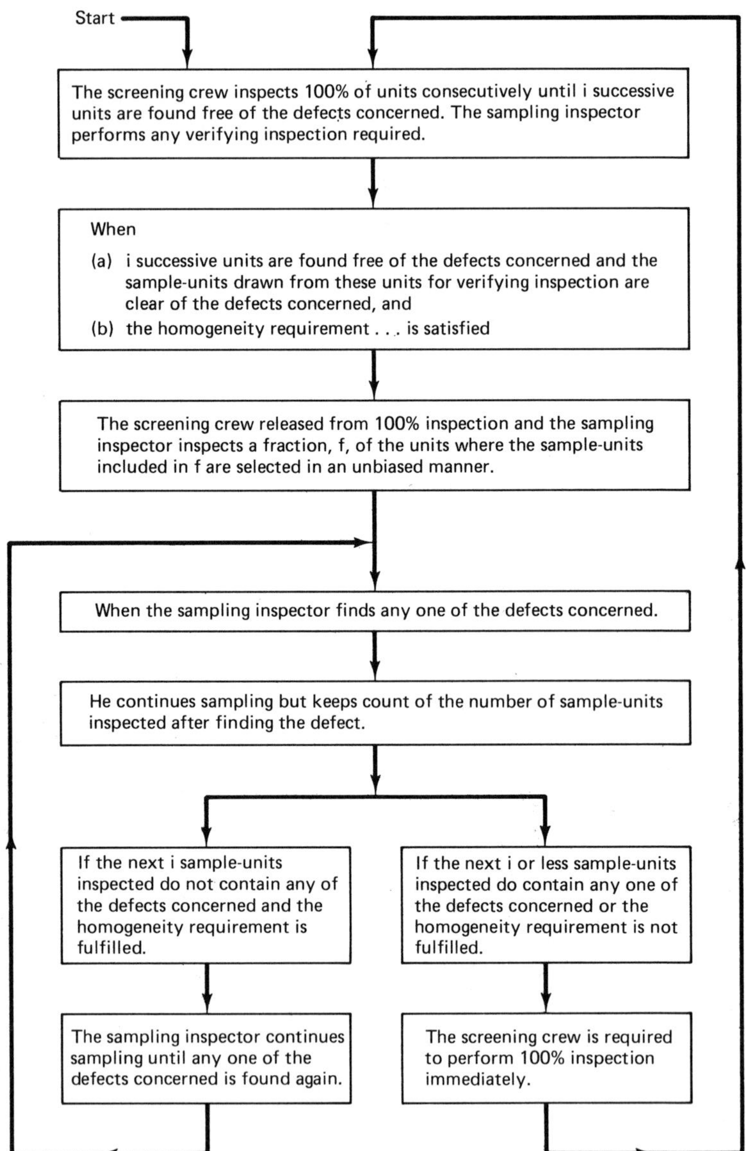

Figure 13.2 Procedure for CSP-2 plans. [From "Single Level Continuous Sampling Procedures and Tables for Inspection by Attributes," *Supply and Logistics Handbook H107* (Washington, D.C.: U.S. Government Printing Office, April 30, 1959).]

a flowchart that depicts the operation of CSP-2 as applied to individual defects and to classes of defects.

Single-Stage Plan CSP-A

Figure 13.3 is a flowchart that depicts the operation of CSP-A. CSP-A operates the same as CSP-1 except that a *stop-inspection* value is included. This type of plan is used normally where the consumer performs the screening inspection in addition to the sampling inspection. CSP-A requires that as soon as the $(a + 1)$th defect is observed during the screening phase, inspection will be curtailed and will not begin again until sufficient corrective action to the process has been taken.

The CSP-A plans provide for alternating sequences of 100% inspection and sampling inspection *with a limit* on the number of such sequences. Placing a limit on the number of alternating sequences provides a procedure whereby the process is rejected when product quality is worse than the AQL. At the same time, assurance is provided that product passing the acceptance requirements meets the AQL. The administration of CSP-A proceeds as follows.

At the start of production each day or of each production interval, each unit is inspected in the order of production by the screening crew until the previously cited qualification requirements are met. Inspection is performed for each defect assigned to the inspection station. Judgment of the product quality may be either by individual defect or by class of defects.

When i successive units have been found to be free of the defect(s) by the screening crew, screening is terminated and sampling at rate f is begun. If one of the defect(s) concerned is found during sampling, an immediate return to 100% inspection is required.

The inspector (consumer quality representative) tallies the number of units of product containing each defect assigned to the station. A new tally is begun at the start of production for each production interval. This tally includes the results of *both* screening inspection and sampling inspection. If only a or fewer tallies [for the defect(s) concerned] are made during the production interval, there will be no interruption of inspection, and all product that has passed the inspector is accepted for the defect(s) concerned. Whenever $a + 1$ tallies [for the defect(s) concerned] are made during the production interval, the inspector stops inspection. At this point all product that has already passed the inspector is accepted for the defect(s) concerned. (The latter does not apply to critical defects, as stated before.)

When the $(a + 1)$st tally has been made, the inspector informs the supplier of the defect(s) involved and indicates that he will no longer inspect product until the supplier locates the source of difficulty and assures him that the causes for defective product have been eliminated. When the inspector is satisfied with this assurance and has verified that all units that had not

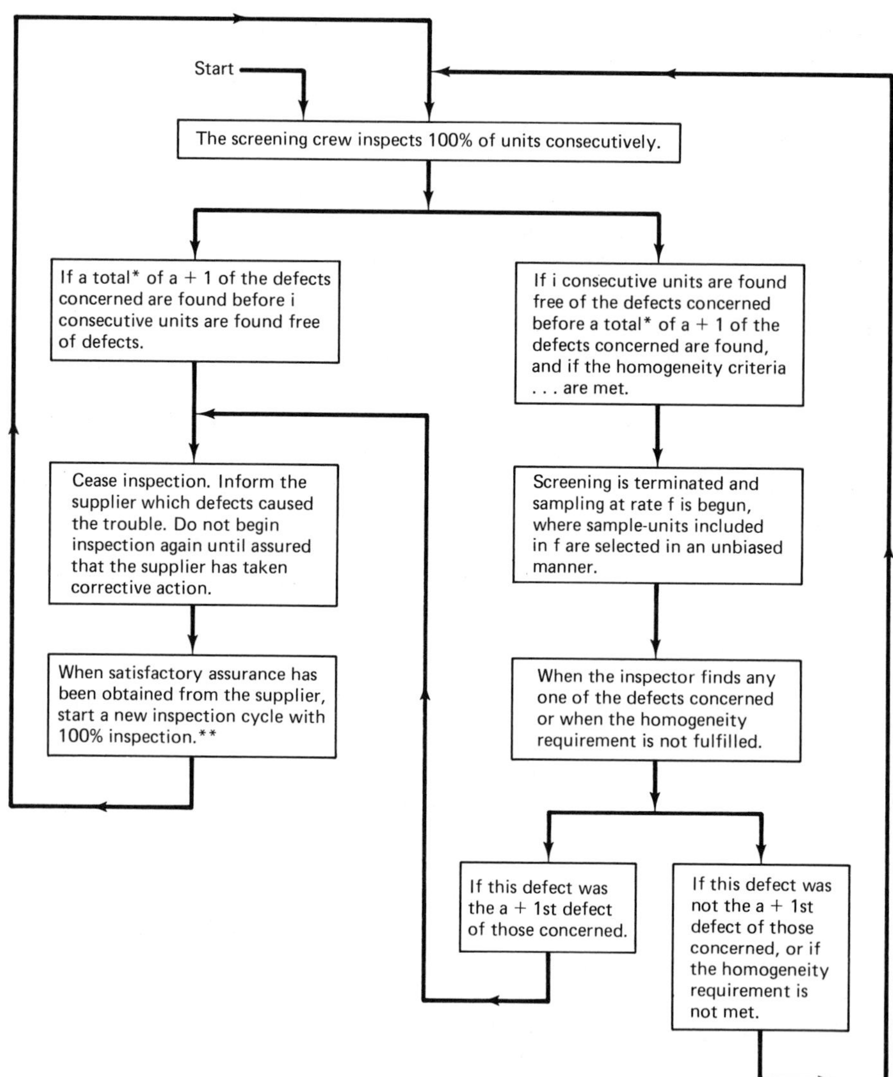

*The total of a + 1 defects includes results of all inspection for the day, both sampling and screening.

**For critical defects the screening should begin with the unit of product just after the last defect-free sample unit.

Figure 13.3 Procedure for CSP-A plans. [From "Single Level Continuous Sampling Procedures and Tables for Inspection by Attributes," *Supply and Logistics Handbook H107* (Washington, D.C.: U.S. Government Printing Office, April 30, 1959).]

reached his station at the time that inspection was stopped have been removed and/or screened and are being presented as resubmitted material, he resumes inspection using a sampling plan based on a new estimate of the production rate. The inspector, at his discretion, may accept screening inspection by the supplier as a basis for resuming his inspection if the problem of location and correcting the source of difficulty will result in an unreasonable delay in production. If the inspector is unable to obtain satisfactory assurance that corrective action has been taken by the supplier when required, he should report the situation to his superiors. The supplier may be required to return to lot-by-lot inspection or take whatever action is deemed necessary to assure receipt of product of an acceptable quality.

Multistage Plan CSP-M

CSP-M sampling plans provide a procedure whereby the fraction inspected of the presented units is decreased or increased by steps of levels, dependent on the quality of the units presented. When the application of the sampling plans is initiated, 100% of the product is inspected or tested until a specified number of consecutive units, i, is found to be free of defects. At that time, the inspection or test is performed on a fraction, f, of the units presented. If i successively inspected units are found to be free of defects, the inspection rate is reduced to a new fraction, f^2, of the units presented. This procedure is continued through the several levels for the plan. However, if at any level a defective unit is found before i successively inspected units are passed, the plan provides a special procedure to determine whether sampling should continue at the present rate or revert to the previous sampling rate.

The special procedure consists of inspecting the next four units produced or processed immediately following the discovery of a defective unit. If no defectives are found in the four consecutive units, sampling is resumed at the same rate as when the defective was found. If no more defectives are found before a total of i successively inspected units (including the four consecutive units) are determined to be acceptable, the sampling rate is reduced to the next smaller fraction (the next level). As soon as a second defective is found, either in the four consecutive units or after resuming the sampling rate, the former level is reverted to immediately and four consecutive units are inspected repeating the procedure just described (except where a defective is found while in state 1^R, then shift to 100% inspection and repeat the procedure of the paragraph above). Thus the sampling rate may be reduced or increased by specific steps as the quality of the presented units varies up and down. At the same time, the plans provide a check to differentiate between the random occurrence of a defective, which can occur even though the overall quality level is acceptable, and inferior or spotty quality.

Figure 13.4 shows the procedure for a three-level plan. The procedure

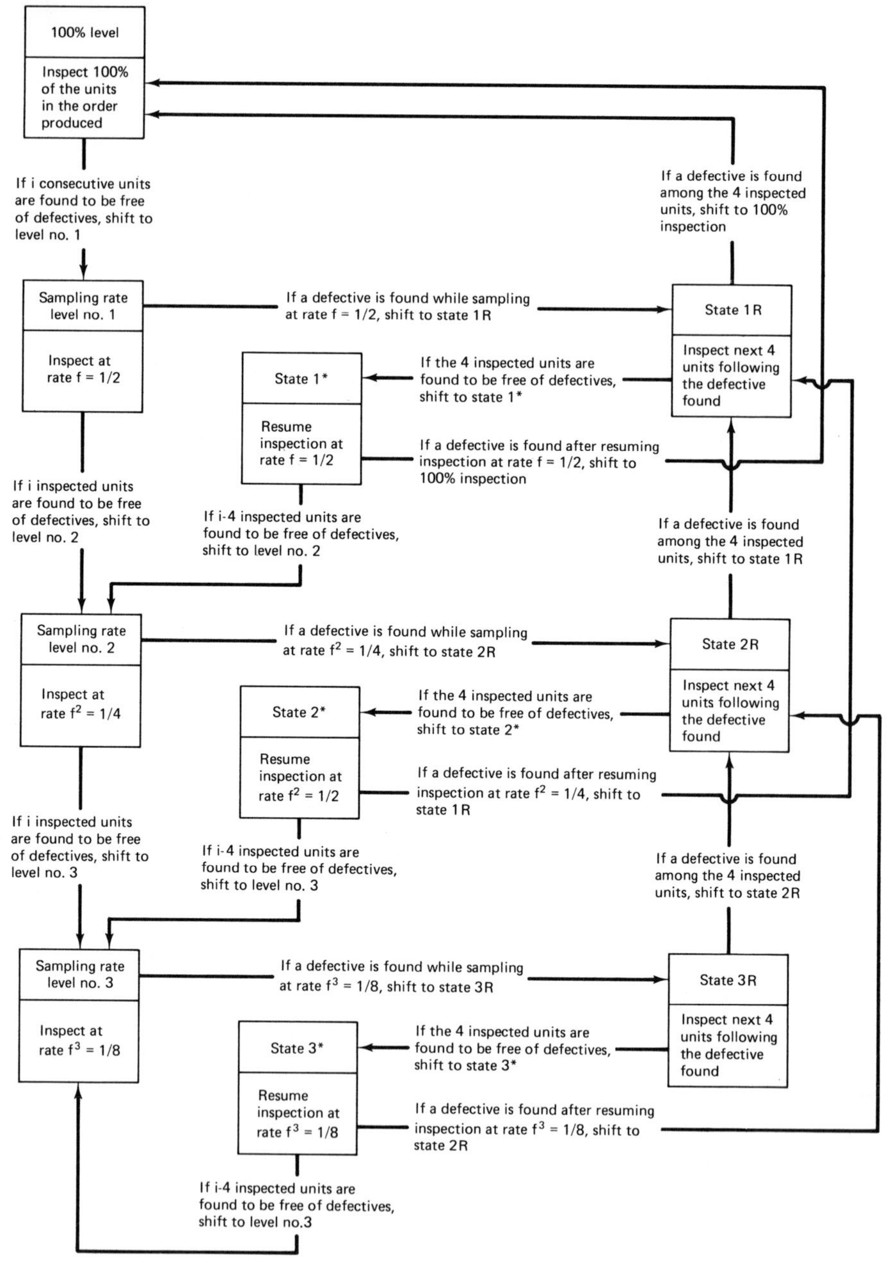

Figure 13.4 Procedure for CSP-M plans, three levels.

is similar for one, two, four, or five levels. It is only necessary to expand or contract the diagram for the proper number of levels, keeping in mind that the last or smallest level always has a procedure similar to that of the third level of Figure 13.4.

TIGHTENED AND REDUCED INSPECTION PLANS

The concept of increasing or decreasing relative inspection according to the observed quality of product submitted for inspection is also carried over to MIL-STD-1235 (ORD). However, master tables are provided only for normal inspection. The parameters for tightened and reduced inspection are defined as certain proportions of parameters in the normal inspection plans.

If the consumer wishes to increase the amount of inspection performed whenever the quality of submitted material is unsatisfactory, the following tightened inspection plan may be utilized. Upon resumption of inspection following a stoppage of inspection, a sampling plan whose AQL and AOQL is one step tighter than that normally specified is used until one full production interval has elapsed without the inspection being stopped. When the latter condition is satisfied, the normally prescribed AQL or AQOL is again used. For critical defects, the tightened sampling plan *uses an i value twice that* for the normal sampling plan.

If the consumer wishes to reduce the amount of inspection done whenever the quality of the submitted material is very good, the following reduced sampling plan may be utilized. A *sampling rate, f, one-fifth of the normal* rate may be used provided that:

1. The preceding 10 full production intervals have been under normal inspection without interruptions in the inspection.
2. The estimated process average is less than the quantity

$$\text{AQL} - 3\sqrt{\frac{\text{AQL}(100 - \text{AQL})}{\text{number inspected}}}$$

3. Production is at a steady rate.

The process quality average may be estimated in the usual manner except that only the results accrued up to and including the occurrence of a defect should be included.

Normal sampling may be reinstated whenever (1) there is an interruption of inspection and/or (2) the estimated process average rises above the AQL and/or (3) the consumer deems that normal inspection should be reinstated. Reduced sampling plans should not be used for critical defects.

With regard to disposition of rejected product, units containing defects, whether found by the sampling inspector or by the screening crew, are turned over to the sampling inspector, who releases them together with all units containing defects found in his own inspection, to the proper agent of the supplier. The supplier may correct the defective units, in which case they are submitted to the sampling inspector separately from the normal flow of product. If the number of resubmitted units is small, the sampling inspector may inspect them under consumer observation and direction. In either event, satisfactory units are rereleased into the flow of product beyond the inspection station; units still containing defects are returned to the supplier for further processing or scrapping.

EFFECTIVENESS OF CONTINUOUS SAMPLING

Let p be defined as the actual quality of the product as it is manufactured. If the product is inspected under a continuous-sampling plan, the protection provided by the plan will depend on p as well as the parameters f, i, and k of the plan. The following formulas (provided without proof) help in analysis of this protection.

(1) $u = \dfrac{1 - (1 - p)^i}{p(1 - p)^i}$ = average number of pieces inspected after a defect is found

(2) $v = \dfrac{1}{f \cdot p}$ = average number of pieces passed by the sampling plan before a defect is discovered

(3) $F = \dfrac{u + f \cdot v}{u + v}$ = average fraction inspected

(4) $P_a = 1 - F$ = average fraction accepted with inspection

(5) $\text{AOQ(CSP-1)} = \dfrac{p(1 - f)(1 - p)^{i-1}}{f + (1 - f)(1 - p)^{i-1}}$ = approximate average outgoing quality under CSP-1

(6) $\text{AOQ(CSP-2)} = \dfrac{P(1 - f)[2(1 - p)^2 - (1 - p)^{2i}]}{f(1 - p) + (1 - f)\,[2(1 - p)^i - (1 - p)^{2i}}$
= approximate average outgoing quality under CSP-2

(7) AOQ(CSP-M)

$$t = \frac{(1 - p)^i}{1 - (1 - p)^i} \qquad f_j = \text{fraction for the } j\text{th level}$$

$$\text{AOQ} = p\,\frac{\sum_{j=1}^{k} t^j(1 - f_j)/f_j}{\sum_{j=0}^{k} t^j/f_j}$$

Earlier versions of military standards for continuous sampling included curves for the values of u and v. An example from ORD-M-608-11 is shown in Figure 13.5.

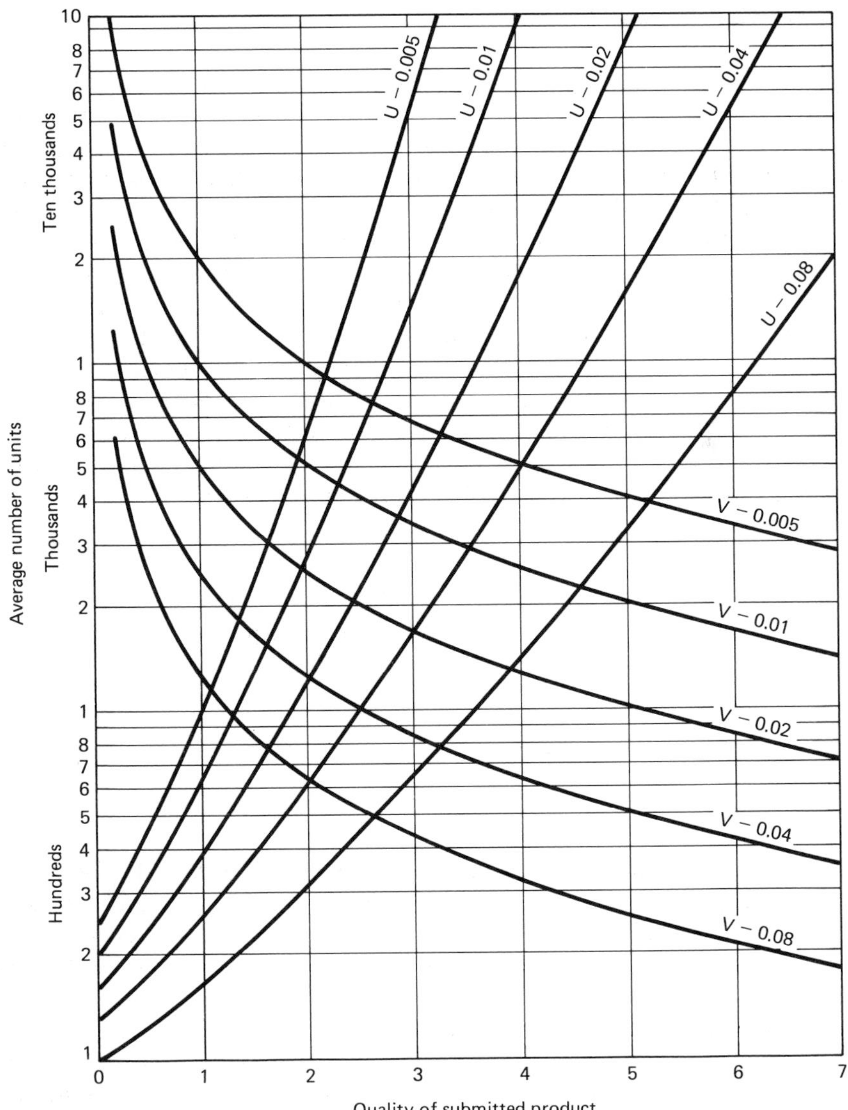

Figure 13.5 *u* and *v* curves for CSP-1, AQL = 1.0, and varying *f* values. [From ORD-M-608-11, "Procedures and Tables for Continuous Sampling by Attributes," *Ordnance Inspection Handbook* (Washington, D.C.: U.S. Government Printing Office, August 1954).]

PLANS FOR SPECIFIC AOQL

In Tables A16.2, A16.3, and A16.6, each column has the value AQL at the top and corresponding value of AOQL at the bottom. This feature implies two things. First, in CSP-1, CSP-2, and CSP-A, there is a fixed relationship between AQL and AOQL. Second, to obtain plans that would guarantee a specific AOQL, these tables can be entered using code letter and AOQL (instead of the code letter and AQL). Maintaining the spirit of MIL-STD-105D the AQL values are usually limited to those in the table. However, linear interpolation is possible for AOQL values in between. For example, in CSP-1 using code letter F the values of i for AQLs 2.5 and 4.0 are given as 35 and 22, respectively. The corresponding AOQL values are 3.09 and 4.96. For using these plans the AQL values would be limited to 2.5 and 4.0 only. If an intermediate value such as 3.0 is desired, it would be either "rounded" down to 2.5 or up to 6.0. On the other hand, it would be possible to determine a plan for AOQL of 4.0 using interpolation.

i	AOQL	
35	3.09	4.0 Desired AOQL
22	4.96	

$$i = 22 + (35 - 22)\frac{4.96 - 4.0}{4.96 - 3.09}$$

$$= 28.67 \quad \text{or} \quad 29$$

The plan $f = \frac{1}{10}$ and $i = 29$ would give an approximate AOQL of 4.0.

For CSP-M the computations for AOQ and AOQL are quite involved. Before the availability of computers, such computations were not feasible at workstations or inspection stations. Handbook H106, now part of MIL-STD-1235 (ORD), provides for alternative tables for obtaining sampling plans for specified AOQL. Two of these tables are shown as Tables A16.9 and A16.10. The computation of average outgoing quality is facilitated by the use of AOQ curves given in Appendices A and D of Handbook H106. For illustration purposes the AOQ and AFI curves for plans with AOQL $= 2.0$ and $f = \frac{1}{2}$ and $f = \frac{1}{3}$ are shown as Figures 13.6 through 13.11.

The decision to use a multi- or single-level plan depends on several factors. The Air Force has made extensive use of multilevel plans. This preference for multilevel over other plans may be explained by one exemplary decision to use it for the acceptance inspection of aircraft engines.

> Due to the slow production rate for aircraft engines, MIL-STD-105 was immediately judged as impractical for the situation. Next, consideration was given to the continuous sampling plans [single-level] developed by Dodge. The Dodge

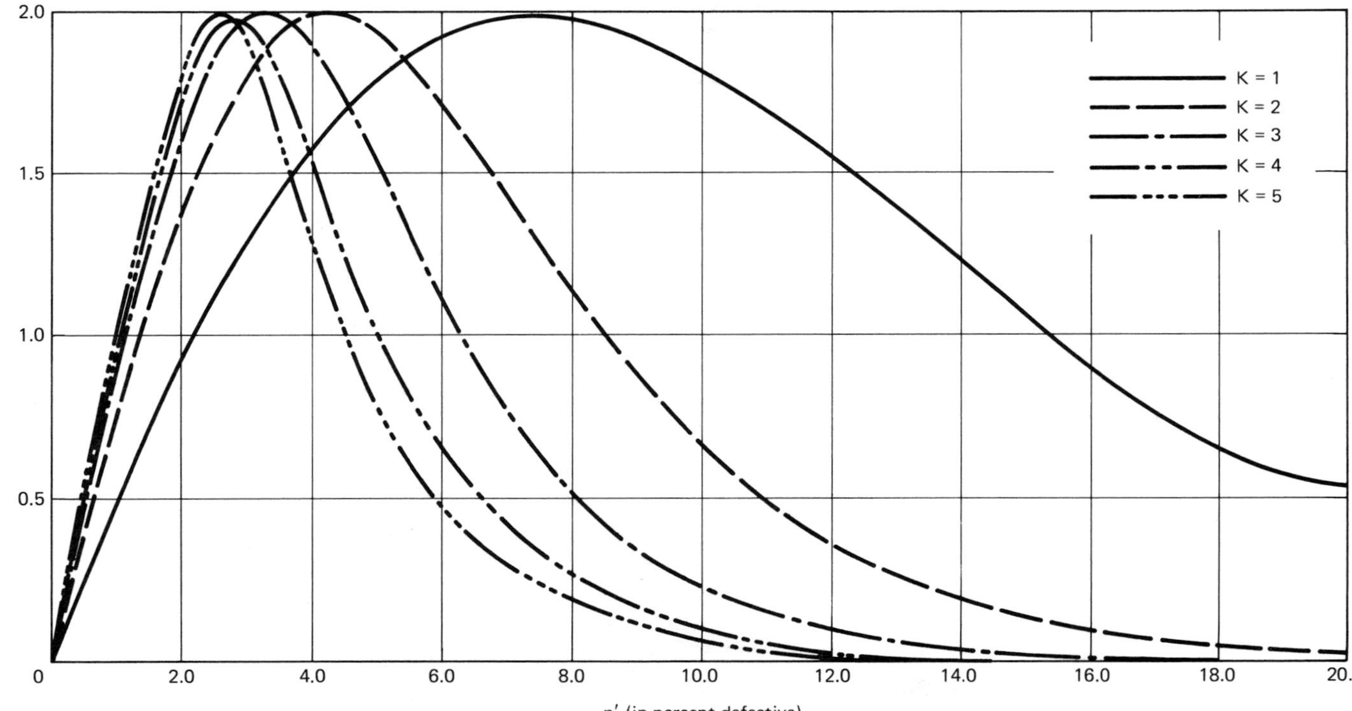

Figure 13.6 Average outgoing quality curves (in percent defective) for AOQL = 2.0 and $f = \frac{1}{2}$. (From Appendix A of H106.)

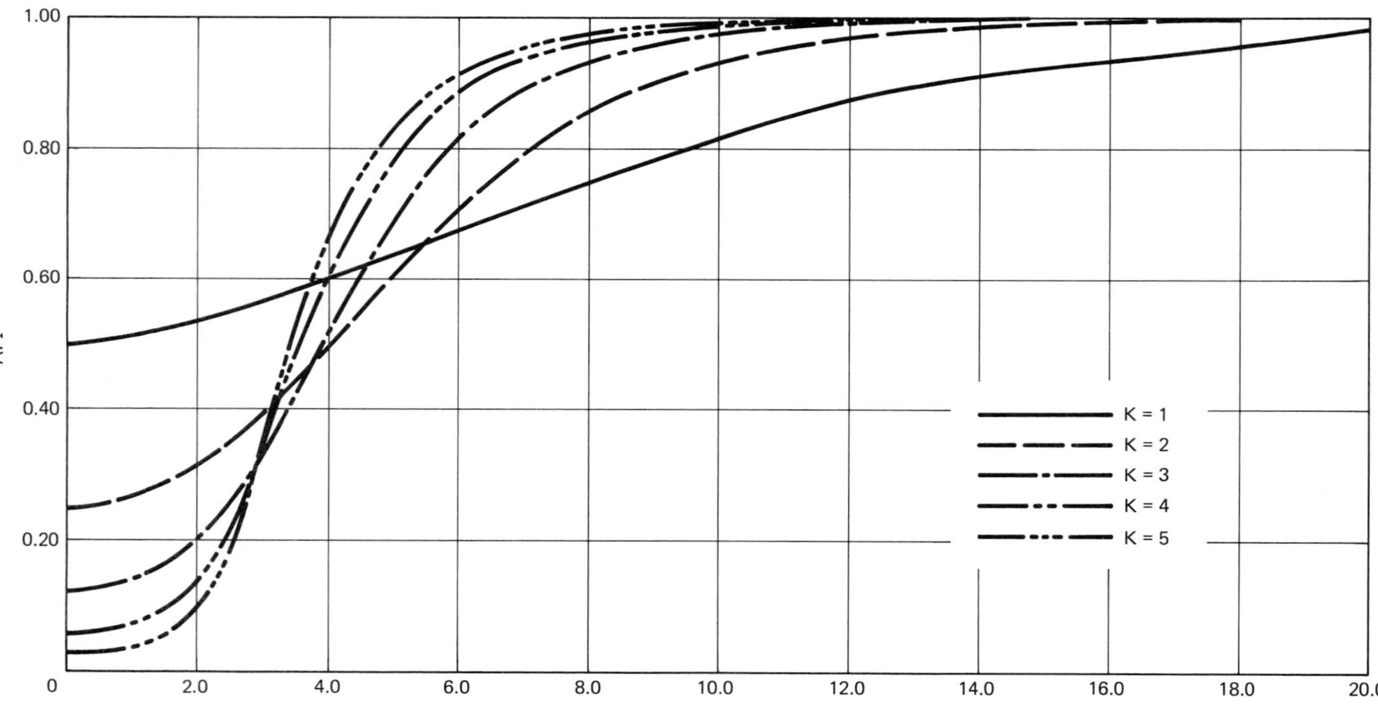

Figure 13.7 Average fraction inspected curves for AOQL = 2.0 and $f = \frac{1}{2}$. (From Appendix B of H106.)

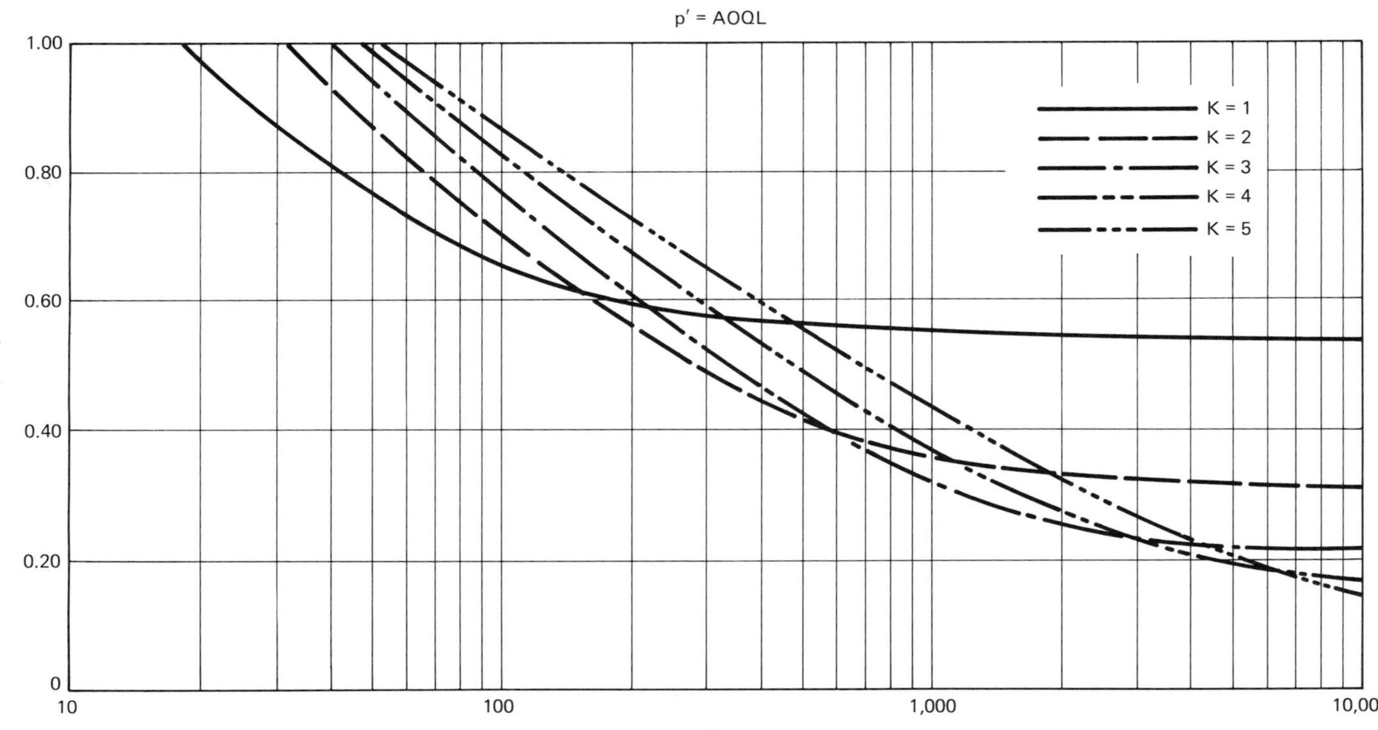

Figure 13.8 Expected average fraction inspected as a function of N. For AOQL = 2.0 and $f = \frac{1}{2}$. (From Appendix C of H106.)

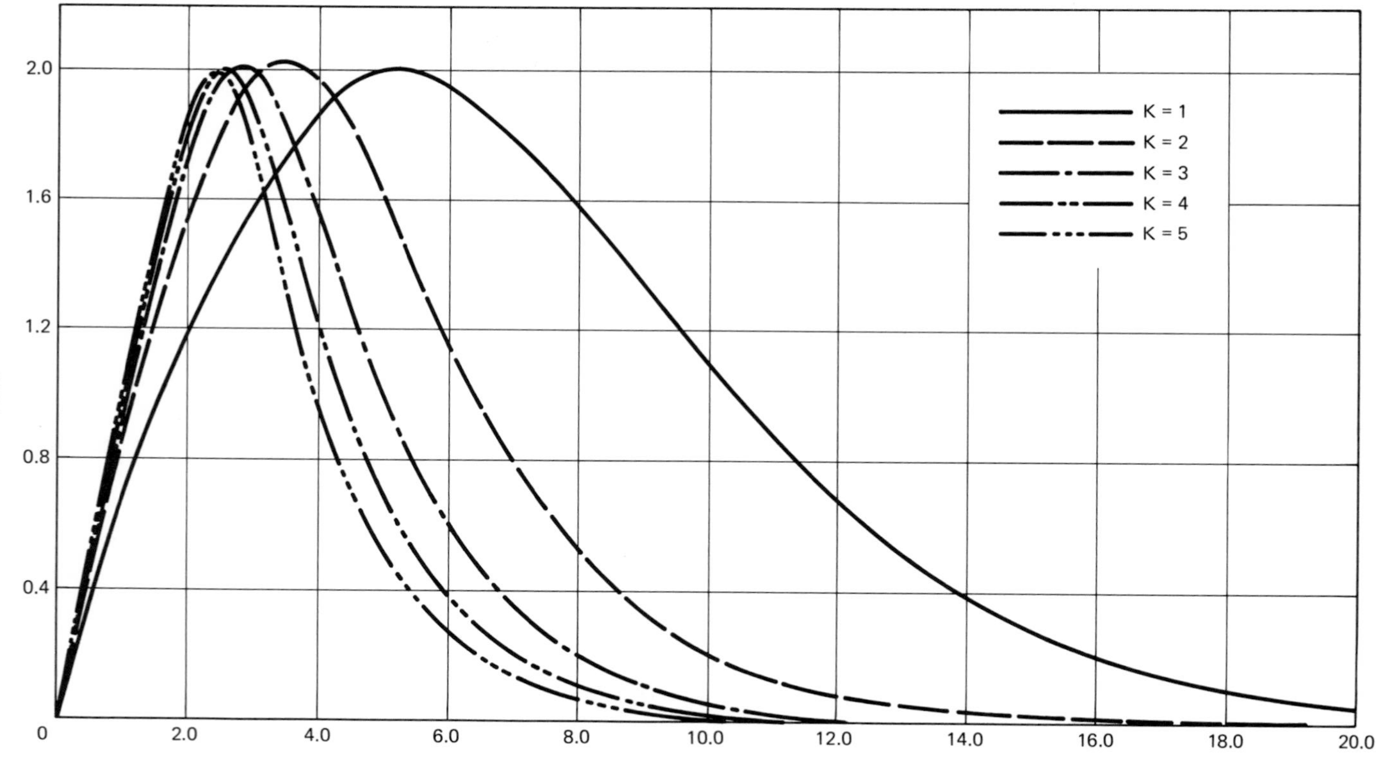

Figure 13.9 Average outgoing quality curves (in percent defective) for AOQL = 2.0 and $f = \frac{1}{3}$. (From Appendix D of H106.)

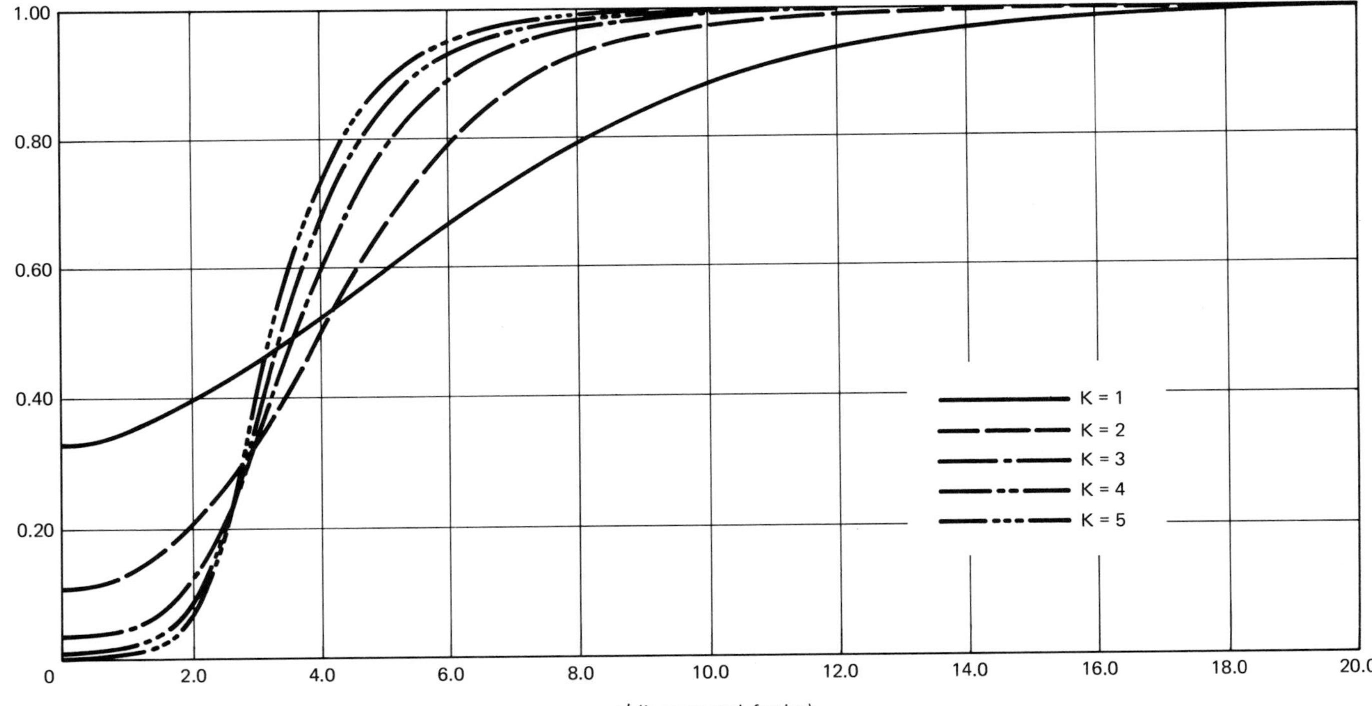

Figure 13.10 Average fraction inspected curves for AOQL = 2.0 and $f = \frac{1}{3}$. (From Appendix E of H106.)

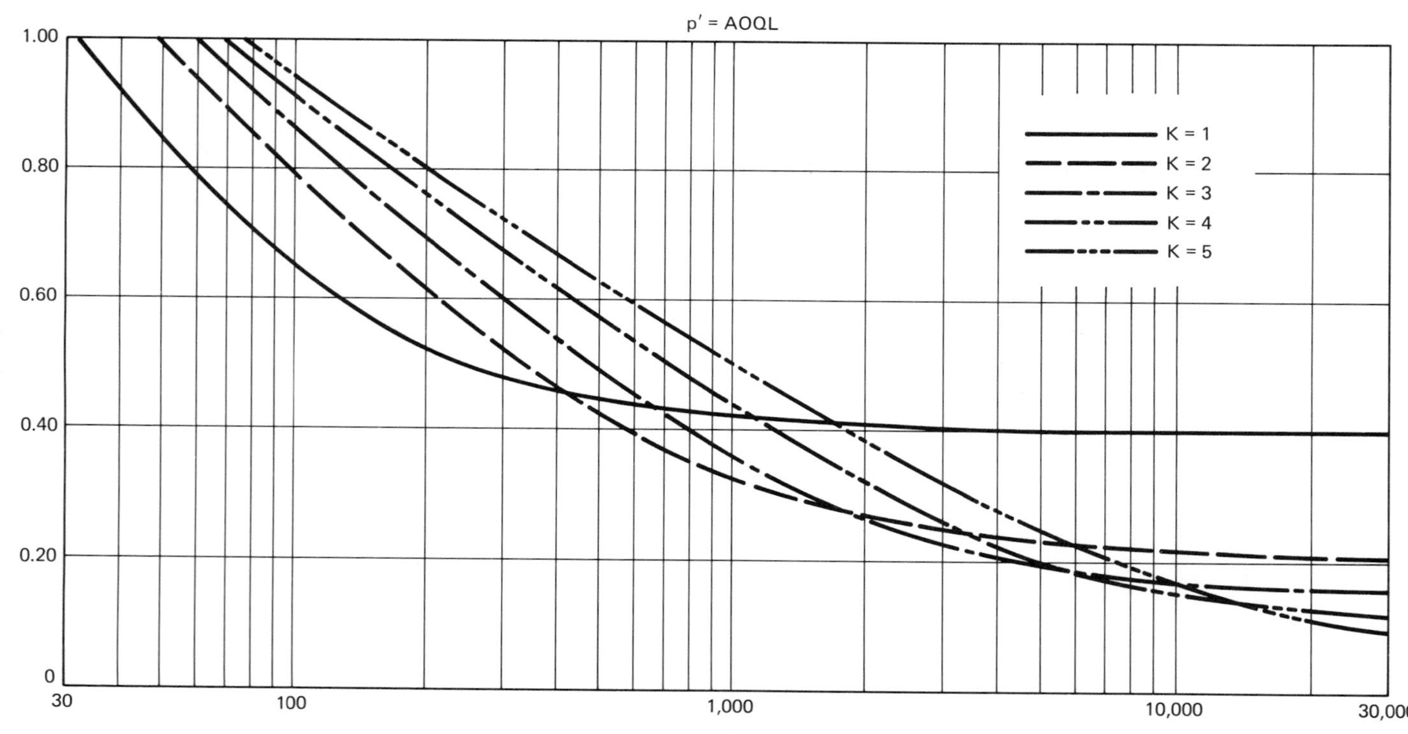

Figure 13.11 Expected average fraction inspected as a function of N for AOQL = 2.0 and $f = \frac{1}{3}$. (From Appendix F of H106.)

plans had certain undesirable features in this application; namely, (1) the sampling fraction was generally rather low [one in ten] and represented a severe change of inspection manpower for 100% inspection, (2) the tight protection [small AQL value] desired against the acceptance of these serious defects would require a very large number of consecutive acceptable engines in order to reach sampling inspection, (3) it was seriously doubted if management would accept a severe change in inspection frequency when past inspection had always been on a 100% basis, and (4) if a high sampling frequency [one in two] were selected then the resulting savings would not be as great as desired. An analysis of these objections indicated that a continuous plan with more than one sampling level would be [desirable]; that is, a plan which would increase or decrease the frequency of inspection by steps or levels dependent on the quality history.[6]

Example 13.1

The production rate for a soft drink is 3000 bottles per hour. The production is continuous. Continuous sampling CSP-1 is to be used. For AQL 1% and inspection level II, determine the sampling plan, assuming an "hour" as the production interval.

From Table A16.1 the code letter is G. From Table A16.2 for code letter G, the sampling fraction f is given as 1/15. Under AQL 1%, the value i is given as 100. In this plan the soft-drink bottles will be inspected continuously until 100 consecutive bottles are found without any intervening defects. When these 100 consecutive defect-free bottles are found, fractional or sampling inspection will be initiated. Under the sampling inspection only 1 out of every 15 bottles will be inspected. The AOQL for this plan is given as 1.35%. From Table A16.4 the limit value L is 475. This means that if 475 bottles are inspected without qualifying for sampling inspection (i.e., without finding 100 consecutive defect-free bottles), the inspection will be stopped. The production will be discontinued and not restarted until the cause for defective product is found and corrected.

Example 13.2

Determine a multilevel plan for the product in Example 13.1 using $f = \frac{1}{2}$ and AOQL = 1%.

In Table A16.7 for AOQL = 1.0% and production rate 3000, there is an arrow pointing down. Therefore, the plan to be used can be found at the end of the arrow $i = 83$, $k = 3$. This means that a three-level plan is indicated.

The inspection will start with continuous (100%) inspection of bottles. When 83 consecutive defect-free bottles are found, the production qualifies for level 1 sampling inspection. At this level $\frac{1}{2}$, or 50%, of the bottles are sampled and inspected. When 83 consecutive samples are found defect-free, the production qualifies for level 2 sampling inspection. At this level $(\frac{1}{2})^2$ or 25% of the bottles are sampled and inspected. When 83 consecutive samples are found defect-free, the production qualifies for level 3 sampling inspection. At this level $(\frac{1}{2})^3$, or 12.5%, of the bottles are

[6] John E. Condon, "Multi-level Continuous Sampling Plans," *Proceedings of the 4th Annual Statistical Engineering Symposium*, U.S. Army Chemical Corps Engineering Command, Army Chemical Center, Md., May 7–8, 1958, p. 145.

sampled and inspected. The third level, being the highest level, there is no further reduction in the sampling fraction.

Example 13.3

Here the illustration in Examples 13.1 and 13.2 is continued further. If the actual quality of production is 0.8%, what is the outgoing quality of the product under (a) CSP-1 and (b) CSP-M?

(a) Under CSP-1, the inspection plan in Example 13.1 is $f = \frac{1}{15}$, $i = 100$, and $p = 0.008$.

$$(1 - p)^i = (1 - 0.008)^{100} = 0.44789$$

$$u = \frac{1 - (1 - p)^i}{p(1 - p)^i} = \frac{1 - 0.44789}{(0.008)(0.44789)} = 154.08$$

$$v = \frac{1}{fp} = \frac{15}{0.008} = 1875$$

$$F = \frac{u + fv}{u + v} = \frac{154.08 + (1/15)(1875)}{154.08 + 1875}$$

$$Pa = 1 - F = 1 - 0.1375 = 0.8625$$

$$\text{AOQ} = \frac{p(1 - f)(1 - p)^{i-1}}{f + (1 - f)(1 - p)^{i-1}}$$

$$1 - f = 1 - \frac{1}{15} = 0.9333$$

$$(1 - p)^{i-1} = (1 - 0.008)^{99} = 0.45150$$

$$(1 - f)(1 - p)^{i-1} = 0.9333 \times 0.4515 = 0.4214$$

$$\text{AOQ} = \frac{0.008 \times 0.4214}{0.0666 + 0.4214} = 0.0069$$

The outgoing quality is 0.69%.

(b) Under CSP-M, the inspection plan in Example 13.2 is $f = 0.5$, $i = 83$, $k = 3$, and $p = 0.008$.

$$t = \frac{(1 - p)^i}{1 - (1 - p)^i}$$

$$= \frac{(1 - 0.008)^{83}}{1 - (1 - 0.008)^{83}} = \frac{0.5134}{1 - 0.5134}$$

$$= 1.055$$

j	t^j	f_j	$1/f_j - 1$
0	1	1	0
1	1.055	0.5	1
2	1.1130	0.25	3
3	1.7424	0.125	7

$$\text{AOQ} = p \frac{\sum_{j=i}^{k} t^j/(1 - f_j)}{\sum_{j=\nu}^{k} t^j/f_j}$$

$$= (0.008) \frac{1.055 + 3(1.1130) + 7(1.7424)}{1 + \frac{1.055}{0.5} + \frac{1.1130}{0.25} + \frac{1.7424}{0.125}}$$

$$= (0.008) \frac{16.5908}{21.501} = 0.00617$$

The average outgoing quality is 0.617%.

PROBLEMS

13.1. Determine the continuous-sampling plans for the following conditions.

	Plan Type	Code Letter	f	AQL
(a)	CSP-1	I	1/50	0.40
(b)	CSP-1	J	1/200	0.40
(c)	CSP-2	G	1/10	1.5
(d)	CSP-2	H	1/25	2.5
(e)	CSP-A	C′	1/5	0.25
(f)	CSP-A	I′	1/10	1.0

13.2. Determine the multilevel continuous sampling plan for the following conditions.

	Production Rate	f	AOQL
(a)	750	1/2	0.35
(b)	1,600	1/2	3.0
(c)	3,600	1/3	1.0
(d)	36,000	1/3	1.0

13.3. Determine the values of AOQL and L for the plans in Problem 13.1a through d.

13.4. Determine the values of AOQL, a, and L for the plans in Problem 13.1e and f.

13.5. A CSP-1 plan, $f = 1/10$, AQL $= 4.0$, and $i = 22$, has been in effect for 10 full production intervals. Of 2500 units inspected, 25 were defective. Production has been at a steady rate. Does the supplier qualify for reduced inspection?

13.6. For plans in Problem 13.1a through c, determine the average fraction accepted without inspection and the average outgoing quality if the incoming quality is 2.0%.

13.7. Determine the probability that the inspection will be stopped under plans in Problem 13.1e and f if the incoming quality is 0.3% and 3.0%, respectively.

13.8. The daily production rate for an item is 800 units. It is desired to maintain an AOQL of 2.0 on this material while using a multilevel continuous plan with a sampling frequency of $\frac{1}{2}$. Give the i and k values of the plan. Under what conditions can the sampling frequency be decreased, and how much can it be decreased? Detail your answer.

13.9. For the plan in Problem 13.8, determine the average outgoing quality if the incoming quality is 4.0%.

13.10. Determine a CSP-M plan with $f = \frac{1}{3}$, AOQL $= 2.0$, and a production rate of 14,000. If the average process quality is 1.0, determine the average outgoing quality:

(a) By direct computation.

(b) Using Figure 13.9.

fourteen

ACCEPTANCE PROCEDURES FOR VARIABLE CHARACTERISTICS

Variable characteristics are those characteristics that can be measured. Examples of such characteristics are lengths, weights, diameters, and so on. Mathematically, it can be said that variable characteristics can be written as *real* numbers, whereas attribute characteristics can only be written as *integer* numbers. In simpler terms this means that a length (variable characteristic) can be a fractional number such as 8.17 cm, whereas the number of defective items in a lot (attribute characteristic) can only be a round number, such as 3 or 4. Variable characteristics are the subject of $\overline{X}$ charts in process control. Acceptance procedures for variable characteristics can be designed in the form of a *variables sampling plan*.

The central limit theorem, which was used as a basis for the $\overline{X}$ chart, can again be referred to and used to determine the approximating distribution of sample averages in a variable sampling plan.

APPLICABILITY OF ACCEPTANCE SAMPLING BY VARIABLES

The usual conditions for applicability of variables sampling for acceptance are as follows:

1. The inspection characteristic under consideration must be a variable or capable of being converted to a variable scale.

2. Attributes inspection is excessively costly (inspection time, destructive nature of test, etc.).
3. Attributes inspection will not give enough information; that is, the extent of the variation is also desired.
4. The distribution of the characteristic should be approximately normal.

The distinguishing features of a variables sampling plan in contrast to an attributes plan are as follows:

1. Equivalent protection is obtained with a smaller sample size.
2. It may only be applied to the acceptance or rejection of *one* inspection characteristic.
3. It usually involves higher administrative cost. More skilled help is required; more computations are required; more errors in calculation are possible; more expensive inspection equipment is required.
4. It usually provides a better basis for improving quality and gives much more information in waiver situations.

VARIABLES SAMPLING PLAN

Let n be the number of items in a sample and x_i, $i = 1, 2, \ldots, n$, be the measured values of the variable characteristic. Let the probability distribution of x_i be constant with a mean μ and variance σ^2.

Then a reference to the central limit theorem indicates that the approximating distribution of the sample average

$$\overline{X} = \frac{1}{n} \sum x_i$$

is normal with mean μ and variance $(1/n)\sigma^2$. As in the case of $\overline{X}$ charts of process control, when the true values of parameters μ and σ^2 are not known, acceptable estimates can be obtained from samples themselves. These estimates are:

estimate of μ = $\overline{\overline{X}}$

= average of sample averages

estimate of σ = either $\bar{s}$, standard deviation of sample, or $\overline{R}/d_2$ as used in $\overline{X}$ and R charts

If the characteristic is subject to an upper limit U, the percentage of items in the lot being not acceptable (exceeding the upper limit) is denoted by the shaded area p_u in Figure 14.1. If the curve in Figure 14.1 were the exact distribution of X, p_u would be the exact fraction defective in the lot.

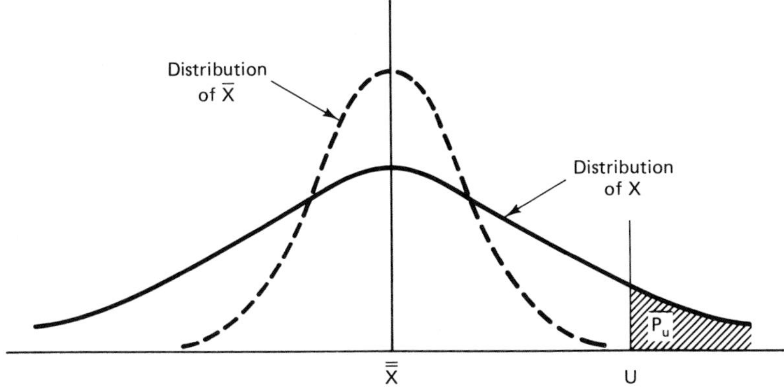

Figure 14.1 Probability of acceptance of a lot.

When the curve is only an estimate based on the observations in a sample, p_u is also an estimate. The criterion for accepting the lot is that p_u must be less than or equal to a designated number M. A variables sampling plan is specified by the two numbers n = sample size and M = maximum allowable fraction defective.

An alternative measure of the fraction of items being defective is z, or how many estimated standard deviations separate the specification limit U and the sample average $\overline{X}$.

$$z = \frac{U - \overline{X}}{\sigma}$$

This gives an alternative definition of variables sampling plan by the two numbers n = sample size and k = minimum standard deviations that must separate U and $\overline{X}$.

OPERATION OF A VARIABLES SAMPLING PLAN

The operation of a variables sampling plan involves the following steps.

1. Determine the sampling plan either as form 1 (n, k) or as form 2 (n, M). The terms form 1 and form 2 are in conformity with the military standard tables, which are usually the source of these sampling plans.
2. Take a sample of size n from the lot and measure the variables characteristic for each item.
3. Determine $\overline{X}$ and either z or p_u. The computational procedure is illustrated in the numerical example that follows.
4. Accept if the lot is $z \geq k$ or $p_u \leq M$; otherwise, reject the lot.

Example 14.1

The acceptable quality level for an item is 1.00% and the upper specification level is $U = 209$. For this AQL and a lot size of 40, two alternative variables sampling plans are found:

Form 1 plan: $n = 5,\ k = 1.53$
Form 2 plan: $n = 5,\ M = 3.32\%$

The two plans are equivalent and have the same OC curve.

A sample of five items yields the following measurements of the characteristic:

197, 188, 184, 205, 201

The computations for both the plans are shown in Table 14.1.

TABLE 14.1 Sampling Plan Computations

Line	Information Needed	Value Obtained: Form 1	Value Obtained: Form 2	Explanation
1	Sample size, n	5	↓	
2	Sum of measurements, ΣX	975		
3	Sum of squared measurements, ΣX^2	190,435		
4	Correction factor (CF), $(\Sigma X)^2/n$	190,125		$(975)^2/5$
5	Corrected sum of squares (SS), $\Sigma X^2 - \text{CF}$	310	Same as form 1	190,435 − 190,125
6	Variance (V), SS/$(n - 1)$	77.5		310/4
7	Estimate of lot standard deviation (s), $\sqrt{V}$	8.81		$\sqrt{77.5}$
8	Sample mean $(\bar{X})$, $(\Sigma X)/n$	195		975/5
9	Specification limit (upper), U	209	↓	
10	The quantity, $(U - \bar{X})/s$	1.59		(209 − 195)/8.81
11	The quality index: $z = (U - \bar{X})/s$		1.59	Same
12	Acceptability constant, k	1.53		From table A15.2
13	Estimate of lot per cent defective, p_u		2.19%	From table A15.4
14	Maximum allowable per cent defective, M		3.32%	
15	Acceptability criterion, $(U - \bar{X})/s$ must be equal to or greater than k	1.59 > 1.53		
16	Acceptability criterion, p_u must be less than or equal to M		2.19 < 3.32	

When both upper and lower specification limits exist, the acceptance criteria are modified as shown below.

1. In form 1 both $(U - \overline{X})/\sigma$ and $(\overline{X} - L)/\sigma$ must exceed k.
2. In form 2 separate values of p_u and p_L are calculated. The total $p_u + p_L$ must be less than M.

MIL-STD-414: SAMPLING PROCEDURES AND TABLES FOR INSPECTION BY VARIABLES FOR PERCENT DEFECTIVE[1]

Although there are many authoritative sources of variables sampling plans for acceptance, only MIL-STD-414 will be discussed in detail in this chapter. Like MIL-STD-105D, this document has become the standard for use by private industry as well as the government. MIL-STD-414 has four sections: A, B, C, and D.

Section A contains a general description of the sampling plans. It sets forth provisions for use of the plans, classification of defects, expression of nonconformance, acceptable quality level (AQL), submittal of product, lot acceptability, sample selection, quality average computation, changes in severity of inspection, and special procedures for application of mixed variables–attributes sampling plans. With the necessary additions and changes necessitated by variables interpretations, the instructions for administration of the plans are substantially the same as MIL-STD-105D.

Section A also contains an AQL conversion table (Table 14.2) and a table for selection of inspection level by lot size (Table A15.1). Unless otherwise specified, level IV is prescribed for use. It is evident that higher levels are associated with tighter plans. The code letters in the body of the table indicate the sample size to be taken. The operating characteristic curves for all the plans are contained in Section A. There are 14 AQLs which may be used. These AQLs are consistent with those contained in MIL-STD-105D. Administrators may, upon determination of the AQL and sample-size code letter, consult this section and observe the risks involved in the application of the plan. Figure 14.2 is a portion of Table A-3 in MIL-STD-414 which shows the OC curves for code letter K with AQLs of 1.0, 1.5, 2.5, 4.0, 6.5, 10.0, and 15.0. The OC curves were derived from the unknown σ plans of Section B but, as stated, are essentially equivalent to range and known σ' plans. In the instructions, use of the unknown σ plans of Section

[1] MIL-STD-414 may be obtained from National Technical Information Service, Washington, DC 20402.

TABLE 14.2 AQL Conversion Table (Table A-1 of MIL-STD-414)

For Specified AQL Values Falling within This Range:	Use This AQL Value:
0–0.049	0.04
0.050–0.069	0.065
0.070–0.109	0.10
0.110–0.164	0.15
0.165–0.279	0.25
0.280–0.439	0.40
0.440–0.699	0.65
0.700–1.09	1.0
1.10–1.64	1.5
1.65–2.79	2.5
2.80–4.39	4.0
4.40–6.99	6.5
7.00–10.9	10.0
11.00–16.4	15.0

B, with standard deviation calculation, is prescribed unless otherwise specified.

Section B contains instructions for application of unknown σ-standard deviation method plans for single and double specification limits; master tables for normal, tightened, and reduced inspection; tables for estimating lot percent defective using the standard deviation method; instructions and tables for estimation of quality average; criteria for reduced and tightened inspection; values of F for MSD (maximum standard deviation); and calculation examples. These are shown as Tables A15.1 through A15.9.

As in the case of MIL-STD-105D, the standard MIL-STD-414 also provides for reduced and tightened inspection. The conditions for instituting reduced inspection are as follows:

Condition A. The preceding ten (10) lots (or such other number of lots designated) have been under normal inspection and none has been rejected.

Condition B. The estimated percent defective for each of these preceding lots is less than the applicable lower limit shown in Table A15.7; or for certain sampling plans, the estimated lot percent defective is equal to zero for a specified number of consecutive lots (see Table A15.7).

Condition C. Production is at a steady rate.

Normal inspection is reinstated if any one of the following conditions occurs under reduced inspection.

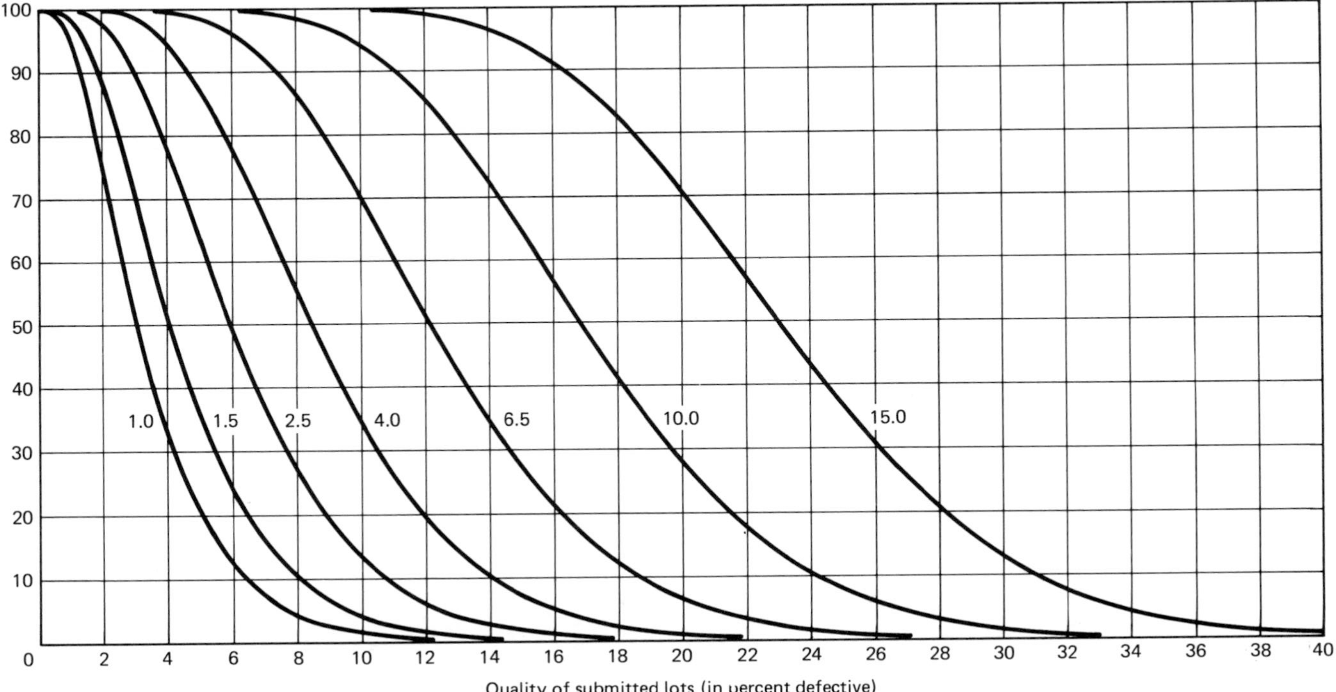

The values of the percent of lots expected to be accepted are valid only when measurements are selected at random from a normal distribution.

Note: Figures on curves are acceptable quality levels for normal inspection.

Figure 14.2 Operating characteristic curves for sampling plans based on standard deviation method. (A portion of Table A-3 of MIL-STD-414.)

Condition D. A lot is rejected.

Condition E. The estimated process average is greater than the AQL.

Condition F. Production becomes irregular or delayed.

Condition G. Other conditions as may warrant that normal inspection should be reinstated.

Tightened inspection is instituted when the estimated process average computed from the preceding 10 lots (or such other number of lots designated) is greater than the AQL, and when more than a certain number, T, of these lots have estimates of the percent defective exceeding the AQL. The estimated process average is the weighted arithmetic mean of the percent defectives of the preceding lots designated. The T values are given in Table A15.8 for the process average computed from 5, 10, or 15 lots. If the sample size code letter is not the same for all samples used, the entry in Table A15.8 is determined by the sample size code letter corresponding to the smallest size used in any of the lots included in the estimation of the process average. Normal inspection is reinstated if the estimated process average of lots under tightened inspection is equal to or less than the AQL.

Tables A15.3 and A15.9 are used for finding sampling plans when double limit specifications are involved. The computation is the same as given for the form 2 example of the single limit example except for the following.

1. For one AQL value for both upper and lower specification limits combined, both Q_U and Q_L are computed. The estimated lot percent defectives associated with the computed Q_U and Q_L are located in Table A15.4. These are designated p_U and p_L, respectively. The sum of $p_U + p_L$ (designated as p) must be less than M for the lot to be acceptable.
2. For different AQL values for upper and lower specification limits, the following three criteria are used:
   a. p_U must be equal to or less than M_U.
   b. p_L must be equal to or less than M_L.
   c. $p_U + p_L$ must be equal to or less than the larger of M_U and M_L.

Form 1 may also be used for the two-sided-limit case. Both of the quantities $(U - \overline{X})/s$ and $(\overline{X} - L)/s$ are compared to k and must be greater than k for the lot to be acceptable. Also, the appropriate F value is located from Table A15.9 to determine the maximum standard deviation (MSD). The MSD is computed by finding the product of F and $(U - L)$. The computed standard deviation should be no larger than the MSD.

Section C is applicable to the unknown variability situation and is exactly the same as Section B except that the tables are based on calculations using the average range as the measure of variability. They are used just as directed by the Section B discussed above.

Section D is applicable to the known variability situation and is organized the same as Sections B and C with the following exceptions:

1. The variability is known, so it is not estimated from the sample data.
2. For the single limit form 2 method and the double limit quality index method, the formulas for the quality indexes are

$$Q_U = \frac{(U - \overline{X})}{\sigma}$$

and

$$Q_L = \frac{(\overline{X} - L)}{\sigma}$$

where σ is the known standard deviation.

The tables are used just as directed in Section B when the known variability plans are prescribed. Tables from Sections C and D are not shown. Any person interested in the use of these sections can refer to the original standard.

It goes without saying that for all the plans, a negative quality index is not acceptable. The way the formulas are set up, the computed quality index must be equal to or greater than the k value. Any negative quality index is algebraically less than the positive k value and thus causes the lot to be unacceptable.

Example 14.2

Air filters are purchased in lots of 600 units. If AQL is 1.0, determine the normal inspection sampling plans using (a) MIL-STD-414 using form 1 and inspection level IV, and (b) MIL-STD-105D using general inspection level II and single sampling.

(a) The code letter is J. From Table A15.2 the sampling plan is $n = 30$ and $k = 1.86$.

(b) The code letter is the same J. From Table A14.2 the sampling plan is $n = 80$ and $c = 2$.

Since both plans are designed to give similar levels of protection, there is an advantage in the use of the variables plan. The sample size is 30 instead of 80 in the attributes plan. However, it would be misleading to jump to the conclusion that variables sampling is always more economical. Sampling inspection is only one of the cost factors. Which procedure is more economical can be decided only after all factors are considered. This is illustrated in Example 14.3.

Example 14.3

Either of the sampling plans shown in Table 14.3 will give equivalent protection. Costs may be classified as follows:

1. *Overhead*. These are independent of the sample size. They include the cost of administration, and part of the recording and computation costs. For a plan

TABLE 14.3

Type of Plan	Sample Size	Acceptance Criterion
Attributes	100	Ac = 4 Re = 5
Two-sided variables	50	$\overline{X} + 1.689\sigma \leq U$
σ unknown		$\overline{X} - 1.689\sigma \geq L$
		$\sigma \leqq 0.0125$
Two-sided variables	20	$\overline{X} + 1.622\sigma' \leq U$
σ known		$\overline{X} - 1.622\sigma' \geq L$

with σ′ known the cost of maintaining up-to-date information concerning the value of σ′ must be included. This could be done by use of a control chart for ranges.

2. *Sampling*. These are the same per unit regardless of the plan.
3. *Inspection*. These will ordinarily be much more expensive per unit for variables, since measuring costs more than making an attributes decision.
4. *Computation*. This involves only the negligible cost of counting for an attribute plan, computing a mean for a variables plan with σ′ known, and a mean and standard deviation (or average range) for a variables plan with σ unknown.

The cost function then is

$$C = a + (b + c + d)n$$

Let the costs shown in Table 14.4 be assumed for this example. The costs per lot of the three plans, then, are as follows:

Attribute: C = 2.50 + (0.022)(100) = \$4.70
σ unknown: C = 3.00 + (0.052)(50) = \$5.60
σ′ known: C = 4.00 + (0.0043)(20) = \$4.86

With the assumptions above, the attributes plan is the most economical.

The foregoing is not intended to demean the contribution of variables sampling for acceptance in the job quality assurance. Rather, it is to place it in proper perspective. If, from a total cost standpoint, it is the most

TABLE 14.4

Plan	Cost per Lot, *a*	Cost per Unit *b*	*c*	*d*	*b* + *c* + *d*
Attributes	\$2.50	\$0.002	\$0.020	\$0.000	\$0.022
σ unknown	\$3.00	0.002	0.040	0.010	0.052
σ′ known	\$4.00	0.002	0.040	0.001	0.043

economical, it should be used. If it is not the most economical, the attributes plan should be used.

Generally speaking, where destructive testing is involved, variables sampling will be the most inexpensive. In most other situations attributes sampling will be the most economical.

DESIGN OF VARIABLES SAMPLING PLANS

Although MIL-STD-414 is a convenient source for variables sampling plans, it is also possible to design sampling plans that approximately satisfy preset risk criteria. (Only the final formulas are presented here without necessary development and derivation.) The risk requirements are defined as

$$p_1 = \text{good or acceptable quality level}$$

$$p_2 = \text{poor or unacceptable quality level}$$

$$1 - \alpha = \text{probability of acceptance when incoming quality is } p_1$$

$$\beta = \text{probability of acceptance when incoming quality is } p_2$$

For one-sided limit plans,

$$k = \frac{K_\alpha K_{P_2} + K_\beta K_{P_1}}{K_\alpha + K_\beta}$$

$$n = \frac{k^2 + 2}{2}\left(\frac{K_\alpha + K_\beta}{K_{P_i} - K_{P_2}}\right)^2$$

where K_α = normal deviate exceeded with probability α
K_β = normal deviate exceeded with probability β
K_{p_1} = normal deviate exceeded with probability P_1
K_{p_2} = normal deviate exceeded with probability P_2

For two-sided limit plans, the formulas for n and k above apply plus[2]

$$\text{MSD} = \frac{U - L}{\max(K_{p'k} + K_{p''k})}$$

where MSD = maximum standard deviation
$KP'_k + KP''_k$ = normal deviate exceeded with the probability $(P'_k + P''_k)$
$P'_k + P''_k$ = probabilities of a normal deviate greater than k

[2] Maximum condition is achieved when $P'_\text{k} = P''_\text{k}$.

The OC curve for the single limit plan is constructed from the following two formulas:

$$K_{p_\alpha} = \frac{k - K_P}{h}$$

$$h = \sqrt{\frac{1}{n} + \frac{k^2}{2(n-1)}}$$

Example 14.4

Design a variables sampling plan to meet the following risk requirements:

$$p_1 = 0.01 \qquad \alpha = 0.05$$

$$p_2 = 0.06 \qquad \beta = 0.10$$

From the normal Table A1, $K_\alpha = 1.65$, $K_\beta = 1.28$, $K_{p_1} = 2.33$, and $K_{p_2} = 1.56$. Thus

$$k = \frac{(1.65)(1.56) + (1.28)(2.33)}{1.65 + 1.28} = 1.89$$

$$n = \frac{(1.89)^2 + 2}{2}\left(\frac{1.65 + 1.28}{2.33 - 1.56}\right)^2 = 41$$

If the reader will check Table A15.2, he or she will find that the code letter L plan for AQL = 1.0% is almost exactly the same.

The OC curve formulas are used to find P_a values for various values of p'. First, h is computed.

$$h = \sqrt{\frac{1}{41} + \frac{(1.89)^2}{2(41-1)}} = 0.263$$

A table is set up for the solution of various values of P_a associated with p values using the other OC curve formula (Table 14.5). An OC curve may be constructed using

TABLE 14.5 P_a and p Values

P_a	K_{Pa}	hK_{Pa}	$k - hK_{Pa} = K_p$	p
0.98	−2.05	−0.540	2.430	0.0075
$(1 - a)$ 0.95	−1.65	−0.434	2.324	0.0100 (p_1)
0.70	−0.52	−0.137	2.027	0.0215
0.50	0.00	0.000	1.890	0.0294 (p_k)
0.30	+0.52	+0.137	1.753	0.0397
(β) 0.10	+1.28	+0.337	1.553	0.0600 (p_2)
0.05	+1.65	+0.434	1.456	0.0727

the first and last columns. Figure 14.3 is the OC curve of the plan $n = 41$, $k = 1.89$ constructed from the coordinates of the P_a and p values.

The acceptance criteria, for two one-sided limits, are

$$\overline{X} + 1.89s \leq U \qquad \text{and} \qquad \overline{X} - 1.89s \geq L$$

or alternatively,

$$\frac{U - \overline{X}}{s} \geq 1.89 \qquad \text{and} \qquad \frac{\overline{X} - L}{s} \geq 1.89$$

and, in addition, for a two-sided limit specification,

$$s \leq \text{MSD} \qquad \text{where} \quad \text{MSD} = 0.23(U - L)$$

The latter criterion results from calculation of the MSD formula above. p_k is the probability of a normal deviate greater than k. Application of the first OC curve formula to this condition yields

$$K_{P_a} = \frac{k - K_p}{h} = \frac{1.89 - 1.89}{0.263} = 0$$

If $K_{P_a} = 0$, then $P_a = 0.50$. Thus $p_k = 0.0294$. For the determination of MSD, p_k is divided into p'_k and p''_k. The maximum condition is achieved when $K_{p'k} = K_{p''k}$, that is, when the normal deviate of p'_k is equal to the normal deviate of p''_k. One-half of p_k of 0.0294 is 0.0145. The normal deviate associated with the p' and p'' values of 0.0145 is approximately 2.18. Substitution in the MSD formula yields

$$\text{MSD} = \frac{U - L}{2.18 + 2.18}$$

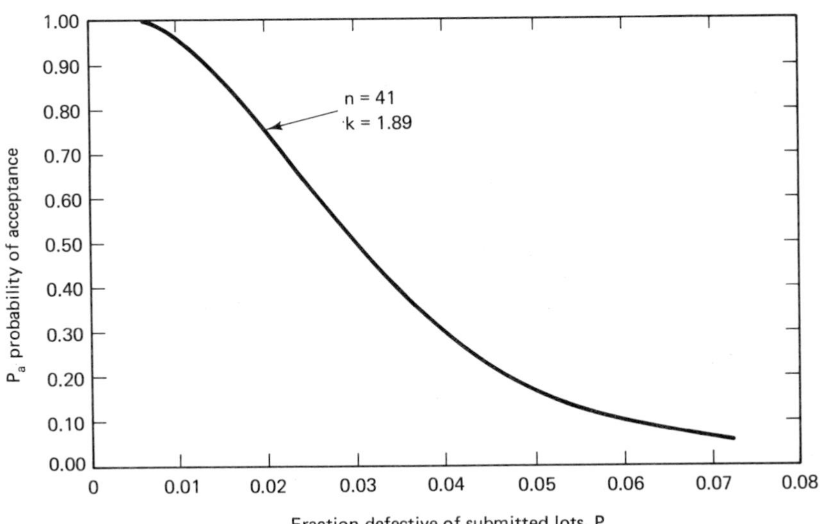

Figure 14.3 Operating characteristic curve of the variables sampling plan $n = 41$, $k = 1.89$.

The reciprocal of 1/4.36 is approximately 0.23, as shown in the two-sided acceptance criterion. This is also the appropriate F value contained in Table A15.9.

More extensive analysis, including graphic portrayal of the acceptance criterion, is beyond the scope of this book. However, sufficient material has been included to enable the practitioner either to select a plan from MIL-STD-414 or to draft one to meet desired quality specifications.

PROBLEMS

14.1. The following sampling plans will give equivalent protection:

Type of Plan	Sample Size	Acceptance Criterion
Attributes	450	Ac = 10, Re = 11
Variables σ unknown	100	k = 2.0
Variables σ known	33	k = 2.0

Given costs as follows:

	Attributes	σ Unknown	σ Known
Unit sampling cost	\$0.02	\$0.02	\$0.02
Unit inspection cost	0.10	0.25	0.30
Unit computation cost	0.00	0.010	0.001
Lot overhead = \$5.00			

Calculate the costs of lot inspection for each method. Which method is most economical?

14.2. The life of a certain type of electron tube has a lower specification limit of 50 hours. A lot of 100 is submitted for inspection. If form 1, inspection level IV, normal inspection, with AQL = 1.5% is used, what are the values of n and k to use?

14.3. If, in Problem 14.2, form 2 of the standard deviation method is to be used, what are the values of n and M? If the lot is 2% defective, what is the probability that it will be accepted?

14.4. The life of a type of equipment is specified to be 70 ± 5 hours. A lot of 60 units is submitted for inspection. Given AQL = 2.0%, normal inspection, inspection level III, what are the proper values of n and M? What are they under tightened and reduced inspection?

14.5. If, in Problem 14.4, the AQL = 0.75% for the lower specification limit and 2.5% for the upper limit, what are the proper values of n, M_u, and M_l?

14.6. The resistance in ohms of an electrical component is specified to be a minimum of 150. A lot of 250 units is submitted for inspection. Given AQL = 1.0%, inspection level IV, and tightened inspection:

(a) With form 1, what are the proper values of n and k? Given the acceptability criterion.

(b) If form 2 is used, what are the values of n, v and M?

14.7. The specifications for weight of a casting are 40 ± 3 lb. Normal inspection, level V, AQL = 1.75% are the sampling specifications. The lot size is 50. A sample of 15 has yielded the following weights in order: 37, 37, 46, 41, 36, 43, 41, 39, 37, 41, 41, 42, 41, 44, and 46. Is the lot acceptable?

14.8. An unknown variability plan with AQL = 1.5%, sample size code letter H, and normal inspection are the sampling specifications for inspection of a product to a double specification limits.

(a) What are the proper values of n and M.

(b) The first five lots have been accepted. The estimated percent defective for each of the lots is as follows: 0.621, 0.357, 0.480, 0.103, and 0.657. If production has been at a steady rate, may reduced inspection be applied? Why? If your answer is yes, what is the reduced plan?

14.9. Derive one-sided limit variables sampling plans that will meet the following criteria:

(a) $\alpha = 0.05, p_1 = 0.02$
$\beta = 0.10, p_2 = 0.05$

(b) $\alpha = 0.05, p_1 = 0.005$
$\beta = 0.10, p_2 = 0.02$

Construct OC curves for each plan. Using the criteria of part (a), calculate F for use with a two-side limit specification.

fifteen

DESIGN FOR QUALITY ASSURANCE

QUALITY ENGINEERING

A dictionary definition of engineering is that it is the art or science of making *practical application* of a pure science. If the theory and principles of economics, probability, and statistics, as well as the sciences of chemistry, physics, biology, and so on, may be considered as pure sciences (and well they may), then engineering for quality assurance may be defined as the coordinated application of these sciences for the assurance and control of quality.

The quality assurance engineer (or quality control engineer, as he or she is often called) is the designer of the plans, procedures, and methods for achieving quality assurance. He[1] may not possess the title, but if he is performing the functions spelled out in this chapter, he is acting in that capacity. Hereafter, he will be referred to as the quality engineer.

What are the functions of the quality engineer?[2] Broadly speaking, any quality function that is characterized by planning or evaluation would fall within the purview of the quality engineer. This means that physical meas-

[1] In this chapter and elsewhere in the discussion of the functionary "quality engineer," the word "he" is used only as an indicative pronoun and does not in any way make "quality engineer" a male position. Obviously a person performing the functions of "quality engineer" could be female or male.

[2] In the elaboration of these functions, the co-author has drawn from his own experience supplemented by the philosophies and practices of the General Electric Company, Bell Telephone Laboratories, and the Department of Defense.

urement and test as well as routine data collection would be excluded from his duties. Also, management decision making regarding quality is not normally a function of the quality engineer. Certain decision-making duties may be delegated to him by management, but this is delegation rather than assignment of a function. Effective managements must depend very heavily on the recommendations of the quality engineer in any case.

The functions of quality engineering may be categorized into two main functions with each having subfunctions. The two main functions are: (1) planning for quality and reliability, and (2) evaluating quality and reliability.

The term *reliability* is used to define the quality of performance or function of the product over time as differentiated from quality of conformance before, during, and immediately after manufacture. Subfunctions are discussed in relation to their importance to the entire function of quality engineering. Because of this, separate chapters are devoted to further discussion of certain of the subfunctions. Others are discussed in this chapter. Taken together with the techniques discussed in previous chapters, these provide the quality engineer with the foundation of a proper design for quality assurance.

PLANNING FOR QUALITY AND RELIABILITY

Quality assurance begins with the design of a product. Innovation usually proceeds in steps as in changes to the design of a product. A new design is developed, tested in the pilot stage, put out for consumption, and modified as dictated by cost, performance, visual appearance, and other considerations affecting rate of consumption.

The quality engineer can be of great service at this stage. It is not intended that he preempt the functions of the design engineer, but he does have certain valuable information at his disposal that will enable the design engineer to do a better job of design engineering. Because of his duties and experience he knows more about the function of a similar product in the field as it relates to the quality effort expended on it during manufacture. He has access to quality histories of vendors and in-plant departments which point up recurring deficiencies as well as efficiencies which are neither economical nor needed. He has access to records of scrap, rework, and field complaints. He keeps the quality assurance budget and thus can relate the cost of quality to the cost of obtaining quality. He has made special process capability studies which can furnish valuable information about the capability of machines and processes. At any time when the cost to obtain quality can make up a large percentage of the cost of the product, he must be consulted at the new design stage for the advice he can give regarding the tools of quality assurance that will be used for this new design and at what stage of manufacture they will be used.

THE PREAWARD QUALITY SURVEY

The quality engineer can be of value before the product has been put into production by conducting preaward surveys of the bidder's production facilities. Quality goes hand in hand with housekeeping and safety, so even a cursory analysis of the production facilities will yield valuable information about the bidder's ability to produce a quality product. A preaward survey may or may not be necessary, depending on whether or not the bidder has been a supplier and, if so, what his quality standards have been. The quality engineer's continuing record of vendor and producer evaluations will be invaluable in the latter event. If the former applies, a preaward quality survey check sheet should be provided for the evaluation. It may also be used for rating the quality efficiency of his own company. The check sheet should provide for a graded check-off rating of the following factors which affect quality in the manufacturing situation:

1. *Provision for and maintenance of adequate tools, gages, and test equipment.* All such equipment is subject to wear and deterioration; therefore, the bidder should have the resources for establishing and maintaining an adequate system of tool and gage control. Each instrument, tool, or test should be identified and undergo a continuing program of inspection for ability to produce a quality product or to measure it. Gages should be calibrated regularly with master calibrating equipment and gages. Adequate records of such calibrations and inspections should be maintained.

2. *Provision for control of subcontracted materials and components.* Quality materials and components make for a quality product. Does the bidder evaluate the quality of product of prospective subcontractors prior to making a purchase? Does he rate his suppliers in any way? Are there quality provisions in the subcontracts? Are certifications required? Does he conduct incoming inspections on materials and supplies? Does he maintain adequate records of quality? What are the policies on defective materials? Do such materials undergo adequate team review for final approval or rejection?

3. *Quality assurance instructions and procedures.* Adequate instructions and procedures are prerequisite to any effective quality assurance program. Are the quality characteristics of the product classified as to seriousness? Are there written instructions on how the characteristics are to be inspected? Is the expenditure of inspection effort proportional to the importance of the quality characteristic? Where sampling is used, is the sampling procedure complete in all respects?

4. *In-process quality controls.* Is quality control in-process planned so as to provide inspections at the most effective and economical stages of manufacture? Is the control adequate? Are the various process sampling quality controls used and, if so, at what percentage of the optimum? Are the processing capabilities known and observed?

5. *Quality record keeping and reporting.* Records of quality inspections and tests, while not in themselves conclusive evidence that quality is controlled, are very good indications of control. Care must be taken to make sure that the bidder is not paying lip service to quality through elaborate manuals, procedures, nice-looking charts, and records which mean nothing, all of which is for the consumption of gullible surveyors. Unfortunately, this passes for quality control in many situations. A fully implemented system of 100% and spot-check inspection, although unscientific, is much to be preferred over this, the most costly and least efficient of all alternatives. Nevertheless, records and reports of quality are necessary. Records should contain evidence that required inspections have been performed. They should indicate the number and types of rejections and their dispositions. Reports of quality should be communicated regularly to top management so that the decision makers know the current quality situation.

6. *Drawing and specification change control.* This is an important aspect of quality control. Drawing and change control are not responsibilities of the quality control organization, but the conduct of this control has much effect on the quality of product. Gross errors may be avoided by a good system of engineering change control. The change control system should provide for an effective means of removing obsolete information from the drawings and specifications and for establishing the effective dates of changes. Records of all changes should be maintained.

7. *Control of special processes and nondestructive testing methods.* Certain special, expensive processing methods and tests may be required by the subcontract. Where this is necessary, evaluation of the end product is possible only through expensive destructive tests for quality evaluation. Typical tests of such processes would be radiographic, magnetic particle, penetrant, ultrasonic, salt spray, spectrographic, mechanical, and chemical tests.

8. *Substandard material control.* A definitive procedure for dealing with materials and parts that depart from standard is very necessary to adequate quality assurance. The procedure should provide for prevention of repeated manufacture of substandard material by outlining specific steps to bring about corrective action. It should provide for a substandard materials review committee composed of representatives of the quality assurance and engineering staffs and the production agency.

9. *Acceptability status.* All materials, parts, and assemblies that have been inspected should be identified by status. Such identification may be applied to individual units or to lots of units. They may be in the form of inspection stamps, labels, tags, or other acceptable means. Lot integrity should be maintained insofar as practicable and all rejected material should be segregated from accepted materials.

10. *Control of preservation, packaging, and packing processes.* It is not unusual to find that for some items the cost of packaging exceeds the cost of the product itself. Improper packaging of product for shipment and storage

can result in traumatic or deteriorating damage which renders the product useless or substandard. To minimize such losses, quality control must be maintained over the packaging materials, cleaning agents, preservative compounds, barriers, cushioning materials, desiccants, containers, adhesives, and soon; over the packaging process, performance, identification, and marketing, and over car loading for shipment.

In general, the attributes that the quality engineer looks for in the preaward survey are the very attributes that he strives for in his own system of quality assurance.

OTHER PLANNING RESPONSIBILITIES

The quality engineer is responsible for establishing quality controls at all stages of manufacture. This responsibility includes the placement of quality control methods at incoming inspection, at stations of manufacture, at finished goods inspection, and at shipping. The types of control will vary depending on the nature of the product and the quantity produced. He identifies critical quality characteristics and classifies all characteristics according to seriousness of a defect. He specifies quality levels and methods of sampling for control and acceptance. He works with engineering and production in establishing standards of quality for appearance, uniformity, color, and so on, to minimize disputes between inspection and production. It is his responsibility to develop the instructions and manuals for quality assurance.

The quality engineer develops vendor and departmental quality rating plans. He devises certification procedures to be used in conjunction with these rating plans. It is his responsibility to develop quality analysis worksheets, quality record and report forms, and to compile quality case histories.

The quality engineer specifies the inspection and test equipment that will be used for quality evaluation at all stages of manufacture and on the end item. He develops new and improved testing methods and techniques. He may or may not design inspection and test equipment. He does design the program of gage surveillance and control which assures that inspection and test equipment is adequately calibrated and otherwise maintained.

The quality engineer is reponsible for special quality studies such as surveys, audits, and process capability analyses. He conducts special studies of manufacturing and processing quality problems as they may arise on a troubleshooting basis. He assists the design engineer by designing a program for feeding back information on complaint analyses, tolerance analyses, and process capability studies. It is his responsibility to conduct special economic studies as they pertain to quality costs, with minimum total cost as the objective. He plans all quality experiments. As mentioned before, he is in charge of the quality assurance budget, and by establishing valid and reliable quantitative measures of the costs of quality, he designs procedures for quality cost variance analysis, measurement, and control. As such, he acts in the capacity of the management engineer for the quality assurance department.

A dynamic quality orientation and training program is essential to an effective quality assurance program. Thus it is necessary in the planning stage to develop a program of quality education which meets the needs of each level of workers and supervision effectively. It should specify the type of education, amount and extent by level of management, follow-up and refresher requirements, and it should be maintained up to date. This is another duty of the quality engineer.

EVALUATION OF QUALITY AND RELIABILITY

In most cases it will be necessary for the quality engineer to evaluate the results of the measures prescribed during the planning stage. He appraises the quality potentials of vendors and departments through the media of quality performance ratings. By evaluating the results and comparing the performances of all vendors and production departments on a standard scale, he can point out those suppliers that are more likely to supply quality materials and products. Special quality studies will require his specialized skills for analysis, interpretation, and evaluation of the data. Such would include studies of process capabilities, tolerances, quality costs, designed quality experiments, and demerit controls, as well as most of the specialized variables and attributes techniques used for control and audit of quality.

The Quality Survey

The term "quality assurance" originated at the Bell Telephone Laboratories. BTL viewed the "quality survey" (a planned program for audit evaluation of quality and reliability) as the most important single element in quality assurance.[3] The quality survey, as used by BTL, is somewhat unique in that it utilizes the team approach to solving quality problems. Thus a team is formed which is charged with the responsibility for making a very thorough study and report of the existing quality situation with recommendations. This approach was used quite successfully in developing a quality assurance program for the Nike missile. The co-author[4] had the honor and pleasure of serving as a member of one of the teams. Briefly reported, the Army Ordnance Department let a contract to BTL for the design of a quality assurance program for the Nike missile. The BTL quality assurance people

[3] E. G. D. Paterson, "An Over-all Quality Assurance Plan," *Industrial Quality Control*, May 1956, p. 34.

[4] B. L. Hansen.

worked on this and several other ordnance projects with "opposite numbers" in the Ordnance Department. This "opposite number" concept provided the continuing follow-up of recommended changes since the Ordnance personnel who were the opposite numbers worked right along with the BTL quality assurance people and could apply the team approach to additional projects. The results proved to be very satisfying and the projects contributed much to quality assurance as it is practiced by the Departments of Defense today. As BTL uses it,

> the Quality Survey includes a comprehensive, critical review of all factors which may have a bearing on product quality, from the design concept through production and use. Its purpose is to disclose any circumstance which may affect quality adversely, and to initiate steps to eliminate any such circumstance. Thus it reviews not only the quality related activities of others, but also the propriety and adequacy of its own activities. Of all the several activities of quality assurance, it is, because of its wide scope, the one which may be expected to contribute most to product reliability. The survey is carried on by a survey committee comprising three members: (1) a quality engineer who is a specialist with respect to the particular type of product under survey (a member of the Laboratories quality assurance organization who acts as chairman of the committee); (2) a member of the Western Electric (the manufacturer) quality assurance organization which functions as the Bell Laboratories' agent in securing the independent inspection results specified by the Laboratories; and (3) a member of the Western Electric shop organization. (In the case of surveys covering products obtained from non-Bell System sources, the third committee member is a representative of the supplier.) A separate committee handles each survey, of which there are about 50 each year covering a wide variety of apparatus, equipments, and systems. The Laboratories member is a specialist on a particular type of product of system. As such, he is familiar with the design, manufacture, and use of the product or system and with its field history. Each Committee member has his particular responsibility and makes his individual contribution to the survey.[5]

A brief coverage of the quality engineer's contribution to the survey follows:

1. *A detailed examination of the design requirements.* "Despite precautions which are taken to avoid them, it is surprising how frequently errors, incompatibilities, and ambiguities may sneak into design specifications. They result not from incompetence but from the sheer complexity of the design problem, from the fact that so many design specialists must be correlated, and from the pressure generated by the time urgency which is so characteristic

[5] E. G. D. Paterson, "The Role of Quality Assurance in Product Reliability," *Industrial Quality Control*, August 1960, p. 19. Reprinted with permission.

of today's development tempo. The survey engineer searches for such irregularities."[6]

2. *Examination of product sample.* A random sample is selected from the product. This sample is examined visually by the survey engineer and the design engineer to determine how closely the design agrees with the intent of the designer. This examination is intended specifically for qualitative characteristics such as design features that present a different appearance than intended or features that were omitted.

3. *Comparison of the design and manufacturing information.* It is common practice to translate the design requirements into manufacturing specifications and drawings. Errors, omissions, and additions occur during and after the translation of the information from design requirements to manufacturing requirements. The survey engineer compares the two sources of information for inconsistencies.

4. *Review of inspection procedures.* This is a complete review of shop and quality assurance inspection procedures for adequacy of planned inspection coverage, quality standards, acceptance criteria, and so on, on the end product and all the components and materials that go to make it up.

5. *Review of inspection results.* The inspection results of both shop inspection and quality assurance are given a complete review for adherence to specifications, adequacy of actual inspection coverage, chronological trends, secular noncomformance, and compatibility.

6. *Review of the results of field performance.* Field performance is the acid test of quality. It is from field complaints that shortcomings in design, manufacture, and quality assurance are detected. "Field results provide a sure road, often a slow road, but in the case of slowly manifested reliability failures, sometimes the only road to learning."[7]

7. *Examination of actual production procedures.* This examination includes a complete review of the production facilities. The production processes for materials, parts, and assemblies are reviewed and evaluated as well as shop and quality assurance testing facilities and practices. The entire committee makes this examination and each member submits a preliminary report of his findings.

8. *The quality survey report.* At the completion of the survey, the committee prepares a report which describes the quality status of the product, cites any significant quality shortcomings disclosed, and recommends to the organization responsible, action necessary to remove these shortcomings. These action items may relate to unsatisfactory features of the design; inadequacies of the manufacturing or inspection processes; improper, incorrectly used, or insufficient-maintained testing and measuring facilities; incom-

[6] Ibid.

[7] Ibid.

plete or incorrect inspection records; oversight, incompatibilities, or improprieties in any phase of the many other possible assignable causes which could lead to substandard quality. The responsible organization must take corrective action which is satisfactory to each of the members of the survey committee before the item is closed; and is followed up diligently until such action has been taken.[8]

It is pointed out that

> as a commentary on the extreme importance of the design phase of reliability, it is of interest to note, in some 1,500 quality surveys covering a wide variety of materials, components, apparatus, and systems, major irregularities in design have been found to outnumber those in production in the order of two to one. . . .[9]

Figure 15.1 is a flowchart depicting the process of making a quality survey. The team survey approach can serve as a model for use by any business interested in quality of product. It may be that a small business could allow no more than a portion of the time of three or even one man to such projects. Even so, the principles and procedure can still be observed no matter how limited the time and talent to be allotted. Moreover, the company has, in the survey committee, a flexible captive consulting organization which can offer benefits not possible from outside firms—namely, a continuing audit by people who are close to and know the design, manufacturing, and quality assurance requirements.

ELEMENTS OF A TOOL, GAGE, AND TEST EQUIPMENT CONTROL PROGRAM[10]

The quality of a product depends, to a large extent, on the accuracy and reliability of the tools, gages, and test equipment used in the manufacturing, inspecting, and testing operations. Tools and gages provide the physical means of attaining volume production and at the same time facilitate the fabrication, inspection, and testing of parts, components, and assemblies to the required degree of uniformity. Suitable gages and other inspecting, measuring, and testing devices necessary to check supplies for conformance to requirements should be provided and maintained. Only with proper design,

[8] Ibid.

[9] Ibid.

[10] Discussion of this portion is reprinted with a few omissions and minor changes, from AMC Manual No. 74-1, *Procurement Quality Control Manual*, Headquarters, Air Material Command, Wright-Patterson Air Force Base, Ohio, October 2, 1958, pp. 3–1 through 3–4. The Air Material Command (now Air Force Logistics Command) has been a leader in application of the concept of quality assurance through surveillance inspection.

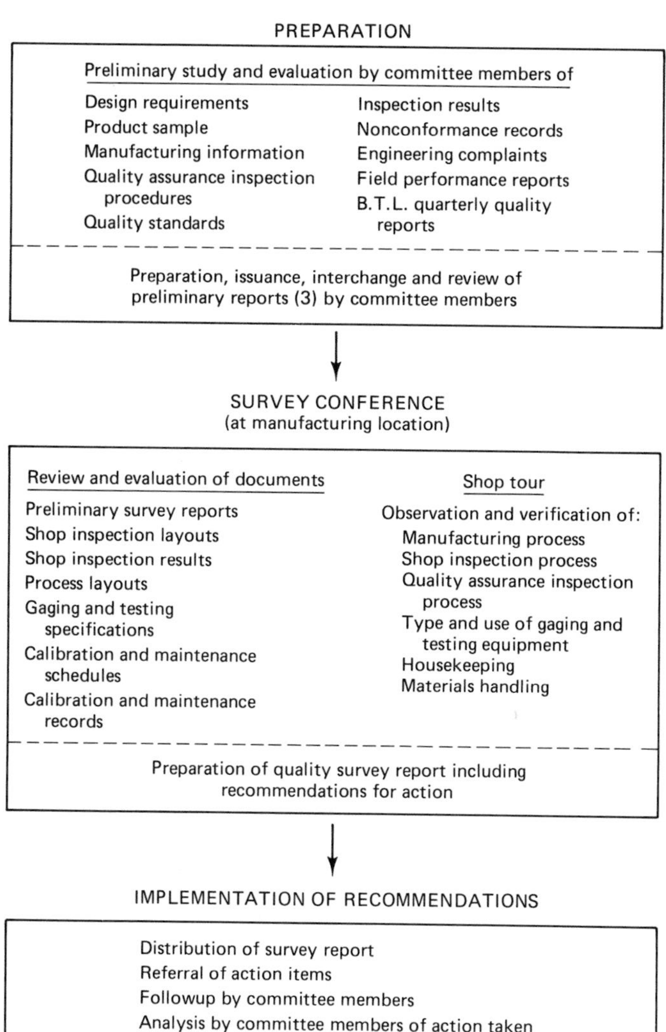

Figure 15.1 Flow process of quality survey procedures. (From E. G. D. Paterson, "The Role of Quality Assurance in Product Reliability," *Industrial Quality Control*, August 1960. Reprinted with permission.)

application, and control will such equipment guarantee continued uniformity and interchangeability within specification requirements. Because such equipment is subjected to constant wear and deterioration, it is essential that a system for tool and gage control be established and maintained to assure the required standards of quality of the product. The equipment should be checked with suitable measuring equipment at established periods to assure continued accuracy. Records or other suitable conclusive evidence should be maintained to assure that proper control is being provided.

For this discussion the terms "tools and gages" will include the following:

Gages and test equipment: measuring and calibrating instruments, masters, templates, meters, and all mechanical, optical, electrical, and electronic devices which are used in determining the conformity of a part, component, or assembly to specified requirements.

Tools: jigs, fixtures, and other devices and appliances which are used in the manufacturing processes to assure the interchangeability and uniformity of either the end product or the components.

Tooling used as media of inspection: fabricating devices which are designed and constructed in a manner that will fix and control the dimensional characteristics of the product without the benefit of parts inspection. The usual procedure to assure the conformity of a part to specified requirements is through the use of measuring or gaging equipment. In some instances, however, such as in the case of complex assemblies, it is not feasible or economical to follow this procedure. Therefore, the tool, by virtue of its design characteristics, fixes and controls the dimensional elements of the part and as such serves as a medium of inspection.

To determine what tools and gages will be necessary and to establish satisfactory controls, the product and the various fabricating, inspecting, and testing processes through which the components of the product progress should be analyzed thoroughly. This is accomplished by first reviewing all applicable governing documents, specifications, and engineering requirements, and then determining the type, quantity, functional characteristics, and important control points of parts and assemblies. Following this, all phases of tool engineering, including the planning, processing, sequence of operations, and manufacturing methods, should be analyzed to determine the extent of control required and the types of tools and gages necessary to assure the final accuracy of the product. The quality engineer must then maintain a continuing surveillance of the tool and gage control system to assure that objectives are being achieved.

The identification of each individual tool, gage, and item of testing equipment is essential to an adequate tool and gage control program. The system of serial numbers, symbols, dates, stamps, and so on, used should reflect such information as equipment name, type, size, initial inspection approved (if applicable), and latest engineering changes. This information is essential in requisitioning and issuing proper devices for specific machine and inspection operations, scheduling of periodic reinspections, maintenance of records, and general cataloging of such devices. Some identification system should be provided that will preclude the use of inaccurate or incorrect tools and gages.

To assure that tools are capable of producing uniform parts and that gages will control the dimensional and functional characteristics of the product within prescribed tolerances, it is necessary that they be initially inspected and proved relative to specification requirements. New, modified, or reworked tools and gages must be inspected and evaluated with reference to the tool or gage drawing as well as to the engineering drawing for the part prior to release for service. Such dual checks are necessary because the tool or gage drawing is representative of the design, function, and operational sequence of the tool or gage but does not enumerate the engineering requirements of the part, which are the ultimate criteria in determining the suitability of these devices.

In order that tools will be cared for properly and to assure satisfactory parts and proper performance, the equipment should be examined periodically for burrs, nicks, malfunctioning, mistreatment, loose and oversize bushings, distorted clamps, and other visible defects. This practice is especially applicable to manufacturers who have a considerable number of fabricating and assembly tools which either do not warrant periodic dimensional reinspections or have long intervals between inspections.

Parts and assemblies manufactured by subcontractors affect the quality of the end product; therefore, the prime contractor should normally require his subcontractors to maintain satisfactory tool and gage control systems.

An effective tool and gage control system cannot exist without precision control over the basic standards and measuring and calibrating instruments that are used to determine the accuracy of tools, gages, and test equipment. Precision gage blocks, masters, setting gages, length measuring rods, master layouts, and similar items form the basis of control over dimensional inspection equipment; standard cells, potentiometers, dead-weight testers, manometers, and similar items form the basis of control over functional testing equipment. Without accurate reference standards, inspections, and calibrations, tools, gages, and test equipment are of little value. The quality engineer must assure that master reference equipment is calibrated at sufficient intervals to guarantee its accuracy.

To preclude the use of worn, faulty, or inaccurate tools, gages, and test equipment, a system for the periodic reinspection and calibration of such devices must be provided. Not only must tools and gages be correct at the start of a job, but they must maintain this accuracy until the completion of the job. The extent and frequency of reinspection depends, to a great extent, on the accuracy requirements, critical dimensions, and interchangeability features of the fabricated parts and on the type, construction, and degree of usage of each particular tool or gage. All types of inspection and test equipment, such as fixed and adjustable gages, hand measuring tools, check fixtures, tools used as media of inspection, and all other mechanical, optical, electrical, and functional characteristics of the product, should be reinspected in accordance with established schedules.

To assure that gaged units are within the specified tolerances and that the accuracy, interchangeability, and uniformity requirements of the product are not jeopardized, the quality assurance group should subscribe to a gage-wear policy which provides for replacement or rework of gages before they wear or change to a point that is beyond the extreme product limits.

This policy, which pertains to fixed-type inspection gages, does not prohibit a normal degree of gage wear if provision is made for proper wear allowance in the gage designs. This is accomplished by the simple expedient of borrowing a relatively small percentage of the product tolerances and transferring it in the form of metal to the gage. For example: A product hole is 0.500 in. with a tolerance of plus 0.002 in. minus 0.000 in.; 0.0002 in. (10% of the tolerance) is borrowed from the total tolerance of the part and applied to the go gage, the basic dimension of which is 0.500 in., thus making it 0.5002 in. (0.0002 in. for wear). During the period it takes the gage to wear to the basic size, the product tolerance is slightly restricted, but this cannot be construed as a hardship on production when the other economical factors, such as gage life, are considered. A substantial portion of any objection can be eliminated by requiring that all units rejected by a fixed gage must be checked by a variables measurement device that does not have this wear allowance buildup on the gage.

Another factor may be introduced which is not considered a departure from the policy above and yet adds to the life of the gage. In actual practice the entering end of gages is subject to the most wear; consequently, a system of control may be established providing for gages to be rechecked for wear at a point back from the entering end equal to approximately 25% of the total gage length. For example, the total length of the gaging surface is 1 in., so check for wear is made $\frac{1}{4}$ in. back from the measuring end. If the gage is within tolerance at this point and for the balance of length, the slight variation from this point to the entering end should not affect the proper dimensional control of the end product. Of course, this procedure is limited by the length or depth of the characteristic being gaged.

If inspection records of the dimensional and functional accuracy of manufactured product are necessary, it follows that records or other conclusive evidence attesting to the continued accuracy of the measuring equipment are also essential to an effective quality assurance system. Not only do records provide the information that proper control is being exercised, but they are a valuable asset in reducing tool and gage inspection cost, estimating life expectancies, and anticipating replacement or repair needs. The system of tool and gage control must provide for the maintenance of records or other evidence that will readily indicate adherence to established procedures. The gage record should contain the following information:[11]

[11] MIL-STD-120, "Gage Inspection," December 12, 1950, p. 76.

1. Name and location of establishment where initial acceptance was conducted
2. Identification number of the gage
3. Gage drawing number and revision date
4. Name of item to which gage is to apply
5. Number and date of drawing showing the item
6. Any identifying letter, number, or symbol for a particular part, shown on the item drawings, to which the gage applies
7. Value of the gage as represented by the cost price
8. Type of the gage
9. Function of the gage
10. Dimensions to be checked by the gage, as represented on the item drawing
11. Actual gage dimensions as determined by the gage inspector
12. Exact information about storage location of the gage
13. Name of the gage inspector and the date the gage was checked
14. Additional remarks deemed necessary

The system of tool and gage control should contain provisions whereby immediate corrective action is taken whenever materials review, inspection and rejection actions, or other evidence indicate product defects that can be attributed to either faulty tools and gages or incorrect manufacturing methods.

Tools, gages, and test equipment, to maintain their inherent built-in accuracies, should be handled and stored in a manner that will not jeopardize their dimensional or functional characteristics. Governing procedures should require that (1) tools and gages receive proper handling to and from the storage areas and during the time of use, (2) tools and gages are prevented from coming into contact with each other or other foreign substances, and (3) in the case of indefinite storage, tools and gages are given proper rust-preventive care.

The Gage Laboratory: Its Equipment and Function[12]

The camera works of the Eastman Kodak Co. implements the objectives cited through control by a gage laboratory. A discussion of some of the most important features of the laboratory follows.

The camera works has a central gage control office where over 100,000 gages are cataloged and where all gaging equipment is checked and accepted. As operations require, the work gages are issued to the operators with the

[12] Clifford A. Wallace, "The Gage Laboratory, Its Equipment and Function," *Industrial Quality Control*, January 1954, pp. 46–50.

tools for the job. Because most of the jobs at the camera works are short run, the gages are allowed to remain at the operation until the job is finished. (This is an example of time-period control.) They are then returned to the gage laboratory for measurement. For long-run jobs, gages are checked at the machine by a traveling gage inspector.

The camera works feels that the gage laboratory is the heart of the gage control program and that precise mechanical control of gages is essential. To assure this control, a gage specialist quality control engineer is assigned to work with the process engineer and others in the review of tool layouts and gage requirements. Tools and gages are then requisitioned together. Any additions to the gaging equipment or orders for replacement gages are handled in the same manner. No gages may be ordered without the knowledge and approval of the gage engineer. This policy has made it possible to enforce the use of universal equipment whenever practicable. Purchase of special-purpose gages results in higher initial cost, higher checking costs at acceptance, and a loss in the time it takes to manufacture the gages. Universal gages are also much more flexible, so there is a tangible reflected economy in lower tooling costs for new models. Another important duty of the gage engineer is to review gage rejection reports and indicate disposition.

Many gages are supplied to subcontractors for inspection of components to be purchased by the camera works. A special group in the gage control section keeps records of all gages furnished to subcontractors. Periodically, they are called in for check.

The camera works feels that a gage control department should have the following responsibilities:

1. Custody and control of all crib gages for inspection of parts
2. Custody of pooled standard gages, responsibility for physical inventory
3. Responsibility for the accuracy of all gages at all times, and authority to require return of gages for checking
4. Accuracy control of all measuring instruments

There are many thousands of dollars wrapped up in the gage control facilities of the camera works. The cost of a suitable air-conditioned and temperature-controlled room is between $30,000 and $40,000, depending on location. The initial equipment consisted of a Swiss S.I.P. (Société Genervoise d'Instruments de Physique) Universal Measuring Instrument, two toolmaker's microscopes, one simple microscope, one supermicrometer, one optical comparator, and miscellaneous equipment, such as one small sine plate, several dial comparators, several sets of gage blocks, standard measuring tools, and the usual small precision measuring tools. Additional equipment was acquired as needed. These included an Electro-limit Universal Internal Comparator, a 48-in. Standard Measuring Machine, several more toolmakers' microscopes, a relatively large number of supermicrometers, a

Vinco Optical Master Dividing Head with Cam Rise checker, monochromatic light source for optical flats, small round super-accurate surface plate, bore gages covering a range of 0.7500 to 6.000 in. inclusive, index master for angular measurements, Cadillac Pla-check, visual gage of the comparator type, sine plate for compound angles, cylindrical standards, more sets of gage blocks, additional optical comparators, and surface finish analyzers.

One gage control person for every 200 production employees is recommended, although the ratio could be even greater if a good tool checking setup existed. Employment of a quality engineer gage specialist to police the gage control system for maintenance of accuracy in the gaging equipment is also highly recommended. The camera works attests to the value of the gage control program by citing quick payoff and accrued savings resulting from the standardization of some $800,000 worth of gages.

PROBLEMS

15.1. Would it be proper to say that one of the big differences between the quality control of today and that of 40 years ago is in the expanded planning function? Explain.

15.2. Develop a job specification for a quality control engineer to include education, experience, and personality characteristics.

15.3. Design a quality survey check sheet.

15.4. Design a feasible attributes sampling plan for acceptance and control of gages. This should include specification of classes of defects, acceptable quality levels, types and amount of sampling (if any), and so on. The problem should be assigned to groups for presentation and critique.

sixteen

QUALITY ASSURANCE METHODS AND STANDARDS

A quality assurance instruction sheet is an absolute necessity for adequate quality assurance. No inspector should be in a position where he has to decide what to inspect, where it is to be inspected, the tools of inspection, quantitative and qualitative quality standards for the item of inspection, and how many, if any, units are to be inspected. These should be defined by the quality assurance instruction sheet.

The author has often heard the complaint that taking the right away from the inspector to make these decisions is, in effect, making him nothing but a machine. This is an understandable reaction but one that has to be overruled by good organization and planning principles. The quality engineer is the specialist in *quality assurance planning*—the inspector is the specialist in *quality measurement*.

This requires, then, that the contract, purchase, or manufacturing order be routed through the quality engineering function for development or specification of a particular quality assurance instruction for the item to be manufactured.

From this point, the development of the instruction sheet may be best described by outlining a step-by-step approach to it using a simple item for illustration purposes. Although the item for illustration would not require the quality planning treatment which it will undergo here, the example serves to illustrate the general procedure. The procedure can then be applied to the items that deserve such extensive planning for quality.

PRODUCT QUALITY VALUE ANALYSIS

The first step is to make a cursory analysis of the quality investment justified for the item. This process may be termed *product quality value analysis*. What is meant is that the item should be viewed in terms of the *total quality cost savings* to be realized by making the investment in planning for and measuring the quality of the item.

The greatest quality costs that can be saved are failure costs. These costs are detailed in Chapter 17. If the quality engineer finds himself in the position where he has to start from the beginning, probably his best bet is to make a quality cost distribution study by product line. To make such a study, failure quality cost data are a necessity. Experience has shown that many companies collect inspection data incident to quality measurement. Unfortunately, too often the data go into a file without analysis. Even so, they are available for historical analysis. Data on the components of failure quality cost are too seldom gathered. Approximation is often a necessity, so where no data are available, the best alternative is to get a committee of people from all affected departments together to make consensus estimates of the failure quality costs for each item.

The quality costs of each item are listed in descending order, with the highest cost at the top and the lowest on the bottom. Assuming for the moment that the investment in quality planning and measurement is the same for each item, the greatest return will come from a quality assurance investment in the items at the top of the list. This assumption is not completely justified, but it illustrates a principle and provides a convenient starting point.

Figure 16.1 is an example of such a breakdown of data in tabular and graphical forms. It is evident that this is the application of Pareto's law to failure costs.[1] The abscissa variable may be inspection characteristic, cost center, departmental unit, or any other applicable variable desired. The ordinate can be total avoidable cost, or any one or a combination of the costs of scrap, repair, rework, returns, investigations, and so on. For these data, arbitrary division lines are drawn as shown and the items fall into either of groups I, II, or III. All other things being equal, the greatest return on investment will be realized by extensive quality assurance planning for, and quality measuring of, the group I items. The failure costs per item of group I items make up 72% of the total costs, although only 25% of the items are in this group. At the other extreme, group III items, although they make up 45% of the product lines, account for only 7% of the failure costs. Quality assurance investment in these items should be low. Group II is the intermediate group which comprises borderline items. Quality investment in these

[1] This is a form of the Lorenz curve currently popularly described as "Pareto's law." See M. O. Lorenz, "Methods of Measuring the Concentration of Wealth," *American Statistical Association*, Vol. 9 (1904–1905), pp. 209–219; and Vilfredo Pareto, *Manuale d'Economia Politica*, 1906.

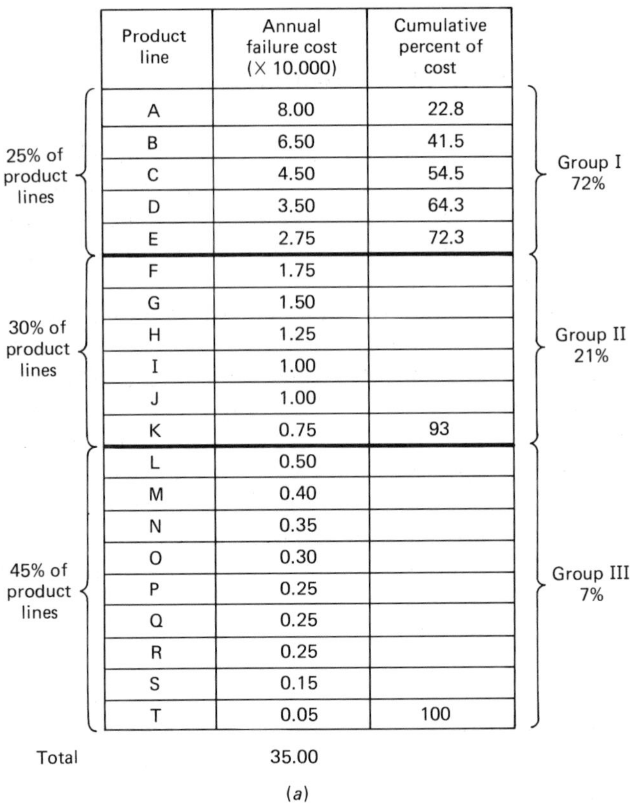

Product line	Annual failure cost (X 10.000)	Cumulative percent of cost
A	8.00	22.8
B	6.50	41.5
C	4.50	54.5
D	3.50	64.3
E	2.75	72.3
F	1.75	
G	1.50	
H	1.25	
I	1.00	
J	1.00	
K	0.75	93
L	0.50	
M	0.40	
N	0.35	
O	0.30	
P	0.25	
Q	0.25	
R	0.25	
S	0.15	
T	0.05	100
Total	35.00	

25% of product lines (A–E): Group I 72%
30% of product lines (F–K): Group II 21%
45% of product lines (L–T): Group III 7%

(a)

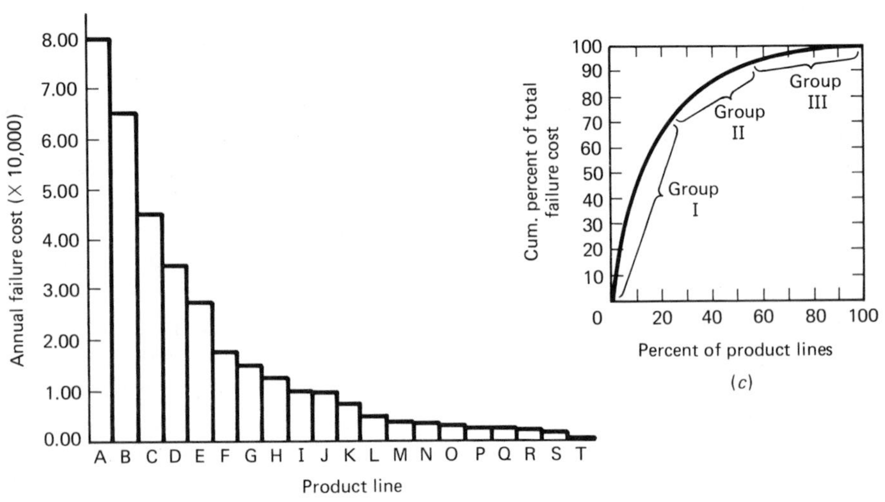

Figure 16.1 Distribution of item failure costs by product line: (a) tabular breakdown; (b) discrete histogram distribution; (c) cumulative percent continuous distribution.

is dependent on the investment in group I; that is, they are second on the priority list.

This method of product quality value analysis lends itself to importance identification of product line manufacturing documents (purchase orders, drawings, and so on) so that the other manufacturing functions may also give attention to the product lines on a proportional basis.

Once the key product lines have been isolated, each of the lines may be broken down into subassemblies and components which are, in effect, inspection points. The same type of analysis may be used within a product line as well as between product lines; that is, there will be a concentration of nonconformance and failures in certain characteristics on the components and subassemblies. At this stage of planning the items for inspection should be viewed in terms of acceptance rather than control. Thus the quality engineer is putting himself in the shoes of the buyer and, in effect, is making decisions about acceptance quality for him. Of course, it is best to have the buyer specify these quality requirements himself, but if he does not, the quality engineer must do it for him. After the acceptance quality requirements have been established, the types of quality control mechanisms needed to meet these requirements may be considered.

CLASSIFICATION OF DEFECTS PROCEDURE

The next step is the development of classifications of defects or demerit lists for each of the items of inspection. A very simple component will be used to illustrate the general procedure.

Figure 16.2 is an exploded view of a common item of ordnance procurement during World War II and the Korean War—the M48 A3 fuse. The Ordnance Corps established 18 stations of acceptance inspection for this product in the same manner as a quality engineer would do for other items of a military or commercial nature. For this illustration assume that the flash tube (the threader cylinder) of the assembly is the item for inspection (inspection station). A classification of defects will now be developed for this item of inspection.

To develop a classification of defects for an item, it is necessary to secure all the contractual material that covers the item. Such material would normally include the contract or purchase order, drawings, specifications, and any other governing documents. Also, the quality engineer should attempt to get all the information he can about the function the item is to serve. If possible, the item itself should be available for examination in addition to the assembly into which it goes. Depending on size and complexity, this may be impossible. If so, the next best bet is a mock-up, or possibly a three-dimensional model of the item. In short, the quality engineer should attempt to get as much information together as possible about the item and its function.

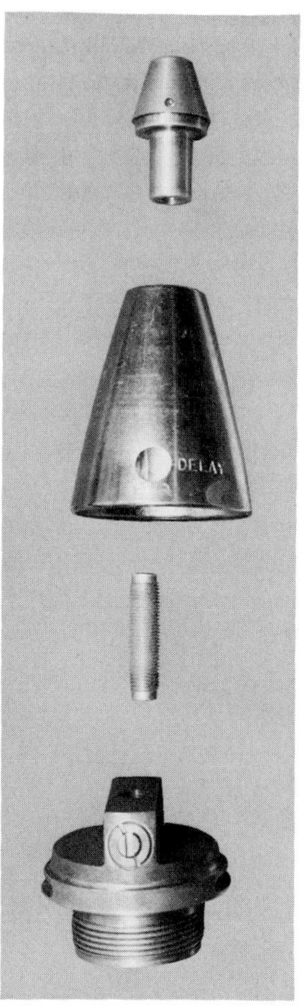

Figure 16.2 Exploded view of the M48A3 fuse.

The complete fuse assembly must be discussed briefly to determine the function of the flash tube. The entire assembly is a point detonation fuse which can be set at either delay or superquick. There is an ignition device in the nose assembly which, upon impact with the objective, causes a spurt of flame to be sent through the flash tube to the body assembly. With a superquick setting the flash is sent directly back to the booster charge, resulting in immediate detonation of the shell to which the fuse is assembled. This is superquick action. If the fuse is set at delay, the flash from the nose assembly at impact is prevented from igniting the booster by a rotation actuated eccentric device which closes up the channel in the body. Instead, there is another ignition device in the body which is actuated at the time of impact of the shell with the objective. However, the ignition flash is directed to a burning powder which causes a delay in detonation until the shell has penetrated the objective. This is termed delay action. Thus the functions of the flash tube are to carry the ignition flash back to the body assembly when the fuse is set at superquick, and to unite the nose and body assemblies of the fuse.

The information given above, the picture of the flash tube as it assembles to the other fuse components and assemblies in the exploded view of Figure 16.2, and an engineering drawing for the flash tube will suffice for setting down the flash tube characteristics for inspection and test. Figure 16.3 is the engineering drawing of the flash tube.

The next step is to list *all* the inspection and test characteristics on the flash tube. Following is a complete listing of the characteristics:

Thread major diameter
Thread pitch diameter, minimum
Thread pitch diameter, maximum
Thread minor diameter
Minimum perfect thread

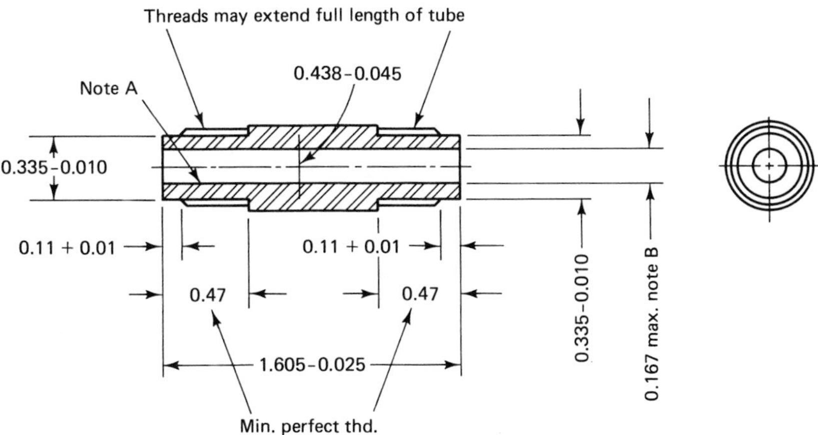

Tube, flash 73-2-268C4
Steel, FS1137 as-cold-finished
Finish all over 125

Note A: Plating of this surface optional.
Note B: Plug 0.1405-0.0005 dia. must pass through flash hole

Min. mechanical properties

TS 90,000	EL 10%
YP 75,000	RED 35%

Figure 16.3 Drawing of flash tube, part 73-2-268C4, for M48A3 fuse. (Courtesy Ordnance Corps, Department of the Army, drawing 73-2-268,ECO18498, 8-1-52.)

Length of pilot
Pilot diameter
Minimum hole size
Maximum hole size
Overall length
Finish
Plating
Chemical properties
Mechanical properties
Burrs
Foreign matter

The last two are usually included in all ammunition items where there is any proximity to explosive or ignition materials. The reasons are obvious.

The next step is to classify the characteristics into categories of seriousness of defects or to assign them to demerit groups. The categories applicable to this item are those contained in MIL-STD-105D. These are, with descriptions, as follows:

> *Critical.* A critical defect is one that judgment and experience indicate could result in hazardous or unsafe conditions for individuals using or maintaining the product; or, for major end item units of product, such as ships, aircraft, or tanks, a defect that would prevent performance of their tactical function.
>
> *Major.* A major defect is a defect, other than critical, that could result in failure, or materially reduced the usability of the unit of product for its intended purpose.
>
> *Minor A.* A minor A defect is one that does not materially reduce the usability of the unit of product for its intended purpose, or is a departure from established standards having no significant bearing on the effective use or operation of the unit.

Classification is logical and necessary. Without it, there could be as many opinions as to what constitutes a serious defect as there are people inspecting the product. The category descriptions above, at the very least, provide a frame of reference for *consistent* viewing of the seriousness of each defect no matter who does the classification job.

For some readers, a word about thread characteristics is in order here. The thread major diameter is the measurement across the apices of the threads. The thread minor diameter is the diameter across the bottom of the grooves of the threads. Each of these three dimensions has a maximum and a minimum. For threads where strength is important, the minimum of these three dimensions is major for external threads and the maximum is major for internal threads. Failure to meet these dimensions causes a sloppy fit which weakens the assembly.

For this item the specification of 0.4-24NS-2 for the thread (0.4000 nominal diameter, 24 threads to the inch, standard class 2 fit) indicates that strength is not an important factor. Hence all thread characteristics are classified as minor A. As it turns out, the only characteristic which could conceivably be classified as a major is the *minimum hole size*. The reason for this is that if the hole were obstructed in any way, or too small, the flash through the tube would be impeded, resulting in a *failure* of the product to perform its intended function. This is not a major end item unit, so the defect does not qualify as critical.

The mechanical and chemical requirements specified for the item also indicate that a high degree of strength is not important. (FS 1137 is a free-cutting steel, and the mechanical requirements for yield point, tensile strength, elongation, and reduction in area are low.) It is common practice to accept certification when these specifications are not severe.

SPECIFICATION OF INSPECTION METHOD

The next step is to specify the inspection method and any pertinent remarks for each characteristic to be measured. For an item such as this, fixed gages and visual inspection are the most logical and economical means. (Actually, if the costs of inspection were balanced against the cost of replacement and repair, the only inspection really justified would be visual, for hole obstruction. The other characteristics would automatically be checked by later assembly. If the item does not assemble, it is cheaper to throw the part away and select another for assembly. However, for this discussion, assume that inspection of the parts as indicated is economically justified.)

Figure 16.4 is the completed classification of defects for the flash tube. When the quality standards have been specified and used in conjunction with standard sampling tables, this provides the instruction sheet for acceptance inspection of the item. Note that verbal descriptions rather than drawing dimensions and tolerances are used on the classification of defects. If the latter were used, engineering drawing changes would require changes in the classifications of defects. With verbal descriptions, such changes are minimized. Drawing dimensions may be indicated, but they should be advisory only. Also, each characteristic has a code number. This is for convenience in recording and reporting inspection data. One method of codification is

Item: Tube, Flash Drawing No. 73-2-268C

Major	AQL 0.10%	Remarks
1. Flash hole obstructed*		Plug 0.1405–0.005 dia. must pass through flash hole

Minor A	AQL 1.50%	Remarks	
41. Pitch diameter of thread, min.		6091100†	DS 2
42. Major diameter of thread, min.		7288366	
43. Pitch diameter of thread, max.		7304003	
44. Major diameter of thread, max.		7388366	
45. Length of thread pilot		7255507	
46. Total length		7288367	
47. Length of perfect thread, min.		7504003	
48. Diameter of thread pilot, max.		7304003	
49. Thread not full		Visual	DS 3
50. Foreign matter		Visual	DS 4
51. Burr		Visual	
52. Exterior protective coating		Visual	DS 5

Defect Standards

DS 2 Determine in accordance with Ammunition Division Order 36–44, Rev. 1 dated 12 May 1945.

DS 3 If any threads are not up to proper height around the thread circumference for the required length of the threads, or if the not-go gage fails to pass over the threads because of a burr or feather edge on a portion of the threads, the assembly will be classed defective.

DS 4 Any part showing evidence of dirt, oil, grease, rust or corrosion or other foreign matter will be classed defective.

DS 5 When the base metal has been exposed, or if the action of a corrosive agent has impaired the effectiveness of the protective coating the part will be classed defective.

* This is slightly different from the original characteristic. Application of a plug is no more difficult than visual inspection here.

† These are gage numbers.

Figure 16.4 Classification of defects for the flash tube example. (From Ordnance Standard Inspection Procedure, ORD-SIP-M7-2 "Fuze, PD, M48A3, Parts," Ordnance Corps, Department of the Army, November 1951.)

to reserve the numbers 1 through 99 for criticals, 100 through 199 for majors, and 200 through 299 for minor A's. Any satisfactory method may be used.

The *remarks* column should be used for clarifying any points about inspection standards, particularly for visual inspection, where room for judgment should be narrowed to as small a zone of error as possible.

SETTING STANDARD QUALITY LEVELS

The next step is to set standard levels of quality for either each characteristic or each class of characteristics. For an item such as this, a standard level of quality for each class is advisable. In the demerit system the defects are classified into weighted demerit groups, but quality is reported as total demerits per unit.

Attempts have been made to arrive at quality levels with minimum total cost formulas, but for the most part these efforts have not met with much success. A rough economic calculation of whether or not to inspect the item can be made and some other economic approximations can be used to arrive at rough estimates. Some of these methods are treated in Chapter 17.

It should also be mentioned that here the concern is with conformance quality rather than design quality. The drawing sets forth the desired design quality—the classification of defects sets forth the desired conformance quality. The former is the manufacturing instruction—the latter is the acceptance inspection instruction. A standard quality level does not constitute a waiver of the drawing requirements. It is, instead, the means by which the process of acceptance and control inspection may be held near an economic minimum.

There are various types of acceptance quality standards. Those most generally used are:

AQL. The acceptable quality level, which is a nominal value expressed in terms of percent defective or defects per 100 units, whichever is applicable, specified for a given group of defects of a product. The AQL is usually in the range 85 to 99% of lots expected to be accepted on the OC curve.

AOQL. The average outgoing quality level, which is the quality level resulting from the acceptance–rectification features of an acceptance sampling plan.

LTPD. The lot tolerance percent defective of the OQL (objectionable quality level), which is a standard with an engineering flavor. It is that quality which will be accepted by the sampling plan no more than β percent of the time. (β is usually set at 10%.)

IQL. The indifference quality level, which is the incoming quality associated with a P_a of 0.50 on the OC curve.

Demerit standard. The acceptable number of demerits per defined unit.

The first two are by far the most popular, with the first being used more than the second. As mentioned before, application of the first results in the second. The AQL, LTPD, IQL, and demerit standard are standards for incoming quality; the AOQL is a standard for outgoing quality.

Several bases are used for arriving at a quality standard. At times each has been used as the single determining factor and, at other times, combinations have been used. The most common bases used for setting quality standards are:

1. *Historical data.* Past data are analyzed to arrive at a historical estimate of the process quality average. The standard is set equal to or at a large fraction of the historical average.
2. *Empirical judgment.* Standard is set at a level approximating a proven satisfactory level for a similar item.
3. *Engineering judgment.* Standard is based on engineering estimates of the quality requirements for function, life, interchangeability, assembly, safety, and so on.
4. *Experimental.* Tentative standard is set and adjusted as indicated by quality performance.
5. *Minimum total cost.* Standard is based on an analysis of the costs of obtaining quality versus the costs of not having quality.
6. *Consistent.* Each category has a set standard which does not change.

Standards can also be set by extrapolating the historical average or the historical trend. Performance in the absence of a standard is usually about 25% poorer than that which can be achieved optimally operating under the same conditions. Thus it may be preferred to set the quality standard at 80% of the adjusted historical average. The historical average should first be adjusted for out-of-control conditions which can be eliminated.

Empirical judgment is one of the preferred methods for setting a quality standard. There are few substitutes for genuine satisfactory experience. The standard based on engineering judgment is used often but, like other engineering judgments, often has an appreciable consumer safety factor in it. The danger in using this method is in specifying too strict a standard and one that is not the economic optimum. Sometimes, of course, cost is no object. In that event, the standard for outgoing quality may be the right one, for the consumer is willing to pay any price to achieve the standard.

The experimental standard is usually used for items where the desire is to accumulate historical evidence so that an equitable standard may be set. Naturally, an experimental standard should be identified as "tentative" because the expectation is that it *will be* adjusted. The minimum total cost standard is discussed in Chapter 17.

Once the acceptance quality standard is set, the process quality standard can be determined. The process quality standard may be set at a value which will assure that the great percentage of lots will be accepted when inspected in accordance with the acceptance quality standard. This may be determined by reference to the OC curve of the acceptance sampling plan. Some rough economic approximations of the proper proportions of sampling and screening inspection can be made here also.

AQL standards were applied to each category of defects on the flash tube, as may be seen by reference to Figure 16.4. A very low AQL of 0.10% was set for the major defect, probably because of the desire for function as intended.

The comparatively low AQL of 1.5% for the minor A category probably reflects application of standard practices of the procurement agency, i.e., the minor category AQL is made to be some multiple function of the major AQL while taking into account also the number of characteristics in the category.

Inclusion of Quality Standards on the Engineering Drawings

Figure 16.5 illustrates an interesting application of the classification of defects and setting of standards. Here, instead of providing a separate instruction sheet, the classification of defects and quality standards are placed

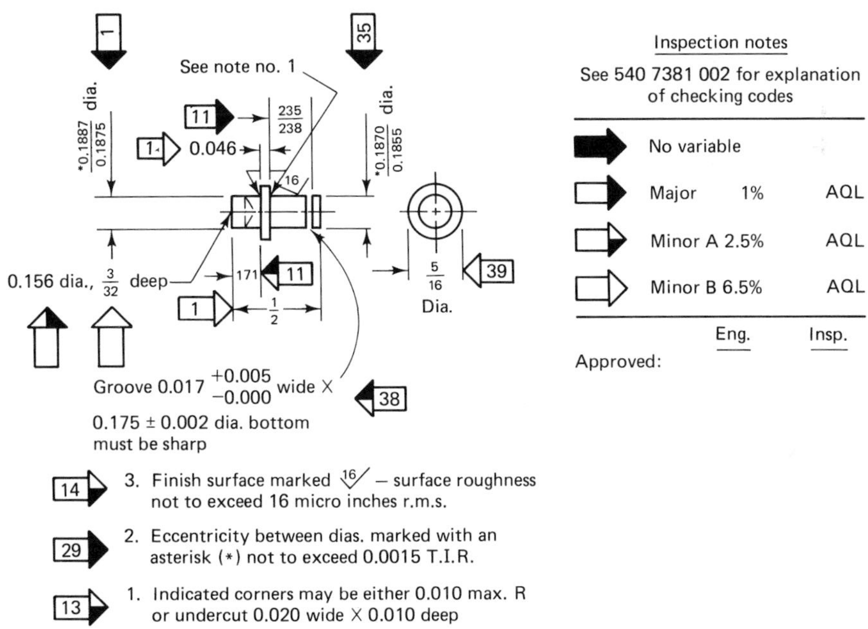

Figure 16.5 Method of classifying dimensions. (From "Statistical Quality Control Will Work on Short Run Jobs," *Industrial Quality Control*, September 1956, p. 11. Reprinted with permission.)

right on the drawing. The users have expressed satisfaction with the method. There appear to be three objections to it. First, there might be a tendency to view the AQLs as waivers on the drawing requirements, which of course, they are not. Second, a change in any of the characteristics or in any of the AQLs could mean a drawing change. Third, is inspection to be for defectives or for defects? There is no indication of this.

Classification of Defects for Complex Assemblies

International Business Machines, Inc. reports an interesting application of classifying defects on complex items for pinpointing need for corrective action. Figure 16.6 is an example of one of their trouble code lists. The list is put on punch cards as indicated by Figure 16.7. It is pointed out that

> recording the quality data on cards which are subsequently processed by means of electric accounting machines equipment not only simplifies the clerical task of computing the average demerits per unit, but it also makes possible detailed analyses which indicate where corrective measures are needed most urgently. The cards may be sorted by defect number and a report prepared which shows the frequency occurrence for each defect and the particular troubles causing the

Trouble codes	
01	Shorted/grounded
02	Sticking/binding
03	Stripped
04	Timing
05	Weak/open
06	Worn
07	Surface finish
08	Damaged
09	Incorrect/missing
10	Adjustment
20	Alignment
30	Bent/warped
40	Broken
50	Blown/burned
60	Dirty/corroded
70	Dry
80	Leaking
90	Loose

Figure 16.6 Trouble code list. (From Paul A. Robert and Michael L. Bugonian, "Quality Control of Complex Assemblies," *Industrial Quality Control*, November 1956. Reprinted with permission.)

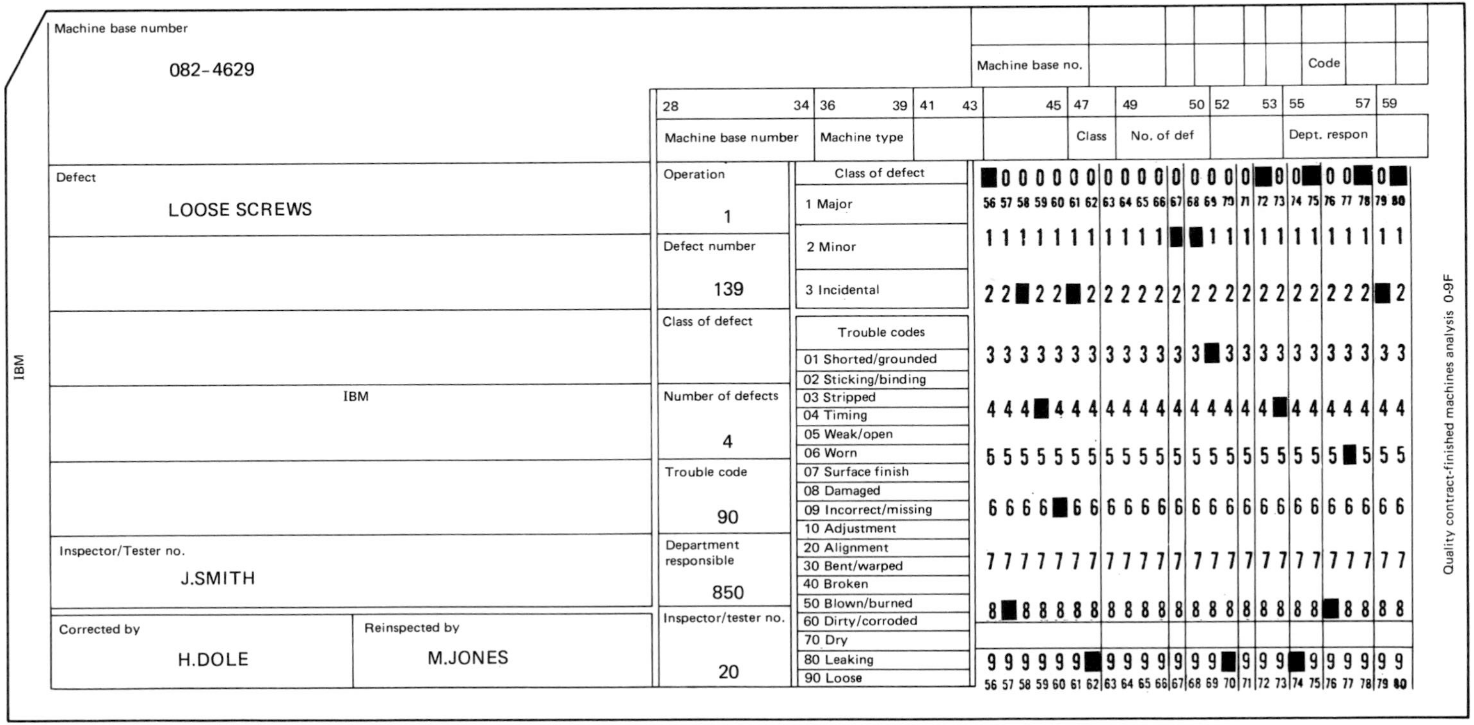

Machine base number

082-4629

Machine base no. | Code

28 34 | 36 39 | 41 43 | 45 | 47 | 49 50 | 52 53 | 55 57 | 59

Machine base number | Machine type | Class | No. of def | Dept. respon

Defect

LOOSE SCREWS

IBM

Inspector/Tester no.

J.SMITH

Corrected by

H.DOLE

Reinspected by

M.JONES

Operation

1

Defect number

139

Class of defect

Number of defects

4

Trouble code

90

Department responsible

850

Inspector/tester no.

20

Class of defect

1 Major

2 Minor

3 Incidental

Trouble codes

01 Shorted/grounded
02 Sticking/binding
03 Stripped
04 Timing
05 Weak/open
06 Worn
07 Surface finish
08 Damaged
09 Incorrect/missing
10 Adjustment
20 Alignment
30 Bent/warped
40 Broken
50 Blown/burned
60 Dirty/corroded
70 Dry
80 Leaking
90 Loose

Quality contract-finished machines analysis 0-9F

IBM

Figure 16.7 Machine accounting card. Punch cards, such as this, were commonly used as devices, both for data entry and data storage, in the early days of computer usage.

defects. The items requiring attention can be determined readily by scanning the report. A portion of a report by defect number is shown in [Figure 16.8].[2]

IBM used the demerit system with 13 to 17 demerits for major defects, 4 to 7 for minor A, and 1 to 2 for minor B. Because of their particular needs they defined the categories as follows:

Major:

1. Defects which, for their correction, require fixtures, tools, or gages not carried in the domestic toolkit
2. Defects which require removal or disassembly of a unit for their correction (units, such as counters, which are designed for easy removal are not included)
3. Poor electrical connections or contacts, which cannot be identified by visual means alone
4. Safety hazards which require exercise of unusual precaution
5. Troubles which require replacement of parts not ordinarily carried by the customer engineer
6. Conditions which, if neglected, could result in defects as outlined in 1, 2, 4, or 5 of this classification within a 90-day period

Minor A:

1. Defects which require corrective action and can be accomplished readily by means of customer engineering tools without disassembly or removal of a major unit
2. Potential safety hazards which could result in slight injuries to the operator
3. Defects which, if neglected, could result in defects as outlined in 1 of this classification within a 90-day period

Minor B:

1. Defects which do not affect the operation of the machine but which, if neglected, could produce a machine malfunction
2. Small imperfections in machine appearance which are not serious enough to cause customer dissatisfaction

It should be noted here that this company has established its own classification definitions. This is as it should be. It is another task of the quality

[2] Paul A. Robert and Michael C. Bugonian, "Quality Control of Complex Assemblies," *Industrial Quality Control*, November 1956, p. 9.

IBM

Finished machines quality analysis

1. By defect number ☐
2. Summary by unit and defect number ☐
3. By department responsible ☐

Weekly   Monthly X X   Period ending: Dec. 31 1953

Class of defect
1 Major
2 Minor
3 Incidental

Trouble code
01 Shorted/grounded
02 Sticking/binding
03 Stripped
04 Timing
05 Weak/open
06 Worn
07 Surface finish
08 Damaged
09 Incorrect/missing
10 Adjustment
20 Alignment
30 Bent/warped
40 Broken
50 Blown/burned
60 Dirty/corroded
70 Dry
80 Leaking
90 Loose

Machine type	Oper. no. or dept. resp.	Defect no.	Defect name	Class of defect	Trouble code	Number of defects
999	2	100	Motor and pump unit			
	2	101	Brushes	2	1	1
	2	101	Brushes	2	6	114
	2	101	Brushes	2	8	69
	2	101	Brushes	2	9	10
	2	101	Brushes	2	10	29
						223
	2	102	Capacitor	2	1	4
	2	102	Capacitor	2	5	11
	2	102	Capacitor	2	8	2
	2	102	Capacitor	2	10	3
	2	102	Capacitor	2	40	1
						21
	2	103	Magnet armature	1	4	4
	2	103	Magnet armature	1	10	4
						8
	2	105	Contact unit	2	4	1
	2	105	Contact unit	2	10	3
						4
	2	107	Magnet latch	2	90	2
						2
	2	108	Contact unit	3	90	5
						5
	2	109	Start contact	1	10	1
	2	109	Start contact	1	90	1
						2
	2	114	Wiring	1	9	3
						3
	2	115	Impellor blade	2	10	30
						30
	2	116	Deflector	2	2	2
						2
	2	117	Guide	2	7	48
	2	117	Guide	2	90	23
						71
	2	118	MP base unit	2	2	1
	2	118	MP base unit	2	4	8
	2	118	MP base unit	2	7	5
	2	118	MP base unit	2	10	4
	2	118	MP base unit	2	90	19
						*390
			Unit name and figures are fictitious			

Class I defects	Class II defects	Class III defects	Number of machines	Number of defects
2594	3817	1718	3390	8129

Figure 16.8 Quality analysis report. (From Paul A. Robert and Michael L. Bugonian, "Quality Control of Complex Assemblies," *Industrial Quality Control*, November 1956. Reprinted with permission.)

engineer to state explicitly the definitions of each classification so that the classifications will properly reflect characteristics which make a defect critical, major, minor A, or B, and to do it in such a way that there will be a minimum of doubt as to which class a defect belongs.

CLASSIFICATION OF DEMERITS[3]

Another guide for the classification of defects using the demerit system for complex items is used for many of the products manufactured within the Bell Telephone System. Defects are broken into four classifications with demerit values appropriate to each classification. The classifications, with definitions, are:

Class A Very serious (demerit value = 100):

1. Will surely cause an operating failure of the unit in service which cannot be readily corrected in the field; for example, open relay winding
2. Will surely cause intermittent operating trouble, difficult to locate in the field; for example, loose connection
3. Will render unit totally unfit for service; for example, dial finger wheel does not return to normal after operation
4. Liable to cause personal injury or property damage under normal conditions of use; for example, exposed part has sharp edges

Class B Serious (demerit value = 50):

1. Will probably cause an operating failure of the unit in service which cannot be readily corrected in the field; for example, protective finish missing from coaxial plug
2. Will surely cause an operating failure of the unit in service which can be readily corrected in the field; for example, relay does not make contact
3. Will surely cause trouble of a nature less serious than an operating failure, such as substandard performance; for example, protector block does not operate at specified voltage
4. Will surely involve increased maintenance or decreased life; for example, single contact disk missing
5. Will cause a major increase in installation effort by the customer; for example, mounting holes in wrong direction

[3] H. F. Dodge and M. N. Torrey, "A Check Inspection and Demerit Rating Plan," *Industrial Quality Control*, July 1956, p. 8.

6. Defects of appearance or finish that are extreme in intensity; for example, finish does not match finish on other parts—requires refinishing

Class C Moderately serious (demerit value = 10):

1. May possibly cause an operating failure of the unit in service; for example, contact follow less than minimum
2. Likely to cause trouble of a nature less serious than an operating failure, such as substandard performance; for example, ringer does not operate within specified limits
3. Likely to involve increased maintenance or decreased life; for example, dirty contact
4. Will cause a minor increase in installation effort by the customer; for example, mounting bracket distorted
5. Major defects of appearance, finish, or workmanship; for example, finish conspicuously scratched, designation omitted or illegible

Class D Not serious (demerit value = 1):

1. Will not affect operation, maintenance, or life of the unit in service (including minor deviations from engineering requirements); for example, sleeving too short
2. Minor defects of appearance, finish, or workmanship; for example, slightly scratched finish

ILLUSTRATION OF CLASSIFICATION OF DEMERITS[4]

This is an example of setting up category definitions for demerit assignment to defects for an item of household furniture, a china cabinet. The defects may be classified as follows:

Critical: those faults that may cause an injury to the user (broken glass) or damage chinaware (breakdown of shelves). In this case the customer most probably will not buy the product. 50 demerits each.

Major: those faults that will decrease the life of the cabinet (inferior quality of wood) or require excessive servicing (loose joints). In this case the customer may buy the product but will not be satisfied with it. 20 demerits each.

[4] This section is based on a paper by Robert Chateauneuf, "Modern Q. C. Pays Off in Woodwork," *Industrial Quality Control*, September 1960, p. 23.

Minor A: those faults that make the product less desirable (poor finishing). 5 demerits each.

Minor B: faults that will not result in injury or damage or decrease life of product.

The acceptable number of demerits per cabinet would be set at 20 demerits.

After the above-mentioned factors have been considered, two additional factors are considered to temper the results:

1. *Cost of inspection.* If the cost of inspection is high, the plan may be relaxed; if low, the plan may be tightened.
2. *Accuracy of inspection.* If there is any question about continuous accuracy, the plan may be tightened to allow for this.

Each dimension is rated in accordance with the above-mentioned factors and listed in order of importance. Ratings are modified so as to have no more than three or four plans on a given part. Plans are subject to periodic review.

EXPERIMENTAL STANDARD QUALITY LEVELS[5]

When there is no quality history on the same or similar item and it is impossible to arrive at a satisfactory engineering judgment, the method of setting experimental standard quality levels on the basis of *number of inspection characteristics* may be worthy of consideration. A nominal value of percent defective or defects per 100 units may be assigned to each inspection characteristic and the standard quality level for the category based on the number of inspection characteristics in it. Generally speaking, the more characteristics there are, the more chance there will be for error, and the more errors there will be. However, due to concentration of deficiencies in accord with Pareto's law, the standard quality level for the category need not be the sum of the nominal values for each characteristic, but a fraction of the sum. For example, one might assign a nominal value of 0.10% to each major characteristic. For a major category of 10 inspection characteristics, the AQL could be 0.65%. A spottiness limit for each defect might be in order for such a plan.

An example of this type of assignment of experimental AQLs for automotive parts is shown in Table 16.1.

Defect classifications were established in accord with MIL-STD-105D with an additional category of incidental for workmanship and defects having

[5] Automative Key Inspector Memorandum 5–54, "Preparation of Tank Automotive Inspection Plans," Ordnance Corps, Detroit Arsenal, May 6, 1954.

TABLE 16.1 Guide for the Assignment of AQL

AQL	Classification	Number of Characteristics
0	Critical	Any number
1.0%	Major	1–5
2.5%	Major	6–10
4.0%	Major	11–15
6.5%	Major	16–20
10.0 defects/100 units	Major	Over 20
2.5%	Minor	1–5
4.0%	Minor	6–10
6.5%	Minor	11–15
10.0 defects/100	Minor	16–20
15.0 defects/100	Minor	Over 20
6.5%	Incidental	1–5
10.0 defects/100	Incidental	6–10
15.0 defects/100	Incidental	11–15
25.0 defects/100	Incidental	16–20
65.0 defects/100	Incidental	Over 20

no effect on functioning, assembly, interchangeability, repair, or life of the unit of product.

Codes were assigned to characteristics of each category with the letters A through M for critical defects, 100 through 199 for minor A defects, and 200 through 299 for minor B defects. When no AQLs were prescribed for a category, Table 16.1 was to be a temporary guide for the assignment of AQLs.

seventeen

QUALITY, PRODUCTIVITY, AND ECONOMY

Economists define *productivity* as the ratio of "output" from a production process to the resource "input" to that process:

$$\text{productivity} = \frac{\text{output}}{\text{input}}$$

This ratio is similar to the engineering concept of efficiency. The concept of productivity is very closely related to the concept of quality. One describes the quantity characteristics of the output and the other describes the quality. Obviously, the twin objectives of productivity growth and improvement of quality are interdependent; one cannot be achieved without the other.

The importance of productivity growth was illustrated by the dramatic emergence of Japan as an industrial power. During the period from 1966 to 1980, Japan achieved a phenomenal growth in productivity while the productivity in Western industrial nations and particularly in United States was stagnating. As a result of this productivity growth, Japanese industry obtained a very strong competitive position in world markets. This competitive dominance spread over all types of manufactured products, ranging from high-technology products such as calculators, television sets, and industrial robots to more traditional products such as automobiles, steel, and shipbuilding.

American industry, as well as government, have somewhat belatedly recognized that productivity growth and improvement of quality are critical to ensure survival in intensely competitive world markets. To face this challenge, leading American companies have adopted a two-pronged approach: first, to learn and to adopt significant Japanese innovations in management, and second, to improve the more traditional American approaches to management and redirect these to the twin goals of productivity growth and quality improvement.

Space limitations prohibit the description of all approaches. This chapter and the next do, however, cover two Japanese innovations, quality control circles and the no-work-in-process inventory (KANBAN) system, as well as two traditional American approaches, budgetary control and economic optimization.

BUDGETARY CONTROL OF QUALITY COSTS

A common method of budgetary control is to measure the cost of quality as a proportion of direct labor. The validity of this method will depend on how frequently the standards are updated. A ratio of one inspector to 10 production workers which was right 30 years ago might be very wrong today. Direct labor, as a fraction of unit cost of product, is steadily decreasing through effects of automation and improved methods. Also, the cost of inspection is only one of the many costs of quality.

In a very challenging article, W. J. Masser of the General Electric Company tells of his company's approach to the problem of budgeting and measuring quality costs.[1] General Electric Company uses three comparison bases to measure the costs of quality: contributed value, net sales billed, and operation labor. The first base is calculated by subtracting the cost of outside purchased materials and services from net sales billed. Thus it is the value contributed by the departments that design, manufacture, and sell the product. The second base is the total amount billed for products sold during a given period, and the third base represents the actual input of money for all planned labor operations.

As General Electric Company views quality costs, they are segregated into three distinct categories. The category descriptions, the elements of cost in each, and two quarters' exemplary percentage results for each of the categories follows.

> *Prevention costs:* costs expended in an effort to prevent poor quality (Table 17.1)
>
> *Appraisal costs:* costs expended on the measurement of quality characteristics to assure conformance to quality requirements (Table 17.2)
>
> *Failure costs:* costs generated by defective product not meeting quality requirements (Table 17.3)

An examination of the 24 cost elements reveals that the largest portion of quality costs may be attributed to just a few of the elements—namely, rework,

[1] W. J. Masser, "The Quality Manager and Quality Costs," *Industrial Quality Control*, October 1957, pp. 5–8.

TABLE 17.1 Prevention Costs

Cost Element Description	First Quarter (%)	Second Quarter (%)
1. Quality control engineering and administration	2.0	2.0
2. Test, inspection, and process control: operating procedures and instruction writing	1.0	1.0
3. Quality assurance equipment: design and development	0.5	0.5
4. Quality training	0.0	0.0
5. Maintenance of patterns, tools, and dies: durable	3.7	2.4
6. Maintenance of nondurable tools: cutting tools, etc.	0.5	0.5
Total prevention	7.7	6.4

scrap, inspection, complaints, and vendor scrap. It is significant that these are either appraisal or failure costs. In other words, the greatest costs arise from correction effort rather than prevention effort.

After several quarters' information has been gathered, short-term objectives and long-term goals may be set for each of the categories and for each of the cost elements. Variance from the standards for each may be measured and evaluated. The three categories are then compared to the comparison bases established previously (Table 17.4). Three bases are used

TABLE 17.2 Appraisal Costs

Cost Element Description	First Quarter (%)	Second Quarter (%)
1. Incoming test and inspection	1.0	1.0
2. Laboratory acceptance testing	0.5	0.5
3. Laboratory or other measurement services	1.0	1.0
4. Inspection	10.0	13.0
5. Test	2.0	1.5
6. Checking labor	2.0	1.5
7. Setup for test and inspection	4.3	1.4
8. Test and inspection material	0.5	0.6
9. Quality audits	1.0	1.0
10. Outside endorsements	0.5	0.5
11. Test and inspection equipment calibration and maintenance	1.0	1.0
Total appraisal	23.8	23.0

TABLE 17.3 Failure Costs

Cost Element Description	First Quarter (%)	Second Quarter (%)
1. Scrap	14.0	14.9
2. Rework	28.0	29.0
3. Scrap and rework: fault of vendor	7.0	7.1
4. Material procurement: formal complaints to vendors, inspection reports, etc.	4.0	4.0
5. Factory contract engineering: use of design or product engineers to solve quality problems	4.5	4.5
6. Complaints: adjustment costs	8.5	8.6
7. Product service: special testing or for correcting imperfections	2.5	2.5
Total failure	68.5	70.6

because short-term events may cause one or two, but seldom all three, of the bases to be thrown out of balance.

In this comparison it is interesting to note that the cost of quality is five percentage points greater than the cost of operation labor. This illustrates the trend of direct labor as a cost. Even so, it is probable that this particular operation of General Electric deals with some very complex items.

The isolation of costs may be carried even further by breaking the cost categories down by product lines. For example, consider two product lines, A and B, and the distribution of quality costs to each (Table 17.5).

In this way, several product lines may be compared to ascertain where the most return for invested prevention money may be obtained. Line B is getting more prevention and appraisal money and shows a lower cost of failure. It also shows up as a lower proportion of each of the measurement bases. If these items could be considered of equal complexity and cost, it is evident that the greater investment in prevention cost for line B is paying dividends.

TABLE 17.4 Costs Comparison

Ratio of Quality Cost to:	First Quarter (%)	Second Quarter (%)
Contributed value	10.2	10.7
Net sales billed	7.8	8.2
Operation labor	105.0	106.0

TABLE 17.5 Quality Costs Distribution

	A, First Quarter (%)	B, Second Quarter (%)
Category		
Prevention	5.0	10.4
Appraisal	16.2	32.0
Failure	78.0	57.6
	100.0	100.0
Ratio of quality costs to:		
Contributed value	11.2	9.2
Net sales billed	9.3	6.3
Operation labor	124.0	86.0

Beech Aircraft Corporation QC people use ratio of quality control costs to direct labor for several interesting and useful purposes.[2] They predict costs of quality control for continuing and new projects by analyzing ratios of quality control to direct labor for such factors as work mix, production phase, product flow, rate, and production phase-out. They have found that different ratios are required for different prime contractors even though the work for each is similar. Also, there is a learning curve pattern of quality costs from the new product through the regular product phase. In an example cited, the ratio for new projects was 21% and for production of several years' duration only 9%.

Regarding whether to do in-process or end-item inspection, it was pointed out that

> most manufacturing people will, at first, prefer that inspection "buy off" each job, operation, or installation as soon as it is completed and signed off by manufacturing. This can be done, but from the inspection cost standpoint, it certainly is not the economical way to do it. Much more efficient use of inspection manpower can be realized if inspection check points are designed which will allow the inspector to check a group of items, a complete system, or a complete installation at one time. Again, it appears that the item-by-item buy-off would have the advantage of early detection; the workman who did the work can be [notified] immediately, before he repeats his error, etc. . . . Studies reveal that in most instances, the apparent gains are again more than cancelled out by the undesirable result of having manufacturing dependent upon inspection for functions which rightly are manufacturing supervision responsibilities.[3]

[2] Paul E. Allen, "Evaluating Inspection Costs," 1959 *Convention Transactions*, American Society for Quality Control, pp. 586–590.

[3] Ibid., p. 586.

It was pointed out that the in-process inspection reference did not include checks for tooling and setup quality or statistical quality control charting.

CONTROL OF QUALITY COSTS IN ENGINEERING

Beech Aircraft also uses an interesting engineering cost control which reduces the cost of quality. A careful analysis of the inspection being performed showed that a substantial portion of inspection time was consumed checking out engineering dimensions and requirements which were noncritical, included purely for the purpose of aiding in jig and tool design, and did not contribute to the quality, serviceability, interchangeability, or reliability of the end product. As a result they negotiated with the engineering department to begin classifying all drawing characteristics as critical, major, minor A, and minor B. This was not the same as classifying defects. Here the intent was to have the engineer actually change the engineering tolerance if it were an unimportant dimension. The results were startling. In one group of machined parts it was found that 43% of the dimensions could be ignored as long as the part made satisfactory assembly. In another case involving sheet metal parts, 62% of the dimensions could be ignored if assembly was satisfactory. The quality control labor-hour savings in the case of one machined part added up to 44%. There were also savings in the engineering time. Some other by-product savings were less rework of product, less rework of tooling, savings on original less-precise tooling, and less rejections to process. Table 17.6 gives the breakdown of engineering characteristics.

ECONOMIC OPTIMIZATION OF QUALITY CONTROL

Defects within an item are seldom uniformly distributed. More likely they will be *maldistributed* and approximate the Lorenz curve of Pareto's law. The items that will cause trouble will follow this law also. Common observations indicate that about 10% of the items contribute 80% of all the quality losses. Further within this group, a smaller group of about 1% could be responsible for up to 60% of the quality losses. This narrows the scope of profitable cost control application enormously and assures maximum return on the investment.

Techniques of economic optimization can be applied identifying the areas that need corrective attention. Some examples of economic optimization have been incorporated in earlier chapters. Two additional examples of economic optimization are discussed in the following sections; one deals with the choice of a proper sampling plan and the other takes into consideration the possibility of inspection error.

TABLE 17.6 Engineering Classification of Characteristics

Engineering Classification	Engineering Action	Inspection Action
Critical: Those characteristics which, when exceeded, vitally affect safety	No change in tolerance	Normal inspection
Major: Those characteristics other than critical which, when exceeded, are important to the function, interchangeability, utility, service life, appearance, etc., of the end product	No change in tolerance	Normal inspection
Minor A: Those characteristics, other than critical or major, whose standard tolerances can be exceeded by a specified amount as long as the part makes up into a satisfactory assembly	Tolerance changed by a specified amount on the drawing *Example:* ±2 (boxed) means tolerance doubled both under and over nominal as long as the part makes up into a satisfactory assembly	Normal inspection using the expanded tolerance
Minor B: Those characteristics, other than critical, major, or minor A which require *only* general adherence to specifications to produce a satisfactory end product	Characteristic specified minor B: dimension tolerance can be ignored as long as the part makes up into a satisfactory assembly	Characteristic is not inspected

Source: Paul E. Allen, "Evaluating Inspection Costs," 1959 *Convention Transactions*, American Society for Quality Control. Reprinted with permission.

ECONOMIC CHOICE OF A SAMPLING PLAN

In acceptance sampling the question of what AQL to use is often a problem. One can use a rule of thumb that the standard level of quality (AQL) for acceptance of a product may be set 20% lower than the historical average of uncontrolled quality. For example, assume that it is desired to set an AQL for an item that has not been quality controlled. The historical average quality over a specified period of time was found to be 3%. Using the 20% rule, this would mean that an AQL of 2.5% would be specified. However, is this the economic standard of quality? That is, does it reject when rejection is cheaper, and does it accept when acceptance is cheaper?

Enell has proposed a method for choosing a sampling plan.[4] When lots are rejected, there is a cost of rejection consisting of the total cost of repair,

[4] John W. Enell, "Which Sampling Plan Should I Choose?" *Industrial Quality Control*, Vol. 10 (May 1954), p. 96.

replacement, and time. Lots accepted by a sampling plan will more than likely contain defective units. These defectives generate extra costs—labor, materials, overhead expenses—by letting them get into the production line or out in service. Also, there is the cost of inspection. The example used by Enell concerns punched pieces of mica film used in certain condensers. Pinholes and conducting inclusions short circuit the finished unit and therefore are considered critical defects. In this case the total cost of manufacture was lost. The part was molded in plastic and it was impracticable to salvage any part of the unit. The following costs and definitions were established:

A = unit cost of acceptance (harm done when a defective piece slips through into subsequent production operations) = 10.5 cents

I = cost of inspecting one piece (good or bad) = 0.1 cent

C = cost of repairing or replacing a defective component once found = 0.5 cent

p = (unknown) fraction defective in the lot

R = unit cost of rejection (cost of finding a defective in a rejected lot, plus expense of correcting it) = $C + I/p$

Figure 17.1 illustrates the relationships graphically. The horizontal line at 10.5 cents is the unit cost of acceptance curve and represents the loss suffered whenever a defective piece of mica is used and causes a condenser to be

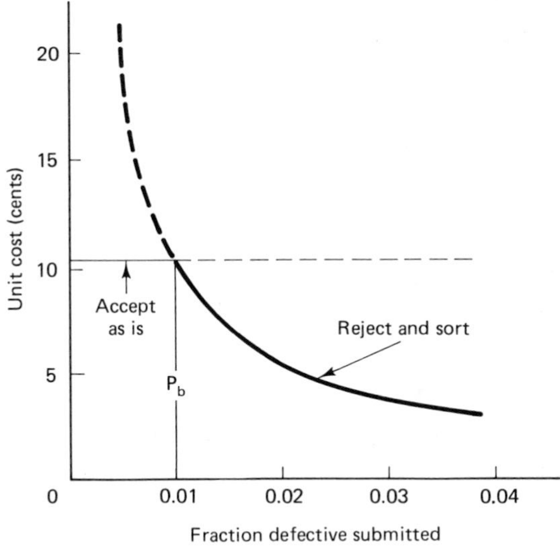

Figure 17.1 Unit cost curve. (From John W. Enell, "Which Sampling Plan Should I Choose?" *Industrial Quality Control*, Vol. 10, No. 6, May 1954, p. 96. Reprinted with permission.)

scrapped. The cost per unit is independent of the number produced. The curved line represents the cost of finding and replacing a defective mica film as a result of sorting after the sampling plan has rejected the lot. This curve is constructed by totaling these costs for given values of percent defective. For example, if the lot happens to be 2% defective, the total cost to find and replace the defective film is

$$C + \frac{I}{p} = 0.5 \text{ cent} + \frac{0.1 \text{ cent}}{0.02} = 5.5 \text{ cents}$$

The $C + I/p$ values are computed for other p and the unit cost of rejection curve results.

The two lines intersect where

$$A = R = C + \frac{I}{p}$$

This is the break-even point and is designated p_b; that is,

$$p_b = \frac{I}{A - C}$$

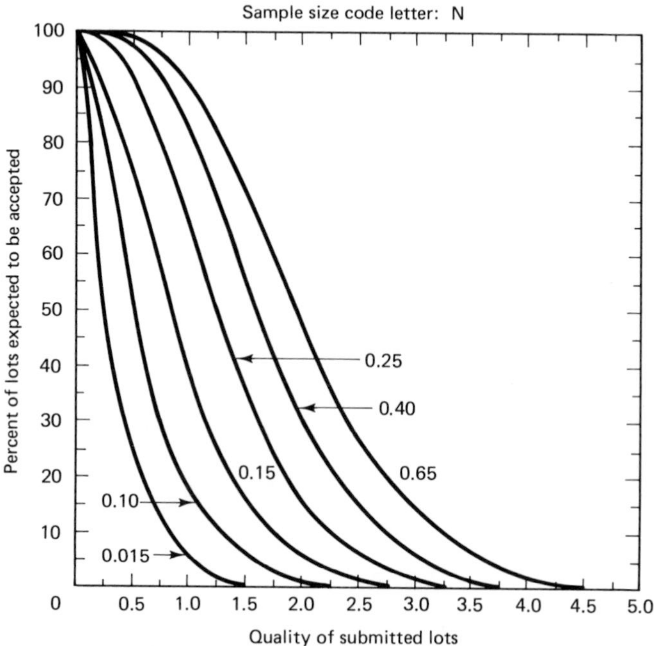

Figure 17.2 Operating characteristic curve, for single sampling plans, code letter N. (From MIL-STD-105.)

TABLE 17.7 AQLs Suggested for Various Ratios of Unit Inspection Costs

For p_b of:	Use AQL of:*
1:900	0.015
1:400	0.035
1:300	0.065
1:200	0.10
1:150	0.15
1:90	0.25
1:65	0.40
1:50	0.40–0.65
1:33	0.65–1
1:25	1–1.5
1:20	1.5–2.5
1:12	2.5–4
1:09	4–6.5

* The smaller (tighter) AQL should be used where normal lot sizes are less than 1000.

Source: John W. Enell, "Which Sampling Plan Should I Choose?" *Industrial Quality Control*, Vol. 10 (May 1954).

Lots worse than 1% defective should be rejected and sorted. Lots better than 1% defective should be accepted as is.

Now, the formula is put to work in the selection of an economic sampling plan. It is applied in this way. Suppose that lots are usually shipped-in in quantities of 15,000 each. For normal inspection, MIL-STD-105[5] specifies code letter N for this size lot. Figure 17.2 shows the operating characteristic curves for the various code letter N plans. Using the indifference probability point on the curve (50% probability of acceptance), the curve is chosen that has this point nearest to the p_b value of 0.01%. The curve labeled 0.15% fits the criterion best. Therefore, this is the plan to adopt.

It is not necessary to set up a curve for each situation. Various ratios of I to $(A - C)$ may be computed, associated AQLs found, and the whole tabulated for ease of selection. Table 17.7 shows this tabulation of AQLs suggested for various ratios of unit inspection cost to unit cost of damage.

The question of when not to inspect is important. If the sampling plan habitually makes the decision to accept, it is more economical to go to audit sampling.

> The crucial factor in deciding whether to use sampling in such instances is not so much the average percent defective as the variability from lot to lot.

[5] This is an earlier version of the military standard and is slightly different from MIL-STD-105D.

If the quality is substantially better than breakeven, and stable as well, no lot-by-lot inspection may be needed. If it is substantially worse then breakeven, and consistently so, it will be cheapest to use 100% inspection without stopping to sample. If the quality is erratic, then sampling will pay for itself.[6]

SIMPLE ILLUSTRATION OF GAME THEORY APPLIED TO AN INSPECTION PROBLEM

Table 17.8 is the simplest form of a game involving two opponents: nature (or the production process) and the inspector. The objective is to find the best strategy for the inspector to use, that is, a probability design for decision making.

The development of the general technique is attributed to the mathematician John von Neumann in the late 1920s.[7] It is often a subject for academic discussion but seldom one that is put to practical use. The dominant principle is that if the player plays the game according to the odds given by the payoff matrix, he will minimize his maximum losses. This is referred to as the *minimax* principle.

The values for insertion in the matrix of Table 17.8 are arbitrary for illustrative purposes and based on a $1.00 per unit cost of inspection and a $5.00 per unit cost of a defective getting further into production. If the inspector inspects a unit and finds it acceptable, the cost is $1.00 (indicated as −$1.00). If he does not inspect the unit and it is a good unit, the cost is $0.00. If he inspects a defective unit, the saving is $4.00 ($5.00 − $1.00 = $4.00). If he does not inspect a unit and it is defective, the cost is $5.00. The odds and payoff on this matrix may be computed; however, it would be somewhat unrealistic since the odds of getting a defective are seldom 50%. In a typical manufacturing situation a figure such as 2% is closer to the mark. Table 17.9 shows the matrix with the 0.98 probability applied to the good

TABLE 17.8 Cost Matrix: Inspector as Decision Maker—Production

	(1) Good Unit	(2) Defective Unit
Inspect	−$1.00	+$4.00
Do not inspect	$0.00	−$5.00

[6] Ibid., p. 100.

[7] For two treatments of the theory of games, see J. von Neumann and O. Morgenstern, *Theory of Games and Economic Behavior* (Princeton, N.J.: Princeton University Press, 1944), and J. D. Williams, *The Compleat Strategist* (New York: McGraw-Hill Book Company, 1954). The latter is written in popularized style for the nontechnical reader.

TABLE 17.9 Cost Matrix: Probability Values Applied—Production

	(1) Good Unit	(2) Defective Unit	(1) − (2)	Disregard Sign and Reverse
Inspect	−$0.98	+$0.08	−$1.06	$0.10
Do not inspect	$0.00	−$0.10	+$0.10	$1.06

column values and 0.02 applied to the defective column values. The odds on the matrix of Table 17.9 are computed by subtracting the right-hand value from the left for both rows, disregarding the sign, and reversing the figures. The computations are shown at the right of the matrix. Thus, if the production process is producing 2% defective, the inspector will minimize his maximum losses by inspecting about 1 out of every 11 at random. The game value is computed by applying the odds to either variable (good or defective). The answer should be the same for each. Thus

$$\frac{(0.10)(-0.98) + (1.06)(0)}{0.10 + 1.06} = -0.08+$$

This means that the average loss with this plan will be 0.08 cent per unit—but it is the least cost of all other proportions of inspection.

The other player is the production process. However, the same values do not apply; that is, the producer does not gain the $1.00 that the inspector loses in the inspection of the good unit situation. Rotating the matrix so that the producer is now the decision maker and introducing some realistic values of unit screening and rework costs yields the matrix of Table 17.10. For this example, the cost values are based on submission of lots of 2000 units per day to the acceptance inspection department. MIL-STD-105 is used for sampling inspection, and samples of 150 are drawn from each lot. The AQL being used is 1.0%. If a lot is rejected, the production department must screen the lot for the defects which rejected the lot and repair all

TABLE 17.10 Cost Matrix: Producer as Decision Maker—Acceptance Inspection

	(1) Accept Lot	(2) Reject Lot
	0.97	0.03
Submit 1% defective lot	−$1.50	−$205.00
	0.30	0.70
Submit 4% defective lot	−$6.00	−$265.00

rejectable units. Also, defective units in the samples must be repaired. The unit cost of screening is 10 cents and the unit cost of repair is $1.00.

The values in the upper left-hand corners of each block of the matrix of Table 17.10 represent the probabilities of acceptance and rejection of lots of 1% and 4% defective. It is assumed here, for purposes of illustration, that the decision maker is concerned with the proportion of each percent defective lot he should submit for inspection. The morality of the decision will not be considered here—although it is of prime importance in the final decision. Reference to the operating characteristic curve of code letter L, AQL 1.0, of MIL-STD-105 gave the indicated probabilities of acceptance and rejection.

The other values in each block represents the cost with each event. If acceptance inspection accepts a 1% defective lot, production will have to bear an average cost of $1.50 for the 1% defective in the sample of 150. If a 1% defective lot is rejected, the total cost will be the cost of screening 1850 units plus the cost of repairing an average of 1% of the 2000 units, or $205.00. The costs for the 4% defective lot are calculated in the same way.

Table 17.11 shows the matrix with the probabilities applied to each value and, to the right of the matrix, the calculations which yield the odds of 39 to 1 in favor of the 1% defective lot. To all intents and purposes, then, the production department should produce to the 1% defective level.

TABLE 17.11 Cost Matrix: Probability Values Applied—Acceptance Inspection

	(1) Accept Lot	(2) Reject Lot	(1) − (2)	Disregard Sign and Reverse
Submit 1% defective lot	−$1.45	−$6.15	+$4.70	$183.70
Submit 4% defective lot	−$1.80	−$185.50	+$183.70	$4.70

eighteen

ORGANIZING FOR QUALITY AND PRODUCTIVITY

Businesses organize to achieve objectives more effectively. The craftsman entrepreneur has a minimum of organization problems since he has to satisfy only himself and his customers. By the same token, his output is limited by the restrictions he puts on productivity by doing all the work himself. If he expands his business and hires more personnel, he will find it necessary to separate out the functions of sales, production, and finance. If he expands still further, functional units of industrial relations, product engineering, purchasing, plant engineering, quality control, and possibly others will emerge. It will be discovered that these "staff" groups are necessary for the success of the enterprise. In the process of this evolution it will also be realized that simple monetary-profit numbers do not reflect the whole performance of the organization. The attention would be increasingly directed toward the productivity of resource utilization as a measure of the efficiency of the organization. As the organization becomes more complex, the productivity of the whole depends on how well the parts work together. In organizations dominated by a central authority, the decision-making process soon outdistances the capabilities of this central authority and the result is stagnation. In successful organizations, enlargement causes the decision making to be more dispersed. Cooperation and consensus become the watchwords. There is a broad agreement that productivity and economic performance are not the sole responsibility of one organizational unit or person. Everybody pitches in and gets the job done. The creative satisfactions come from solving problems, which, by the way, basically stem from a lack of objectives and organization. Nevertheless, the concerted efforts of everyone toward solving the problem do yield results.

OBJECTIVES OF AN ENTERPRISE

What are or should be the objectives of an enterprise? The authors believe that there is one overriding objective, and that is to provide a continuing acceptable service to the public while yielding a satisfactory long-term return on the stockholders' investment. Chester I. Barnard[1] identifies the principal goal of any organization as "to continue itself." This continuation would be endangered in the absence of incentives for cooperation being provided to the public (satisfaction of a need for goods or services) and to the investor (economic return). Quality and productivity are two measures of the ability of the organization to provide these incentives.

Whether or not there should be a separate functional units responsible for quality and productivity should be considered in terms of the primary objective. Will it help to provide an acceptable service, and will it help to yield a better return on the investment in quality? Before the widespread acceptance of the concept that every unit within the organization bears responsibility for quality and productivity, separate organizational units used to be the norm. More recently there has been a tendency to consider this as an integral *function* of very organizational unit. This transition is facilitated by specialized techniques such as quality control circles. A few general principles of organization will be considered before detailing specific techniques devoted to the twin objectives of increased productivity and improved quality.

MANAGEMENT GUIDELINES FOR IMPROVING QUALITY AND PRODUCTIVITY

Shetty and Beuhler[2] describe the following guidelines for developing and instituting a "productivity and quality" program and for making it function effectively.

1. Managers must take responsibility for improving quality and productivity.
2. Productivity and quality improvement should become a strategic issue.
3. Employee ideas should be solicited and acted on.
4. Managers must recognize that quality improvement is a catalyst for improving productivity.

[1] Chester I. Barnard, *Functions of an Executive* (Cambridge Massachusetts: Harvard University Press, 1938).

[2] Y. K. Shetty and V. M. Beuhler, "Some Guidelines for Improving Quality and Productivity," Chapter 21 in Y. K. Shetty and V. M. Beuhler, eds., *Quality and Productivity Improvements* (Chicago: Manufacturing Productivity Center, 1983).

5. Managers should carefully measure quality and productivity levels before designing and implementing improvements.
6. Recognize that a wide variety of techniques and tools have the potential for improving quality and productivity.
7. Innovation, not imitation, is the route to successful productivity and quality efforts.

STRUCTURE OF AN ORGANIZATION[3]

Organization results from the division and delegation of work. The work to be accomplished may be divided in two ways: vertically, which is known as *scalar division*, and horizontally, which is *functional division*. To illustrate the former, a craftsman expanding his business by adding more *operative* craftsmen would be making a primary scalar division. He would now have to supervise operative employees. He might find later on that it is necessary to break out the craft work into two or more functional work centers. This would be a primary functional division. Thus he would now find himself supervising supervisors, since the separate work centers would require adequate supervisory control. This is secondary scalar division. And later he would find that the problems of sales, engineering, personnel, finance, research, and purchasing were so many as to require additional functionalization. Either process of division creates communications and human relations problems. The division of work means that different people will have different problems and will have little time for someone else's.

There is a chain of levels from top to bottom in an organization and each change implies further division and delegation of work. What is the most desirable number of levels is a matter of a trade-off between the benefits of increasingly fine division of work and the disadvantage of widening the separation between policymakers and production workers. A relatively small business organization, employing 20 to 30 persons, may have only three levels of organization (Figure 18.1). Any further division and delegation would be neither desirable nor affordable in economic terms. On the other hand, modern American corporations tend to be of gigantic dimensions. The sales of these corporations run into billions of dollars and employment into hundreds of thousands. Many of the corporate giants have as many as 11 levels of organization. Generally speaking, the top three levels, with personnel titles such as CEO, chairman, president, vice president, and so on, determine the strategies and overall objectives of the organizations. At the other extreme the bottom three levels, which include the operative worker, foremen, and

[3] The authors are indebted to Keith Davis for some of the principles presented here. Chapters 4, 5, and 6 of his book *Human Relations in Business* (New York: McGraw-Hill Book Company, 1957) are recommended reading for the human behavior aspects of organization.

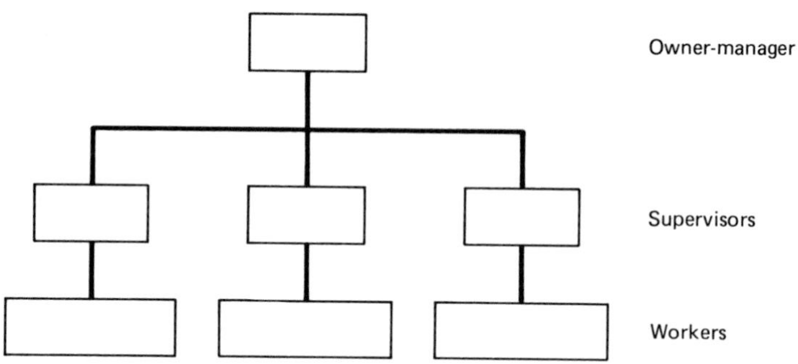

Figure 18.1 Three levels of organization for a small business.

first-line supervisors, deal with the day-to-day, or even hour-to-hour, problems of scheduling, work assignments, and the actual production of goods and services. In between is a large multilevel group which can loosely be termed "middle management." This group is involved in the smooth running of the corporation and faces all the problems of making and implementing the policies. Effectively, they are performing the same functions as the owner-manager of a small corporation. However, they do not have the equity ownership or controlling authority enjoyed by the owner-manager. On the other side, they cannot be as close to the production workers as the owner-manager can. Persons at these middle levels are in the "no-man's land" of management. They supervise supervisors. They are neither close to the employees technologically, socially, or in any other way, nor are they close to upper management.

DIVISION OF WORK AND FUNCTIONALIZATION

The division of work requires that there be delegation of duties, authority, and responsibility. An inadequate apportionment of the three can, and usually does, create problems. For example, to tell a machine operator that he is responsible for quality and not allow enough time for quality check in the standard is unfair and unrealistic. To give a supervisor authority to reward an employee with a pay raise and then not make the money available would be silly. In one case, an inspector was assigned the duty of inspecting gun tubes for acceptance. He rejected every one for one reason or another and every one was passed on waiver at a higher level. Under such conditions it would be hard to conceive of one's job as important.

Generally, duties should not be either overlapping or disjoint. Every element must be the responsibility of one and only one person. If a production supervisor is responsible for the quality of work turned out by his work center, he should not have a policeman inspector overruling quality decisions that he or his staff make—at least not at the same work station.

At the other extreme are duties which are not specifically assigned to anybody. Undefined duties essential to successful operation cause frustrations in people who want to get work done and cannot find out who is supposed to do it. These are duties which are likely to be pulled in by "empire" builders who are anxious to enhance the importance of the services of their particular organizational units. The duty elements end up in organizational units that were never intended locations orginally. In many instances this causes both organizational and personal problems.

The exception principle should be used in the delegation of duties; that is, routine tasks should be delegated to subordinates and only the exceptional tasks retained by the superior. Exceptional here does not necessarily refer to the technical nature of the work, since tasks of this type would probably be assigned to the technical staff specialists. It does apply to the general work for which the superior is getting paid. One cannot properly delegate in a haphazard manner. Like any other management operation, delegation should be well planned.

Table 18.1 is a convenient breakdown of supervisory time. The regular duties depend on the level. Regular duties for operative or lower management are oriented in the direction of human relations and work methods. Regular duties of middle management involve the integration of the resources of men, material, and machines. Regular duties of top management are primarily of a strategic and policymaking nature.

Functionalization introduces other problems. The reasons for having it are economic, but the human relations problems that result from it can make it uneconomic. By tradition, in a manufacturing organization the organization that produces the item for distribution is the *line* organization. Specialist groups such as personnel, purchasing, and quality control may be formed to support the line. Such specialist groups are known as *staff*. A staff specialist is one whose regular duties embrace a small but important aspect of the business. It is his responsibility to furnish technical guidance on matters in the purview of this specialty. The section supervisor is, or should be, a specialist in handling people. Middle and departmental managers are specialists in integrating human, material, and equipment resources. The farther one proceeds up the management scale the more one becomes a

TABLE 18.1 Breakdown of Supervisory Time

Duties	Percent of Time	Disposition
Creative	>20	So you *can* work smarter
Regular	60	Work smarter—not harder
Special	10	Some of these tasks are used as a test for promotion
Routine	<10	A subordinate can do a better job at this than you

generalist. Finally, at the top, one becomes an anomaly—a specialist in generalism.

Most organizational units have both line and staff functions. If a line function is thought of as that which produces the end item for distribution and the staff as technical support, any of the classifications shown in Table 18.2 would be true. It is seen that there is no such thing as all line or all staff. How one looks at one or the other is more a matter of where one works than anything else.

The traditional explanations about staff that one hears and reads are that there are two main types: general staff and specialist staff. *General staff* is that staff which is essentially an arm of the manager. Assistant VPs and "assistants to" fall in this category. The specialist staff has specialized functions to perform. There are many of these functions in a large corporation and it is here where the great problems of communication and human relations exist.

There are three types of *specialist staff:* advisory, service, and control. *Advisory staff* usually causes no problem. This is the expert called in to handle a special problem, such as the outside consultant or the legal advisor. His advice can be taken or not taken as desired. Seeking advice from advisory staff may be mandatory or left to the discretion of the manager. A supervisor may be able to discipline a worker but he may be *required* to seek the advice of the personnel staff prior to taking the action. Whether he takes the advice is up to him. He will, in the majority of cases, or it will be found that one or the other is not doing his job properly.

Service staff, as the name implies, provides a service to line and other staffs. Duplicating and reproduction offices are pure examples of service staff. Purchasing, maintenance, and janitorial functions are additional examples of service staffs. Actually, there can be considerable overlap of service and control functions.

TABLE 18.2 Line and Staff Functions

Departmental Unit	End Product	Line Function	Possible Staff Support
Purchasing	Purchasing document	Write purchase order	Production scheduling
Quality control planning	Inspection plan	Write inspection plan	Gage control
Industrial engineering	Method	Develop and write up method	Tooling department
Payroll	Paycheck	Write up the paycheck	Standards department

Many of the human relations conflicts due to organization can be traced to conflicts between line management and *control staff*. Line management, as defined here, means any management activity that had dealings with a staff control group. Examples of staff control groups are: production control, quality control, inventory control, salary and wage administration and control, industrial engineering, and cost accounting.

Control implies command. However, command is a line responsibility. Therefore, staff control is in the peculiar position of controlling the line indirectly through the chain of command. Normally, command proceeds from top to bottom within the organizational unit and never laterally between organizational units. Thus, in the scalar chain represented here, E should never be commanding (or controlling) O, or vice versa.

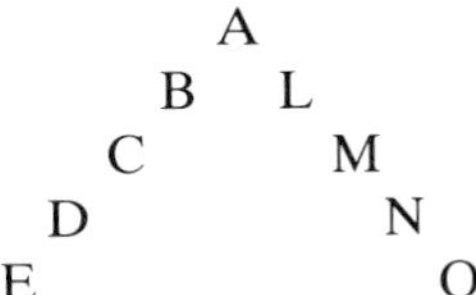

However, if E is a staff control group, it is foolish to require that every measure of control proposed go up the ladder DCBA and down the ladder LMNO. Things would just not get done. Therefore, through proper working relationships between D and N, and E and O, the implication is that the control measure proposed by E is the same as a command coming down the chain from A. In the military this is accomplished by signing "for the commanding officer." Mutual respect is a necessity for an effective lateral working relationship within the industrial organization. The burden is on the staff person. He must *gain* the respect of the line manager.

There are ways that the parent organization can help to achieve this working relationship. First, line experience can be made a prerequisite for staff work. Where this is not practicable, the prospective staff specialist should serve an apprenticeship as an "assistant to" the line manager. Second, he can be sent to seminars and training conferences with the line manager so that they are forced to see the other sides of problems. Third, he can be a member of a work center or work simplification team headed up by the line manager.

There are several predominant attributes that distinguish an effective staff person. He uses persuasion and negotiation rather than authority. He is tactful and diplomatic. He shows good timing in making his suggestions and he makes them in languages that can be understood. He is flexible and recognizes that time and patience are of the essence. In short, he is a subtle technological salesperson.

ORGANIZATION FOR QUALITY AND PRODUCTIVITY

Increasing productivity and improving quality are essential components of the long-term objectives of any industrial organization. This rules out formation of a short-term organization for advertising purposes. It is sad but true that many management initiatives are faddish, overexploited in the first blush of introduction to industry, and used primarily for advertising purposes. Both productivity and quality control have been provided lip service, served as advertising gimmicks, been used as a medium to gain recognition and status both within the firm and in technical societies, and for many other devious purposes.

From a total management viewpoint the organizational effort directed toward quality and/or productivity must show an acceptable return on the investment in it and it must provide a continuing acceptable service. It may be all right to get there by devious ways, but it will have to produce to remain there. And after the initial cost savings are realized, it will have to justify its savings on the grounds of costs being avoided.

Traditionally, the organizational effort for quality involved separate delegation units or persons in line or staff capacity or a combination. More recently, with increasing recognition of the interdependence of quality and productivity and the widespread responsibility for these efforts ("Quality is everybody's job"), the entire organization is redirected with quality and productivity in view. This chapter provides first an overview of the more traditional quality organization, then an example of organization-wide effort, commonly called quality control circles, and finally a discussion of the *kanban* system for production and inventory control.

TRADITIONAL QUALITY ORGANIZATION

There are essentially four types of quality organizations. They are listed in Table 18.3 in terms of responsibility. The organization most suited to a company depends on the type and volume of product manufactured. In a

TABLE 18.3 Types of Quality Organizations

Type	Characteristics
1	No quality control or inspection organization; operator performs quality checks; supervisor has final authority
2	Definite inspection organization with inspection hierarchy; reports to production supervisor; responsible for quality; production supervisor has final authority
3	Quality control organization on a level with the production (shops) organization; quality control represents the buyer—does all quality planning; in-process quality is a responsibility of shops
4	Quality control autonomous in all matters of quality; does in-process inspection

high-volume assembly operation, where it is impossible for the operators to identify defects, it would be wise to have an autonomous quality control organization. High precision, low volume, and highly engineered products requiring skilled craft workers might do better under the type 1 system.

Generally, the primary objectives of business will be best served if the quality control organization will view itself as the representative of the customer in matters of quality. It attempts to ensure that the customer will receive quality equal to or better than the standard he specifies. A customer can be the outside customer or another unit of the same organization. A producer can be an outside supplier or a production organization within the plant. If the quality organization will simply view itself in this way, it will minimize the human conflicts that result with line–staff relationships.

Why cannot the internal production organization be viewed as just another supplier and held *responsible* for the quality of its products? There would naturally be more intercourse for geographical reasons alone. However, the relationship could be maintained in principle and also in practice. Quality is a generally nebulous area of responsibility. The production department is said to be responsible, yet it has only partial authority and lacks the tools with which to carry out this responsibility. The final decision usually rests with the quality organization.

It is believed that where the type 3 organization applies, the best interests of the entire organization are served by giving the production department the responsibility, authority, and tools to carry out the responsibility. Figure 18.2 presents an organizational arrangement of this type. Also shown are the relationships between the quality control department, the customers it represents, and the producers whose quality it assures.

The quality assurance unit develops all quality control, acceptance sampling, and auditing plans subject to ad hoc approval of the quality standards committee. Once they have been approved, either by signatory or tacit agreement, adherence to the plans is mandatory. All producers, internal and external, are responsible for quality in accordance with the plan. All will be represented by a quality assurance plan specified by them or specified for them by the quality assurance organization.

The initial effect of this arrangement will be a duplication of work. However, gradually the need for this duplication will disappear. Theoretically, the ideal situation would be where all produced items are so good as to eliminate the need for an acceptance control organization. This is an ideal that is impossible to achieve. However, the ultimate aim should be to reduce it to the economic minimum—and this economic minimum exists when the producing organizations have accepted the full responsibility for production of quality units and have the proper tools with which to do the job.

The quality organization of Figure 18.2 is outsized in comparison to the other organizational units. This was done merely to show the interrelationships between quality, other units in the organization, and external suppliers

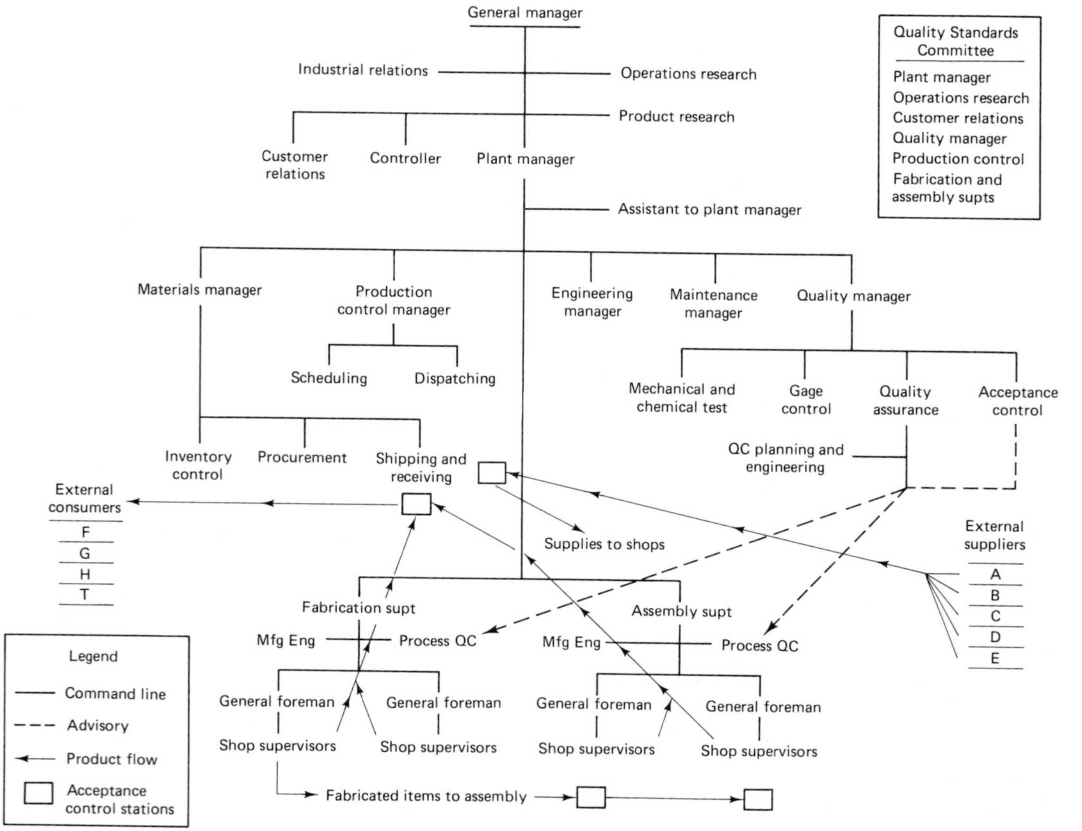

Figure 18.2 "Ideal" type 3 organization.

and consumers. In some companies quality will be at a higher level, answering to the general manager. However, it is always desirable to delegate the responsibility to lower levels. The intent should be always to delegate the responsibility for quality at the lowest level that is feasible economically. Feigenbaum expresses this point very well as follows:

> First, quality is everybody's job in business. There have been many experiments over the years that have run counter to this principle. They take this form: a company, or a product line, or a plant is in serious quality trouble. In desperation, management hires or assigns a man to be quality control manager with job assignments vaguely stated—makes him responsible for all factors affecting product quality. [Author's note: Typical brushfire management.] In my experience these men last 6 to 9 months, if that. They are doomed to failure because of these facts: the marketing man is in the best position to evaluate customer quality preference; the design engineer is the only man who can adequately determine specifications; and so on.
>
> So the first job required to set up a program of total quality control is for management to dovetail it with the structure and interests of the total organization, to accept the fact that quality is everybody's job in the business, and to recognize quality responsibilities and accountabilities across the board.
>
> That leads to the second principle: Because quality is everybody's job, it may become nobody's job. This means that top management's second job is to buttress and service the many responsibilities for quality throughout the organization. How? By establishing a fully effective, truly professional quality-control organization whose specialized activity is product quality and whose only area of operation is in quality control.
>
> This quality control function has two basic responsibilities. First, to provide quality assurance for the company's products. That is, simply, to be sure that the products shipped are right. Second, to assist in assuring optimum quality costs.[4]

QUALITY CONTROL CIRCLES

A *quality control circle* is a small group of persons within an organization who meet regularly to discuss production and operation problems. Their objective is to pinpoint specific problems, devise possible methods for solving these problems, analyze the implications of these methods, and recommend solutions. An alternative name for quality control circles is *quality circle*. Both names are prevalent in the United States. Japanese corporations tend to use "quality control circle" more often, whereas European corporations tend toward "quality circle."

Although the name refers only to quality, the groups discuss all problems related to quality and productivity (e.g., problems involving design of prod-

[4] A. V. Feigenbaum, "New Approach to Quality Control," *Factory*, March 1957, pp. 12–16.

ucts, production methods, human relations, or safety). Philosophically, the quality control circle approach is based on two hypotheses. The first hypothesis recognizes that creativity is not limited to upper management; everyone working within the corporation from president all the way down to an assistant janitor is capable of creative thought. The second hypothesis postulates that solutions to production problems are clearer to and better understood by persons closest to the problem. An operator would probably be as capable of understanding problems with the machine he operates as the best expert brought in from outside the firm.

The formation of groups is the beginning of any quality control circle program. In some companies the formation is structured. Each group invites the participation of persons closest to the operations. Each organizational unit has its own group and the structure of the groups parallels the structure of the organization itself. Such formally organized effort is sometimes called *participative management.*

More commonly the groups do not have a formalized structure. Persons involved in each group are in some way involved with the immediate problems concerned. Participation is encouraged from production workers, supervisors, and representatives of unions. Each group has a group leader or organizer. This person may be, but does not have to be, the supervisor. The group meets regularly at some predetermined interval, the most common frequency being once every week.

QC circles limit themselves to problems related to work. They are not organized to discuss salaries, employment practices, personalities, grievances, or collective bargaining issues, but are designed to boost productivity, improve quality, increase communication between management and workers, and get the workers involved in the operations of a company. A large automobile company goes as far as calling QC circles "employee involvement groups."

In the middle of the year 1983 it was estimated that 1.75 to 2.00 million U.S. workers were involved in QC circle programs organized under a variety of names. By the end of 1984, this number was expected to grow to 5 million. However, even this rapid growth failed to catch up with the organization in Japan. In mid-year 1983, with a labor force of only half the size of the U.S. labor force, Japan had over 10 million workers organized in QC circle programs.

Basics of a Quality Control Circle

Members. Members of a QC circle come from the persons immediately concerned with a problem area or work area. In structured organizations these are persons from the same department. There is no definite optimum number of members. However, groups smaller than 5 or larger than 20 find it difficult to function effectively.

Resources. Resources such as meeting rooms, initial training, members time, and so on, are furnished by the company.

Scope. Within its problem area (or work area) the group itself decides which specific problems need to be considered. As a result of the discussions, the group makes recommendations to another group (usually called as a "steering group" or "control group").

Authority. A QC circle normally does not have any authority for investments, this authority normally resting with the upper management. However, all suggestions coming from QC circle need to be given proper consideration by management. If these suggestions are routinely neglected by management, the QC circle program is apt to wither and disintegrate. In companies with successful QC circle programs there is a three-level approach. Suggestions that need no investment can be implemented by the group itself. Those needing "small" investments can be authorized by the control group. Only those suggestions that need "substantial" investment decisions go to the upper management for considerations. The management may, if needed, ask members of either the control group or the QC circle to make formal presentations in the form of a "proposed project."

Starting a Quality Control Circle

QC circles are based on the precepts that persons closest to the problems have the clearest understanding of the problem and that all persons are capable of creative thinking. The principal difficulties in starting a QC circle program involve the diffidence of members to express themselves and the lack of training in problem solving techniques. Initially, any QC circle program needs assistance from an outsider "expert," usually called a facilitator. The facilitator must be a person with certain special qualities. He/she must be:

1. Experienced in the process of QC circles
2. Familiar with the industry, the organization, and its products
3. Able to communicate
4. Comfortable in dealing with people
5. Enthusiastic

In addition to these characteristics, this person must be able to generate an atmosphere of trust and free and open discussion of problems.

There are two ways of introducing a QC circle program to a company. One is to start a "model QC circle." The facilitator acts as a leader to start a QC circle in a department or division chosen by the management. While this group is being developed, two persons work with the facilitator; one is an apprentice leader, who takes over the leadership of the group after the facilitator leaves, and the second is an apprentice later to be appointed QC circle program coordinator. This second person works with the facilitator to develop company-wide guidelines for QC circles. After the model QC circle is operating successfully, it is imitated, in light of the guidelines developed, by other departments, divisions, or interdepartmental groups within the company.

A second approach is to offer a "circle leader course" to the potential QC circle leaders. The facilitator offers instruction in the development and operation of a QC circle, using the group of potential leaders as a model. The course includes training in the technical aspects of QC circles as well as in communications, human relations, and creative thinking.

Each program evolves in the manner found most suitable by its participants. However, the following common elements need to be included in the first few sessions.

1. General discussion about the QC circle concept
2. Identification of problems in production environment
3. Training in brainstorming technique
4. Creating a problem inventory by brainstorming
5. Establishment of a priority list
6. Training in creative problem solving
7. Training in logical identification of possible causes of problems and in cause-and-effect diagrams
8. Selection of first problem and analysis of this problem

Orjan Alexanderson[5] describes some useful guidelines for the proper functioning of a QC circle. These are listed in three categories: problem-solving techniques, steps in problem solving, and proper methods of presentation of final recommendations.

Problem-solving techniques

1. Brainstorming is our most important creative instrument.
2. The cause and effect diagram is a way of showing the relation between a problem and its possible causes. Listing all possible causes in a systematic manner makes the analysis more convenient. The cause and effect (C & E) diagram is such a systematic listing. You may have seen other

[5] Orjan Alexanderson, "Productivity Innovations in Sweden," Chapter 11 in Y. K. Shetty and V. M. Beuhler, eds., *Quality and Productivity Improvements* (Chicago: Manufacturing Productivity Center, 1983).

names of the C & E diagram, e.g., "Fishbone-diagram", as the shape of the diagram reminds you of a fishbone. Even more often, it is called, "Ishikawa-diagram" after its orginator, the Japanese professor and quality expert, Kaoru Ishikawa.

3. The Pareto diagram is a way of presenting data, that makes it obvious what is important and what is less important. When you analyze the causes of a problem, it is often found that a few causes give rise to the major part of the problem. A majority of the number of defects, e.g., can be explained by a few major causes. Obviously the problem solving is more efficient if we start by tackling the most important causes.
4. A histogram is a way of presenting data, e.g., in order to compare the outcome of a production process with the existing tolerance limits.
5. A large number of data may sometimes be described by using only a measure of position and a measure of variability. Knowledge about the most common measures of position and variability can be of good help in the circle work.
6. A simple decision model for choosing between different alternatives is useful. The factors that should be decisive (the decision criteria) are often differently important. Therefore a method for calculation of weight factors is needed. The most simple way of doing this is to make a matrix where the criteria form the columns and the alternatives form the rows.

Steps in problem solving

We try to be systematic when we solve problems in the circle. The relative importance of the different steps of the following model can, of course, vary from one problem to another:

1. *Priority*. We wish to tackle the most important problem first.
2. *Objective and limitations*. It is important to agree on the goal, but also to make sure that the task is neither too narrow and specialized nor too broad and general.
3. *Cause and effect analysis*. We must find the real causes, not only the superficial symptoms.
4. *Ideas*. Use old experience as well as new combinations in order to find good solutions.
5. *Choice*. Decide which solution is best with respect to the objective.
6. *Practical tests*. If possible, every serious idea or assumption should be verified in practice.
7. *Presentation and decision*. Many simple problems fall within the circle's own authority to decide about. Sometimes, however, the idea must be sold to some higher level of the organization.
8. *Implementation*.
9. *Follow-up*. Do not let go until the objective is reached.

Presenting recommendations

Primarily the quality circle is supposed to solve the many small problems, closely related to the circle's own work area. But nevertheless it quite often happens, that the circle must ask for a decision higher up in the organization. This is almost always the case when an investment is involved. It is then important to realize that the decision-maker was not present during the creative process, so he has consequently no idea about how brilliant the proposal is. He must be convinced—you must sell your idea to him. Below you will find some simple pieces of advice concerning sales promotion:

1. Build on available and accepted facts and analyze the consequences of the proposal:

   "We registered the occurrence of this kind of failure during a period of four weeks. The frequency was found to be 12 percent. The cost of rework amounts to $14,000 per year. By means of the proposed investment of $5,600 the failure will be eliminated. The pay-off time thus is less than six months."

2. Sometimes you cannot prove your figures 100 percent. You must then openly state the assumptions you have made:

   "We think that the failure will be eliminated, but we have cautiously assumed that every fourth failure will still remain. The yearly savings would then be approximately $10,500, which should be compared to the investment of $5,600."

3. Involve the whole group:

   There are two reasons for this. The presentation becomes more interesting and varied for the listener and it contributes to the personal development of the group members.

4. Use pictures:

   It is easier to remember things you have both seen and heard. An adequate graph underlines the point you want to make. In addition, it is easier for the listener to stay awake if you do not just talk all the time.

5. Do not short-cut the organization:

   The whole circle program may be damaged if the medium level managers feel that the circle goes around them in order to get a decision on a higher level. On the contrary the circle must rely as much as possible on the line organization. Every level of managers should have a task in the circle program. And even if you are talking to the manager who has the line responsibility for the discussed matter, never press him for a decision right away. A person under pressure easily becomes defensive. Give reasonable time for consideration.

EXAMPLE OF A NEW QUALITY CONTROL CIRCLE PROGRAM

Blackman Shoe Company[6] is a family-owned business in southwestern Virginia employing approximately 300 in two plants. In 1978 and 1979 the company operated at full capacity, working two shifts in both plants. By 1981, the combination of general recession and tightening of credit severely depressed the demand for the high-quality shoes produced by the company. Mr. Matson, the president of the company, decided to introduce QC circle program as a means of improving productivity, lowering unit costs, and becoming more competitive.

Dr. Goldstein was invited as a facilitator. He visited the company to obtain a broad view of the operations and the interpersonal behavior that was considered normal at Blackman Shoe Company. He noticed two important features. First, the managers and operators did not talk to each other freely. Second, although QC circles are normally oriented towards solutions to operating problems, in this instance there was a need for identifying the problems before addressing the solutions. He suggested a two-day "circle leadership course" to train potential leaders and subsequent monitoring visits to observe the operation of the circles. This arrangement had proved to be effective in Goldstein's previous experience with quality control circles.

Since production was slack, Matson could assemble and designate 18 potential group leaders for this leadership course. Persons from both the plants were represented and their titles ranged from director of manufacturing to machine operator.

During the leadership course, Goldstein arranged the group to go through two sets of exercises. Most of the available time was spent on these exercises; Goldstein limited his lectures to an introductory exposition of QC circles and a review including suggestions regarding the formation of individual circles. He believed the role of a true facilitator is to facilitate group discussion among the participants. A good facilitator needs to avoid the temptation to adopt the role of a professor lecturing to students. The first set of exercises was called "Team Development Exercises." The objective was twofold. Many individuals are reticent in public and need some "loosening of reserve." Once a person does speak a few words on *any* topic it becomes easier for him/her to speak on the *specific* topic. Further, if any QC circle is to be successful all participants must think of each other as fellow participants instead of superior-subordinate, white collar–blue collar, technician–unskilled, or even male–female. These exercises are described in Figure 18.3. For the purposes of these exercises the participants were divided in small groups of two or three people each.

[6] The name and nature of the company is disguised to protect the privacy of the real company involved. The persons mentioned are fictitious stand-ins for their real counterparts.

Exercise 1:

Members paired off as instructed.

Each person is to introduce his/her "partner" to the group and should cover the following:

1. His/her name, job title, and short job description
2. *Short* summary of his/her work history

Time: 10 minutes for interviewing; 2–3 minutes of introduction

Exercise 2:

Members paired off as instructed.

Paired persons to list areas of disagreement of conflict experienced between themselves which they feel adversely affects productivity. List these in approximate order of importance and suggest ways by which these problems can be resolved.

Time: 15–20 minutes for interviews and discussions; 10 minutes for presentation (i.e., for listing and describing the nature of the disagreements of conflicts)

Exercise 3:

Members grouped as instructed.

Each group is to list *as many* problems as possible that they believe exist in their plant (a short statement for each will do). Rank these in approximate order of importance.

Time: 15–20 minutes for listing problems; 10 minutes for presentation

Exercise 4:

The whole group together.

Classification, elimination, and extension of the "problems" list.

Time: 30 minutes

Exercise 5:

Members grouped as instructed. Copies of the problem listing should be available to each member.

Prepare two ranked lists:

A. Rank the problems from the viewpoint of *utility* to the company.

B. Rank the problems in order of *ease* of solution.

Time: 15 minutes for discussion; 5 minutes for presentation of ranking

Exercise 6:

The whole group together.

An agreed ranking of problems.

Selection of two problems for investigation.

Time: 20 minutes

Exercises 7 and 8:

Members grouped as instructed. Same group for both exercises. Each exercise deals with one of the two problems selected in Exercise 6.

The team generates ideas for solving the particular problem under consideration. A different member of the team will present the group findings for each problem in turn.

Time: 15 minutes for discussion and ideas generation; 5 minutes for presentation; 15 minutes for group summary

Figure 18.3 Team development exercises.

The objective of these exercises was twofold. First, it helped break down the barriers of reserve. Second, it enabled the participants to start thinking in terms of "solutions to problems" rather than "unpleasant situations to be complained about." On the second day of the leadership course the group devoted some time to free-form thinking about factors in the workplace that were hindering the growth of productivity. To everybody's surprise many problems were apparent to a large number of persons. When this happens in a group, the participants start becoming more and more confident about their own thought processes. After identifying the problems, participants were asked to rank these problems according to two criteria:

1. *Benefits to the company.* The problems whose solution would benefit the company most would be ranked number 1.
2. *Ease of solution.* The problem easiest to solve would be ranked number 1.

The rankings are summarized in Table 18.4. A weighted sum of the rankings was used to decide the areas that could be most fruitful to deal in quality control circles. The top three were:

1. Lack of communications Rank 1.2
2. Scheduling Rank 1.4
3. Lack of personnel (high turnover) Rank 1.5

Following the two-day leadership course, four QC circles were formed with the help and leadership of the persons participating in the course. The three problems identified as most important became the first problems to be handled by the circles. When Mr. Matson reviewed the findings he was mildly surprised. He was aware of the shortage of personnel, but the other two problems were revelations to him. He was encouraged by the start and was convinced of the benefits of QC circles.

KANBAN SYSTEM

A *kanban* is a card or a tag usually attached to a product and is used to facilitate the proper movement of this product; the movement may be within the same manufacturing plant or between plants. A *kanban system* is a system of inventory and production control which uses kanbans as the principal information transmission device. There are two major advantages of using kanbans: first, the level of in-process inventories is reduced, and second, the production system can respond very quickly to changes in production schedule.

TABLE 18.4 Summary of Rankings

Problems Grouped under General Topics	Ranking A, Company Benefits						Ranking B, Ease of Solution						Rank on Sum	
Staffing													A	B
1. Lack of personnel, turnover	1	1	2	5	1	7	4	2	3	3	8	3	1	5
2. High absenteeism	2	2	1	6	3	5	8	3	5	6	5	2	2	7
3. Better housekeeping	8	7	7	7	8	8	1	1	1	1	1	5	8	1
4. Lack of trained people	5	3	8	3	2	4	6	7	4	5	4	1	5	4
5. Overtime maintenance not allowed	7	8	6	8	5	6	2	8	8	2	3	4	7	3
6. Poor work attitude	3	4	4	2	6	1	7	5	7	8	7	2	3	8
7. Lack of employee motivation	4	5	3	1	7	2	3	4	6	7	6	2	4	6
8. Lack of training programs	6	6	5	4	4	3	5	6	2	4	2	1	6	2
Scheduling														
1. Not time to produce samples	5	8	7	7	5	7	4	6	5	6	3	10	7	6
2. Need two bills on each order	8	10	9	8	7	8	2	1	1	1	1	1	10	1
3. Split order	6	3	8	10	6	6	3	5	6	3	4	2	8	3
4. Scheduling	1	2	5	3	4	1	5	2	3	9	5	3	1	4
5. Handwritten bills	9	7	10	9	9	5	1	3	2	2	7	7	9	2
6. Late bills for new customers	2	6	4	6	8	9	9	4	7	4	2	4	5	5
7. Late delivery of purchased parts	4	1	2	5	3	3	10	7	8	8	8	5	2	9
8. Purchasing delayed	3	4	3	4	2	4	8	8	9	7	6	6	3	8
9. Foreman overloaded	10	5	6	2	1	2	6	9	4	5	9	9	4	7
10. Inadequate production schedule	7	9	1	1	10	10	7	10	10	10	10	8	6	10
Communications														
1. Delays in information	4	2	4	2	2	2	3	3	1	1	4	1	2	1
2. Lack of communication	1	3	1	1	1	1	1	2	4	4	3	1	1	2
3. Inaccurate production reporting	3	4	2	4	4	4	2	4	3	2	2	3	4	4
4. Too much passing the buck	2	1	3	3	3	3	4	1	2	3	1	4	3	2

Quality problems														
1. Inferior leather	2	1	1	4	1	1	5	6	9	3	9	7	1	8
2. Bad roof, leaking rainwater	9	5	9	9	9	7	8	9	8	2	1	9	9	7
3. Damaged product	4	8	6	8	2	4	3	3	3	1	8	6	5	3
4. Shortage, incorrect count and quality	5	3	8	5	3	3	2	2	2	5	3	4	3	2
5. Lack of trained people	1	6	2	2	4	2	6	4	4	9	4	1	2	4
6. Inspection scheduling	3	4	3	6	8	5	4	5	7	7	5	5	5	5
7. Coordination between plants 1 and 2	7	4	4	3	5	6	7	7	5	6	7	2	4	6
8. No separation of product by quality	6	9	7	7	6	8	1	1	1	4	2	3	8	1
9. Product design	8	2	5	1	7	9	9	8	6	8	6	8	5	9

Facilities/Equipment														
1. Bad roof	8	2	7	11	1	7	8	13		2	1	12	6	8
2. Machine breakdowns	2	3	6	4	12	1	4	8		10	12	5	3	9
3. Temperature (working conditions)	13	10	11	10	2	13	13	1		3	11	13	12	10
4. Removal of dust particles from machinery area	9	8	10	6	11	3	9	2		4	10	4	7	4
5. Better housekeeping	12	9	9	8	13	12	1	3		5	2	11	13	2
6. Obsolete machines	1	1	1	2	3	6	11	12		11	9	3	1	11
7. Bad floors	6	11	8	9	10	4	12	11		6	3	2	9	6
8. New tool needed not ordered	5	5	2	5	8	9	3	7		7	8	6	4	5
9. Correct tools not available at all workstations	10	12	5	12	8	9	7	6		8	7	7	10	7
10. Late delivery on maintenance parts	3	4	3	7	7	10	6	9		12	13	9	4	13
11. Between plant transportation	7	13	12	13	6	5	5	5		1	6	1	10	1
12. Lack of energy source	11	7	12	1	4	11	10	10		13	5	10	7	12
13. Lack of functional small hand tools	4	6	4	3	5	2	2	4		9	4	8	2	3

TABLE 18.4 Continued

Problems Grouped under General Topics	Ranking A, Company Benefits						Ranking B, Ease of Solution					Rank on Sum	
Organizational												A	B
1. No time to produce samples	8	4	8	12	1	8	4	2	5	5	6	7	2
2. Information delays	5	10	11	4	2	1	3	3	4	6	5	3	1
3. Temperature (working conditions)	14	13	12	14	7	12	14	1	1	7	13	14	6
4. Too many samples to make	3	3	7	13	3	7	5	4	6	8	6	4	4
5. Obsolete machines	4	1	4	10	8	3	10	14	13	14	7	2	14
6. Bad floors	7	12	13	11	12	11	9	13	2	1	12	13	7
7. New tools needed not ordered	11	2	10	9	9	13	2	12	3	2	11	10	5
8. Lack of communication	1	6	1	2	4	2	1	5	12	9	1	1	3
9. Lack of training programs	13	5	5	5	10	4	6	11	10	12	2	8	10
10. No I.E. support on floor	12	14	6	8	11	5	8	9	8	10	3	11	8
11. Estimated costs not equal to actual costs	10	9	14	3	14	14	7	10	7	13	8	12	12
12. Lack of employee motivation	2	11	9	1	13	6	12	8	14	11	4	8	13
13. Product design	9	7	3	6	5	9	14	6	11	4	9	5	11
14. Too much passing the buck	6	8	2	7	6	10	11	7	9	3	10	5	9

Feedforward and Feedback Systems of Production Control

In a *feedforward system*, the information would be passed from the initial stages of production to the later stages and finally to the assembly line. Information travels in the same direction as the product. Most traditional production control systems are feedforward systems. Within such a system, whenever an order is received by the plant, a master schedule is prepared and every workstation and assembly line is assigned a schedule of production. Each workstation is informed *how many* units are to be processed and the time *when* the preceding station would be delivering these units. The schedule of processing at the workstation would be estimated as an amount of time (hours, shifts, or days) after the receipt from the preceding workstation. Only the first workstation would control the start of each item being processed This system leads to two kinds of operational problems: first, there is a need for in-process inventory between all workstations, and second, any change in the schedule must be implemented simultaneously at all workstations involved in any assembly. The first problem leads to a high cost of in-process inventory, and the second problem makes it difficult to introduce frequent changes in schedule.

In a *feedback system*, information travels in the opposite direction. Each succeeding workstation will withdraw items partially processed by the preceding workstation. Figure 18.4 shows the use of kanbans for such withdrawals. The succeeding workstation withdraws only the items needed for immediate processing and the preceding workstation will then replace the items withdrawn. In this manner, even though all workstations would have the necessary drawings and specifications for processing, only the final as-

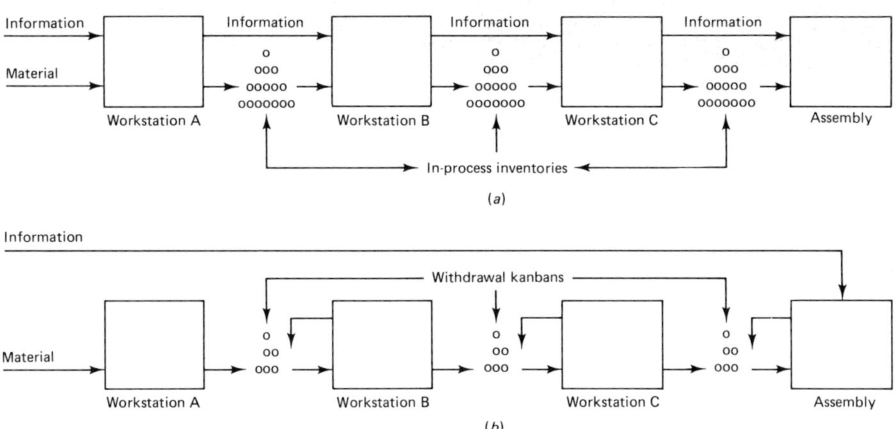

Figure 18.4 (a) Feedforward and (b) feedback systems of production control.

sembly needs to have the master schedule. Since withdrawals are made only for items needed immediately, each withdrawal lot is small and the in-process inventory between workstations is also small. If any changes are to be introduced in the master schedule, only the final workstation (or final assembly) needs to be informed of the schedule changes.

Feedback systems are inherent in systems referred to as kanban systems or *just-in-time systems*. Feedback systems had been used in U.S. manufacturing under the name "just-in-time production." More recently, Japanese manufacturers have revived the use of feedback systems under the name "kanban systems."

The Basic Kanban System

The operation of the basic kanban system can be described using the interchange between a preceding workstation supplying partially processed items or components to a succeeding workstation. Two types of kanbans are used: a *withdrawal kanban*, used by the succeeding workstation to specify the item and the quantity to be withdrawn, and a *production kanban*, used by the preceding workstation as a signal to specify the item and the quantity to be produced. A withdrawal kanban would include the following information:

1. Preceding and succeeding workstations and/or processes
2. Name and identification number of the item
3. Quantity in each box or container and its type
4. Store shelf location
5. Name or identification number of the final product where this item would be used
6. Sequence number of kanban

The last is written as "3/10" to indicate that there are a total of 10 kanbans of this type and this is third in the sequence. A production kanban that does not immediately initiate production would contain the same information, except items 5 and 6. Even the name of the succeeding workstation may be omitted. The production kanban which indicates the need for starting production of the next production lot is usually of a different shape and is called a *signal kanban*. A signal kanban would also contain the following additional information:

1. Production lot size and reorder level
2. Machines to be used for production

Suppose that an item is produced in lots of 80, the reorder level is 30, and each box contains 10 units. The preceding workstation will attach a production kanban to each box as it is filled with processed units. A stack of 8 boxes containing a total of 80 (production lot) items will be taken to the appropriate storage place. Seven boxes will have production kanbans and one box will have the signal kanban attached to it. In this case it will be the third box ($3 \times 10 = 30 =$ reorder level) from the bottom or from the end.

A person, a carrier from the subsequent workstation, will come with a withdrawal kanban (and transporting equipment) whenever the subsequent workstation needs this item. The person will take one box, attach the withdrawal kanban to it, and withdraw the production kanban. At the time of exchange the information on the two kanbans is carefully compared to avoid misdirected items. Then the carrier leaves the production kanban at the designated place and takes the box to the subsequent workstation. When the signal kanban arrives at this place, the preceding workstation initiates production of the next production lot. The reorder level is adapted to the processing times in the two departments so that the next production lot will arrive at the storage place when the last box of the preceding lot is withdrawn.

When the box arrives at the subsequent workstation the worker(s) would remove the withdrawal kanban and leave it at a designated place and use the items in the box for processing. The withdrawal kanban would then return to the storage place with the carrier, in sequential order. The carrier may be designated to make rounds at predetermined times or according to the number of kanbans waiting. After processing the workers at the subsequent workstation will attach their own production kanban to the product.

This sequence is illustrated in Figure 18.5.

Other Types of Kanban

Besides the two basic types of kanban, withdrawal and production (signal kanban is considered as a specific type of production kanban), several other types of kanbans can be used in specific circumstances. The principal ones are supplier kanban, express kanban, and cart kanban.

A *supplier kanban* is used instead of production kanban when the preceding workstation is an outside supplier. There is no corresponding signal kanban. Instead, the supplier is given a fixed delivery frequency. The information on a supplier kanban would include:

1. Name and identification number of the item
2. Quality to be delivered in each lot
3. Quantity in each box or container and its type
4. Store shelf location where the item would be withdrawn
5. Store of the supplier delivering the item

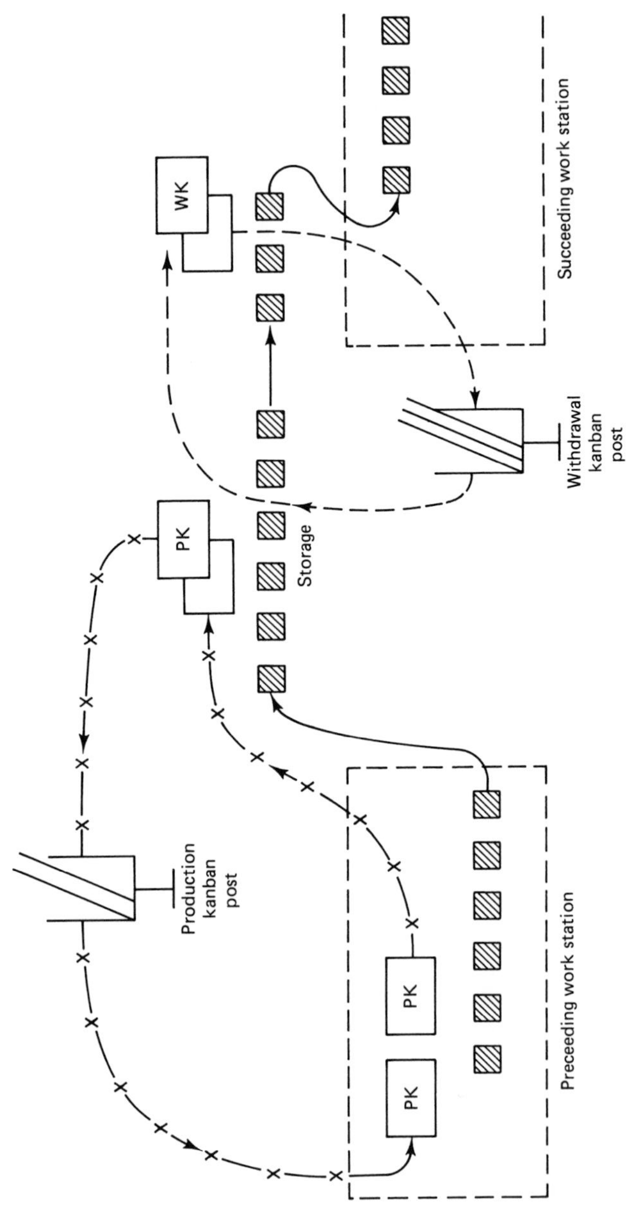

Figure 18.5 Basic kanban system.

6. Delivery frequency, usually given as a string of times of the day; for example, for an item to be delivered: 8:00 A.M., 1:00 P.M., 5:00 P.M., 10:00 P.M.—four times within a two-shift operation
7. Names of supplier and receiver companies

An *express kanban* is used when a subsequent workstation or assembly line is in danger of having to stop due to the shortage of one out of many items being used: for example, if an assembly uses five different components and item 381 is short. When the carrier arrives at the storage place with a withdrawal kanban, there is no box or lot to withdraw. If the shortage is deemed to be critical, the carrier issues an express kanban. This kanban is left in a separate place, not with the usual production kanbans. The carrier also activates a button at this post, marked 381. This lights up a red light at the line, which produces 381, indicating the arrival of an express kanban. The line or workstation will take two actions. First, they will expressly produce a normal withdrawal lot of 381 and take it directly to the assembly line, not to the storage place, along with the express kanban (in Japan, accompanied by an apology). Next, they will find and correct the reasons that caused the shortage. Express kanbans are not circulated and are to be used as few times as possible.

A *cart kanban* is used for the withdrawal of large items, such as complete engines, where the cart would normally be used to transport the item. After using each engine, the subsequent workstation will send the empty cart to the preceding workstation. The preceding workstation will continue to assemble engines as long as there is at least one empty cart to load.

Operational Procedures

The principal difference introduced by the kanban system is inherent in the withdrawal kanban. A withdrawal kanban determines the quantity of the items received by the subsequent workstation, and this quantity is usually much smaller than the entire production lot from the preceding workstation. For workers accustomed to working with full racks or bins of unfinished items, the smaller quantities of the kanban system would appear inappropriate. It would take a considerable amount of training and understanding for the workers to believe that there would be no interruptions. Once fully implemented, the kanban system leads to very smooth and steady production, but it is very difficult to imagine this before it is in operation.

Similar confusion is likely to affect the previous workstation. Instead of receiving a master schedule of what items are to be produced when, the workstation receives its production orders through kanbans and the start of production is indicated only by the signal kanban. The workers at this workstation may have a feeling of working in the dark, never knowing what production order may pop up next. Again, this does not happen in the kanban system once it is fully implemented, but it would be difficult to convince the workers of this before implementation. Actually, the kanban system permits the workers of the preceding workstation to concentrate fully on the production lot in hand without having to think of the next production lot.

Although the kanban system is described in terms of preceding and succeeding workstations, it must be remembered that the production system really is built up of chains of such workstations. In each chain a workstation is a "succeeding workstation" for workstation(s) preceding and at the same time is a "preceding workstation" for workstation(s) that follow. This can be seen in Figure 18.6.

Kanbans and Quality Control

A kanban is really an instrument of production control. At the same time it promotes quality control, as *fine-tuned, steady* production processes facilitate better product quality. In a well-run production process this is achieved through several intricate but important factors. Some of these are as follows.

Since the material from the preceding workstation is withdrawn in very small units, that of a single withdrawal kanban lot, the production horizon is

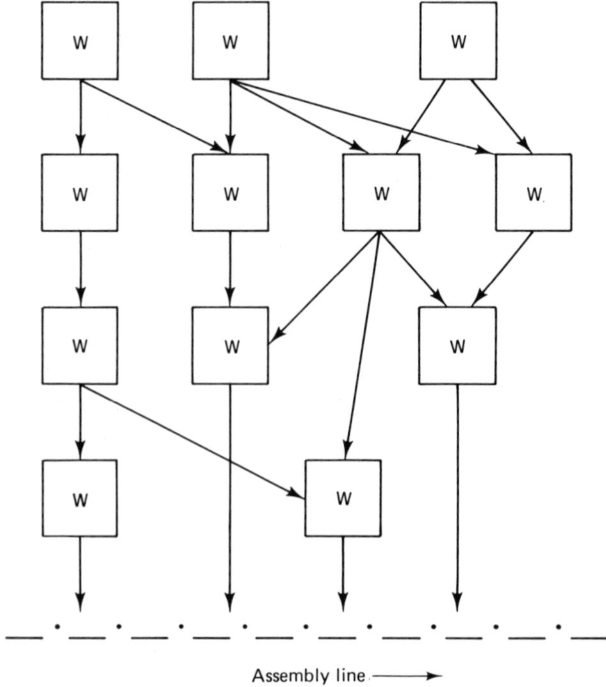

Figure 18.6 Network of workstations.

short, and the production process is finely tuned. Any deviation from the norm, either in the incoming material or in the process itself, would clearly stand out and be noticed. Further, every time a kanban lot is loaded in a box, there is a visual inspection of all items. Although this would be natural for most skilled workers, many companies make this a formal work procedure. Such visual inspection is not sufficient as a "measurement and test," but usually is good enough to detect many types of obvious defects. This visual inspection takes place at every interface of preceding and succeeding workstations. The carrier has the responsibility of carefully comparing the information on withdrawal and production kanbans at the time of withdrawal. This avoids possible errors of supplying incorrect items to succeeding processes. The most important contribution to quality comes from the steady rate of production. When there is no "rush" or "delay," the operator can concentrate on proper ways of producing the product. Naturally, the production is more defect-free and of an even and superior quality.

nineteen

RELIABILITY[1]

Reliability is that aspect of quality assurance that is concerned with the quality of performance. One definition of reliability is that it is "the probability of performing without failure a specified function under given conditions for a specified period of time."[2] In contrasting it to traditional quality control, reliability is associated with quality over the long term, whereas quality control is associated with the relatively short period of time required for manufacture of the product.

The causes of unreliability of product are many. One of the major causes is the increasing complexity of product. The multiplication law of probability illustrates this fact very simply. Given an assembly made up of five components, each of which has a reliability of 0.95, the reliability of the assembly is $(0.95)^5$, or about 0.77. Many complex electronic assemblies involve thousands of parts. It does not take too much reflection to realize what the component reliabilities must be to have a reasonable chance of successful performance by such assemblies.

Attempts to assess the causes of component unreliability have resulted in the percentage breakdown given in Table 19.1.

The breakdown shows that the causes of unreliability are fairly well

[1] Recognizing the complexity of acceptance control and process control based on reliability, this chapter provides somewhat more elaborations of the development of formulas and test plan. The reader is advised to read this chapter in conjunction with Chapter 2.

[2] AGREE Report, *Reliability of Military Electronic Equipment* (Washington, D.C.: National Technical Information Service, June 1957).

TABLE 19.1 Sources of Unreliability

Source	Percent of Trouble
Engineering	
Electrical	30
Mechanical	10
Field operations	30
Manufacturing	20
Other	10

F. M. Gryna, Jr., N. J. McAfee, C. M. Ryerson, and S. Zwerling, "Reliability Training Text," Institute of Radio Engineers, Inc., March 1960, p. 1.

distributed among the sources, with engineering design being the primary souce of trouble. It would follow that the reliability control effort should be apportioned much as the trouble is distributed.

DISTRIBUTIONS ENCOUNTERED IN CONTROLLING RELIABILITY

The basic elements required for an adequate specification or definition of reliability are as follows:

1. Numerical value of probability
2. Statement defining successful product performance
3. Statement defining the environment in which the equipment must operate
4. Statement of the required operating time

Thus a specification for the reliability of a product might be 0.99 probability of performance without failure at 30°C for a period of 48 hours.

To measure or estimate the probability of performance it becomes necessary to understand the probability distribution of "failure." The word *failure* indicates incorrect, insufficient, inadequate, or unsatisfactory performance. The event of failure in this sense occurs when the system fails to conform to the specifications. In some instances this use of the word "failure" may differ from the more common use.

The failure rate can be considered as the probability of failure of one of the units that has not failed up to that time. The relationship between the failure rate, failure probability, and reliability can be estimated as follows.

Let $h(t)$ = failure rate at time t
$f(t)$ = probability density of failure
$R(t)$ = reliability of the system

Then

$$F(t) = \int_0^t f(t)\, dt$$

$$= \text{probability of failure at or before time } t$$

$$R(t) = 1 - F(t)$$

$$n = \text{number of failures between the interval } t \text{ and } t + \Delta t$$

$$= \text{number of units operating at time } t \times \text{failure rate} \times \Delta t$$

$$= R(t)h(t)\, \Delta t$$

However, n is also given by the probability distribution of failure as

$$n = f(t) \times \Delta t$$

Therefore,

$$h(t)R(t) = f(t)$$

or alternatively,

$$h(t) = \frac{f(t)}{1 - F(t)}$$

Figure 19.1 illustrates the typical failure pattern for units of a complex product. The first phase is the *debugging* period. The presence of marginal

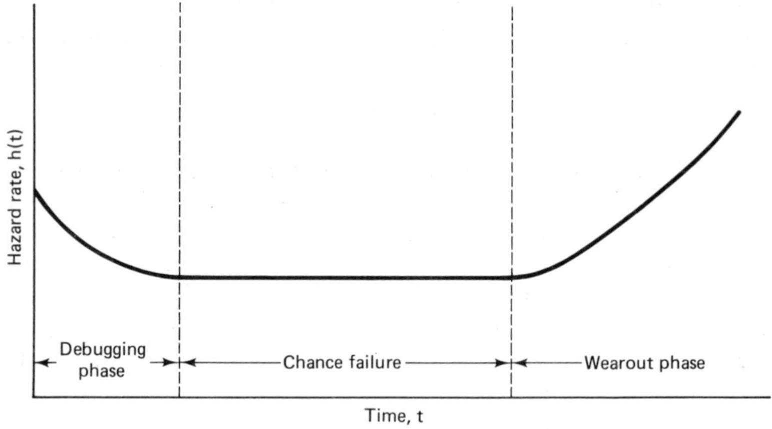

Figure 19.1 Typical failure rates for a complex product. (Not to scale.)

and short-life parts at original operation (burn-in) is characterized by a decreasing rate of failure per time period. The next phase is characterized by a relatively constant chance failure-rate period, which is the effective life of the product. This is followed by the last phase, a period of increasing failure rate which indicates the beginning of wear-out failures in the population. The probability models for these three phases are commonly referred to as the DFR, CFR, and IFR models, respectively.

Much work has been done in recent years on the analysis of failure distributions. Figure 19.2 illustrates the forms of distributions applicable during these three phases. It may be generalized that the distribution of actual test results will usually be approximated by one of the distributions of Figure 19.2.

Figure 19.2a depicts the possible distributions of the debugging phase. Either the gamma or Weibull distributions with shape parameters less than 1 may be used to describe the occurrence of failures during this phase. Since this is a phase that is not intended to be an operational phase, it is normally not a subject for failure study, at least not in the reliability sense.

Figure 19.2b is the chance or random failure phase. Either the exponential, or gamma and Weibull distributions with shape parameters of 1, may be used to describe this phase. A great many reliability studies are concerned with this phase.

Figure 19.2c is the wear-out failure phase. The usual distribution applied here is the normal, although the gamma and Weibull with shape parameters greater than 1 may be applied. The modal similarity between these distributions is evident, and in fact, either the Weibull or gamma may be used in lieu of the normal. The test, of course, is which distribution best describes the data. These distributions may apply where deterioration is the cause of failure and where the mean life is large in relation to the measure of dispersion. Lamp bulbs and electron tubes are examples of items which have failure times that follow the normal law.

To develop a mathematical model for the probability of failure, consider the operation of an item subject to the specified environment. Let the random variable T be defined as the time the item performs satisfactorily before a failure. The probability that the item would be delivering satisfactory performance at time t can be defined as *reliability*:

$$R(t) = \Pr(T > t) \tag{19.1}$$

If $f(t)$ denotes the probability density function of failures,

$$\begin{aligned} R(t) &= \Pr(T > t) \\ &= 1 - F(t) \end{aligned} \tag{19.2}$$

The conditional failure rate of an item which has not failed prior to time t is called the *hazard rate* or *hazard function* $h(t)$.

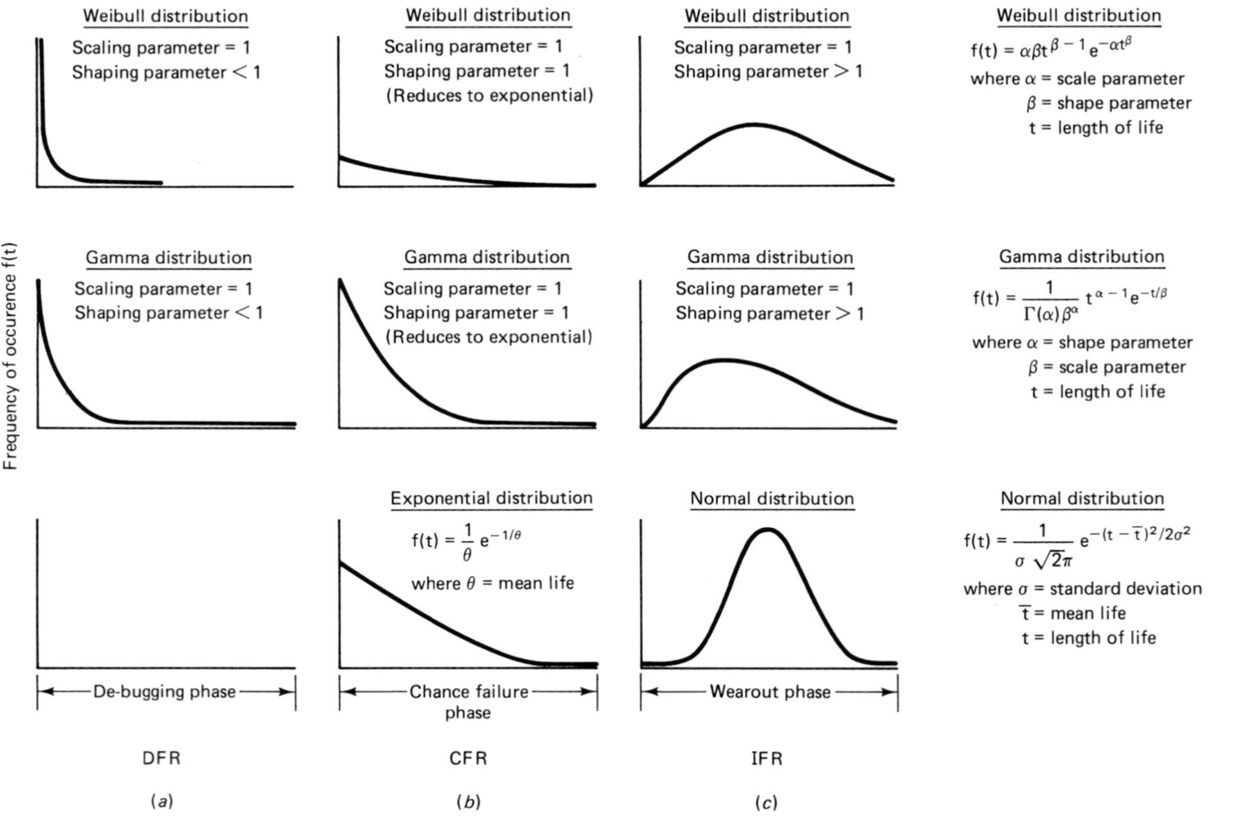

Figure 19.2 Possible life distributions by phase.

The probability of a failure in an interval from t to $t + \Delta t$ is given by

$$\Pr(t \leq T \leq t + \Delta t) = \frac{R(t) - R(t + \Delta t)}{R(t)}$$

$$= h(t)\,\Delta t \tag{19.3}$$

$$h(t) = \frac{R(t) - R(t + \Delta t)}{R(t)\,\Delta t}$$

In the limit,

$$h(t) = \frac{\frac{d}{dt}R(t)}{R(t)} \tag{19.4}$$

$$= \frac{f(t)}{R(t)} \tag{19.5}$$

Another way of expressing equation (19.4) is

$$R(t) = exp\left[-\int_0^t h(x)\,dx\right]$$
$$= e^{-H(t)} \tag{19.6}$$

MEAN TIME TO FAILURE

The quality of performance of an item would in general be indicated by the time the item is expected to perform in a satisfactory manner. Using the reliability model described in the preceding section, it is possible to obtain a statistical expectation of this time, the time until a failure occurs. This expectation is called the *mean time to failure* (MTTF). Alternatively, for systems that are continually repaired after failures and reused, the expectation may be called the *mean time between failures* (MTBF). In either case the "time" may be real time, operational time, or number of operations.

Since the failure density is $f(t)$, the expected time to failure would be given by

$$E(T) = \text{MTTF} = \int_0^\infty t \cdot f(t)\,dt \tag{19.7}$$

where T is the time of failure. Alternatively, reliability at time t can be viewed as the probability of survival up to time t. Hence the expected duration of survival, which is the same as expected time to failure would be given by

$$E(T) = \text{MTTF} = \int_0^\infty R(t)\,dt \tag{19.8}$$

t	θ	$1/\theta$	t/θ	$e^{-t/\theta}$	$\frac{1}{\theta}e^{-t/\theta}$
0	10	1/10	0	1.000	0.1000
1	↓	↓	0.1	0.905	0.0905
2			0.2	0.819	0.0819
4			0.4	0.670	0.0670
8			0.8	0.449	0.0449
12			1.2	0.301	0.0301
16			1.6	0.202	0.0202
20			2.0	0.315	0.0135
24			2.4	0.091	0.0091
28			2.8	0.061	0.0061
32			3.2	0.041	0.0041
36			3.6	0.027	0.0027

t	θ	$1/\theta$	t/θ	$e^{-t/\theta}$	$\frac{1}{\theta}e^{-t/\theta}$
0	20	1/20	0	1.000	0.050
5	↓	↓	0.25	0.779	0.039
10			0.50	0.607	0.030
20			1.00	0.368	0.018
30			1.50	0.223	0.012
40			2.00	0.135	0.007
50			2.50	0.082	0.004
60			3.00	0.050	0.0025
70			3.50	0.030	0.0015
80			4.00	0.018	0.0009

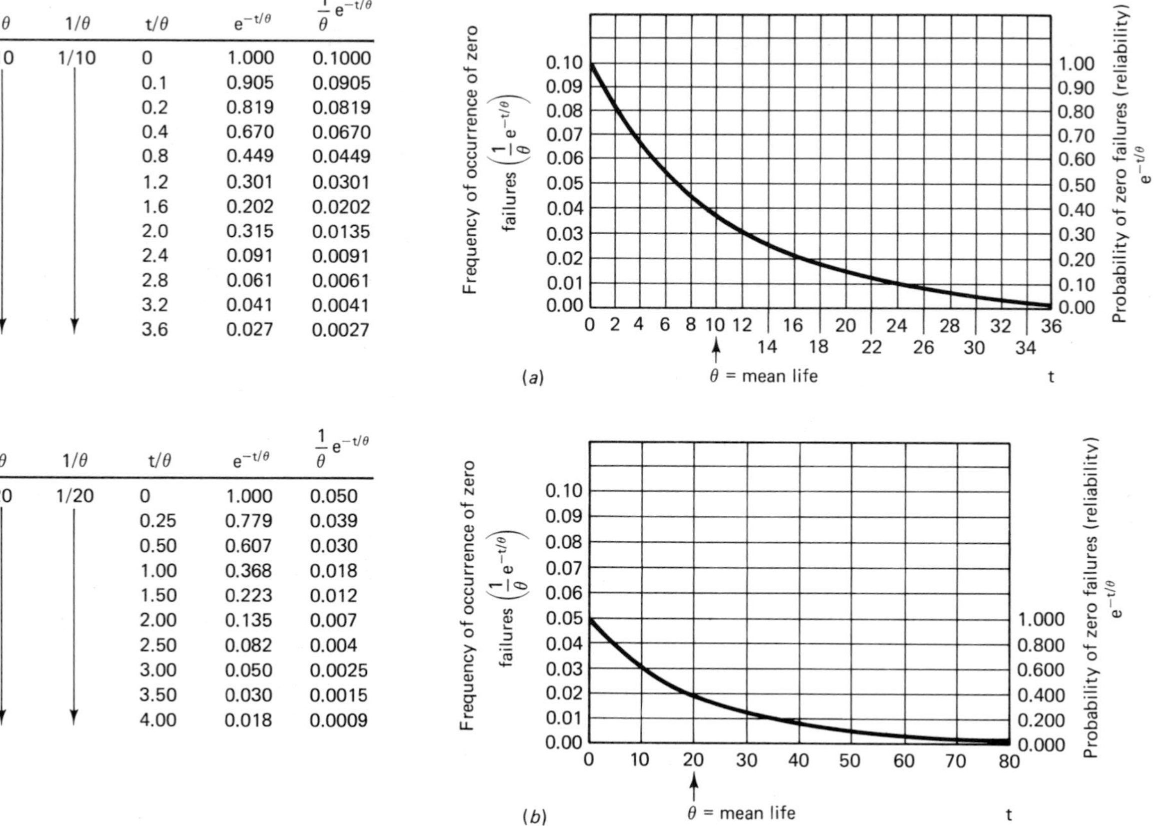

Figure 19.3 Exponential distributions: (a) θ = mean life = 10; (b) θ = 20; (c) scaled exponential density.

The product specifications for reliability are usually stated in terms of MTTF or MTBF.

In the testing for reliability of short-life items such as ballistic missiles or other items that are destroyed early with test, wear-out failure distributions do not apply. For such items the failure distribution may be of a form similar to the exponential or of the allied gamma and Weibull distributions; or in fact, none of these, but of other distributions as yet not described by empirical evidence. Assuming that the exponential applies, it is evident that an increase in mean life will cause a reduction in the probability of failure (the height of the curve at $t = 0$ during the change-failure phase will be lowered) and therefore will result in a more reliable item.

Figure 19.3a and b illustrate this statement graphically. Figure 19.3a is an exponential with mean life θ equal to 10. Figure 19.3b is an exponential with mean life equal to 20. The familiar shape of the exponential is seen in both cases, but as θ is increased, the corresponding ordinate values are decreased. For example, assume that an item with a mean life of 10 hours is tested for 20 hours. What is the probability that no failure will occur? This probability is given by height of the ordinate of Figure 19-3a at $t = 20$, which is 0.135. Assume now that a design change increased the mean life to 20 hours. Now, what is the probability of failure at 20 hours? The height of the ordinate at 20 hours on Figure 19.3b is 0.368, which is the probability of no failure when the mean life is 20. This means that the reliability of the item has been improved. In reliability practice the abscissa is usually expressed as the ratio of t to θ, as in Figure 19.3c. This way the same horizontal scale can be used in all situations.

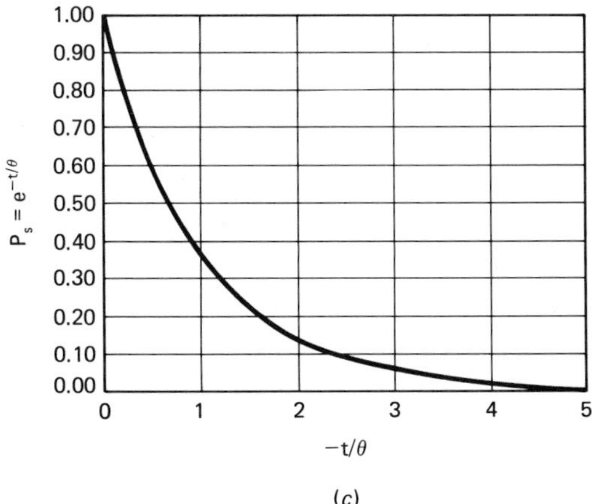

(c)

Figure 19.3 Continued.

EXPONENTIAL FAILURE DENSITY

The exponential probability density function for failure is stated as

$$f(t) = \lambda e^{-\lambda t} \quad \text{when } t \geq 0 \qquad (19.9)$$
$$= 0 \quad \text{when } t < 0$$

For this density function the cumulative function is

$$F(t) = \int_0^t \lambda e^{-\lambda \phi}\, d\phi \qquad (19.10)$$
$$= 1 - e^{-\lambda t} \quad t \geq 0$$

From equation (19.2) the reliability function can be obtained as

$$R(t) = 1 - F(t) \qquad (19.11)$$
$$= e^{-\lambda t} \quad t \geq 0$$

From equation (19.5) the hazard function can be obtained as

$$h(t) = \frac{f(t)}{R(t)}$$
$$= \frac{\lambda e^{-\lambda t}}{e^{-\lambda t}} \qquad (19.12)$$
$$= \lambda \quad t \geq 0$$

It can be noticed that $h(t)$ does not depend on t. In other words, the hazard rate is constant. Whenever the hazard rate can be assumed to be constant, the exponential density function can be used to describe the failure rate. Sometimes a constant hazard rate is described as a "failure process that has no memory." If an item has not failed up to time t, the probability that it will fail during t and $t + \Delta t$ is given by

$$\Pr(t \leq T \leq t + \Delta t \mid T > t) = \frac{\Pr(T \leq t + \Delta t) - \Pr(T \leq t)}{\Pr(T > t)} \qquad (19.13)$$
$$= \frac{F(t + \Delta t) - F(t)}{1 - F(t)}$$

Substituting from equation (19.10) yields

$$\Pr(t \leq T \leq t + \Delta t \mid T > t) = \frac{(1 - e^{-\lambda(t + \Delta t)}) - (1 - e^{-\lambda t})}{1 - (1 - e^{-\lambda t})}$$
$$= \frac{e^{-\lambda t} - e^{-\lambda t - \lambda \Delta t}}{e^{-\lambda t}} \qquad (19.14)$$
$$= 1 - e^{-\lambda \Delta t} \quad \text{for finite } t$$

This probability does not depend on t.

Figure 19.3 shows the typical failure density, reliability, and hazard functions when the failure density is exponential.

ESTIMATION OF MTTF: EXPONENTIAL FAILURE DENSITY

When the failure density is exponential, MTTF would be given by

$$\begin{aligned} E(T) &= \int_0^\infty tf(t)\,dt \\ &= \int_0^\infty \lambda t e^{-\lambda t}\,dt \\ &= -te^{-\lambda t}\Big|_{t=0}^{t=\infty} + \int_0^\infty e^{-\lambda t}\,dt \\ &= 0 + \frac{1}{\lambda}\int_0^\infty e^{-\lambda t}\,d(\lambda t) \\ &= \frac{1}{\lambda} e^{-\lambda t}\Big|_{t=0}^{t=\infty} \\ &= \frac{1}{\lambda} \end{aligned} \tag{19.15}$$

Hence the parameter λ of the exponential failure density and the MTTF of the item are related by equation (19.15) and are reciprocals of each other. Epstein[3] developed a procedure for estimating MTTF and for determining a confidence interval for this estimate. In a simplified form the procedure works as follows. The test is started with n units at time $t = 0$. The time of failure of each item is noted, t_i being the time when ith failure occurs. The test is terminated when either the predetermined number of units r^* fail or at a predetermined time t^*. The statistic being measured is Q, the total test time, measured as (unit in operation) $\times$ (time of operation).

Case 1: Failed units are not replaced. In this case

$$Q = \sum_{i=1}^{r} t_i + (n - r)t^* \tag{19.16}$$

The estimate $\hat{\theta}$ of θ is obtained as a maximum likelihood estimator. At time t^*, units $1, 2, \ldots, r$ have failed at times $t_1, t_2, \ldots, t_r$, and $n - r$

[3] Epstein B. "Estimation of Life Test Data" IRE Transactions on Reliability, Vol. RQC-9, 1960.

units are still operating. The likelihood function

$$L = \prod_{i=1}^{r} f(t_i) \prod_{i=r}^{n} R(t^*)$$

Let

$$\theta = \text{MTTF} = \frac{1}{\lambda}$$

$$r = \text{number of failures up to time } t$$

Then

$$f(t) = \lambda e^{-\lambda t} \tag{19.17}$$
$$= \frac{1}{\theta} e^{-t/\theta}$$

From equations (19.6) and (19.11),

$$L = \prod_{i=1}^{r} \frac{1}{\theta} e^{-t_i/\theta} \prod_{i=r}^{n} \mathrm{e}^{-t^*/\theta}$$

$$= \left(\frac{1}{\theta}\right)^{\mathrm{r}} e^{(-1/\theta)} \sum_{i=1}^{r} t_i e^{-(n-r)t^*/\theta} \tag{19.18}$$

$$\text{Log } L = r \log \theta - \frac{1}{\theta}\left[\sum_{i=1}^{r} t_i + (n - r)t^*\right]$$

$$= -r \log \theta - \frac{1}{\theta} Q$$

Minimizing log L with respect to θ yields

$$\hat{\theta} = \frac{Q}{r} \tag{19.19}$$

Case 2: Failed units are replaced. Since each failed unit is replaced as soon as it fails, there are n units operating at all times.

$$Q = nt^* \tag{19.20}$$

The maximum likelihood estimator can be obtained as in case 1 and is also given as

$$\hat{\theta} = \frac{Q}{r} \tag{19.19}$$

For both case 1 and case 2, Epstein[4] has shown that the statistic $k = 2r\,\hat{\theta}/\theta$ has a chi-square distribution. The degrees of freedom are $2r^*$

[4] Ibid.

when the test is terminated after predetermined number of failures and are $2r + 2$ when the test is terminated after predetermined time t^*.

Example 19.1

A sample of 10 electronic components were tested. The time to failure for first four components to fail were 1900, 2650, 2810, and 2820 hours, respectively. The test was terminated at 3000 hours. There was no replacement of failed units and the remaining six units were functioning properly at the time of termination.

This is an example of case 1. Using equation (19.16), the total test time Q is obtained as

$$Q = \sum_{i=1}^{4} t_i + (10 - 4)3000$$

$$= 1900 + 2650 + 2810 + 2820 + 18{,}000$$

$$= 28{,}180 \text{ hours}$$

Estimated mean time to failure

$$\hat{\theta} = \frac{Q}{r}$$

$$= \frac{28{,}180}{4} = 7045 \text{ hours}$$

Example 19.2

Can the components in Example 19.1 be accepted if the specification for these items is MTTF = 8000 hours?

Here the hypothesis to be tested is

$$H_0\text{: } \theta = 8000$$

against

$$H_1\text{: } \theta < 8000$$

$$\text{Test statistic } k = \frac{2r\hat{\theta}}{\theta}$$

$$= \frac{2Q}{\theta}$$

$$= \frac{2 \times 28{,}180}{8000} = 7.045$$

As the test is terminated at the predetermined time, the degrees of freedom are $2r + 2 = 2(4) + 2 = 10$.

As the statistic k lies outside the rejection region (see Figure 19.4) the hypothesis H_0 is not rejected and the lot may be accepted. It may be noticed that a one-tailed test has been used, as the alternative hypothesis is H_1: $\theta < 8000$.

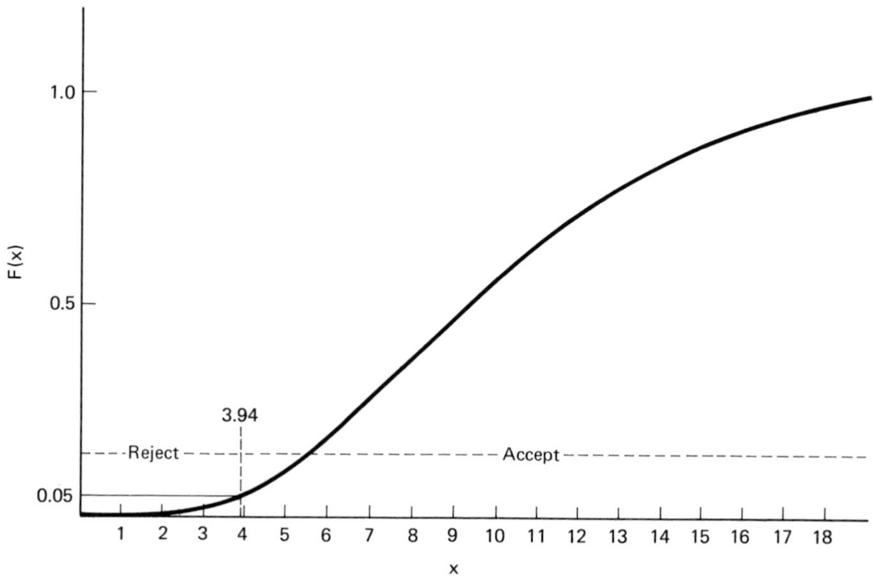

Figure 19.4 Rejection region at 5% level for chi-square with 10 df.

WEIBULL FAILURE DENSITY

The Weibull probability density function for failure is stated as

$$\begin{aligned} f(t) &= \alpha\beta t^{\beta-1}\, e^{-\alpha t^{\beta}} && \text{when } t \geq 0 \\ &= 0 && \text{when } t < 0 \end{aligned} \tag{19.21}$$

In equation (19.21) the parameter β is referred to as the *shape parameter* and α as the *scale parameter*. For this density function the cumulative function is

$$\begin{aligned} F(t) &= \int_0^t \alpha\beta\theta^{\beta-1}e^{-\alpha\theta^{\beta}} \quad d\theta \\ &= 1 - e^{-\alpha\theta^{\beta}} \qquad t \geq 0 \end{aligned} \tag{19.22}$$

From equation (19.2) the reliability function is

$$\begin{aligned} R(t) &= 1 - F(t) \\ &= e^{-\alpha t^{\beta}} \qquad t \geq 0 \end{aligned} \tag{19.23}$$

From equation (19.5) the hazard function is

$$\begin{aligned} h(t) &= \frac{f(t)}{R(t)} \\ &= \frac{\alpha\beta t^{\beta-1}e^{-\alpha\beta^{\theta-1}}}{e^{-\alpha\beta^{\theta-1}}} \\ &= \alpha\beta t^{\beta-1} \qquad t \geq 0 \end{aligned} \tag{19.24}$$

Further,

$$h'(t) = \frac{d}{dt} h(t) \\ = \alpha\beta(\beta - 1)t^{\beta-2} \qquad t \geq 0 \tag{19.25}$$

Equations (19.24) and (19.25) give an indication of the type of hazard rate function to be expected for any shape parameter β.

1. When $\beta = 0$, both $h'(t)$ and $h(t)$ are always zero. Obviously, the shape parameter cannot be zero for any system subject to failures.
2. When $\beta = 1$, $h'(\mathrm{t}) = 0$ and $h(t) = \alpha$. This is a constant hazard rate. The failure density is

$$f(t) = \alpha e^{-\alpha}$$

   which is an exponential density.
3. When $0 < \beta < 1$, $h'(t) < 0$. This implies that the hazard rate is decreasing as time progresses.
4. When $\beta > 1$, $h'(t) > 0$. This implies that the hazard rate is increasing as time progresses.

The reliability models under conditions 2, 3, and 4 are described as *constant failure rate* (CFR) *model*, *decreasing failure rate* (DFR) *model*, and *increasing failure rate* (IFR) *model*, respectively. Referring to Figure 19.1, it can be seen that the debugging phase can be described as a DFR model, the chance failure phase as a CFR model, and the wearout phase as an IFR model.

Although Weibull failure density can represent a wide variety of situations, it is very difficult to devise acceptance procedures based on Weibull failure density, due to the difficulties involved in obtaining estimates for the parameters.

ACHIEVEMENT OF RELIABILITY

There are five key areas of effort affecting the achievement of a reliable product. They are design, production, measurement and test, maintenance, and field operation. One could break each of these down into various subareas, but for purposes of general discussion, these will suffice.

It has been mentioned that design is the most important of the key areas and that the greater percentage of causes of unreliability can be traced to this area. E. G. D. Paterson has this to say about it:

> Except by pure chance, a product will not have a greater reliability than the designer has engineered into it. He, himself, doesn't know what degree of

> reliability he has obtained until the stages of production and substantial usage has passed. He builds a model, perhaps several if he is so fortunately circumstanced; he subjects the model to tests, usually very limited tests in terms of actual service requirements; and, unless he is an extraordinary genius or is unusually blessed by good luck, he revises his design to correct its deficiencies. When he has repeated this performance until he arrives at a result with which he is satisfied, he takes the next difficult and critical step: he tries to define his design in terms of words, lines, and figures by which a second party, without the benefit of the designer's knowledge as to why, can build in quantity, under commercial conditions duplicates of his prototype. If the design requirements are complete and the producer follows them to the letter, we end up with a product whose reliability is predicted largely upon the results obtained on a very small sample of a model subjected to limited tests. These critical limitations lead me to regard with apprehension any reliability prediction which assumes the guise of a solemn promise.[5]

Notwithstanding this, there are several common methods used to achieve a reliable design. Prior to designing for reliability, standards of reliability must be established; that is, some benchmarks of reliability required should be set. There is no economic sense in designing one component to last for 1000 hours when another that it is dependent on cannot possibly last beyond 10 hours. So, in a sense, component reliability standards are dependent on each other, and all are dependent on the reliability requirement of the end item.

DESIGNING FOR RELIABILITY

The design should be as simple as possible. The error rate is directly proportional to complexity. The greater the number of components, the greater the chance of failure. The new technique of value engineering *is* compatible with reliability. Value engineering is the analysis of function versus cost and involves the study of operating functions (procurement, installation, operation, maintenance, logistics) to determine their contributions to the overall worth of the equipment.

> Each characteristic is evaluated to optimize reliability and is reviewed to determine if modifications can be made that will substantially reduce the cost of providing that degree of operability, level of reliability, etc., which was originally thought necessary. Increased reliability is a natural byproduct of equipment simplification, a value engineering analysis goal, hence it is an indication that value engineering and reliability go hand in hand.[6]

[5] E. G. D. Paterson, "The Role of Quality Assurance in Product Reliability," *Industrial Quality Control*, August 1960, p. 24. Reprinted by permission.

[6] Richard M. Jacobs, "The Compatibility of Value Engineering Analysis and Reliability," *Journal of Industrial Engineering*, January–February, 1959, p. 54.

It has been stated that economic goals have no place in a reliability problem. Nothing could be further from the truth. There has always been a necessity for trade-off, and this necessity will remain. One relatively unimportant component will have to sacrifice to another, more important, money which has been allocated to it. This holds true for operations, programs, and so on. It is true of life itself. And it makes sense. It may be that a very high budget figure for a very reliable end item has been allocated; however, the apportioning of portions of the budget will not be on an equal but on an *economic* basis.

Derating (providing a large safety margin) is also used as a method of achieving design reliability. This method is analogous to using a significance level of 0.0001 when 0.05 is thought to be sufficient. For example, a material with tensile strength of 150,000 psi might be prescribed where only 100,000 psi is required.

Parts should be designed with consideration for possible failures. How the component fails is of importance. If possible, failure should occur in a noncatastrophic manner and should do no harm to operating personnel. In an other-than-combat situation, an airplane starter is an example of a fail-safe device. A starter failure happens on the ground, where it causes no harm to the pilot.

Redundancy is another way of achieving reliability. This is the provision of standby or parallel components or assemblies to take over in the event of failure of the primary item. Auxiliary power generators are examples of redundant items. They are put into service when the primary system fails. For a simple illustration of improvement in reliability by providing redundant units, consider a 90% reliable unit which is backed up by another unit of equal reliability. Using the multiplication theorem, the reliability of the system of the two is now 0.99 [reliability of a system is roughly equal to $1 - (1 - R_i)^n$, assuming, of course, that the R_i are independent of each other].

An item protected from extremes of environmental conditions will have increased reliability. The item must be able to withstand environmental stresses to which it will be subjected throughout its service life. Frequently, it cannot withstand these extremes without some type of protection. Thus the pilots of supersonic aircraft are protected from the effects of extremes of heat and load. Electric motors of common household appliances are rubber mounted to protect them from vibration.

Maintainability and *serviceability* are important considerations in designing for reliability. Ease of maintenance and service contributes to higher field reliability. The easier and faster necessary maintenance becomes, the longer an item of known reliability may remain in effective service. Also, it is evident that an item which is easy to maintain will naturally receive better maintenance and service. Items should be designed with these characteristics in mind.

As pointed out before, the desires for a high degree of reliability in each of the characteristics cited above must be considered in terms of the cost of obtaining the reliability desired. It may be that adding another component will be adding too much weight. Thus there is a trade-off of decrease in weight for the decrease in reliability. Or, it may be that a desired degree of comfort may have to be traded off to obtain a greater degree of operator movement. For example, it would be possible to insulate a pilot from almost any extreme of temperature, but the suit might be so bulky that he would not be able to manipulate the controls properly. Another example of trade-off would be trading length of service life between services for a greater frequency of service and maintenance. Components would have shorter life and would be exchanged more often.

Figure 19.5 illustrates a general model for trade-off of reliability for reduced cost. Total cost can be the criterion in any case. It may be that a particular cost is difficult to quantify. For instance, the cost of serious injury to operating personnel is very high, but just how high? There has to be some probability point where one must make the decision to pay no more for a very slight improvement in reliability. If it were possible to get equal return

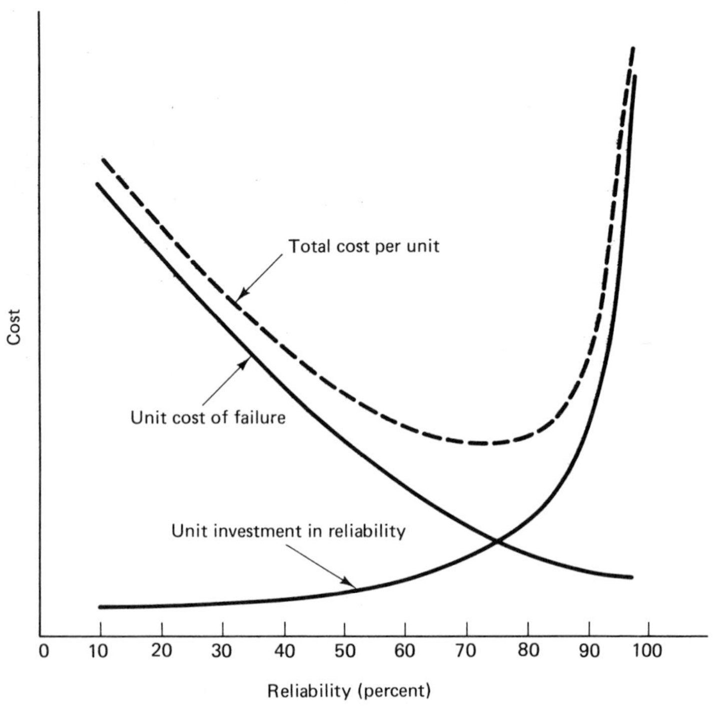

Figure 19.5 Basic model of optimum reliability determination with total cost as determining factor.

in safety for equal investment in reliability, there might be little reason for argument. However, the investment in reliability increases exponentially; that is, it becomes increasingly more expensive to obtain reliability.

Example 19.3

A $20 component in a system has a reliability of 0.50. The provision of a redundant component at equal cost improves the reliability to 0.75; another to 0.875, a fourth to 0.9375, a fifth to 0.9575, and a sixth to approximately 0.98. Figure 19.6 depicts the relationship in graphic form. It is quite evident that there is a decreasing reliability return on the investment in redundancy. Also, if the increase in weight were added in as another cost (as it should be), the return would be much less.

This redundancy example may also be used to illustrate that it may be economically more feasible to manufacture two of an item than to try to make the one item nearly perfect. For example, given an interceptor missile with a hit capability of 0.50, it follows that the hit capability of a combination of two of these missiles is 0.75. In some situations it may make more sense to get improved reliability in this way. This is what is done by most manufac-

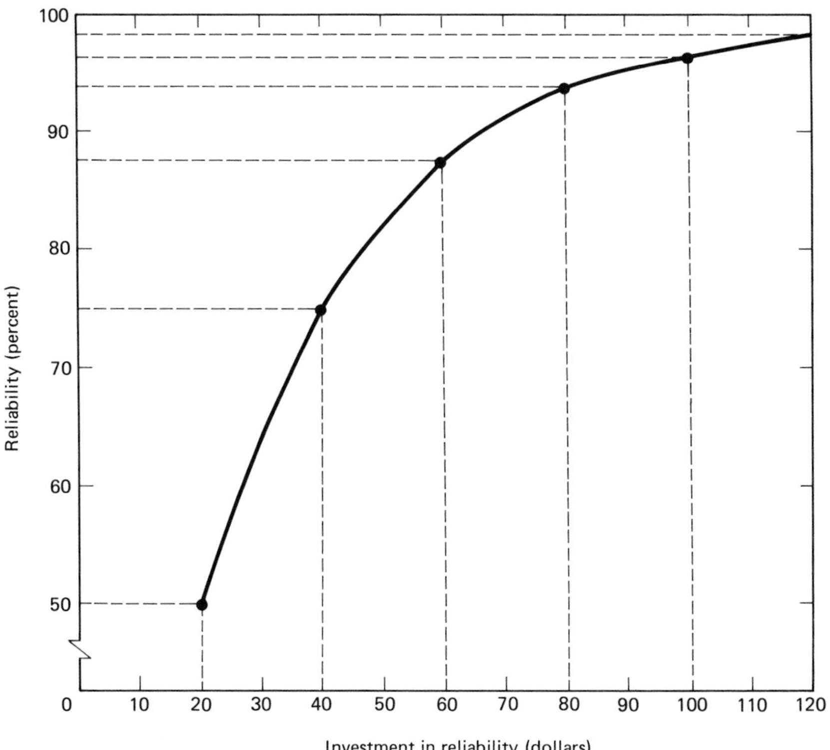

Figure 19.6 Graph of reliability return on investment in redundancy.

turers of consumer items. They would rather manufacture quantities of components and replace free of charge than have a component which is guaranteed not to fail for a long period of time. The feeling here is that consumer tastes are such that there is no requirement for a long-lasting item. "Planned failure time" may be an apt way to term this view. However, this view could become too costly very soon when the rising cost of service is considered.

RELIABILITY MEASUREMENT AND TESTS

The primary measurement tools of reliability are functional, environmental, life, and reliability tests. Prior to the existence of the concept of reliability as a separate phase of quality assurance, these were considered as just a few of the measurement tools in the arsenal of quality control engineers. With the breakout of the reliability phase of quality assurance as a separate functional and sometimes organizational unit, these tests quite naturally came to be considered as the measurement tools of the reliability technician. Also, with increasing emphasis on reliability, increasingly more work was devoted to the development of reliability, environmental, and life-testing plans.

Considering the definition of reliability, it is evident that reliability testing is merely an extension of functional, environmental, and life testing. *Functional testing* involves a test to determine if the product will function at time zero. An *environmental test* is a functional test with the added condition of some environmental stress, such as temperature, pressure, vibration, or other extreme. A *life test* is to determine the mean life of a product. Combine the three types of test and the result is a reliability test.

Acceptance sampling plans where specifications are based on mean life or MTTF (life testing) or on reliability (life testing under stipulated environmental conditions) can be designed in the same manner as the sampling plans for product acceptance. Most of these plans are based on the assumption of exponential failure density (constant hazard). It is worth bearing in mind that these plans are not likely to yield satisfactory results when the failure density is not exponential.[7]

As in the case of lot-by-lot acceptance sampling, documents produced by the U.S. Department of Defense provide an excellent source for ready-to-use plans. Three principal documents that can be used for the purpose are:

1. Handbook H108
2. MIL-STD-690B
3. MIL-STD-718C

[7] See National Bureau of Standards Summary Technical Report, November 1960, "Are Statistical Life-Testing Procedures Robust?" *Industrial Quality Control*, February 1961.

Acceptance plans in all three are similar to each other. It is proposed to describe the use of Handbook H108 first and then illustrate the use of the other two standards by means of examples.

USE OF HANDBOOK H108[8]

This handbook is designed for determining the acceptability of lots of product with regard to length of life and reliability. The lot of product may consist of one or more units of product. The lot is accepted or rejected depending on the results of a life test on a sample of n representative units selected at random from the lot.

H108 has four sections. Section A provides procedures and description of life-test sampling plans contained in the handbook. Section B describes procedures and applications of sampling plans when life tests are terminated on the occurrence of a preassigned number of failures. Section C provides sampling plans when life tests are ended at a preassigned time. Section D contains sequential life-test sampling plans.

Section B is divided into three parts. Part I contains acceptance procedures. Part II contains methods and tables for calculating expected duration of life tests and costs associated with the selection of various sample sizes. Part III contains life-testing plans for certain specified values of α, β, and θ_1/θ_0, producer's risk, consumer's risk, and ratio of unacceptable to acceptable mean life, respectively. Section C of the handbook is also divided into three parts. Part I of Section C contains acceptance procedures. Part II contains life-testing plans for certain specified values of α, β, θ_1/θ_0, and T/θ_0, where the latter term is the ratio of test time to acceptable mean life. Part III contains life-testing plans based on proportion of lot failing before specified time. The acceptance procedures of Part I of both Sections B and C provide for life testing both with replacement and without replacement of failed units. Section D consists of only the one part on sequential life testing.

Operating characteristic (OC) curves for the life-testing sampling plans are contained in the handbook. They were computed for the life-testing sampling plans of Section B, Part I, but are equally applicable to acceptance procedures of Part I of Section C and of Section D. An example of these OC curves is shown in Figure 19.7. The risk values shown by the curves apply only if the underlying distribution approximates the exponential. Chi-square tests may be used to monitor the life testing so as to verify the validity of the exponential assumption.

[8] Handbook H108 is published by the Office of the Assistant Secretary of Defense (Supply and Logistics), April 29, 1960. For sale by the National Technical Information Service, Washington, DC 20402. Another useful handbook source of plans for life testing based on the Weibull distribution is available from the same source, titled *Quality Control and Technical Report* TR3, "Sampling Procedures and Tables for Life and Reliability Testing Based on the Weibull Distribution," September 30, 1961.

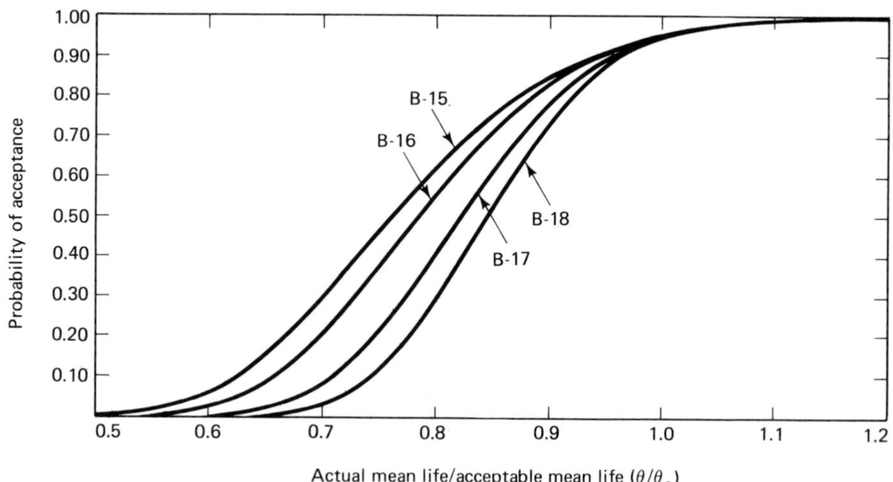

Figure 19.7 Operating characteristic curves for life tests terminated upon occurrence of preassigned number of failures. (Table 2A-2 of H108.) Reprinted from H108, "Sampling Procedures and Tables for Life and Reliability Testing." (Curves for sequential plans and tests terminated at preassigned time are essentially equivalent.)

Some representative tables from the handbook are reproduced in the Appendix as Tables A18.x. These are:

A18.1. Index of Life-Testing Plans of Section 2B part I, 2C part I, and 2D

A18.2. Master Table for Life Tests Terminated upon Predetermined Number of Failures

A18.3. Life Tests for Predetermined Number of Failures based on α, β, and θ_1/θ_0

A18.4. Master Table for Life Tests Terminated at Predetermined Time (without Replacement)

A18.5. Master Table for Life Tests Terminated at Predetermined Time (with Replacement)

A18.6. Life Tests for Predetermined Time Based on α, β, and θ_1/θ_0 (without Replacement)

A18.7. Life Tests for Predetermined Time Based on α, β, and θ_1/θ_0 (with Replacement)

A18.8. Life Tests Acceptance Sampling Plans Based on α, β, and p_1/p_0 (without Replacement)

A18.9. Master Table for Sequential Life Tests

The use of these tables is illustrated by means of Examples 19.4 through 19.11.

Example 19.4

Determine a test plan that will have a producer's risk $\alpha = 0.05$, acceptable mean life 1000 hours, and will be terminated after the fourth failure.

Here $r = 4$. From Table A18.2, for producer's risk 0.05 and $r = 4$, the code is B-4. For this test plan $c/\theta_0 = 0.342$. Hence $c = 342$. The test procedure would be to start the test with some number $n \geq 4$ of units. The times of failures would be noted sequentially. At the fourth failure the test would be terminated. If the estimated mean life computed by equation (19.19) is more than 342 hours, the lot would be considered acceptable. The sample size does not affect the critical level, 342 hours, but does influence the computation of the estimated mean life.

To illustrate, assume that the failure occurs at times 175, 250, 300, and 425 hours. Two possible situations are considered.

1. There were only 4 units in the test and the failed units were not replaced. From equations (19.19) and (19.16),

$$\theta_{r,n} = \hat{\theta} = \frac{1}{r}\left[\sum_{i=1}^{r} t_i + (n - r)t^*\right]$$

$$= \frac{1}{4}[175 + 250 + 300 + 425 + 0(425)]$$

$$= \frac{1150}{4} = 287.5$$

The lot fails the test.

2. There were 10 units at the start of the test and failed units were not replaced.

$$\theta_{r,n} = \hat{\theta} = \frac{1}{r}\left[\sum_{i=1}^{r} t_i + (n - r)t^*\right]$$

$$= \frac{1}{4}[175 + 250 + 300 + 425 + 6(425)]$$

$$= \frac{3700}{4} = 925$$

The lot passes the test.

The reason the same test results lead to apparently conflicting conclusions can be explained by looking at the total unit-hours of operation (Table 19.2).

Part II of Section 2B of the handbook contains methods for considering expected waiting times and testing costs in the selection of n, the sample size. It is obvious that a larger sample size will yield a quicker decision, but it will also cost more, due to placing more units of the product on test. When

TABLE 19.2 Comparison of Test Results

		Situation 1		Situation 2	
Time Period	Hours	Units	Unit-Hours	Units	Unit-Hours
0–175	175	4	700	10	1750
175–250	75	3	225	9	675
250–300	50	2	100	8	400
300–425	125	1	125	7	875
Total	425		1150		3700

testing without replacement, the total expected cost of any of the life-test plans in the referenced section is given by

$$\text{total cost} = c_1\theta_0\left(\frac{1}{n} + \frac{1}{n-1} + \cdots + \frac{1}{n-r+1}\right) + c_2 n \qquad (19.26)$$

where c_1 = cost of waiting per unit time
c_2 = cost of placing a unit of product on test
θ_0 = acceptable mean life
r = termination number
n = sample size

The value of n that minimizes the total cost, as calculated from equation (19.26), is the optimum sample size. An example taken directly from H108 follows.

Example 19.5

Consider the case where $r = 10$, $\theta_0 = 1000$ hours, $c_1 = \$1$ per hour, and $c_2 = \$100$ per unit of product tested. Using the total cost formula, determine the optimum sample size if failed units are not replaced.

Using equation (19.26), the costs for the various values of n are as given in Table 19.3. Tables to facilitate the calculations have been provided in the handbook.

When testing with replacement,

$$\text{total cost} = c_1\theta_0\frac{r}{n} + c_2(n + r - 1) \qquad (19.27)$$

The value of n that minimizes the total cost is the optimum sample size. Generally, the optimum n, when testing with replacement, is the integer closest to

$$\sqrt{\frac{c_1\theta_0 r}{c_2} + \frac{1}{4}}$$

TABLE 19.3 Costs Summary

n	Expected Cost Due to Waiting	Cost of Units Tested	Total Cost
10	2929	1000	3929
11	2020	1100	3120
12	1603	1200	2803
13	1346	1300	2646
14	1168	1400	2568
15	1035	1500	2535
16	931	1600	2531*
17	847	1700	2547

*The optimum sample size is $n = 16$.

Using the data from the foregoing example yields 10, the integer closest to

$$\sqrt{\frac{1(1000)(10)}{100}} + \frac{1}{4} = 10.25$$

Part III of Section 2B of H108 is an extension of Part II for the case where it is desired to specify values of α, β, and θ_1/θ_0. Both tables and formulas are provided.

Example 19.6

Determine a test plan that possesses the following characteristics. If the mean life $\theta_0 = 900$ hours, the lot is accepted with probability at least 0.95; if the mean life $\theta_1 = 300$ hours, it is accepted with probability, at most, 0.10. In this case $\alpha = 0.05$, $\beta = 0.10$, and $\theta_1/\theta_0 = 1/3$.

From Table A18.3 the following test plan is obtained. $r = 8$ and $c/\theta_0 = 0.498$. Hence $c = 0.498 \times 900 = 448.2$. The test procedure would be to start the test with some number $n \geq 8$ of units. The test would be terminated after the eighth failure. If the estimated mean life $\theta_{8,n}$ is greater than 448.2, the lot would be considered acceptable.

To supplement the tabled values, for values of θ_1/θ_0 greater than $\frac{2}{3}$, the following formulas may be used:

$$r = \left[\frac{K_\beta + (\theta_0/\theta_1)K_\alpha}{(\theta_0/\theta_1) - 1}\right]^2 \tag{19.28}$$

$$C = \theta_0\left(1 - \frac{K_\alpha}{\sqrt{r}}\right) \tag{19.29}$$

K_α and K_β may be determined from tables of the cumulative normal distribution. For example, assume that it is desired to find a sampling plan that will have a 0.95 probability of accepting lots with mean life quality of 1000 hours, and a 0.10 probability of accepting lots with mean life quality of 750 hours. The normal deviate (K) values for $\alpha = 0.05$ and $\beta = 0.10$ are 1.645 and 1.282, respectively. Solution yields

$$r = \frac{1.282 + \frac{4}{3}(1.645)}{\frac{4}{3} - 1} = 110$$

$$C = 1000\left(1 - \frac{1.645}{110}\right) = 985 \text{ hours}$$

Part I of Section 2C of H108 contains tables and procedures for determining lot acceptability when the test is terminated at a preassigned time—for testing with or without replacement. Tables A18.4 through A18.7 have been reproduced from H108 to illustrate the procedures for finding sampling plans from this portion of the handbook.

Example 19.7

Determine a predetermined time test plan, without replacement, for the data in Example 19.4:

$$\alpha = 0.05 \qquad \theta_0 = 1000 \text{ hours} \qquad r = 4$$

From Table A18.4 the code is B-4 (same as in Example 19.4). If the sample size is taken as $5r = 20$, the value T/θ_0 is 0.074. The test procedure would be to start the test with 20 units. If after time $T = \theta_0(T/\theta_0) = 74$ hours the number of failures is less than 4, the lot is acceptable. In this case the test may possibly be terminated before 74 hours if the fourth failure occurs earlier.

Example 19.8

Determine a predetermined time test plan, with replacement, for the data in Example 19.4. Again, $\theta = 0.05$, $\theta_0 = 1000$ hours, $r = 4$, and $n = 20$.

From Table A18.5 the code is once again B-4 and $T/\theta_0 = 0.068$. The test procedure would be to start the test with 20 units. As each unit fails, replace it with a good unit. The test terminates after 68 hours (or earlier if the fourth failure occurs earlier). If the fourth failure has not occurred by 68 hours of testing, the lot is considered acceptable.

Part II of Section 2C contains sampling plans for specified α, β, θ_1/θ_0, and T/θ_0, for testing without and with replacement.

Example 19.9

Determine a predetermined time test plan for the following parameters (a) without replacement and (b) with replacement:

$$\alpha = 0.05,\ \theta_0 = 500; \quad \beta = 0.10,\ \theta_1 = 250,\ T = 50$$

Here $T/\theta_0 = 50/500 = 1/10$, and $\theta_1/\theta_0 = 250/500 = 1/2$.

(a) The test plan obtained from the section $\alpha = 0.05$, $\beta = 0.10$ of Table A18.6 is sample size $n = 134$ and termination number $r = 19$. The test procedure would be to start the test with 134 units. There is no replacement of failed units. If the nineteenth failure has not occurred by 50 hours, the lot is considered acceptable.

(b) For test plan with replacement, Table A18.7 is used. The test plan is sample size $n = 124$ and $r = 19$. The test procedure would be to start the test with 124 units. As each unit fails, replace it with a good unit. If the nineteenth failure has not occurred by 50 hours, the lot is considered acceptable.

Part III of Section 2C of H108 provides tables and procedures for nonreplacement life-test sampling plans based on failure rates. Table A18.8 gives values of the termination number, r, and the sample size factor, D, for various values of α, β, and p_1/p_0. The sampling plans in this part of the handbook may be used when either the proportion of the lot failing before the specified time, or the failure rate during the time period, is specified. That is, $p = GT$, where p is the proportion of lot failing before specified time T, and G is the failure rate during period of time T. In this case it must be remembered that the specification is not in terms of acceptable mean life. It is in terms of the proportion of the lot that may fail before a specified time. For example, the user of an item may require an acceptable mean life of 1000 hours and at the same time specify that not more than 2% may fail before 400 hours.

Example 19.10

Determine a predetermined time test plan that will accept at least 95% of the lots where 2% or fewer items fail before 400 hours and reject at least 90% of the lots where 8% or more items fail before 400 hours.

Table A18.8 gives the test plan without replacement. Here $p_1/p_0 = 0.08/0.02 = 4$, $\alpha = 0.05$, and $\beta = 0.10$. The test plan from Table A18.8 is $r = 6$ and $D = 2.61$. Hence the sample size $n = D/p_0 = 131$ (rounded upward). The test procedure would be to start the test with 131 units. The test is run for 400 hours. If the sixth failure has not occurred by 400 hours, the lot is acceptable.

SEQUENTIAL ACCEPTANCE PROCEDURES BASED ON MTTF

As in the case of acceptance procedures described in Chapter 12, sequential procedures can be developed for life testing. The development parallels the development in Chapter 12.

Here the hypothesis being tested is

$$H_0\colon \theta = \text{a satisfactory value } \theta$$

against

$$H_1\colon \theta_1 = \text{an unsatisfactory value } \theta_1$$

If at time t the total test time is Q as given by equation (19.16) for test without replacement and by (19.20) for test with replacement, and ϕ is the event that r failures have occurred, then

$$\Pr(\phi \mid H_0) = \left(\frac{1}{\theta_0}\right)^r e^{-\theta/\theta_0}$$

$$\Pr(\phi \mid H_1) = \left(\frac{1}{\theta_1}\right)^r e^{-\theta/\theta_1}$$

Hence the probability ratio is

$$\begin{aligned} R &= \frac{\Pr(\phi \mid H_0)}{\Pr(\phi \mid H_1)} \\ &= \left(\frac{\theta_1}{\theta_0}\right) \exp\left[-Q\left(\frac{1}{\theta_0} - \frac{1}{\theta_1}\right)\right] \end{aligned} \tag{19.30}$$

The lot would be considered acceptable when R exceeds $(1 - \alpha)/\beta$ and be rejected when R falls below $\alpha/(1 - \beta)$. For values of R in between these limits, the test continues. MIL-STD-781C provides for explicit truncation of the test by specifying both the maximum number of failures r^* and the maximum duration t^*. In practice the test is conducted by plotting the number of failures r versus the relative total test time Q/θ_1.

The acceptance and rejection criteria become straight lines.

$$\begin{aligned} \text{Rejection line: } r &= s\frac{Q}{\theta_1} + h_2 \\ \text{Acceptance line: } r &= s\frac{Q}{\theta_1} - h_1 \end{aligned} \tag{19.31}$$

The formulas necessary for finding the parameters are as follows:

$$\begin{aligned} h_1 &= \frac{b}{g_1} \\ h_2 &= \frac{a}{g_1} \\ s &= \frac{g_2}{g_1}\cdot\theta_1 \end{aligned} \tag{19.32}$$

where

$$g = \log \frac{\theta_0}{\theta_1}$$

$$g_2 = \frac{1}{\theta_1} - \frac{1}{\theta_0} \tag{19.33}$$

$$a = \log \frac{1 - \beta}{\alpha}$$

$$b = \log \frac{1 - \alpha}{\beta}$$

All logarithms in equation 19.33 are natural logarithms or logarithms to the base e.

Example 19.11

Determine a sequential sampling plan for the following specifications:

$$\alpha = 0.05,\ \beta = 0.10,\ \theta_0 = 900 \text{ and } \theta_1 = 300$$

$$g_i = \log \frac{\theta_0}{\theta_1} = \log \frac{900}{300}$$

$$= 1.0986$$

$$g_2 = \frac{1}{\theta_1} - \frac{1}{\theta_0} = \frac{1}{300} - \frac{1}{900}$$

$$= 0.0022$$

$$a = \log \frac{1 - \beta}{\alpha} = \log \frac{0.9}{0.05}$$

$$= 2.8904$$

$$b = \log \frac{1 - \alpha}{\beta} = \log \frac{0.95}{0.1}$$

$$= 2.2513$$

$$h_1 = \frac{b}{g_1} = \frac{2.2513}{1.0986} = 2.0492$$

$$h_2 = \frac{a}{g_1} = \frac{2.8904}{1.0986} = 2.6310$$

$$s = \frac{g_2}{g_1}\theta_1 = \frac{0.0022}{1.0986} \times 300$$

$$= 0.6068$$

$$\text{Rejection line: } r = 0.6068\left(\frac{Q}{\theta_1}\right) + 2.6310$$

$$\text{Acceptance line: } r = 0.6068\left(\frac{Q}{\theta_1}\right) - 2.0492$$

Figure 19.8 shows this test plan in operation. Nine units are tested sequentially without replacement. First two failures occur after 100 and 250 hours, respectively.

Time Period	Units	Unit-Hours	Q
0–100	9	900	900
100–250	8	1200	2100

The point for the second failure is below the acceptance line, indicating the lot to be acceptable.

There are two points to note in the case of sequential plan. First, the horizontal scale is in units of θ_1 or the unacceptable mean life. Second, the logarithm in the computation is the natural logarithm. A conversion is needed if logarithm to the base 10 is used.

Figure 19.8 is drawn according to the convention used in MIL-STD-781C. Handbook H108 uses the alternative convention, where Q is placed on the vertical axis and r on the horizontal axis. According to Handbook H108 the acceptance and rejection lines would be

$$\text{Acceptance line: } \frac{Q}{\theta_1} = 1.648r + 3.377$$

$$\text{Rejection line: } \frac{Q}{\theta_1} = 1.648r - 4.336$$

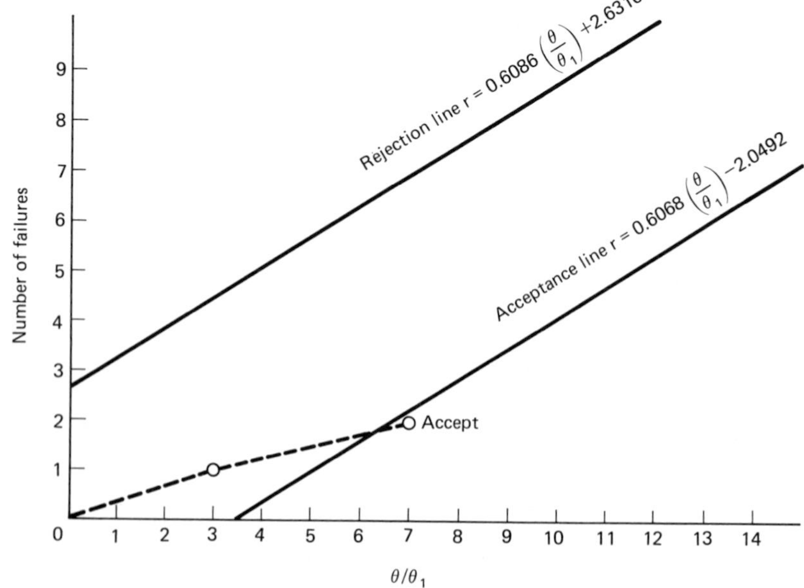

Figure 19.8 Sequential test plan.

No tables are provided for sequential test plans and the reader is advised to use equations (19.32) and (19.33) to compute the necessary test plan procedures.

MAINTENANCE AND RELIABILITY

Approximately twice the original cost of complex equipment is expended each year to support the equipment. Much of this cost is the result of upkeep and maintenance. The total reliability of the equipment in the field is a function of design, maintenance, and field operation reliability; that is,

$$P_s = f(D, M, \text{FO})$$

Maintainability plays an important part in the job of achieving reliability in the use system. Simply stated, it refers to the relative ease with which an item may be kept in operation. An item with high maintainability is one that is easy to keep in operation; one with low maintainability is exactly the opposite. An item that is difficult to maintain will not be maintained as well and will require much more time for necessary maintenance. Modular design (design for replacement of entire subsystems) is one example of designing for ease of maintenance. In addition to the inherent design effect on maintainability, the environment, conditions, and operating personnel at the place of use also have a substantial effect. In effect, maintenance is a production-type operation at or near the place of use, where production is confined to repair or replacement of failed, marginal, or time-change units. Thus it should be susceptible to the same types of reliability controls as the manufacturing operation.

There are three types of maintenance performed:

1. *Corrective*: repair, adjustment, or replacement as a result of unsatisfactory equipment operation
2. *Preventive*: repair, adjustment, or replacement on satisfactory equipment to prevent future occurrences of unsatisfactory operation; acts to expand the random failure phase of the "bathtub" curve
3. *Monitor*: check for condition of equipment to determine the need for preventive or corrective maintenance; essentially an inspection operation

The most significant maintenance and field support factors are the following.[9]

[9] F. M. Gryna, Jr., N. J. McAfee, C. M. Ryerson, and S. Zwerling, "Reliability Training Text," Institute of Radio Engineers, Inc., March 1960, pp. 150–151. Criteria are taken from the text with abridged descriptions furnished by the authors.

Criteria of Adequate Performance

Both operators and maintenance personnel must possess the necessary skills and knowledge to make correct decisions about the performance of equipment. Maintainability is dependent on correct and consistent decisions regarding whether or not maintenance is required. These decisions can be made in the monitoring phase, the preventive phase, or by the operator as a result of actual unsatisfactory operation. Maintainability may be enhanced by designing into the equipment various measuring devices to detect unsatisfactory performance as soon as it occurs. Estimates of availability of equipment and preventive maintenance downtime requirements must be realistic.

Marginal Testing

Marginal testing is a technique for detecting potential failures so as to shortcut them. It consists of testing at maximum and minimum values required by the specifications. This testing at the "margins" of the acceptable specification range will often be helpful in detecting whether a deteriorating unit will fail before the next maintenance period. A weak semi-conductor in a home television set is a good example for illustrating the marginal test. It may be replaced as a result of marginal failure, or it may be put back into the set until an actual failure results. Of course, the seriousness of a failure is of prime importance in the decision of whether to replace "now" or at the next maintenance period.

Spares Provisioning

If a replacement is needed, factors of spares provisioning are introduced. The right spare parts must be available in sufficient quantity and of equal or better quality. Reliability of equipment does not necessarily dictate requirements for spares. Normally, only true random failures are included in the calculations for reliability. Replacements resulting from marginal testing, parts damaged in maintenance, and secondary failures (failure as a result of a primary failure) are usually not included in the estimate of the reliability of a system. Total replacements over a given time period may exceed the true random failures by as much as three or four times. Thus it is not only the failure rate that must be considered in planning for spares but these other replacements also.

Training

Random, sequential replacement of parts until trouble disappears is very undesirable. Unfortunately, field maintenance sometimes consists of this method. The total effect is a serious reduction in reliability through accidental damage, improper reassembly, misalignment, and other malpractices. Detailed step-by-step procedures for locating trouble sources are mandatory. For each type of failure, maintenance handbooks should contain instructions on how to trace the failure and the corrective action that should be taken. Maintenance training programs should provide for thorough indoctrination in the various methods.

Manuals and Technical Instructions

Simple, adequate, understandable maintenance instructions are essential to proper maintenance of equipment and to proper operation. They should be clear, concise, and sufficiently direct to allow the maintenance person to proceed through a step-by-step routine toward fault isolation. Whenever possible, requirements for maintenance quality should be expressed in quantitative rather than qualitative terms. Since maintenance is a form of a production operation, the same principles should apply. Also, prior to issue, manuals and technical instructions should be checked by having a typical maintenance worker run through all the requirements, reporting forms, tests, and so on, to eliminate bugs in them. This is analogous to having a pilot run on a new item and from a relative cost standpoint is just as desirable.

Test Equipment and Facilities

Maintenance of equipment may require the use of precision test equipment for a variety of measurements. Such equipment should be at least as accurate as the test equipment used in original production and test. There should be calibration as often as necessary and the standards from maintenance area to maintenance area should be uniform. Finally, the test equipment should be adequate to perform the necessary test, and it should be available at the time of need.

PROBLEMS

19.1. Given the component reliabilities indicated below, calculate the probability of survival of the assembly.

Component	Reliability
A	0.999
B	0.98
C	0.99
D	0.87
E	0.92
F	0.84

19.2. A lightweight component in an electrical assembly has a reliability of 0.70. Provision of two redundant units can be tolerated with no appreciable effect on weight specifications. If two redundant units of the same component are installed, what will be the compound reliability of the three?

19.3. An assembly, through simplification, can be reduced from six components to three components. The reliability of each of the six components is 0.98. Presuming no change in component reliabilities, what would be the change in the assembly reliability with reduction of components?

19.4. A sample of 10 neon bulbs used in a console were observed by a status reporting system. The times to failure, without replacement, were 2935, 3658, 3868, 3870, 4102, 4119, 4320, 4719, 4923, and 5100, respectively. What is the estimated mean life?

19.5. If the specification for these bulbs requires the MTTF to be equal to or greater than 5000 hours, can these bulbs be accepted? Use a chi-square test.

19.6. How would your answers to Problems 19.4 and 19.5 differ if you are given further information that the console had 20 more bulbs and all of these were functioning at the end of 5100 hours?

19.7. Sketch the reliability function and the hazard function for the following Weibull failure densities.

(a) $\alpha = 1$, $\beta = 2$
(b) $\alpha = 10$, $\beta = 1$

19.8. Determine a life-testing plan which would terminate after the sixth failure and would have a producer's risk of 0.05 for an acceptable mean life of 500 hours. Ten units were tested without replacement and the first six units to fail did so after 200, 270, 290, 310, 320, and 330 hours, respectively. Would the lot be acceptable?

19.9. What would be the conclusion in Problem 19.8 if the same failure times were observed in a test of 10 units with replacement?

19.10. Determine a life-testing plan for the following conditions. $\alpha = 0.05$, $\beta = 0.10$, acceptable mean life 600 hours, unacceptable mean life 400.

19.11. The acceptable mean life of a product is 1000 hours. The consumer wishes to limit the probability of accepting items with mean life of 500 hours or less to 0.05. If the producer's risk is to be 0.05 and the test is to be concluded in 200 hours, how many units should be tested without replacement? What is the termination number of failures?

19.12. Determine a sampling plan that will accept at least 90% of the lots when no more than 2% of the items in the lot fail in 200 hours, and will reject at least 90% of the lots when 10% or more of the items in the lot fail before 200.

19.13. Using Table A18.8, find the nonreplacement life-testing sampling plan that will accept at least 95% of lots for which the failure rate for a period of time, expressed as a percentage, is less than or equal to 5% per 1000 hours, and will reject at least 90% of lots that have a failure rate greater than or equal to 10% per 1000 hours.

19.14. How would you calculate the OC curve of a plan from Table A18.2? Assume exponential failure density, replacement of failed units, and a sample size equal to $4r$.

19.15. Determine a sequential life-testing plan when the acceptable mean life is 5000 hours and unacceptable mean life is 3000 hours. α and β are both 0.10.

19.16. Calculate the significant points on the OC curve for the plan in Problem 19.15.

BIBLIOGRAPHY

Statistics

BROWNLEE, K. A. *Statistical Theory and Methodology*. 2d ed. New York: John Wiley, 1965.

DIXON, WILFRED J., AND MASSEY, F. J. *Introduction to Statistical Analysis*. 3rd ed. New York: McGraw-Hill, 1969.

FREUND, JOHN E. *Statistics, A First Course*. 2d ed. Englewood Cliffs, N.J.: Prentice-Hall, 1976.

GUTTMAN, IRWIN; WILKS, S. S.; AND HUNTER, J. S. *Introductory Engineering Statistics*, 3d ed. New York: John Wiley, 1982.

HINES, W. W. AND MONTGOMERY, D. C. *Probability and Statistics in Engineering and Statistics*. 2d ed. New York: John Wiley, 1980.

HOEL, PAUL G. *Elementary Statistics*. 3d ed. New York: John Wiley, 1971.

HOEL, PAUL G. *Introduction to Mathematical Statistics*. 5th ed. New York: John Wiley, 1984.

MOOD, AND GRAYBILL. *Introduction to the Theory of Statistics*. 3d ed. New York: McGraw-Hill, 1974.

MOSTELLER, F. R.; ROURKE, R. E. K.; AND THOMAS, C. B. *Probability with Statistical Applications*. Reading, Mass.: Addison-Wesley, 1970.

PARZEN, EMANUEL. *Modern Probability and its Applications*. New York: John Wiley, 1960.

SNEDECOR, G. W., AND COCHRAN, W. G. *Statistical Methods*. 7th ed. Ames, Iowa: Iowa State University, 1980.

Quality Control

COWDEN, D. J. *Statistical Methods in Quality Control*. Englewood Cliffs, N.J.: Prentice-Hall, 1957.

DEMING, W. EDWARD. *Quality, Productivity and Competitive Position*. Cambridge, Mass.: Massachusetts Institute of Technology, Center for Advanced Engineering Studies, 1982.

DODGE, H. F., AND ROMIG, H. G. *Sampling Inspection Tables—Single and Double Sampling*. 2d ed. New York: John Wiley, 1959.

DUNCAN, ACHESON, J. *Quality Control and Industrial Statistics*. 3d ed. New York: Irwin, 1974.

FEIGENBAUM, A. V. *Total Quality Control*. 3d ed. New York: McGraw-Hill, 1983.

GRANT, E. L., AND LEAVENWORTH, R. S. *Statistical Quality Control*. 5th ed. New York: McGraw-Hill, 1980.

HANSEN, B. L. *Quality Control: Theory and Applications*. Englewood Cliffs, N.J.: Prentice-Hall, 1963.

JURAN, J. M., AND GRYNA, F. M. *Quality Planning and Analysis*. 2d ed. New York: McGraw-Hill, 1980.

MONTGOMERY, DOUGLAS C. *Introduction to Statistical Quality Control*. New York: John Wiley, 1985.

Reliability

BAZOWSKY, I. *Reliability: Theory and Practice*. Englewood Cliffs, N.J.: Prentice-Hall, 1961.

HAVILAND, ROBERT P. *Engineering Reliability and Long Life Design*. Princeton, N.J.: J. Van Nostrand, 1964.

HENLEY, ERNEST J., AND KAVMAMOTO, H. *Reliability Engineering and Risk Assessment*. Englewood Cliffs, N.J.: Prentice-Hall, 1981.

KAPUR, K. *Reliability in Engineering Design*. New York: John Wiley, 1977.

LLOYD, D. K., AND LIPOW, MYRON. *Reliability: Management, Methods and Mathematics*. Englewood Cliffs, N.J.: Prentice-Hall, 1962.

SHOOMAN, M. L. *Probabilistic Reliability: An Engineering Approach*. New York: McGraw-Hill, 1968.

SINHA, S. K. AND KALE, B. K. *Life Testing and Reliability Estimation*. New York: John Wiley, 1980.

SMITH, DAVID J. *Reliability and Maintainability in Perspective*. 2d ed. New York: John Wiley, 1985.

U.S. Government Publications

NOTE: An excellent and exhaustive source for standardized quality control procedures can be found in the publications of the U.S. Government. Some examples of these tables are illustrated in the text. The complete documents would prove very useful to any quality control engineer. All these publications are available from National Technical Information Service, Washington D.C. 20402.

1. MIL-STD-105D
2. MIL-STD-414
3. MIL-STD-441
4. MIL-STD-690B
5. MIL-STD-781C
6. MIL-STD-1235(ORD)
7. Handbook H106
8. Handbook H107
9. Handbook H108

appendix

TABLES

A1 Areas under the Normal Curve
A2 Standard Normal Density Function
A3 Cumulative Poisson Distribution
A4 Chi-Square Distribution
A5 Student's t Distribution
A6 F Distribution
A7 Factors to Estimate σ from $\overline{R}$ and $\overline{S}$
A8 Factors for Control Limits for $\overline{X}$, S, and R Charts
A9 Formulas for Control Charts
A10 Formulas and Factors for Median and Midrange Charts
A11 Control Limits for p Charts
A12 Average Run Length, Known σ
A13 Average Run Length, Based on $\overline{R}$
A14 MIL-STD-105D Tables
A15 MIL-STD-414 Tables
A16 MIL-STD-1235 ORD Tables
A17 Dodge–Romig Sampling Plans
A18 Handbook H108 Tables

TABLE A1 Areas under the Normal Curve

$$P = 10000 \cdot \int_{-\infty}^{z} \frac{1}{\sqrt{2\pi}} \exp(-z^2/2)dz$$

$z = \frac{x - \mu}{\sigma}$	0.09	0.08	0.07	0.06	0.05	0.04	0.03	0.02	0.01	0.00
−3.40	2	2	3	3	3	3	3	3	3	3
−3.30	3	4	4	4	4	4	4	4	5	5
−3.20	5	5	5	6	6	6	6	6	7	7
−3.10	7	7	8	8	8	8	9	9	9	10
−3.00	10	10	11	11	11	12	12	13	13	13
−2.90	14	14	15	15	16	16	17	17	18	19
−2.80	19	20	20	21	22	23	23	24	25	26
−2.70	26	27	28	29	30	31	32	33	34	35
−2.60	36	37	38	39	40	41	43	44	45	47
−2.50	48	49	51	52	54	55	57	59	60	62
−2.40	64	66	68	69	71	73	75	78	80	82
−2.30	84	87	89	91	94	96	99	102	104	107
−2.20	110	113	116	119	122	125	129	132	136	139
−2.10	143	146	150	154	158	162	166	170	174	179
−2.00	183	188	192	197	202	207	212	217	222	227
−1.90	233	239	244	250	256	262	268	274	281	287
−1.80	294	301	307	314	322	329	336	344	351	359
−1.70	367	375	384	392	401	409	418	427	436	446
−1.60	455	465	475	485	495	505	515	526	537	548
−1.50	559	571	582	594	606	618	630	643	655	668
−1.40	681	694	708	721	735	749	764	778	793	808
−1.30	823	838	853	869	885	901	918	934	951	968
−1.20	985	1003	1020	1038	1056	1075	1093	1112	1131	1151
−1.10	1170	1190	1210	1230	1251	1271	1292	1314	1335	1357
−1.00	1379	1401	1423	1446	1469	1492	1515	1539	1562	1587
−0.90	1611	1635	1660	1685	1711	1736	1762	1788	1814	1841
−0.80	1867	1894	1921	1949	1977	2005	2033	2061	2090	2119
−0.70	2148	2177	2206	2236	2266	2296	2327	2358	2389	2420
−0.60	2451	2483	2514	2546	2578	2611	2643	2676	2709	2743
−0.50	2776	2810	2843	2877	2912	2946	2981	3015	3050	3085
−0.40	3121	3156	3192	3228	3264	3300	3336	3372	3409	3446
−0.30	3483	3520	3557	3594	3632	3669	3707	3745	3783	3821
−0.20	3859	3897	3936	3974	4013	4052	4090	4129	4168	4207
−0.10	4247	4286	4325	4364	4404	4443	4483	4522	4562	4602
0.00	4641	4681	4721	4761	4801	4840	4880	4920	4960	5000

TABLE A1 Areas under the Normal Curve *(Continued)*

$$P = 10000 \cdot \int_{-\infty}^{z} \frac{1}{\sqrt{2\pi}} \exp(-z^2/2)dz$$

$z = \frac{x - \mu}{\sigma}$	0.00	0.01	0.02	0.03	0.04	0.05	0.06	0.07	0.08	0.09
0	5000	5039	5079	5119	5159	5199	5239	5279	5318	5358
.1	5398	5437	5477	5517	5556	5596	5635	5674	5714	5753
.2	5792	5831	5870	5909	5948	5987	6025	6064	6102	6140
.3	6179	6217	6255	6292	6330	6368	6405	6443	6480	6517
.4	6554	6590	6627	6664	6700	6736	6772	6808	6843	6879
.5	6914	6949	6984	7019	7054	7088	7122	7156	7190	7224
.6	7257	7290	7323	7356	7389	7421	7453	7485	7517	7549
.7	7580	7611	7642	7673	7703	7733	7763	7793	7823	7852
.8	7881	7910	7938	7967	7995	8023	8051	8078	8105	8132
.9	8159	8185	8212	8238	8263	8289	8314	8339	8364	8389
1	8413	8437	8461	8484	8508	8531	8554	8576	8599	8621
1.1	8643	8664	8686	8707	8728	8749	8769	8789	8809	8829
1.2	8849	8868	8887	8906	8925	8943	8961	8979	8997	9014
1.3	9031	9049	9065	9082	9098	9114	9130	9146	9162	9177
1.4	9192	9207	9221	9236	9250	9264	9278	9292	9305	9318
1.5	9331	9344	9357	9369	9382	9394	9406	9417	9429	9440
1.6	9451	9462	9473	9484	9494	9505	9515	9525	9535	9544
1.7	9554	9563	9572	9581	9590	9599	9607	9616	9624	9632
1.8	9640	9648	9656	9663	9671	9678	9685	9692	9699	9706
1.9	9712	9719	9725	9731	9738	9744	9750	9755	9761	9767
2	9772	9777	9783	9788	9793	9798	9803	9807	9812	9816
2.1	9821	9825	9829	9834	9838	9842	9846	9849	9853	9857
2.2	9860	9864	9867	9871	9874	9877	9880	9883	9886	9889
2.3	9892	9895	9898	9900	9903	9906	9908	9911	9913	9915
2.4	9918	9920	9922	9924	9926	9928	9930	9932	9934	9936
2.5	9937	9939	9941	9942	9944	9946	9947	9949	9950	9952
2.6	9953	9954	9956	9957	9958	9959	9960	9962	9963	9964
2.7	9965	9966	9967	9968	9969	9970	9971	9971	9972	9973
2.8	9974	9975	9975	9976	9977	9978	9978	9979	9980	9980
2.9	9981	9981	9982	9983	9983	9984	9984	9985	9985	9986
3	9986	9986	9987	9987	9988	9988	9988	9989	9989	9989
3.1	9990	9990	9990	9991	9991	9991	9992	9992	9992	9992
3.2	9993	9993	9993	9993	9994	9994	9994	9994	9994	9994
3.3	9995	9995	9995	9995	9995	9995	9996	9996	9996	9996
3.4	9996	9996	9996	9996	9997	9997	9997	9997	9997	9997

TABLE A2 Standard Normal Density Function

$$f(x) = f(-x) = \frac{1}{\sqrt{2\pi}} e^{-x^2/2}$$

x	0	1	2	3	4	5	6	7	8	9
0	0.3989	0.3989	0.3989	0.3988	0.3986	0.3984	0.3982	0.3980	0.3977	0.3973
0.1	0.3970	0.3965	0.3961	0.3956	0.3951	0.3945	0.3939	0.3932	0.3925	0.3918
0.2	0.3910	0.3902	0.3894	0.3885	0.3876	0.3867	0.3857	0.3847	0.3836	0.3825
0.3	0.3814	0.3802	0.3790	0.3778	0.3765	0.3752	0.3739	0.3725	0.3712	0.3697
0.4	0.3683	0.3668	0.3653	0.3637	0.3621	0.3605	0.3589	0.3572	0.3555	0.3538
0.5	0.3521	0.3503	0.3485	0.3467	0.3448	0.3429	0.3410	0.3391	0.3372	0.3352
0.6	0.3332	0.3312	0.3292	0.3271	0.3251	0.3230	0.3209	0.3187	0.3166	0.3144
0.7	0.3123	0.3101	0.3079	0.3056	0.3034	0.3011	0.2989	0.2966	0.2943	0.2920
0.8	0.2897	0.2874	0.2850	0.2827	0.2803	0.2780	0.2756	0.2732	0.2709	0.2685
0.9	0.2661	0.2637	0.2613	0.2589	0.2565	0.2541	0.2516	0.2492	0.2468	0.2444
1	0.2420	0.2396	0.2371	0.2347	0.2323	0.2299	0.2275	0.2251	0.2227	0.2203
1.1	0.2179	0.2155	0.2131	0.2107	0.2083	0.2059	0.2036	0.2012	0.1989	0.1965
1.2	0.1942	0.1919	0.1895	0.1872	0.1849	0.1826	0.1804	0.1781	0.1758	0.1736
1.3	0.1714	0.1691	0.1669	0.1647	0.1626	0.1604	0.1582	0.1561	0.1539	0.1518
1.4	0.1497	0.1476	0.1456	0.1435	0.1415	0.1394	0.1374	0.1354	0.1334	0.1315

1.5	0.1295	0.1276	0.1257	0.1238	0.1219	0.1200	0.1182	0.1163	0.1145	0.1127
1.6	0.1109	0.1092	0.1074	0.1057	0.1040	0.1023	0.1006	0.0989	0.0973	0.0957
1.7	0.0957	0.0940	0.0909	0.0893	0.0878	0.0863	0.0848	0.0833	0.0818	0.0804
1.8	0.0790	0.0775	0.0761	0.0748	0.0734	0.0721	0.0707	0.0694	0.0681	0.0669
1.9	0.0656	0.0644	0.0632	0.0620	0.0608	0.0596	0.0584	0.0573	0.0562	0.0551
2	0.0540	0.0529	0.0519	0.0508	0.0498	0.0488	0.0478	0.0468	0.0459	0.0449
2.1	0.0440	0.0431	0.0422	0.0413	0.0404	0.0396	0.0387	0.0379	0.0371	0.0363
2.2	0.0355	0.3470	0.3390	0.0332	0.0325	0.0317	0.0310	0.0303	0.0297	0.0290
2.3	0.0283	0.0277	0.0270	0.0264	0.0258	0.0252	0.0246	0.0241	0.0235	0.0229
2.4	0.0224	0.0219	0.0213	0.0208	0.0203	0.0198	0.0194	0.0189	0.0184	0.0180
2.5	0.0175	0.0171	0.0167	0.0163	0.0158	0.0154	0.0151	0.0147	0.0143	0.0139
2.6	0.0136	0.0132	0.0129	0.0126	0.0122	0.0119	0.0116	0.0113	0.0110	0.0107
2.7	0.0104	0.0101	0.0099	0.0096	0.0093	0.0091	0.0088	0.0086	0.0084	0.0081
2.8	0.0079	0.0077	0.0075	0.0073	0.0071	0.0069	0.0067	0.0065	0.0063	0.0061
2.9	0.0060	0.0058	0.0056	0.0055	0.0053	0.0051	0.0050	0.0048	0.0047	0.0046
3	0.0044	0.0043	0.0042	0.0040	0.0039	0.0038	0.0037	0.0036	0.0035	0.0034
3.1	0.0033	0.0032	0.0031	0.0030	0.0029	0.0028	0.0027	0.0026	0.0025	0.0025
3.2	0.0024	0.0023	0.0022	0.0022	0.0021	0.0020	0.0020	0.0019	0.0018	0.0018
3.3	0.0017	0.0017	0.0016	0.0016	0.0015	0.0015	0.0014	0.0014	0.0013	0.0013
3.4	0.0012	0.0012	0.0012	0.0011	0.0011	0.0010	0.0010	0.0010	0.0009	0.0009
3.5	0.0009	0.0008	0.0008	0.0008	0.0008	0.0007	0.0007	0.0007	0.0007	0.0006

TABLE A3.1 Cumulative Poisson Distribution

Values in body of Table give the probability (x 1000) of c or less defectives (defects), when the expected number is that represented by the c′ or np′ value.

c / c′ or np′	0	1	2	3	4	5	6	7	8	c / c′ or np′
0.02	980	1000	....	....	....	....	....	....	....	0.02
0.04	961	999	1000	....	....	....	....	....	....	0.04
0.06	942	998	1000	....	....	....	....	....	....	0.06
0.08	923	997	1000	....	....	....	....	....	....	0.08
0.10	905	995	1000	....	....	....	....	....	....	0.10
0.15	861	990	999	1000	....	....	....	....	....	0.15
0.20	819	982	999	1000	....	....	....	....	....	0.20
0.25	779	974	998	1000	....	....	....	....	....	0.25
0.30	741	963	996	1000	....	....	....	....	....	0.30
0.35	705	951	994	1000	....	....	....	....	....	0.35
0.40	670	938	992	999	1000	....	....	....	....	0.40
0.45	638	925	989	999	1000	....	....	....	....	0.45
0.50	607	910	986	998	1000	....	....	....	....	0.50
0.55	577	894	982	998	1000	....	....	....	....	0.55
0.60	549	878	977	997	1000	....	....	....	....	0.60
0.65	522	861	972	996	999	1000	....	....	....	0.65
0.70	497	844	966	994	999	1000	....	....	....	0.70
0.75	472	827	959	993	999	1000	....	....	....	0.75
0.80	449	809	953	991	999	1000	....	....	....	0.80
0.90	407	772	937	987	998	1000	....	....	....	0.90
1.00	368	736	920	981	996	999	1000	....	....	1.00
1.10	333	699	900	974	995	999	1000	....	....	1.10
1.20	301	663	879	966	992	998	1000	....	....	1.20
1.30	273	627	857	957	989	998	1000	....	....	1.30
1.40	247	592	833	946	986	997	999	1000	....	1.40
1.50	223	558	809	934	981	996	999	1000	....	1.50
1.60	202	525	783	921	976	994	999	1000	....	1.60
1.70	183	493	757	907	970	992	998	1000	....	1.70
1.80	165	463	731	891	964	990	997	999	1000	1.80
1.90	150	434	704	875	956	987	997	999	1000	1.90
2.00	135	406	677	857	947	983	995	999	1000	2.00
2.10	122	380	650	839	938	980	994	999	1000	2.10
2.20	110	354	622	819	927	974	993	998	1000	2.20
2.30	100	331	596	799	916	970	991	997	999	2.30
2.40	091	308	570	779	904	964	988	997	999	2.40
2.50	082	287	544	758	891	958	986	996	999	2.50
2.60	074	267	518	736	877	951	983	995	999	2.60
2.70	067	249	494	714	863	943	979	993	998	2.70
2.80	061	231	469	692	848	935	976	992	998	2.80
2.90	055	215	[illegible]	670	832	926	971	990	997	2.90
3.00	050	199	423	647	815	916	966	988	996	3.00
3.10	045	185	401	625	798	906	961	986	995	3.10
3.20	041	171	380	603	781	895	955	983	994	3.20
3.30	037	159	359	580	763	883	949	980	993	3.30
3.40	033	147	340	558	744	871	942	977	992	3.40
3.50	030	136	321	537	725	858	935	973	991	3.50
3.60	027	126	303	515	706	844	927	969	988	3.60
3.70	025	116	285	494	687	830	918	965	986	3.70
3.80	022	107	269	473	668	816	909	960	984	3.80
3.90	020	099	253	453	648	801	899	955	981	3.90
4.00	018	092	238	433	629	785	889	949	979	4.00
4.10	017	085	224	414	609	769	879	943	976	4.10
4.20	015	078	210	395	590	753	867	936	972	4.20
4.30	014	072	197	377	570	737	856	929	968	4.30
4.40	012	066	185	359	551	720	844	921	964	4.40
4.50	011	061	174	342	532	703	831	913	960	4.50
4.60	010	056	163	326	513	686	818	905	955	4.60
4.70	009	052	152	310	495	668	805	896	950	4.70
4.80	008	048	143	294	476	651	791	887	944	4.80
4.90	007	044	133	279	458	634	777	877	938	4.90

TABLE A3.1 Cumulative Poisson Distribution *(Continued)*

c / c′ or np′	0	1	2	3	4	5	6	7	8	c / c′ or np′
5.00	007	040	125	265	440	616	762	867	932	5.00
5.10	006	037	116	251	423	598	747	856	925	5.10
5.20	006	034	109	238	406	581	732	845	918	5.20
5.30	005	031	102	225	390	563	717	833	911	5.30
5.40	004	029	095	213	373	546	702	822	903	5.40
5.50	004	027	088	202	358	529	686	809	894	5.50
5.60	004	024	082	191	342	512	670	797	886	5.60
5.70	003	022	077	180	327	495	654	784	877	5.70
5.80	003	021	072	170	313	478	638	771	867	5.80
5.90	003	019	067	160	299	462	622	758	857	5.90
6.00	002	017	062	151	285	446	606	744	847	6.00
6.10	002	016	058	143	272	430	590	730	837	6.10
6.20	002	015	054	134	259	414	574	716	826	6.20
6.30	002	013	050	126	247	399	558	702	815	6.30
6.40	002	012	046	119	235	384	542	687	803	6.40
6.50	002	011	043	112	224	369	527	673	792	6.50
6.60	001	010	040	105	213	355	511	658	780	6.60
6.70	001	009	037	099	202	341	495	643	767	6.70
6.80	001	009	034	093	192	327	480	628	755	6.80
6.90	001	008	032	087	182	314	465	614	742	6.90
7.00	001	007	030	082	173	301	450	599	729	7.00
7.20	001	006	025	072	156	276	420	569	703	7.20
7.40	001	005	022	063	140	253	392	539	676	7.40
7.60	000	004	019	055	125	231	365	510	648	7.60
7.80	...	004	016	048	112	210	338	481	620	7.80
8.00	...	003	014	042	100	191	313	453	593	8.00
8.20	...	003	012	037	089	174	290	425	565	8.20
8.40	...	002	010	032	079	157	267	399	537	8.40
8.60	...	002	009	028	070	142	246	373	509	8.60
8.80	...	001	007	024	062	128	226	348	482	8.80
9.00	...	001	006	021	055	116	207	324	456	9.00
9.20	...	001	005	018	049	104	189	301	430	9.20
9.40	...	001	005	016	043	093	173	279	404	9.40
9.60	...	001	004	014	038	084	157	258	380	9.60
9.80	...	001	003	012	033	075	143	239	356	9.80
10.00	...	001	003	010	029	067	130	220	333	10.00
10.20	...	000	002	009	026	060	118	203	311	10.20
10.40	...	...	002	008	023	053	107	186	290	10.40
10.60	...	...	002	007	020	048	097	171	269	10.60
10.80	...	...	001	006	017	042	087	157	250	10.80
11.00	...	...	001	005	015	037	079	143	232	11.00
11.20	...	...	001	004	013	033	071	131	215	11.20
11.40	...	...	001	004	012	029	064	119	198	11.40
11.60	...	...	001	003	010	026	057	108	183	11.60
11.80	...	...	001	003	009	023	051	099	169	11.80
12.00	...	...	001	002	008	020	046	089	155	12.00
12.20	...	...	000	002	007	018	041	081	143	12.20
12.40	...	...	...	002	006	016	037	073	131	12.40
12.60	...	...	...	001	005	014	033	066	120	12.60
12.80	...	...	...	001	004	012	029	060	109	12.80
13.00	...	...	...	001	004	011	026	054	100	13.00
13.20	...	...	...	001	003	009	023	049	091	13.20
13.40	...	...	...	001	003	008	020	044	083	13.40
13.60	...	...	...	001	002	007	017	039	075	13.60
13.80	...	...	...	001	002	006	016	035	068	13.80
14.00	...	...	...	000	002	006	014	032	062	14.00
14.20	...	...	...	...	002	005	013	028	056	14.20
14.40	...	...	...	...	0Q1	004	011	025	051	14.40
14.60	...	...	...	...	001	004	010	023	046	14.60
14.80	...	...	...	...	001	003	009	020	042	14.80
15.00	...	...	...	...	001	003	008	018	037	15.00

TABLE A3.2 Mean Values to Obtain Desired Cumulative Poisson Probabilities*

c	0.99	0.95	0.90	0.50	0.10	0.05
0	0.010	0.051	0.105	0.693	2.303	2.996
1	0.149	0.355	0.532	1.678	3.890	4.744
2	0.436	0.818	1.102	2.674	5.322	6.296
3	0.823	1.366	1.745	3.672	6.681	7.754
4	1.279	1.970	2.433	4.671	7.994	9.154
5	1.785	2.613	3.152	5.670	9.275	10.513
6	2.330	3.286	3.895	6.670	10.532	11.842
7	2.906	3.981	4.656	7.669	11.771	13.148
8	3.507	4.695	5.432	8.669	12.995	14.434
9	4.130	5.426	6.221	9.669	14.206	15.705
10	4.771	6.169	7.021	10.668	15.407	16.962
11	5.428	6.924	7.829	11.668	16.598	18.208
12	6.099	7.690	8.646	12.668	17.782	19.442
13	6.782	8.464	9.470	13.668	18.958	20.668
14	7.477	9.246	10.300	14.668	20.128	21.886
15	8.181	10.035	11.135	15.668	21.292	23.098
16	8.895	10.831	11.976	16.668	22.452	24.302
17	9.616	11.633	12.822	17.668	23.606	25.500
18	10.346	12.442	13.672	18.668	24.756	26.692
19	11.082	13.254	14.525	19.668	25.902	27.879
20	11.825	14.072	15.383	20.668	27.045	29.062
21	12.574	14.894	16.244	21.668	28.184	30.241
22	13.329	15.719	17.108	22.668	29.320	31.416
23	14.088	16.548	17.975	23.668	30.453	32.586
24	14.853	17.382	18.844	24.668	31.584	33.752
25	15.623	18.218	19.717	25.667	32.711	34.916
30	19.532	22.444	24.113	30.667	38.315	40.690
35	23.525	26.731	28.556	35.667	43.872	46.404
40	27.587	31.066	33.038	40.667	49.390	52.069
45	31.704	35.441	37.550	45.667	54.878	57.695
50	35.867	39.849	42.089	50.667	60.339	63.287

* Tabulated values are the means of Poisson distribution. The value $c = 2$, $pr = 0.90$ is 1.102. This means that

$$\sum_{i=0}^{2} \frac{e^{-\lambda}\lambda^i}{i!} = 0.90$$

when $\lambda = 1.102$.

df	Probability													
	0.99	0.98	0.95	0.90	0.80	0.70	0.50	0.30	0.20	0.10	0.05	0.02	0.01	0.001
1	0.0^3157	0.0^3628	0.00393	0.0158	0.0642	0.148	0.455	1.074	1.642	0.706	3.841	5.412	6.635	10.827
2	0.0201	0.0404	0.103	0.211	0.446	0.713	1.386	2.408	3.219	4.605	5.991	7.824	9.210	13.815
3	0.115	0.185	0.352	0.584	1.005	1.424	2.366	3.665	4.642	6.251	7.815	9.837	11.341	16.268
4	0.297	0.429	0.711	1.064	1.649	2.195	3.357	4.878	5.989	7.779	9.488	11.668	13.277	18.465
5	0.554	0.752	1.145	1.610	2.343	3.000	4.351	6.064	7.289	9.236	11.070	13.388	15.086	20.517
6	0.872	1.134	1.635	2.204	3.070	3.828	5.348	7.231	8.558	10.645	12.592	15.033	16.812	22.457
7	1.239	1.564	2.167	2.833	3.822	4.671	6.346	8.383	9.803	12.017	14.067	16.622	18.475	24.322
8	1.646	2.032	2.733	3.490	4.594	5.527	7.344	9.524	11.030	13.362	15.507	18.168	20.090	26.125
9	2.088	2.532	3.325	4.168	5.380	6.393	8.343	10.656	12.242	14.684	16.919	19.679	21.666	27.877
10	2.558	3.059	3.940	4.865	6.179	7.267	9.342	11.781	13.442	15.987	18.307	21.161	23.209	29.588
11	3.053	3.609	4.575	5.578	6.989	8.148	10.341	12.899	14.631	17.275	19.675	22.618	24.725	31.264
12	3.571	4.178	5.226	6.304	7.807	9.034	11.340	14.011	15.812	18.549	21.026	24.054	26.217	32.909
13	4.107	4.765	5.892	7.042	8.634	9.926	12.340	15.119	16.985	19.812	22.362	25.472	27.688	34.528
14	4.660	5.368	6.571	7.790	9.467	10.821	13.339	16.222	18.151	21.064	23.685	26.873	29.141	36.123
15	5.229	5.985	7.261	8.547	10.307	11.721	14.339	17.322	19.311	22.307	24.996	28.259	30.578	37.697
16	5.812	6.614	7.962	9.312	11.152	12.624	15.338	18.418	20.465	23.542	26.296	29.663	32.000	39.252
17	6.408	7.255	8.762	10.085	12.002	13.531	16.338	19.511	21.615	24.769	27.587	30.995	33.409	40.790
18	7.015	7.906	9.390	10.865	12.857	14.440	17.338	20.601	22.760	25.989	28.869	32.346	34.805	42.312
19	7.633	8.567	10.117	11.651	13.716	15.352	18.338	21.689	23.900	27.204	30.144	33.687	36.191	43.820
20	8.260	9.237	10.851	12.443	14.578	16.266	19.337	22.775	25.038	28.412	31.410	35.020	37.566	45.315
21	8.897	9.915	11.591	13.240	15.445	17.182	20.337	23.858	26.171	29.615	32.671	36.343	38.932	46.797
22	9.542	10.600	12.338	14.041	16.314	18.101	21.337	24.939	27.301	30.813	33.924	37.659	40.289	48.268
23	10.196	11.293	13.091	14.848	17.187	19.021	22.337	26.018	28.429	32.007	35.172	38.968	41.638	49.728
24	10.856	11.992	13.848	15.659	18.062	19.943	23.337	27.096	29.553	33.196	36.415	40.270	42.980	51.179
25	11.524	12.697	14.611	16.473	18.940	20.867	24.337	28.172	30.675	34.382	37.652	41.566	44.314	52.620
26	12.198	13.409	15.379	17.292	19.820	21.792	25.336	29.246	31.795	35.563	38.885	42.856	45.642	54.052
27	12.879	14.125	16.151	18.114	20.703	22.719	26.336	30.319	32.912	36.741	40.113	44.140	46.963	55.476
28	13.565	14.847	16.928	18.939	21.588	23.647	27.336	31.391	34.027	37.916	41.337	45.419	48.278	56.893
29	14.256	15.574	17.708	19.768	22.475	24.577	28.336	32.461	35.139	39.087	42.557	46.693	49.588	58.302
30	14.953	16.306	18.493	20.599	23.364	25.508	29.336	33.530	36.250	40.256	43.773	47.962	50.892	59.703

From Fisher & Yates, *Statistical Tables for Biological, Agricultural and Medical Research* (London: Oliver and Boyd, 1943.)

TABLE A5 Student's *t* Distribution*

df	Probability (single tail)							
	0.40	0.20	0.10	0.05	0.025	0.010	0.005	0.0005
1	0.325	1.376	3.078	6.314	12.706	31.821	63.657	636.619
2	0.289	1.061	1.886	2.290	4.303	6.965	9.925	31.598
3	0.277	0.978	1.638	2.353	3.182	4.541	5.841	12.941
4	0.271	0.941	1.533	2.132	2.776	3.747	4.604	8.610
5	0.267	0.920	1.476	2.015	2.571	3.365	4.032	6.859
6	0.265	0.906	1.440	1.943	2.447	3.143	3.707	5.959
7	0.263	0.896	1.415	1.895	2.365	2.998	3.499	5.405
8	0.262	0.889	1.397	1.860	2.306	2.896	3.355	5.041
9	0.261	0.883	1.383	1.833	2.262	2.821	3.250	4.781
10	0.260	0.879	1.372	1.812	2.228	2.764	3.169	4.587
11	0.260	0.876	1.363	1.796	2.201	2.718	3.106	4.437
12	0.259	0.873	1.356	1.782	2.179	2.681	3.055	4.318
13	0.259	0.870	1.350	1.771	2.160	2.650	3.012	4.221
14	0.258	0.868	1.345	1.761	2.145	2.624	2.977	4.140
15	0.258	0.866	1.341	1.753	2.131	2.602	2.947	4.073
16	0.258	0.865	1.337	1.746	2.120	2.583	2.921	4.015
17	0.257	0.863	1.333	1.740	2.110	2.567	2.898	3.965
18	0.257	0.862	1.330	1.734	2.101	2.552	2.878	3.922
19	0.257	0.861	1.328	1.729	2.093	2.539	2.861	3.883
20	0.257	0.860	1.325	1.725	2.086	2.528	2.845	3.850
21	0.257	0.859	1.323	1.721	2.080	2.518	2.831	3.819
22	0.256	0.858	1.321	1.717	2.074	2.508	2.819	3.792
23	0.256	0.858	1.319	1.714	2.069	2.500	2.807	3.767
24	0.256	0.857	1.318	1.711	2.064	2.492	2.797	3.745
25	0.256	0.856	1.316	1.708	2.060	2.485	2.787	3.725
26	0.256	0.856	1.315	1.706	2.056	2.479	2.779	3.707
27	0.256	0.855	1.314	1.703	2.052	2.473	2.771	3.690
28	0.256	0.855	1.313	1.701	2.048	2.467	2.763	3.674
29	0.256	0.854	1.311	1.699	2.045	2.462	2.756	3.659
30	0.256	0.854	1.310	1.697	2.042	2.457	2.750	3.646
40	0.255	0.851	1.303	1.684	2.021	2.423	2.704	3.551
60	.254	0.848	1.296	1.671	2.000	2.390	2.660	3.460
120	0.254	0.845	1.289	1.658	1.980	2.358	2.617	3.373
∞	0.253	0.842	1.282	1.645	1.960	2.326	2.576	3.291
df		0.40	0.20	0.10	0.05	0.02	0.01	0.001
	Probability (two-tail)							

* Adapted and abridged from Fisher & Yates, *Statistical Tables for Biological, Agricultural and Medical Research* (London: Oliver and Boyd, 1943.)

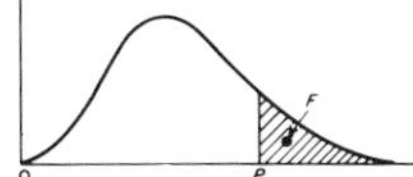

TABLE A6 *F* Distribution

	Values of df_1, the number of degrees of freedom of the greater variance															
	1		2		3		4		5		6		7		8	
$P \rightarrow$	0.05	0.01	0.05	0.01	0.05	0.01	0.05	0.01	0.05	0.01	0.05	0.01	0.05	0.01	0.05	0.01
Values of df_2 1	161	4,052	200	4,999	216	5,403	225	5,625	230	5,764	234	5,859	237	5,928	239	5,981
2	18.51	98.49	19.00	99.01	19.16	99.17	19.25	99.25	19.30	99.30	19.33	99.33	19.36	99.34	19.37	99.36
3	10.13	34.12	9.55	30.81	9.28	29.46	9.12	28.71	9.01	28.24	8.94	27.91	8.88	27.67	8.84	27.49
4	7.71	21.20	6.94	18.00	6.59	16.69	6.39	15.98	6.26	15.52	6.16	15.21	6.09	14.98	6.04	14.80
5	6.61	16.26	5.79	13.27	5.41	12.06	5.19	11.39	5.05	10.97	4.95	10.67	4.88	10.45	4.82	10.27
6	5.99	13.74	5.14	10.92	4.76	9.78	4.53	9.15	4.39	8.75	4.28	8.47	4.21	8.26	4.15	8.10
7	5.59	12.25	4.74	9.55	4.35	8.45	4.12	7.85	3.97	7.46	3.87	7.19	3.79	7.00	3.73	6.84
8	5.32	11.26	4.46	8.65	4.07	7.59	3.84	7.01	3.69	6.63	3.58	6.37	3.50	6.19	3.44	6.03
9	5.12	10.56	4.26	8.02	3.86	6.99	3.63	6.42	3.48	6.06	3.37	5.80	3.29	5.62	3.23	5.47
10	4.96	10.04	4.10	7.56	3.71	6.55	3.48	5.99	3.33	5.64	3.22	5.39	3.14	5.21	3.07	5.06
11	4.84	9.65	3.98	7.20	3.59	6.22	3.36	5.67	3.20	5.32	3.09	5.07	3.01	4.88	2.95	4.74
12	4.75	9.33	3.88	6.93	3.49	5.95	3.26	5.41	3.11	5.06	3.00	4.82	2.92	4.65	2.85	4.50
13	4.67	9.07	3.80	6.70	3.41	5.74	3.18	5.20	3.02	4.86	2.92	4.62	2.84	4.44	2.77	4.30
14	4.60	8.86	3.74	6.51	3.34	5.56	3.11	5.03	2.96	4.69	2.85	4.46	2.77	4.28	2.70	4.14
15	4.54	8.68	3.68	6.36	3.29	5.42	3.06	4.89	2.90	4.58	2.79	4.32	2.70	4.14	2.64	4.00
16	4.49	8.53	3.63	6.23	3.24	5.29	3.01	4.77	2.85	4.44	2.74	4.20	2.68	4.03	2.59	3.89
17	4.45	8.40	3.59	6.11	3.20	5.18	2.96	4.67	2.81	4.34	2.70	4.10	2.63	3.93	2.55	3.79
18	4.41	8.28	3.55	6.01	3.16	5.09	2.93	4.58	2.77	4.25	2.66	4.01	2.58	3.85	2.51	3.71
19	4.38	8.18	3.52	5.93	3.13	5.01	2.90	4.50	2.74	4.17	2.63	3.94	2.55	3.77	2.48	3.63
20	4.35	8.10	3.49	5.85	3.10	4.94	2.87	4.43	2.71	4.10	2.60	3.87	2.52	3.71	2.45	3.56
21	4.32	8.02	3.47	5.78	3.07	4.87	2.84	4.37	2.68	4.04	2.57	3.81	2.49	3.65	2.42	3.51
22	4.30	7.94	3.44	5.72	3.05	4.82	2.82	4.31	2.66	3.99	2.55	3.76	2.47	3.59	2.40	3.45
23	4.28	7.83	3.42	5.66	3.03	4.76	2.80	4.26	2.64	3.94	2.53	3.71	2.45	3.54	2.38	3.41
24	4.26	7.82	3.40	5.61	3.01	4.72	2.78	4.22	2.62	3.90	2.51	3.67	2.43	3.50	2.36	3.36
25	4.24	7.77	3.38	5.57	2.99	4.68	2.76	4.18	2.60	3.86	2.49	3.63	2.41	3.46	2.34	3.32
26	4.22	7.72	3.37	5.53	2.98	4.64	2.74	4.14	2.59	3.82	2.47	3.59	2.39	3.42	2.32	3.29
27	4.21	7.68	3.35	5.49	2.96	4.60	2.73	4.11	2.57	3.79	2.46	3.56	2.37	3.39	2.30	3.26
28	4.20	7.64	3.34	5.45	2.95	4.57	2.71	4.07	2.56	3.76	2.44	3.53	2.36	3.36	2.29	3.23
29	4.18	7.60	3.33	5.42	2.93	4.54	2.70	4.04	2.54	3.73	2.43	3.50	2.35	3.33	2.28	3.20
30	4.17	7.56	3.32	5.39	2.92	4.51	2.69	4.02	2.53	3.70	2.42	3.47	2.34	3.30	2.27	3.17
32	4.15	7.50	3.30	5.34	2.90	4.46	2.67	3.97	2.51	3.66	2.40	3.42	2.32	3.25	2.25	3.12
34	4.13	7.44	3.28	5.29	2.88	4.42	2.65	3.93	2.49	3.61	2.38	3.38	2.30	3.21	2.23	3.08
38	4.10	7.35	3.25	5.21	2.85	4.34	2.62	3.86	2.46	3.54	2.35	3.32	2.26	3.15	2.19	3.02
42	4.07	7.27	3.22	5.15	2.83	4.29	2.59	3.80	2.44	3.49	2.32	3.26	2.24	3.10	2.17	2.96
46	4.05	7.21	3.20	5.10	2.81	4.24	2.57	3.76	2.42	3.44	2.30	3.22	2.22	3.05	2.14	2.92
50	4.03	7.17	3.18	5.06	2.79	4.20	2.56	3.72	2.40	3.41	2.29	3.18	2.20	3.02	2.13	2.88
60	4.00	7.08	3.15	4.98	2.76	4.13	2.52	3.65	2.37	3.34	2.25	3.12	2.17	2.93	2.10	2.82
80	3.96	6.96	3.11	4.88	2.72	4.04	2.48	3.56	2.33	3.25	2.21	3.04	2.12	2.87	2.05	2.74
100	3.94	6.90	3.09	4.82	2.70	3.98	2.46	3.51	2.30	3.20	2.19	2.99	2.10	2.82	2.03	2.69
200	3.89	6.76	3.04	4.71	2.65	3.88	2.41	3.41	2.26	3.11	2.14	2.90	2.05	2.73	1.98	2.60
1,000	3.85	6.68	3.00	4.62	2.61	3.80	2.38	3.34	2.22	3.04	2.10	2.82	2.02	2.66	1.95	2.53
∞	3.84	6.64	2.99	4.60	2.60	3.78	2.37	3.32	2.21	3.02	2.09	2.80	2.01	2.64	1.94	2.51

TABLE A6 ***F* Distribution** (*Continued*)

	Values of df_1, the number of degrees of freedom of the greater variance															
	10		12		16		20		30		50		100		∞	
$P \rightarrow$	0.05	0.01	0.05	0.01	0.05	0.01	0.05	0.01	0.05	0.01	0.05	0.01	0.05	0.01	0.05	0.0[illegible]
Values of df_2: 1	242	6,056	244	6,106	246	6,169	248	6,208	230	6,258	252	6,302	253	6,334	254	6,3[illegible]
2	19.39	99.40	19.41	99.42	19.43	99.44	19.44	99.45	19.46	99.47	19.47	99.48	19.49	99.49	19.50	99.[illegible]
3	8.78	27.23	8.74	27.05	8.69	26.83	8.66	26.69	8.62	26.50	8.58	26.35	8.56	26.23	8.53	26.[illegible]
4	5.96	14.54	5.91	14.37	4.85	14.15	5.80	14.02	5.74	13.83	5.70	13.69	5.66	13.57	5.63	13.[illegible]
5	4.74	10.05	4.68	9.89	4.60	9.68	4.56	9.55	4.50	9.38	4.44	9.24	4.40	9.13	4.36	9.[illegible]
6	4.06	7.87	4.00	7.72	3.92	7.52	3.87	7.39	3.81	7.23	3.75	7.09	3.71	6.99	3.67	6.[illegible]
7	3.63	6.62	3.57	6.47	3.49	6.27	3.44	6.15	3.38	5.98	3.32	5.85	3.28	5.75	3.23	5.[illegible]
8	3.34	5.82	3.28	5.67	3.20	5.48	3.15	5.36	3.08	5.20	3.03	5.06	2.98	4.96	2.93	4.[illegible]
9	3.13	5.26	3.07	5.11	2.98	4.92	2.93	4.80	2.86	4.64	2.80	4.51	2.76	4.41	2.71	4.[illegible]
10	2.97	4.85	2.91	4.71	2.82	4.52	2.77	4.41	2.70	4.25	2.64	4.12	2.59	4.01	2.54	3.[illegible]
11	2.86	4.54	2.79	4.40	2.70	4.21	2.65	4.10	2.57	3.94	2.50	3.80	2.45	3.70	2.40	3.[illegible]
12	2.77	4.30	2.69	4.16	2.60	3.98	2.54	3.86	2.46	3.70	2.40	3.56	2.35	3.46	2.30	3.[illegible]
13	2.67	4.10	2.60	3.96	2.51	3.78	2.46	3.67	2.38	3.51	2.32	3.37	2.26	3.27	2.21	3.[illegible]
14	2.50	3.94	2.53	3.80	2.44	3.62	2.39	3.51	2.31	3.34	2.24	3.21	2.19	3.11	2.13	3.[illegible]
15	2.55	3.30	2.48	3.67	2.39	3.48	2.33	3.36	2.25	3.20	2.18	3.07	2.12	2.97	2.07	2.[illegible]
16	2.49	3.69	2.42	3.55	2.33	3.37	2.28	3.25	2.20	3.10	2.13	2.96	2.07	2.86	2.01	2.[illegible]
17	2.45	3.59	2.38	3.45	2.20	3.27	2.23	3.16	2.15	3.00	2.08	2.86	2.02	2.76	1.96	2.[illegible]
18	2.41	3.51	2.34	3.37	2.25	3.19	2.19	3.07	2.11	2.91	2.04	2.78	1.98	2.68	1.92	2.[illegible]
19	2.38	3.43	2.31	3.30	2.21	3.12	2.15	3.00	2.07	2.84	2.00	2.70	1.94	2.60	1.88	2.[illegible]
20	2.35	3.37	2.28	3.23	2.18	3.05	2.12	2.94	2.04	2.71	1.96	2.63	1.90	2.53	1.84	2.[illegible]
21	2.32	3.31	2.25	3.17	2.15	2.99	2.09	2.88	2.00	2.72	1.93	2.58	1.87	2.47	1.81	2.[illegible]
22	2.30	3.26	2.23	3.12	2.13	2.94	2.07	2.83	1.98	2.67	1.91	2.53	1.84	2.42	1.78	2.[illegible]
23	2.28	3.21	2.20	3.07	2.10	2.89	2.04	2.78	1.96	2.62	1.88	2.48	1.82	2.37	1.76	2.[illegible]
24	2.26	3.17	2.18	3.03	2.09	2.85	2.02	2.74	1.94	2.58	1.86	2.44	1.80	2.33	1.73	2.[illegible]
25	2.24	3.13	2.16	2.99	2.06	2.81	2.00	2.70	1.92	2.54	1.84	2.40	1.77	2.29	1.71	2.[illegible]
26	2.22	3.09	2.15	2.96	2.05	2.77	1.99	2.66	1.90	2.50	1.82	2.36	1.76	2.23	1.69	2.[illegible]
27	2.20	3.06	2.13	2.93	2.03	2.74	1.97	2.63	1.88	2.47	1.80	2.33	1.74	2.21	1.67	2.[illegible]
28	2.19	3.03	2.12	2.90	2.02	2.71	1.96	2.60	1.87	2.44	1.78	2.30	1.72	2.18	1.65	2.[illegible]
29	2.18	3.00	2.10	2.87	2.00	2.68	1.94	2.57	1.85	2.41	1.77	2.27	1.71	2.15	1.64	2.[illegible]
30	2.16	2.98	2.09	2.84	1.99	2.66	1.93	2.55	1.84	2.38	1.76	2.24	1.69	2.13	1.62	2.[illegible]
32	2.14	2.94	2.07	2.80	1.97	2.62	1.91	2.51	1.82	2.34	1.74	2.20	1.67	2.08	1.59	1.[illegible]
34	2.12	2.89	2.05	2.76	1.95	2.58	1.89	2.47	1.80	2.30	1.71	2.15	1.64	2.04	1.57	1.[illegible]
38	2.09	2.82	2.02	2.69	1.92	2.51	1.85	2.40	1.76	2.22	1.67	2.08	1.60	1.97	1.53	1.[illegible]
42	2.06	2.77	1.99	2.64	1.89	2.46	1.82	2.35	1.73	2.17	1.64	2.02	1.57	1.91	1.49	1.[illegible]
46	2.04	2.73	1.97	2.60	1.87	2.42	1.80	2.30	1.71	2.13	1.62	1.98	1.54	1.86	1.46	1.[illegible]
50	2.02	2.70	1.95	2.56	1.85	2.39	1.78	2.26	1.69	2.10	1.60	1.94	1.52	1.82	1.44	1.[illegible]
60	1.99	2.63	1.92	2.50	1.81	2.32	1.75	2.20	1.65	2.03	1.56	1.87	1.48	1.74	1.39	1.[illegible]
80	1.95	2.55	1.88	2.41	1.77	2.24	1.70	2.11	1.60	1.94	1.51	1.78	1.42	1.65	1.32	1.[illegible]
100	1.92	2.51	1.35	2.36	1.75	2.19	1.68	2.06	1.57	1.89	1.48	1.73	1.39	1.59	1.28	1.[illegible]
200	1.87	2.41	1.80	2.28	1.69	2.09	1.62	1.97	1.52	1.79	1.42	1.62	1.32	1.48	1.19	1.[illegible]
1,000	1.84	2.34	1.76	2.20	1.65	2.01	1.58	1.89	1.47	1.71	1.36	1.54	1.26	1.38	1.08	1.[illegible]
∞	1.83	2.32	1.75	2.18	1.64	1.99	1.57	1.87	1.46	1.69	1.35	1.52	1.24	1.36	1.00	1.[illegible]

Reproduced from *Statistical Methods*, by G. W. Snedecor (Collegiate Press, Iowa, 1937).

TABLE A7 Factors to Estimate σ from $\bar{R}$ and $\bar{S}$

Number of observations, n	$d_1 = R/\sigma$	$c_2 = \bar{S}/\sigma$	Number of observations, n	$d_2 = \bar{R}/\sigma$	$c_2 = \bar{S}/\sigma$
2	1.128	0.5642	21	3.778	0.9638
3	1.693	0.7236	22	3.819	0.9655
4	2.059	0.7979	23	3.858	0.9670
5	2.326	0.8407	24	3.895	0.9684
6	2.534	0.8686	25	3.931	0.9696
7	2.704	0.8882	30	4.086	0.9748
8	2.847	0.9027	35	4.213	0.9784
9	2.970	0.9139	40	4.322	0.9811
10	3.078	0.9227	45	4.415	0.9832
11	3.173	0.9300	50	4.498	0.9849
12	3.258	0.9359	55	4.572	0.9863
13	3.336	0.9410	60	4.639	0.9874
14	3.407	0.9453	65	4.699	0.9884
15	3.472	0.9490	70	4.755	0.9892
16	3.532	0.9523	75	4.806	0.9900
17	3.588	0.9551	80	4.854	0.9906
18	3.640	0.9576	85	4.898	0.9912
19	3.689	0.9599	90	4.939	0.9916
20	3.735	0.9619	95	4.978	0.9921
			100	5.015	0.9925

TABLE A8 Factors for Control Limits for $\overline{X}$, S, and R Charts

Number of Observations in Sample, n	$\overline{X}$ Chart			S Chart						R Chart								Chart for Observations	
	Factors for Control Limits			Factors for Central Line		Factors for Control Limits				Factors for Central Line		Factors for Control Limits						Factors for Control Limits	
	A	A_1	A_2	c_2	$1/c_2$	B_1	B_2	B_3	B_4	d_2	$1/d_2$	d_3	D_1	D_2	D_3	D_4	E_1	E_2
2	2.121	3.760	1.880	0.5642	1.7725	0	1.843	0	3.267	1.128	0.8865	0.853	0	3.686	0	3.267	5.318	2.660
3	1.732	2.394	1.023	0.7236	1.3820	0	1.858	0	2.568	1.693	0.5907	0.888	0	4.358	0	2.575	4.146	1.772
4	1.500	1.880	0.729	0.7979	1.2533	0	1.808	0	2.266	2.059	0.4857	0.880	0	4.698	0	2.282	3.760	1.457
5	1.342	1.596	0.577	0.8407	1.1894	0	1.756	0	2.089	2.326	0.4299	0.864	0	4.918	0	2.115	3.568	1.290
6	1.225	1.410	0.483	0.8686	1.1512	0.026	1.711	0.030	1.970	2.534	0.3946	0.848	0	5.078	0	2.004	3.454	1.184
7	1.134	1.277	0.419	0.8882	1.1259	0.105	1.672	0.118	1.882	2.704	0.3698	0.833	0.205	5.203	0.076	1.924	3.378	1.109
8	1.061	1.175	0.373	0.9027	1.1078	0.167	1.638	0.185	1.815	2.847	0.3512	0.820	0.387	5.307	0.136	1.864	3.323	1.054
9	1.000	1.094	0.337	0.9139	1.0942	0.219	1.609	0.239	1.761	2.970	0.3367	0.808	0.546	5.394	0.184	1.816	3.283	1.010
10	0.949	1.028	0.308	0.9227	1.0837	0.262	1.584	0.284	1.716	3.078	0.3249	0.797	0.687	5.469	0.223	1.777	3.251	0.975

11	0.905	0.973	0.285	0.9300	1.0753	0.299	1.561	0.321	1.679	3.173	0.3152	0.787	0.812	5.534	0.256	1.744	3.226	0.946
12	0.866	0.925	0.266	0.9359	1.0684	0.331	1.541	0.354	1.646	3.258	0.3069	0.778	0.924	5.592	0.284	1.716	3.205	0.921
13	0.832	0.884	0.249	0.9410	1.0627	0.359	1.523	0.382	1.618	3.336	0.2998	0.770	1.026	5.646	0.308	1.692	3.188	0.899
14	0.802	0.848	0.235	0.9453	1.0579	0.384	1.507	0.406	1.594	3.407	0.2935	0.762	1.121	5.693	0.329	1.671	3.174	0.881
15	0.775	0.816	0.223	0.9490	1.0537	0.406	1.492	0.428	1.572	3.472	0.2880	0.755	1.207	5.737	0.348	1.652	3.161	0.864
16	0.750	0.788	0.212	0.9523	1.0501	0.427	1.478	0.448	1.552	3.532	0.2831	0.749	1.285	5.779	0.364	1.636	3.150	0.849
17	0.728	0.762	0.203	0.9551	1.0470	0.445	1.465	0.466	1.534	3.588	0.2787	0.743	1.359	5.817	0.379	1.621	3.141	0.836
18	0.707	0.738	0.194	0.9576	1.0442	0.461	1.454	0.482	1.518	3.640	0.2747	0.738	1.426	5.854	0.392	1.608	3.133	0.824
19	0.688	0.717	0.187	0.9599	1.0418	0.477	1.443	0.497	1.503	3.689	0.2711	0.733	1.490	5.888	0.404	1.596	3.125	0.813
20	0.671	0.697	0.180	0.9619	1.0396	0.491	1.433	0.510	1.490	3.735	0.2677	0.729	1.548	5.922	0.144	1.586	3.119	0.803
21	0.655	0.679	0.173	0.9638	1.0376	0.504	1.424	0.523	1.477	3.778	0.2647	0.724	1.606	5.950	0.425	1.575	3.113	0.794
22	0.640	0.662	0.167	0.9655	1.0358	0.516	1.415	0.534	1.466	3.819	0.2618	0.720	1.659	5.979	0.434	1.566	3.107	0.785
23	0.626	0.647	0.162	0.9670	1.0342	0.527	1.407	0.545	1.455	3.858	0.2592	0.716	1.710	6.006	0.443	1.557	3.103	0.778
24	0.612	0.632	0.157	0.9684	1.0327	0.538	1.399	0.555	1.445	3.895	0.2567	0.712	1.759	6.031	0.452	1.548	3.098	0.770
25	0.600	0.619	0.153	0.9696	1.0313	0.548	1.392	0.565	1.435	3.931	0.2544	0.709	1.804	6.058	0.459	1.541	3.094	0.763
Over 25	$\frac{3}{\sqrt{n}}$	$\frac{3}{\sqrt{n}}$				*	**	*	**								3	$\frac{3}{d_2}$

$* \ 1 - \frac{3}{\sqrt{2n}}$ $** \ 1 + \frac{3}{\sqrt{2n}}$

TABLE A9 Formulas for Control Charts

I–variables (measurements)

Condition	For	Measure of Dispersion	Central Line	Control Limits
No standard given	Averages ($\bar{X}$)	$\bar{\sigma}$	$\bar{\bar{X}}$	$\bar{\bar{X}} \pm A_1\bar{\sigma}$
	Averages ($\bar{X}$)	$\bar{R}$	$\bar{\bar{X}}$	$\bar{\bar{X}} \pm A_2\bar{R}$
	Ranges (R)	$\bar{R}$	$\bar{R}$	$D_4\bar{R}$ and $D_3\bar{R}$
	Standard deviations (σ)	$\bar{\sigma}$	$\bar{\sigma}$	$B_4\bar{\sigma}$ and $B_3\bar{\sigma}$
	Individuals (X)	$\bar{\sigma}$	$\bar{\bar{X}}$	$\bar{\bar{X}} \pm E_1\bar{\sigma}$
		$\bar{R}$	$\bar{\bar{X}}$	$\bar{\bar{X}} \pm E_2R$
Standard given	Averages ($\bar{X}$)	σ'	$\bar{X}'$	$\bar{X}' \pm A\sigma'$
	Ranges (R)	σ'	$d_2\sigma'$	$D_2\sigma'$ and $D_1\sigma'$
	Standard deviations (σ)	σ'	$c_2\sigma'$	$B_2\sigma'$ and $B_1\sigma'$
	Individuals (X)	σ'	$\bar{X}'$	$\bar{X}' \pm 3\sigma'$

II—attributes (go–not go)

Condition	For	Central Line	Control Limits
No standard given	Fraction defective (p)	$\bar{p}$	$\bar{p} \pm \frac{3\sqrt{\bar{p}(1-\bar{p})}}{\sqrt{n}}$
	Number defective (pn)	$\bar{p}n$	$\bar{p}n \pm 3\sqrt{\bar{p}n(1-\bar{p})}$
	Number of defects (c)	$\bar{c}$	$\bar{c} \pm 3\sqrt{\bar{c}}$
	Number of defects per unit (u)	$\bar{u}$	$\bar{u} \pm \frac{3\sqrt{\bar{u}}}{\sqrt{n}}$
Standard given	Fraction defective (p)	p'	$p' \pm \frac{3\sqrt{p'(1-p')}}{\sqrt{n}}$
	Number defective (pn)	$p'n$	$p'n \pm 3\sqrt{p'n(1-p')}$
	Number of defects (c)	c'	$c' \pm 3\sqrt{c'}$
	Number of defects per unit (u)	u'	$u' \pm \frac{3\sqrt{u'}}{\sqrt{n}}$

TABLE A10 Formulas and Factors for Median and Midrange Charts*

$\tilde{X}'$ = median of parent universe

$\tilde{X}$ = median of sub-group

$\overset{\sqcap}{X}$ = mid-range of sub-group

$\tilde{X}_i$ = median of all individuals in sample

$\overset{\approx}{X}$ = median of sub-group medians

$\tilde{\overset{\sqcap}{X}}$ = median of sub-group mid-ranges

$\tilde{R}$ = median of sub-group ranges

Standards Given:

$$\tilde{d}_2\sigma' = \tilde{R}'$$

$$\tilde{A}_2\tilde{R}' = 3\sigma_{\tilde{x}}, \qquad \overset{\sqcap}{A}_2\tilde{R}' = 3\sigma_{\tilde{x}}, \qquad \tilde{A} = \frac{A}{\sqrt{E_{\tilde{x}}}}$$

$$\tilde{D}_3\tilde{R} = D_3R, \qquad \tilde{D}_4\tilde{R} = D_4R, \qquad \overset{\sqcap}{A} = \frac{A}{\sqrt{E_{\overset{\sqcap}{x}}}}$$

Estimates:

$$\tilde{X}' = \overset{\approx}{X} \quad \text{or} \quad \tilde{X}_i \quad \text{or} \quad \overset{\sqcap}{X}$$

$$\sigma = \frac{\tilde{R}}{\tilde{d}_2}$$

3σ Limits for

$\tilde{X}$	$\overset{\approx}{X} \pm \tilde{A}_2\tilde{R}$ or $\tilde{X}_i \pm \tilde{A}_2\tilde{R}$
$\overset{\sqcap}{X}$	$\tilde{\overset{\sqcap}{X}} \pm \overset{\sqcap}{A}_2\tilde{R}$
R	$\tilde{D}_3\tilde{R}$ and $\tilde{D}_4\tilde{R}$

Note: $E_{\tilde{x}} = \sigma_x{}^2/\sigma_{\tilde{x}}{}^2$.

n	$\tilde{A}$	$\overset{\sqcap}{A}$	$\tilde{A}_2$	$\overset{\sqcap}{A}_2$	$\tilde{d}_2$	$\tilde{D}_3$	$\tilde{D}_4$
2	2.121	2.121	2.224	2.224	0.954	0	3.865
3	2.014	1.806	1.265	1.137	1.588	0	2.745
4	1.637	1.637	0.829	0.829	1.978	0	2.375
5	1.615	1.532	0.712	0.679	2.257	0	2.179
6	1.387	1.458	0.562	0.590	2.472	0	2.055
7	1.385	1.402	0.520	0.530	2.645	0.078	1.967
8	1.233	1.358	0.441	0.486	2.791	0.139	1.901
9	1.240	1.322	0.419	0.453	2.916	0.187	1.850
10	1.216	1.293	0.369	0.427	3.024	0.227	1.809

* From Paul C. Clifford, "Control Charts Without Calculations," *Industrial Quality Control*, May 1959, p. 44. Reprinted with permission.

TABLE A11.1 Control Limits for p Charts, UCL

p	100	150	200	300	500	600	800	1000	2000	5000	10000	20000
0.10	1.04	0.87	0.77	0.64	0.52	0.48	0.43	0.39	0.31	0.23	0.19	0.16
0.20	1.54	1.29	1.14	0.97	0.79	0.74	0.67	0.62	0.49	0.38	0.33	0.29
0.30	1.94	1.63	1.46	1.24	1.03	0.96	0.88	0.81	0.66	0.53	0.46	0.41
0.50	2.61	2.22	1.99	1.72	1.44	1.36	1.24	1.16	0.97	0.79	0.71	0.64
0.80	3.47	2.98	2.68	2.34	1.99	1.89	1.74	1.64	1.39	1.17	1.06	0.98
1.00	3.98	3.43	3.11	2.72	2.33	2.21	2.05	1.94	1.66	1.42	1.29	1.21
1.25	4.58	3.97	3.60	3.17	2.74	2.61	2.42	2.30	1.99	1.72	1.58	1.48
1.50	5.14	4.47	4.07	3.60	3.13	2.98	2.78	2.65	2.31	2.01	1.86	1.75
1.75	5.68	4.96	4.53	4.02	3.50	3.35	3.14	2.99	2.62	2.30	2.14	2.02
2.00	6.20	5.42	4.96	4.42	3.87	3.71	3.48	3.32	2.93	2.59	2.42	2.29
2.50	7.18	6.32	5.81	5.20	4.59	4.41	4.15	3.98	3.54	3.16	2.96	2.83
3.00	8.11	7.17	6.61	5.95	5.28	5.08	4.80	4.61	4.14	3.72	3.51	3.36
3.50	9.01	8.00	7.39	6.68	5.96	5.75	5.44	5.24	4.73	4.27	4.05	3.88
4.00	9.87	8.80	8.15	7.39	6.62	6.39	6.07	5.85	5.31	4.83	4.58	4.41
4.50	10.71	9.57	8.89	8.09	7.28	7.03	6.69	6.46	5.89	5.37	5.12	4.93
5.00	11.53	10.33	9.62	8.77	7.92	7.66	7.31	7.06	6.46	5.92	5.65	5.46
5.50	12.33	11.08	10.33	9.44	8.55	8.29	7.91	7.66	7.02	6.46	6.18	5.98
6.00	13.12	11.81	11.03	10.11	9.18	8.90	8.51	8.25	7.59	7.00	6.71	6.50
6.50	13.89	12.53	11.72	10.76	9.80	9.51	9.11	8.83	8.15	7.54	7.23	7.02
7.00	14.65	13.24	12.41	11.41	10.42	10.12	9.70	9.42	8.71	8.08	7.76	7.54
7.50	15.40	13.95	13.08	12.06	11.03	10.72	10.29	9.99	9.26	8.61	8.29	8.05
8.00	16.13	14.64	13.75	12.69	11.63	11.32	10.87	10.57	9.81	9.15	8.81	8.57
8.50	16.86	15.33	14.41	13.33	12.24	11.91	11.45	11.14	10.37	9.68	9.33	9.09
9.00	17.58	16.00	15.07	13.95	12.83	12.50	12.03	11.71	10.91	10.21	9.85	9.60
9.50	18.29	16.68	15.72	14.57	13.43	13.09	12.61	12.28	11.46	10.74	10.37	10.12
10.00	19.00	17.34	16.36	15.19	14.02	13.67	13.18	12.84	12.01	11.27	10.90	10.63
11.00	20.38	18.66	17.63	16.41	15.19	14.83	14.31	13.96	13.09	12.32	11.93	11.66
12.00	21.74	19.95	18.89	17.62	16.35	15.97	15.44	15.08	14.17	13.37	12.97	12.68
13.00	23.08	21.23	20.13	18.82	17.51	17.11	16.56	16.19	15.25	14.42	14.00	13.71
14.00	24.40	22.49	21.36	20.00	18.65	18.24	17.68	17.29	16.32	15.47	15.04	14.73
15.00	25.71	23.74	22.57	21.18	19.79	19.37	18.78	18.38	17.39	16.51	16.07	15.75
20.00	32.00	29.79	28.48	26.92	25.36	24.89	24.24	23.79	22.68	21.69	21.20	20.84
25.00	37.99	35.60	34.18	32.50	30.80	30.30	29.59	29.10	27.90	26.83	26.29	25.91
30.00	43.74	41.22	39.72	37.93	36.14	35.61	34.86	34.34	33.07	31.94	31.37	30.97
35.00	49.30	46.68	45.11	43.26	41.39	40.84	40.05	39.52	38.19	37.02	36.43	36.01

TABLE A11.2 Control Limits for p Charts, LCL

p	100	150	200	300	500	600	800	1000	2000	5000	10000	20000
0.10	0.00	0.00	0.00	0.00	0.00	0.00	0.00	0.00	0.00	0.00	0.00	0.03
0.20	0.00	0.00	0.00	0.00	0.00	0.00	0.00	0.00	0.00	0.01	0.06	0.10
0.30	0.00	0.00	0.00	0.00	0.00	0.00	0.00	0.00	0.00	0.06	0.13	0.18
0.50	0.00	0.00	0.00	0.00	0.00	0.00	0.00	0.00	0.02	0.20	0.28	0.35
0.80	0.00	0.00	0.00	0.00	0.00	0.00	0.00	0.00	0.20	0.42	0.53	0.61
1.00	0.00	0.00	0.00	0.00	0.00	0.00	0.00	0.05	0.33	0.57	0.70	0.78
1.25	0.00	0.00	0.00	0.00	0.00	0.00	0.07	0.19	0.50	0.77	0.91	1.01
1.50	0.00	0.00	0.00	0.00	0.00	0.01	0.21	0.34	0.68	0.98	1.13	1.24
1.75	0.00	0.00	0.00	0.00	0.00	0.14	0.35	0.50	0.87	1.19	1.35	1.47
2.00	0.00	0.00	0.00	0.00	0.12	0.28	0.51	0.67	1.06	1.40	1.58	1.70
2.50	0.00	0.00	0.00	0.00	0.40	0.58	0.84	1.01	1.45	1.83	2.03	2.16
3.00	0.00	0.00	0.00	0.04	0.71	0.91	1.19	1.38	1.85	2.27	2.48	2.63
3.50	0.00	0.00	0.00	0.31	1.03	1.24	1.55	1.75	2.26	2.72	2.94	3.11
4.00	0.00	0.00	0.00	0.60	1.37	1.60	1.92	2.14	2.68	3.16	3.41	3.58
4.50	0.00	0.00	0.10	0.90	1.71	1.96	2.30	2.53	3.10	3.62	3.87	4.06
5.00	0.00	0.00	0.37	1.22	2.07	2.33	2.68	2.93	3.53	4.07	4.34	4.53
5.50	0.00	0.00	0.66	1.55	2.44	2.70	3.08	3.33	3.97	4.53	4.81	5.01
6.00	0.00	0.18	0.96	1.88	2.81	3.09	3.48	3.74	4.40	4.99	5.28	5.49
6.50	0.00	0.46	1.27	2.23	3.19	3.48	3.88	4.16	4.84	5.45	5.76	5.97
7.00	0.00	0.75	1.58	2.58	3.57	3.87	4.29	4.57	5.28	5.91	6.23	6.45
7.50	0.00	1.04	1.91	2.93	3.96	4.27	4.70	5.00	5.73	6.38	6.70	6.94
8.00	0.00	1.35	2.24	3.30	4.36	4.67	5.12	5.42	6.18	6.84	7.18	7.42
8.50	0.13	1.66	2.58	3.66	4.75	5.08	5.54	5.85	6.62	7.31	7.66	7.90
9.00	0.41	1.99	2.92	4.04	5.16	5.49	5.96	6.28	7.08	7.78	8.14	8.39
9.50	0.70	2.31	3.27	4.42	5.56	5.90	6.38	6.71	7.53	8.25	8.62	8.87
10.00	1.00	2.65	3.63	4.80	5.97	6.32	6.81	7.15	7.98	8.72	9.10	9.36
11.00	1.61	3.33	4.36	5.58	6.80	7.16	7.68	8.03	8.90	9.67	10.06	10.33
12.00	2.25	4.04	5.10	6.37	7.64	8.02	8.55	8.91	9.82	10.62	11.02	11.31
13.00	2.91	4.76	5.86	7.17	8.48	8.88	9.43	9.80	10.74	11.57	11.99	12.28
14.00	3.59	5.50	6.63	7.99	9.34	9.75	10.31	10.70	11.67	12.52	12.95	13.26
15.00	4.28	6.25	7.42	8.81	10.20	10.62	11.21	11.61	12.60	13.48	13.92	14.24
20.00	8.00	10.20	11.51	13.07	14.63	15.10	15.75	16.20	17.31	18.30	18.79	19.15
25.00	12.00	14.39	15.81	17.50	19.19	19.69	20.40	20.89	22.09	23.16	23.70	24.08
30.00	16.25	18.77	20.27	22.06	23.85	24.38	25.13	25.65	26.92	28.05	28.62	29.02
35.00	20.69	23.31	24.88	26.73	28.60	29.15	29.94	30.47	31.80	32.97	33.56	33.98

TABLE A12 Average Run Length* of $\overline{X}$ Charts, Known σ

Sample Size	d/σ						
	0.1	0.2	0.5	1.0	1.5	2.0	3.0
3	314.8	223.9	54.7	9.1	2.9	1.5	1.0
4	303.9	192.1	42.9	6.3	2.0	1.2	1.0
5	289.3	175.6	33.4	4.5	1.6	1.1	1.0
6	277.8	159.0	26.3	3.4	1.3	1.0	1.0
7	267.5	147.5	21.3	2.8	1.2	1.0	1.0
8	258.9	133.0	17.7	2.3	1.1	1.0	1.0
9	251.3	122.0	15.0	2.0	1.1	1.0	1.0
10	244.0	111.1	12.8	1.8	1.0	1.0	1.0
15	203.9	76.4	6.9	1.2	1.0	1.0	1.0
20	175.6	56.6	4.5	1.1	1.0	1.0	1.0
25	155.5	41.1	3.2	1.0	1.0	1.0	1.0

* ARL = 1.0 means ARL less than 1.05.

TABLE A13 Average Run Length* of $\overline{X}$ Charts, Based on $\overline{R}$

Sample Size	$d/\overline{R}$					
	0.05	0.10	0.20	0.30	0.50	0.100
3	326.2	254.3	126.1	58.5	15.9	2.1
4	300.3	192.4	67.5	25.7	5.8	1.2
5	277.0	151.6	39.9	13.3	2.9	1.0
6	244.1	114.4	25.2	7.8	1.8	1.0
7	217.6	89.2	17.1	5.1	1.4	1.0
8	197.6	71.1	12.2	3.6	1.2	1.0
9	177.5	57.1	9.0	2.7	1.1	1.0
10	160.0	36.6	6.8	2.1	1.0	1.0
15	99.8	20.3	2.6	1.2	1.0	1.0
20	65.7	10.9	1.6	1.0	1.0	1.0
25	46.0	6.7	1.2	1.0	1.0	1.0

* ARL = 1.0 means ARL less than 1.05.

TABLE A14.1 Sample Size Code Letters (MIL-STD-105D)

Lot or batch size	Special inspection levels				General inspection levels		
	S-1	S-2	S-3	S-4	I	II	III
2–8	A	A	A	A	A	A	B
9–15	A	A	A	A	A	B	C
16–25	A	A	B	B	B	C	D
26–50	A	B	B	C	C	D	E
51–90	B	B	C	C	C	E	F
91–150	B	B	C	D	D	F	G
151–280	B	C	D	E	E	G	H
281–500	B	C	D	E	F	H	J
501–1,200	C	C	E	F	G	J	K
1,201–3,200	C	D	E	G	H	K	L
3,201–10,000	C	D	F	G	J	L	M
10,001–35,000	C	D	F	H	K	M	N
35,001–150,000	D	E	G	J	L	N	P
150,001–500,000	D	E	G	J	M	P	Q
500,001 and over	D	E	H	K	N	Q	R

TABLE A14.2 Master Table for Normal Inspection: Single Sampling (MIL-STD-105D)

Sample size code letter	Sample size	Acceptable quality levels (normal inspection)																									
		0.010	0.015	0.025	0.040	0.065	0.10	0.15	0.25	0.40	0.65	1.0	1.5	2.5	4.0	6.5	10	15	25	40	65	100	150	250	400	650	1,000
		Ac Re	Ac Re	Ac Re	Ac Re	Ac Re	Ac Re	Ac Re	Ac Re	Ac Re	Ac Re	Ac Re	Ac Re	Ac Re	Ac Re	Ac Re	Ac Re	Ac Re	Ac Re	Ac Re	Ac Re	Ac Re	Ac Re	Ac Re	Ac Re	Ac Re	Ac Re
A	2	↓	↓	↓	↓	↓	↓	↓	↓	↓	↓	↓	↓	↓	↓	0 1	↓	↓	1 2	2 3	3 4	5 6	7 8	10 11	14 15	21 22	30 31
B	3	↓	↓	↓	↓	↓	↓	↓	↓	↓	↓	↓	↓	↓	0 1	↑	↓	1 2	2 3	3 4	5 6	7 8	10 11	14 15	21 22	30 31	44 45
C	5	↓	↓	↓	↓	↓	↓	↓	↓	↓	↓	↓	↓	0 1	↑	↓	1 2	2 3	3 4	5 6	7 8	10 11	14 15	21 22	30 31	44 45	↑
D	8	↓	↓	↓	↓	↓	↓	↓	↓	↓	↓	↓	0 1	↑	↓	1 2	2 3	3 4	5 6	7 8	10 11	14 15	21 22	30 31	44 45	↑	↑
E	13	↓	↓	↓	↓	↓	↓	↓	↓	↓	↓	0 1	↑	↓	1 2	2 3	3 4	5 6	7 8	10 11	14 15	21 22	30 31	44 45	↑	↑	↑
F	20	↓	↓	↓	↓	↓	↓	↓	↓	↓	0 1	↑	↓	1 2	2 3	3 4	5 6	7 8	10 11	14 15	21 22	↑	↑	↑	↑	↑	↑
G	32	↓	↓	↓	↓	↓	↓	↓	↓	0 1	↑	↓	1 2	2 3	3 4	5 6	7 8	10 11	14 15	21 22	↑	↑	↑	↑	↑	↑	↑
H	50	↓	↓	↓	↓	↓	↓	↓	0 1	↑	↓	1 2	2 3	3 4	5 6	7 8	10 11	14 15	21 22	↑	↑	↑	↑	↑	↑	↑	↑
J	80	↓	↓	↓	↓	↓	↓	0 1	↑	↓	1 2	2 3	3 4	5 6	7 8	10 11	14 15	21 22	↑	↑	↑	↑	↑	↑	↑	↑	↑
K	125	↓	↓	↓	↓	↓	0 1	↑	↓	1 2	2 3	3 4	5 6	7 8	10 11	14 15	21 22	↑	↑	↑	↑	↑	↑	↑	↑	↑	↑
L	200	↓	↓	↓	↓	0 1	↑	↓	1 2	2 3	3 4	5 6	7 8	10 11	14 15	21 22	↑	↑	↑	↑	↑	↑	↑	↑	↑	↑	↑
M	315	↓	↓	↓	0 1	↑	↓	1 2	2 3	3 4	5 6	7 8	10 11	14 15	21 22	↑	↑	↑	↑	↑	↑	↑	↑	↑	↑	↑	↑
N	500	↓	↓	0 1	↑	↓	1 2	2 3	3 4	5 6	7 8	10 11	14 15	21 22	↑	↑	↑	↑	↑	↑	↑	↑	↑	↑	↑	↑	↑
P	800	↓	0 1	↑	↓	1 2	2 3	3 4	5 6	7 8	10 11	14 15	21 22	↑	↑	↑	↑	↑	↑	↑	↑	↑	↑	↑	↑	↑	↑
Q	1,250	0 1	↑	↓	1 2	2 3	3 4	5 6	7 8	10 11	14 15	21 22	↑	↑	↑	↑	↑	↑	↑	↑	↑	↑	↑	↑	↑	↑	↑
R	2,000	↑	↑	1 2	2 3	3 4	5 6	7 8	10 11	14 15	21 22	↑	↑	↑	↑	↑	↑	↑	↑	↑	↑	↑	↑	↑	↑	↑	↑

TABLE A14.3 Master Table for Tightened Inspection: Single Sampling (MIL-STD-105D)

Sample size code letter	Sample size	Acceptable quality levels (tightened inspection)																									
		0.010	0.015	0.025	0.040	0.065	0.10	0.15	0.25	0.40	0.65	1.0	1.5	2.5	4.0	6.5	10	15	25	40	65	100	150	250	400	650	1,000
		Ac Re	Ac Re	Ac Re	Ac Re	Ac Re	Ac Re	Ac Re	Ac Re	Ac Re	Ac Re	Ac Re	Ac Re	Ac Re	Ac Re	Ac Re	Ac Re	Ac Re	Ac Re	Ac Re	Ac Re	Ac Re	Ac Re	Ac Re	Ac Re	Ac Re	Ac Re
A	2	↓	↓	↓	↓	↓	↓	↓	↓	↓	↓	↓	↓	↓	↓	↓	↓	↓	↓	1 2	2 3	3 4	5 6	8 9	12 13	18 19	27 28
B	3	↓	↓	↓	↓	↓	↓	↓	↓	↓	↓	↓	↓	↓	↓	0 1	↓	↓	1 2	2 3	3 4	5 6	8 9	12 13	18 19	27 28	41 42
C	5	↓	↓	↓	↓	↓	↓	↓	↓	↓	↓	↓	↓	↓	0 1	↓	↓	1 2	2 3	3 4	5 6	8 9	12 13	18 19	27 28	41 42	↑
D	8	↓	↓	↓	↓	↓	↓	↓	↓	↓	↓	↓	↓	0 1	↓	↓	1 2	2 3	3 4	5 6	8 9	12 13	18 19	27 28	41 42	↑	↑
E	13	↓	↓	↓	↓	↓	↓	↓	↓	↓	↓	↓	0 1	↓	↓	1 2	2 3	3 4	5 6	8 9	12 13	18 19	27 28	41 42	↑	↑	↑
F	20	↓	↓	↓	↓	↓	↓	↓	↓	↓	↓	0 1	↓	↓	1 2	2 3	3 4	5 6	8 9	12 13	18 19	↑	↑	↑	↑	↑	↑
G	32	↓	↓	↓	↓	↓	↓	↓	↓	↓	0 1	↓	↓	1 2	2 3	3 4	5 6	8 9	12 13	18 19	↑	↑	↑	↑	↑	↑	↑
H	50	↓	↓	↓	↓	↓	↓	↓	↓	0 1	↓	↓	1 2	2 3	3 4	5 6	8 9	12 13	18 19	↑	↑	↑	↑	↑	↑	↑	↑
J	80	↓	↓	↓	↓	↓	↓	↓	0 1	↓	↓	1 2	2 3	3 4	5 6	8 9	12 13	18 19	↑	↑	↑	↑	↑	↑	↑	↑	↑
K	125	↓	↓	↓	↓	↓	↓	0 1	↓	↓	1 2	2 3	3 4	5 6	8 9	12 13	18 19	↑	↑	↑	↑	↑	↑	↑	↑	↑	↑
L	200	↓	↓	↓	↓	↓	0 1	↓	↓	1 2	2 3	3 4	5 6	8 9	12 13	18 19	↑	↑	↑	↑	↑	↑	↑	↑	↑	↑	↑
M	315	↓	↓	↓	↓	0 1	↓	↓	1 2	2 3	3 4	5 6	8 9	12 13	18 19	↑	↑	↑	↑	↑	↑	↑	↑	↑	↑	↑	↑
N	500	↓	↓	↓	0 1	↓	↓	1 2	2 3	3 4	5 6	8 9	12 13	18 19	↑	↑	↑	↑	↑	↑	↑	↑	↑	↑	↑	↑	↑
P	800	↓	↓	0 1	↓	↓	1 2	2 3	3 4	5 6	8 9	12 13	18 19	↑	↑	↑	↑	↑	↑	↑	↑	↑	↑	↑	↑	↑	↑
Q	1,250	↓	0 1	↓	↓	1 2	2 3	3 4	5 6	8 9	12 13	18 19	↑	↑	↑	↑	↑	↑	↑	↑	↑	↑	↑	↑	↑	↑	↑
R	2,000	0 1	↑	↓	1 2	2 3	3 4	5 6	8 9	12 13	18 19	↑	↑	↑	↑	↑	↑	↑	↑	↑	↑	↑	↑	↑	↑	↑	↑
S	3,150			1 2																							

TABLE A14.4 Master Table for Reduced Inspection: Single Sampling (MIL-STD-105D)

Sample size code letter	Sample size	Acceptable quality levels (reduced inspection)																									
		0.010	0.015	0.025	0.040	0.065	0.10	0.15	0.25	0.40	0.65	1.0	1.5	2.5	4.0	6.5	10	15	25	40	65	100	150	250	400	650	1,000
		Ac Re	Ac Re	Ac Re	Ac Re	Ac Re	Ac Re	Ac Re	Ac Re	Ac Re	Ac Re	Ac Re	Ac Re	Ac Re	Ac Re	Ac Re	Ac Re	Ac Re	Ac Re	Ac Re	Ac Re	Ac Re	Ac Re	Ac Re	Ac Re	Ac Re	Ac Re
A	2	↓	↓	↓	↓	↓	↓	↓	↓	↓	↓	↓	↓	↓	↓	0 1	↓	↓	1 2	2 3	3 4	5 6	7 8	10 11	14 15	21 22	30 31
B	2	↓	↓	↓	↓	↓	↓	↓	↓	↓	↓	↓	↓	↓	0 1	↑	↓	0 2	1 3	2 4	3 5	5 6	7 8	10 11	14 15	21 22	30 31
C	2	↓	↓	↓	↓	↓	↓	↓	↓	↓	↓	↓	↓	0 1	↑	↓	0 2	1 3	1 4	2 5	3 6	5 8	7 10	10 13	14 17	21 24	↑
D	3	↓	↓	↓	↓	↓	↓	↓	↓	↓	↓	↓	0 1	↑	↓	0 2	1 3	1 4	2 5	3 6	5 8	7 10	10 13	14 17	21 24	↑	↑
E	5	↓	↓	↓	↓	↓	↓	↓	↓	↓	↓	0 1	↑	↓	0 2	1 3	1 4	2 5	3 6	5 8	7 10	10 13	14 17	21 24	↑	↑	↑
F	8	↓	↓	↓	↓	↓	↓	↓	↓	↓	0 1	↑	↓	0 2	1 3	1 4	2 5	3 6	5 8	7 10	10 13	↑	↑	↑	↑	↑	↑
G	13	↓	↓	↓	↓	↓	↓	↓	↓	0 1	↑	↓	0 2	1 3	1 4	2 5	3 6	5 8	7 10	10 13	↑	↑	↑	↑	↑	↑	↑
H	20	↓	↓	↓	↓	↓	↓	↓	0 1	↑	↓	0 2	1 3	1 4	2 5	3 6	5 8	7 10	10 13	↑	↑	↑	↑	↑	↑	↑	↑
J	32	↓	↓	↓	↓	↓	↓	0 1	↑	↓	0 2	1 3	1 4	2 5	3 6	5 8	7 10	10 13	↑	↑	↑	↑	↑	↑	↑	↑	↑
K	50	↓	↓	↓	↓	↓	0 1	↑	↓	0 2	1 3	1 4	2 5	3 6	5 8	7 10	10 13	↑	↑	↑	↑	↑	↑	↑	↑	↑	↑
L	80	↓	↓	↓	↓	0 1	↑	↓	0 2	1 3	1 4	2 5	3 6	5 8	7 10	10 13	↑	↑	↑	↑	↑	↑	↑	↑	↑	↑	↑
M	125	↓	↓	↓	0 1	↑	↓	0 2	1 3	1 4	2 5	3 6	5 8	7 10	10 13	↑	↑	↑	↑	↑	↑	↑	↑	↑	↑	↑	↑
N	200	↓	↓	0 1	↑	↓	0 2	1 3	1 4	2 5	3 6	5 8	7 10	10 13	↑	↑	↑	↑	↑	↑	↑	↑	↑	↑	↑	↑	↑
P	315	↓	0 1	↑	↓	0 2	1 3	1 4	2 5	3 6	5 8	7 10	10 13	↑	↑	↑	↑	↑	↑	↑	↑	↑	↑	↑	↑	↑	↑
Q	500	0 1	↑	↓	0 2	1 3	1 4	2 5	3 6	5 8	7 10	10 13	↑	↑	↑	↑	↑	↑	↑	↑	↑	↑	↑	↑	↑	↑	↑
R	800	↑	↑	0 2	1 3	1 4	2 5	3 6	5 8	7 10	10 13	↑	↑	↑	↑	↑	↑	↑	↑	↑	↑	↑	↑	↑	↑	↑	↑

TABLE A14.5 Master Table for Normal Inspection: Double Sampling (MIL-STD-105D)

Sample size code letter	Sample	Sample size	Cumulative sample size	Acceptable quality levels (normal inspection)																									
				0.010	0.015	0.025	0.040	0.065	0.10	0.15	0.25	0.40	0.65	1.0	1.5	2.5	4.0	6.5	10	15	25	40	65	100	150	250	400	650	1,000
				Ac Re	Ac Re	Ac Re	Ac Re	Ac Re	Ac Re	Ac Re	Ac Re	Ac Re	Ac Re	Ac Re	Ac Re	Ac Re	Ac Re	Ac Re	Ac Re	Ac Re	Ac Re	Ac Re	Ac Re	Ac Re	Ac Re	Ac Re	Ac Re	Ac Re	Ac Re
A				↓	↓	↓	↓	↓	↓	↓	↓	↓	↓	↓	↓	↓	↓	†	↓	↓	†	†	†	†	†	†	†	†	†
B	First Second	2 2	2 4	↓	↓	↓	↓	↓	↓	↓	↓	↓	↓	↓	↓	↓	†	↑	↓	0 2 1 2	0 3 3 4	1 4 4 5	2 5 6 7	3 7 8 9	5 9 12 13	7 11 18 19	11 16 26 27	17 22 37 38	25 31 56 57
C	First Second	3 3	3 6	↓	↓	↓	↓	↓	↓	↓	↓	↓	↓	↓	↓	†	↑	↓	0 2 1 2	0 3 3 4	1 4 4 5	2 5 6 7	3 7 8 9	5 9 12 13	7 11 18 19	11 16 26 27	17 22 37 38	25 31 56 57	↑
D	First Second	5 5	5 10	↓	↓	↓	↓	↓	↓	↓	↓	↓	↓	↓	†	↑	↓	0 2 1 2	0 3 3 4	1 4 4 5	2 5 6 7	3 7 8 9	5 9 12 13	7 11 18 19	11 16 26 27	17 22 37 38	25 31 56 57	↑	↑
E	First Second	8 8	8 16	↓	↓	↓	↓	↓	↓	↓	↓	↓	↓	†	↑	↓	0 2 1 2	0 3 3 4	1 4 4 5	2 5 6 7	3 7 8 9	5 9 12 13	7 11 18 19	11 16 26 27	17 22 37 38	25 31 56 57	↑	↑	↑
F	First Second	13 13	13 26	↓	↓	↓	↓	↓	↓	↓	↓	↓	†	↑	↓	0 2 1 2	0 3 3 4	1 4 4 5	2 5 6 7	3 7 8 9	5 9 12 13	7 11 18 19	11 16 26 27	↑	↑	↑	↑	↑	↑
G	First Second	20 20	20 40	↓	↓	↓	↓	↓	↓	↓	↓	†	↑	↓	0 2 1 2	0 3 3 4	1 4 4 5	2 5 6 7	3 7 8 9	5 9 12 13	7 11 18 19	11 16 26 27	↑	↑	↑	↑	↑	↑	↑

H	First	32	32	↓	↓	↓	↓	↓	↓	↓	†	↑	↓	0 2	0 3	1 4	2 5	3 7	5 9	7 11	11 16	↑	↑	↑	↑	↑	↑	↑	↑
	Second	32	64											1 2	3 4	4 5	6 7	8 9	12 13	18 19	26 27								
J	First	50	50	↓	↓	↓	↓	↓	↓	†	↑	↓	0 2	0 3	1 4	2 5	3 7	5 9	7 11	11 16	↑	↑	↑	↑	↑	↑	↑	↑	↑
	Second	50	100										1 2	3 4	4 5	6 7	8 9	12 13	18 19	26 27									
K	First	80	80	↓	↓	↓	↓	↓	†	↑	↓	0 2	0 3	1 4	2 5	3 7	5 9	7 11	11 16	↑	↑	↑	↑	↑	↑	↑	↑	↑	↑
	Second	80	160									1 2	3 4	4 5	6 7	8 9	12 13	18 19	26 27										
L	First	125	125	↓	↓	↓	↓	†	↑	↓	0 2	0 3	1 4	2 5	3 7	5 9	7 11	11 16	↑	↑	↑	↑	↑	↑	↑	↑	↑	↑	↑
	Second	125	250								1 2	3 4	4 5	6 7	8 9	12 13	18 19	26 27											
M	First	200	200	↓	↓	↓	†	↑	↓	0 2	0 3	1 4	2 5	3 7	5 9	7 11	11 16	↑	↑	↑	↑	↑	↑	↑	↑	↑	↑	↑	↑
	Second	200	400							1 2	3 4	4 5	6 7	8 9	12 13	18 19	26 27												
N	First	315	315	↓	↓	†	↑	↓	0 2	0 3	1 4	2 5	3 7	5 9	7 11	11 16	↑	↑	↑	↑	↑	↑	↑	↑	↑	↑	↑	↑	↑
	Second	315	630						1 2	3 4	4 5	6 7	8 9	12 13	18 19	26 27													
P	First	500	500	↓	†	↑	↓	0 2	0 3	1 4	2 5	3 7	5 9	7 11	11 16	↑	↑	↑	↑	↑	↑	↑	↑	↑	↑	↑	↑	↑	↑
	Second	500	1,000					1 2	3 4	4 5	6 7	8 9	12 13	18 19	26 27														
Q	First	800	800	†	↑	↓	0 2	0 3	1 4	2 5	3 7	5 9	7 11	11 16	↑	↑	↑	↑	↑	↑	↑	↑	↑	↑	↑	↑	↑	↑	↑
	Second	800	1,600				1 2	3 4	4 5	6 7	8 9	12 13	18 19	26 27															
R	First	1,250	1,250	↑	↑	0 2	0 3	1 4	2 5	3 7	5 9	7 11	11 16	↑	↑	↑	↑	↑	↑	↑	↑	↑	↑	↑	↑	↑	↑	↑	↑
	Second	1,250	2,500			1 2	3 4	4 5	6 7	8 9	12 13	18 19	26 27																

† means the use of corresponding single sampling plan is recommended.

TABLE A14.6 Master Table for Tightened Inspection: Double Sampling (MIL-STD-105D)

Sample size code letter	Sample	Sample size	Cumulative sample size	Acceptance quality levels (tightened inspection)																									
				0.010	0.015	0.025	0.040	0.065	0.10	0.15	0.25	0.40	0.65	1.0	1.5	2.5	4.0	6.5	10	15	25	40	65	100	150	250	400	650	1,000
				Ac Re	Ac Re	Ac Re	Ac Re	Ac Re	Ac Re	Ac Re	Ac Re	Ac Re	Ac Re	Ac Re	Ac Re	Ac Re	Ac Re	Ac Re	Ac Re	Ac Re	Ac Re	Ac Re	Ac Re	Ac Re	Ac Re	Ac Re	Ac Re	Ac Re	Ac Re
A				↓	↓	↓	↓	↓	↓	↓	↓	↓	↓	↓	↓	↓	↓	↓	↓	↓	↓	†	†	†	†	†	†	†	†
B	First Second	2 2	2 4	↓	↓	↓	↓	↓	↓	↓	↓	↓	↓	↓	↓	↓	↓	†	↓	↓	0 2 1 2	0 3 3 4	1 4 4 5	2 5 6 7	3 7 11 12	6 10 15 16	9 14 23 24	15 20 34 35	23 29 52 53
C	First Second	3 3	3 6	↓	↓	↓	↓	↓	↓	↓	↓	↓	↓	↓	↓	↓	†	↓	↓	0 2 1 2	0 3 3 4	1 4 4 5	2 5 6 7	3 7 11 12	6 10 15 16	9 14 23 24	15 20 34 35	23 29 52 53	↑
D	First Second	5 5	5 10	↓	↓	↓	↓	↓	↓	↓	↓	↓	↓	↓	↓	†	↓	↓	0 2 1 2	0 3 3 4	1 4 4 5	2 5 6 7	3 7 11 12	6 10 15 16	9 14 23 24	15 20 34 35	23 29 52 53	↑	↑
E	First Second	8 8	8 16	↓	↓	↓	↓	↓	↓	↓	↓	↓	↓	↓	†	↓	↓	0 2 1 2	0 3 3 4	1 4 4 5	2 5 6 7	3 7 11 12	6 10 15 16	9 14 23 24	15 20 34 35	23 39 52 53	↑	↑	↑
F	First Second	13 13	13 26	↓	↓	↓	↓	↓	↓	↓	↓	↓	↓	†	↓	↓	0 2 1 2	0 3 3 4	1 4 4 5	2 5 6 7	3 7 11 12	6 10 15 16	9 14 23 24	↑	↑	↑	↑	↑	↑
G	First Second	20 20	20 40	↓	↓	↓	↓	↓	↓	↓	↓	↓	†	↓	↓	0 2 1 2	0 3 3 4	1 4 4 5	2 5 6 7	3 7 11 12	6 10 15 16	9 14 23 24	↑	↑	↑	↑	↑	↑	↑

H	First	32	32	↓	↓	↓	↓	↓	↓	↓	↓	†	↓	↓	0 2	0 3	1 4	2 5	3 7	6 10	9 14	↑	↑	↑	↑	↑	↑	↑	↑
	Second	32	64												1 2	3 4	4 5	6 7	11 12	15 16	23 24								
J	First	50	50	↓	↓	↓	↓	↓	↓	↓	†	↓	↓	0 2	0 3	1 4	2 5	3 7	6 10	9 14	↑	↑	↑	↑	↑	↑	↑	↑	↑
	Second	50	100											1 2	3 4	4 5	6 7	11 12	15 16	23 24									
K	First	80	80	↓	↓	↓	↓	↓	↓	†	↓	↓	0 2	0 3	1 4	2 5	3 7	6 10	9 14	↑	↑	↑	↑	↑	↑	↑	↑	↑	↑
	Second	80	160										1 2	3 4	4 5	6 7	11 12	15 16	23 24										
L	First	125	125	↓	↓	↓	↓	↓	†	↓	↓	0 2	0 3	1 4	2 5	3 7	6 10	9 14	↑	↑	↑	↑	↑	↑	↑	↑	↑	↑	↑
	Second	125	250									1 2	3 4	4 5	6 7	11 12	15 16	23 24											
M	First	200	200	↓	↓	↓	↓	†	↓	↓	0 2	0 3	1 4	2 5	3 7	6 10	9 14	↑	↑	↑	↑	↑	↑	↑	↑	↑	↑	↑	↑
	Second	200	400								1 2	3 4	4 5	6 7	11 12	15 16	23 24												
N	First	315	315	↓	↓	↓	†	↓	↓	0 2	0 3	1 4	2 5	3 7	6 10	9 14	↑	↑	↑	↑	↑	↑	↑	↑	↑	↑	↑	↑	↑
	Second	315	630							1 2	3 4	4 5	6 7	11 12	15 16	23 24													
P	First	500	500	↓	↓	†	↓	↓	0 2	0 3	1 4	2 5	3 7	6 10	9 14	↑	↑	↑	↑	↑	↑	↑	↑	↑	↑	↑	↑	↑	↑
	Second	500	1,000						1 2	3 4	4 5	6 7	11 12	15 16	23 24														
Q	First	800	800	↓	†	↓	↓	0 2	0 3	1 4	2 5	3 7	6 10	9 14	↑	↑	↑	↑	↑	↑	↑	↑	↑	↑	↑	↑	↑	↑	↑
	Second	800	1,600					1 2	3 4	4 5	6 7	11 12	15 16	23 24															
R	First	1,250	1,250	†	↑	↓	0 2	0 3	1 4	2 5	3 7	6 10	9 14	↑	↑	↑	↑	↑	↑	↑	↑	↑	↑	↑	↑	↑	↑	↑	↑
	Second	1,250	2,500				1 2	3 4	4 5	6 7	11 12	15 16	23 24																
S	First	2,000	2,000			0 2																							
	Second	2,000	4,000			1 2																							

† means the use of corresponding single sampling plan is recommended.

TABLE A14.7 Master Table for Reduced Inspection: Double Sampling (MIL-STD-105D)

Sample size code letter	Sample	Sample size	Cumulative sample size	Acceptable quality levels (reduced inspection)																									
				0.010	0.015	0.025	0.040	0.065	0.10	0.15	0.25	0.40	0.65	1.0	1.5	2.5	4.0	6.5	10	15	25	40	65	100	150	250	400	650	1,000
				Ac Re	Ac Re	Ac Re	Ac Re	Ac Re	Ac Re	Ac Re	Ac Re	Ac Re	Ac Re	Ac Re	Ac Re	Ac Re	Ac Re	Ac Re	Ac Re	Ac Re	Ac Re	Ac Re	Ac Re	Ac Re	Ac Re	Ac Re	Ac Re	Ac Re	Ac Re
A				↓	↓	↓	↓	↓	↓	↓	↓	↓	↓	↓	↓	↓	↓	‡	↓	↓	‡	‡	‡	‡	‡	‡	‡	‡	‡
B				↓	↓	↓	↓	↓	↓	↓	↓	↓	↓	↓	↓	↓	‡	↓	↓	‡	‡	‡	‡	‡	‡	‡	‡	‡	‡
C				↓	↓	↓	↓	↓	↓	↓	↓	↓	↓	↓	↓	‡	↑	↓	‡	‡	‡	‡	‡	‡	‡	‡	‡	‡	↑
D	First	2	2	↓	↓	↓	↓	↓	↓	↓	↓	↓	↓	↓	‡	↑	↓	0 2	0 3	0 4	0 4	1 5	2 7	3 8	5 10	7 12	11 17	↑	↑
	Second	2	4															0 2	0 4	1 5	3 6	4 7	6 9	8 12	12 16	18 21	26 30		
E	First	3	3	↓	↓	↓	↓	↓	↓	↓	↓	↓	↓	‡	↑	↓	0 2	0 3	0 4	0 4	1 5	2 7	3 8	5 10	7 12	11 17	↑	↑	↑
	Second	3	6														0 2	0 4	1 5	3 6	4 7	6 9	8 12	12 16	18 21	26 30			
F	First	5	5	↓	↓	↓	↓	↓	↓	↓	↓	↓	‡	↑	↓	0 2	0 3	0 4	0 4	1 5	2 7	3 8	5 10	↑	↑	↑	↑	↑	↑
	Second	5	10													0 2	0 4	1 5	3 6	4 7	6 9	8 12	12 16						
G	First	8	8	↓	↓	↓	↓	↓	↓	↓	↓	‡	↑	↓	0 2	0 3	0 4	0 4	1 5	2 7	3 8	5 10	↑	↑	↑	↑	↑	↑	↑
	Second	8	16												0 2	0 4	1 5	3 6	4 7	6 9	8 12	12 16							
H	First	13	13	↓	↓	↓	↓	↓	↓	↓	‡	↑	↓	0 2	0 3	0 4	0 4	1 5	2 7	3 8	5 10	↑	↑	↑	↑	↑	↑	↑	↑
	Second	13	26											0 2	0 4	1 5	3 6	4 7	6 9	8 12	12 16								

J	First Second	20 20	20 40						↓	‡	↑	↓	0 2 0 2	0 3 0 4	0 4 1 5	0 4 3 6	1 5 4 7	2 7 6 9	3 8 8 12	5 10 12 16	↑								
K	First Second	32 32	32 64					↓	‡	↑	↓	0 2 0 2	0 3 0 4	0 4 1 5	0 4 3 6	1 5 4 7	2 7 6 9	3 8 8 12	5 10 12 16	↑									
L	First Second	50 50	50 100				↓	‡	↑	↓	0 2 0 2	0 3 0 4	0 4 1 5	0 4 3 6	1 5 4 7	2 7 6 9	3 8 8 12	5 10 12 16	↑										
M	First Second	80 80	80 160			↓	‡	↑	↓	0 2 0 2	0 3 0 4	0 4 1 5	0 4 3 6	1 5 4 7	2 7 6 9	3 8 8 12	5 10 12 16	↑											
N	First Second	125 125	125 250		↓	‡	↑	↓	0 2 0 2	0 3 0 4	0 4 1 5	0 4 3 6	1 5 4 7	2 7 6 9	3 8 8 12	5 10 12 16	↑												
P	First Second	200 200	200 400	↓	‡	↑	↓	0 2 0 2	0 3 0 4	0 4 1 5	0 4 3 6	1 5 4 7	2 7 6 9	3 8 8 12	5 10 12 16	↑													
Q	First Second	315 315	315 630	‡	↑	↓	0 2 0 2	0 3 0 4	0 4 1 5	0 4 3 6	1 5 4 7	2 7 6 9	3 8 8 12	5 10 12 16	↑														
R	First Second	500 1,000	500 1,500	↑		0 2 0 2	0 3 0 4	0 4 1 5	0 4 3 6	1 5 4 7	2 7 6 9	3 8 8 12	5 10 12 16	↑															

‡ means the use of corresponding single sampling plan is recommended.

TABLE A14.8 Master Table for Normal Inspection: Multiple Sampling (MIL-STD-105D)

Sample size code letter	Sample	Sample size	Cumulative sample size	Acceptable quality levels (reduced inspection)																									
				0.010	0.015	0.025	0.040	0.065	0.10	0.15	0.25	0.40	0.65	1.0	1.5	2.5	4.0	6.5	10	15	25	40	65	100	150	250	400	650	1,000
				Ac Re	Ac Re	Ac Re	Ac Re	Ac Re	Ac Re	Ac Re	Ac Re	Ac Re	Ac Re	Ac Re	Ac Re	Ac Re	Ac Re	Ac Re	Ac Re	Ac Re	Ac Re	Ac Re	Ac Re	Ac Re	Ac Re	Ac Re	Ac Re	Ac Re	Ac Re
A																	↓	†		↓	†	†	†	†	†	†	†	†	†
B																↓	†	↑	↓	‡	‡	‡	‡	‡	‡	‡	‡	‡	‡
C															↓	†	↑	↓	‡	‡	‡	‡	‡	‡	‡	‡	‡	‡	↑
D	First	2	2												†	↑		§ 2	§ 2	§ 3	§ 4	0 4	0 5	1 7	2 9	4 12	6 16	↑	
	Second	2	4															§ 2	0 3	0 3	1 5	1 6	3 8	4 10	7 14	11 19	17 27		
	Third	2	6															0 2	0 3	1 4	2 6	3 8	6 10	8 13	13 19	19 27	29 39		
	Fourth	2	8															0 3	1 4	2 5	3 7	5 10	8 13	12 17	19 25	27 34	40 49		
	Fifth	2	10															1 3	2 4	3 6	5 8	7 11	11 15	17 20	25 39	36 40	53 58		
	Sixth	2	12															1 3	3 5	4 6	7 9	10 12	14 17	21 23	31 33	45 47	65 68		
	Seventh	2	14											↓			↓	2 3	4 5	6 7	9 10	13 14	18 19	25 26	37 38	53 54	77 78		
E	First	3	3											†	↑		§ 2	§ 2	§ 3	§ 4	0 4	0 5	1 7	2 9	4 12	6 16	↑		
	Second	3	6														§ 2	0 3	0 3	1 5	1 6	3 8	4 10	7 14	11 19	17 27			
	Third	3	9														0 2	0 3	1 4	2 6	3 8	6 10	8 13	13 19	19 27	29 39			
	Fourth	3	12														0 3	1 4	3 5	3 7	5 10	8 13	12 17	19 25	27 34	40 49			
	Fifth	3	15														1 3	2 4	3 6	5 8	7 11	11 15	17 20	25 29	36 40	53 58			
	Sixth	3	18														1 3	3 5	4 6	7 9	10 12	14 17	21 23	31 33	45 47	65 68			
	Seventh	3	21										↓			↓	2 3	4 5	6 7	9 10	13 14	18 19	25 26	37 38	53 54	77 78			
F	First	5	5										†	↑		§ 2	§ 2	§ 3	§ 4	0 4	0 5	1 7	2 9	↑	↑	↑			
	Second	5	10													§ 2	0 3	0 3	1 5	1 6	3 8	4 10	7 14						
	Third	5	15													0 2	0 3	1 4	2 6	3 8	6 10	8 13	13 19						
	Fourth	5	20													0 3	1 4	2 5	3 7	5 10	8 13	12 17	19 25						
	Fifth	5	25													1 3	2 4	3 6	5 8	7 11	11 15	17 20	25 29						
	Sixth	5	30													1 3	3 5	4 6	7 9	10 12	14 17	21 23	31 33						
	Seventh	5	35							↓				↓		2 3	4 5	6 7	9 10	13 14	18 19	25 26	37 38						

G	First	8	8	↓	↓	↓	↓	↓	↓	↓	↓	†	↑	↓	§ 2	§ 2	§ 3	§ 4	0 4	0 5	1 7	2 9	↑						
	Second	8	16												§ 2	0 3	0 3	1 5	1 6	3 8	4 10	7 14							
	Third	8	24												0 2	0 3	1 4	2 6	3 8	6 10	8 13	13 19							
	Fourth	8	32												0 3	1 4	2 5	3 7	5 10	8 13	12 17	19 25							
	Fifth	8	40												1 3	2 4	3 6	5 8	7 11	11 15	17 20	25 29							
	Sixth	8	48												1 3	3 5	4 6	7 9	10 12	14 17	21 23	31 33							
	Seventh	8	52												2 3	4 5	6 7	9 10	13 14	18 19	25 26	37 38							
H	First	13	13	↓	↓	↓	↓	↓	↓	↓	†	↑	↓	§ 2	§ 2	§ 3	§ 4	0 4	0 5	1 7	2 9	↑							
	Second	13	26											§ 2	0 3	0 3	1 5	1 6	3 8	4 10	7 14								
	Third	13	39											0 2	0 3	1 4	2 6	3 8	6 10	8 13	13 19								
	Fourth	13	52											0 3	1 4	2 5	3 7	5 10	8 13	12 17	19 25								
	Fifth	13	65											1 3	2 4	3 6	5 8	7 11	11 15	17 20	25 29								
	Sixth	13	78											1 3	3 5	4 6	7 9	10 12	14 17	21 23	31 33								
	Seventh	13	91											2 3	4 5	6 7	9 10	13 14	18 19	25 26	37 38								
J	First	20	20	↓	↓	↓	↓	↓	↓	†	↑	↓	§ 2	§ 2	§ 3	§ 4	0 4	0 5	1 7	2 9	↑								
	Second	20	40										§ 2	0 3	0 3	1 5	1 6	3 8	4 10	7 14									
	Third	20	60										0 2	0 3	1 4	2 6	3 8	6 10	8 13	13 19									
	Fourth	20	70										0 3	1 4	2 5	3 7	5 10	8 13	12 17	19 25									
	Fifth	20	100										1 3	2 4	3 6	5 8	7 11	11 15	17 20	25 29									
	Sixth	20	120										1 3	3 5	4 6	7 9	10 12	14 17	21 23	31 33									
	Seventh	20	140										2 3	4 5	6 7	9 10	13 14	18 19	25 26	37 38									

† means the use of corresponding single sampling plan is recommended.

‡ means the use of corresponding double sampling plan is recommended.

§ means no acceptance is possible for this sample.

TABLE A14.8 Master Table for Normal Inspection: Multiple Sampling (*Continued*)

Sample size code letter	Sample	Sample size	Cumulative sample size	Acceptable quality levels (reduced inspection)																					
				0.010	0.015	0.025	0.040	0.065	0.10	0.15	0.25	0.40	0.65	1.0	1.5	2.5	4.0	6.5	10	15	25	40	65	100	150	250	400	650	1,000
				Ac Re	Ac Re	Ac Re	Ac Re	Ac Re	Ac Re	Ac Re	Ac Re	Ac Re	Ac Re	Ac Re	Ac Re	Ac Re	Ac Re	Ac Re	Ac Re	Ac Re	Ac Re	Ac Re	Ac Re	Ac Re	Ac Re	Ac Re	Ac Re	Ac Re	Ac Re
K	First	32	32	↓	↓	↓	↓	↓	†	↑	↓	§ 2	§ 2	§ 3	§ 4	0 4	0 5	1 7	2 9	↑	↑	↑	↑	↑	↑	↑	↑	↑	↑
	Second	32	64									§ 2	0 3	0 3	1 5	1 6	3 8	4 10	7 14										
	Third	32	96									0 2	0 3	1 4	2 6	3 8	6 10	8 13	13 19										
	Fourth	32	128									0 3	1 4	2 5	3 7	5 10	8 13	12 17	19 25										
	Fifth	32	160									1 3	2 4	3 6	5 8	7 11	11 15	17 20	25 29										
	Sixth	32	192									1 3	3 5	4 6	7 9	10 12	14 17	21 23	31 33										
	Seventh	32	224									2 3	4 5	6 7	9 10	13 14	18 19	25 26	37 38										
L	First	50	50	↓	↓	↓	↓	†	↑	↓	§ 2	§ 2	§ 3	§ 4	0 4	0 5	1 7	2 9	↑	↑	↑	↑	↑	↑	↑	↑	↑	↑	↑
	Second	50	100								§ 2	0 3	0 3	1 5	1 6	3 8	4 10	7 14											
	Third	50	150								0 2	0 3	1 4	2 6	3 8	6 10	8 13	13 19											
	Fourth	50	200								0 3	1 4	2 5	3 7	5 10	8 13	12 17	19 25											
	Fifth	50	250								1 3	2 4	3 6	5 8	7 11	11 15	17 20	25 29											
	Sixth	50	300								1 3	3 5	4 6	7 9	10 12	14 17	21 23	31 33											
	Seventh	50	350								2 3	4 5	6 7	9 10	13 14	18 19	25 26	37 38											
M	First	80	80	↓	↓	↓	†	↑	↓	§ 2	§ 2	§ 3	‡ 4	0 4	0 5	1 7	2 9	↑	↑	↑	↑	↑	↑	↑	↑	↑	↑	↑	↑
	Second	80	160							§ 2	0 3	0 3	1 5	1 6	3 8	4 10	7 14												
	Third	80	240							0 2	0 3	1 4	2 6	3 8	6 10	8 13	13 19												
	Fourth	80	320							0 3	1 4	2 5	3 7	5 10	8 13	12 17	19 25												
	Fifth	80	400							1 3	2 4	3 6	5 8	7 11	11 15	17 20	25 29												
	Sixth	80	480							1 3	3 5	4 6	7 9	10 12	14 17	21 23	31 33												
	Seventh	80	560							2 3	4 5	6 7	9 10	13 14	18 19	25 26	37 38												

N	First	125	125	↓	↓	†	↑	↓	§ 2	§ 2	§ 3	§ 4	0 4	0 5	1 7	2 9	↑												
	Second	125	250						§ 2	0 3	0 3	1 5	1 6	3 8	4 10	7 14													
	Third	125	375						0 2	0 3	1 4	2 6	3 8	6 10	8 13	13 19													
	Fourth	125	500						0 3	1 4	2 5	3 7	5 10	8 13	12 17	19 25													
	Fifth	125	625						1 3	2 4	3 6	5 8	7 11	11 15	17 20	25 29													
	Sixth	125	750						1 3	3 5	4 6	7 9	10 12	14 17	21 23	31 33													
	Seventh	125	875						2 3	4 5	6 7	9 10	13 14	18 19	25 26	37 38													
P	First	200	200	↓	†	↑	↓	§ 2	§ 2	§ 3	§ 4	0 4	0 5	1 7	2 9	↑													
	Second	200	400					§ 2	0 3	0 3	1 5	1 6	3 8	4 10	7 14														
	Third	200	600					0 2	0 3	1 4	2 6	3 8	6 10	8 13	13 19														
	Fourth	200	800					0 3	1 4	2 5	3 7	5 10	8 13	12 17	19 25														
	Fifth	200	1,000					1 3	2 4	3 6	5 8	7 11	11 15	17 20	25 29														
	Sixth	200	1,200					1 3	3 5	4 6	7 9	10 12	14 17	21 23	31 33														
	Seventh	200	1,400					2 3	4 5	6 7	9 10	13 14	18 19	25 26	37 38														
Q	First	315	315	†	↑	↓	§ 2	§ 2	§ 3	§ 4	0 4	0 5	1 7	2 9	↑														
	Second	315	630				§ 2	0 3	0 3	1 5	1 6	3 8	4 10	7 14															
	Third	315	945				0 2	0 3	1 4	2 6	3 8	6 10	8 13	13 19															
	Fourth	315	1,260				0 3	1 4	2 5	3 7	5 10	8 13	12 17	19 25															
	Fifth	315	1,575				1 3	2 4	3 6	5 8	7 11	11 15	17 20	25 29															
	Sixth	315	1,890				1 3	3 5	4 6	7 9	10 12	14 17	21 23	31 33															
	Seventh	315	2,205				2 3	4 5	6 7	9 10	13 14	18 19	25 26	37 38															
R	First	500	500	↑	↑	§ 2	§ 2	§ 3	§ 4	0 4	0 5	1 7	2 9	↑															
	Second	500	1,000			§ 2	0 3	0 3	1 5	1 6	3 8	4 10	7 14																
	Third	500	1,500			0 2	0 3	1 4	2 6	3 8	6 10	8 13	13 19																
	Fourth	500	2,000			0 3	1 4	2 5	3 7	5 10	8 13	12 17	19 25																
	Fifth	500	2,500			1 3	2 4	3 6	5 8	7 11	11 15	17 20	25 29																
	Sixth	500	3,000			1 3	3 5	4 6	7 9	10 12	14 17	21 23	31 33																
	Seventh	500	3,500			2 3	4 5	6 7	9 10	13 14	18 19	25 26	37 38																

† means the use of corresponding single sampling plan is recommended.

‡ means the use of corresponding double sampling plan is recommended.

§ means no acceptance is possible for this sample.

TABLE A14.9 Master Table for Tightened Inspection: Multiple Sampling (MIL-STD-105D)

Sample size code letter	Sample	Sample size	Cumulative sample size	Acceptable quality levels (tightened inspection) 0.010	0.015	0.025	0.040	0.065	0.10	0.15	0.25	0.40	0.65	1.0	1.5	2.5	4.0	6.5	10	15	25	40	65	100	150	250	400	650	1,000
				Ac Re	Ac Re	Ac Re	Ac Re	Ac Re	Ac Re	Ac Re	Ac Re	Ac Re	Ac Re	Ac Re	Ac Re	Ac Re	Ac Re	Ac Re	Ac Re	Ac Re	Ac Re	Ac Re	Ac Re	Ac Re	Ac Re	Ac Re	Ac Re	Ac Re	Ac Re
A				↓	↓	↓	↓	↓	↓	↓	↓	↓	↓	↓	↓	↓	↓	↓	↓	↓	↓	†	†	†	†	†	†	†	†
B																	↓	†		↓	‡	‡	‡	‡	‡	‡	‡	‡	‡
C																↓	†		↓	‡	‡	‡	‡	‡	‡	‡	‡	‡	↑
D	First	2	2													↑			§ 2	§ 2	§ 3	§ 4	0 4	0 6	1 8	3 10	6 15	↑	
	Second	2	4																§ 2	0 3	0 3	1 5	2 7	3 9	6 12	10 17	16 25		
	Third	2	6																0 2	0 3	1 4	2 6	4 9	7 12	11 17	17 24	26 36		
	Fourth	2	8																0 3	1 4	2 5	3 7	6 11	10 15	16 22	24 31	37 46		
	Fifth	2	10																1 3	2 4	3 6	5 8	9 12	14 17	22 25	32 37	49 55		
	Sixth	2	12																1 3	3 5	4 6	7 9	12 14	18 20	27 29	40 43	61 64		
	Seventh	2	14												↓			↓	2 3	4 5	6 7	9 10	14 15	21 22	32 33	48 49	72 73		
E	First	3	3												†			§ 2	§ 2	§ 3	§ 4	0 4	0 6	1 8	3 10	6 15	↑		
	Second	3	6															§ 2	0 3	0 3	1 5	2 7	3 9	6 12	10 17	16 25			
	Third	3	9															0 2	0 3	1 4	2 6	4 9	7 12	11 17	17 24	26 36			
	Fourth	3	12															0 3	1 4	2 5	3 7	6 11	10 15	16 22	24 31	37 46			
	Fifth	3	15															1 3	2 4	3 6	5 8	9 12	14 17	22 25	32 37	49 55			
	Sixth	3	18															1 3	3 5	4 6	7 9	12 14	18 20	27 29	40 43	61 64			
	Seventh	3	21										↓			↓	2 3	4 5	6 7	9 10	14 15	21 22	32 33	48 49	72 73				
F	First	5	5											†			§ 2	§ 2	§ 3	§ 4	0 4	0 6	1 8	↑	↑	↑			
	Second	5	10														§ 2	0 3	0 4	1 5	2 7	3 9	6 12						
	Third	5	15														0 2	0 3	1 4	2 6	4 9	7 12	11 17						
	Fourth	5	20														0 3	1 4	2 5	3 7	6 11	10 15	16 22						
	Fifth	5	25														1 3	2 4	3 6	5 8	9 12	14 17	22 25						
	Sixth	5	30														1 3	3 5	4 6	7 9	12 14	18 20	27 29						
	Seventh	5	35									↓			↓		2 3	4 5	6 7	9 10	14 15	21 22	32 33						

G	First	8	8	↓	↓	↓	↓	↓	↓	↓	↓	↓	†	↓	↓	§ 2	§ 2	§ 3	§ 4	0 4	0 6	1 8	↑						
	Second	8	16													§ 2	0 3	0 3	1 5	2 7	3 9	6 12							
	Third	8	24													0 2	0 3	1 4	2 6	4 9	7 12	11 17							
	Fourth	8	32													0 3	1 4	2 5	3 7	6 11	10 15	16 22							
	Fifth	8	40													1 3	2 4	3 6	5 8	9 12	14 17	22 25							
	Sixth	8	48													1 3	3 5	4 6	7 9	12 14	18 20	27 29							
	Seventh	8	56													2 3	4 5	6 7	9 10	14 15	21 22	32 33							
H	First	13	13	↓	↓	↓	↓	↓	↓	↓	↓	†	↓	↓	§ 2	§ 2	§ 3	§ 4	0 4	0 6	1 8	↑							
	Second	13	26												§ 2	0 3	0 3	1 5	2 7	3 9	6 12								
	Third	13	39												0 2	0 3	1 4	2 6	4 9	7 12	11 17								
	Fourth	13	52												0 3	1 4	2 5	3 7	6 11	10 15	16 22								
	Fifth	13	65												1 3	2 4	3 6	5 8	9 12	14 17	22 25								
	Sixth	13	78												1 3	3 5	4 6	7 9	12 14	18 20	27 29								
	Seventh	13	91												2 3	4 5	6 7	9 10	14 15	21 22	32 33								
J	First	20	20	↓	↓	↓	↓	↓	↓	↓	†	↓	↓	§ 2	§ 2	§ 3	§ 4	0 4	0 6	1 8	↑								
	Second	20	40											§ 2	0 3	0 3	1 5	2 7	3 9	6 12									
	Third	20	60											0 2	0 3	1 4	2 6	4 9	7 12	11 17									
	Fourth	20	80											0 3	1 4	2 5	3 7	6 11	10 15	16 22									
	Fifth	20	100											1 3	2 4	3 6	5 8	9 12	14 17	22 25									
	Sixth	20	120											1 3	3 5	4 6	7 9	12 14	18 20	27 29									
	Seventh	20	140											2 3	4 5	6 7	9 10	14 15	21 22	32 33									

† means the use of corresponding single sampling plan is recommended.

‡ means the use of corresponding double sampling plan is recommended.

§ means no acceptance is possible for this sample.

TABLE A14.9 Master Table for Tightened Inspection: Multiple Sampling (*Continued*)

Sample size code letter	Sample	Sample size	Cumulative sample size	Acceptable quality levels (tightened inspection)																									
				0.010	0.015	0.025	0.040	0.065	0.10	0.15	0.25	0.40	0.65	1.0	1.5	2.5	4.0	6.5	10	15	25	40	65	100	150	250	400	650	1,000
				Ac Re	Ac Re	Ac Re	Ac Re	Ac Re	Ac Re	Ac Re	Ac Re	Ac Re	Ac Re	Ac Re	Ac Re	Ac Re	Ac Re	Ac Re	Ac Re	Ac Re	Ac Re	Ac Re	Ac Re	Ac Re	Ac Re	Ac Re	Ac Re	Ac Re	Ac Re
K	First	32	32	↓	↓	↓	↓	↓	↓	†	↓	↓	§ 2	§ 2	§ 3	§ 4	0 4	0 6	1 8	↑	↑	↑	↑	↑	↑	↑	↑	↑	↑
	Second	32	64										§ 2	0 3	0 3	1 5	2 7	3 9	6 12										
	Third	32	96										0 2	0 3	1 4	2 6	4 9	7 12	11 17										
	Fourth	32	128										0 3	1 4	2 5	3 7	6 11	10 15	16 22										
	Fifth	32	160										1 3	2 4	3 6	5 8	9 12	14 17	22 25										
	Sixth	32	192										1 3	3 5	4 6	7 9	12 14	18 20	27 29										
	Seventh	32	224										2 3	4 5	6 7	9 10	14 15	21 22	32 33										
L	First	50	50	↓	↓	↓	↓	↓	†	↓	↓	§ 2	§ 2	§ 3	§ 4	0 4	0 6	1 8	↑	↑	↑	↑	↑	↑	↑	↑	↑	↑	↑
	Second	50	100									§ 2	0 3	0 3	1 5	2 7	3 9	6 12											
	Third	50	150									0 2	0 3	1 4	2 6	4 9	7 12	11 17											
	Fourth	50	200									0 3	1 4	2 5	3 7	6 11	10 15	16 22											
	Fifth	50	250									1 3	2 4	3 6	5 8	9 12	14 17	22 25											
	Sixth	50	300									1 3	3 5	4 6	7 9	12 14	18 20	27 29											
	Seventh	50	350									2 3	4 5	6 7	9 10	14 15	21 22	32 33											
M	First	80	80	↓	↓	↓	↓	†	↓	↓	§ 2	§ 2	§ 3	§ 4	0 4	0 6	1 8	↑	↑	↑	↑	↑	↑	↑	↑	↑	↑	↑	↑
	Second	80	160								§ 2	0 3	0 3	1 5	2 7	3 9	6 12												
	Third	80	240								0 2	0 3	1 4	2 6	4 9	7 12	11 17												
	Fourth	80	320								0 3	1 4	2 5	3 7	6 11	10 15	16 22												
	Fifth	80	400								1 3	2 4	3 6	5 8	9 12	14 17	22 25												
	Sixth	80	480								1 3	3 5	4 6	7 9	12 14	18 20	27 29												
	Seventh	80	560								2 3	4 5	6 7	9 10	14 15	21 22	32 33												
N	First	125	125	↓	↓	↓	†	↓	↓	§ 2	§ 2	§ 3	§ 4	0 4	0 6	1 8	↑	↑	↑	↑	↑	↑	↑	↑	↑	↑	↑	↑	↑
	Second	125	250							§ 2	0 3	0 3	1 5	2 7	3 9	6 12													
	Third	125	375							0 2	0 3	1 4	2 6	4 9	7 12	11 17													
	Fourth	125	500							0 3	1 4	2 5	3 7	6 11	10 15	16 22													
	Fifth	125	625							1 3	2 4	3 6	5 8	9 12	14 17	22 25													
	Sixth	125	750							1 3	3 5	4 6	7 9	12 14	18 20	27 29													
	Seventh	125	875							2 3	4 5	6 7	9 10	14 15	21 22	32 33													

P	First	200	200	↓	↓	†	↓	↓	§ 2	§ 2	§ 3	§ 4	0 4	0 6	1 8	↑													
	Second	200	400						§ 2	0 3	0 3	1 5	2 7	3 9	6 12														
	Third	200	600						0 2	0 3	1 4	2 6	4 9	7 12	11 17														
	Fourth	200	800						0 3	1 4	2 5	3 7	6 11	10 15	16 22														
	Fifth	200	1,000						1 3	2 4	3 6	5 8	9 12	14 17	22 25														
	Sixth	200	1,200						1 3	3 5	4 6	7 9	12 14	18 20	27 29														
	Seventh	200	1,400						2 3	4 5	6 7	9 10	14 15	21 22	32 33														
Q	First	315	315	↓	†	↓	↓	§ 2	§ 2	§ 3	§ 4	0 4	0 6	1 8	↑	↑													
	Second	315	630					§ 2	0 3	0 3	1 5	2 7	3 9	6 12															
	Third	315	945					0 2	0 3	1 4	2 6	4 9	7 12	11 17															
	Fourth	315	1,260					0 3	1 4	2 5	3 7	6 11	10 15	16 22															
	Fifth	315	1,575					1 3	2 4	3 6	5 8	9 12	14 17	22 25															
	Sixth	315	1,890					1 3	3 5	4 6	7 9	12 14	18 20	27 29															
	Seventh	315	2,205					2 3	4 5	6 7	9 10	14 15	21 22	32 33															
R	First	500	500	†	↑	↓	§ 2	§ 2	§ 3	§ 4	0 4	0 6	1 8	↑	↑	↑													
	Second	500	1,000				§ 2	0 3	0 3	1 5	2 7	3 9	6 12																
	Third	500	1,500				0 2	0 3	1 4	2 6	4 9	7 12	11 17																
	Fourth	500	2,000				0 3	1 4	2 5	3 7	6 11	10 15	16 22																
	Fifth	500	2,500				1 3	2 4	3 6	5 8	9 12	14 17	22 25																
	Sixth	500	3,000				1 3	3 5	4 6	7 9	12 14	18 20	27 29																
	Seventh	500	3,500				2 3	4 5	6 7	9 10	14 15	21 22	32 33																
S	First	800	800			§ 2																							
	Second	800	1,600			§ 2																							
	Third	800	2,400			0 2																							
	Fourth	800	3,200			0 3																							
	Fifth	800	4,000			1 3																							
	Sixth	800	4,800			1 3																							
	Seventh	800	5,600			2 3																							

† means the use of corresponding single sampling plan is recommended.

‡ means the use of corresponding double sampling plan is recommended.

§ means no acceptance is possible for this sample.

TABLE A14.10 Master Table for Reduced Inspection: Multiple Sampling (MIL-STD-105D)

Sample size code letter	Sample	Sample size	Cumulative sample size	Acceptable quality levels (reduced inspection)																									
				0.010	0.015	0.025	0.040	0.065	0.10	0.15	0.25	0.40	0.65	1.0	1.5	2.5	4.0	6.5	10	15	25	40	65	100	150	250	400	650	1,000
				Ac Re	Ac Re	Ac Re	Ac Re	Ac Re	Ac Re	Ac Re	Ac Re	Ac Re	Ac Re	Ac Re	Ac Re	Ac Re	Ac Re	Ac Re	Ac Re	Ac Re	Ac Re	Ac Re	Ac Re	Ac Re	Ac Re	Ac Re	Ac Re	Ac Re	Ac Re
A				↓	↓	↓	↓	↓	↓	↓							↓	†		↓	†	†	†	†	†	†	†	†	†
B																↓	†	↑	↓	†	†	†	†	†	†	†	†	†	†
C															↓	†	↑	↓	†	†	†	†	†	†	†	†	†	†	↑
D														↓	†	↑	↓	‡	‡	‡	‡	‡	‡	‡	‡	‡	‡	↑	
E													↓	†	↑	↓	‡	‡	‡	‡	‡	‡	‡	‡	‡	‡	↑		
F	First	2	2										†	↑		§ 2	§ 2	§ 3	§ 3	§ 4	§ 4	0 5	0 6	↑	↑	↑			
	Second	2	4													§ 2	§ 3	§ 3	0 4	0 5	1 6	1 7	3 9						
	Third	2	6													0 2	0 3	0 4	0 5	1 6	2 8	3 9	6 12						
	Fourth	2	8													0 3	0 4	0 5	1 6	2 7	3 10	5 12	8 15						
	Fifth	2	10													0 3	0 4	1 6	2 7	3 8	5 11	7 13	11 17						
	Sixth	2	12													0 3	1 5	1 6	3 7	4 9	7 12	10 15	14 20						
	Seventh	2	14									↓			↓	1 3	1 5	2 7	4 8	6 10	9 14	13 17	18 22						
G	First	3	3									‡	↑		§ 2	§ 2	§ 3	§ 3	§ 4	§ 4	0 5	0 6	↑						
	Second	3	6												§ 2	§ 3	§ 3	0 4	0 5	1 6	1 7	3 9							
	Third	3	9												0 2	0 3	0 4	0 5	1 6	2 8	3 9	6 12							
	Fourth	3	12												0 3	0 4	0 5	1 6	2 7	3 10	5 12	8 15							
	Fifth	3	15												0 3	0 4	1 6	2 7	3 8	5 11	7 13	11 17							
	Sixth	3	18												0 3	1 5	1 6	3 7	4 9	7 12	10 15	14 20							
	Seventh	3	21								↓			↓	1 3	1 5	2 7	4 8	6 10	9 14	13 17	18 22							

H	First	5	5	↓	↓	↓	↓	↓	↓	↓	‡	↑	↓	§ 2	§ 2	§ 3	§ 3	§ 4	§ 4	0 5	0 6	↑							
	Second	5	10											§ 2	§ 3	§ 3	0 4	0 5	1 6	1 7	3 9								
	Third	5	15											0 2	0 3	0 4	0 5	1 6	2 8	3 9	6 12								
	Fourth	5	20											0 3	0 4	0 5	1 6	2 7	3 10	5 12	8 15								
	Fifth	5	25											0 3	0 4	1 6	2 7	3 8	5 11	7 13	11 17								
	Sixth	5	30											0 3	1 5	1 6	3 7	4 9	7 12	10 15	14 20								
	Seventh	5	35											1 3	1 5	2 7	4 8	6 10	9 14	13 17	18 22								
J	First	8	8							‡	↑	↓	§ 2	§ 2	§ 3	§ 3	§ 4	§ 4	0 5	0 6	↑								
	Second	8	16										§ 2	§ 3	§ 3	0 4	0 5	1 6	1 7	3 9									
	Third	8	24										0 2	0 3	0 4	0 5	1 6	2 8	3 9	6 12									
	Fourth	8	32										0 3	0 4	0 5	1 6	2 7	3 10	5 12	8 15									
	Fifth	8	40										0 3	0 4	1 6	2 7	3 8	5 11	7 13	11 17									
	Sixth	8	48										0 3	1 5	1 6	3 7	4 9	7 12	10 15	14 20									
	Seventh	8	56										1 3	1 5	2 7	4 8	6 10	9 14	13 17	18 22									
K	First	13	13						‡	↑	↓	§ 2	§ 2	§ 3	§ 3	§ 4	§ 4	0 5	0 6	↑									
	Second	13	26									§ 2	§ 3	§ 3	0 4	0 5	1 6	1 7	3 9										
	Third	13	39									0 2	0 3	0 4	0 5	1 6	2 8	3 9	6 12										
	Fourth	13	52									0 3	0 4	0 5	1 6	2 7	3 10	5 12	8 15										
	Fifth	13	65									0 3	0 4	1 6	2 7	3 8	5 11	7 13	11 17										
	Sixth	13	78									0 3	1 5	1 6	3 7	4 9	7 12	10 15	14 20										
	Seventh	13	91									1 3	1 5	2 7	4 8	6 10	9 14	13 17	18 22										

† means the use of corresponding single sampling plan is recommended.

‡ means the use of corresponding double sampling plan is recommended.

§ means no acceptance is possible for this sample.

TABLE A14.10 Master Table for Reduced Inspection: Multiple Sampling (*Continued*)

Sample size code letter	Sample	Sample size	Cumulative sample size	0.010	0.015	0.025	0.040	0.065	0.10	0.15	0.25	0.40	0.65	1.0	1.5	2.5	4.0	6.5	10	15	25	40	65	100	150	250	400	650	1,000
				Ac Re	Ac Re	Ac Re	Ac Re	Ac Re	Ac Re	Ac Re	Ac Re	Ac Re	Ac Re	Ac Re	Ac Re	Ac Re	Ac Re	Ac Re	Ac Re	Ac Re	Ac Re	Ac Re	Ac Re	Ac Re	Ac Re	Ac Re	Ac Re	Ac Re	Ac Re
L	First	20	20	↓	↓	↓	↓	‡	↑	↓	§ 2	§ 2	§ 3	§ 3	§ 4	§ 4	0 5	0 6	↑	↑	↑	↑	↑	↑	↑	↑	↑	↑	↑
	Second	20	40								§ 2	§ 3	§ 3	0 4	0 5	1 6	1 7	3 9											
	Third	20	60								0 2	0 3	0 4	0 5	1 6	2 8	3 9	6 12											
	Fourth	20	80								0 3	0 4	0 5	1 6	2 7	3 10	5 12	8 15											
	Fifth	20	100								0 3	0 4	1 6	2 7	3 8	5 11	7 13	11 17											
	Sixth	20	120								0 3	1 5	1 6	3 7	4 9	7 12	10 15	14 20											
	Seventh	20	140								1 3	1 5	2 7	4 8	6 10	9 14	13 17	18 22											
M	First	32	32	↓	↓	↓	†	↑	↓	§ 2	§ 2	§ 3	§ 3	§ 4	§ 4	0 5	0 6	↑	↑	↑	↑	↑	↑	↑	↑	↑	↑	↑	↑
	Second	32	64							§ 2	§ 3	§ 3	0 4	0 5	1 6	1 7	3 9												
	Third	32	96							0 2	0 3	0 4	0 5	1 6	2 8	3 9	6 12												
	Fourth	32	128							0 3	0 4	0 5	1 6	2 7	3 10	5 12	8 15												
	Fifth	32	160							0 3	0 4	1 6	2 7	3 8	5 11	7 13	11 17												
	Sixth	32	192							0 3	1 5	1 6	3 7	4 9	7 12	10 15	14 20												
	Seventh	32	224							1 3	1 5	2 7	4 8	6 10	9 14	13 17	18 22												
N	First	50	50	↓	↓	†	↑	↓	§ 2	§ 2	§ 3	§ 3	§ 4	§ 4	0 5	0 6	↑	↑	↑	↑	↑	↑	↑	↑	↑	↑	↑	↑	↑
	Second	50	100						§ 2	§ 3	§ 3	0 4	0 5	1 6	1 7	3 9													
	Third	50	150						0 2	0 3	0 4	0 5	1 6	2 8	3 9	6 12													
	Fourth	50	200						0 3	0 4	0 5	1 6	2 7	3 10	5 12	8 15													
	Fifth	50	250						0 3	0 4	1 6	2 7	3 8	5 11	7 13	11 17													
	Sixth	50	300						0 3	1 5	1 6	3 7	4 9	7 12	10 15	14 20													
	Seventh	50	350						1 3	1 5	2 7	4 8	6 10	9 14	13 17	18 22													

P	First	80	80	↓	‡	↑	↓	§ 2	§ 2	§ 3	§ 3	§ 4	§ 4	0 5	0 6	↑													
	Second	80	160					§ 2	§ 3	§ 3	0 4	0 5	1 6	1 7	3 9														
	Third	80	240					0 2	0 3	0 4	0 5	1 6	2 8	3 9	6 12														
	Fourth	80	320					0 3	0 4	0 5	1 6	2 7	3 10	5 12	8 15														
	Fifth	80	400					0 3	0 4	1 6	2 7	3 8	5 11	7 13	11 17														
	Sixth	80	480					0 3	1 5	1 6	3 7	4 9	7 12	10 15	14 20														
	Seventh	80	560					1 3	1 5	2 7	4 8	6 10	9 14	13 17	18 22														
Q	First	125	125	‡	↑	↓	§ 2	§ 2	§ 3	§ 3	§ 4	§ 4	0 5	0 6	↑														
	Second	125	250				§ 2	§ 3	§ 3	0 4	0 5	1 6	1 7	3 9															
	Third	125	375				0 2	0 3	0 4	0 5	1 6	2 8	3 9	6 12															
	Fourth	125	500				0 3	0 4	0 5	1 6	2 7	3 10	5 12	8 15															
	Fifth	125	625				0 3	0 4	1 6	2 7	3 8	5 11	7 13	11 17															
	Sixth	125	750				0 3	1 5	1 6	3 7	4 9	7 12	10 15	14 20															
	Seventh	125	875				1 3	1 5	2 7	4 8	6 10	9 14	13 17	18 22															
R	First	200	200	↑		§ 2	§ 2	§ 3	§ 3	§ 4	§ 4	0 5	0 6	↑															
	Second	200	400			§ 2	§ 3	§ 3	0 4	0 5	1 6	1 7	3 9																
	Third	200	600			0 2	0 3	0 4	0 5	1 6	2 8	3 9	6 12																
	Fourth	200	800			0 3	0 4	0 5	1 6	2 7	3 10	5 12	8 15																
	Fifth	200	1,000			0 3	0 4	1 6	2 7	3 8	5 11	7 13	11 17																
	Sixth	200	1,200			0 3	1 5	1 6	3 7	4 9	7 12	10 15	14 20																
	Seventh	200	1,400			1 3	1 5	2 7	4 8	6 10	9 14	13 17	18 22																

† means the use of corresponding single sampling plan is recommended.

‡ means the use of corresponding double sampling plan is recommended.

§ means no acceptance is possible for this sample.

TABLE A14.11 Average Outgoing Quality Limit Factors for Normal Inspection: Single Sampling (MIL-STD-105D)*

Code letter	Sample size	Acceptable quality level																									
		0.010	0.015	0.025	0.040	0.065	0.10	0.15	0.25	0.40	0.65	1.0	1.5	2.5	4.0	6.5	10	15	25	40	65	100	150	250	400	650	1,000
A	2															18			42	69	97	160	220	330	470	730	1,100
B	3														12			28	46	65	110	150	220	310	490	720	1,100
C	5													7.4			17	27	39	63	90	130	190	290	430	660	
D	8												4.6			11	17	24	40	56	82	120	180	270	410		
E	13											2.8			6.5	11	15	24	34	50	72	110	170	250			
F	20										1.8			4.2	6.9	9.7	16	22	33	47	73						
G	32									1.2			2.6	4.3	6.1	9.9	14	21	29	46							
H	50								0.74			1.7	2.7	3.9	6.3	9.0	13	19	29								
J	80							0.46			1.1	1.7	2.4	4.0	5.6	8.2	12	18									
K	125						0.29			0.67	1.1	1.6	2.5	3.6	5.2	7.5	12										
L	200					0.18			0.42	0.69	0.97	1.6	2.2	3.3	4.7	7.3											
M	315				0.12			0.27	0.44	0.62	1.00	1.4	2.1	3.0	4.7												
N	500			0.074			0.17	0.27	0.39	0.63	0.90	1.3	1.9	2.9													
P	800		0.046			0.11	0.17	0.24	0.40	0.56	0.82	1.2	1.8														
Q	1,250	0.029			0.067	0.11	0.16	0.25	0.36	0.52	0.75	1.2															
R	2,000			0.042	0.069	0.097	0.16	0.22	0.33	0.47	0.73																

* For the exact AOQL, these values must be multiplied by $\left(1 - \frac{\text{sample size}}{\text{lot or batch size}}\right)$.

TABLE A14.12 Average Outgoing Quality Limit Factors for Tightened Inspection: Single Sampling (MIL-STD-105D)*

Code letter	Sample size	Acceptable quality level																									
		0.010	0.015	0.025	0.040	0.065	0.10	0.15	0.25	0.40	0.65	1.0	1.5	2.5	4.0	6.5	10	15	25	40	65	100	150	250	400	650	1,000
A	2																			42	69	97	160	260	400	620	970
B	3															12			28	46	65	110	170	270	410	650	1,100
C	5														7.4			17	27	39	63	100	160	250	390	610	
D	8													4.6			11	17	24	40	64	99	160	240	380		
E	13												2.8			6.5	11	15	24	40	61	95	150	240			
F	20											1.8			4.2	6.9	9.7	16	26	40	62						
G	32										1.2			2.6	4.3	6.1	9.9	16	25	39							
H	50									0.74			1.7	2.7	3.9	6.3	10	16	25								
J	80								0.46			1.1	1.7	2.4	4.0	6.4	9.9	16									
K	125							0.29			0.67	1.1	1.6	2.5	4.1	6.4	9.9										
L	200						0.18			0.42	0.69	0.97	1.6	2.6	4.0	6.2											
M	315					0.12			0.27	0.44	0.62	1.0	1.6	2.5	3.9												
N	500				0.074			0.17	0.27	0.39	0.63	1.0	1.6	2.5													
P	800			0.046			0.11	0.17	0.24	0.40	0.64	0.99	1.6														
Q	1,250		0.029			0.067	0.11	0.16	0.25	0.41	0.64	0.99															
R	2,000	0.018			0.042	0.069	0.097	0.16	0.26	0.40	0.62																
S	3,150			0.027																							

* For the exact AOQL, these values must be multiplied by $\left(1 - \frac{\text{sample size}}{\text{lot or batch size}}\right)$

TABLE A14.13 Limit Numbers for Reduced Inspection (MIL-STD-105D)

Number of sample units from last 10 lots or batches	Acceptable quality level																									
	0.010	0.015	0.025	0.040	0.065	0.10	0.15	0.25	0.40	0.65	1.0	1.5	2.5	4.0	6.5	10	15	25	40	65	100	150	250	400	650	1,000
20–29	†	†	†	†	†	†	†	†	†	†	†	†	†	†	†	0	0	2	4	8	14	22	40	68	115	181
30–49	†	†	†	†	†	†	†	†	†	†	†	†	†	†	0	0	1	3	7	13	22	36	63	105	178	277
50–79	†	†	†	†	†	†	†	†	†	†	†	†	†	0	0	2	3	7	14	25	40	63	110	181	301	
80–129	†	†	†	†	†	†	†	†	†	†	†	†	0	0	2	4	7	14	24	42	68	105	181	207		
130–199	†	†	†	†	†	†	†	†	†	†	†	0	0	2	4	7	13	25	42	72	115	177	301	490		
200–319	†	†	†	†	†	†	†	†	†	†	0	0	2	4	8	14	22	40	68	115	181	277	471			
320–499	†	†	†	†	†	†	†	†	†	0	0	1	4	8	14	24	39	68	113	189						
500–799	†	†	†	†	†	†	†	†	0	0	2	3	7	14	25	40	63	110	181							
800–1,249	†	†	†	†	†	†	†	0	0	2	4	7	14	24	42	68	105	181								
1,250–1,999	†	†	†	†	†	†	0	0	2	4	7	13	24	40	69	110	169									
2,000–3,149	†	†	†	†	†	0	0	2	4	8	14	22	40	68	115	181										
3,150–4,999	†	†	†	†	0	0	1	4	8	14	24	38	67	111	186											
5,000–7,999	†	†	†	0	0	2	3	7	14	25	40	63	110	181												
8,000–12,499	†	†	0	0	2	4	7	14	24	42	68	105	181													
12,500–19,999	†	0	0	2	4	7	13	24	40	69	110	169														
20,000–31,499	0	0	2	4	8	14	22	46	68	115	181															
31,500–49,999	0	1	4	8	14	24	38	67	111	185																
50,000 and over	2	3	7	14	25	40	63	110	181	301																

† Denotes that the number of sample units from the last 10 lots or batches is not sufficient for reduced inspection for this AQL. In this instance more than 10 lots or batches may be used for the calculation, provided that the lots or batches used are the most recent ones in sequence, that they have all been on normal inspection, and that none has been rejected while on original inspection.

TABLE A14.14 Limiting Quality Tables for which $P_a = 10\%$: Normal Inspection, Single Sampling (MIL-STD-105D)

In percent defective ($100p_{0.1}i0$)

Code letter	Sample size	Acceptable quality level															
		0.010	0.015	0.025	0.040	0.065	0.0	0.15	0.25	0.40	0.65	1.0	1.5	2.5	4.0	6.5	10
A	2															68	
B	3														54		
C	5													37			58
D	8												25			41	54
E	13											16			27	36	44
F	20										11			18	25	30	42
G	32									6.9			12	16	20	27	34
H	50								4.5			7.6	10	13	18	22	29
J	80							2.8			4.8	6.5	8.2	11	14	19	24
K	125						1.8			3.1	4.3	5.4	7.4	9.4	12	16	23
L	200					1.2			2.0	2.7	3.3	4.6	5.9	7.7	10	14	
M	315				0.73			1.2	1.7	2.1	2.9	3.7	4.9	6.4	9.0		
N	500			0.46			0.78	1.1	1.3	1.9	2.4	3.1	4.0	5.6			
P	800		0.29			0.49	0.67	0.84	1.2	1.5	1.9	2.5	3.5				
Q	1,250	0.18			0.31	0.43	0.53	0.74	0.94	1.2	1.6	2.3					
R	2,000			0.20	0.27	0.33	0.46	0.59	0.77	1.0	1.4						

TABLE A14.14 Limiting Quality Tables for which $P_a = 10\%$: Normal Inspection, Single Sampling (*Continued*)

In defects per 100 units

Code letter	Sample size	Acceptable quality level																									
		0.010	0.015	0.025	0.040	0.065	0.10	0.15	0.25	0.40	0.65	1.0	1.5	2.5	4.0	6.5	10	15	25	40	65	100	150	250	400	650	1,000
A	2															120			200	270	330	460	590	770	1000	1400	1900
B	3														77			130	180	220	310	390	510	670	940	1300	1800
C	5													46			78	110	130	190	240	310	400	560	770	1100	
D	8												29			49	67	84	120	150	190	250	350	480	670		
E	13											18			30	41	51	71	91	120	160	220	300	410			
F	20										12			20	27	33	46	59	77	100	140						
G	32									7.2			12	17	21	29	37	48	63	88							
H	50								4.6			7.8	11	13	19	24	31	40	56								
J	80							2.9			4.9	6.7	8.4	12	15	19	25	35									
K	125						1.8			3.1	4.3	5.4	7.4	9.4	12	16	23										
L	200					1.2			2.0	2.7	3.3	4.6	5.9	7.7	10	14											
M	315				0.73			1.2	1.7	2.1	2.9	3.7	4.9	6.4	9.0												
N	500			0.46			0.78	1.1	1.3	1.9	2.4	3.1	4.0	5.6													
P	800		0.29			0.49	0.67	0.84	1.2	1.5	1.9	2.5	3.5														
Q	1,250	0.18			0.31	0.43	0.53	0.74	0.94	1.2	1.6	2.3															
R	2,000			0.20	0.27	0.33	0.46	0.59	0.77	1.0	1.4																

TABLE A15.1 Sample Size Code Letters* (Table A–2 of MIL-STD-414)

Lot Size	Inspection Levels				
	I	II	III	IV	V
3 to 8	B	B	B	B	C
9 to 15	B	B	B	B	D
16 to 25	B	B	B	C	E
26 to 40	B	B	B	D	F
41 to 65	B	B	C	E	G
66 to 110	B	B	D	F	H
111 to 180	B	C	E	G	I
181 to 300	B	D	F	H	J
301 to 500	C	E	G	I	K
501 to 800	D	F	H	J	L
801 to 1,300	E	G	I	K	L
1,301 to 3,200	F	H	J	L	M
3,201 to 8,000	G	I	L	M	N
8,001 to 22,000	H	J	M	N	O
22,001 to 110,000	I	K	N	O	P
110,001 to 550,000	I	K	O	P	Q
550,001 and over	I	K	P	Q	Q

*Sample size code letters given in body of table are applicable when the indicated inspection levels are to be used.

TABLE A15.2 Master Table for Normal and Tightened Inspection for Plans Based on Variability Unknown (Single Specification Limit—Form 1), Standard Deviation Method (Table B–1 of MIL-STD-414)

Sample size code letter	Sample size	Acceptable quality levels (normal inspection)													
		0.04	0.065	0.10	0.15	0.25	0.40	0.65	1.00	1.50	2.50	4.00	6.50	10.00	15.00
		k	k	k	k	k	k	k	k	k	k	k	k	k	k
B	3	↓	↓	↓	↓	↓	↓	↓	↓	↓	1.12	0.958	0.765	0.566	0.341
C	4	↓	↓	↓	↓	↓	↓	↓	1.45	1.34	1.17	1.01	0.814	0.617	0.393
D	5	↓	↓	↓	↓	↓	↓	1.65	1.53	1.40	1.24	1.07	0.874	0.675	0.455
E	7	↓	↓	↓	↓	2.00	1.88	1.75	1.62	1.50	1.33	1.15	0.955	0.755	0.536
F	10	↓	↓	↓	2.24	2.11	1.98	1.84	1.72	1.58	1.41	1.23	1.03	0.828	0.611
G	15	2.64	2.53	2.42	2.32	2.20	2.06	1.91	1.79	1.65	1.47	1.30	1.09	0.886	0.664
H	20	2.69	2.58	2.47	2.36	2.24	2.11	1.96	1.82	1.69	1.51	1.33	1.12	0.917	0.695
I	25	2.72	2.61	2.50	2.40	2.26	2.14	1.98	1.85	1.72	1.53	1.35	1.14	0.936	0.712
J	30	2.73	2.61	2.51	2.41	2.28	2.15	2.00	1.86	1.73	1.55	1.36	1.15	0.946	0.723
K	35	2.77	2.65	2.54	2.45	2.31	2.18	2.03	1.89	1.76	1.57	1.39	1.18	0.969	0.745
L	40	2.77	2.66	2.55	2.44	2.31	2.18	2.03	1.89	1.76	1.58	1.39	1.18	0.971	0.746
M	50	2.83	2.71	2.60	2.50	2.35	2.22	2.08	1.93	1.80	1.61	1.42	1.21	1.00	0.774
N	75	2.90	2.77	2.66	2.55	2.41	2.27	2.12	1.98	1.84	1.65	1.46	1.24	1.03	0.804
O	100	2.92	2.80	2.69	2.58	2.43	2.29	2.14	2.00	1.86	1.67	1.48	1.26	1.05	0.819
P	150	2.96	2.84	2.73	2.61	2.47	2.33	2.18	2.03	1.89	1.70	1.51	1.29	1.07	0.841
Q	200	2.97	2.85	2.73	2.62	2.47	2.33	2.18	2.04	1.89	1.70	1.51	1.29	1.07	0.845
		0.065	0.10	0.15	0.25	0.40	0.65	1.00	1.50	2.50	4.00	6.50	10.00	15.00	
		Acceptable quality levels (tightened inspection)													

All AQL values are in percent defective.

Use first sampling plan below arrow, that is, both sample size as well as k value. When sample size equals or exceeds lot size, every item in the lot must be inspected.

TABLE A15.3 Master Table for Normal and Tightened Inspection for Plans Based on Variability Unknown (Double Specification Limit and Form 2 —Single Specification Limit), Standard Deviation Method (Table B–3 of MIL-STD-414)

Sample size code letter	Sample size	Acceptable quality levels (normal inspection)													
		0.04	0.065	0.10	0.15	0.25	0.40	0.65	1.00	1.50	2.50	4.00	6.50	10.00	15.00
		M	*M*	*M*	*M*	*M*	*M*	*M*	*M*	*M*	*M*	*M*	*M*	*M*	*M*
B	3	↓	↓	↓	↓	↓	↓	↓	↓	↓	7.59	18.86	26.94	33.69	40.47
C	4	↓	↓	↓	↓	↓	↓	↓	1.53	5.50	10.92	16.45	22.86	29.45	36.90
D	5	↓	↓	↓	↓	↓	↓	1.33	3.32	5.83	9.80	14.39	20.19	26.56	33.99
E	7	↓	↓	↓	↓	0.422	1.06	2.14	3.55	5.35	8.40	12.20	17.35	23.29	30.50
F	10	↓	↓	↓	0.349	0.716	1.30	2.17	3.26	4.77	7.29	10.54	15.17	20.74	27.57
G	15	0.099	0.186	0.312	0.503	0.818	1.31	2.11	3.05	4.31	6.56	9.46	13.71	18.94	25.61
H	20	0.135	0.228	0.365	0.544	0.846	1.29	2.05	2.95	4.09	6.17	8.92	12.99	18.03	24.53
I	25	0.155	0.250	0.380	0.551	0.877	1.29	2.00	2.86	3.97	5.97	8.63	12.57	17.51	23.97
J	30	0.179	0.280	0.413	0.581	0.879	1.29	1.98	2.83	3.91	5.86	8.47	12.36	17.24	23.58
K	35	0.170	0.264	0.388	0.535	0.847	1.23	1.87	2.68	3.70	5.57	8.10	11.87	16.65	22.91
L	40	0.179	0.275	0.401	0.566	0.873	1.26	1.88	2.71	3.72	5.58	8.09	11.85	16.61	22.86
M	50	0.163	0.250	0.363	0.503	0.789	1.17	1.71	2.49	3.45	5.20	7.61	11.23	15.87	22.00
N	75	0.147	0.228	0.330	0.467	0.720	1.07	1.60	2.29	3.20	4.87	7.15	10.63	15.13	21.11
O	100	0.145	0.220	0.317	0.447	0.689	1.02	1.53	2.20	3.07	4.69	6.91	10.32	14.75	20.66
P	150	0.134	0.203	0.293	0.413	0.638	0.949	1.43	2.05	2.89	4.43	6.57	9.88	14.20	20.02
Q	200	0.135	0.204	0.294	0.414	0.637	0.945	1.42	2.04	2.87	4.40	6.53	9.81	14.12	19.92
		0.065	0.10	0.15	0.25	0.40	0.65	1.00	1.50	2.50	4.00	6.50	10.00	15.00	
		Acceptable quality levels (tightened inspection)													

All AQL and table values are in percent defective.

Use first sampling plan below arrow, that is, both sample size as well as *M* value. When sample size equals or exceeds lot size, every item in the lot must be inspected.

TABLE A15.4 Table for Estimating the Lot Percent Defective Using Standard Deviation Method (Table B–5 of MIL-STD-414)

Q_L or Q_U	Sample Size															
	3	4	5	7	10	15	20	25	30	35	40	50	75	100	150	200
0	50.00	50.00	50.00	50.00	50.00	50.00	50.00	50.00	50.00	50.00	50.00	50.00	50.00	50.00	50.00	50.00
.1	47.24	46.67	46.44	46.26	46.16	46.10	46.08	46.06	46.05	46.05	46.04	46.04	46.03	46.03	46.02	46.02
.2	44.46	43.33	42.90	42.54	42.35	42.24	42.19	42.16	42.15	42.13	42.13	42.11	42.10	42.09	42.08	42.08
.3	41.63	40.00	39.37	38.87	38.60	38.44	38.37	38.33	38.31	38.29	38.28	38.27	38.25	38.24	38.22	38.22
.31	41.35	39.67	39.02	38.50	38.23	38.06	37.99	37.95	37.93	37.91	37.90	37.89	37.87	37.86	37.84	37.84
.32	41.06	39.33	38.67	38.14	37.86	37.69	37.62	37.58	37.55	37.54	37.52	37.51	37.49	37.48	37.46	37.46
.33	40.77	39.00	38.32	37.78	37.49	37.31	37.24	37.20	37.18	37.16	37.15	37.13	37.11	37.10	37.09	37.08
.34	40.49	38.67	37.97	37.42	37.12	36.94	36.87	36.83	36.80	36.78	36.77	36.75	36.73	36.72	36.71	36.71
.35	40.20	38.33	37.62	37.06	36.75	36.57	36.49	36.45	36.43	36.41	36.40	36.38	36.36	36.35	36.33	36.33
.36	39.91	38.00	37.28	36.69	36.38	36.20	36.12	36.08	36.05	36.04	36.02	36.01	35.98	35.97	35.96	35.96
.37	39.62	37.67	36.93	36.33	36.02	35.83	35.75	35.71	35.68	35.66	35.65	35.63	35.61	35.60	35.59	35.58
.38	39.33	37.33	36.58	35.98	35.65	35.46	35.38	35.34	35.31	35.29	35.28	35.26	35.24	35.23	35.22	35.21
.39	39.03	37.00	36.23	35.62	35.29	35.10	35.01	34.97	34.94	34.93	34.91	34.89	34.87	34.86	34.85	34.84
.40	38.74	36.67	35.88	35.26	34.93	34.73	34.65	34.60	34.58	34.56	34.54	34.53	34.50	34.49	34.48	34.47
.41	38.45	36.33	35.54	34.90	34.57	34.37	34.28	34.24	34.21	34.19	34.18	34.16	34.13	34.12	34.11	34.10
.42	38.15	36.00	35.19	34.55	34.21	34.00	33.92	33.87	33.85	33.83	33.81	33.79	33.77	33.76	33.74	33.74
.43	37.85	35.67	34.85	34.19	33.85	33.64	33.56	33.51	33.48	33.46	33.45	33.43	33.40	33.39	33.38	33.37
.44	37.56	35.33	34.50	33.84	33.49	33.28	33.20	33.15	33.12	33.10	33.09	33.07	33.04	33.03	33.02	33.01
.45	37.26	35.00	34.16	33.49	33.13	32.92	32.84	32.79	32.76	32.74	32.73	32.71	32.68	32.67	32.66	32.65
.46	36.96	34.67	33.81	33.13	32.78	32.57	32.48	32.43	32.40	32.38	32.37	32.35	32.32	32.31	32.30	32.29
.47	36.66	34.33	33.47	32.78	32.42	32.21	32.12	32.07	32.04	32.02	32.01	31.99	31.96	31.95	31.94	31.93
.48	36.35	34.00	33.12	32.43	32.07	31.85	31.77	31.72	31.69	31.67	31.65	31.63	31.61	31.60	31.58	31.58
.49	36.05	33.67	32.78	32.08	31.72	31.50	31.41	31.36	31.33	31.31	31.30	31.28	31.25	31.24	31.23	31.22
.50	35.75	33.33	32.44	31.74	31.37	31.15	31.06	31.01	30.98	30.96	30.95	30.93	30.90	30.89	30.87	30.87
.51	35.44	33.00	32.10	31.39	31.02	30.80	30.71	30.66	30.63	30.61	30.60	30.57	30.55	30.54	30.52	30.52
.52	35.13	32.67	31.76	31.04	30.67	30.45	30.36	30.31	30.28	30.26	30.25	30.23	30.20	30.19	30.17	30.17
.53	34.82	32.33	31.42	30.70	30.32	30.10	30.01	29.96	29.93	29.91	29.90	29.88	29.85	29.84	29.83	29.82
.54	34.51	32.00	31.08	30.36	29.98	29.76	29.67	29.62	29.59	29.57	29.55	29.53	29.51	29.49	29.48	29.48
.55	34.20	31.67	30.74	30.01	29.64	29.41	29.32	29.27	29.24	29.22	29.21	29.19	29.16	29.15	29.14	29.13
.56	33.88	31.33	30.40	29.67	29.29	29.07	28.98	28.93	28.90	28.88	28.87	28.85	28.82	28.81	28.79	28.79
.57	33.57	31.00	30.06	29.33	28.95	28.73	28.64	28.59	28.56	28.54	28.53	28.51	28.48	28.47	28.45	28.45
.58	33.25	30.67	29.73	28.99	28.61	28.39	28.30	28.25	28.22	28.20	28.19	28.17	28.14	28.13	28.12	28.11
.59	32.93	30.33	29.39	28.66	28.28	28.05	27.96	27.92	27.89	27.87	27.85	27.83	27.81	27.79	27.78	27.77
.60	32.61	30.00	29.05	28.32	27.94	27.72	27.63	27.58	27.55	27.53	27.52	27.50	27.47	27.46	27.45	27.44
.61	32.28	29.67	28.72	27.98	27.60	27.39	27.30	27.25	27.22	27.20	27.18	27.16	27.14	27.13	27.11	27.11
.62	31.96	29.33	28.39	27.65	27.27	27.05	26.96	26.92	26.89	26.87	26.85	27.83	26.81	26.80	26.78	26.78
.63	31.63	29.00	28.05	27.32	26.94	26.72	26.63	26.59	26.56	26.54	26.52	26.50	26.48	26.47	26.45	26.45
.64	31.30	28.67	27.72	26.99	26.61	26.39	26.31	26.26	26.23	26.21	26.20	26.18	26.15	26.14	26.13	26.12
.65	30.97	28.33	27.39	26.66	26.28	26.07	25.98	25.93	25.90	25.88	25.87	25.85	25.83	25.82	25.80	25.80
.66	30.63	28.00	27.06	26.33	25.96	25.74	25.66	25.61	25.58	25.56	25.55	25.53	25.51	25.49	25.48	25.48
.67	30.30	27.67	26.73	26.00	25.63	25.42	25.33	25.29	25.26	25.24	25.23	25.21	25.19	25.17	25.16	25.16
.68	29.96	27.33	26.40	25.68	25.31	25.10	25.01	24.97	24.94	24.92	24.91	24.89	24.87	24.86	24.84	24.84
.69	29.61	27.00	26.07	25.35	24.99	24.78	24.70	24.65	24.62	24.60	24.59	24.57	24.55	24.54	24.53	24.52
.70	29.27	26.67	25.74	25.03	24.67	24.46	24.38	24.33	24.31	24.29	24.28	24.26	24.24	24.23	24.21	24.21
.71	28.92	26.33	25.41	24.71	24.35	24.15	24.06	24.02	23.99	23.98	23.96	23.95	23.92	23.91	23.90	23.90
.72	28.57	26.00	25.09	24.39	24.03	23.83	23.75	23.71	23.68	23.67	23.65	23.64	23.61	23.60	23.59	23.59
.73	28.22	25.67	24.76	24.07	23.72	23.52	23.44	23.40	23.37	23.36	23.34	23.33	23.31	23.30	23.29	23.28
.74	27.86	25.33	24.44	23.75	23.41	23.21	23.13	23.09	23.07	23.05	23.04	23.02	23.00	22.99	22.98	22.98

TABLE A15.4 Table for Estimating the Lot Percent Defective Using Standard Deviation Method (*Continued*)

Q_L or Q_U	Sample Size															
	3	4	5	7	10	15	20	25	30	35	40	50	75	100	150	200
.75	27.50	25.00	24.11	23.44	23.10	22.90	22.83	22.79	22.76	22.75	22.73	22.72	22.70	22.69	22.68	22.67
.76	27.13	24.67	23.79	23.12	22.79	22.60	22.52	22.48	22.46	22.44	22.43	22.42	22.40	22.39	22.38	22.37
.77	26.77	24.33	23.47	22.81	22.48	22.30	22.22	22.18	22.16	22.14	22.13	22.12	22.10	22.09	22.08	22.08
.78	26.39	24.00	23.15	22.50	22.18	21.99	21.92	21.89	21.86	21.85	21.84	21.82	21.80	21.79	21.78	21.78
.79	26.02	23.67	22.83	22.19	21.87	21.70	21.63	21.59	21.57	21.55	21.54	21.53	21.51	21.50	21.49	21.49
.80	25.64	23.33	22.51	21.88	21.57	21.40	21.33	21.29	21.27	21.26	21.25	21.23	21.22	21.21	21.20	21.20
.81	25.25	23.00	22.19	21.58	21.27	21.10	21.04	21.00	20.98	20.97	20.96	20.94	20.93	20.92	20.91	20.91
.82	24.86	22.67	21.87	21.27	20.98	20.81	20.75	20.71	20.69	20.68	20.67	20.65	20.64	20.63	20.62	20.62
.83	24.47	22.33	21.56	20.97	20.68	20.52	20.46	20.42	20.40	20.39	20.38	20.37	20.35	20.35	20.34	20.34
.84	24.07	22.00	21.24	20.67	20.39	20.23	20.17	20.14	20.12	20.11	20.10	20.09	20.07	20.06	20.06	20.05
.85	23.67	21.67	20.93	20.37	20.10	19.94	19.89	19.86	19.84	19.82	19.82	19.80	19.79	19.78	19.78	19.77
.86	23.26	21.33	20.62	20.07	19.81	19.66	19.60	19.57	19.56	19.54	19.54	19.53	19.51	19.51	19.50	19.50
.87	22.84	21.00	20.31	19.78	19.52	19.38	19.32	19.30	19.28	19.27	19.26	19.25	19.24	19.23	19.22	19.22
.88	22.62	20.67	20.00	19.48	19.23	19.10	19.04	19.02	19.00	18.99	18.98	18.98	18.96	18.96	18.95	18.65
.89	21.99	20.33	19.69	19.19	18.95	18.82	18.77	18.74	18.73	18.72	18.71	18.70	18.69	18.69	18.68	18.68
.90	21.55	20.00	19.38	18.90	18.67	18.54	18.50	18.47	18.46	18.45	18.44	18.43	18.42	18.42	18.41	18.41
.91	21.11	19.67	19.07	18.61	18.39	18.27	18.22	18.20	18.19	18.18	18.17	18.17	18.16	18.15	18.15	18.15
.92	20.66	19.33	18.77	18.33	18.11	18.00	17.96	17.94	17.92	17.92	17.91	17.90	17.89	17.89	17.88	17.88
.93	20.20	19.00	18.46	18.04	17.84	17.73	17.69	17.67	17.66	17.65	17.65	17.64	17.63	17.63	17.62	17.62
.94	19.74	18.67	18.16	17.76	17.57	17.46	17.43	17.41	17.40	17.39	17.39	17.38	17.37	17.37	17.36	17.36
.95	19.25	18.33	17.86	17.48	17.29	17.20	17.17	17.15	17.14	17.13	17.13	17.12	17.12	17.11	17.11	17.11
.96	18.76	18.00	17.56	17.20	17.03	16.94	16.91	16.89	16.88	16.88	16.87	16.87	16.86	16.86	16.86	16.85
.97	18.25	17.67	17.25	16.92	16.76	16.68	16.65	16.63	16.63	16.62	16.62	16.61	16.61	16.61	16.60	16.60
.98	17.74	17.33	16.96	16.65	16.49	16.42	16.39	16.38	16.37	16.37	16.37	16.36	16.36	16.36	16.36	16.36
.99	17.21	17.00	16.66	16.37	16.23	16.16	16.14	16.13	16.12	16.12	16.12	16.12	16.11	16.11	16.11	16.11
1.00	16.67	16.67	16.36	16.10	15.97	15.91	15.89	15.88	15.88	15.87	15.87	15.87	15.87	15.87	15.87	15.87
1.01	16.11	16.33	16.07	15.83	15.72	15.66	15.64	15.63	15.63	15.63	15.63	15.63	15.62	15.62	15.62	15.62
1.02	15.53	16.00	15.78	15.56	15.46	15.41	15.40	15.39	15.39	15.39	15.39	15.38	15.38	15.38	15.38	15.38
1.03	14.93	15.67	15.48	15.30	15.21	15.17	15.15	15.15	15.15	15.15	15.15	15.15	15.15	15.15	15.15	15.15
1.04	14.31	15.33	15.19	15.03	14.96	14.92	14.91	14.91	14.91	14.91	14.91	14.91	14.91	14.91	14.91	14.91
1.05	13.66	15.00	14.91	14.77	14.71	14.66	14.67	14.67	14.67	14.67	14.68	14.68	14.68	14.68	14.68	14.68
1.06	12.98	14.67	14.62	14.51	14.46	14.44	14.44	14.44	14.44	14.44	14.44	14.45	14.45	14.45	14.45	14.45
1.07	12.27	14.33	14.33	14.26	14.22	14.20	14.20	14.21	14.21	14.21	14.21	14.22	14.22	14.22	14.22	14.23
1.08	11.51	14.00	14.05	14.00	13.97	13.97	13.97	13.98	13.91	13.98	13.99	13.99	13.99	14.00	14.00	14.00
1.09	10.71	13.67	13.76	13.75	13.73	13.74	13.74	13.75	13.75	13.76	13.76	13.77	13.77	13.77	13.78	13.78
1.10	9.84	13.33	13.48	13.49	13.50	13.51	13.52	13.52	13.53	13.54	13.54	13.54	13.55	13.55	13.56	13.56
1.11	8.89	13.00	13.20	13.25	13.26	13.28	13.29	13.30	13.31	13.31	13.32	13.32	13.33	13.34	13.34	13.34
1.12	7.82	12.67	12.93	13.00	13.03	13.05	13.07	13.08	13.09	13.10	13.10	13.11	13.12	13.12	13.12	13.13
1.13	6.60	12.33	12.65	12.75	12.80	12.83	12.85	12.86	12.87	12.88	12.89	12.89	12.90	12.91	12.91	12.92
1.14	5.08	12.00	12.37	12.51	12.57	12.61	12.63	12.65	12.66	12.67	12.67	12.68	12.69	12.70	12.70	12.70
1.15	0.29	11.67	12.10	12.27	12.34	12.39	12.42	12.44	12.45	12.46	12.46	12.47	12.48	12.49	12.49	12.50
1.16	0.00	11.33	11.83	12.03	12.12	12.18	12.21	12.22	12.24	12.25	12.25	12.26	12.28	12.28	12.29	12.29
1.17	0.00	11.00	11.56	11.79	11.90	11.96	12.00	12.02	12.03	12.04	12.05	12.06	12.07	12.08	12.08	12.09
1.18	0.00	10.67	11.29	11.56	11.68	11.75	11.79	11.81	11.82	11.84	11.84	11.85	11.87	11.88	11.88	11.89
1.19	0.00	10.33	11.02	11.33	11.46	11.54	11.58	11.61	11.62	11.63	11.64	11.65	11.67	11.68	11.69	11.69

TABLE A15.4 Table for Estimating the Lot Percent Defective Using Standard Deviation Method *(Continued)*

Q_L or Q_U	Sample Size															
	3	4	5	7	10	15	20	25	30	35	40	50	75	100	150	200
1.20	0.00	10.00	10.76	11.10	11.24	11.34	11.38	11.41	11.42	11.43	11.44	11.46	11.47	11.48	11.49	11.49
1.21	0.00	9.67	10.50	10.87	11.03	11.13	11.18	11.21	11.22	11.24	11.25	11.26	11.28	11.29	11.30	11.30
1.22	0.00	9.33	10.23	10.65	10.82	10.93	10.98	11.01	11.03	11.04	11.05	11.07	11.09	11.09	11.10	11.11
1.23	0.00	9.00	9.97	10.42	10.61	10.73	10.78	10.81	10.84	10.85	10.86	10.88	10.90	10.91	10.91	10.92
1.24	0.00	8.67	9.72	10.20	10.41	10.53	10.59	10.62	10.64	10.66	10.67	10.69	10.71	10.72	10.73	10.73
1.25	0.00	8.33	9.46	9.98	10.21	10.34	10.40	10.43	10.46	10.47	10.48	10.50	10.52	10.53	10.54	10.55
1.26	0.00	8.00	9.21	9.77	10.00	10.15	10.21	10.25	10.27	10.29	10.30	10.32	10.34	10.35	10.36	10.37
1.27	0.00	7.67	8.96	9.55	9.81	9.96	10.02	10.06	10.09	10.10	10.12	10.13	10.16	10.17	10.18	10.19
1.28	0.00	7.33	8.71	9.34	9.61	9.77	9.84	9.88	9.90	9.92	9.94	9.95	9.98	9.99	10.00	10.01
1.29	0.00	7.00	8.46	9.13	9.42	9.58	9.65	9.70	9.72	9.74	9.76	9.78	9.80	9.82	9.83	9.83
1.30	0.00	6.67	8.21	8.93	9.22	9.40	9.48	9.52	9.55	9.57	9.58	9.60	9.63	9.64	9.65	9.66
1.31	0.00	6.33	7.97	8.72	9.03	9.22	9.30	9.34	9.37	9.39	9.41	9.43	9.46	9.47	9.48	9.49
1.32	0.00	6.00	7.73	8.52	8.85	9.04	9.12	9.17	9.20	9.22	9.24	9.26	9.29	9.30	9.31	9.32
1.33	0.00	5.67	7.49	8.32	8.66	8.86	8.95	9.00	9.03	9.05	9.07	9.09	9.12	9.13	9.15	9.15
1.34	0.00	5.33	7.25	8.12	8.48	8.69	8.78	8.83	8.86	8.88	8.90	8.92	8.95	8.97	8.98	8.99
1.35	0.00	5.00	7.02	7.92	8.30	8.52	8.61	8.66	8.69	8.72	8.74	8.76	8.79	8.81	8.82	8.83
1.36	0.00	4.67	6.79	7.73	8.12	8.35	8.44	8.50	8.53	8.55	8.57	8.60	8.63	8.65	8.66	8.67
1.37	0.00	4.33	6.56	7.54	7.95	8.18	8.28	8.33	8.37	8.39	8.41	8.44	8.47	8.49	8.50	8.51
1.38	0.00	4.00	6.33	7.35	7.77	8.01	8.12	8.17	8.21	8.24	8.25	8.28	8.31	8.33	8.35	8.35
1.39	0.00	3.67	6.10	7.17	7.60	7.85	7.96	8.01	8.05	8.08	8.10	8.12	8.16	8.18	8.19	8.20
1.40	0.00	3.33	5.88	6.98	7.44	7.69	7.80	7.86	7.90	7.92	7.94	7.97	8.01	8.02	8.04	8.05
1.41	0.00	3.00	5.66	6.80	7.27	7.53	7.64	7.70	7.74	7.77	7.79	7.82	7.86	7.87	7.89	7.90
1.42	0.00	2.67	5.44	6.62	7.10	7.37	7.49	7.55	7.59	7.62	7.64	7.67	7.71	7.73	7.74	7.75
1.43	0.00	2.33	5.23	6.45	6.94	7.22	7.34	7.40	7.44	7.47	7.50	7.52	7.56	7.58	7.60	7.61
1.44	0.00	2.00	5.01	6.27	6.78	7.07	7.19	7.26	7.30	7.33	7.35	7.38	7.42	7.44	7.46	7.47
1.45	0.00	1.67	4.81	6.10	6.63	6.92	7.04	7.11	7.15	7.18	7.21	7.24	7.28	7.30	7.31	7.33
1.46	0.00	1.33	4.60	5.93	6.47	6.77	6.90	6.97	7.01	7.04	7.07	7.10	7.14	7.16	7.18	7.19
1.47	0.00	1.00	4.39	5.77	6.32	6.63	6.75	6.83	6.87	6.90	6.93	6.96	7.00	7.02	7.04	7.05
1.48	0.00	0.67	4.19	5.60	6.17	6.48	6.61	6.69	6.73	6.77	6.79	6.82	6.86	6.88	6.90	6.91
1.49	0.00	0.33	3.99	5.44	6.02	6.34	6.48	6.55	6.60	6.63	6.65	6.69	6.73	6.75	6.77	6.78
1.50	0.00	0.00	3.80	5.28	5.87	6.20	6.34	6.41	6.46	6.50	6.52	6.55	6.60	6.62	6.64	6.65
1.51	0.00	0.00	3.61	5.13	5.73	6.06	6.20	6.28	6.33	6.36	6.39	6.42	6.47	6.49	6.51	6.52
1.52	0.00	0.00	3.42	4.97	5.59	5.93	6.07	6.15	6.20	6.23	6.26	6.29	6.34	6.36	6.38	6.39
1.53	0.00	0.00	3.23	4.82	5.45	5.80	5.94	6.02	6.07	6.11	6.13	6.17	6.21	6.24	6.26	6.27
1.54	0.00	0.00	3.05	4.67	5.31	5.67	5.81	5.89	5.95	5.98	6.01	6.04	6.09	6.11	6.13	3.15
1.55	0.00	0.00	2.87	4.52	5.18	5.54	5.69	5.77	5.82	5.86	5.88	5.92	5.97	5.99	6.01	6.02
1.56	0.00	0.00	2.69	4.38	5.05	5.41	5.56	5.65	5.70	5.74	5.76	5.80	5.85	5.87	5.89	5.90
1.57	0.00	0.00	2.52	4.24	4.92	5.29	5.44	5.53	5.58	5.62	5.64	5.68	5.73	5.75	5.78	5.79
1.58	0.00	0.00	2.35	4.10	4.79	5.16	5.32	5.41	5.46	5.50	5.53	5.56	5.61	5.64	5.66	5.67
1.59	0.00	0.00	2.19	3.96	4.66	5.04	5.20	5.29	5.34	5.38	5.41	5.45	5.50	5.52	5.54	5.56
1.60	0.00	0.00	2.03	3.83	4.54	4.92	5.09	5.17	5.23	5.27	5.30	5.33	5.38	5.41	5.43	5.44
1.61	0.00	0.00	1.87	3.69	4.41	4.81	4.97	5.06	5.12	5.16	5.18	5.22	5.27	5.30	5.32	5.33
1.62	0.00	0.00	1.72	3.57	4.30	4.69	4.86	4.95	5.01	5.04	5.07	5.11	5.16	5.19	5.21	5.23
1.63	0.00	0.00	1.57	3.44	4.18	4.58	4.75	4.84	4.90	4.94	4.97	5.01	5.06	5.08	5.11	5.12
1.64	0.00	0.00	1.42	3.31	4.06	4.47	4.64	4.73	4.79	4.83	4.86	4.90	4.95	4.98	5.00	5.01

TABLE A15.4 Table for Estimating the Lot Percent Defective Using Standard Deviation Method *(Continued)*

Q_L or Q_U	Sample Size															
	3	4	5	7	10	15	20	25	30	35	40	50	75	100	150	200
1.65	0.00	0.00	1.28	3.19	3.95	4.36	4.53	4.62	4.68	4.72	4.75	4.79	4.85	4.87	4.90	4.91
1.66	0.00	0.00	1.15	3.07	3.84	4.25	4.43	4.52	4.58	4.62	4.65	4.69	4.74	4.77	4.80	4.81
1.67	0.00	0.00	1.02	2.95	3.73	4.15	4.32	4.42	4.48	4.52	4.55	4.59	4.64	4.67	4.70	4.71
1.68	0.00	0.00	0.89	2.84	3.62	4.05	4.22	4.32	4.38	4.42	4.45	4.49	4.55	4.57	4.60	4.61
1.69	0.00	0.00	0.77	2.73	3.52	3.94	4.12	4.22	4.28	4.32	4.35	4.39	4.45	4.47	4.50	4.51
1.70	0.00	0.00	0.66	2.62	3.41	3.84	4.02	4.12	4.18	4.22	4.25	4.30	4.35	4.38	4.41	4.42
1.71	0.00	0.00	0.55	2.51	3.31	3.75	3.93	4.02	4.09	4.13	4.16	4.20	4.26	4.29	4.31	4.32
1.72	0.00	0.00	0.45	2.41	3.21	3.65	3.83	3.93	3.99	4.04	4.07	4.11	4.17	4.19	4.22	4.23
1.73	0.00	0.00	0.36	2.30	3.11	3.56	3.74	3.84	3.90	3.94	3.98	4.02	4.08	4.10	4.13	4.14
1.74	0.00	0.00	0.27	2.20	3.02	3.46	3.65	3.75	3.81	3.85	3.89	3.93	3.99	4.01	4.04	4.05
1.75	0.00	0.00	0.19	2.11	2.93	3.37	3.56	3.66	3.72	3.77	3.80	3.84	3.90	3.93	3.95	3.97
1.76	0.00	0.00	0.12	2.01	2.83	3.28	3.47	3.57	3.63	3.68	3.71	3.76	3.81	3.84	3.87	3.88
1.77	0.00	0.00	0.06	1.92	2.74	3.20	3.38	3.48	3.55	3.59	3.63	3.67	3.73	3.76	3.78	3.80
1.78	0.00	0.00	0.02	1.83	2.66	3.11	3.30	3.40	3.47	3.51	3.54	3.59	3.64	3.67	3.70	3.71
1.79	0.00	0.00	0.00	1.74	2.57	3.03	3.21	3.32	3.38	3.43	3.46	3.51	3.56	3.59	3.62	3.63
1.80	0.00	0.00	0.00	1.65	2.49	2.94	3.13	3.24	3.30	3.35	3.38	3.43	3.48	3.51	3.54	3.55
1.81	0.00	0.00	0.00	1.57	2.40	2.86	3.05	3.16	3.22	3.27	3.30	3.35	3.40	3.43	3.46	3.47
1.82	0.00	0.00	0.00	1.49	2.32	2.79	2.98	3.08	3.15	3.19	3.22	3.27	3.33	3.36	3.38	3.40
1.83	0.00	0.00	0.00	1.41	2.25	2.71	2.90	3.00	3.07	3.11	3.15	3.19	3.25	3.28	3.31	3.32
1.84	0.00	0.00	0.00	1.34	2.17	2.63	2.82	2.93	2.99	3.04	3.07	3.12	3.18	3.21	3.23	3.25
1.85	0.00	0.00	0.00	1.26	2.09	2.56	2.75	2.85	2.92	2.97	3.00	3.05	3.10	3.13	3.16	3.17
1.86	0.00	0.00	0.00	1.19	2.02	2.48	2.68	2.78	2.85	2.89	2.93	2.97	3.03	3.06	3.09	3.10
1.87	0.00	0.00	0.00	1.12	1.95	2.41	2.61	2.71	2.78	2.82	2.86	2.90	2.96	2.99	3.02	3.03
1.88	0.00	0.00	0.00	1.06	1.88	2.34	2.54	2.64	2.71	2.75	2.79	2.83	2.89	2.92	2.95	2.96
1.89	0.00	0.00	0.00	0.99	1.81	2.28	2.47	2.57	2.64	2.69	2.72	2.77	2.83	2.85	2.88	2.90
1.90	0.00	0.00	0.00	0.93	1.75	2.21	2.40	2.51	2.57	2.62	2.65	2.70	2.76	2.79	2.82	2.83
1.91	0.00	0.00	0.00	0.87	1.68	2.14	2.34	2.44	2.51	2.56	2.59	2.63	2.69	2.72	2.75	2.77
1.92	0.00	0.00	0.00	0.81	1.62	2.08	2.27	2.38	2.45	2.49	2.52	2.57	2.63	2.66	2.69	2.70
1.93	0.00	0.00	0.00	0.76	1.56	2.02	2.21	2.32	2.38	2.43	2.46	2.51	2.57	2.60	2.62	2.64
1.94	0.00	0.00	0.00	0.70	1.50	1.96	2.15	2.25	2.32	2.37	2.40	2.45	2.51	2.54	2.56	2.58
1.95	0.00	0.00	0.00	0.65	1.44	1.90	2.09	2.19	2.26	2.31	2.34	2.39	2.45	2.48	2.50	2.52
1.96	0.00	0.00	0.00	0.60	1.38	1.84	2.03	2.14	2.20	2.25	2.28	2.33	2.39	2.42	2.44	2.46
1.97	0.00	0.00	0.00	0.56	1.33	1.78	1.97	2.08	2.14	2.19	2.22	2.27	2.33	2.36	2.39	2.40
1.98	0.00	0.00	0.00	0.51	1.27	1.73	1.92	2.02	2.09	2.13	2.17	2.21	2.27	2.30	2.33	2.34
1.99	0.00	0.00	0.00	0.47	1.22	1.67	1.86	1.97	2.03	2.08	2.11	2.16	2.22	2.25	2.27	2.29
2.00	0.00	0.00	0.00	0.43	1.17	1.62	1.81	1.91	1.98	2.03	2.06	2.10	2.16	2.19	2.22	2.23
2.01	0.00	0.00	0.00	0.39	1.12	1.57	1.76	1.86	1.93	1.97	2.01	2.05	2.11	2.14	2.17	2.18
2.02	0.00	0.00	0.00	0.36	1.07	1.52	1.71	1.81	1.87	1.92	1.95	2.00	2.06	2.09	2.11	2.13
2.03	0.00	0.00	0.00	0.32	1.03	1.47	1.66	1.76	1.82	1.87	1.90	1.95	2.01	2.04	2.06	2.08
2.04	0.00	0.00	0.00	0.29	0.98	1.42	1.61	1.71	1.77	1.82	1.85	1.90	1.96	1.99	2.01	2.03
2.05	0.00	0.00	0.00	0.26	0.94	1.37	1.56	1.66	1.73	1.77	1.80	1.85	1.91	1.94	1.96	1.98
2.06	0.00	0.00	0.00	0.23	0.90	1.33	1.51	1.61	1.68	1.72	1.76	1.80	1.86	1.89	1.92	1.93
2.07	0.00	0.00	0.00	0.21	0.86	1.28	1.47	1.57	1.63	1.68	1.71	1.76	1.81	1.84	1.87	1.88
2.08	0.00	0.00	0.00	0.18	0.82	1.24	1.42	1.52	1.59	1.63	1.66	1.71	1.77	1.79	1.82	1.84
2.09	0.00	0.00	0.00	0.16	0.78	1.20	1.38	1.48	1.54	1.59	1.62	1.66	1.72	1.75	1.78	1.79

TABLE A15.4 **Table for Estimating the Lot Percent Defective Using Standard Deviation Method** (*Continued*)

Q_L or Q_U	Sample Size														
	3	4	5	7	10	15	20	25	30	35	40	50	75	100	150	200
2.10	0.00	0.00	0.00	0.14	0.74	1.16	1.34	1.44	1.50	1.54	1.58	1.62	1.68	1.71	1.73	1.75
2.11	0.00	0.00	0.00	0.12	0.71	1.12	1.30	1.39	1.46	1.50	1.53	1.58	1.63	1.66	1.69	1.70
2.12	0.00	0.00	0.00	0.10	0.67	1.08	1.26	1.35	1.42	1.46	1.49	1.54	1.59	1.62	1.65	1.66
2.13	0.00	0.00	0.00	0.08	0.64	1.04	1.22	1.31	1.38	1.42	1.45	1.50	1.55	1.58	1.61	1.62
2.14	0.00	0.00	0.00	0.07	0.61	1.00	1.18	1.28	1.34	1.38	1.41	1.46	1.51	1.54	1.57	1.58
2.15	0.00	0.00	0.00	0.06	0.58	0.97	1.14	1.24	1.30	1.34	1.37	1.42	1.47	1.50	1.53	1.54
2.16	0.00	0.00	0.00	0.05	0.55	0.93	1.10	1.20	1.26	1.30	1.34	1.38	1.43	1.46	1.49	1.50
2.17	0.00	0.00	0.00	0.04	0.52	0.90	1.07	1.16	1.22	1.27	1.30	1.34	1.40	1.42	1.45	1.46
2.18	0.00	0.00	0.00	0.03	0.49	0.87	1.03	1.13	1.19	1.23	1.26	1.30	1.36	1.39	1.41	1.42
2.19	0.00	0.00	0.00	0.02	0.46	0.83	1.00	1.09	1.15	1.20	1.23	1.27	1.32	1.35	1.38	1.39
2.20	0.000	0.000	0.000	0.015	0.437	0.803	0.968	1.061	1.120	1.161	1.192	1.233	1.287	1.314	1.340	1.352
2.21	0.000	0.000	0.000	0.010	0.413	0.772	0.936	1.028	1.087	1.128	1.158	1.199	1.253	1.279	1.305	1.318
2.22	0.000	0.000	0.000	0.006	0.389	0.743	0.905	0.996	1.054	1.095	1.125	1.166	1.219	1.245	1.271	1.283
2.23	0.000	0.000	0.000	0.003	0.366	0.715	0.875	0.965	1.023	1.063	1.093	1.134	1.186	1.212	1.238	1.250
2.24	0.000	0.000	0.000	0.002	0.345	0.687	0.845	0.935	0.992	1.032	1.061	1.102	1.154	1.180	1.205	1.218
2.25	0.000	0.000	0.000	0.001	0.324	0.660	0.816	0.905	0.962	1.002	1.031	1.071	1.123	1.148	1.173	1.186
2.26	0.000	0.000	0.000	0.000	0.304	0.634	0.789	0.876	0.933	0.972	1.001	1.041	1.092	1.117	1.142	1.155
2.27	0.000	0.000	0.000	0.000	0.285	0.609	0.762	0.848	0.904	0.943	0.972	1.011	1.062	1.087	1.112	1.124
2.28	0.000	0.000	0.000	0.000	0.267	0.585	0.735	0.821	0.876	0.915	0.943	0.982	1.033	1.058	1.082	1.094
2.29	0.000	0.000	0.000	0.000	0.250	0.561	0.710	0.794	0.849	0.887	0.915	0.954	1.004	1.029	1.053	1.065
2.30	0.000	0.000	0.000	0.000	0.233	0.538	0.685	0.769	0.823	0.861	0.888	0.927	0.977	1.001	1.025	1.037
2.31	0.000	0.000	0.000	0.000	0.218	0.516	0.661	0.743	0.797	0.834	0.862	0.900	0.949	0.974	0.997	1.009
2.32	0.000	0.000	0.000	0.000	0.203	0.495	0.637	0.719	0.772	0.809	0.836	0.874	0.923	0.947	0.971	0.982
2.33	0.000	0.000	0.000	0.000	0.189	0.474	0.614	0.695	0.748	0.784	0.811	0.848	0.897	0.921	0.944	0.956
2.34	0.000	0.000	0.000	0.000	0.175	0.454	0.592	0.672	0.724	0.760	0.787	0.824	0.872	0.895	0.915	0.930
2.35	0.000	0.000	0.000	0.000	0.163	0.435	0.571	0.650	0.701	0.736	0.763	0.799	0.847	0.870	0.893	0.905
2.36	0.000	0.000	0.000	0.000	0.151	0.416	0.550	0.628	0.678	0.714	0.740	0.776	0.823	0.846	0.869	0.880
2.37	0.000	0.000	0.000	0.000	0.139	0.398	0.530	0.606	0.656	0.691	0.717	0.753	0.799	0.822	0.845	0.856
2.38	0.000	0.000	0.000	0.000	0.128	0.381	0.510	0.586	0.635	0.670	0.695	0.730	0.777	0.799	0.822	0.833
2.39	0.000	0.000	0.000	0.000	0.118	0.364	0.491	0.566	0.614	0.648	0.674	0.709	0.754	0.777	0.799	0.810
2.40	0.000	0.000	0.000	0.000	0.109	0.348	0.473	0.546	0.594	0.628	0.653	0.687	0.732	0.755	0.777	0.787
2.41	0.000	0.000	0.000	0.000	0.100	0.332	0.455	0.527	0.575	0.608	0.633	0.667	0.711	0.733	0.755	0.766
2.42	0.000	0.000	0.000	0.000	0.091	0.317	0.437	0.509	0.555	0.588	0.613	0.646	0.691	0.712	0.734	0.744
2.43	0.000	0.000	0.000	0.000	0.083	0.302	0.421	0.491	0.537	0.569	0.593	0.627	0.670	0.692	0.713	0.724
2.44	0.000	0.000	0.000	0.000	0.076	0.288	0.404	0.474	0.519	0.551	0.575	0.608	0.651	0.672	0.693	0.703
2.45	0.000	0.000	0.000	0.000	0.069	0.275	0.389	0.457	0.501	0.533	0.556	0.589	0.632	0.653	0.673	0.684
2.46	0.000	0.000	0.000	0.000	0.063	0.262	0.373	0.440	0.484	0.516	0.539	0.571	0.613	0.634	0.654	0.664
2.47	0.000	0.000	0.000	0.000	0.057	0.249	0.339	0.425	0.468	0.499	0.521	0.553	0.595	0.615	0.635	0.646
2.48	0.000	0.000	0.000	0.000	0.051	0.237	0.344	0.409	0.452	0.482	0.505	0.536	0.577	0.597	0.617	0.627
2.49	0.000	0.000	0.000	0.000	0.046	0.226	0.331	0.394	0.436	0.466	0.488	0.519	0.560	0.580	0.600	0.609
2.50	0.000	0.000	0.000	0.000	0.041	0.214	0.317	0.380	0.421	0.451	0.473	0.503	0.543	0.563	0.582	0.592
2.51	0.000	0.000	0.000	0.000	0.037	0.204	0.304	0.366	0.407	0.436	0.457	0.487	0.527	0.546	0.565	0.575
2.52	0.000	0.000	0.000	0.000	0.033	0.193	0.292	0.352	0.392	0.421	0.442	0.472	0.511	0.530	0.549	0.558
2.53	0.000	0.000	0.000	0.000	0.029	0.184	0.280	0.339	0.379	0.407	0.428	0.457	0.495	0.514	0.533	0.542
2.54	0.000	0.000	0.000	0.000	0.026	0.174	0.268	0.326	0.365	0.393	0.413	0.442	0.480	0.499	0.517	0.527

TABLE A15.4 Table for Estimating the Lot Percent Defective Using Standard Deviation Method *(Continued)*

Q_L or Q_U	Sample Size															
	3	4	5	7	10	15	20	25	30	35	40	50	75	100	150	200
2.55	0.000	0.000	0.000	0.000	0.023	0.165	0.257	0.314	0.352	0.379	0.400	0.428	0.465	0.484	0.502	0.511
2.56	0.000	0.000	0.000	0.000	0.020	0.156	0.246	0.302	0.340	0.366	0.386	0.414	0.451	0.469	0.487	0.496
2.57	0.000	0.000	0.000	0.000	0.017	0.148	0.236	0.291	0.327	0.354	0.373	0.401	0.437	0.455	0.473	0.482
2.58	0.000	0.000	0.000	0.000	0.015	0.140	0.226	0.279	0.316	0.341	0.361	0.388	0.424	0.441	0.459	0.468
2.59	0.000	0.000	0.000	0.000	0.013	0.133	0.216	0.269	0.304	0.330	0.349	0.375	0.410	0.428	0.445	0.454
2.60	0.000	0.000	0.000	0.000	0.011	0.125	0.207	0.258	0.293	0.318	0.337	0.363	0.398	0.415	0.432	0.441
2.61	0.000	0.000	0.000	0.000	0.009	0.118	0.198	0.248	0.282	0.307	0.325	0.351	0.385	0.402	0.419	0.428
2.62	0.000	0.000	0.000	0.000	0.008	0.112	0.189	0.238	0.272	0.296	0.314	0.339	0.373	0.390	0.406	0.415
2.63	0.000	0.000	0.000	0.000	0.007	0.105	0.181	0.229	0.262	0.285	0.303	0.328	0.361	0.378	0.394	0.402
2.64	0.000	0.000	0.000	0.000	0.005	0.099	0.172	0.220	0.252	0.275	0.293	0.317	0.350	0.366	0.382	0.390
2.65	0.000	0.000	0.000	0.000	0.005	0.094	0.165	0.211	0.243	0.265	0.282	0.307	0.339	0.355	0.371	0.379
2.66	0.000	0.000	0.000	0.000	0.004	0.088	0.157	0.202	0.233	0.256	0.273	0.296	0.328	0.344	0.359	0.367
2.67	0.000	0.000	0.000	0.000	0.003	0.083	0.150	0.194	0.224	0.246	0.263	0.286	0.317	0.333	0.348	0.356
2.68	0.000	0.000	0.000	0.000	0.002	0.078	0.143	0.186	0.216	0.237	0.254	0.277	0.307	0.322	0.338	0.345
2.69	0.000	0.000	0.000	0.000	0.002	0.073	0.136	0.179	0.208	0.229	0.245	0.267	0.297	0.312	0.327	0.335
2.70	0.000	0.000	0.000	0.000	0.001	0.069	0.130	0.171	0.200	0.220	0.236	0.258	0.288	0.302	0.317	0.325
2.71	0.000	0.000	0.000	0.000	0.001	0.064	0.124	0.164	0.192	0.212	0.227	0.249	0.278	0.293	0.307	0.315
2.72	0.000	0.000	0.000	0.000	0.000	0.060	0.118	0.157	0.184	0.204	0.219	0.241	0.269	0.283	0.298	0.305
2.73	0.000	0.000	0.000	0.000	0.000	0.057	0.112	0.151	0.177	0.197	0.211	0.232	0.260	0.274	0.288	0.296
2.74	0.000	0.000	0.000	0.000	0.000	0.053	0.107	0.144	0.170	0.189	0.204	0.224	0.252	0.266	0.279	0.286
2.75	0.000	0.000	0.000	0.000	0.000	0.049	0.102	0.138	0.163	0.182	0.196	0.216	0.243	0.257	0.271	0.277
2.76	0.000	0.000	0.000	0.000	0.000	0.046	0.087	0.132	0.157	0.175	0.189	0.209	0.235	0.249	0.262	0.269
2.77	0.000	0.000	0.000	0.000	0.000	0.043	0.092	0.126	0.151	0.168	0.182	0.201	0.227	0.241	0.254	0.260
2.78	0.000	0.000	0.000	0.000	0.000	0.040	0.087	0.121	0.145	0.162	0.175	0.194	0.220	0.233	0.246	0.252
2.79	0.000	0.000	0.000	0.000	0.000	0.037	0.083	0.115	0.139	0.156	0.169	0.187	0.212	0.225	0.238	0.244
2.80	0.000	0.000	0.000	0.000	0.000	0.035	0.079	0.110	0.133	0.150	0.162	0.181	0.205	0.218	0.230	0.237
2.81	0.000	0.000	0.000	0.000	0.000	0.032	0.075	0.105	0.128	0.144	0.156	0.174	0.198	0.211	0.223	0.229
2.82	0.000	0.000	0.000	0.000	0.000	0.030	0.071	0.101	0.122	0.138	0.150	0.168	0.192	0.204	0.216	0.222
2.83	0.000	0.000	0.000	0.000	0.000	0.028	0.067	0.096	0.117	0.133	0.145	0.162	0.185	0.197	0.209	0.215
2.84	0.000	0.000	0.000	0.000	0.000	0.026	0.064	0.092	0.112	0.128	0.139	0.156	0.179	0.190	0.202	0.208
2.85	0.000	0.000	0.000	0.000	0.000	0.024	0.060	0.088	0.108	0.122	0.134	0.150	0.173	0.184	0.195	0.201
2.86	0.000	0.000	0.000	0.000	0.000	0.022	0.057	0.084	0.103	0.118	0.129	0.145	0.167	0.178	0.189	0.195
2.87	0.000	0.000	0.000	0.000	0.000	0.020	0.054	0.080	0.099	0.113	0.124	0.139	0.161	0.172	0.183	0.188
2.88	0.000	0.000	0.000	0.000	0.000	0.019	0.051	0.076	0.094	0.108	0.119	0.134	0.155	0.166	0.177	0.182
2.89	0.000	0.000	0.000	0.000	0.000	0.017	0.048	0.073	0.090	0.104	0.114	0.129	0.150	0.160	0.171	0.176
2.90	0.000	0.000	0.000	0.000	0.000	0.016	0.046	0.069	0.087	0.100	0.110	0.125	0.145	0.155	0.165	0.171
2.91	0.000	0.000	0.000	0.000	0.000	0.015	0.043	0.066	0.083	0.096	0.106	0.120	0.140	0.150	0.160	0.165
2.92	0.000	0.000	0.000	0.000	0.000	0.013	0.041	0.063	0.079	0.092	0.101	0.115	0.135	0.145	0.155	0.160
2.93	0.000	0.000	0.000	0.000	0.000	0.012	0.038	0.060	0.076	0.088	0.097	0.111	0.130	0.140	0.149	0.154
2.94	0.000	0.000	0.000	0.000	0.000	0.011	0.036	0.057	0.072	0.084	0.093	0.107	0.125	0.135	0.144	0.149
2.95	0.000	0.000	0.000	0.000	0.000	0.010	0.034	0.054	0.069	0.081	0.090	0.103	0.121	0.130	0.140	0.144
2.96	0.000	0.000	0.000	0.000	0.000	0.009	0.032	0.051	0.066	0.077	0.086	0.099	0.117	0.126	0.135	0.140
2.97	0.000	0.000	0.000	0.000	0.000	0.009	0.030	0.049	0.063	0.074	0.083	0.095	0.112	0.121	0.130	0.135
2.98	0.000	0.000	0.000	0.000	0.000	0.008	0.028	0.046	0.060	0.071	0.079	0.091	0.108	0.117	0.126	0.130
2.99	0.000	0.000	0.000	0.000	0.000	0.007	0.027	0.044	0.057	0.068	0.076	0.088	0.104	0.113	0.122	0.126

TABLE A15.4 Table for Estimating the Lot Percent Defective Using Standard Deviation Method (*Continued*)

Q_L or Q_U	Sample Size															
	3	4	5	7	10	15	20	25	30	35	40	50	75	100	150	200
3.00	0.000	0.000	0.000	0.000	0.000	0.006	0.025	0.042	0.055	0.065	0.073	0.084	0.101	0.109	0.118	0.122
3.01	0.000	0.000	0.000	0.000	0.000	0.006	0.024	0.040	0.052	0.062	0.070	0.081	0.097	0.105	0.114	0.118
3.02	0.000	0.000	0.000	0.000	0.000	0.005	0.022	0.038	0.050	0.059	0.067	0.078	0.093	0.101	0.110	0.114
3.03	0.000	0.000	0.000	0.000	0.000	0.005	0.021	0.036	0.048	0.057	0.064	0.075	0.090	0.098	0.106	0.110
3.04	0.000	0.000	0.000	0.000	0.000	0.004	0.019	0.034	0.045	0.054	0.061	0.072	0.087	0.094	0.102	0.106
3.05	0.000	0.000	0.000	0.000	0.000	0.004	0.018	0.032	0.043	0.052	0.059	0.069	0.083	0.091	0.099	0.103
3.06	0.000	0.000	0.000	0.000	0.000	0.003	0.017	0.030	0.041	0.050	0.056	0.066	0.080	0.088	0.095	0.099
3.07	0.000	0.000	0.000	0.000	0.000	0.003	0.016	0.029	0.039	0.047	0.054	0.064	0.077	0.085	0.092	0.096
3.08	0.000	0.000	0.000	0.000	0.000	0.003	0.015	0.027	0.037	0.045	0.052	0.061	0.074	0.081	0.089	0.092
3.09	0.000	0.000	0.000	0.000	0.000	0.002	0.014	0.026	0.036	0.043	0.049	0.059	0.072	0.079	0.086	0.089
3.10	0.000	0.000	0.000	0.000	0.000	0.002	0.013	0.024	0.034	0.041	0.047	0.056	0.069	0.076	0.083	0.086
3.11	0.000	0.000	0.000	0.000	0.000	0.002	0.012	0.023	0.032	0.039	0.045	0.054	0.066	0.073	0.080	0.083
3.12	0.000	0.000	0.000	0.000	0.000	0.002	0.011	0.022	0.031	0.038	0.043	0.052	0.064	0.070	0.077	0.080
3.13	0.000	0.000	0.000	0.000	0.000	0.002	0.011	0.021	0.029	0.036	0.041	0.050	0.061	0.068	0.044	0.077
3.14	0.000	0.000	0.000	0.000	0.000	0.001	0.010	0.019	0.028	0.034	0.040	0.048	0.059	0.065	0.071	0.075
3.15	0.000	0.000	0.000	0.000	0.000	0.001	0.009	0.018	0.026	0.033	0.038	0.046	0.057	0.063	0.069	0.072
3.16	0.000	0.000	0.000	0.000	0.000	0.001	0.009	0.017	0.025	0.031	0.036	0.044	0.055	0.060	0.066	0.069
3.17	0.000	0.000	0.000	0.000	0.000	0.001	0.008	0.016	0.024	0.030	0.035	0.042	0.053	0.058	0.064	0.067
3.18	0.000	0.000	0.000	0.000	0.000	0.001	0.007	0.015	0.022	0.028	0.033	0.040	0.050	0.056	0.062	0.065
3.19	0.000	0.000	0.000	0.000	0.000	0.001	0.007	0.015	0.021	0.027	0.032	0.038	0.049	0.054	0.059	0.062
3.20	0.000	0.000	0.000	0.000	0.000	0.001	0.006	0.014	0.020	0.026	0.030	0.037	0.047	0.052	0.057	0.060
3.21	0.000	0.000	0.000	0.000	0.000	0.000	0.006	0.013	0.019	0.024	0.029	0.035	0.045	0.050	0.055	0.058
3.22	0.000	0.000	0.000	0.000	0.000	0.000	0.005	0.012	0.018	0.023	0.027	0.034	0.043	0.048	0.053	0.056
3.23	0.000	0.000	0.000	0.000	0.000	0.000	0.005	0.011	0.017	0.022	0.026	0.032	0.041	0.046	0.051	0.054
3.24	0.000	0.000	0.000	0.000	0.000	0.000	0.005	0.011	0.016	0.021	0.025	0.031	0.040	0.044	0.049	0.052
3.25	0.000	0.000	0.000	0.000	0.000	0.000	0.004	0.010	0.015	0.020	0.024	0.030	0.038	0.043	0.048	0.050
3.26	0.000	0.000	0.000	0.000	0.000	0.000	0.004	0.009	0.015	0.019	0.023	0.028	0.037	0.041	0.046	0.048
3.27	0.000	0.000	0.000	0.000	0.000	0.000	0.004	0.009	0.014	0.019	0.022	0.027	0.035	0.040	0.044	0.046
3.28	0.000	0.000	0.000	0.000	0.000	0.000	0.003	0.008	0.013	0.017	0.021	0.026	0.034	0.038	0.042	0.045
3.29	0.000	0.000	0.000	0.000	0.000	0.000	0.003	0.008	0.012	0.016	0.020	0.025	0.032	0.037	0.041	0.043
3.30	0.000	0.000	0.000	0.000	0.000	0.000	0.003	0.007	0.012	0.015	0.019	0.024	0.031	0.035	0.039	0.042
3.31	0.000	0.000	0.000	0.000	0.000	0.000	0.003	0.007	0.011	0.015	0.018	0.023	0.030	0.034	0.038	0.040
3.32	0.000	0.000	0.000	0.000	0.000	0.000	0.002	0.006	0.010	0.014	0.017	0.022	0.029	0.032	0.036	0.039
3.33	0.000	0.000	0.000	0.000	0.000	0.000	0.002	0.006	0.010	0.013	0.015	0.021	0.027	0.031	0.035	0.037
3.34	0.000	0.000	0.000	0.000	0.000	0.000	0.002	0.006	0.009	0.013	0.015	0.020	0.026	0.030	0.034	0.036
3.35	0.000	0.000	0.000	0.000	0.000	0.000	0.002	0.005	0.009	0.012	0.015	0.019	0.025	0.029	0.032	0.034
3.36	0.000	0.000	0.000	0.000	0.000	0.000	0.002	0.005	0.008	0.011	0.014	0.018	0.024	0.028	0.031	0.033
3.37	0.000	0.000	0.000	0.000	0.000	0.000	0.002	0.005	0.008	0.011	0.013	0.017	0.023	0.026	0.030	0.032
3.38	0.000	0.000	0.000	0.000	0.000	0.000	0.001	0.004	0.007	0.010	0.013	0.016	0.022	0.025	0.029	0.031
3.39	0.000	0.000	0.000	0.000	0.000	0.000	0.001	0.004	0.007	0.010	0.012	0.016	0.021	0.024	0.028	0.029
3.40	0.000	0.000	0.000	0.000	0.000	0.000	0.001	0.004	0.007	0.009	0.011	0.015	0.020	0.023	0.027	0.028
3.41	0.000	0.000	0.000	0.000	0.000	0.000	0.001	0.003	0.006	0.009	0.011	0.014	0.020	0.022	0.026	0.027
3.42	0.000	0.000	0.000	0.000	0.000	0.000	0.001	0.003	0.006	0.008	0.010	0.014	0.019	0.022	0.025	0.026
3.43	0.000	0.000	0.000	0.000	0.000	0.000	0.001	0.003	0.005	0.008	0.010	0.013	0.018	0.021	0.024	0.025
3.44	0.000	0.000	0.000	0.000	0.000	0.000	0.001	0.003	0.005	0.007	0.009	0.012	0.017	0.020	0.023	0.024

TABLE A15.4 Table for Estimating the Lot Percent Defective Using Standard Deviation Method (*Continued*)

Q_L or Q_U	Sample Size															
	3	4	5	7	10	15	20	25	30	35	40	50	75	100	150	200
3.45	0.000	0.000	0.000	0.000	0.000	0.000	0.001	0.003	0.005	0.007	0.009	0.012	0.016	0.019	0.022	0.023
3.46	0.000	0.000	0.000	0.000	0.000	0.000	0.001	0.002	0.005	0.007	0.008	0.011	0.016	0.018	0.021	0.022
3.47	0.000	0.000	0.000	0.000	0.000	0.000	0.001	0.002	0.004	0.006	0.008	0.011	0.015	0.017	0.020	0.022
3.48	0.000	0.000	0.000	0.000	0.000	0.000	0.001	0.002	0.004	0.006	0.007	0.010	0.014	0.017	0.019	0.021
3.49	0.000	0.000	0.000	0.000	0.000	0.000	0.000	0.002	0.004	0.005	0.007	0.010	0.014	0.016	0.019	0.020
3.50	0.000	0.000	0.000	0.000	0.000	0.000	0.000	0.002	0.003	0.005	0.007	0.009	0.013	0.015	0.018	0.019
3.51	0.000	0.000	0.000	0.000	0.000	0.000	0.000	0.002	0.003	0.005	0.006	0.009	0.013	0.015	0.017	0.018
3.52	0.000	0.000	0.000	0.000	0.000	0.000	0.000	0.002	0.003	0.005	0.006	0.008	0.012	0.014	0.017	0.018
3.53	0.000	0.000	0.000	0.000	0.000	0.000	0.000	0.001	0.003	0.004	0.006	0.008	0.012	0.014	0.016	0.017
3.54	0.000	0.000	0.000	0.000	0.000	0.000	0.000	0.001	0.003	0.004	0.005	0.008	0.011	0.013	0.015	0.016
3.55	0.000	0.000	0.000	0.000	0.000	0.000	0.000	0.001	0.003	0.004	0.005	0.007	0.011	0.012	0.015	0.016
3.56	0.000	0.000	0.000	0.000	0.000	0.000	0.000	0.001	0.002	0.004	0.005	0.007	0.010	0.012	0.014	0.015
3.57	0.000	0.000	0.000	0.000	0.000	0.000	0.000	0.001	0.002	0.003	0.005	0.006	0.010	0.011	0.013	0.014
3.58	0.000	0.000	0.000	0.000	0.000	0.000	0.000	0.001	0.002	0.003	0.004	0.006	0.009	0.011	0.013	0.014
3.59	0.000	0.000	0.000	0.000	0.000	0.000	0.000	0.001	0.002	0.003	0.004	0.006	0.009	0.010	0.012	0.013
3.60	0.000	0.000	0.000	0.000	0.000	0.000	0.000	0.001	0.002	0.003	0.004	0.006	0.008	0.010	0.012	0.013
3.61	0.000	0.000	0.000	0.000	0.000	0.000	0.000	0.001	0.002	0.003	0.004	0.005	0.008	0.010	0.011	0.012
3.62	0.000	0.000	0.000	0.000	0.000	0.000	0.000	0.001	0.002	0.003	0.003	0.005	0.008	0.009	0.011	0.012
3.63	0.000	0.000	0.000	0.000	0.000	0.000	0.000	0.001	0.001	0.002	0.003	0.005	0.007	0.009	0.010	0.011
3.64	0.000	0.000	0.000	0.000	0.000	0.000	0.000	0.001	0.001	0.002	0.003	0.004	0.007	0.008	0.010	0.011
3.65	0.000	0.000	0.000	0.000	0.000	0.000	0.000	0.001	0.001	0.002	0.003	0.004	0.007	0.008	0.010	0.010
3.66	0.000	0.000	0.000	0.000	0.000	0.000	0.000	0.000	0.001	0.002	0.003	0.004	0.006	0.008	0.009	0.010
3.67	0.000	0.000	0.000	0.000	0.000	0.000	0.000	0.000	0.001	0.002	0.003	0.004	0.006	0.007	0.009	0.010
3.68	0.000	0.000	0.000	0.000	0.000	0.000	0.000	0.000	0.001	0.002	0.002	0.004	0.006	0.007	0.008	0.009
3.69	0.000	0.000	0.000	0.000	0.000	0.000	0.000	0.000	0.001	0.002	0.002	0.003	0.005	0.007	0.008	0.009
3.70	0.000	0.000	0.000	0.000	0.000	0.000	0.000	0.000	0.001	0.002	0.002	0.003	0.005	0.006	0.008	0.008
3.71	0.000	0.000	0.000	0.000	0.000	0.000	0.000	0.000	0.001	0.001	0.002	0.003	0.005	0.006	0.007	0.008
3.72	0.000	0.000	0.000	0.000	0.000	0.000	0.000	0.000	0.001	0.001	0.002	0.003	0.005	0.006	0.007	0.008
3.73	0.000	0.000	0.000	0.000	0.000	0.000	0.000	0.000	0.001	0.001	0.002	0.003	0.005	0.006	0.007	0.007
3.74	0.000	0.000	0.000	0.000	0.000	0.000	0.000	0.000	0.001	0.001	0.002	0.003	0.004	0.005	0.007	0.007
3.75	0.000	0.000	0.000	0.000	0.000	0.000	0.000	0.000	0.001	0.001	0.002	0.002	0.004	0.005	0.006	0.007
3.76	0.000	0.000	0.000	0.000	0.000	0.000	0.000	0.000	0.001	0.001	0.001	0.002	0.004	0.005	0.006	0.007
3.77	0.000	0.000	0.000	0.000	0.000	0.000	0.000	0.000	0.001	0.001	0.001	0.002	0.004	0.005	0.006	0.006
3.78	0.000	0.000	0.000	0.000	0.000	0.000	0.000	0.000	0.000	0.001	0.001	0.002	0.004	0.004	0.005	0.006
3.79	0.000	0.000	0.000	0.000	0.000	0.000	0.000	0.000	0.000	0.001	0.001	0.002	0.003	0.004	0.005	0.006
3.80	0.000	0.000	0.000	0.000	0.000	0.000	0.000	0.000	0.000	0.001	0.001	0.002	0.003	0.004	0.005	0.006
3.81	0.000	0.000	0.000	0.000	0.000	0.000	0.000	0.000	0.000	0.001	0.001	0.002	0.003	0.004	0.005	0.005
3.82	0.000	0.000	0.000	0.000	0.000	0.000	0.000	0.000	0.000	0.001	0.001	0.002	0.003	0.004	0.005	0.005
3.83	0.000	0.000	0.000	0.000	0.000	0.000	0.000	0.000	0.000	0.001	0.001	0.002	0.003	0.004	0.004	0.005
3.84	0.000	0.000	0.000	0.000	0.000	0.000	0.000	0.000	0.000	0.001	0.001	0.001	0.003	0.003	0.004	0.005
3.85	0.000	0.000	0.000	0.000	0.000	0.000	0.000	0.000	0.000	0.001	0.001	0.001	0.002	0.003	0.004	0.004
3.86	0.000	0.000	0.000	0.000	0.000	0.000	0.000	0.000	0.000	0.000	0.001	0.001	0.002	0.003	0.004	0.004
3.87	0.000	0.000	0.000	0.000	0.000	0.000	0.000	0.000	0.000	0.000	0.001	0.001	0.002	0.003	0.004	0.004
3.88	0.000	0.000	0.000	0.000	0.000	0.000	0.000	0.000	0.000	0.000	0.001	0.001	0.002	0.003	0.004	0.004
3.89	0.000	0.000	0.000	0.000	0.000	0.000	0.000	0.000	0.000	0.000	0.001	0.001	0.002	0.003	0.003	0.004
3.90	0.000	0.000	0.000	0.000	0.000	0.000	0.000	0.000	0.000	0.000	0.001	0.001	0.002	0.003	0.003	0.004

TABLE A15.5 Master Table for Reduced Inspection for Plans Based on Variability Unknown (Single Specification Limit—Form 1), Standard Deviation Method (Table B–2 of MIL-STD-414)

Sample size code letter	Sample size	Acceptable quality levels												
		0.04	0.065	0.10	0.15	0.25	0.40	0.65	1.00	1.50	2.50	4.00	6.50	10.00
		k	k	k	k	k	k	k	k	k	k	k	k	k
B	3	↓	↓	↓	↓	↓	↓	↓	↓	1.12	0.958	0.765	0.566	0.341
C	3	↓	↓	↓	↓	↓	↓	↓	↓	1.12	0.958	0.765	0.566	0.341
D	3	↓	↓	↓	↓	↓	↓	↓	↓	1.12	0.958	0.765	0.566	0.341
E	3	↓	↓	↓	↓	↓	↓	↓	↓	1.12	0.958	0.765	0.566	0.341
F	4	↓	↓	↓	↓	↓	↓	1.45	1.34	1.17	1.01	0.814	0.617	0.393
G	5	↓	↓	↓	↓	↓	1.65	1.53	1.40	1.24	1.07	0.874	0.675	0.455
H	7	↓	↓	↓	2.00	1.88	1.75	1.62	1.50	1.33	1.15	0.955	0.755	0.536
I	10	↓	↓	2.24	2.11	1.98	1.84	1.72	1.58	1.41	1.23	1.03	0.828	0.611
J	10	↓	↓	2.24	2.11	1.98	1.84	1.72	1.58	1.41	1.23	1.03	0.828	0.611
K	15	2.53	2.42	2.32	2.20	2.06	1.91	1.79	1.65	1.47	1.30	1.09	0.886	0.664
L	20	2.58	2.47	2.36	2.24	2.11	1.96	1.82	1.69	1.51	1.33	1.12	0.917	0.695
M	20	2.58	2.47	2.36	2.24	2.11	1.96	1.82	1.69	1.51	1.33	1.12	0.917	0.695
N	25	2.61	2.50	2.40	2.26	2.14	1.98	1.85	1.72	1.53	1.35	1.14	0.936	0.712
O	30	2.61	2.51	2.41	2.28	2.15	2.00	1.86	1.73	1.55	1.36	1.15	0.946	0.723
P	50	2.71	2.60	2.50	2.35	2.22	2.08	1.93	1.80	1.61	1.42	1.21	1.00	0.774
Q	75	2.77	2.66	2.55	2.41	2.27	2.12	1.98	1.84	1.65	1.46	1.24	1.03	0.804

All AQL values are in percent defective.

Use first sampling plan below arrow, that is, both sample size as well as k value. When sample size equals or exceeds lot size, every item in the lot must be inspected.

TABLE A15.6 Master Table for Reduced Inspection for Plans Based on Variability Unknown (Double Specification Limit and Form 2—Single Specification Limit), Standard Deviation Method (Table B–4 of MIL-STD-414)

Sample size code letter	Sample size	Acceptable quality levels												
		0.04	0.065	0.10	0.15	0.25	0.40	0.65	1.00	1.50	2.50	4.00	6.50	10.00
		M	***M***	***M***	***M***	***M***	***M***	***M***	***M***	***M***	***M***	***M***	***M***	***M***
B	3									7.59	18.86	26.94	33.69	40.47
C	3									7.59	18.86	26.94	33.69	40.47
D	3									7.59	18.86	26.94	33.69	40.47
E	3							↓	↓	7.59	18.86	26.94	33.69	40.47
F	4						↓	1.53	5.50	10.92	16.45	22.86	29.45	36.90
G	5				↓	↓	1.33	3.32	5.83	9.80	14.39	20.19	26.56	33.99
H	7			↓	0.422	1.06	2.14	3.55	5.35	8.40	12.20	17.35	23.29	30.50
I	10			0.349	0.716	1.30	2.17	3.26	4.77	7.29	10.54	15.17	20.74	27.57
J	10	↓	↓	0.349	0.716	1.30	2.17	3.26	4.77	7.29	10.54	15.17	20.74	27.57
K	15	0.186	0.312	0.503	0.818	1.31	2.11	3.05	4.31	6.56	9.46	13.71	18.94	25.61
L	20	0.228	0.365	0.544	0.846	1.29	2.05	2.95	4.09	6.17	8.92	12.99	18.03	24.53
M	20	0.228	0.365	0.544	0.846	1.29	2.05	2.95	4.09	6.17	8.92	12.99	18.03	24.53
N	25	0.250	0.380	0.551	0.877	1.29	2.00	2.86	3.97	5.97	8.63	12.57	17.51	23.97
O	30	0.280	0.413	0.581	0.879	1.29	1.98	2.83	3.91	5.86	8.47	12.36	17.24	23.58
P	50	0.250	0.363	0.503	0.789	1.17	1.71	2.49	3.45	5.20	7.61	11.23	15.87	22.00
Q	75	0.228	0.330	0.467	0.720	1.07	1.60	2.29	3.20	4.87	7.15	10.63	15.13	21.11

All AQL and table values are in percent defective.

Use first sampling plan below arrow, that is, both sample size as well as ***M*** value. When sample size equals or exceeds lot size, every item in the lot must be inspected.

TABLE A15.7 Limits of Estimated Lot Percent Defective for Reduced Inspection, Standard Deviation Method (Table B–7 of MIL-STD-414)

Code letter	Acceptable quality level														Number of lots
	.04	.065	.10	.15	.25	.40	.65	1.0	1.5	2.5	4.0	6.5	10.0	15.0	
B	*	*	*	*	*	*	*	*	*	** [40]	** [30]	** [20]	** [12]	** [8]	
C	*	*	*	*	*	*	*	** [35]	** [25]	↓ ↓ 0	↓ ↓ .57	** [8]	** [6]	0 ↑ ↑	5 10 15
D	*	*	*	*	*	*	** [35]	** [25]	** [20]	↓ ↓ .77	↓ .53 3.95	↓ 4.40 ↑	.74 9.96 ↑	6.06 ↑ ↑	5 10 15
E	*	*	*	*	** [25]	** [20]	↓ ↓ .02	↓ 0 .25	↓ .10 .88	↓ .88 2.49	.13 2.65 ↑	1.38 5.96 ↑	4.24 10.00 ↑	9.09 ↑ ↑	5 10 15
F	*	*	*	↓ ↓ .002	↓ .001 .029	↓ .016 .123	↓ .101 .369	.003 .317 .81	.044 .74 1.50	.306 1.80 ↑	1.05 3.56 ↑	2.81 6.50 ↑	5.79 10.00 ↑	10.47 ↑ ↑	5 10 15
G	↓ ↓ .003	↓ .002 .010	↓ .006 .028	↓ .018 .062	.002 .057 .151	.011 .143 .315	.047 .330 .626	.136 .643 1.00	.323 1.14 ↑	.84 2.23 ↑	1.84 3.94 ↑	3.80 6.50 ↑	6.86 10.00 ↑	11.52 15.00 ↑	5 10 15
H	↓ .004 .013	↓ .010 .029	.002 .023 .058	.005 .048 .105	.017 .111 .215	.048 .225 .396	.123 .445 ↑	.266 .785 ↑	.521 1.31 ↑	1.14 2.40 ↑	2.24 4.00 ↑	4.29 6.50 ↑	7.40 10.00 ↑	12.07 15.00 ↑	5 10 15
I	.001 .009 .021	.002 .020 .043	.006 .039 .077	.014 .071 .133	.037 .146 .248	.083 .274 .40	.185 .509 ↑	.360 .863 ↑	.653 1.39 ↑	1.33 2.48 ↑	2.49 4.00 ↑	4.59 6.50 ↑	7.74 10.00 ↑	12.43 15.00 ↑	5 10 15
J	.002 .013 .027	.005 .027 .052	.012 .050 .089	.023 .087 .146	.054 .169 .25	.113 .306 ↑	.233 .550 ↑	.431 .909 ↑	.750 1.44 ↑	1.47 2.50 ↑	2.66 4.00 ↑	4.81 6.50 ↑	7.98 10.00 ↑	12.69 15.00 ↑	5 10 15
K	.004 .017 .032	.008 .033 .058	.017 .059 .097	.032 .099 .15	.069 .186 ↑	.137 .328 ↑	.270 .577 ↑	.483 .940 ↑	.821 1.47 ↑	1.57 2.50 ↑	2.79 4.00 ↑	4.96 6.50 ↑	8.15 10.00 ↑	12.88 15.00 ↑	5 10 15
L	.005 .020 .035	.011 .038 .063	.022 .065 .10	.040 .108 .15	.082 .199 ↑	.157 .343 ↑	.300 .596 ↑	.525 .961 ↑	.876 1.49 ↑	1.64 2.50 ↑	2.88 4.00 ↑	5.08 6.50 ↑	8.29 10.00 ↑	13.03 15.00 ↑	5 10 15
M	.008 .025 .040	.016 .045 .065	.030 .075 .10	.052 .120 ↑	.102 .215 ↑	.187 .364 ↑	.345 .621 ↑	.587 .989 ↑	.959 1.50 ↑	1.76 2.50 ↑	3.03 4.00 ↑	5.27 6.50 ↑	8.50 10.00 ↑	13.25 15.00 ↑	5 10 15
N	.014 .031 .04	.026 .054 ↑	.044 .087 ↑	.072 .136 ↑	.134 .236 ↑	.235 .389 ↑	.414 .650 ↑	.681 1.00 ↑	1.082 1.50 ↑	1.92 2.50 ↓	3.24 4.00 ↑	5.52 6.50 ↑	8.81 10.00 ↑	13.60 15.00 ↑	5 10 15
O	.018 .034 ↑	.032 .058 ↑	.053 .093 ↑	.085 .143 ↑	.153 .245 ↑	.261 .400 ↑	.453 .65 ↑	.733 1.00 ↑	1.149 1.50 ↑	2.01 2.50 ↑	3.36 4.00 ↑	5.67 6.50 ↑	8.98 10.00 ↑	13.80 15.00 ↑	5 10 15
P	.023 .038 ↑	.039 .064 ↑	.064 .100 ↑	.101 .15 ↑	.177 .25 ↑	.296 .40 ↑	.501 .65 ↑	.799 1.00 ↑	1.237 1.50 ↑	2.13 2.50 ↑	3.52 4.00 ↑	5.87 6.50 ↑	9.22 10.00 ↑	14.07 15.00 ↑	5 10 15
Q	.025 .040 ↑	.044 .065 ↑	.069 .10 ↑	.108 .15 ↑	.188 .25 ↑	.312 .40 ↑	.525 .65 ↑	.830 1.00 ↑	1.276 1.50 ↑	2.19 2.50 ↑	3.59 4.00 ↑	5.96 6.50 ↑	9.32 10.00 ↑	14.19 15.00 ↑	5 10 15

* There are no sampling plans provided in this Standard for these code letters and AQL values.

↑ ↓ Use the first figure in direction of arrow and corresponding number of lots. In each block the top figure refers to the preceding 5 lots, the middle figure to the preceding 10 lots, and the bottom figure to the preceding 15 lots.

Reduced inspection may be instituted when every estimated lot percent defective from the preceding 5, 10, or 15 lots is below the figure given in the table; reduced inspection for sampling plans marked (**) in the table requires that the estimated lot percent defective is equal to zero for the number of consecutive lots indicated in brackets. In addition, all other conditions for reduced inspection must be satisfied.

All estimates of the lot percent defective are obtained from Table A15.4 (Table B-5 of MIL-STD-414).

TABLE A15.8 **Standard Deviation Method, Values of *T* for Tightened Inspection, (Table B–6 of MIL-STD-414)**

Code letter	Acceptable quality level														Number of lots
	.04	.065	.10	.15	.25	.40	.65	1.0	1.5	2.5	4.0	6.5	10.0	15.0	
B	*	*	*	*	*	*	*	*	*	2	3	4	4	4	5
										4	5	6	7	8	10
										5	6	8	9	11	15
C	*	*	*	*	*	*	*	2	2	3	3	4	4	4	5
								3	4	5	6	7	7	8	10
								5	6	7	8	9	10	11	15
D	*	*	*	*	*	*	2	3	3	3	4	4	4	4	5
							4	4	5	6	6	7	8	8	10
							5	6	7	8	9	10	11	11	15
E	*	*	*	*	2	3	3	3	4	4	4	4	4	4	5
					4	4	5	5	6	6	7	7	8	8	10
					5	6	6	7	8	9	9	10	11	11	15
F	*	*	*	3	3	3	3	4	4	4	4	4	4	4	5
				4	5	5	6	6	6	7	7	8	8	8	10
				6	6	7	8	8	9	9	10	11	11	11	15
G	3	3	3	3	3	4	4	4	4	4	4	4	4	4	5
	4	5	5	5	6	6	6	7	7	7	7	8	8	8	10
	6	6	6	7	7	8	9	9	9	10	10	11	11	11	15
H	3	3	3	3	4	4	4	4	4	4	4	4	4	4	5
	5	5	5	6	6	6	7	7	7	7	8	8	8	8	10
	6	7	7	8	8	9	9	9	10	10	11	11	11	11	15
I	3	3	4	4	4	4	4	4	4	4	4	4	4	4	5
	5	6	6	6	6	7	7	7	7	7	8	8	8	8	10
	7	7	8	8	9	9	9	10	10	10	11	11	11	11	15
J	3	4	4	4	4	4	4	4	4	4	4	4	4	4	5
	6	6	6	6	7	7	7	7	7	8	8	8	8	8	10
	8	8	8	9	9	9	10	10	10	11	11	11	11	11	15
K	4	4	4	4	4	4	4	4	4	4	4	4	4	4	5
	6	6	6	6	7	7	7	7	8	8	8	8	8	8	10
	8	8	9	9	9	9	10	10	10	11	11	11	11	11	15
L	4	4	4	4	4	4	4	4	4	4	4	4	4	4	5
	6	6	6	7	7	7	7	7	8	8	8	8	8	8	10
	8	9	9	9	9	10	10	10	10	11	11	11	11	11	15
M	4	4	4	4	4	4	4	4	4	4	4	4	4	4	5
	6	7	7	7	7	7	7	7	8	8	8	8	8	8	10
	9	9	9	9	10	10	10	10	11	11	11	11	11	11	15
N	4	4	4	4	4	4	4	4	4	4	4	4	4	4	5
	7	7	7	7	7	7	8	8	8	8	8	8	8	8	10
	9	9	10	10	10	10	11	11	11	11	11	11	11	11	15
O	4	4	4	4	4	4	4	4	4	4	4	4	4	4	5
	7	7	7	7	7	8	8	8	8	8	8	8	8	8	10
	10	10	10	10	10	11	11	11	11	11	11	11	11	11	15
P	4	4	4	4	4	4	4	4	4	4	4	4	4	4	5
	7	7	7	8	8	8	8	8	8	8	8	8	8	8	10
	10	10	10	10	11	11	11	11	11	11	11	11	11	12	15
Q	4	4	4	4	4	4	4	4	4	4	4	4	4	4	5
	7	8	8	8	8	8	8	8	8	8	8	8	8	8	10
	10	11	11	11	11	11	11	11	11	11	11	11	11	12	15

* There are no sampling plans provided in this Standard for these code letters and AQL values.

The top figure in each block refers to the preceding 5 lots, the middle figure to the preceding 10 lots and the bottom figure to the preceding 15 lots.

Tightened inspection is required when the number of lots with estimates of percent defective above the AQL from the preceding 5, 10, or 15 lots is greater than the given value of *T* in the table, and the process average from these lots exceeds the AQL.

All estimates of the lot percent defective are obtained from Table A15.4 (Table B–5 of MIL-STD-414).

TABLE A15.9 Values of F for Maximum Standard Deviation (MSD) (Table B–8 of MIL-STD-414)

Sample Size Code Letter	Sample Size	AQL (per cent defective)													
		0.04	0.065	0.10	0.15	0.25	0.40	0.65	1.00	1.50	2.50	4.00	6.50	10.00	15.00
B	3										0.436	0.453	0.475	0.502	0.538
C	4								0.339	0.353	0.374	0.399	0.432	0.472	0.528
D	5							0.294	0.308	0.323	0.346	0.372	0.408	0.452	0.511
E	7					0.242	0.253	0.266	0.280	0.295	0.318	0.345	0.381	0.425	0.485
F	10				0.214	0.224	0.235	0.248	0.261	0.276	0.298	0.324	0.359	0.403	0.460
G	15	0.182	0.188	0.195	0.202	0.211	0.222	0.235	0.248	0.262	0.284	0.309	0.344	0.386	0.442
H	20	0.177	0.183	0.190	0.197	0.206	0.216	0.229	0.242	0.255	0.277	0.302	0.336	0.377	0.432
I	25	0.174	0.180	0.187	0.193	0.203	0.212	0.225	0.238	0.251	0.273	0.297	0.331	0.372	0.426
J	30	0.173	0.179	0.185	0.192	0.201	0.210	0.223	0.236	0.249	0.270	0.295	0.328	0.369	0.423
K	35	0.170	0.176	0.183	0.189	0.198	0.208	0.220	0.232	0.245	0.266	0.291	0.323	0.364	0.416
L	40	0.169	0.176	0.182	0.188	0.198	0.207	0.219	0.232	0.245	0.266	0.290	0.323	0.363	0.416
M	50	0.166	0.172	0.178	0.184	0.194	0.203	0.214	0.227	0.241	0.261	0.284	0.317	0.356	0.408
N	75	0.162	0.168	0.174	0.181	0.189	0.199	0.211	0.223	0.235	0.255	0.279	0.310	0.348	0.399
O	100	0.160	0.166	0.172	0.179	0.187	0.197	0.208	0.220	0.233	0.253	0.276	0.307	0.345	0.395
P	150	0.158	0.163	0.170	0.175	0.185	0.193	0.206	0.216	0.230	0.249	0.271	0.302	0.341	0.388
Q	200	0.157	0.163	0.168	0.175	0.183	0.193	0.203	0.215	0.228	0.248	0.269	0.302	0.338	0.386

TABLE A16.1 Sampling Frequency Code Letters (Table II of H107)

Number of Units of Product Produced in a Production Interval*	Inspection [Levels]			
	I	II		III
	CSP–1 & CSP–2	CSP–1 & CSP–2	CSP–A	CSP–1 & CSP–2
2–8	C	B	A′	A
9–25	D	C	B′	A
26–65	E	D	C′	B
66–110	F	E	D′	B
111–180	F	E	E′	C
181–300	G	E	F′	C
301–500	G	F	G′	D
501–800	G	F	H′	E
801–1300	H	F	I′	E
1301–3200	H	G	J′	F
3201–8000	I	H	K′	G
8001–22,000	J	I	L′	H
22,001–110,000	K	J	M′	I
110,001–up	K	K	N′	J

* The production interval is the period of time, usually a shift or a day, during which a number of units of product or a homogeneous batch of product is produced. The choice of the number of units of product or of the duration of the production interval must be estimated from prior information.

TABLE A16.2 Values of *i* for CSP-1 Plans (Table III-1 of H107)

Sampling Frequency Code Letter	f	AQL (per cent)													
		0.015	0.035	0.065	0.10	0.15	0.25	0.40	0.65	1.0	1.5	2.5	4.0	6.5	10.0
A	$\frac{1}{2}$	240	180	120	100	75	50	33	25	20	12	9	5	4	2
B	$\frac{1}{3}$	390	290	200	170	130	80	55	43	34	20	15	9	6	4
C	$\frac{1}{4}$	500	380	260	220	170	100	75	55	45	27	19	12	8	5
D	$\frac{1}{5}$	600	450	320	270	200	130	90	70	55	33	23	14	9	6
E	$\frac{1}{7}$	750	560	390	330	250	150	110	85	65	40	29	17	12	8
F	$\frac{1}{10}$	920	690	480	410	310	190	140	100	80	50	35	22	15	10
G	$\frac{1}{15}$	1,110	840	590	500	380	230	170	130	100	65	43	27	18	12
H	$\frac{1}{25}$	1,380	1,040	730	620	470	290	210	160	130	75	55	34	22	15
I	$\frac{1}{50}$	1,780	1,340	940	800	600	370	260	200	160	100	70	42	29	19
J	$\frac{1}{100}$	2,210	1,660	1,150	980	740	450	320	250	200	120	85	55	36	24
K	$\frac{1}{200}$	2,630	1,970	1,370	1,170	880	530	380	300	240	150	100	65	43	28
		0.12	0.16	0.23	0.27	0.36	0.59	0.83	1.08	1.35	2.20	3.09	4.96	7.24	10.70
		AOQL (per cent)													

TABLE A16.3 Values of *i* for CSP-2 Plans (Table III-2 of H107)

Sampling Frequency Code Letter	f	AQL (per cent)													
		0.015	0.035	0.065	0.10	0.15	0.25	0.40	0.65	1.0	1.5	2.5	4.0	6.5	10.0
A	$\frac{1}{2}$	360	270	190	160	120	75	50	39	31	19	13	8	5	3
B	$\frac{1}{3}$	590	500	310	260	200	120	90	65	50	31	22	13	9	6
C	$\frac{1}{4}$	730	550	380	320	240	150	110	80	65	39	27	17	11	7
D	$\frac{1}{5}$	850	640	440	380	280	170	120	95	75	45	32	20	13	9
E	$\frac{1}{7}$	1,020	760	530	450	340	210	150	110	90	55	39	24	16	11
F	$\frac{1}{10}$	1,220	920	640	540	410	250	180	140	110	70	47	29	19	13
G	$\frac{1}{15}$	1,440	1,090	760	650	490	300	210	170	130	80	55	35	23	16
H	$\frac{1}{25}$	1,750	1,320	920	780	590	360	260	200	160	95	65	42	28	19
I	$\frac{1}{50}$	2,200	1,650	1,150	980	730	450	320	250	200	120	85	55	35	23
J	$\frac{1}{100}$	2,650	2,000	1,380	1,180	880	540	380	290	230	150	110	65	42	27
K	$\frac{1}{200}$	3,200	2,400	1,660	1,410	1,060	640	460	360	290	180	130	75	55	33
		0.12	0.16	0.23	0.27	0.36	0.59	0.83	1.08	1.35	2.20	3.09	4.96	7.24	10.70
		AOQL (per cent)													

Note: CSP–2 plans will not be used for inspection of critical defects.

TABLE A16.4 Values of L for CSP-1 Plans (Table IV-A of H107)

Sampling Frequency Code Letter	f	AQL (per cent)													
		0.015	0.035	0.065	0.10	0.15	0.25	0.40	0.65	1.0	1.5	2.5	4.0	6.5	10.0
A	$\frac{1}{2}$	575	425	300	250	175	125	80	60	50	30	23	13	11	6
B	$\frac{1}{3}$	1,075	800	550	475	375	225	150	125	95	60	45	27	19	13
C	$\frac{1}{4}$	1,550	1,200	800	700	525	325	250	175	150	90	60	40	27	18
D	$\frac{1}{5}$	1,800	1,350	1,000	800	600	400	275	225	175	100	70	45	30	20
E	$\frac{1}{7}$	2,350	1,750	1,200	1,050	800	475	350	275	200	125	90	55	40	25
F	$\frac{1}{10}$	3,450	2,600	1,800	1,550	1,175	725	550	400	300	200	150	90	60	40
G	$\frac{1}{15}$	5,250	3,950	2,800	2,350	1,800	1,100	800	625	475	325	225	125	90	60
H	$\frac{1}{25}$	6,800	5,100	3,600	3,050	2,300	1,425	1,050	800	650	375	275	175	110	80
I	$\frac{1}{50}$	13,600	10,200	7,200	6,100	4,600	2,825	2,000	1,550	1,225	775	550	350	250	150
J	$\frac{1}{100}$	22,200	16,700	11,500	9,850	7,450	4,525	3,225	2,525	2,025	1,225	875	575	375	275
K	$\frac{1}{200}$	39,500	29,600	20,600	17,600	13,250	8,000	5,750	4,525	3,625	2,275	1,525	1,000	675	450
		0.12	0.16	0.23	0.27	0.36	0.59	0.83	1.08	1.35	2.20	3.09	4.96	7.24	10.70
		AOQL (per cent)													

TABLE A16.5 Values of L for CSP-2 Plans (Table IV-B of H107)

Sampling Frequency Code Letter	f	AQL (per cent)													
		0.015	0.035	0.065	0.10	0.15	0.25	0.40	0.65	1.0	1.5	2.5	4.0	6.5	10.0
A	$\frac{1}{2}$	1,300	975	700	600	450	275	200	150	125	75	50	32	21	14
B	$\frac{1}{5}$	2,700	2,275	1,400	1,175	900	550	425	300	250	150	105	70	44	31
C	$\frac{1}{4}$	3,675	2,775	1,925	1,625	1,225	775	575	425	350	200	150	90	60	40
D	$\frac{1}{5}$	3,400	2,575	1,775	1,525	1,125	700	500	400	325	200	150	90	55	40
E	$\frac{1}{7}$	5,125	3,825	2,675	2,275	1,725	1,075	775	575	475	300	200	125	85	60
F	$\frac{1}{10}$	7,200	5,450	3,800	3,200	2,425	1,475	1,075	850	650	425	300	175	125	80
G	$\frac{1}{15}$	10,950	8,300	5,800	4,950	3,725	2,300	1,600	1,300	1,000	625	425	275	175	125
H	$\frac{1}{25}$	14,000	10,600	7,400	6,250	4,725	3,000	2,100	1,600	1,300	775	525	350	225	175
I	$\frac{1}{50}$	28,600	21,450	14,950	12,750	9,500	5,850	4,175	3,250	2,600	1,575	1,125	725	475	300
J	$\frac{1}{100}$	39,800	30,050	20,750	17,750	13,250	8,125	5,725	4,375	3,475	2,275	1,675	1,000	675	450
K	$\frac{1}{200}$	80,100	60,100	41,600	35,300	26,600	16,100	11,600	9,050	7,250	4,550	3,300	1,925	1,425	875
		0.12	0.16	0.23	0.27	0.36	0.59	0.83	1.08	1.35	2.20	3.09	4.96	7.24	10.7
		AOQL (per cent)													

TABLE A16.6 **Values of i and a for CSP-A Plans (Table III-A of H107)**

Sampling Frequency Code Letter	f	AQL (per cent)									
		0.015		0.10		0.15		0.25		0.40	
		i	a	i	a	i	a	i	a	i	a
A′	$\frac{1}{1}$	100	0	←		←		←		←	
B′	$\frac{1}{1}$	100	0	←		←		←		←	
C′	$\frac{1}{5}$	100	0	←		←		←		25	0
D′	$\frac{1}{10}$	100	0	←		65	0	35	0	25	0
E′	$\frac{1}{10}$	105	0	80	0	50	0	25	0	15	0
F′	$\frac{1}{10}$	100	0	60	0	40	0	20	0	←	
G′	$\frac{1}{10}$	80	0	50	0	20	0	←		40	1
H′	$\frac{1}{10}$	80	0	30	0	←		40	1	20	1
I′	$\frac{1}{10}$	80	0	←		50	1	35	1	25	2
J′	$\frac{1}{15}$	100	0	135	1	50	1	40	2	40	3
K′	$\frac{1}{25}$	120	0	100	1	60	2	50	3	40	4
L′	$\frac{1}{50}$	160	0	80	1	90	2	80	3	50	5
M′	$\frac{1}{100}$	200	0	110	3	100	4	80	5	65	7
N′	$\frac{1}{200}$	240	0	120	6	100	8	80	11	60	15
		0.12		0.27		0.36		0.59		0.73	
		AOQL (per cent)									

TABLE A16.6 Values of *i* and *a* for CSP-A Plans (*Continued*)

AQL (per cent)													
0.65		1.0		1.5		2.5		4.0		6.5		10.0	
i	*a*	*i*	*a*	*i*	*a*	*i*	*a*	*i*	*a*	*i*	*a*	*i*	*a*
100	0	←		←		←		←		100	0	←	
100	0	←		←		←		100	1	100	2	100	3
25	0	←		20	1	10	1	4	1	3	2	3	3
25	0	30	1	20	1	8	1	6	2	4	2	4	3
15	0	20	1	10	1	8	2	6	3	4	3	4	5
30	1	14	1	10	2	10	3	8	4	6	5	4	7
20	1	15	2	15	3	10	4	8	6	6	8	4	11
20	2	15	3	15	4	10	6	8	8	6	12	4	16
25	3	20	4	15	5	10	7	8	11	6	17	4	24
30	4	25	5	20	7	10	9	9	15	7	25	5	37
30	5	30	8	25	11	15	17	9	24	7	34	5	53
40	7	30	10	20	14	16	20	12	32	9	57	9	108
50	13	35	18	25	15	20	43	12	62	15	180	12	300
45	26	30	35	25	53	15	81	10	126	7	207	5	326
1.08		1.35		2.20		3.09		4.96		7.24		10.70	
AOQL (per cent)													

TABLE A16.7 Multilevel Continuous-Sampling Plans for $f = \frac{1}{2}$ (Table II of H 106)

N		AOQL (per cent defective)													
Contract Size or Production Rate		0.10	0.15	0.25	0.35	0.50	0.75	1.0	1.5	2.0	3.0	5.0	7.5	10.0	15.0
4–65	i k	↓	↓	↓	↓	↓	↓	↓	↓	↓	↓	5 1	↓	4 2	↓
66–135	i k	↓	↓	↓	↓	↓	↓	↓	↓	18 1	11 1	↓	↓	↓	↓
136–200	i k	↓	↓	↓	↓	↓	↓	↓	25 1	↓	↓	↓	6 2	↓	↓
201–300	i k	↓	↓	↓	↓	↓	↓	39 1	↓	↓	↓	11 2	↓	↓	↓
301–400	i k	↓	↓	↓	↓	↓	↓	↓	↓	↓	20 2	↓	↓	↓	↓
401–500	i k	↓	↓	↓	↓	↓	54 1	↓	↓	31 2	↓	↓	↓	6 3	↓
501–700	i k	↓	↓	↓	↓	82 1	↓	↓	43 2	↓	↓	↓	9 3	↓	4 4
701–1,100	i k	↓	↓	↓	119 1	↓	↓	65 2	↓	↓	↓	15 3	↓	↓	↓
1,101–1,500	i k	↓	↓	167 1	↓	↓	↓	↓	↓	↓	26 3	↓	↓	8 4	↓
1,501–2,700	i k	↓	218 1		↓	↓	88 2	↓	↓	40 3	↓	18 4	11 4	↓	↓

TABLE A16.7 Multilevel Continuous-Sampling Plans for $f = \frac{1}{2}$ *(Continued)*

2,701–4,000	i	421			197	132			55		31				
	k	1		↓	2	2			3	↓	4				
4,001–5,500	i			269						47					
	k		↓	2				↓	↓	4					
5,501–8,500	i		446					83	63						
	k		2			↓	↓	3	4						
8,501–10,500	i					168	112								
	k	↓			↓	3	3	↓							
10,501–15,000	i	675			241			95							
	k	2		↓	3	↓	↓	4							
15,001–21,000	i			337		193	128								
	k		↓	3	↓	4	4								
21,001–32,000	i		564		275										
	k	↓	3	↓	4										
32,001–50,000	i	847		386											
	k	3	↓	4											
50,001–80,000	i		636												
	k	↓	4												
80,001–150,000	i	969													
	k	4	↓	↓	↓	↓	↓	↓	↓	↓	↓	↓	↓	↓	↓
150,001 and over	i	1059	706	422	302	210	140	104	69	51	34	20	13	9	5
	k	5	5	5	5	5	5	5	5	5	5	5	5	5	5

Use the sampling below, or at the point of, the arrow. When the value of i equals or exceeds N, every unit must be inspected. (In such cases, sampling in accordance with MIL-STD-105D may be preferable.)

TABLE A16.8 Multilevel Continuous-Sampling Plans for $f = \frac{1}{3}$ (Table IV of H106)

N		AOQL (per cent defective)													
Contract Size or Production Rate		0.10	0.15	0.25	0.35	0.50	0.75	1.0	1.5	2.0	3.0	5.0	7.5	10.0	5.0
4–75	i k											↓	6 1		↓
76–200	i k										↓	10 1		↓	4 2
201–325	i k								↓	↓	19 1			7 2	
326–450	i k								42 1	31 1			↓		
451–600	i k							↓					11 2		
601–750	i k							64 1				↓			
751–1,000	i k						↓				↓	18 2			↓
1,001–1,300	i k					↓	87 1			↓	32 2			↓	6 3
1,301–1,900	i k				↓	133 1			↓	48 2			↓	10 3	
1,901–2,700	i k				190 1			↓	66 2		↓	↓	14 3		↓
2,701–3,500	i k			↓				100 2		↓	39 3	22 3		↓	7 4
3,501–3,500	i k	↓	↓	269 1	↓	↓	↓	↓	↓	59 3	↓	↓	↓	12 4	↓

Lot size															
4,501–6,000	i	↓	↓	↓	↓	↓	↓	↓	80	↓	↓	↓	16	↓	↓
	k								3				4		
6,001–7,500	i	↓	450	↓	↓	↓	134	120	↓	↓	↓	↓	↓	↓	↓
	k		1				2	3							
7,501–9,000	i	↓	↓	↓	↓	↓	↓	↓	↓	↓	↓	25	↓	↓	↓
	k											4			
9,001–12,000	i	677	↓	↓	↓	202	↓	↓	↓	↓	43	↓	↓	↓	↓
	k	1				2					4				
12,001–15,000	i	↓	↓	↓	290	↓	↓	↓	↓	66	↓	↓	↓	↓	↓
	k				2					4					
15,001–22,000	i	↓	↓	406	↓	↓	161	↓	89	↓	↓	↓	↓	↓	↓
	k			2			3		4						
22,001–30,000	i	↓	680	↓	↓	243	↓	134	↓	↓	↓	↓	↓	↓	↓
	k		2			3		4							
30,001–40,000	i	1022	↓	↓	349	↓	↓	↓	↓	↓	↓	↓	↓	↓	↓
	k	2			3										
40,001–55,000	i	↓	↓	488	↓	↓	179	↓	↓	↓	↓	↓	↓	↓	↓
	k			3			4								
55,001–75,000	i	↓	815	↓	↓	269	↓	↓	↓	↓	↓	↓	↓	↓	↓
	k		3			4									
75,001–120,000	i	1224	↓	540	386	↓	↓	↓	↓	↓	↓	↓	↓	↓	↓
	k	3		4	4										
120,001–200,000	i	↓	903	↓	↓	↓	↓	↓	↓	↓	↓	↓	↓	↓	↓
	k		4												
200,001–350,000	i	1354	↓	↓	↓	↓	↓	↓	↓	↓	↓	↓	↓	↓	↓
	k	4													
350,001 and over	i	1443	960	576	408	287	191	142	95	71	46	27	18	13	8
	k	5	5	5	5	5	5	5	5	5	5	4	5	5	5

Use the sampling below, or at the point of, the arrow. When the value of i equals or exceeds N, every unit must be inspected. (In such cases, sampling in accordance with MIL-STD-105D may be preferable.)

TABLE A16.9 Table of *i* Values for Multilevel Continuous-Sampling Plans Based on $f = \frac{1}{2}$ (Table III of H106)

AOQL (per cent defective)	$k = 1$	$k = 2$	$k = 3$	$k = 4$	$k = 5$
15.0	*	*	*	4	5
10.0	*	4	6	8	9
7.5	*	6	9	11	13
5.0	5	11	15	18	20
3.0	11	20	26	31	34
2.0	18	31	40	47	51
1.5	25	43	55	63	69
1.0	39	65	83	95	104
0.75	54	88	112	128	140
0.50	82	133	168	193	210
0.35	119	197	241	275	302
0.25	167	269	337	386	422
0.15	281	446	564	636	706
0.10	421	675	847	969	1059

k = number of sampling levels

* Sampling plan not available for values of *i* less than 4.

TABLE A16.10 Table of *i* Values for Multilevel Continuous-Sampling Plans Based on $f = \frac{1}{3}$ (Table V of H106)

AOQL (per cent defective)	$k = 1$	$k = 2$	$k = 3$	$k = 4$	$k = 5$
15.0	*	4	6	7	8
10.0	*	7	10	12	13
7.5	6	11	14	16	18
5.0	10	18	22	25	27
3.0	19	32	39	43	46
2.0	31	48	59	66	71
1.5	42	66	80	89	95
1.0	64	100	120	134	142
0.75	87	134	161	179	191
0.50	133	202	243	269	287
0.35	190	290	349	386	408
0.25	269	406	488	540	576
0.15	450	680	815	903	960
0.10	677	1022	1224	1354	1443

k = number of sampling levels

* Sampling plans not available for values of *i* less than 4.

TABLE A17.1 Example of Dodge–Romig Single Sampling Lot Tolerance Tables

Lot tolerance percent defective = 5.0%
Consumer's risk = 0.10

Process Average %	0–.05			.06–.50			.51–1.00			1.01–1.50			1.51–2.00			2.01–2.50		
Lot Size	n	c	AOQL	n	c	AOQL	n	c	AOQL	n	c	AOQL	n	c	AOQL	n	c	AOQL
1–30	All	0	0	All	0	0	All	0	0	All	0	0	All	0	0	All	0	0
31–50	30	0	.49	30	0	.49	30	0	.49	30	0	.49	30	0	.49	30	0	.49
51–100	37	0	.63	37	0	.63	37	0	.63	37	0	.63	37	0	.63	37	0	.63
101–200	40	0	.74	40	0	.74	40	0	.74	40	0	.74	40	0	.74	40	0	.74
201–300	43	0	.74	43	0	.74	70	1	.92	70	1	.92	95	2	.99	95	2	.99
301–400	44	0	.74	44	0	.74	70	1	.99	100	2	1.0	120	3	1.1	145	4	1.1
401–500	45	0	.75	75	1	.95	100	2	1.1	100	2	1.1	125	3	1.2	150	4	1.2
501–600	45	0	.76	75	1	.98	100	2	1.1	125	3	1.2	150	4	1.3	175	5	1.3
601–800	45	0	.77	75	1	1.0	100	2	1.2	130	3	1.2	175	5	1.4	200	6	1.4
801–1000	45	0	.78	75	1	1.0	105	2	1.2	155	4	1.4	180	5	1.4	225	7	1.5
1001–2000	45	0	.80	75	1	1.0	130	3	1.4	180	5	1.6	230	7	1.7	280	9	1.8
2001–3000	75	1	1.1	105	2	1.3	135	3	1.4	210	6	1.7	280	9	1.9	370	13	2.1
3001–4000	75	1	1.1	105	2	1.3	160	4	1.5	210	6	1.7	305	10	2.0	420	15	2.2
4001–5000	75	1	1.1	105	2	1.3	160	4	1.5	235	7	1.8	330	11	2.0	440	10	2.2
5001–7000	75	1	1.1	105	2	1.3	185	5	1.7	260	8	1.9	350	12	2.2	490	18	2.4
7001–10,000	75	1	1.1	105	2	1.3	185	5	1.7	260	8	1.9	380	13	2.2	535	20	2.5
0,001–20,000	75	1	1.1	135	3	1.4	210	6	1.8	285	9	2.0	425	15	2.3	610	23	2.6
0,001–50,000	75	1	1.1	135	3	1.4	235	7	1.9	305	10	2.1	470	17	2.4	700	27	2.7
0,001–100,000	75	1	1.1	160	4	1.6	235	7	1.9	355	12	2.2	515	19	2.5	770	30	2.8

rce: H. F. Dodge and H. G. Romig, *Sampling Inspection Tables—Single and Double Sampling*, 2nd ed. (New York: John Wiley & Sons, ., 1959). Reprinted by permission.

TABLE A17.2 Example of Dodge–Romig Double Sampling Lot Tolerance Tables

Lot tolerance percent defective = 5.0%
Consumer's risk = 0.10

Process Average %	0–.05						.06–.50						.51–1.00					
Lot Size	Trial 1		Trial 2			AOQL in %	Trial 1		Trial 2			AOQL in %	Trial 1		Trial 2			AOQL in %
	n_1	c_1	n_2	n_1+n_2	c_2		n_1	c_1	n_2	n_1+n_2	c_2		n_1	c_1	n_2	n_1+n_2	c_2	
1–30	All	0	—	—	—	0	All	0	—	—	—	0	All	0	—	—	—	0
31–50	30	0	—	—	—	.49	30	0	—	—	—	.49	30	0	—	—	—	.49
51–75	38	0	—	—	—	.59	38	0	—	—	—	.59	38	0	—	—	—	.59
76–100	44	0	21	65	1	.64	44	0	21	65	1	.64	44	0	21	65	1	.64
101–200	49	0	26	75	1	.84	49	0	26	75	1	.84	49	0	26	75	1	.84
201–300	50	0	30	80	1	.91	50	0	30	80	1	.91	50	0	55	105	2	1.0
301–400	55	0	30	85	1	.92	55	0	55	110	2	1.1	55	0	55	110	2	1.1
401–500	55	0	30	85	1	.93	55	0	55	110	2	1.1	55	0	80	135	3	1.2
501–600	55	0	30	85	1	.94	55	0	60	115	2	1.1	55	0	85	140	3	1.2
601–800	55	0	35	90	1	.95	55	0	65	120	2	1.1	55	0	85	140	3	1.3
801–1000	55	0	35	90	1	.96	55	0	65	120	2	1.1	55	0	115	170	4	1.4
1001–2000	55	0	35	90	1	.98	55	0	95	150	3	1.3	55	0	120	175	4	1.4
2001–3000	55	0	65	120	2	1.2	55	0	95	150	3	1.3	55	0	150	205	5	1.5
3001–4000	55	0	65	120	2	1.2	55	0	85	150	3	1.3	90	1	140	230	6	1.6
4001–5000	55	0	65	120	2	1.2	55	0	95	150	3	1.4	90	1	165	255	7	1.8
5001–7000	55	0	65	120	2	1.2	55	0	95	150	3	1.4	90	1	165	255	7	1.8
7001–10,000	55	0	65	120	2	1.2	55	0	120	175	4	1.5	90	1	190	280	8	1.9
10,001–20,000	55	0	65	120	2	1.2	55	0	120	175	4	1.5	90	1	190	280	8	1.9
20,001–50,000	55	0	65	120	2	1.2	55	0	150	205	5	1.7	90	1	215	305	9	2.0
50,001–100,000	55	0	65	120	2	1.2	55	0	150	205	5	1.7	90	1	240	330	10	2.1

Process Average %	1.01–1.50						1.51–2.00						2.01–2.50					
Lot Size	Trial 1		Trial 2			AOQL in %	Trial 1		Trial 2			AOQL in %	Trial 1		Trial 2			AOQL in %
	n_1	c_1	n_2	n_1+n_2	c_2		n_1	c_1	n_2	n_1+n_2	c_2		n_1	c_1	n_2	n_1+n_2	c_2	
1–30	All	0	—	—	—	0	All	0	—	—	—	0	All	0	—	—	—	0
31–50	30	0	—	—	—	.49	30	0	—	—	—	.49	30	0	—	—	—	.49
51–75	38	0	—	—	—	.59	38	0	—	—	—	.59	38	0	—	—	—	.59
76–100	44	0	21	65	1	.64	44	0	21	65	1	.64	44	0	21	65	1	.64
101–200	49	0	51	100	2	.91	49	0	51	100	2	.91	49	0	51	100	2	.91
201–300	50	0	55	105	2	1.0	50	0	80	130	3	1.1	50	0	100	150	4	1.1
301–400	55	0	80	135	3	1.1	55	0	100	155	4	1.2	85	1	105	190	6	1.3
401–500	55	0	105	160	4	1.3	85	1	120	205	6	1.4	85	1	140	225	7	1.4
501–600	55	0	110	165	4	1.3	85	1	145	230	7	1.4	85	1	165	250	8	1.5
601–800	90	1	125	215	6	1.5	90	1	170	260	8	1.5	120	2	185	305	10	1.6
801–1000	90	1	150	240	7	1.5	90	1	200	290	9	1.6	120	2	210	330	11	1.7
1001–2000	90	1	185	275	8	1.7	120	2	225	345	11	1.9	175	4	260	435	15	2.0
2001–3000	120	2	180	300	9	1.9	150	3	270	420	14	2.1	205	5	375	580	21	2.3
3001–4000	120	2	210	330	10	2.0	150	3	295	445	15	2.3	230	6	420	650	24	2.4
4001–5000	120	2	255	375	12	2.1	150	3	345	495	17	2.3	255	7	445	700	26	2.5
5001–7000	120	2	260	380	12	2.1	150	3	370	520	18	2.3	255	7	495	750	28	2.6
7001–10,000	120	2	285	405	13	2.1	175	4	370	545	19	2.4	280	8	540	820	31	2.7
10,001–20,000	120	2	310	430	14	2.2	175	4	420	595	21	2.4	280	8	660	940	36	2.8
20,001–50,000	120	2	335	455	15	2.2	205	5	485	690	25	2.5	305	9	745	1050	41	2.9
50,001–100,000	120	2	360	480	16	2.3	205	5	555	760	28	2.6	330	10	810	1140	45	3.0

Source: H. F. Dodge and H. G. Romig, *Sampling Inspection Tables—Single and Double Sampling*, 2nd ed. (New York: John Wiley & Sons, Inc., 1959). Reprinted by permission.

TABLE A17.3 Example of Dodge-Romig Single Sampling AOQL Tables

Average outgoing quality limit = 2.0%

Process Average %	0–.04			.05–.40			.41–.80			.81–1.20			1.21–1.60			1.61–2.00		
Lot Size	n	c	$100p_{0.10}$	n	c	$100p_{0.10}$	n	c	$100p_{0.10}$	n	c	$100p_{0.10}$	n	c	$100p_{0.10}$	n	c	$100p_{0.10}$
1–15	All	0	—	All	0	—	All	0	—	All	0	—	All	0	—	All	0	—
16–50	14	0	13.6	14	0	13.6	14	0	13.6	14	0	13.6	14	0	13.6	14	0	13.6
51–100	16	0	12.4	16	0	12.4	16	0	12.4	16	0	12.4	16	0	12.4	16	0	12.4
101–200	17	0	12.2	17	0	12.2	17	0	12.2	17	0	12.2	35	1	10.5	35	1	10.5
201–300	17	0	12.3	17	0	12.3	17	0	12.3	37	1	10.2	37	1	10.2	37	1	10.2
301–400	18	0	11.8	18	0	11.8	38	1	10.0	38	1	10.0	38	1	10.0	60	2	8.5
401–500	18	0	11.9	18	0	11.9	39	1	9.8	39	1	9.8	60	2	8.6	60	2	8.6
501–600	18	0	11.9	18	0	11.9	39	1	9.8	39	1	9.8	60	2	8.6	60	2	8.6
601–800	18	0	11.9	40	1	9.6	40	1	9.6	65	2	8.0	65	2	8.0	85	3	7.5
801–1000	18	0	12.0	40	1	9.6	40	1	9.6	65	2	8.1	65	2	8.1	90	3	7.4
1001–2000	18	0	12.0	41	1	9.4	65	2	8.2	65	2	8.2	95	3	7.0	120	4	6.5
2001–3000	18	0	12.0	41	1	9.4	65	2	8.2	95	3	7.0	120	4	6.5	180	6	5.8
3001–4000	18	0	12.0	42	1	9.3	65	2	8.2	95	3	7.0	155	5	6.0	210	7	5.5
4001–5000	18	0	12.0	42	1	9.3	70	2	7.5	125	4	6.4	155	5	6.0	245	8	5.3
5001–7000	18	0	12.0	42	1	9.3	95	3	7.0	125	4	6.4	185	6	5.6	280	9	5.1
7001–10,000	42	1	9.3	70	2	7.5	95	3	7.0	155	5	6.0	220	7	5.4	350	11	4.8
10,001–20,000	42	1	9.3	70	2	7.6	95	3	7.0	190	6	5.6	290	9	4.9	460	14	4.4
20,001–50,000	42	1	9.3	70	2	7.6	125	4	6.4	220	7	5.4	395	12	4.5	720	21	3.9
50,001–100,000	42	1	9.3	95	3	7.0	160	5	5.9	290	9	4.9	505	15	4.2	955	27	3.7

Source: H. F. Dodge and H. G. Romig, *Sampling Inspection Tables—Single and Double Sampling*, 2nd ed. (New York: John Wiley & Sons, Inc., 1959). Reprinted by permission.

TABLE A17.4 Example of Dodge–Romig Double AOQL Tables

Average outgoing quality limit = 2.0%

Process Average %	0–.04						.05–.40						.41–.80						.81–1.20						1.21–1.60						1.61–2.00					
Lot Size	Trial 1		Trial 2			$100p_{0.10}$	Trial 1		Trial 2			$100p_{0.10}$	Trial 1		Trial 2			$100p_{0.10}$	Trial 1		Trial 2			$100p_{0.10}$	Trial 1		Trial 2			$100p_{0.10}$	Trial 1		Trial 2			$100p_{0.10}$
	n_1	c_1	n_2	n_1+n_2	c_2		n_1	c_1	n_2	n_1+n_2	c_2		n_1	c_1	n_2	n_1+n_2	c_2		n_1	c_1	n_2	n_1+n_2	c_2		n_1	c_1	n_2	n_1+n_2	c_2		n_1	c_1	n_2	n_1+n_2	c_2	
1–15	All	0	—	—	—	—	All	0	—	—	—	—	All	0	—	—	—	—	All	0	—	—	—	—	All	0	—	—	—	—	All	0	—	—	—	—
16–50	14	0	—	—	—	13.6	14	0	—	—	—	13.6	14	0	—	—	—	13.6	14	0	—	—	—	13.6	14	0	—	—	—	13.6	14	0	—	—	—	13.6
51–100	21	0	12	33	1	11.7	21	0	12	33	1	11.7	21	0	12	33	1	11.7	21	0	12	33	1	11.7	21	0	12	33	1	11.7	23	0	23	46	2	10.9
101–200	24	0	13	37	1	11.0	24	0	13	37	1	11.0	24	0	13	37	1	11.0	27	0	28	55	2	9.6	27	0	28	55	2	9.6	27	0	28	55	2	9.6
201–300	26	0	15	41	1	10.4	26	0	15	41	1	10.4	29	0	31	60	2	9.1	29	0	31	60	2	9.1	32	0	48	80	3	8.4	32	0	48	80	3	8.4
301–400	26	0	16	42	1	10.3	26	0	16	42	1	10.3	30	0	35	65	2	9.0	33	0	52	85	3	8.2	33	0	52	85	3	8.2	36	0	69	105	4	7.6
401–500	27	0	16	43	1	10.3	30	0	35	65	2	9.0	30	0	35	65	2	9.0	34	0	56	90	3	7.9	36	0	74	110	4	7.5	60	1	90	150	6	7.0
501–600	27	0	16	43	1	10.3	31	0	34	65	2	8.9	35	0	55	90	3	7.9	35	0	55	90	3	7.9	37	0	78	115	4	7.4	65	1	95	160	6	6.8
601–800	27	0	17	44	1	10.2	31	0	39	70	2	8.8	35	0	60	95	3	7.7	38	0	82	120	4	7.3	38	0	82	120	4	7.3	70	1	120	190	7	6.4
801–1000	27	0	17	44	1	10.2	32	0	38	70	2	8.7	36	0	59	95	3	7.6	38	0	87	125	4	7.2	70	1	100	170	6	6.5	70	1	145	215	8	6.2
1001–2000	33	0	37	70	2	8.5	33	0	37	70	2	8.5	37	0	63	100	3	7.5	43	0	112	155	5	6.5	80	1	160	240	8	5.8	110	2	205	315	11	5.5
2001–3000	34	0	41	75	2	8.2	34	0	41	75	2	8.2	41	0	84	125	4	7.0	75	1	115	190	6	6.1	115	2	195	310	10	5.3	160	3	310	470	15	4.7
3001–4000	34	0	41	75	2	8.2	38	0	62	100	3	7.3	41	0	89	130	4	6.9	80	1	140	220	7	5.8	120	2	255	375	12	5.0	235	5	415	650	20	4.3
4001–5000	34	0	41	75	2	8.2	38	0	62	100	3	7.3	42	0	88	130	4	6.9	80	1	175	255	8	5.5	125	2	285	410	13	4.9	275	6	475	750	23	4.2
5001–7000	35	0	40	75	2	8.1	38	0	62	100	3	7.3	44	0	116	160	5	6.4	85	1	205	290	9	5.3	125	2	320	445	14	4.8	280	6	575	855	26	4.1
7001–10,000	35	0	40	75	2	8.1	38	0	62	100	3	7.3	45	0	115	160	5	6.3	85	1	210	295	9	5.2	165	3	335	500	15	4.5	320	7	645	965	29	4.0
10,001–20,000	35	0	40	75	2	8.1	39	0	66	105	3	7.2	45	0	115	160	5	6.3	90	1	260	350	11	5.1	170	3	425	595	18	4.4	395	9	835	1230	37	3.9
20,001–50,000	35	0	40	75	2	8.1	43	0	92	135	4	6.6	47	0	148	195	6	6.0	130	2	300	430	13	4.7	205	4	515	720	22	4.3	480	11	1090	1570	46	3.7
50,001–100,000	35	0	45	80	2	8.0	43	0	92	135	4	6.6	85	1	185	270	8	5.2	135	2	345	480	14	4.5	250	5	615	865	26	4.1	580	13	1460	2040	58	3.5

Source: H. F. Dodge and H. G. Romig, *Sampling Inspection Tables—Single and Double Sampling*, 2nd ed. (New York: John Wiley & Sons, Inc., 1959). Reprinted by permission.

TABLE A18.1 Index of Life-Testing Plans of Section 2B part I, 2C part I, and 2D

$\alpha=0.01$ $\beta=0.10$		$\alpha=0.05$ $\beta=0.10$		$\alpha=0.10$ $\beta=0.10$		$\alpha=0.25$ $\beta=0.10$		$\alpha=0.50$ $\beta=0.10$	
Code	θ_1/θ_0	Code	θ_1/θ_0	Code	θ_1/θ_0	Code	θ_1/θ_0	Code	θ_1/θ_0
A–1	0. 004	B–1	0. 022	C–1	0. 046	D–1	0. 125	E–1	0. 301
A–2	. 038	B–2	. 091	C–2	. 137	D–2	. 247	E–2	. 432
A–3	. 082	B–3	. 154	C–3	. 207	D–3	. 325	E–3	. 502
A–4	. 123	B–4	. 205	C–4	. 261	D–4	. 379	E–4	. 550
A–5	. 160	B–5	. 246	C–5	. 304	D–5	. 421	E–5	. 584
A–6	. 193	B–6	. 282	C–6	. 340	D–6	. 455	E–6	. 611
A–7	. 221	B–7	. 312	C–7	. 370	D–7	. 483	E–7	. 633
A–8	. 247	B–8	. 338	C–8	. 396	D–8	. 506	E–8	. 652
A–9	. 270	B–9	. 361	C–9	. 418	D–9	. 526	E–9	. 667
A–10	. 291	B–10	. 382	C–10	. 438	D–10	. 544	E–10	. 681
A–11	. 371	B–11	. 459	C–11	. 512	D–11	. 608	E–11	. 729
A–12	. 428	B–12	. 512	C–12	. 561	D–12	. 650	E–12	. 759
A–13	. 470	B–13	. 550	C–13	. 597	D–13	. 680	E–13	. 781
A–14	. 504	B–14	. 581	C–14	. 624	D–14	. 703	E–14	. 798
A–15	. 554	B–15	. 625	C–15	. 666	D–15	. 737	E–15	. 821
A–16	. 591	B–16	. 658	C–16	. 695	D–16	. 761	E–16	. 838
A–17	. 653	B–17	. 711	C–17	. 743	D–17	. 800	E–17	. 865
A–18	. 692	B–18	. 745	C–18	. 774	D–18	. 824	E–18	. 882

Producer's risk α is the probability of rejecting lots with mean life θ_0.
Consumer's risk β is the probability of accepting lots with mean life θ_1.

TABLE A18.2 Master Table for Life Tests Terminated upon Predetermined Number of Failures

r	Producer's risk (α)									
	0.01		0.05		0.10		0.25		0.50	
	Code	C/θ_0	Code	C/θ_0	Code	C/θ_0	Code	C/θ_0	Code	C/θ_0
1	A–1	0.010	B–1	0.052	C–1	0.106	D–1	0.288	E–1	0.693
2	A–2	.074	B–2	.178	C–2	.266	D–2	.481	E–2	.839
3	A–3	.145	B–3	.272	C–3	.367	D–3	.576	E–3	.891
4	A–4	.206	B–4	.342	C–4	.436	D–4	.634	E–4	.918
5	A–5	.256	B–5	.394	C–5	.487	D–5	.674	E–5	.934
6	A–6	.298	B–6	.436	C–6	.525	D–6	.703	E–6	.945
7	A–7	.333	B–7	.469	C–7	.556	D–7	.726	E–7	.953
8	A–8	.363	B–8	.498	C–8	.582	D–8	.744	E–8	.959
9	A–9	.390	B–9	.522	C–9	.604	D–9	.760	E–9	.963
10	A–10	.413	B–10	.543	C–10	.622	D–10	.773	E–10	.967
15	A–11	.498	B–11	.616	C–11	.687	D–11	.816	E–11	.978
20	A–12	.554	B–12	.663	C–12	.726	D–12	.842	E–12	.983
25	A–13	.594	B–13	.695	C–13	.754	D–13	.859	E–13	.987
30	A–14	.625	B–14	.720	C–14	.774	D–14	.872	E–14	.989
40	A–15	.669	B–15	.755	C–15	.803	D–15	.889	E–15	.992
50	A–16	.701	B–16	.779	C–16	.824	D–16	.901	E–16	.993
75	A–17	.751	B–17	.818	C–17	.855	D–17	.920	E–17	.996
100	A–18	.782	B–18	.841	C–18	.874	D–18	.931	E–18	.997

Producer's risk α is the probability of rejecting lots with mean life θ_0.
Acceptance criterion: Accept lot if $\hat{\theta}_{r,n} \geqq \theta_0(C/\theta_0)$.

TABLE A18.3 Life Tests for Predetermined Number of Failures Based on α, β, and θ_1/θ_0

θ_1/θ_0	$\alpha=.01$ $\beta=.01$		$\alpha=.01$ $\beta=.05$		$\alpha=.01$ $\beta=.10$		$\alpha=.01$ $\beta=.25$	
	r	C/θ_0	r	C/θ_0	r	C/θ_0	r	C/θ_0
2/3	136	.811	101	.783	83	.762	60	.724
1/2	46	.689	35	.649	30*	.625	22	.572
1/3	19	.544	15*	.498	13	.469	10*	.413
1/5	9*	.390	8*	.363	7*	.333	5*	.256
1/10	5*	.256	4*	.206	4*	.206	3*	.145

θ_1/θ_0	$\alpha=.05$ $\beta=.01$		$\alpha=.05$ $\beta=.05$		$\alpha=.05$ $\beta=.10$		$\alpha=.05$ $\beta=.25$	
	r	C/θ_0	r	C/θ_0	r	C/θ_0	r	C/θ_0
2/3	95	.837	67	.808	55	.789	35	.739
1/2	33	.732	23	.683	19	.655	13	.592
1/3	13	.592	10*	.543	8*	.498	6*	.436
1/5	7*	.469	5*	.394	4*	.342	3*	.272
1/10	4*	.342	3*	.272	3*	.272	2*	.178

θ_1/θ_0	$\alpha=.10$ $\beta=.01$		$\alpha=.10$ $\beta=.05$		$\alpha=.10$ $\beta=.10$		$\alpha=.10$ $\beta=.25$	
	r	C/θ_0	r	C/θ_0	r	C/θ_0	r	C/θ_0
2/3	77	.857	52	.827	41	.806	25*	.754
1/2	26	.758	18	.712	15*	.687	9*	.604
1/3	11	.638	8*	.582	6*	.525	4*	.436
1/5	5*	.487	4*	.436	3*	.367	3*	.367
1/10	3*	.367	2*	.266	2*	.266	2*	.266

θ_1/θ_0	$\alpha=.25$ $\beta=.01$		$\alpha=.25$ $\beta=.05$		$\alpha=.25$ $\beta=.10$		$\alpha=.25$ $\beta=.25$	
	r	C/θ_0	r	C/θ_0	r	C/θ_0	r	C/θ_0
2/3	52	.903	32	.876	23	.853	12	.793
1/2	17	.827	11	.784	8*	.744	5*	.674
1/3	7*	.726	5*	.674	4*	.634	2*	.481
1/5	3*	.576	2*	.481	2*	.481	1*	.288
1/10	2*	.481	2*	.481	1*	.288	1*	.288

Note. A complete set of OC curves is not provided for the sampling plans of this table. For those sampling plans marked (*), the appropriate OC curves in table 2A-2 may be used by determining, from table 2B-1, the sample code designation corresponding to the same values of α and r. For the sampling plans that are not marked (*), two points $(1, 1-\alpha)$ and $(\theta_1/\theta_0, \beta)$ on the OC curves are given.

TABLE A18.4 Master Table for Life Tests Terminated at Predetermined Time (without Replacement)

Values of T/θ_o for $\alpha = 0.05$

Code	r	Sample size									
		$2r$	$3r$	$4r$	$5r$	$6r$	$7r$	$8r$	$9r$	$10r$	$20r$
B–1	1	0. 026	0. 017	0. 013	0. 010	0. 009	0. 007	0. 006	0. 006	0. 005	0. 003
B–2	2	. 104	. 065	. 048	. 038	. 031	. 026	. 023	. 020	. 018	. 009
B–3	3	. 168	. 103	. 075	. 058	. 048	. 041	. 036	. 031	. 028	. 014
B–4	4	. 217	. 132	. 095	. 074	. 061	. 052	. 045	. 040	. 036	. 017
B–5	5	. 254	. 153	. 110	. 086	. 071	. 060	. 052	. 046	. 041	. 020
B–6	6	. 284	. 170	. 122	. 095	. 078	. 066	. 057	. 051	. 045	. 022
B–7	7	. 309	. 185	. 132	. 103	. 084	. 072	. 062	. 055	. 049	. 024
B–8	8	. 330	. 197	. 141	. 110	. 090	. 076	. 066	. 058	. 052	. 025
B–9	9	. 348	. 207	. 148	. 115	. 094	. 080	. 069	. 061	. 055	. 027
B–10	10	. 363	. 216	. 154	. 120	. 098	. 083	. 072	. 064	. 057	. 028
B–11	15	. 417	. 246	. 175	. 136	. 112	. 094	. 082	. 072	. 065	. 032
B–12	20	. 451	. 266	. 189	. 147	. 120	. 102	. 088	. 078	. 070	. 034
B–13	25	. 475	. 280	. 199	. 154	. 126	. 107	. 093	. 082	. 073	. 036
B–14	30	. 493	. 290	. 206	. 160	. 131	. 111	. 096	. 085	. 076	. 037
B–15	40	. 519	. 305	. 216	. 168	. 137	. 116	. 101	. 089	. 079	. 039
B–16	50	. 536	. 315	. 223	. 173	. 142	. 120	. 104	. 092	. 082	. 040
B–17	75	. 564	. 331	. 235	. 182	. 149	. 126	. 109	. 096	. 086	. 042
B–18	100	. 581	. 340	. 242	. 187	. 153	. 130	. 112	. 099	. 089	. 043

TABLE A18.5 Master Table for Life Tests Terminated at Predetermined Time (with Replacement)

Values of T/θ_o for $\alpha=0.05$

Code	r	Sample size									
		$2r$	$3r$	$4r$	$5r$	$6r$	$7r$	$8r$	$9r$	$10r$	$20r$
B–1	1	0.026	0.017	0.013	0.010	0.009	0.007	0.006	0.006	0.005	0.003
B–2	2	.089	.059	.044	.036	.030	.025	.022	.020	.018	.009
B–3	3	.136	.091	.068	.055	.045	.039	.034	.030	.027	.014
B–4	4	.171	.114	.085	.068	.057	.049	.043	.038	.034	.017
B–5	5	.197	.131	.099	.079	.066	.056	.049	.044	.039	.020
B–6	6	.218	.145	.109	.087	.073	.062	.054	.048	.044	.022
B–7	7	.235	.156	.117	.094	.078	.067	.059	.052	.047	.023
B–8	8	.249	.166	.124	.100	.083	.071	.062	.055	.050	.025
B–9	9	.261	.174	.130	.104	.087	.075	.065	.058	.052	.026
B–10	10	.271	.181	.136	.109	.090	.078	.068	.060	.054	.027
B–11	15	.308	.205	.154	.123	.103	.088	.077	.068	.062	.031
B–12	20	.331	.221	.166	.133	.110	.095	.083	.074	.066	.033
B–13	25	.348	.232	.174	.139	.116	.099	.087	.077	.070	.035
B–14	30	.360	.240	.180	.144	.120	.103	.090	.080	.072	.036
B–15	40	.377	.252	.189	.151	.126	.108	.094	.084	.075	.038
B–16	50	.390	.260	.195	.156	.130	.111	.097	.087	.078	.039
B–17	75	.409	.273	.204	.164	.136	.117	.102	.091	.082	.041
B–18	100	.421	.280	.210	.168	.140	.120	.105	.093	.084	.042

TABLE A18.6 Life Tests for Predetermined Time Based on α, β, and θ_1/θ_0 (without Replacement)

θ_1/θ_0	r	T/θ_0 1/3	1/5	1/10	1/20	r	T/θ_0 1/3	1/5	1/10	1/20
		n	n	n	n		n	n	n	n
		$\alpha=0.01$		$\beta=0.01$			$\alpha=0.05$		$\beta=0.01$	
2/3	136	403	622	1172	2275	95	289	447	843	1639
1/2	46	119	182	340	657	33	90	138	258	499
1/3	19	41	61	113	216	13	30	45	83	160
1/5	9	15	22	39	74	7	13	20	36	69
1/10	5	6	9	15	28	4	6	9	15	29
		$\alpha=0.01$		$\beta=0.05$			$\alpha=0.05$		$\beta=0.05$	
2/3	101	291	448	842	1632	67	198	305	575	1116
1/2	35	87	132	245	472	23	59	90	168	326
1/3	15	30	45	82	157	10	21	32	59	113
1/5	8	13	18	33	62	5	8	12	22	41
1/10	4	4	6	10	18	3	4	5	9	17
		$\alpha=0.01$		$\beta=0.10$			$\alpha=0.05$		$\beta=0.10$	
2/3	83	234	359	675	1307	55	159	245	462	895
1/2	30	72	109	202	390	19	47	72	134	258
1/3	13	25	37	67	128	8	16	24	43	83
1/5	7	11	15	26	50	4	6	9	15	29
1/10	4	4	6	10	18	3	4	5	9	17
		$\alpha=0.01$		$\beta=0.25$			$\alpha=0.05$		$\beta=0.25$	
2/3	60	162	248	465	899	35	96	147	276	535
1/2	22	49	74	137	262	13	30	45	83	160
1/3	10	18	26	46	87	6	11	16	29	55
1/5	5	6	9	15	28	3	4	5	9	17
1/10	3	3	4	6	10	2	2	2	4	8

TABLE A18.6 Life Tests for Predetermined Time Based on α, β, and θ_1/θ_0 (without Replacement) (*Continued*)

θ_1/θ_0	r	T/θ_0 1/3	1/5	1/10	1/20	r	T/θ_0 1/3	1/5	1/10	1/20
		n	n	n	n		n	n	n	n
		$\alpha=0.10$		$\beta=0.01$			$\alpha=0.25$		$\beta=0.01$	
2/3	77	238	369	699	1358	52	168	261	496	965
1/2	26	73	112	210	407	17	51	79	149	289
1/3	11	27	40	75	145	7	19	29	54	105
1/5	5	10	14	26	51	3	6	10	18	36
1/10	3	5	7	12	23	2	3	5	10	20
		$\alpha=0.10$		$\beta=0.05$			$\alpha=0.25$		$\beta=0.05$	
2/3	52	156	242	456	886	32	101	156	296	576
1/2	18	48	73	137	265	11	31	48	91	177
1/3	8	18	27	50	97	5	12	19	36	69
1/5	4	7	10	19	36	2	3	5	10	20
1/10	2	2	3	6	11	2	3	5	10	20
		$\alpha=0.10$		$\beta=0.10$			$\alpha=0.25$		$\beta=0.10$	
2/3	41	121	186	351	681	23	71	110	207	403
1/2	15	39	59	110	213	8	22	33	63	123
1/3	6	12	18	34	66	4	9	14	27	52
1/5	3	5	7	12	23	2	3	5	10	20
1/10	2	2	3	6	11	1	1	1	3	6
		$\alpha=0.10$		$\beta=0.25$			$\alpha=0.25$		$\beta=0.25$	
2/3	25	69	107	201	389	12	34	53	101	196
1/2	9	21	31	58	113	5	12	19	36	69
1/3	4	7	10	19	36	2	3	5	10	20
1/5	3	5	7	12	23	1	1	1	3	6
1/10	2	2	3	6	11	1	1	1	3	6

No operating characteristic curves are provided for these sampling plans. However, two points on the OC curves $(1, 1-\alpha)$ and $(\theta_1/\theta_0, \beta)$ are given.

TABLE A18.7 Life Tests for Predetermined Time Based on α, β, and θ_1/θ_0 (with Replacement)

θ_1/θ_0	r	T/θ_0				r	T/θ_0			
		1/3	1/5	1/10	1/20		1/3	1/5	1/10	1/20
		n	n	n	n		n	n	n	n
		$\alpha=0.01$		$\beta=0.01$			$\alpha=0.05$		$\beta=0.01$	
2/3	136	331	551	1103	2207	95	238	397	795	1591
1/2	46	95	158	317	634	33	72	120	241	483
1/3	19	31	51	103	206	13	23	38	76	153
1/5	9	10	17	35	70	7	9	16	32	65
1/10	5	4	6	12	25	4	4	6	13	27
		$\alpha=0.01$		$\beta=0.05$			$\alpha=0.05$		$\beta=0.05$	
2/3	101	237	395	790	1581	67	162	270	541	1082
1/2	35	68	113	227	454	23	47	78	157	314
1/3	15	22	37	74	149	10	16	27	54	108
1/5	8	8	14	29	58	5	6	10	19	39
1/10	4	3	4	8	16	3	3	4	8	16
		$\alpha=0.01$		$\beta=0.10$			$\alpha=0.05$		$\beta=0.10$	
2/3	83	189	316	632	1265	55	130	216	433	867
1/2	30	56	93	187	374	19	37	62	124	248
1/3	13	18	30	60	121	8	11	19	39	79
1/5	7	7	11	23	46	4	4	7	13	27
1/10	4	2	4	8	16	3	3	4	8	16
		$\alpha=0.01$		$\beta=0.25$			$\alpha=0.05$		$\beta=0.25$	
2/3	60	130	217	434	869	35	77	129	258	517
1/2	22	37	62	125	251	13	23	38	76	153
1/3	10	12	20	41	82	6	7	13	26	52
1/5	5	4	7	13	25	3	3	4	8	16
1/10	3	2	2	4	8	2	1	2	3	7

TABLE A18.7 Life Tests for Predetermined Time Based on α, β, and θ_1/θ_0 (with Replacement) (*Continued*)

θ_1/θ_0	r	T/θ_0 1/3 n	1/5 n	1/10 n	1/20 n	r	T/θ_0 1/3 n	1/5 n	1/10 n	1/20 n
		$\alpha=0.10$		$\beta=0.01$			$\alpha=0.25$		$\beta=0.01$	
2/3	77	197	329	659	1319	52	140	234	469	939
1/2	26	59	98	197	394	17	42	70	140	281
1/3	11	21	35	70	140	7	15	25	50	101
1/5	5	7	12	24	48	3	5	8	17	34
1/10	3	3	5	11	22	2	2	4	9	19
		$\alpha=0.10$		$\beta=0.05$			$\alpha=0.25$		$\beta=0.05$	
2/3	52	128	214	429	859	32	84	140	280	560
1/2	18	38	64	128	256	11	25	43	86	172
1/3	8	13	23	46	93	5	10	16	33	67
1/5	4	5	8	17	34	2	3	5	10	19
1/10	2	2	3	5	10	2	2	4	9	19
		$\alpha=0.10$		$\beta=0.10$			$\alpha=0.25$		$\beta=0.10$	
2/3	41	99	165	330	660	23	58	98	196	392
1/2	15	30	51	102	205	8	17	29	59	119
1/3	6	9	15	31	63	4	7	12	25	50
1/5	3	4	6	11	22	2	3	4	9	19
1/10	2	2	2	5	10	1	1	2	3	5
		$\alpha=0.10$		$\beta=0.25$			$\alpha=0.25$		$\beta=0.25$	
2/3	25	56	94	188	376	12	28	47	95	190
1/2	9	16	27	54	108	5	10	16	33	67
1/3	4	5	8	17	34	2	2	4	9	19
1/5	3	3	5	11	22	1	1	2	3	6
1/10	2	1	2	5	10	1	1	1	2	5

No operating characteristic curves are provided for these sampling plans. However, two points on the OC curves $(1, 1-\alpha)$ and $(\theta_1/\theta_0, \beta)$ are given.

TABLE A18.8 **Life Tests Acceptance Sampling Plans Based on α, β, and p_1/p_0 (without Replacement)**

Values of r (upper numbers) and of D (lower numbers)*

p_1/p_0	$\alpha=0.01$			$\alpha=0.05$			$\alpha=0.10$		
	$\beta=0.01$	0.05	0.10	0.01	0.05	0.10	0.01	0.05	0.10
3/2	136	101	83	95	67	55	77	52	41
	110. 4	79. 1	63. 3	79. 6	54. 1	43. 4	66. 0	43. 0	33. 0
2	46	35	30	33	23	19	26	18	15
	31. 7	22. 7	18. 7	24. 2	15. 7	12. 4	19. 7	12. 8	10. 3
5/2	27	21	18	19	14	11	15	11	9
	16. 4	11. 8	9. 62	12. 4	8. 46	6. 17	10. 3	7. 02	5. 43
3	19	15	13	13	10	8	11	8	6
	10. 3	7. 48	6. 10	7. 69	5. 43	3. 98	7. 02	4. 66	3. 15
4	12	10	9	9	7	6	7	5	4
	5. 43	4. 13	3. 51	4. 70	3. 29	2. 61	3. 90	2. 43	1. 75
5	9	8	7	7	5	4	5	4	3
	3. 51	2. 91	2. 33	3. 29	1. 97	1. 37	2. 43	1. 75	1. 10
10	5	4	4	4	3	3	3	2	2
	1. 28	. 823	. 823	1. 37	. 818	. 818	1. 10	. 532	. 532

*The sample size n is obtained by taking the largest integer less than or equal to the tabled value divided by p_0, i.e., $n=[D/p_0]$.
Producer's risk α is the probability of rejecting lots with acceptable proportion of lot failing before specified time, p_0.
Consumer's risk β is the probability of accepting lots with unacceptable proportion of lot failing before specified time, p_1.

TABLE A18.9 Master Table for Sequential Life Tests

$\alpha = 0.05$

Code	r_0	h_0/θ_0	h_1/θ_0	s/θ_0	$F_0(r)$	$E_{\theta_1}(r)$	$E_s(r)$	$E_{\theta_0}(r)$
B–1	3	0. 0506	−0. 0650	0. 0859	0. 8	0. 8	0. 4	0. 0
B–2	6	. 2254	−. 2894	. 2400	1. 2	1. 6	1. 1	. 3
B–3	9	. 4098	−. 5261	. 3405	1. 5	2. 3	1. 9	. 6
B–4	12	. 5805	−. 7453	. 4086	1. 8	3. 0	2. 6	. 9
B–5	15	. 7345	−. 9430	. 4576	2. 1	3. 7	3. 3	1. 2
B–6	18	. 8842	−1. 1352	. 4972	2. 3	4. 3	4. 1	1. 6
B–7	21	1. 0209	−1. 3107	. 5282	2. 5	5. 0	4. 8	1. 9
B–8	24	1. 1495	−1. 4757	. 5538	2. 7	5. 6	5. 5	2. 3
B–9	27	1. 2719	−1. 6329	. 5756	2. 8	6. 3	6. 3	2. 7
B–10	30	1. 3916	−1. 7866	. 5948	3. 0	6. 9	7. 0	3. 0
B–11	45	1. 9101	−2. 4523	. 6607	3. 7	10. 0	10. 7	5. 0
B–12	60	2. 3620	−3. 0325	. 7024	4. 3	13. 1	14. 5	7. 0
B–13	75	2. 7516	−3. 5327	. 7307	4. 8	16. 1	18. 2	9. 1
B–14	90	3. 1217	−4. 0079	. 7530	5. 3	19. 2	22. 1	11. 2
B–15	120	3. 7522	−4. 8173	. 7833	6. 2	25. 0	29. 5	15. 3
B–16	150	4. 3314	−5. 5610	. 8053	6. 9	31. 0	37. 1	19. 7
B–17	225	5. 5386	−7. 1109	. 8391	8. 5	45. 6	55. 9	30. 5
B–18	300	6. 5773	−8. 4444	. 8600	9. 8	60. 4	75. 1	41. 6

INDEX

A

Acceptable quality level (AQL), 357
  acceptance procedures based on, 245–67
  circumstances for using, 246–47
  history of, 247
  procedures:
    applicability of, 248
    initial decisions of, 248–50
  specification of, 249, 251
Acceptance:
  procedure(s):
    based on AQL, 245–67
    for defects, 262–63
    indifference quality, 272–75
  sequential, 278–83
    based on MTTF, 435–39
Acceptance control:
  hypothesis testing in, 227–28
    objectives of, 222–23
Acceptance number of zero, and sampling plans, 254
Acceptance quality q_1, 230
Acceptance sampling, 228
  continuous, by attributes, 291–315
  lot-by-lot, by attributes, 236–44
  quality of conformance to design and, 14–16
  by variables, applicability of, 317–18
Accuracy, of inspection, 366
Adequate performance, criteria of, 440
Adjustment, for within study trend, 208–9
Adjustment action, responsibilities for chart maintenance and, 95
Administration:
  procedures of, for submission and resubmission of lots, 266–67
  of sampling plan(s), 253
    criteria for, 258–60
Advisory staff, 386
Algebra, of probabilities, 24
AOQL, *see* Average outgoing quality level (limit)
Appraisal costs, 369–70
Approximations, hierarchy of, 40–43
AQL. *see* Acceptable quality level
Array, frequency, 43–44
Assemblies, complex, classification of defects for, 360–64
Assurance, quality. *see* Quality assurance
Attribute(s), 164
  acceptance sampling by
    continuous, 291–315
    lot-by-lot, 236–44
  control charts for, 164–93
Attributes chart, 164
  for performance control, 183–84
  for quality troubleshooting, 181–83
Attributes control, job shop application of, 171–78
Attributes sampling plan, simple:
  development of, 241–42

Attributes sampling plan, simple (*cont.*)
OC curve of, analysis and interpretation of, 243–44
Attributes single sampling plan, OC curve of, construction of, 237–41
Audit sampling, for quality assurance, 288
Authority, of quality control circle, 393
Availability, lot, for sample selection, 253
Average(s):
moving, charts for, 131–33
process, *see* Process average
sample, significance tests for, 65–69
Average defects, chart for, 180
Average outgoing quality, 231–32
Average outgoing quality level (limit) (AOQL), 232, 357
plans for specific, 306–15
Average run length:
OC curve and, 159–60
for $\bar{X}$, charts for, 151–54
Average sample number (ASN), 265
Average total inspection (ATI), 232–33

B

Base period, 93–94, 107
process not stable during, 109–12
Binomial distribution, 32–33
of estimates, 49
Budgetary control, of quality costs, 369–73

C

Capability:
machine, 81, 199
process. *see* Process capability *entries*
Cart Kanban, 407
Central limit theorem, 41
Central moments, 29
Central tendency, 29
Chart(s):
attributes. *see* Attributes chart
for average defects, 180
control. *see* Control chart(s)
CUSUM, 131, 133–40
floor, 173
index, for performance control, 184–90
moving average (sum), 131–33
p. *see* Percentage control chart
Shewhart, 12
supervision, 174
for variable quality characteristics, 98–114
specifics of, 102–4
$\bar{X}$ and R, 12
Circle, quality control. *see* Quality control circle(s)
Classification:
of defects:
for complex assemblies, 360–64
illustration of, 365–66
procedure for, 351–55
of demerits, 364–65
Complex assemblies, classification of defects for, 360–64
Computation, of OC curve, 145–47
Conditional probability, 23
Conformance to design. *see* Design, conformance to
Consistency, and quality standard, 358
Constant failure rate (CFR) model, 423
Construction, of OC curve of attributes single sampling plan, 237–41
Continuous acceptance sampling, by attributes, 291–315
advantages of, 292
description of, 296–302
effectiveness of, 304–5
historical note on, 294
Continuous event space, 26
Control:
acceptance:
hypothesis testing in, 227–28
objectives of, 222–23
attributes, job shop application of, 171–78
budgetary, of quality costs, 369–73
defects per unit, application of, 179–81
performance. *see* Performance control
point of, 272
process, 95
special procedures in, 120–40
production, feedforward and feedback systems of, 403–4
quality. *see* Quality control
of quality costs in engineering, 373
of reliability, distribution in, 411–15
statistical, of processes, 80–96
Control chart(s):
for attributes, 164–93
basic form of, 88–91
basics of, 99–101
defect-cause, 177
defects, 178–79
departmental data and overall, 176
development of, 93–94
for individual measurements, 123–28
maintenance of, and adjustment action, responsibilities for, 95
in monitoring period, 108, 112–14
operating characteristic (OC) of, 143–45
percentage, 165–70
properties of, 143–62

starting of, 106–9
use of, 91–93, 101–2
for $\bar{X}$ and s, 120–23
Control chart factors, derivation of, 105–6
Control limit, 11
Control program, for tools, gages and test equipment, 340–47
Control staff, 387
Control variable quality characteristics, charts for, 98–114
specifics of, 102–4
Corrective maintenance, 439
Cost(s):
appraisal, 369–70
failure, 369, 371
of inspection, 366
prevention, 369–70
quality. *see* Quality cost(s)
total, minimum, and quality standard, 358
unit inspection, and sampling plans, 254
Critical defect(s), 262, 354, 365
Cumulative probability function, 28
Current quality performance, 181
CUSUM charts, 131, 133–40

D

Data:
historical, and quality standard, 358
from paired specimens, variance unknown, and significance of difference between sample means, 67–69
test, 50–51
Decreasing failure rate (DFR) model, 423
Defect(s), 248
acceptance procedure for, 262–63
classification of:
for complex assemblies, 360–64
illustration of, 365–66
procedure for, 351–55
critical, 262, 354, 365
major, 262, 354, 362, 365
Military-Standard-105D for, 263–64
minor A, 262, 354, 362, 366
minor B, 262, 362, 366
in sample, number of, and number specified by standard, significance of difference between, 70
Defect-cause control chart, 177
Defective item(s), 248
percent of, inspection by variables for, sampling procedures and tables for, 321–27
production of, before shift in process average is detected, 160–62
Defects control chart, 178–79
Defects per unit control, application of, 179–81
Degrees of freedom, 60–62
Demerit rating system, 190–93
Demerit sampling, 272, 283–87
Demerit standard, 357
Demerits, classification of, 364–65
Departmental data and overall control chart, 176
Derating, 425
Design:
conformance to, quality of, 3
acceptance sampling and, 14–16
process monitoring and, 10–14
quality, 3, 5–10
for quality assurance, 332–47
of variables sampling plans, 327–30
Design specifications and tolerances, 209–10
Designing, for reliability, 424–28
Determination of process capability. *see* Process capability, determination of
Development:
of control chart, 93–94
of simple attributes sampling plan, 241–42
Deviation, standard, 29
Difference(s), significance of. *see* Significance of difference(s)
Discrete event space, 26
Distribution(s):
binomial, 32–33
of estimates, 49
in controlling reliability, 411–15
estimates, 47–50
exponential and Weibull, 38–39
frequency, graphic representation of, 45–47
of functions of sample observations, 49–50
hypergeometric, 30–32
normal, 36–38
of estimates, 49
parameters and their, 47–48
Poisson, 33–36
of estimates, 49
probability, 27
in QC studies, 30–39
run-length, 57
in quality control, 149–51
Division(s):
scalar and functional, 383
of work, and functionalization, 384–87
Dodge-Romig tables, 275–77
Double sampling plan, 233–34, 252–55
Drawing limits, 81
Drawings, engineering, inclusion of quality standards on, 359–60

E

Economic choice of sampling plan, 374–78
Economic optimization of quality control, 373–74
Empirical judgment, and quality standard, 358
Engineering:
  quality, 332–33
  quality costs in, control of, 373
Engineering drawings, inclusion of quality standards on, 359–60
Engineering judgment, and quality standard, 358
Enterprise, objectives of, 382
Environmental test, 428
Error(s):
  of estimation, 48
  type I and type II, 53–57
Estimated process average, inspection records and, 260–62
Estimates, and their distributions, 47–50
Estimation:
  error of, 48
  interval, 48
  of mean, $\overline{\overline{X}}$ used in, R used in estimation of variance, 153–54
  of MTTF, exponential failure density and, 419–22
  point, 48
  process average, 277–78
  of variance, $\overline{R}$ used in, mean known and, 151–54
Estimator function, 48
Estimators, 47–48
Evaluation, of quality and reliability, 337–41
Event space, 26
Events:
  mutually exclusive, 25
  and probability, 22–23
Ex post facto analysis, 181
Expectation, 28–29
Expected value, 28–29
Experimental basis for quality standard, 358
Experimental standard quality levels, 366–67
Exponential distribution, 38–39
Exponential failure density, 418–19
  estimation of MTTF and, 419–22
Express Kanban, 407

F

Factors, control chart, derivation of, 105–6
Failure(s), 355
  mean time between, 415
  mean time to, 415–17
    estimation of, and exponential failure density, 419–22
Failure costs, 369, 371
Failure density:
  exponential, 418–19
    estimation of MTTF and, 419–22
  Weibull, 422–23
Feedback system, 403–4
Feedforward system, 403
Finite event space, 26
Fit, interference and tolerance of, 215–18
Floor chart, 173
Freedom, degrees of, 60–62
Frequency, 26–28
Frequency distribution, graphic representation of, 45–47
Function(s):
  estimator, 48
  hazard, 413
  power:
    of control chart, 145–46
    of test, 55–56
  probability. *see* Probability function(s)
  probability density, 27
  of sample observations, distributions of, 49–50
Functional division, 383
Functional testing, 428
Functionalization, division of work and, 384–87

G

Gage(s):
  control program for, 340–47
  definition of, 342
  go/no-go, 164
Gage laboratory, 345–47
Gage theory, applied to inspection problem, 378–80
General inspection levels, 251
General staff, 386
Go/no-go gages, 164
Graphic representation, of frequency distribution, 45–47
Gross process quality control, 164
Growth, of quality control, 4–5

H

Handbook H108, use of, 429–35
Hazard rate (function), 413
Hierarchy of approximations, 40–43
Histogram, 45–46
Historical data, and quality standard, 358
Hypergeometric distribution, 30–32
Hypothesis, 50
  simple, 62

Hypothesis testing, 50–57
in acceptance control, 227–28

I

Incoming quality, 231
Increasing failure rate (IFR) model, 423
Index chart, for performance control, 184–90
Indifference quality acceptance procedures, 272–75
Indifference quality level (IQL), 357
Indifference quality q_1, 230
Individual measurements, control charts for, 123–28
Infinite event space, 26
Information, lot, and sampling plans, 253
Inherent variability, 80
In-plant relationships, 224–25
Inspection:
accuracy of, 366
AQL and, 248
cost of, 366
normal, 252, 258
one hundred percent, 14
rectifying, 230–31
total inspection under, 232–33
reduced, plan for, 252, 303–4
sampling, 32
total amount of, 264–66
tightened, plan for, 252, 258, 303–4
tooling used as media of, 342
total, under rectifying inspection, 232–33
unit, cost of, and sampling plans, 254
by variables, for percent defective, sampling procedures and tables for, 321–27
Inspection characteristics, number of, and experimental standard quality levels, 366
Inspection daily total sheet, 172
Inspection level, specification of, 251–52
Inspection method, specification of, 355–56
Inspection problem, game theory applied to, 378–80
Inspection records, and estimated process average, 260–62
Intercompany relationships, 224–25
Interdivision relationships, 224–25
Interference, and tolerance, of fit, 215–18
Intermediate steps, in production, setting tolerances for, 213–15
Interval estimation, 48
Investigation, causes for, 94–95
IQL. *see* Indifference quality level
Items, defective:
percent of, inspection by variables for, sampling procedures and tables for, 321–27
production of, before shift in process average is detected, 160–62

J

Job shop application, of attributes control, 171–78
Job shop process quality control, 169, 171
Judgment, empirical and engineering, and quality standard, 358
Just-in time systems, 404

K

Kanban system, 399, 403–9

L

Laboratory, gage, 345–47
Law(s):
Poisson, 15
of probability, 23–26
Level of significance, 107
Life cycle, 5
Life test, 428
Limit(s):
central, theorem of, 41
control, 11
drawing, 81
natural, 81
specification, 81
warning, 128–30
use of, 154–59
Line organization, 385
Location parameter, 39
Lot availability for sample selection, 253
Lot-by-lot acceptance sampling, by attributes, 236–44
Lot information, and sampling plans, 253
Lot tolerance percent defective (LTPD), 357
Lots:
moving, 292–94
submission and resubmission of, administrative procedures for, 266–67

M

Machine accounting card, 361
Machine capability, 81, 199. *See also* Process capability
Machines, variability in, 80–84
Maintainability, 425
Maintenance:
control chart, and adjustment action, responsibilities for, 95
corrective, 439
monitor, 439

Maintenance (*cont.*)
preventive, 439
and reliability, 439–41
Major defect(s), 262, 354, 362, 365
Maldistributed defects, 373
Management:
participative, 392
of quality, 18
Management guidelines, for improving quality and productivity, 382–83
Manuals, maintenance, 441
Marginal quality influence, and sampling plans, 253–54
Marginal testing, 440
Materials, variability in, 80–84
Mean(s):
estimation of, $\overline{\overline{X}}$ used in, $\overline{R}$ used in estimation of variance, 153–54
known:
and known variance, and charts for average run length for $\overline{X}$, 151–52
and $\overline{R}$ used to estimate variance, 151–54
sample. *see* Sample mean(s)
Mean time between failures (MTBF), 415
Mean time to failure (MTTF), 415–17
estimation of, and exponential failure density, 419–22
sequential acceptance procedures based on, 435–39
Measurement(s):
individual, control charts for, 123–28
quality, 348
and tests, for reliability, 428–29
Members, of quality control circle, 392
Men, variability in, 80–84
Methods, and standards, of quality assurance, 348–67
MIL-STD-105D, use of, for defects, 263–64
MIL-STD-414, and sampling procedures and tables for inspection by variables, for percent defective, 321–27
MIL-STD-1235 (ORD), and continuous acceptance sampling by attributes, 294–96
Minimum hole size, 355
Minimum total cost, and quality standard, 358
Minor A defects, 262, 354, 362, 366
Minor B defects, 262, 362, 366
Moments, 29
Monitor maintenance, 439
Monitoring, process:
quality of conformance to design and, 10–14
run length of, 57–60
Monitoring period, 93–94
control chart in, 108, 112–14
Moving average (sum) charts, 131–33
Moving lots, 292–94
MTTF. *see* Mean time to failure
Multiple sampling plan, 233–35, 252–55
Multistage plan CSP-M, 301–2
Mutually exclusive events, 25

N

n large:
and p' small, and significance of difference between proportion and standard, 70
and significance of difference between proportion and standard, 70
n_1 and n_2 and $np'>5$ in each sample, and significance of difference between two proportions, 70–71
Natural limits, 81
Natural tolerances, 12
Natural variability, 80
Natural variation of process, variation over time versus, 88–89
Normal distribution, 36–38
of estimates, 49
Normal inspection, 252, 258
Normal probability function, 46–47
Number:
of defects in sample, and number specified by standard, significance of difference between, 70
of inspection characteristics, and experimental standard quality levels, 366
Numerically valued event space, 26

O

Objectives, of enterprise, 382
Observations, sample:
determination of process capability using, 203–6
functions of, distributions of, 49–50
OC curve. *see* Operating characteristic curve
Ogive, 46
One hundred percent inspection, 14
One-tailed test, 62
Operating characteristic:
of control chart, 143–45
of sampling plan, 228–30
Operating characteristic curve(s) (OC curve[s]), 15, 145, 271
in acceptance sampling, analysis and interpretation of, 243–44

of attributes single sampling plan, construction of, 237–41
and average run length, 159–60
computation of, 145–47
producer's risk and, 257–58
of sampling plan, 229–30
and subgroup size, 147–49
of test, 55–56
Operation, of variables sampling plan, 319–21
Operations:
of sampling plan, results of, 9–10
Operative craftsmen, 383
Optimal in the strong sense, 57
Optimum quality of performance, 3
Organization:
line, 385
quality:
for productivity, 388
traditional, 388–91
structure of, 383–84
Outgoing quality, average, 231–32

P

p chart. *see* Percentage control chart
Paired specimens, data from; variance unknown, and significance of difference between sample means, 67–69
Parameter(s):
location, 39
sample, 47–48
scale, 39, 422
shape, 39, 422
and their distributions, 47–48
Participative management, 392
Percent defective, inspection by variables for, sampling procedures and tables for, 321–27
Percentage control chart (*p* chart), 165–70
Percentage spot check, 225
Performance:
adequate, criteria of, 440
quality of, 3–5
reliability and, 16–17
Performance control:
attribute chart for, 183–84
index chart for, 184–90
possible applications of, 193
Philips standard sampling system, 272
Planning:
for quality and reliability, 333
quality assurance, 348
Planning responsibilities, 336–37
Point estimation, 48
Point of control, 272
Poisson distribution, 33–36
of estimates, 49
Poisson law, 15
Polygon, 45–46
Population, 29, 47
Power, of test, 53–57
Power function:
of control chart, 145–46
of test, 55–56
Preaward quality survey, 334–36
Prevention costs, 369–70
Preventive maintenance, 439
Probability(ies):
of A and B, 24
of A complement, 24
of A or B, 24
algebra of, 24
events and, 22–23
laws of, 23–26
relative frequency concept of, 23
Probability density function (PDF), 27
Probability distribution, 27
Probability function(s), 27
cumulative, 28
normal, 46–47
in practice, 43–45
Probability ratio, 281
Problem(s):
inspection, game theory applied to, 378–80
quality, simple, as probability problems, 25–26
Problem-solving, in QC circle, steps in, 395
Problem-solving techniques, in QC circle, 394–95
Process(es):
gross, quality control of, 164
job shop, quality control of, 169, 171
monitoring of. *see* Monitoring, process
natural variation of, variation over time versus, 88–89
not stable during base period, 109–12
production, 57
statistical control of, 80–96
Process average:
estimated, inspection records and, 260–62
estimation of, 277–78
shift in, detection of, production of defective items before, 160–62
Process capability, 81, 95
determination of, 199–202
single-range method of, 206–8
using sample observations, 203–6
and tolerances, 210–11
Process capability analysis, 199–218
Process control, 95
special procedures in, 120–40

Process monitoring. *see* Monitoring, process
Process out of control, 11
Process sampling, 95–96
Process variability, statistical inference of, 84–87
Producer's risk, and OC curves, 257–58
Product quality value analysis, 349–51
Production:
  of defective items, before shift in process average is detected, 160–62
  intermediate steps in, setting tolerances for, 213–15
Production control, feedforward and feedback systems of, 403–4
Production process, 57
Productivity, 2
  definition of, 368
  quality and, 19
    and economy, 368–80
    management guidelines for improving, 382–83
    organization for, 388
Promotion, of quality control, 5
Proportions:
  (n_1 and n_2 large and $np'>5$ in each sample), significance of difference between two, 70–71
  significance of differnce involving, t test for, 69–71
Provisioning, spares, 440
Psychological considerations, and sampling plans, 255

Q

QC. *see* Quality control
Quality, 1–2
  average outgoing, 231–32
  of conformance to design. *see* Design, conformance to
  of design, 3, 5–10
  incoming, 231
  indifference. *see* Indifference *entries*
  management of, 18
  marginal, influence of, and sampling plans, 253–54
  of performance, 3–5
    reliability and, 16–17
  and productivity, 19
    management guidelines for improving, 382–83
    organization for, 388
  and reliability:
    evaluation of, 337–41
    planning for, 333
Quality analysis report, 363
Quality assurance:
  audit sampling for, 288
  design for, 332–47
  methods of, 5
    standards and, 348–67
  responsibilities for, 223–24
Quality assurance planning, 348
Quality characteristics, variable, 98–114
  specifics of, 102–4
Quality circle. *see* Quality control circle(s)
Quality control (QC)
  definition of, 2
  economic optimization of, 373–74
  gross process, 164
  growth of, 4–5
  job shop process, 169, 171
  kanbans and, 408–9
  in perspective, 1–20
  run-length distribution in, 149–51
  statistical, 22
Quality control circle(s), 391–96
  basics of, 392–93
  presenting recommendations in, 396
  problem solving in, steps in, 395
  problem-solving techniques in, 394–95
  starting of, 393–94
Quality control circle program, new, 397–402
Quality control project study, results of, 8–9
Quality control studies, distribution useful in, 30–39
Quality cost(s):
  budgetary control of, 369–73
  in engineering, control of, 373
  savings in, total, 349
Quality engineering, 332–33
Quality levels, standard:
  experimental, 366–67
  setting of, 357–64
Quality measurement, 348
Quality organization, traditional, 388–91
Quality problems, simple, as probability problems, 25–26
Quality q_1, 230
Quality standards, inclusion of,
  on engineering drawings, 359–60. *See also* Standards
Quality survey, 337–41
  preaward, 334–36
Quality troubleshooting, attributes chart for, 181–83
Quality value, product, analysis of, 349–51
Quality value analysis, 182

R

$\overline{R}$, used to estimate variance:
  mean known and, 151–54
  $\overline{\overline{X}}$ in estimation of mean, 153–54
Random variable, values of, 26–27

Random variation, 94
Rating system, demerit, 190–93
Receiver-producer relationships, 224–25
Recommendations, presenting of, in QC circle, 396
Records, inspection, and estimated process average, 260–62
Rectifying inspection, 230–31
  total inspection under, 232–33
Reduced inspection plan, 252, 303–4
Redundancy, 425
Relative frequency concept of probability, 23
Reliability, 333, 410–41
  achievement of, 423–24
  designing for, 424–28
  distributions in, 411–15
  maintenance and, 439–41
  measurement and tests for, 428–29
  quality and:
    evaluation of, 337–41
    planning for, 333
  quality of performance and, 16–17
Remarks column, 356
Representation sample, 95
Resources, of quality control circle, 393
Risk, of producer, and OC curves, 257–58
Run length:
  average:
    OC curve and, 159–60
    for $\overline{X}$, charts for, 151–54
  of monitoring process, 57–60
Run-length distribution, 57
  in quality control, 149–51

S

Sample(s), 47
  defects in, number of, and number specified by standard, significance of difference between, 70
  representative, 95
  sample variances from two, significance of difference between, 72–74
Sample averages, significance tests for, 65–69
Sample mean(s):
  difference between, significance of, data from paired specimens; variance unknown, 67–69
  difference between two, significance of:
    equal but unknown σ', 67
    variances known and equal, 66–67
  from standard, significance of:
    variability unknown, 65–66
    variance known, 65
Sample observations:
  determination of process capability using, 203–6
  functions of, distributions of, 49–50
Sample parameters, 47–48
Sample selection, lot availability for, 253
Sample size, 106–7
Sample-size variation, 253
Sample variances:
  and standard, significance of difference between, 71–72
  from two samples, significance of difference between, 72–74
Sampling:
  acceptance. *see* Acceptance sampling
  audit, for quality assurance, 288
  continuous. *see* Continuous acceptance sampling
  demerit, 272, 283–87
  double, plan for, 233–34, 252–55
  multiple, plan for, 233–35, 252–55
  process, 95–96
  sequential, 272
  spot-check method of, fallacies of, 225–26
  See also Sampling plan(s)
Sampling inspection, 32
  total amount of, 264–66
Sampling plan(s), 228
  attributes. *see* Attributes sampling plan *entries*
  economic choice of, 374–78
  operating characteristic of, 228–30
  results of operation of, 9–10
  single, 233, 252–55
    attributes, OC curve of, construction of, 237–41
  variables, 318–19
    design of, 327–30
    operation of, 319–21
  See also Sampling
Sampling procedures, and tables, for inspection by variables for percent defective, 321–27
Sampling system, Philips standard, 272
Scalar divison, 383
Scale parameter, 39, 422
Scope, of quality control circle, 393
Screening, 100 percent, 14
Second central moment, 29
Sequential acceptance procedures, 278–83
  based on MTTF, 435–39
Sequential probability ratio test (SPRT), 279
Sequential sampling, 272
Service staff, 386
Serviceability, 425
Setting:
  of standard quality levels, 357–64
  of tolerance, for intermediate steps in production, 213–15
Shape parameter, 39, 422

Shewhart charts, 12
Shift in process average, detection of, production of defective items before, 160–62
Signal Kanban, 404–6
Significance:
  of difference(s):
    between number of defects in sample and number specified by standard, 70
    involving proportions, *t* test for, 69–71
    between proportion and standard:
      (n large), 69
      (n large and p' small), 70
    between sample means, data from:
      paired specimens; variance unknown, 67–69
    between sample variances:
      and standard, 71–72
      from two samples, 72–74
    between two proportions (n_1 and n_2 large and $np'>5$ in each sample), 70–71
    between two sample means:
      variances known and equal, 66–67
      equal but unknown σ', 67
    between variances, test for, 71–74
  level of, 63, 107
  of sample mean from standard:
    variability unknown, 65–66
    variance known, 65
Significance tests, 62–64
  for sample averages, 65–69
Simple attributes sampling plan, development of, 241–42
Simple hypothesis, 62
Single-range method, for determination of process capability, 206–8
Single sampling plan, 233, 252–55
  attributes, OC curve of, construction of, 237–41
Single-stage plan CSP-1, 296–97
Single-stage plan CSP-2, 297–99
Single-stage plan CSP-A, 299–301
Size:
  minimum hole, 355
  sample, 106–7
  subgroup, OC curve and, 147–49
Spares provisioning, 440
Special inspection levels, 251
Specialist staff, 386
Specification(s), 199
  of AQL, 249, 251
  of inspection level, 251–52
  of inspection method, 355–56
  and tolerances, design, 209–10
Specification limits, 81
Specimens, paired, data from; variance unknown, and significance of difference between sample means, 67–69
Spot check, 225
Spot-check method of sampling, fallacies of, 225–26
Stability of process, lack of, during base period, 109–12
Staff, 385–87
Standard(s):
  demerit, 357
  experimental, quality levels of, 366–67
  methods and, of quality assurance, 348–67
  (n large and p' small), significance of differenc between proportion and, 70
  number of defects in sample and number specified by, significance of difference between, 70
  Philips, sampling system of, 272
  quality, inclusion of, on engineering drawings, 359–60
  sample mean from, significance of:
    variance known, 65
    variability unknown, 65–66
  sample variances and, significance of difference between, 71–72
  significance of difference between proportion and, (n large), 69
Standard deviation, 29
Standard normal deviation, 38
Standard normal variate, 38
Standard quality levels, setting of, 357–64
Stated tolerances, 12
Statistic(s):
  and probability, in quality control, 21–74
  test, 51
Statistical control of processes, 80–96
Statistical inference of process variability, 84–87
Statistical quality control, 22
Statistically dependent events, 24
Stochastically larger random variable, 58
Structure, of organization, 383–84
Subassemblies, tolerances for, 211–13
Subgroup, 131
Subgroup size, OC curve and, 147–49
Submission and resubmission of lots, administrative procedures for, 266–67
Sum, moving, charts for, 131–33
Supervision chart, 174
Supervisor's deviation report, 175
Supplier kanban, 405, 407

T

t test(s), 65–69
  for significance of difference involving proportions, 69–71

Tables:
  Dodge-Romig, 275–77
  for sampling plans, description and use of, 255–57
  sampling procedures and, for inspection by variables for percent defective, 321–27
Technical instructions, for maintenance, 441
Tendency, central, 29
Test(s):
  environmental, 428
  life, 428
  measurement and, for reliability, 428–29
  one-tailed, 62
  power of, 53–57
  sequential probability ratio, 279
  significance, 62–64
    for sample averages, 65–69
  for significance of differences between variances, 71–74
  t, 65–69
    for significance of difference involving proportions, 69–71
  two-tailed, 62–63
Test data, 50–51
Test equipment:
  control program for, 340–47
  definition of, 342
  and facilities, for maintenance, 441
Test statistic, 51
Testing:
  functional, 428
  hypothesis, 50–57
    in acceptance control, 227–28
  marginal, 440
Tightened inspection plan, 252, 258, 303–4
Time:
  mean, to failure, 415–17
    estimation of, and exponential failure density, 419–22
  variation over, versus natural variation of process, 88–89
Tolerance(s), 199
  design specifications and, 209–10
  of fit, interference and, 215–18
  natural, 12
  process capability and, 210–11
  setting of, for intermediate steps in production, 213–15
  stated, 12
  for subassemblies, 211–13
Tool(s):
  control program for, 340–47
  definition of, 342
Tooling, used as media of inspection, 342
Total amount of sampling inspection, 264–66
Total cost, minimum, and quality standard, 358
Total inspection, under rectifying inspection, 232–33
Total quality cost savings, 349
Traditional quality organization, 388–91
Training, and reliability, 440–41
Trend, within study, adjustment for, 208–9
Trouble code list, 360
Troubleshooting, quality, attributes chart for, 181–83
Two-tailed test, 62
Type I and type II errors, 53–57

U

Unacceptable quality q_1, 230
Uniformly most powerful test, 55, 57
Unit, defects per, control of, application of, 179–81
Unit inspection cost, and sampling plans, 254
Universe, 47

V

Value(s):
  expected, 28–29
  product quality, analysis of, 349–51
  of random variable, 26–27
Value analysis, 182
Variability, 29
  inherent, 80
  in materials, machines and men, 80–84
  natural, 80
  process, statistical inference of, 84–87
  unknown, in significance of sample mean from standard, 65–66
Variable(s):
  acceptance sampling by, applicability of, 317–18
  inspection by, for percent defective, sampling procedures and tables for, 321–27
  quality characteristics, charts for, 98–114
  random, values of, 26–27
  specifics of, 102–4
Variables sampling plan(s), 318–19
  design of, 327–30
  operation of, 319–21
Variance(s):
  equal but unknown, significance of difference between two sample means and, 67
  estimation of, $\overline{R}$ used in, mean known and, 151–54
  known:
    known mean and, charts for average run length for $\overline{X}$, 151–52

Variance(s) (*cont.*)
in significance of sample mean from standard, 65
and equal, in significance of difference between two sample means, 66–67
sample, and standard, significance of difference between, 71–72
significance of differences between, test for, 71–74
$\overline{R}$ in estimation of, $\overline{\overline{X}}$ in estimation of mean, 153–54
unknown, data from paired specimens and, significance of difference between sample means, 67–69
Variation:
over time, versus natural variation of process, 88–89
random, 94
sample-size, 253

W

Warning limits, 128–30
use of, 154–59
Weibull distribution, 38–39
Weibull failure density, 422–23
Withdrawal kanban, 404
Within study trend, adjustment for, 208–9
Work, division of, and functionalization, 384–87

X

$\overline{X}$:
average run length for, charts for, 151–54
and R, charts for, 12
and s', control charts for, 120–23
$\overline{\overline{X}}$, used to estimate mean, $\overline{R}$ used to estimate variance, 153–54

Z

Zero, acceptance number of, and sampling plans, 254